STARTING AND MANAGING
A SMALL BUSINESS

STARTING AND MANAGING A SMALL BUSINESS

FRANS BEKKER

With consulting editor
GAVIN STAUDE
Professor of Business Administration
Rhodes University

SINCE 1853

JUTA & CO, LTD

First Published 1988
Third Impression 1990

© Juta & Co, Ltd 1988
PO Box 14373, Kenwyn 7790

ISBN 0 7021 2128 2

PRINTED AND BOUND IN THE REPUBLIC OF SOUTH AFRICA
BY THE RUSTICA PRESS (PTY) LTD, WYNBERG, CAPE
C846

PREFACE

The extensive emphasis on the importance of economic development and the establishment of viable enterprises in Southern Africa has made me acutely aware of the need for a comprehensive body of knowledge aimed at serving both as a theoretical and as a practical guide to business. The main object of this book, then, is to assist you, whether you are planning to go into business, or are running an existing one, in organizing your thoughts and actions in an effective and efficient way.

The successful entrepreneur is made, not born, and he is made by his willingness to respect sound, basic business principles enough to master them. This book is written on the assumption that this is your attitude.

It is my hope that you will find this book not only interesting, but also valuable to you in your business enterprise. I would thus appreciate receiving your comments on the book, as well as any further ideas you may have on topics presented, criticisms, and recommendations that may improve the contents. Letters can be sent to P.O. Box 207, Nelspruit, 1200, RSA.

Frans Bekker

1988

ACKNOWLEDGEMENTS

This book could not have been written without the inspiration received from above. I praise Him. To Florence, my wife, for her support and encouragement—never has she failed to cheer me on. Also of much importance was the contribution of Noreen Smit, who worked long hours on the typescript. A special thanks must go to Tienie Briers for all the five-minute 'consultations' to confirm, deny, or sharpen an argument; I had to have someone help me get the facts straight. To my father (and mother) who fulfilled their obligations ['Has the leader a right to mold and shape? Of what use is aging, experience and wisdom if not to be the leaven for those who are younger? Of what use is pain if not to teach others to avoid it? The leader not only has the right; if he is a leader, he has the obligation.'*]

I must also thank Dr Willie Conradie whose knowledge helped much to frame the effort in fundamental ways. I also thank other writers for their kind consent to the use of some of their material, as referred to in quotations, footnotes and bibliographies.

Last, but certainly not least, to Sally Anderson for subediting the manuscript, and to the Juta team for taking care of the book during the process of publication.

*Harry Levinson, THE EXCEPTIONAL EXECUTIVE.

CONTENTS

Preface

Introduction

Acknowledgements

1 **Know about business ownership** 1
  ★ Introduction 1
  ★ Going into business for yourself 2
  ★ Personal qualities of the successful
    entrepreneur 8
  ★ Self-analysis 12
  ★ Assessing your investment capabilities 15
  ★ What is a business? 16
  ★ Objectives of business 19
  ★ Summary and conclusions 22

2 **Entering the business world** 25
  ★ Introduction 25
  ★ Choosing the right type of business 27
  ★ Choosing a specific business opportunity 28
  ★ Entering an established business 28
  ★ Advantages and disadvantages of buying a
    business 31
  ★ Evaluating the business for sale 33
  ★ How much to pay for the business 40
  ★ Closing the deal 50
  ★ Franchising 51
  ★ Advantages to the Franchisee 52
  ★ Disadvantages to the Franchisee 55
  ★ Types of Franchising systems 57

★ Getting to know the Franchisor...................... 59
★ Getting to know the Franchise business......... 61
★ The Franchise Agreement 63
★ Starting a business from scratch.................... 66
★ Assessing your market..................................... 68
★ Think creatively when assessing your business
  opportunity... 73
★ The location decision.. 77
★ Using a traffic study 81
★ A name for your business................................ 84
★ How to get a trading licence 84
★ Preparing the business plan............................ 88
★ What form of business? 102
★ Financing the business 106
★ Source of finance... 107
★ Arranging insurance... 118
★ The grand opening... 120
★ Summary and conclusions............................... 121

3 **Your managerial functions** 126
★ Introduction... 126
★ Planning... 128
★ Types of planning... 128
★ Barriers to planning 128
★ What to plan for.. 129
★ Checklist for decision-making.......................... 132
★ Forecasting 134
★ Developing objectives....................................... 135
★ Developing strategies 137
★ Developing programmes.................................. 138
★ Scheduling... 138
★ Budgeting... 139
★ Developing policies 141
★ Developing procedures..................................... 142
★ Organizing 143
★ Developing an organization structure 143
★ Symptoms of poor organization 144

★ How to organize.. 145
★ Delegation of responsibility and authority...... 146
★ Developing relationships................................... 147
★ Leading 147
★ Communication 149
★ Motivating 150
★ Selecting people... 155
★ Developing people's skills 155
★ Controlling.. 157
★ Developing performance standards.................. 158
★ Measuring performance 158
★ Evaluating performance.................................... 160
★ Correcting performance.................................... 160
★ Summary and conclusion 160

4 **Your business team** 164
★ Introduction... 164
★ Your employees 166
★ The value of human resources in business 169
★ Suggestions for better employee relations....... 170
★ Your employees as contributors 172
★ Training 173
★ Tracking down the right training course 177
★ Productivity in small business......................... 180
★ Summary and conclusion 184

5 **Staffing the business** 187
★ Introduction... 187
★ Prepare job descriptions 189
★ Personal characteristics and qualities 192
★ Recruiting new employees................................ 192
★ Interviewing new employees............................ 193
★ Checking references 197
★ Compensation.. 198
★ Statutory points according to the basic
  conditions of the employment act................... 199
★ Terminations.. 200
★ Summary and conclusions................................ 200

6 **Purchasing**.. 203
 ★ Introduction 203
 ★ The importance of the purchasing function ... 204
 ★ What to buy..................................... 207
 ★ When to buy.................................... 211
 ★ How much to buy............................ 213
 ★ Economic evaluation of retail purchasing....... 214
 ★ Buy the right quality 216
 ★ Selecting suppliers............................. 216
 ★ Summary and conclusions.................... 219

7 **Pricing**.. 221
 ★ Introduction..................................... 221
 ★ Simple formulae to find profitable mark-ups ... 222
 ★ Special factors to consider in setting prices..... 232
 ★ Pricing in the service business.......................... 234
 ★ Avoiding price competition............................. 234
 ★ Summary and conclusions.................... 236

8 **Shop layout, display and improving external and internal images**............................. 238
 ★ Introduction..................................... 238
 ★ Issues to consider in planning the layout 240
 ★ Floor space..................................... 240
 ★ Checkout area.................................. 240
 ★ Accessibility of merchandise.................. 242
 ★ Visibility of merchandise..................... 242
 ★ Security.. 244
 ★ Signs 245
 ★ Housekeeping................................... 245
 ★ Customer service 245
 ★ Summary and conclusions.................... 247

9 **Customer relations and service** 249
 ★ Introduction..................................... 249
 ★ The marketing concept....................... 251
 ★ Quality and value.............................. 257
 ★ Summary and conclusions.................... 266

10   **Advertising and promotions**...................... 269
★ Introduction.. 269
★ Promoting sale of products and services........ 271
★ How much to spend on advertising............... 272
★ Media selection..................................... 274
★ Measuring the results of advertising.............. 275
★ Types of advertising 277
★ Planning for, and developing an advertisement..... 279
★ Sales promotion.................................... 284
★ Publicity... 286
★ Summary and conclusions........................ 289

11   **Salesmanship and selling**........................ 292
★ Introduction.. 292
★ The salesman....................................... 293
★ The knowledge salesman must have.............. 295
★ Buying behaviour................................... 299
★ Sales presentation and demonstration............. 301
★ Selling benefits 304
★ Measuring sales performance 305
★ Sales letters.. 307
★ How to correspond by letter....................... 314
★ Summary and conclusions........................ 318

12   **Stock control** 321
★ Introduction.. 321
★ Having the right goods............................. 324
★ Having the goods at the right time................ 327
★ Having the goods at the right place 328
★ Having the goods at the right price.............. 329
★ Having the goods displayed in the right
   manner 330
★ How to increase your range of stock............. 331
★ Stocktaking... 333
★ Inflation 335
★ Checklist for the administration of stock........ 338
★ Summary and conclusions........................ 343

13 **Security** 346
  ★ Introduction 346
  ★ Why do people steal? 347
  ★ How people steal 349
  ★ Spotting shoplifters 351
  ★ Anti-shoplifting methods and safeguard
    procedures 352
  ★ Apprehension and prosecution 357
  ★ Burglary and robbery 359
  ★ Comments on security by experts in
    the field 360
  ★ Screening the applicant 361
  ★ Set the tone 362
  ★ Provide incentives 362
  ★ Summary and conclusions 365

14 **Setting up a record-keeping system** 368
  ★ Introduction 368
  ★ The cash book 370
  ★ Cash control system 373
  ★ Asset register 375
  ★ Debtors record 376
  ★ Creditors record 377
  ★ Bank reconciliation 377
  ★ Summary and conclusions 379

15 **Financial fundamentals** 381
  ★ Introduction 381
  ★ Financial statements 382
  ★ Ratio analysis 383
  ★ Liquidity ratios 384
  ★ Survival during a liquidity crisis 387
  ★ Leverage ratios 384
  ★ Activity ratios 392
  ★ Profitability ratios 396
  ★ Other ratios 403
  ★ Measuring against standard ratios 406

    ★ Depreciation 410

    ★ Summary and conclusions 414

16 **Profit planning and budgeting** 416

    ★ Introduction 416

    ★ Profit planning 417

    ★ Budgeting 421

    ★ Action plans 423

    ★ Break-even analysis 427

    ★ Summary and conclusions 435

17 **Credit Controlling** 438

    ★ Introduction 438

    ★ Making a decision on extending credit 439

    ★ Credit policy 441

    ★ Preparing a credit application 443

    ★ Investigating the credit application 445

    ★ Monitoring accounts 447

    ★ Following up accounts in arrears 448

    ★ The credit collection letter 448

    ★ Bank's credit cards 453

    ★ Summary and conclusions 454

18 **Development of entrepreneurship** 456

    ★ Introduction 456

    ★ Consultation services 457

    ★ Meaning of a consultation service 458

    ★ The role of the consultant 459

    ★ Operation of a consultation service 459

    ★ Where to find assistance 460

    ★ Self-development 470

    ★ Summary and conclusions 472

19 **Maintaining a dynamic business** 475

    ★ Introduction 475

    ★ Why does a business succeed? 476

    ★ Why a business fails 501

    ★ The quest for growth 508

★ Survival comes first... 508
★ Your business is ready for growth when:
(8 attributes).. 510
★ Thinking about growth...................................... 524
★ Planned growth.. 530
★ Summary and conclusions................................ 544

Index.. 551

(Notes and bibliographies appear at the end
of each chapter.)

INTRODUCTION

Thinking about investing your energy and financial resources in a small business is like going into battle. Firstly, it is essential to get all the information and knowledge and skills you need because operating a small business is a practical but challenging occupation. The high rate of failure is indicative of the fact that such undertakings may be unrewarding for the unwary and the unknowledgeable. The adage that 'fortune favours the prepared mind' is particularly relevant to the complexities of small business management. Since financial rewards do not accrue automatically, knowledge of the steps which leads to profits is as important as the desire for profitability. It is thus a prerequisite of success that you meet this challenge with knowledge and understanding. Once in business, you of course want to see the business stay open and make money. Therefore your objectives should be longevity and profitability, and you should utilize your business acumen optimally in accomplishing them. Secondly, keep your ears, eyes, mind and attitude open. Tenacity is essential. Go after what you believe in. Believe that you are capable of accomplishing what you set out to do. The confidence will come across. The small business sector is an open opportunity, and not too many people should listen to others and allow themselves to be dissuaded from what they want in life. All of us have the capacity to accomplish anything we want, only few realize it. Thirdly, planning for everything you intend to accomplish in business is essential. Planning is hard work — it involves creative thinking. Careful planning will help you 'expect the unexpected' and will give you a secure feeling from one activity to another. Your chances of making the desired return on your investment are so much greater when you have planned and managed your business into a position of strength. Fourthly, business is punctuated by failures. The important thing is to learn from those failures and not to become discouraged by them. The saying 'it is always darkest before the dawn' is certainly true in business. If you put in the effort, you will make it. Concentrate on opportunities that can be to the advantage of the business. That necessitates a different approach and method of thinking — be positive. Identify the real problem and get sound advice on it, then do what you did incorrectly differently and profitably. I cannot think of anything that is more fulfilling, exciting, or creative than running your own business. You can move it any way you want to, and it can be financially rewarding.

May entrepreneurship be alive and well in Southern Africa through your efforts to succeed in business.

W. VERNON SMITH

1988

1 | KNOW ABOUT BUSINESS OWNERSHIP

'The finest part of courage is prudence.'

Shakespeare

'Never acquire a business you don't know how to run.'

Robert W. Johnson[1]
Former Chairman of Johnson & Johnson

'Thinking of owning and managing your own business? It's a good idea — provided you know what it takes and have what it takes.'

U.S. Small Business Administration
Management Aids No. 2.016

INTRODUCTION

Most businesses in Southern Africa are classified as small,[2] and, because they are so prevalent and perform such a valuable function in the economy of Southern Africa, it is important that this book should begin with some indication of the unique challenges involved in owning a small business. To become the owner of a small business is for some a dream come true. However, the dream can easily become a nightmare if you do not know how to cope, and do not do the correct thing in the right way. Being the owner, you will have to accept responsibility for all final decisions concerning the business. Therefore, the first questions you should find answers to are whether owning a business is the 'right thing' for you, and whether you are the type of person that could make a success of it. One thing is certain: in order to succeed in business you have to perform at your best consistently, and to be in a position to do this you must rate yourself objectively by considering and appraising your strengths and weaknesses. As a business-owner, you must be able to acknowledge that you are weak in some areas. Once

1

you do this, you can take action to cover the deficiency, through personal training or through employing someone with the necessary skills.

GOING INTO BUSINESS FOR YOURSELF

Whether to go into business for yourself or to work for someone else is a major decision. At some time or another almost everyone thinks about being self-employed. As M. McCormack says:[3]

'If everyone who has talked about starting a business actually went out and did it, the whole nation would be self-employed.'

If you wish to become self-employed you must decide whether you know what it takes and have what it takes to manage a business effectively. One of the greatest opportunities almost anyone has is the chance to own and manage a small business. But for many indulging in such a fanciful idea, reality seems too imaginative. The question is why? The answer could probably be because of some recurring myths that discourage them from 'taking charge'. In my opinion these myths need to be destroyed. Two major ones are:

Entrepreneurs are born, not made. Nothing could be further from the truth. Biographies of entrepreneurs sometimes read as if they had entered the world with an extraordinary endowment, that somehow their future was preordained. Don't believe it. The truth is that the successful entrepreneur is made, and not born; and he is made by his willingness to respect each sound and basic business principle enough to master it. In other words, essential capacities and competencies of entrepreneurship can be learned, and we are all educable, at least if the basic desire to learn is there and we do not suffer from serious learning disorders. Also, whatever natural endowments you have, can be enhanced. Books can help you understand what is going on, but for most of us learning takes place during the experience itself. Thus, you must make the first move.

Someone has to supply you with a job. This is perhaps the most damaging myth of all. It seems that the only vision many people have is a specific list of employers who might employ them rather than a clear picture of a specific list of likely customers who need and will pay for a specific set of products and services.

One cannot help to ask: How else can one devise a small business development strategy that will create the most needed jobs if entrepreneurship is described as a set of psychological drives reserved for titans? Almost all of us have a latent entrepreneurial drive waiting to be inspired. Look around you. The people behind those businesses with which you have dealings every day are entrepreneurs — the pharmacist, the supermarket manager, the hawker selling vegetables, etc. And the truth is that very few of them will ever see their pictures on the front cover of the *Financial Mail*. From an economic development point of view it would of course be most stimulating to the economy if more people became self-employed — and if fewer businesses failed. But of course, no one goes into business to stimulate the economy and provide people with jobs. A person goes into business for maximum personal gain — in terms of money and pride. Thus, individuals are pulled towards entrepreneurship by various powerful incentives, or rewards. The abovementioned two factors are probably the most important ones for people who decide to be 'their own bosses', for example, people like Billy J. (Red) McCombs of San Antonio whose objective is simply to make as much money as he can. Even as a boy, Red McCombs possessed an obvious entrepreneurial instinct, as noted by one writer's account:

This single-mindedness baffled and sometimes distressed his gentle, middle-class parents. 'When I was 11, I'd wash dishes in a café downtown from 4 p.m. until midnight and deliver newspapers at 5 a.m.', he recalls. 'My mother would get tears in her eyes. "You don't need to do this," she'd say, and of course she was right. My father was an auto mechanic and we never wanted for anything. But I wanted to make money'. ('Red McCombs; Making Money's Fun,' Forbes, Vol. 126 (September 15, 1980) p. 124)

Certainly the strongest force in achieving a bright future for small business is the unflinching spirit of the entrepreneur — the one who brings new firms into existance and provides leadership for them. Entrepreneurs are creative, talented individuals who provide the backbone for the small business system. They are the tough individuals who face business problems but who look beyond those problems to find solutions and success in economic endeavour. However, a characteristic common in entrepreneurs is that they 'self-elect' — the ability to inspire themselves as to initiate action. Nobody demands that they take the entrepreneurial course, and it is thus a difficult task to persuade people to go into business for themselves if they are not 'natural' entrepreneurs.

Some other myths about entrepreneurs that should also be dispelled are:[4]

1. The first great obstacle is the myth that entrepreneurs are larger-than-life characters — an innately special breed who form new businesses every 90 days and stay just one step ahead of the Receiver of Revenue.
2. Many people assume that only the gifted and aggressive can become entrepreneurs.
3. The third myth is that entrepreneurs are money-hungry sharks, out for a quick return. Venture-capitalists call such people 'promoters', and avoid them like the plague.

Larry Farrell, president of the Farrell Consulting Corporation of Princeton, thinks that the public, ever-fuelled by the popular press, sees the entrepreneur in a very different light from the truth. Business literature discusses the characteristics of the entrepreneur *ad infinitum*, exploring his every psychological and social trait. He is described as a risk-taker, driver, dreamer, deal-maker and over-achiever. Sometimes this can be dangerously misleading.[5]

The object of this book is not to call upon all people to become entrepreneurs, but to encourage those who feel they have the necessary entrepreneurial traits. Understandably, some are simply not suited to the task; some would not enjoy it; and others would not succeed. But to encourage would-be entrepreneurs, the myths must be destroyed. There is nothing new or mysterious about entrepreneurship and businessmen are not an unfathomable, risk-seeking breed far removed from you and me. Most are rather ordinary people. Farrell comments:[6]

'In reality, modern entrepreneurs are a fairly average lot. As a group, they are not smarter than the rest of us, they are not less honest than most of us, they are not neurotics and they haven't invented 21st-century products beyond the grasp of mortal man. Their pursuits range from starting a garbage collection service to baking bread.

Every shred of serious research indicates that entrepreneurs are cautious business people, driven by their products and their customers. Yes, cautious. Almost all of them became entrepreneurs because their environments went sour, and they perceived starting their own businesses as being less risky than starving, or than fighting bureaucratic politics for another 20 years. A lesson learned from B.F. Skinner and Company is that human beings are very adaptive in acting in their own self-interest. The irrefutable rule of human behaviour is that people behave in ways they believe will result in positive consequences to themselves, and they avoid behaviour that results in negative consequences to themselves.

Entrepreneurs, like all other human beings, are motivated by their perception of the likely consequences of their action. Entrepreneurs, like the bygone craftsmen who made and sold their own goods, exist on the most basic level of enterprise, where customers obviously are the only means of survival.'

Professor Oliver Galbraith III, of San Diego State University, California, puts the case in this way:[7]

'The person who wouldn't think of starting a business, might call you a plunger, a gambler, a high risk taker. Yet you probably don't feel that about yourself. Studies have shown that very often the small business owner doesn't differ from anyone else in risk avoidance or aversion when measured on tests. At first thought this seems unreasonable since logic tells us that it is risky to open your own business. An Ohio State Professor once explained this apparent contradiction very simply; "When a person starts and manages his own business he doesn't see the risks, he sees only factors that he can control to his advantage." '

David C. McClelland[8] discovered in his studies where he questioned the extent to which entrepreneurial risk-taking propensities differ from those of managers and the general population, that individuals with a high need for achievement also have moderate risk-taking propensities. This means that they prefer risky situations in which they can exert some control on the outcome in contrast to gambling situations in which the outcome depends on pure luck. This preference for moderate risk reflects self-confidence.

What are your motives for going into business? Are you searching for an alternative that offers independence and satisfaction, or just money? Are you perhaps frustrated or unfulfilled in your present job? Perhaps you envy someone who is successful in business and wish to do as he did. Perhaps, like many others, you seek a self-determined life-style, personal achievement, status and recognition, and enjoyable and meaningful work. Freedom to operate

5

independently is certainly another basic reward of entrepreneurship. Many of us have a strong, even fierce, desire to make our own decisions, take risks, and reap the rewards for ourselves. Being one's own boss seems an attractive ideal. And those who are in business for themselves have, to a considerable extent, realized this ideal. One example of an individual who was drawn to entrepreneurship more by the reward of independence than any other incentive is Richard Blasco. He left corporate employment in 1980 at the age of 33 to become an independent consultant in the electronics industry. Although he expected to earn less money — at least initially — than he would earn as a salaried employee, he valued the independence of entrepreneurship when he stated:[9]

'Being independent is what I have always wanted, and I am prepared to tighten my belt for a while in order to make it. If I'm still in business a year from now, I will consider myself a success. And after that, I intend to see things get better and better.'

Of course, independence does not guarantee an easy life. Most entrepreneurs work very hard for long hours. But they do have the satisfaction of making their own decisions within the constraints imposed by economic and other environmental factors.

Whatever your motives for going into business for yourself, it stands to reason that you want to achieve something. If you think that you are wasting your time and energy building a career in a field you don't enjoy or will not enjoy in the future, entering a business for yourself could be justified if you can find an opportunity which will exercise all your abilities, skills, knowledge and energy to their fullest. Kenneth J. Albert says the following about choosing the right business:[10]

'... Most importantly, picking the right business means first of all choosing an opportunity that suits your capabilities, and that provides an enjoyable, challenging, and fulfilling environment. Then the work will seem like fun and will lead to success because if you enjoy and find fulfilment in your work, you are much more likely to do an outstanding job. And if you do an outstanding job, you are much more likely to succeed. And success means money and much more.'

If you like new challenges, are not afraid of hard work or of making decisions, and are willing to accept responsibility for the consequences of your actions, business is for you. Hard work does not necessarily mean physical labour, it means that you will have to devise a set of attainable objectives, draw up plans to achieve them, and then work towards your goals. Mark H. McCormack puts this into perspective:[11]

'Most successful entrepreneurs spend twenty-four hours a day either working or thinking about their businesses. But it is how they fill those hours that makes the difference between success and failure. The cliché is: Don't work hard, work smart. The truth is: Work hard, work long, and work smart.'

Managing a small business suits the personalities, characteristics and independent attitude of many, but obviously an owner is just a little more willing to take a chance in order to achieve full benefit. With a little bit of capital and a lot of courage, such a person will find the sense of achievement and independence managing a business can bring.

It must be borne in mind, however, that starting a business is a financial as well as a professional commitment. If you are thinking of starting a business as a stop-gap until you have found another job, or with some other short-term goal, don't start at all. Rather start the business with the attitude to manage for the consistency of the business as you want it to provide you with security comparable to employment, and even better. But to manage for its consistency, you have to behave consistently. That is: to firstly become brilliant on the basic sound business principles and then put them to practice through consistent, particular behaviour demanded for success. It is these basic business principles that form the basis for all decisions to be made, and adhering to them will help you make your 'courage pay off' in the long run.

Being committed is crucial, even when failure seems to be close. An investment consultant, Arnold van den Bergh, has watched many businesses go under, and he says: 'Just when things seem the most difficult, just when you begin to wonder what you are doing in business, it will all turn around.' Never give up. Think positively. Negative thinking never did anyone any good.

In the highly competitive world of business today, poor judgement, lack of attention to detail, and other incompetencies can easily cause failure. The trouble usually lies in the fact that the new owner-manager is not fully prepared, and is not able to apply the principles and methods of business operation which for years have spelt success. Those who plan to start a service business, for example, such as pharmacists or plumbers, will usually be applying professional knowledge acquired through education and study in formal training courses. However, the acquisition of sound business skills is not often a feature of their professional training. This is true in numerous other fields, e.g. hairdressing, building, managing a consultancy and so on. Without this business background people are quite unprepared for self-employment. The remedy can lie in taking courses in basic management skills before you enter the business world. The key word in business is 'preparation'.

You must also bear in mind the disadvantages of owning a business. There is a great risk of failure, and with it loss of money, business reputation and prestige. You have a responsibility towards employees, customers, your family, lenders and creditors. Therefore, apply sound managerial principles and narrow the odds of suffering such a set-back.

Furthermore, risk is also related to the impact of economic conditions and competitive pressures. In addition: income is often small in the beginning; there are longer hours and perhaps more worries; you may lose some immediate perks, a steady routine and regular holidays; and you may also lose the security of a regular income. However, most of these things will affect you only in the early stages.

PERSONAL QUALITIES OF THE SUCCESSFUL ENTREPRENEUR

A number of studies have been made of small business managers in an attempt to identify the common characteristics in those who start their own businesses and in those who manage businesses successfully. Psychologists at Western Reserve University, using tests, questionnaires and in-depth interviews studied the managers of several successful small businesses and prepared this report:[12]

'1. The successful small businessman is a moderate risk-taker, not a gambler. He is an adventurer, but with a combination of daring and caution. His motivation for independence of action is stronger than his need for security. He shows an exceptional willingness to make more than ordinary effort to achieve. Financial gain is not his driving power.

His risk-taking is not for the sake of "the fast buck". His desire for acquisition is not as high as his passion for achievement. It is a deeper, more elemental, creative urge to leave his mark on something he alone brought from an idea to reality. His satisfaction is not in plaudits or rewards. He finds it in accomplishment. To achieve, he will lay security on the line.

2. The successful small businessman is decisive. He expects and covets the part of decision maker. Most of the chief executive officers tested and interviewed kept a tight grip on the reins of all phases of management, though not by any means in a tyrannical way. His sense of responsibility for the business is so overpowering he feels that important decisions of policy and day-to-day operations should be made by him or referred to him for discussion. Curiously enough, though the popular concept of an efficient executive is a willingness to delegate authority, little resentment was found among subordinates interviewed. This is probably because in a small, closely-knit operation teamwork is not a slogan on a poster, but a natural outgrowth of limited size. Thus subordinates, thrown into daily close contact with the "boss" on a multiplicity of problems, feel a sense of participation in the exercise of authority. The point is, however, that the man who runs a successful small firm is not a vacillator or a "referrer to committee". He faces problems as they come, is not afraid to make decisions, in fact, prefers to do so. After all, his first decision — to risk security for independence — is indicative of the kind of man who expects to make the decisions.

3. The successful small businessman is versatile. In business matters, rather than being confined in his scope of activities to one area of the business, he constantly strives to become competent in all areas. In many instances if his background had been in sales, marketing, production or engineering, he took courses in other phases of business operation if he felt he lacked adequate knowledge. Unless a man is interested in not only the planning function, but also the business details, the technical aspects of marketing and production, and is genuinely concerned for the quality of his product or service, leading to the reputation of his firm, he might think twice before launching his own venture, for he is not typical of successful small businessmen who were studied. Studies of causes of failure consistently point to three things: inadequate capital, poor accounting, and lack of know-how.

4. The successful small businessman is a "finisher". Many people start a project with wild enthusiasm, high hopes and banners waving. To a man, the group studied had not only strong motives to achieve, but equally strong motives to endure, to finish the task at hand. When this is accompanied by a need to dominate, things get done. We were often told by the subordinates of these men, whom we interviewed to

get their appraisal of their chief, "if we're in a bind on a job the boss rolls up his sleeves and slugs it out right with us, evenings, Sundays, holidays if necessary, until the job is complete".

5. The successful small businessman is self-confident. Rated on fifteen psychological needs the executive scored lowest on "abasement" (admitting error or defeat) and "deference" (following suggestions or instructions from others). This indicated a person with a strong belief in his own capabilities, with unpleasantly aggressive tendencies. Yet our table showed that "aggression" (or hostility) scored thirteenth, just above "abasement" and "deference". Thus a mature belief in one's self is a requisite to head up a small business operation successfully, but it must not be teamed with an overbearing or hostile manner.

6. The successful small businessman is a benevolent despot. The chief executive officers who were studied viewed themselves as versatile, energetic workers whose primary concern was the success and continuity of the business. Giving freely of his time and energy, the small business owner-manager expects subordinates to do likewise. His subordinates view him as generally friendly, willing to listen to suggestions but not always accepting them, not insisting on standard ways of doing things or over-concerned with the details of their work, not expecting rigid conformity. His expectations are for productivity and competence; he is flexible as to the method of doing a job. He is more interested in getting it done and done right.'

Another study was carried out by Dr. H. B. Pickle of Southwest Texas State University. He identified five significant characteristics:[13]

1. 'Drive: composed of responsibility, vigor, initiative, persistence and health.

2. Thinking ability: comprised of original (creative) and critical (analytical) thinking.

3. Human relation ability: competency in human relations means emotional stability, sociability, good personal relations, consideration, cheerfulness, cooperation, tactfulness and cautiousness.

4. Communications ability: verbal comprehension and oral and written communications.

5. Technical knowledge: comprehension of the physical process of producing goods or services (selling, marketing, accounting, financing, purchasing, etc.)'

The most outstanding characteristic of the successful entrepreneur is his urge to achieve. To do this he sets himself high, but realistic and attainable goals, and conducts himself and manages the business in a way that will achieve these objectives. Thus, he is motivated by his desire to achieve, rather than by fear of failure.

If there is one word which is missing from the successful businessman's vocabulary, it is 'failure'. Two Americans, Warren Bennis and Burt Nanus, interviewed successful leaders in business and other spheres and found euphemisms, such as 'mistake', 'setback', 'error' and countless others, but never 'failure'. If you worry too much about failing, you place obstacles in the way of clear thinking. This point is illustrated by Bennis and Nanus in their book *Leaders: Strategies for Taking Charge:*[14]

'Shortly after Wallenda fell to his death in 1978 (traversing a 75-foot high wire in downtown San Juan, Puerto Rico), his wife, also an aerialist, discussed that fateful San Juan walk, "perhaps his most dangerous". She recalled: "All Karl thought about for three straight months prior to it was falling. It was the first time he'd ever thought about that and it seemed to me that he put all his energies into not falling rather than walking the tightrope." Mrs Wallenda added that her husband even went so far as to personally supervise the installation of the tightrope, making certain that the guy wires were secure, "something he had never even thought of doing before".'

What's the point? The point is that when Karl Wallenda poured his energies into not falling rather than walking the tightrope, he was virtually destined to fail. His perception of the outcome of the event made him fail because he seriously doubted that he could do what was required. Or he may have been assured of his competencies but gave up trying because he expected his effort to produce no result whatsoever. He thought failure, not success. He was not incompetent, he lacked self-confidence.

Acting confidently is vitally important in the business world, in order that you may secure financial backing, credit, selling of your products and/or services, and the loyalty of your employees. Numerous studies done brought to light that individuals who possess self-confidence feel that they can meet the challenge which confront them. They have a sense of mastery over the types of problems that they might encounter. These studies have shown that successful entrepreneurs tend to be self-reliant individuals who see the problems in launching a new venture but believe in their own ability to overcome these problems.

Now that you are aware of some of the qualities which make a good entrepreneur, you can begin to prepare yourself for going into business. Try to absorb as much information about starting out as possible, by reading, attending courses, listening to experts and talking to other businessmen. In addition, get as much managerial experience as you can, and study the modern principles and practices presented in this book.

Self-analysis is important Below are 21 of the original 140 test statements used in the Western Reserve Study for the appraisal of chief executives of small businesses. If the statement is only rarely or slightly descriptive of your behaviour, score 1. If it is applicable under some circumstances, but is only partially true, score 2. If it describes you perfectly, score 3.

' 1. I relish competing with others. ....   _____
  2. I compete intensely to win regardless of the rewards. ......   _____
  3. I compete with some caution, but will often "bluff." .....   _____
  4. I do not hesitate to take a calculated risk for future gain. ....   _____
  5. I do a job so effectively that I get a definite feeling of accomplishment. ....   _____
  6. I want to be "tops" in whatever I elect to do. ....   _____
  7. I am not bound by tradition. ....   _____
  8. I am inclined to forge ahead and discuss later. ....   _____
  9. Reward or praise means less to me than a job well done. ....   _____
 10. I usually go my own way regardless of others' opinions. ....   _____
 11. I find it difficult to admit error or defeat. ....   _____
 12. I am a self-starter — I need little urging from others. ....   _____
 13. I am not easily discouraged. ....   _____
 14. I work out my own answers to problems. ....   _____
 15. I am inquisitive. ....   _____
 16. I am not patient with interference from others. ....   _____
 17. I have an aversion to taking orders from others. ....   _____
 18. I can take criticism without hurt feelings. ....   _____
 19. I insist on seeing a job through to the finish. ....   _____
 20. I expect associates to work as hard as I do. ....   _____
 21. I read to improve my knowledge in all business activities. ....   _____
       TOTAL ....   _____ '

A score of 63 is 'perfect'; 52 – 62 is 'good'; 42 – 51 is 'fair'; and under 42 is 'poor'.

A high score should encourage you to pursue the matter further. You stand a good chance of success — if you have been honest with yourself. To make sure that you have been objective in your self-analysis, have your spouse or a good friend check your answers. Another worksheet, from *Management Aids No. 2016* U.S. Small Business Administration, may be helpful:

'Are you a self-starter?

☐ I do things on my own. Nobody has to tell me to get going.

☐ If someone gets me started, I keep going all right.

☐ Easy does it. I don't put myself out until I have to.

How do you feel about other people?

☐ I like people. I can get along with just about anybody.

☐ I have plenty of friends — I don't need anyone else.

☐ Most people irritate me.

Can you lead others?

☐ I can get most people to go along when I start something.

☐ I can give the orders if someone tells me what we should do.

☐ I let someone else get things moving. Then I go along if I feel like it.

Can you take responsibility?

☐ I like to take charge of things and see them through.

☐ I'll take over if I have to, but I'd rather let someone else be responsible.

☐ There's always some eager beaver wanting to show how smart he is. I say let him.

How good an organizer are you?

☐ I like to have a plan before I start. I'm usually the one to get things lined up when the group wants to do something.

☐ I do all right unless things get too confused. Then I quit.

☐ You get all set and then something comes along and presents too many problems. So I just take things as they come.

How good a worker are you?

☐ I can keep going as long as I need to. I don't mind working hard for something I want.

☐ I'll work hard for a while, but when I've had enough, that's it.

☐ I can't see that hard work gets you anywhere.

Can you make decisions?

☐ I can make up my mind in a hurry if I have to. It usually turns out O.K., too.

☐ I can if I have plenty of time. If I have to make up my mind fast, I think later I should have decided the other way.

☐ I don't like to be the one who has to decide things.

Can people trust what you say?

☐ You bet they can. I don't say things I don't mean.

☐ I try to be on the level most of the time, but sometimes I just say what's easiest.

☐ Why bother if the other fellow doesn't know the difference?

Can you stick with it?

☐ If I make up my mind to do something, I don't let anything stop me.

☐ I usually finish what I start — if it goes well.

☐ If it doesn't go right away, I quit. Why beat your brains out?

How good is your health?

☐ I never run down!

☐ I have enough energy for most things I want to do.

☐ I run out of energy sooner than most of my friends seem to.

Now count the checks you made.

How many checks are there beside the first

answer to each question?   _____

How many checks are there beside the second
answer to each question? _____
How many checks are there beside the third
answer to each question? _____

If most of your checks are beside the first answers, you
probably have what it takes to run a business. If not, you're
likely to have more trouble than you can handle by yourself.
Better find a partner who is strong on the points you're weak
on. If many checks are beside the third answer, not even a
good partner will be able to shore you up.'

ASSESSING YOUR INVESTMENT CAPABILITIES

Do you know how much money you will need to get your
business started? Have you counted up the amount of money
you can put into it yourself? These are important questions,
as the amounts of money needed to start various different
sorts of businesses differ greatly. Some businesses have been
started with as little as R1 000, but others may need as much
as R50 000 or more. The simplest way to assess how much of
a financial commitment you can make is to calculate your
net worth. Below is a table to assist you:

Assets		Liabilities	
Cash on hand and in bank	____	Property mortgages	____
Amounts due to me	____	Other debts	____
Properties owned	____		
Motor vehicles	____		
Cash surrender value of life insurance	____		
Fixed investments	____		
Savings	____		
Other assets	====		====
Total assets	____	Total liabilities	____

Net worth calculation	
Total assets	____
Less: Total liabilities	____
Net worth	====

You may find after doing this calculation that your net worth is not as large as you would like it to be. Furthermore, you probably cannot invest all of it in a new business. You need a contingency fund for your family. Most advisers recommend the equivalent of one year's net income, but you could of course reduce this if your family had some other income, for instance if your spouse is employed.

Take some steps to improve your investment potential. The most logical and sensible thing to do is to set up a formal savings plan. By cutting down on some of your expenses, you may be able to save up to 15% more of your net income. Another source of income is life insurance policies. You can eventually borrow against their cash values.

WHAT IS A BUSINESS?

A business can be defined as the transformation of an idea into a saleable product or service to provide benefit (to both consumer and owner), and to generate profit (to ensure its continued existence), using some or all of the following: men (manpower), money (capital), materials (stock), machines (equipment, tools), methods (ways of conducting the business), and a market (customers). These are better known as the 6 m's of business.

It should be borne in mind that no business starts on its own. It always requires initiative on the part of someone, and if the idea is not saleable and if the profit does not benefit the consumer and owner, then it is a waste of time. Furthermore, ideas are useless; they need to be put into practice. Ideas have been called 'funny little things that don't work unless you do'. Probably the very point this person tried to make was that the proof of an idea's value is in its implementation. Peter Drucker stresses this:[15]

'Opportunity is where you find it; says an old proverb. It does not say: ... where it finds you.'

The point is that people would rather fantasize about it than actually try to make it happen. It is thus a case of 'It is easier said than done'. A question to then seriously consider, if you have a strong urge to enter business for yourself is: are you a dreamer or a doer? Have you ever seen a new business going like a house on fire and thought to yourself: I had that idea myself; or, why didn't I think of that? This ability to see a need and how to fill it, is the beginning of a small idea, which in time, can grow into a prosperous enterprise. And unfilled needs there will always be. There will always be some aspect or a combination of aspects to improve or to be improved. Room for any improvement will never cease and the entrepreneur can make a major contribution to the lives of people. Dreams are dreams, but actions are better than dreams. The best way to make your dreams come true is to wake up — even if you have a sound business idea, you may get beaten by someone else implementing your idea while you are still asleep. However, the matter of importance is to firstly discover a genuine business opportunity which means a need for your proposed product(s) or service(s) in sufficient volume and at a high enough price to operate at a profit.[16] This is a vital factor, as you don't want to put up a sign after a few months in business — 'Opened by mistake'.

In South Africa everyone has the opportunity of going into business. So why not try it? The worst that can happen is that you fail, but what better way is there to learn than through your mistakes? When Bennis and Nanus studied the qualities of successful leaders, one of the conclusions they came to was that these leaders never mentioned charisma, dressing for success, time management, or any of the other glib formulas that pass for wisdom in the popular press. Instead they talked about persistence and self-knowledge, about willingness to take risks and accept losses, about commitment, consistency and challenge. Above all they talked about learning. The authors sum up:[17]

'Learning is the essential fuel for the leader, the source of high-octane energy that keeps up the momentum by continually sparking new understanding, new ideas, and new challenges. It is absolutely indispensable under today's conditions of rapid change and complexity. Very simply, those who do not learn do not long survive as leaders.'

The problem is often that those who have failed are unwilling to face the reasons for their failure. This is usually the result of their own shortcomings or the fact that knowledge was applied incorrectly in the business. For a lot of people the word 'failure' means the end of things, while for the successful leader it means a new beginning.

Bennis and Nanus also illustrate this with an example:[18]

'... Ray Meyer — perhaps the winningest coach in college basketball, who led DePaul University to forty-two consecutive years of winning seasons. When his team dropped its first game after twenty-nine straight home court victories, we called to see how he felt about it. His response was: "Great! Now we can start concentrating on winning, not on losing." '

That is what is meant by positive thinking — throwing all your energies into 'believing you can do it'. Your mind and thoughts should not wander, and that takes discipline.

All businessmen start with the same expectations — acquiring a decent income in a satisfying manner. They have the 6 Ms to work with and it is their task to make sure that they are all available in balanced quantities, to devise a programme of action to achieve goals and to execute controls that will keep the business running comfortably. These three functions of an owner-manager are also the three overall requirements of being in business. And money is the scoring system by which you measured how successfully you are performing these tasks.

Never lose sight of the fact that any business is in the 'business' of anticipating and satisfying the wants and needs of people. And, should you be deficient in this respect, your business will cease as an economic institution contributing to the welfare of society. You must control your business in a way which keeps it economically viable. 'In every action you take and in every decision you make, you must put economic performance first.'[19] You must ask yourself before taking action on any issue: how does the customer benefit; do I benefit; and does the business benefit? You must satisfy the needs of your market effectively, economically and profitably, otherwise your business will fail. 'It has failed if it does not supply goods and services desired by the consumer at the price and quality the consumer is willing to pay for. You have failed if you don't improve, or at least maintain the economic resources (capital invested) entrusted to your business.'[20]

Being in business means more than having the title of entrepreneur. Being in business is not a position, it is a function. It also means being accountable for the capital invested in it and being held repsonsible for its progress. Thus your basic goal is to take care of the money — your own and that borrowed — invested in the business and to utilize it as profitable as possible.

OBJECTIVES OF BUSINESS

The objectives of a business are the ends towards which all the activities of the business are aimed. They are supposed to be the focal points of all your decisions for economic performance. The three objectives are:

The service objective The overall objective of your business must be to perform a useful service for society by selling goods or services to the public at a fair price and adequate profit to you. Peter F. Drucker puts it this way:[21]

'If we want to know what a business is we have to start with its purpose. And its purpose must lie outside of the business itself. In fact, it must lie in society since a business enterprise is an organ of society. There is only one valid definition of business purpose: to create a customer.'

An investment consultant, Arnold van den Bergh, looks at the service objective like this:[22]

'If you are in business strictly to make money, and you do not want to help people, business is not for you. Forget the money and remember the service. With that philosophy, the money comes automatically.'

Good service can give your business that extra edge over your competitors. It uncovers and satisfies your customers' constantly changing needs. In order to monitor these needs, close contact is essential. If you satisfy needs, you will earn a reputation of dependability and quality performance which pays off handsomely. So, 'stay close' to your customers as a great deal of business success rests on something called a sale.

The profit objective The generation of profits is a legitimate reward for taking the risks involved in setting up a business. Profits are not, however, self-generating and become a reality only if your business satisfies the demand for a certain product or service.

Profit is determined by three factors: costs, selling prices and sales volume, and they are all interrelated (see pages 222 – 231 for an illustration of this phenomenon). In order to expand your business or equip it in a more advanced fashion, you need to make more money than you are paying out. Of course, you could borrow extra money, but if you are not making a profit it gets harder and harder to borrow for things you and your business may need.

Because income minus expenses equals profit, you need to raise the income or lower the expenses, or both, to increase the profit of the business. To do this, you must watch every aspect of the business. Be on the alert in all areas, take note of the employees' attitudes, their work habits, your stock (both on the shelves and in the storeroom), customers' acceptance of your products and/or services and prices, etc. Learn to observe and measure every activity and how it will affect profit. Profit must be planned for, not hoped for. 'When you fail to plan ... you plan to fail.'[23]

How much profit?

When a businessman says he is going to make all the profits he can ... how much is that? Some reasons why businesses are not more profitable are: businessmen do not determine how much profit to make; they fail to set a profit goal; they never plan how much profit is needed; or they develop a plan but cannot apply it effectively.[24]

Peter Drucker has the following to say about profit:[25]

'It is the first duty of the business to survive. The guiding principle of business economics, in other words, is not the maximization of profits; it is the avoidance of loss. Business enterprise must produce the premium to cover the risks inevitably involved in its own operation. And there is only one source for this risk premium: profits. It is the "risk premium" that covers the costs of staying in business — replacement, obsolescence, market risk and uncertainty. Seen from this point of view, there is no such thing as "profit"; there are only "costs of being in business" and "costs of staying in business". And the task of a business is to provide adequately for these "costs of staying in business" by earning an adequate profit — which not enough businesses do.

Profit serves three purposes. It measures the net effectiveness and the soundness of a business's efforts (and is the ultimate test of business performance); it is the "risk premium" that covers the costs of staying in business, and it ensures the supply of future capital for innovation and expansion (either directly, by providing the means of self-financing out of retained earnings; or indirectly, through providing sufficient inducement for new outside capital in the form in which it is best suited to the enterprise's objectives).

To summarize, whether it is the motive of the businessman to maximize profits is debatable. But it is an absolute necessity for the business to produce at the very least the profit required to cover its own risks, the profit required to enable it to stay in business and to maintain intact the wealth-producing capacity of its resources. This "required minimum profit" affects business behaviour and business decisions — both by setting rigid limits to them and by testing their validity. Management, in order to manage needs a profit objective at least equal to the required minimum profit, and yardsticks to measure its profit performance against this requirement.'

The most important thing, however, is to have a set target. Your profit goal should not be a 'pie in the sky' figure, but a carefully calculated target which is achievable through efficient operations.[26]

To make your business venture worthwhile, it is essential that you should make a greater return on your investment than the yearly inflation rate, and higher than you would if you had invested the money elsewhere. The return should be enough to be an incentive. (For a full discussion of the return on investment ratios, see chapter 15, p. 400; and for their application, see the chapter on 'Profit planning and budgeting')

The growth You should set a growth objective for your business as early
objective as possible. Some of the questions you need to ask yourself are:[27]

'1. Do I seek relative stability or merely survival?
2. Do I seek a rate of profit which is "satisfactory" considering my efforts and investments?
3. Do I seek to maximize profits?
4. Will I be satisfied to remain small?
5. Do I want to grow and challenge larger shops?'

The element of growth alone does not ensure success, but it is a necessary ingredient. Consider growth as a factor in the quest for longevity and profitability. Many consultants believe that small businessmen often do not achieve real success because they fail to see the opportunities for growth. Some business analysts have gone as far as saying that a business must either grow or die. There may be some danger in this statement in the sense that owner-managers tend to prize growth for growth's sake without evaluating its impact on the profits of the business. Any growth can strain a business's capital position and damage current operations. It can also spread managerial skills too thinly. The point is that all growth opportunities should be scrutinized carefully. But below are some reasons why you should become growth-oriented:

'If the economy as a whole is progressing and your business is in a relatively stable position, you will find it increasingly difficult to maintain the same level of profits, year after year. Inflation, you see, accounts for a significant part of our economic "growth" in a country each year. Thus your operating expenses are likely to be increasing, due to cost increases and salary hikes, even though your sales may continue at the same level.

Even if you manage to obtain sales increases of 2 or 3 percent per year, your profits may still decline if other companies in the industry are achieving sales gains of 6, 8, or 10 percent. In addition, more intense competition can make sales harder to come by, thereby forcing your selling and promotional expenses upward.

And even if you are able to increase your net income from the business each year, unless the rate of increase is higher than the general rise in the cost of living, your "purchasing power" income will actually have declined.'

SUMMARY AND CONCLUSIONS

Many people think about getting into business for themselves but are waiting for the right opportunity to come along. Others become so well-established in careers that they tend to get 'locked into' salaried employment. They achieve promotion to positions of greater responsibility and higher salaries. Others again look back over their careers as salaried personnel, thinking of 'what might have been' if only they had gone into business for themselves, but recognize that is now too late.

Business decisions are not easy, and the most difficult of them all is whether to embark on owning your own business in the first place. Prepare yourself for making this decision by finding out what you will be letting yourself in for, and doing some objective personal analysis. Do not let your judgement be clouded by dreams of success or by fears of failure. Listen to suggestions from your banker and other outsiders, and then consider the future calmly and coolly.

Even when biographies of entrepreneurs are 'blown up' in business magazines, they still are proof of the stunning successes achieved by normal people and provides readers with dramatic examples of the unlimited opportunities available in this country. These entrepreneurs frequently speak of the personal satisfaction they experience in their own businesses. Some even refer to business as 'fun'. Part of this enjoyment may derive from the independence described, whilst some of it come also from the peculiar nature of the business, the entrepreneur's role in the business, and the entrepreneur's opportunity to be of service.

NOTES

[1] Thomas J. Peters, Robert H. Waterman Jr. *In Search of Excellence.* 1982. Harper & Row, New York: 15.

[2] A business can generally be deemed small when it is privately owned; independently managed; with an annual turnover of not more than R3 million; with total assets not exceeding R500 000 (excluding land and buildings but including capital goods acquired on lease agreements); and employing not more than 100 people on a full-time basis. (Prof. J. Smith, Director, Small Business Advisory Bureau, Potchefstroom University of C.H.E. *Entrepreneur* 1982; 1(2): 7.

[3] Mark H. McCormack. *What They Don't Teach You at Harvard Business School.* 1984. Collins, London: 235.

[4] Larry Farrell. Building entrepreneurship: a global perspective. *Training, the Magazine of Human Resources Development* 1986; July: 49. (Reprinted with permission.)

[5] Idem, 46.

[6] Idem, 49-50.

[7] O. Wendell, O. Metcalf. Starting and managing a small business of your own. *Starting and Managing Series,* Vol. 1. 1982. Small Business Administration, Washington, D.C.: 3-4.

[8] David C. McClelland, "Achievement Motivation Can Be Developed," Harvard Business Review, Vo. 43, No. 6 (November–December, 1965), pp. 6-24ff.

[9] 'Free-Lance Engineers,' Venture, Vol. 2, No. 12 (December, 1980) p. 46.

[10] Kenneth J. Albert. *How to Pick the Right Small Business Opportunity.* 1977. McGraw-Hill, New York.

[11] Mark H. McCormack. *What They Don't Teach You at Harvard Business School.* 1984. Collins, London: 244.

[12] Baumback, Lawyer. *How to Organize and Operate a Small Business.* 1979. Prentice-Hall, Englewood Cliffs, NJ: 56-57. (Reprinted with permission.)

[13] Idem, 57-58.

[14] Warren Bennis, Burt Nanus. *Leaders: The Strategies for Taking Charge.* 1985. Harper & Row, New York: 70, 77.

[15] Peter F. Drucker. *Managing for Results.* 1964. Pan, London: 175.

[16] Baumback, Lawyer. *How to Organize and Operate a Small Business.* 1979. Prentice-Hall, Englewood Cliffs, NJ: 37. (Reprinted with permission.)

[17] Warren Bennis, Burt Nanus, *Leaders, The Strategies for Taking Charge.* 1985. Harper & Row, New York: 188.

[18] Idem, 71.

[19] Peter F. Drucker. *The Practice of Management.* 1969. Heinemann, London: 7. (Reprinted by permission of William Heinemann Limited.)

[20] Idem, 35.

[21] Ron Tepper. *Become a Top Consultant.* 1985. John Wiley, Canada: 143.

[22] William H. Day. *Maximizing Small Business Profits.* 1978. Prentice-Hall, Englewood Cliffs, NJ: 121.

[23] Idem, 19.

[24] Peter F. Drucker. *The Practice of Management.* 1969. Heinemann, London: 44–45, 73–74. (Reprinted with permission of William Heinemann Limited.)

[25] William H. Day. *Maximizing Small Business Profits.* 1978. Prentice-Hall, Englewood Cliffs, NJ: 20.

[26] Curtis E. Tate Jr. *et al. Successful Small Business Management.* 1985. Business Publication, Plano, Texas: 10. (Reprinted with permission.)

[27] John V. Petrof, Peter S. Carusone, John E. McDavid. *Small Business Management: Concepts and Techniques for Improving Decisions.* 1972. McGraw-Hill, New York: 375. (Reprinted with permission.)

2 | ENTERING THE BUSINESS WORLD

'You have to discover what the people are short of, then commit yourself in making it your "business" to fill the shortage, obtain the required capital to exploit the opportunity and thus bring your business into existence.'

Frans Bekker

'If you are unsure of your income prospects, you are really not going into business, you are gambling — betting against the odds.'

J.K. Lasser Tax Institute[1]

'Whatever type of business opportunity is involved, it must be genuine. This means that the new business must have some type of advantage that will provide a competitive edge. The prospective entrepreneur must visualize some new product or service or location or 'angle' that will not only 'get the foot in the door' but keep it there.'[2]

Broom, Longenecker, Moore.

INTRODUCTION

In the preceding part we looked upon some challenges in starting your own business, certain business and personal objectives, and entrepreneurial characteristics that lead to success in owning and managing a small business. We now assume you are of the entrepreneurial type as well as having the will to succeed when taking on a business challenge. If so, the contents of this chapter will be of great value to you in planning and organizing your own business. In doing so you have two alternatives: establish a new business from scratch, or buy an already existing business.

There is no doubt that success in business rests a great deal on an opportunity which has a potential to generate profit. As already explained, a genuine business opportunity is based on a need for the proposed goods or services in sufficient volume, and a high enough mark-up on cost to allow you to generate a certain amount of profit. It means selecting the right business opportunity which implies making sure, before either starting from scratch or buying an established business, that you choose a viable and profitable concern. It also means that your choice must preferably fall on a business with growth potential so as to expand in the future.

When starting a new business or acquiring an established one, you may ask yourself: 'What type of business will suit me best?' Some people may think that a certain type of business is more profitable than others, and thus enter into that line of business. Many people envy another who made a success of a certain type of business and eventually they also venture into that kind of business operation. The fact that somebody made a success of one kind of business is no guarantee that you will also succeed, or will enjoy being in that particular type of business. Some experts agree that many a business fails because the owners went into the wrong type of business rather than 'did business wrong'. It is better to choose an opportunity that fits in with your capabilities and which will provide you with an enjoyable, challenging and personally fulfilling opportunity. One should therefore choose the kind of business in which you would be prepared to put all your very best efforts and talents. Only then will being in business be a pleasure, which will also enhance your chances to make a success thereof. The opposite is also true — if you don't like what you are doing, the chances of success are greatly reduced, because success is only to be found in making your will the will of your business. Therefore, select a business opportunity that will help to achieve your objectives, while also satisfying all your personal needs. Remember, too, no matter how happy you are with your choice of business, you will not make money (and profit) if your products or services are not needed by other people (your market).

This part will thus be devoted to the various aspects applicable to buying an established business or starting a new one from scratch. These aspects will include: a price to be paid for an established business; creative thinking in setting up a new business; assessing the market; drawing up of a business plan framework; selecting a location for the new business; how to approach a financial institution for borrowing the money; and sources of finance.

An important distinction must be made at this point between an idea and an opportnity. An idea is just what the word implies — an idea. It cannot yet make you any money. A business opportunity, on the other hand, can provide the basis for investment and so lead to a profitable business. This part therefore also deals with the question: Do you have a business idea that can be translated into a viable business opportunity?

CHOOSING THE RIGHT TYPE OF BUSINESS

Your decision in choosing a particular type of business involves making a commitment to yourself for the eventual establishment or acquisition of that type of business, whether it be in retailing, service, food, consulting or manufacturing. A few matters of concern are of course to know whether the current condition and outlook for your type of business is prosperous, whether you can develop it or have the attributes and capabilities that are required for success in that kind of venture, and whether the business will satisfy most of your important wants and desires.

The first step is to compile a list of types of businesses you are interested in. You have to evaluate this list in order to find out which business will meet your desires for the kind of work you really want to do, or are interested in, and the kind of life-style you are prepared to live. To get all these facts together plays an important role in the evaluation process. It means getting out and speak to people about it, as your mind will be filled with questions, and what you need is stimulation in order to get your thoughts organized. You could get a group of friends together and ask them what kind of product or services they need and whether their needs are being met adequately. If not, what would be necessary for their needs to be satisfied? It is a fact that there is always room for another business where the people (or market) are not being adequately served for various reasons, and to then put your effort into this business by providing a better service than those presently in operation.

Other sources of information are business owners, commercial banks, management consultants, estate agents, development corporations and existing or potential suppliers of the merchandise to that type of business. However, when you obtain advice and information from these people, bear in mind that it is your resources that are at stake when a commitment is to be made. You can't afford not to talk to people, especially to those who 'have been there'. This will help to avoid the costly error of choosing a business opportunity without enough objective thinking and reasoning. In other words, let your mind and not your emotions rule your decisions. Speak to people and find out as much as you possibly can before investing your money, time and energy. This exercise of speaking to others is of absolute necessity because, not only will you learn much from it, you might just also spot other opportunities to be exploited. Listen, ask and observe must be your 'keys' to the start of owning a profitable business, as many unsatisfied needs might be revealed in the process.

CHOOSING A SPECIFIC BUSINESS OPPORTUNITY

At this point there is little left to do but make a decision, as you have already determined what type of business you want to enter. The decision to be made boils down to choosing whether you will be entering an established business or conceiving, planning, organizing and operating a new business of your own. It is an important decision indeed. You must select the alternative that seems to provide the best opportunity of accomplishing success.

ENTERING AN ESTABLISHED BUSINESS

Buying a business can be a complicated transaction. The business's performance must be evaluated, a price must be determined and the deal should be closed in a legal and fair manner. It is of importance that you, as the prospective buyer, should study the business and the local conditions wherein it operates in order to make sure that certain factors, such as increased competition, rerouting of traffic, obsolete products and equipment, and problems with creditors and debtors, are not forcing the business into decline. In such a declining situation, even the best of management skills will not be sufficient to put the business back on the road to profits.

Your main concern should be of whether the business is doing well. Is it a profitable business? If not, why not? What is the problem? What is the cause of the problem? What can be done about it? Do you have the ability to do something about it? Many potential entrepreneurs reason that because the failure rate of new businesses is high, the next best thing is to buy a business already in operation and in doing so avoid many of the beginner's problems. However, the past success of an established business is not always enough to justify a decision whether or not to buy the business. You still need to make a thorough analysis of its present condition (an examination of its profitability) as well as its future potential. In other words: is the business profitable? If the answer is 'yes', then investigate how profitable.

A fact not to be overlooked is that there are far more 'dying' businesses for sale than profitable ones. When I asked a friend who is in business why he didn't sell it as he had family problems, and he was considering leaving to be closer to his family, he answered: 'One does not make money by selling a business, but you do make money by staying in business.' That confirms the particular uncertainty of whether your decision to buy will be a good or a bad one, and this has to be kept in mind as you study the business you wish to buy. You must make sure that you do not take on any more problems than necessary. Be thus always aware of the following when coming across an advertisement in the local newspaper where a business for sale is advertized;

BUSINESS FOR SALE!!!
AVERAGE TURNOVER OF R358 000,00!!!!

The seller may claim that the business's average annual sales over the five years was R358 000,00. Assume, for example, that two similar businesses are to be compared. Their annual sales for the past 5 years have been as follows;

Year	Business A	Business B
1	R 570 000	R 160 000
2	460 000	210 000
3	390 000	390 000
4	210 000	460 000
5	160 000	570 000
	R1 790 000	R1 790 000

Both businesses show the same average sales over the 5 years, namely, R358 000,00. But with the difference that business A has been declining and business B has been growing. Make sure you are not buying a Business A which is on its way down. If any analysis of the financial records indicates that the business is not profitable, as buyer, you should determine why and whether you are able to turn the operation around. If your management skills are not substantially better, chances for improvement may be slight unless an expanding population in the trading area, a growth trend in the industry, or some other outside market factor promises to improve the business.

The point is that the opportunity to buy a business already in operation always appear attractive when advertized in local newspapers. You think; perhaps it is a proven success, the typical start-up hazards can be avoided – the 'bugs' are out of it and it is apparently running nicely. You think; the business for sale is running like a new motorcar after the usual small adjustments have been made. Or is it, in fact, more like a used car? Most owners do not sell their cars until they feel it needs considerable mechanical attention.

The lesson is of course threefold; (1) If you are not 100% satisfied with the future prospects of the business, do not spend your money yet; and (2), appreciate the need for outside assistance (that of a reputable business advisor who is familiar with the methods of evaluating a business's potential) in evaluating the business for sale, and then be willing and able to take the time to profit by it; and (3), you should rely largely on past results of the business operation when it is evaluated. Do not take anything for granted.

One of your major tasks in the process of investigating the purchase of a business is to ascertain the owner's reasons for selling. Always be specific in your questioning, and ask the question 'why are you selling' many times. You may find that every time you ask, there is a different reason. Remember, you are searching for information that will allow you to form your own opinion, and all important facts you hear, must be taken notice of — critically at times. Sometimes, the seller may know of future developments you don't know of, such as a new road to be built which endangers the present business because of its present location. If poor health is brought up as a reason, it will be necessary, if possible, to verify this statement by consulting the doctor of the seller. Make sure that it is physical poor health and not economic poor health. Another reason people may put up a business for sale can be the desire to retire. As far as future competition from the seller is concerned, it may be wise to engage your lawyer to draw up an agreement stating that the seller will not conduct a similar business in the same area for a reasonable period of time.

When interviewing the owner of a business you are interested in, the secret lies in getting the seller to talk — you just listen. If you ask all you are talking to why he is selling, it might be that they will confirm the seller's reasons for selling or lead you to the real reason. However, you may not get an answer from everybody you ask, as some may not yet know that the business is for sale. Remember though, that for some it is not so easy to part with their businesses, while others would be only too happy to get rid of theirs as quickly as possible — at a minimum loss or maximum gain. And of course, you don't intend paying for his mistakes. If the seller is at fault and you know it, you could then bring it to his notice in order to negotiate and thus get the business for a better price.

Just about every day we make decisions that have a bearing on our lives and sometimes we have to live with the consequences of those decisions. Buying or starting up a new business is a serious decision because not only is there a great deal of money involved, but also your future and that of your family. You need to proceed cautiously as both parties want to secure full value in the transaction. Last but not least, you and your family will feel better if you have left no stone unturned in your preparation and in so doing, you must have the patience to learn all there is to know about the particular business you want to purchase.

ADVANTAGES AND DISADVANTAGES OF BUYING A BUSINESS

Advantages • There is reduced risk, as buying a business that is already successful is less risky than starting one from scratch. It

31

may already have an established and proven share of the market.

- The location could be good, and there might be doubt about the potential of other locations for a new business.
- A successful business could generate profit much faster than a new business. The established business can provide you with a reasonable income right from the start.
- It involves a single financial transaction, while a new business would involve many before being ready to sell the products.
- It would be easier to plan for the future, as past records provide a firm basis for projecting the future of a business. Strengths can be built on and weaknesses can be rectified.
- You could be inheriting already competent personnel.
- You could gain customers accustomed to trading with the established business.
- The 'goodwill' created by the previous owner may be a valuable asset.
- You may be able to buy the business at a bargain price.

Disadvantages
- You may inherit 'ill-will'. When you take ownership, 'ill-will' can get you off to a bad start.
- You might be inheriting the incompetencies of employees. Consider whether you are acquiring an asset of great worth or a liability. You need competent people to build a business.
- Old facilities and equipment may not be up to date and may be inadequate for your purpose, such as the image you wish to create.
- You may inherit 'dead' stock. The seller may be carrying 'dead' stock on his books at original value when in fact it may be worthless. If you don't make the effort to check it out, you might pay good money for worthless stock.
- You run the risk of overpaying for the business which will limit profits as more might be expended to recover.
- You may find an uncooperative lessor renting the premises. If major repairs won't be attended to, you may

32

have to spend unnecessary time and money in arguments to reach a satsifactory solution.

- The location may change to your disadvantage.

EVALUATING THE BUSINESS FOR SALE

An established business can be evaluated with reasonable accuracy. The first thing to do is pay a visit to the business in order to take a closer look — pretend you are a customer and observe how they treat you as well as others in the business. A more formal visit could be planned afterwards in order to discuss more serious matters concerning the purchase of the business. The purpose of your initial visit with the seller is to learn enough so that after the visit you will be able to make your first critical decision; in other words, to determine exactly what you are planning to let yourself in for. Purchasing a business is much more complicated than, for instance buying a car, as many different things are involved — equipment, vehicles, a building and people. You must find out how much it is worth and if you will be rewarded for taking the risk. It is also important to talk to people in order to know more about the overall operation of the business to be purchased. Below are some matters to. talk to people about:

Customers

- How many products they are buying and from whom.
- The reputation and reliability of the seller and competitors.
- Whether their support for the business is going to increase or decrease in the future.
- The prices asked by the seller and competitors. Are they fair?
- The quality of the products or services offered by the seller.
- How the services can be improved.
- What type of products are in need, and not supplied by the seller?
- The general attitude towards the business and employees.

Suppliers

- How promptly the seller pays accounts.
- Does the supplier have liens against the assets of the business? Is the business committed to any of the suppliers through contracts, and if so, for how long?
- How much and what the seller buys compared to competition.
- If the seller is fair and equitable in dealings.
- If the quantity purchased by the seller has increased or decreased.
- Why is the business for sale?
- If the seller keeps up with changes in the market.
- Whether there are special arrangements between supplier and seller.
- Will supplies continue and on what terms?

Competitors

- The overall size of the market.
- Who the market is and the type of customer supporting the business.
- Why is the business for sale?
- The reputation of the seller.
- Strengths and weaknesses of other competitors.
- Changes and likely changes of population in the market.
- Who are potential customers for this kind of business?
- Success rate of competing businesses.
- Unscrupulous competition — 'pirate' shops. How many are there?
- Is the market growing?

Financial Institution (Bank)

- How profitable is the business?
- Why is the business for sale?
- Reputation of seller.
- How many businesses have been there? What types? How successful were they? How long has this business been for sale?
- Potential of business.
- Would they consider assisting you financially in buying the business?

Once you have spoken to some people who in the past have had dealings with the business, you should examine its main financial documents closely. Also remember that not all financial statements are a true reflection of the business's past operations. There may be various reasons why the accounts were drawn up that way. They may, for instance, reflect poor performance such as bad management. If this is the case, you may be able to bargain with the seller for a better price, provided, however, that you are convinced that with your management, the situation will be improved.

Excellent financial statements should not tempt or persuade you too easily to pay too large an amount for the business. Your main task will be to verify the validity of the financial statements. Always insist on seeing accurate records reflecting the true financial situation. It has been found that some businesses keep more than one set of financial statements — one for the Receiver of Revenue, reflecting poor results so as to pay less tax; one for the bank, with excellent results so that they can borrow more money easily; an accurate one for the owner-manager, reflecting the true position; and sometimes yet another set of accounts to be used by the seller to persuade a prospective buyer to pay a price in excess of the business's real worth! You should reconsider buying the business if the seller refuses to disclose its true financial records.

In most cases a close study of the financial statements, bank records and other documents will enable you to establish whether the business you intend to acquire has rewarded its owner or not. Also consider whether this amount of income will provide a satisfactory living for you and your family, and if not, whether you could do something to improve the situation. The following questions should serve to remind you that you must seek both a return on your investment if the business is bought by you, as well as reasonable remuneration for the time you will have to spend in operating that particular type of business:

1. How much income do you want?
2. What minimum income will you require?
3. How much could you earn elsewhere, if you invested the money asked by the seller for the business?
4. What is the average return on investment for a business of the kind you wish to purchase?

5. How much could you earn by working for someone else?
6. Add the amounts in 3 and 5. If this total is more than what you can realistically expect in profit from the business, are you prepared to forego this additional income just to be your own boss, possibly with only remote prospects of more substantial income (profit) in future years?

The return on investment ratio is applied to answer the question of whether the net result of your findings compare favourably with the rate of income you can obtain from other investment opportunities.

To estimate future profits, you should begin by analysing the business's income statement. The seller can also be asked to hand over to you his projected cash flow statement for the present and forthcoming financial year (his budget), and those figures are then compared with the actual results obtained by him. The same exercise can be done for the previous three or four years. Close scrutinization of the business's past performance will give an indication whether sales have been going down or up. In both cases find out why.

In addition to return on investment you need to know the income and expenses of the business, so that you can compare the operating ratios with those of similar businesses in that particular trade. Operating ratios are expressed as percentages of net sales in relationship to the various types of expenses. For example, R90 000 in net sales equals 100% of sales income. Net profit after tax equals 4% of net sales. The industry average (or proven trade average) after tax might leave a net profit of 7% in a given year for a similar business with net sales of R90 000. You must then find out why there is a discrepancy of 3% in net profit after tax. Other differences should also be analysed to establish why this particular business is doing better or worse than its competitors. Below follows a simple illustration of how operating expense ratios are used in appraising the business:

A hardware shop for sale had average net sales of R160 000 per year for the previous three years. Analysis of the financial statements show the following operating expense ratios (expressed as a percentage of sales), for the previous three years.

	1980	1981	1982
Total expenses	26%	28%	32%
Salaries	16%	18%	20%
Rent	5%	5%	5%
Advertising	1%	1%	1%

However, the operating expense ratios for this kind and size of business for the years covered were as follows:

Total expenses	22%
Salaries	13%
Rent	3%
Advertising	1,5%

It is obvious that the rent is too high, as are personnel expenses. As the prospective new owner of the business you could negotiate more favourable terms with the lessor. You could furthermore bring the salary expense into line either by increasing the sales (higher productivity) or eventually by reducing the number of employees. You could also come to decide that advertising expenses remained pretty much the same — no significant increase over the three years. And you could give more attention to bring it into line with the standard ratio of the trade and so boost your sales — provided you know how to advertise.

Financial ratios are used to evaluate the economic health of a business and also to assist management with up-to-date performance information. When investigating the possibility of buying a business, other main concerns must also be to establish whether the business is still solvent and viable. By solvent is meant that the present value of the net assets of the business must exceed the net liabilities by a ratio of at least 2:1. If you are to take over the business's existing debts, you will have to check every outstanding amount in detail. Ask for proof of how every debt was incurred, inspect all legal documents, such as hire-purchase agreements, credit sales contracts, lease agreements (premises), etc. By doing this you can establish the business's total financial obligations, and determine whether there are any hidden liabilities. Sound advice is to get your accountant or a consultant to consult with the seller's accountant and attorney. All liabilities to be taken over by you should be specified in an agreement to purchase.

You should then check on the age analysis of debtors. Some businesses continue to carry debtor accounts that should already have been regarded as bad debts. Compare total debtor amounts outstanding over periods of 30, 60, 90, 120 or more days. This should give a good indication of the effectiveness of the existing management's credit policies, and also how successful the seller has been in collecting outstanding amounts. When checking the debtors position, you can at the same time assess the creditworthiness of the business's customers and its total sales volume. Large amounts of working capital can be tied up in outstanding debtors accounts. In some instances it has become standard practice not to take over debtor accounts that have been outstanding for longer than 60 days, which mean that the seller must keep on trying to collect the older amounts for his own benefit.

Arrange with the seller for proper stocktaking to establish the true value of all merchandise to be taken over. Compare stock on hand with that of competitors, especially in terms of quality, price and assortment. Stock on hand should also be examined for age, saleability, style, condition and freshness. Check on cost prices and mark-up methods by scrutinizing the supplier's invoices. No unsaleable stock should be taken over.

Inspect all equipment, fixtures and fittings, furniture and the premises from which trading is done. All equipment to be taken over should be checked for its usable value. Also establish whether you really want to take over all the equipment. Redundant equipment or equipment in bad condition should be deleted. Also check which equipment is fully paid for, and which not yet paid for, the respective amounts outstanding, and payment periods or terms of lease. If any renovations are to be done to premises, proper quotations must be obtained. Also determine whether maximum use is made of all space available.

The purchase price is not the only factor to be considered. You must also think about the additional capital requirements for the proper running of the business you wish to purchase. Sufficient cash reserves must be available to pay for renovations, new equipment, stock, opening day and other expenses. If additional capital will be needed to run the business profitably, such an amount should then be deducted from the calculated purchase price. The price for the business which gives you the highest return on investment with which you will be satisfied, is the maximum price you should offer the seller.

The intangibles The seller will most probably include goodwill in his price for the business. Goodwill normally includes such things as a favourable location, a good profit history, capable personnel, advantageous contracts with lessor and customers, etc. Goodwill can thus be described as an amount or value the seller is asking in excess of the tangible assets of the business resulting from the business's superior past and future capacity to provide profits. Care should be taken to determine whether the business has earned 'goodwill or ill-will'. Goodwill is created mostly by the attitude of the consumers. It is easier to ruin the reputation of a business than make a bad reputation good or build up and maintain a good reputation. Buying an established business may also include a valuable public acceptance attitude towards the business. The attitude of various other parties is also impor-tant, such as employees, suppliers, the lessor, banks, etc. Establish whether the business is selling an asset or a liability. You can find out by talking to people with whom you will have dealings in the future or with those the seller dealt with before. In short, goodwill can be thought of as the difference between an established successful business and one that has yet to establish itself and achieve success.

A point that does need attention under this heading is the question of trading rights. Trading rights are contained in a document issued by the governments of the national states and they confer a 'right to trade'. The issuing of these documents are only applicable to businesses in the self-governing national states. The lack of proper understanding about this matter has in the past caused considerable confu-sion as people consider it their right to ask ridiculous amounts for those rights when they sell their businesses.

Trading rights are not goodwill and the truth is that they can only be sold at the price which the seller paid for them, if any.

HOW MUCH TO PAY FOR THE BUSINESS

As mentioned earlier in this part, you as buyer want to pay as little as possible for the business of your choice, and you have already calculated the price. What you are not yet sure of is the fair market price and specifically, what amount you can offer the seller. When you are purchasing a business, you are in effect acquiring a combination of productive things. Before making an offer to purchase such a combination, you must arrive at a realistic assessment of the aggregate worth of the assets of the business to establish whether you are buying a bargain or not. Normally, the price will be based on the fair market value[3] of the assets of the business plus an amount set for the goodwill. In calculating the purchase price of a business, two valuations are normally used: valuation of the business's expected future earnings and the asset appraisal method.

Valuation of expected future earnings The valuation of expected future earnings is based on two estimates. The first being an estimate of future annual earnings of the business, usually five years into the future, and the second being a quantification of the risk associated with the business. The risk factor is usually estimated by comparing the risk of going into business with the risks of other types of investments. A business risk is that uncertainty involved in going into business and standing a chance of failing. Business risks also arise from the possibility that the volume of sales may fluctuate widely or that costs may be higher than expected. In deciding whether to invest or not, you compare the amount of business risk involved in a proposed venture with prospective profit, and thus base the price on the expected value of future annual earnings (usually five years into the future). If the business in question is very stable, for example, the risk might be similar to that of a bank savings account. Say this return is 16% per year. Then if the business has a five-year estimated future profit of R20 000 a year (before tax and after deducting the owner's salary), this approach would suggest a fair market price of R125 000 (R20 000 divided by 0,16%). However, if the risk factor is much higher (the business being a little unstable) the risk factor might be estimated at 26%. Then the business would be valued at R76 923 (R20 000 divided by 0,26%). The business is now valued at a much lower price because of the higher risk involved in taking over the business. Of course, a low offer might not be realistic, but if the seller is eager to sell, he may agree to it and you would thus be able to recover your investment in about five years. Furthermore this figure provides you with a starting point in your bargaining. It may sound confusing, but return on investment is the same process as the risk factor. In the last example, this business was to be purchased for R76 923 as it was to earn R20 000 per year. Its annual return on investment would be R20 000 divided by R76 923, or 26%. Either way, with risk factor or return on investment, the results are the same. This method (valuation of expected future earnings) requires that both future earnings and a risk factor be estimated. Determining the risk factor is in fact nothing more than guessing.

Seen from yet another viewpoint, above-average earnings are normally considered the best evidence of the existence of goodwill, and the value placed on the goodwill at the time of its sale is often determined by capitalizing these extra earnings. For example, a business in a field in which the average return on investment is 16 percent. Suppose the business has a capital investment of R180 000,00 and an annual return on investment of R32 000,00. The average return on investment on R180 000,00 for this type of business would be R28 800 (16% of R180 000,00) a year. Therefore the business has above-average earnings of R3 200,00 (R32 000,00 minus R28 800,00). Capitalizing these above-average earnings at 16% (R3 200,00 ÷ 16) gives R20 000 as the investment needed to earn R3 200. Therefore R20 000,00 may be taken as the value of the goodwill of this business. Many people feel that unless a business has above-average earnings, it does not have any goodwill. Thus, a business might appear to have an excellent location, enlightened customer policies, and a superb product and/or service; yet this business will not have goodwill attaching to it unless its earnings exceed the normal earnings for that type of business. As you may have realized by now, goodwill has many pitfalls. For a start, normal earnings is a relevant concept. So, a decision must be made as to what normal earnings are (industry averages will probably be available, but average earnings for the industry are not necessarily normal earnings). Secondly, once this decision has been made, the percent at which the above-normal earnings will be capitalized must be decided, which is based on personal opinion. In the example given, 16 percent was used. This means that you (the buyer) should recover your investment in 6 years and three months (R180 000 ÷ R28 800,00). If you want to recover your investment more quickly, you will want to use a higher percent, which will give a lower capitalized value, and if you are willing to wait longer, you will accept a lower percent, which will raise the capitalized value.

The following is a list of factors to be considered in determining the risk factor. These factors have an influence on the 'risk factor estimation':[4]

* Profit of the business

Increased profits are an indication of stability in the business. The risk factor in such a business is low. By using the method of ratio analysis and comparing it with the trade averages it can be determined whether a business is in a good liquidity situation, and whether it is solvent and profitable. If the condition of the business is poor, the risk factor would be high. Consider the following examples; profit trend of business X and business Y.

	1983	1984	1985	1986
Business X	R 3 700	R 4 995	R 6 743	R 9 103
Business Y	R14 000	R10 500	R 7 875	R 5 906

In the case of business X there is a steady increase of profits of 35% every year and business Y's profits have decreased by 25% every year. If there is an indication that growth (growth means higher profits) has taken place as in the case of business X, the risk factor will be reduced, but in the case of business Y, the risk factor will be increased.

* The location:

The location of the business with consideration to population tendencies and buying power of the market it is serving must be considered. The buying habits of the population must be taken into consideration. In studying the market area, you should ascertain the number of similar businesses that have been liquidated. When the number is high, it is usually a sign of economic weakness. The demand for a business's products may be declining for reasons such as: changing neighbourhood — there may be a change from one age group to another or in the life-style of the inhabitants; and declining population — the movement of population in areas can have a devastating economic effect on some businesses (new roads, residential areas, etc.), a changing birthrate can affect many businesses orientated toward the baby (toys, clothes, etc.) In such cases the risk factor would be high.

* *The nature, age, accessibility, customer parking facilities of the business.*

These factors and the construction and appearance of the business building should be considered. In the case of the fixed assets being old and not able to be replaced, potential profits are threatened and much has to be done to fix or improve the assets, which costs money. This will increase the risk factor.

* *The availability of manpower.*

Where competent labour is abundant, the risk factor will be reduced.

* *The quality and competency of management and employees.*

If this is poor, the risk factor would increase. Employee attitudes and skills are important to the productivity of the business. Attitudes can be judged by measuring employee turnover and absenteeism, by the business's record of resolving employee-management conflicts and by the tenure of employees.

* *The market.*

The market for the particular type of products you sell should be considered. The nature of the product can determine the risk factor, for example: will luxurious articles have a higher risk factor than groceries? What is the relationship between the small business of this type and larger businesses — there may be adverse features associated with this relationship, for example, tyres or petrol sales are solely dependent on the motor industry for customers and subject to the fluctuations of motor sales, condition of roads and other relative factors that could increase the risk factor in such a situation.

* Geographic distribution.

What is the geographic distribution of the suppliers of the business? Are they close or widely distributed? What is their service and reliability like? Rising transportation expenses (costs) have increased the importance of this factor. If transportation costs are high or there are other obstacles, this will increase the risk factor. If these are easily available, and close to the business and dependable suppliers, the risk factor is reduced.

* The community's attitude.

What is the community's attitude toward the business? This can be determined by interviewing customers — even just people in the street. What do they think about the business? Do they have dealings with the business and what was it like? Answers to such questions and many others can help you find facts about many aspects affecting the risk factor. If there is an unfavourable attitude, the risk factor will increase.

Agreeing on a price for the business is often the most difficult aspect of the buy/sell process for both parties because the buyer and seller look at the business from different viewpoints. The buyer looks at the business for its ability to earn a fair return on investment, after deducting his salary. Thus, if the business is not at least equal in earning power to other investments, the buyer will not be willing to pay more than the price of the tangible assets. The seller, in contrast, has generally put time and money into the business and would like to recover something for this investment. A price on the tangibles can usually be agreed on quite easily but determining a price for goodwill is more difficult.

The Bank of America offers a formula for arriving at a price of a business. Although there may be a variety of formulas that can be used to set the price, this formula is based on an evaluation of the business's existing earning power and profit potential. The approach is from the buyer's point of view but should also be helpful to the seller. Because each business sale transaction is different, the formula should be used only to indicate some of the major considerations in pricing a business. The steps are presented for your consideration:[5]

Step 1. Determine the tangible net worth of the business on the basis of its liquidation value (the total market value of all current and long-term assets less liabilities).

Step 2. Estimate how much the buyer could earn annually with an amount equal to the value of the tangible net worth if he invested it elsewhere. A reasonable figure depends on the stability and relative risks of the business and the investment picture generally. The rate of return should be similar to that which could be earned elsewhere with the approximate risk.

Step 3. Add to this a salary normal for an owner-manager of the business. This combined figure provides a reasonable estimate of the income the buyer can earn elsewhere with the investment and effort involved in working in the business.

Step 4. Determine the average annual net earnings of the business (net profit before subtracting owner's salary) over the past few years. This is taken before income tax, to make it comparable with earnings from other sources or by individuals in different tax brackets. The tax implications of alternate investments should be carefully considered. The trend of earnings is a key factor. Have they been rising steadily, falling steadily, remaining constant, or fluctuating widely? The earnings figure should be adjusted to reflect these trends.

Step 5. Subtract the total of earning power (2) and reasonable salary (3) from the average net earnings (4). This gives the extra earning power of the business.

Step 6. Use this extra, or excess, earning figure to estimate the value of the intangibles (or goodwill). This is done by multiplying the extra earnings by what is termed the 'years of profit' figure. This 'years of profit' multiplyer pivots on these points: how unique are the intangibles offered by the business?; how long would it take to set up a similar business and bring it to this stage of development?; what expenses and risks would be involved?; what is the price of goodwill in similar businesses?; and will the seller be signing an agreement with a covenant not to compete? If the business is well established, a factor of five or more might be used, especially if the business has a valuable name, patent or location. A multiplier of three might be reasonable for a moderately seasoned business. A younger, but profitable business might merely have a one-year profit figure.

Step 7. Final price = tangible net worth + value of intangibles (extra earnings × 'years of profit').

The application of these steps can be better explained by an example, and in making the following assumptions:

- Suppose the liquidation or market value of the business's net assets is R70 000.

- Assume that the present owner's return on investment (before tax) was or is 9%,[*] or R6 300.

- Assume that the actual yearly profit during the past few years has averaged R21 000 (excluding the seller's salary or drawings).

- From this profit figure of R21 000, you should deduct a reasonable salary for yourself. In other words, what you might earn managing this type of business for someone else or what you could get working for somebody else, or the amount of the current salary you would be giving up to run the business. If you worked for an annual salary of R11 000, then the excess profits can be capitalized, that is, the amount of profit based on goodwill is R3 700 (R21 000 minus R11 000 minus R6 300).

- Assume a 20% rate of return on estimated earnings attributable to goodwill, then the calculated value to you (buyer) of the business's intangible assets is R3 700 divided by 0,20, or R18 500.

[*] Nine percent is an arbitrary figure used for illustration. A reasonable figure depends on the stability and relative risks of the business and the investment picture generally. The rate of return should be similar to that which could be earned elsewhere with the same approximate risk.

Calculation of the above according to the steps developed by the Bank of America is as follows:[6]

1.	Value of tangible net worth (assets less liabilities)		R70 000
2.	Earning power at 9%	R 6 300	
3.	Reasonable salary for owner-manager	R11 000	
		R17 300	
4.	Average annual net earnings before subtracting owner's salary	R21 000	
5.	Extra earning power of the business (line 4 minus lines 2 and 3)	R 3 700	
6.	Value of intangibles, using a 5-year profit figure for a well-established business (5 × line 5)		R18 500
7.	Final price (line 1 plus line 6)		R88 500

In the example above the seller receives a value for goodwill because the business is moderately well established and earning more than the buyer could earn elsewhere with similar risks and effort. Within five years, the buyer should have recovered the amount paid for goodwill in this example.

If the average annual net earnings of the business, before subtracting the owner's salary (line 4) were only R17 300 or lower, the seller would receive no value for goodwill because the business is not earning as much as the buyer could earn through other investments and efforts. The calculation below illustrates this:[7]

1.	Value of tangible net worth (assets less liabilities)		R70 000
2.	Earning power at 9%	R 6 300	
3.	Reasonable salary for owner-manager	R11 000	
		R17 300	

4. Average annual net earnings before subtracting owner's salary   R17 300

5. Extra earning power of the business (line 4 minus lines 2 and 3)   R   0

6. Value of intangibles — using 5-
year profit figure for a well-established business (5 × line 5)   R   0

7. Final price (line 1 plus line 6)   R70 000

In the example above the seller receives no value for goodwill because the business, even though it may have existed for some time, is not earning as much as the buyer could earn through outside investment and efforts. In fact, the buyer may feel that even an investment of R70 000 (the current appraised value of the net assets), is too much because it cannot earn a sufficient return.

Let us consider yet another example based on the above situation and figures. Suppose the earning power of the business is lower, for example, only 7% (instead of 9%), or R4 900. Assume further that the business averaged a profit of only R13 000 (instead of R21 000), then the excess profits would be negative (R13 000 less R4 900 return on investment and less R11 000 salary = –R2 900).

1. Value of intangible net worth
(assets less liabilities)   R70 000

2. Earning power at 7%   R 4 900

3. Reasonable salary for owner-
manager   R11 000

                               R15 900

4. Average annual net earnings before subtracting owner's salary   R13 000

5. Extra earning power of the
business (line 4 minus lines 2
and 3)   (R 2 900)

6. Value of intangible, using 3-year
profit figure for a moderately
seasoned business (3 × line 5)   (R 8 700)

7. Final price (line 1 minus line 6)   R61 300

Negative profits can mean one of several things: all the assets are not capable of generating the required return on investment; there are too many unproductive assets; assets have been valued too highly; the business is incapable of providing you with the salary you desire; or the business's potential has not been fully utilized or exploited because of the present manager's inability to do so. This does not mean that you must not buy the business, it merely gives you a thorough opinion about the business. You can still buy it, if you consider your own capabilities and other abilities sufficient to improve the business. Maybe, after your investigation the real problem will have been identified, and the causes established. You may already know the solution!

The last example implies that the business is worth less than the appraised asset value of R70 000, and furthermore that if the potential for profit cannot be improved, it will not meet the buyer's return on investment and salary requirements. The advantage in this method of setting the price is thus that it shows you, the buyer, the profitability of the business and a price to start on for bargaining purposes.

The asset Frequently used terms to express the value of an asset
appraised are:[8]
method
1. *Book value:* What it cost or is worth to the present owner from an accounting viewpoint; the amount shown on the books as representing its value as part of the business's worth.

2. *Replacement value:* What it would cost to go into the current market and buy the same stock, equipment, etc. Relative availability and desirability of newer items must be considered here.

3. *Liquidation value:* How much the seller could get for this business, or any part of it, if it were suddenly put on the market to be bid for by sophisticated buyers.

The method of asset appraisal involves the tangible assets most commonly found in a small business such as stock, office furniture, equipment, and the building. The only intangible asset is goodwill. In evaluating the assets, book value is not the most reliable figure to work on because equipment may have depreciated below its market value, and buildings may have been appreciated above their original cost. Consider this example: What is a butchery cold room worth after twelve months? Amos thinks it has a 7-year lifespan, so it is worth 85% of its original cost. Thomas agrees with Amos about its lifespan, but thinks it loses half its value in the first twelve months of operation, so it is worth 50% of its original cost. Both are right in their assumptions but note the difference in value of the cold room. Many people can say and calculate what they believe it is worth as well as giving valid reasons therefor from their own experiences with a particular asset, technological changes, new developments, etc. Neither is replacement value a reliable figure to work on as its shortcoming lies in the prospective owner's opportunity to buy used equipment which will obviously be less than new equipment. This leaves us with liquidation value which is considered the most reliable and realistic method of appraising assets. It is the price no one would dream of buying for, and the price no one would dream of selling for.

CLOSING THE DEAL

Whatever formula you use to set a price, you still have an opportunity to negotiate a fair price for the business. If you have to pay for goodwill, make sure that you can earn the goodwill as well as having the ability and other necessary requirements such as competent personnel and other things to retain it. Both parties bring personal reasons for wanting to sell and to buy. But you are the buyer and negotiations will depend on facts such as: how badly the seller wants to sell; how serious you are about wanting to buy it; what the price is of similar businesses for sale; whether there are other buyers involved; whether you wish to live in the area or town where the business is located; what the financial institutions say; and whether they will assist you financially. Assuming that you have done your homework, are happy with your analysis of the business's financial situation and market, and have considered all requirements such as the ability to operate the business, financing, family and others, you are ready to close the deal. Don't work on this deal alone — expert counsel is important. Consult an attorney, an auditor, consultants, or a financial institution before closing the deal. Always seek the best counsel you can to safeguard your interests.

FRANCHISING

The franchising concept is booming into many different types of businesses, and is an attractive option for operating a small business. Franchising does offer genuine business opportunities to many prospective entrepreneurs, but be careful of reaching the opinion that a franchise is a gold mine, or at least earn a higher than normal income as compared to other non-franchise operations. Many assume so just because a franchise may have a valuable name or patent. It should be remembered that it is still the jockey that makes the horse win or lose. Although a great advantage of franchising is that of receiving initial training, you should not 'completely' believe that franchising is the route to quick, easy money. Franchising merely reduces the risk of failure and consequently makes your investment safer. Franchising can be defined as a marketing system which revolves around a mutual agreement whereby one party is granted the privilege to conduct business as an individual business owner but is required to operate according to certain methods and terms specified by the other party. This legal agreement is known as the franchise contract, and the privileges it contains is known as the franchise. The sponsor of the privileges is the franchisor, and the individual receiving the privileges is called the franchisee.

There are several reasons why franchising has grown so rapidly in recent years of which the most important of these are that it provides opportunities for the establishment of new small businesses as well as a method of financing corporate growth that would otherwise be much slower. While the franchising concept has merits, there are also those individuals who had some experience of unscrupulous exploitation. Instances are where franchisors demand that prospective franchisees make sizable deposits before seeing the contract which contained clauses such as 'subsequent refusal of the franchise results in forfeiture of the deposit'. In some cases prospective franchise buyers are not receiving all information from a franchisor that will allow them to make a sound decision on whether to buy or not. In other instances the exaggeration of a franchise's prospects has caused only pain to those after the deposit was paid. For prospective entrepreneurs thinking about the acquisition of a franchise, the answer to avoiding pitfalls is 'look before you leap'. Follow this advice:

* Call or visit the South African Franchise Association and ask for a business responsibility report on the franchise promotor.
* Have your lawyer or management consultant go over all provisions of the franchise contract.
* Personally contact several of the company's franchise holders and find out how they liked the deal.

The South African Franchise Association (SAFA) was formed in 1979 by a group of franchise company executives who saw a need for an organization that would:

* Provide a forum for the exchange of experience among member companies;
* Serve as a central point for the collection and dissemination of franchise data and information;
* Speak on behalf of franchising before government bodies and the general public.
* Offer educational programmes for executives and managers.

Today, SAFA carries out these functions. The Association is affiliated to the International Franchise Association in Washington D.C. SAFA's membership is continually growing and has earned the reputation as the spokesman for the franchise system of distribution.

Before you can assess any franchise opportunity you should firstly understand the advantages and disadvantages of franchising from the Franchisee's viewpoint so that you can put the relationship and its legal form into proper perspective.

Advantages to the Franchisee

1. The Franchisee's lack of basic or specialized knowledge is overcome by the training programme of the Franchisor. While some franchising systems have

developed excellent training programmes, this is by no means universal. The following example is illustrative of an unfortunate consequence of a franchise arrangement which lacked proper training programmes. (Robert M Dias and Stanley I. Gurnick, Franchising: The Investor's Complete Handbook, New York: Hastings House, 1969, pp. 73–74.)

John Smith worked nearly 10 years with the same company before a magazine advertisement caught his eye. The ad read: 'Be your own boss. Earn a living in the profitable carpeting business. No previous experience is necessary. We'll teach you all the ropes.'

John talked it over with his wife and decided to take the big step into self-employment.

John sent in the clipping and in turn was invited for an interview by the company. After a red carpet tour of the city, franchisor-paid, and an elaborate slide presentation at the franchisor's 'Executive Offices', John could hardly wait to get home and start selling carpets. He signed the franchise agreement, which did not mention training, assured by the soothing tone of the company vice-president's words: 'Don't worry about a thing,' he said. 'We'll teach and train you in every aspect of carpet merchandising at one of our best outlets.' John returned home after investing the required R8 000 and revamped his personal affairs – and waited for the franchisor's call to report for training. Finally, the call came in the form of a "Do-It-Yourself' book on carpet installation and merchandising. Having signed leases, ordered merchandise, and invested R8 000, he could do little but try it on his own. Even with the help of fairly experienced 'carpeting men' he was in deep trouble within 3 months. After a few more weeks, John was approached by a company representative. 'Look Mr. Smith, let's face it. The carpet business is not for you. Our company is prepared to make you an offer of R4 700 for your franchise.' John, bewildered and frightened at the prospects of bankruptcy, accepted the offer — a considerable loss from his original R8 000 investment.

2. The Franchisee has the incentive of owning his own business, despite the background of assistance from the Franchisor. That is, becoming an independent businessman within the framework of the Franchise Agreement and can, by hard work and effort, maximize the value of the investment made.

3. The Franchisee's business opens with the benefit of a name already well established in the mind and eye of the public.

4. The Franchisee invariably requires less capital of his own than is required in setting up independently by reason of the assistance given by the Franchisor in obtaining finance, as leases. However, many franchised businesses are organised in a highly sophisticated way and a Franchisee may well have to make a larger investment than he would if he were to open for business totally independently.

   On the other hand, a more modest investment may jeopardise the success of the business.

5. The Franchisee should, where appropriate, receive assistance in:

   5.1 Site selection
   5.2 Preparation of plans for remodelling the business premises, including the obtaining of any necessary town planning or bye-laws consents.
   5.3 Obtaining finance for the acquisition of the franchised business.
   5.4 The training of his staff.
   5.5 Purchase of equipment.
   5.6 Selection and purchase of stock.
   5.7 Getting the business open and running smoothly.

6. The Franchise receives the benefit of national and/or regional franchisor's advertising and promotional activities.

7. The Franchisee receives the benefit of the bulk purchasing and negotiating capacity of the Franchisor on behalf of all the Franchisees.

8. The Franchisee has at his fingertips the specialised and highly skilled knowledge and experience of the Franchisor's head office organisation and management

in all aspects of his business, while continuing in a self-employed capacity.

9. The Franchisee's business risk is reduced. However, no Franchisee should consider that because he is coming under the umbrella of the Franchisor he is not going to be exposed to any risk at all. Any business undertaking involves risk and a franchised business is no exception. To be successful the Franchisee will have to work hard, perhaps harder than ever before. The Franchisor will never be able to promise rewards for little effort.

   The blueprint for carrying on business successfully and profitably can rarely be the blueprint for carrying on business successfully without working.

10. The Franchisee has the services of 'trouble-shooters' provided by the Franchisor to assist him with the problems that may arise from time to time in the course of his business.

11. The Franchisee has the benefit of the use of the Franchisor's patents, trademarks, copyrights, trade secrets and any secret processes or formulae.

12. The Franchisee has the benefit of the Franchisor's continuous research and development programmes which are designed to improve the business, keep it up to date and competitive.

13. The Franchisor obtains the maximum amount of market information and experience which is assembled for the benefit of all the Franchisees in his system. This should give the Franchisee information which would not otherwise be available to him because of its cost or inaccessibility.

14. There are sometimes territorial guarantees to ensure that no competitive Franchisee is set up in a competing business within a defined area around the Franchisee's business address.

Disadvantages to the Franchisee

1. Inevitably, the relationship between the Franchisor and the Franchisee will involve the imposition of controls. These controls will regulate the quality of the goods or

service to be provided or sold by the Franchisee. It has been mentioned previously that the Franchisee will own his own business. He will, but he must accept that for the advantages enjoyed by him, by virtue of his association with the Franchisor and all the other Franchisees, the control of quality and standard is essential. Each weak Franchisee has an adverse effect not only on his own business, but indirectly on the whole of the franchised chain and all other Franchisees in the system.

The Franchisor will, therefore, demand that standards are maintained so that the maximum benefit is derived by the Franchisee, and indirectly by the whole franchised chain, from the operation of the Franchisee's business.

This is not to say that the Franchisee will not be able to make any contribution, or to impose his own personality on his business. Most Franchisors do encourage their Franchisees to make their contribution to the development of the business of the franchise chain, and they hold seminars and meetings to assist in this process.

2. The Franchise will have to pay the Franchisor for the services provided and for the use of the corporate blueprint i.e. the franchise fee and continuing royalties.

3. The difficulty of assessing the Franchisor. This factor must be weighed very carefully by the potential Franchisee for it can affect the franchise in two ways:
   3.1 The Franchisor's offer of a package may well not amount to what it appears to be on the surface.
   3.2 The Franchisor may be unable to maintain the continuing services which the Franchisee may need in order to sustain his business.

4. The franchise contract will contain some restrictions against the assignment of the franchised business. This is a clear inhibition on the Franchisee's ability to sell his own business but, as with most of the restrictions, there is a reason for it.

The reason is that the Franchisor will already have been most meticulous in his choice of the Franchisee as his original Franchisee for this particular unit. Why then should he be any less meticulous in his approval of a replacement? Naturally, he will wish to be satisfied that any successor to the Franchisee is equally suitable for that purpose.

In practice, there is normally very little difficulty in the achievement of successful assignments of franchised businesses.

5. The Franchisee may find himself becoming too dependent upon the Franchisor. This can affect him in a number of ways.

   For example, he may rely too heavily on the Franchisor and fail to produce the personal drive that is necessary to build up a successful business to take full advantage of the foundations that the blueprint provides.

6. The Franchisor's policies may affect the Franchisee's profitability. For example, the Franchisor may wish to see his Franchisee build up to a higher gross sales level, from which the Franchisor normally acquires his royalty, whilst the Franchisee may be more concerned with increasing his profitability, which does not always necessarily follow from increased turnover.

7. The Franchisor may make mistakes in his policy. He may make decisions relating to innovations in the business which turn out to be unsuccessful and operate to the detriment of the Franchisee.

8. The good name of the franchised business, or its brand image, may become less reputable for reasons beyond the Franchisee's control.

TYPES OF FRANCHISING SYSTEMS

Franchise systems can be classified according to distribution functions:

   I   *Manufacturer – Retailer.* The manufacturer of a product contracts with local independent businessmen to distribute its product to the final consumer.

Well-known examples are new car dealers and petrol stations.

II *Manufacturer – Wholesaler.* Manufacturers grant franchises to wholesalers who in turn sell to retailers. An example is Coca-Cola franchising to bottlers (who are independent mid-line manufacturer/wholesaler franchisees) who in turn sell to retailers.

III *Wholesaler – Retailer.* Here the retailer retains the advantage of independence while enjoying the benefits of a chain with bulk-buying discounts and co-ordinated national advertising efforts. Example: Spar supermarkets.

IV *Service/Trademark Holder – Retailer.* The real value of the franchise lies in the trademark, image and method of operation. The franchisor is not a manufacturer, but is in the business of selling a business system. Normally the franchisor has operated several successful outlets and then expands by selling the system to others who wish to start their own business.

Fast food establishments are the most visible form of this type as in Wimpy, Kentucky Fried Chicken and Juicy Lucy.

Which field of business The market within which the franchise operates is another vital consideration. You should not only look at the specific business in relation to its own field, but also make an assessment of the prospects for the overall industry or trade of which it forms a part.

The franchise will either be dealing in goods or products, or the provision of services. If a product is involved, is it stable or seasonal, new or nearly obsolescent? Is it proven and is there a market for it generally and in the territory in which you will operate? Is the product untested, speculative or a gimmick? How long has it been on the market? Is the product manufactured by the franchisor or a third party? How strong and reputable is the source? Check the reliability of delivery and availability.

Determine who controls product price to you and whether prices have been and are competitive. Is any suggested or projected selling price realistic in the light of competitive product conditions and anticipated returns? What is the competition?

Are there governmental standards and regulations governing the product? Does it meet the standards? Are there government restrictions on use?

Are there product warranties or guarantees? Who makes them and who backs them? Are there arrangements for repair or replacement? At who's cost are repairs done and warranties honoured? If the franchisor assumes warranty responsibility, what are the mechanics for and what is the franchisor's track record on warranty servicing?

Is there some product line diversification existing or planned? What new products if any are to be added? When?

Do the product and the supplier enjoy a good reputation?

Is the product patented? Is it protected by trademarks or copyrights? Does it involve formulas and trade secrets not available to others?

After you have determined the product line, industry, or business area in which you are interested and for which you are suited by training, ability, temperament and desire, then begin investigating prospective franchisors.

GETTING TO KNOW THE FRANCHISOR

The following are the type of questions you should put to the Franchisor to enable you to assess him, his financial involvement and the quality of his personnel.

1. How long have you been franchising?
2. Did you run your own pilot operation before franchising?
3. If not, why not? If you did not run a pilot operation what do you really have to sell?
4. Whether you did or not, what is the extent of your own cash investment in the business?

5. How many franchised businesses are you running at the moment?
6. What are the addresses of these businesses?
7. May I please interview any number of these Franchisees. May I choose whom I interview?
8. How many outlets do you yourself run at the present time?
9. What does your head office organisation consist of?
10. Can I meet your senior executive staff? How long have they each been with you and do they have service contracts which will ensure continuity?
11. Can you demonstrate your capacity to provide the necessary follow-up services? Is your organization developed sufficiently well to cope with the expansion of the size and area of operations?
12. May I follow up your bank references?
13. Are there any other referees whom I may approach?
14. How many business failures have been experienced by your Franchisees?
15. On what basis do you choose your Franchisees — how selective are you?
16. What is the business background of the directors and executives of your company?
17. Have you or any of your directors or executives ever experienced any business failures; if so, please provide details.
18. Has any of your directors or executives within the last ten years:
    a. Been bankrupt?
    b. Entered into an arrangement with his creditors?
    c. Been convicted of any criminal offence?
    d. Been involved as a shareholder or director in any company, which during his term of office or shortly thereafter went into liquidation?

    If so, please provide details.

19. Have you or any of your directors or executives been involved in litigation with Franchisees?

    If so, please provide details.

    In assessing the reply to this question, you should bear in mind that many reputable Franchisors will from time to time be involved in litigations with Franchisees over failure to perform contractual obligations, or in order to maintain the standards and integrity of their franchise system.

GETTING TO KNOW THE FRANCHISE BUSINESS

There are various aspects of the Franchisor's business which should be investigated in detail. The following questions should be asked.

A. *Operational Details*

1. What is the initial cost of your franchise? What does this price include? What capital costs will be incurred in addition to this price?
2. How much working capital do I need? How long will I have to spend in training and setting up the business before it actually opens?
3. What are the costs incurred in the business likely to be, broken down into gross and nett profit?
4. May I see actual accounts which confirm, or fail to confirm, your projections? Can they be relied upon, or are they merely illustrations?
5. What financing arrangements can you make and what terms for repayment will there be? What rate of interest will be charged and will the finance company want security?
6. Is the business seasonal?
7. When is the best time to open up?
8. How do you make your money?
9. Do you charge royalties?
10. Do you make a mark-up on product sales to Franchisees?
11. If so, how much? And what protection do I have against an unjustified increase?
12. Do you take any commission on supplies of goods or materials to a Franchisee?
13 Do you receive any other commissions from any other source? If so, please provide details.
14. Will I be obliged to maintain a minimum royalty, or a minimum purchase volume of goods? What happens if I fail to meet this commitment?

15. What advertising and promotional support do you provide? Does this cost the Franchisee anything? If so, please provide details.
16. Do I have to contribute to Advertising? If so, how much?
17. What initial services do you offer?
18. Do you train me? Who pays for my training? What about the training of my staff?
19. Will I be able to obtain and motivate sufficient able staff?
20. What continuing services do you provide after the business has commenced?

B. *The Franchise Contract*

1. May I have a copy of your franchise contract? May I have it evalutated by my lawyer?
2. Does this contract permit me to sell my business? What restrictions are there affecting my rights to sell the business?
3. For what time period is the Franchise granted?
4. What do I get at the end of this period? Do I get automatic renewal?
5. What will happen if I do not like the business? Upon what basis can I terminate the contract?
6. What happens if I die?

C. *Other Aspects*

1. Who will be my link with you after I have opened for business? Can I meet some of your operational staff? How long have they each been with you and do they have service contracts to ensure continuity?
2. What point-of-sale aids and promotional literature do you supply and what do I have to pay for it?
3. What will be the opening hours of business?
4. Will I own the equipment necessary to operate the business when I have cleared the finance company?
5. How soon will I have to spend money on replacing equipment?
6. Will you find me a site, or do I have to find it?
7. What systems do you have for keeping Franchisees in touch with you and each other? Do you publish a newsletter? Hold seminars?

8. What help will I receive in local advertising and promotions?
9. What exclusive rights do I get?
10. How will I cope with my bookkeeping?
11. What can I sell and not sell?
12. Do you provide Operational and Management Training manuals?
13. What would happen if you misjudged the site and it did not produce the anticipated figures but resulted in a loss?
14. What would happen if I ran into operational problems that I was not able to solve? What help would I receive?

THE FRANCHISE AGREEMENT

Your first contact with the Franchisor will, if you follow the usual pattern, have come about in one of the following three ways:

1. You will be attracted to the business by a friend who has a Franchise, or by talking to an existing Franchisee.
2. You will be responding to a report about a successful franchise in a newspaper or magazine
3. You will have seen an advertisement in a business magazine or business section of a newspaper.

You will then either write to or telephone the Franchise company concerned and they will send you a package which will invariably contain:

1. A glossy presentation describing the Franchise company and its success story. Often this is presented in a question and answer form.
2. Another presentation explaining briefly what Franchising is and setting out in particular what the Franchisor does for his Franchisees in terms of setting them up and continuing to service them thereafter.
3. Financial projections. These are very rarely presented as suggestions of what you *will achieve*. Rather they are to illustrate what profits can be achieved if certain levels of turnover are reached.
4. A letter inviting you to contact the Franchisor to discuss the matter further.

5. A preliminary information sheet for you to return which provides the Franchisor with some details about yourself.

Assuming that you follow up and get together with the Franchise company, you will in due course be handed a copy of the Franchise Agreement to read. Hopefully you will also have made an assessment in the light of your contact to date with the Franchisor.

The Franchisor, or his representative, will probably go through the provisions of the contract with you in detail to explain what they mean and the reason why each provision is inserted.

He will probably suggest that you see your own lawyer with the contract. It is most important that you understand the reason why the contract reads as it does because what might otherwise seem unreasonable on the face of it, is not so unreasonable when the nature of the Franchise relationship is taken into account and other relevant factors considered.

These factors are:

1. The Franchisee is to be licensed to conduct a business only in accordance with the Franchisor's business format and not otherwise.
2. That each Franchisee owes a duty to all other Franchisees to maintain the standards associated with the Franchise scheme. The misdeeds of one Franchisee can affect the others.
3. The Franchisor needs to be in a position to ensure that the business which is being operated with the benefit of his tradename and the associated goodwill is being run strictly in accordance with the format which has been established.
4. The Franchisor is quite reasonably entitled to protect himself against someone who may be inclined to learn all about the Franchise and then steal the ideas and set up in competition.

In the course of your investigation of the Franchisor and the franchised business a number of facts about the Franchise will emerge. These must be properly secured and reflected in the contract.

1. You will wish to see that the initial obligations of the Franchisor are correctly detailed.
2. The initial package and setting up will probably cost something. What is costs and what it includes should be clearly stated in the contract.
3. Be sure that you understand what your working capital requirement, in addition to the initial package and setting-up costs, will be.
4. The initial package will undoubtedly include training in all aspects of the business and in the preparations for opening, plus appropriate assistance with shopfitting, the opening promotion and start up assistance.
5. The contract will also specify exactly what the Franchisee is being licensed to do. The grant of exclusive territorial trading rights must be provided for.
6. The franchise fees will be identified and the method of payment established. The Franchisor will also have the machinery available to enable him to verify the calculation of fees and to monitor the financial performance of the business.
7. Advertising and promotional support is often provided by establishing a fund, which is administered by a Co-operative Committee, made up of an equal number of Franchisee and Franchisor members, which has complete discretion over how the fund is spent.

In conclusion we offer this advice: Protect yourself and investigate with the aim to evaluate the nature and characteristics of a particular franchise operation; and if the franchise company is not a member of SAFA, ask them 'Why not?' Valuable assistance can be rendered by a Franchisor (a management consultant or the South African Franchise Association) such as introductions to suitable franchisor companies; explanations of franchising procedures; negotiating the Franchise Agreement; assistance in site location and in raising finance.

Most of the material as presented in this section was reproduced with permission of the South African Franchise Association (SAFA). See the South African Franchise Association Handbook, 1985/86. Should you have any general queries relating to Franchising, please feel free to approach SAFA. They can be contacted by writing to: The Secretary, SAFA, P.O. Box 18398, Hillbrow, 2038: Telephone (011)726-5300 or 642-2921.

STARTING A BUSINESS FROM SCRATCH

As already mentioned, another way to enter the business world is to start a business from scratch. Both methods of getting involved in a business of your own have unique advantages as well as disadvantages which you must weigh against each other in order to see whether you have the abilities to withstand or eliminate the disadvantages or not. Advantages or reasons for starting a business of your own instead of buying one may include the opportunity: to purchase 'fresh' stock of your own customer's choice; to have a free hand in selecting and training personnel to your liking; to take advantage of, and have a free hand in selecting equipment of your own choice and of the latest technology; to create the atmosphere and layout you prefer; to choose the name of your business as well as its location; and generally to be able to say at the end of the day 'I built this business'.

However, where there are advantages there are always disadvantages. These may include the following: it will take too long to get the business established; no performance records are available for sales and profit in order to present a convincing case to possible financial institutions (lenders); lack of knowledge in doing a market survey and a feasibility study; difficulties in drawing up a business plan; etc. However, there is no fixed way of getting into business as some may prefer and believe in starting from scratch. Only you can make a final decision.

An opportunity for a new business in a specific town or area could develop through poor management of existing businesses. If in such a situation you decide to capitalize thereon, you can start by offering better prices, better services, better quality products and a wider range of products. However, before you start a business this way, a proper market analysis is important and should be carried out thoroughly. Such a market analysis will reveal whether

66

your business and its products are wanted by the people you intend to sell to. In other words, first determine what your market requires so that you could offer them the right items.

Let's organize a market analysis (also known as a market survey). How and where do you start? You always start by setting up a work plan with a list of questions to be asked in order to gather information concerning the market you intend to enter as well as what you need to know about starting a business. The work plan mainly concerns identifying the sources from which certain information can be obtained. There are many methods of collecting market and other information, such as personal contact with customers, personal contact surveys, questionaire surveys and statistical analyses and projections. Sources from which such information can be obtained are the local or other magistrates offices (depending on the scope of your market); town councils and development corporations in the respective national states who provide information which is applicable to the respective geographical areas; and potential suppliers and consumers. When speaking to them it is imperative that you get true answers as they may tend to provide you with information which will not hurt your feelings, which is the last thing you want to hear. Always ask whether they would buy the products or services and then dig deeper for the reasons behind their answers. Some more valuable information can be obtained from the information bank of the SBDC (Small Business Development Corporation[9]). The SBDC information bank is a data centre for small business knowledge and information from both local and foreign sources. It consists of a library of books, periodicals, pamphlets, articles, research and technical reports relating to small business. Information on such factors as statistics, performance indicators, new developments, management practices, technology and legal aspects in specific businesses and industries is available. This service is free to anyone promoting or personally involved in small business. For example, if you want to open a hardware shop, the SBDC's information bank can provide you with the following information:

- the growth of the market over a relatively long period;

- projected growth rate per annum;
- structure of the trade (industrial, domestic, farmers, builders; which of these markets are the most stable and profitable);
- an owner's profile (experience, the cause of failure for such a business, vital management know-how for operating such a business);
- consumer demand information (average annual expenditure per person);
- a typical hardware marketing strategy (important matters relating to price and promotions);
- where to locate a hardware shop;
- capital requirements per square metre (size of business);
- a profit profile (rent percentage to sales, personnel expenses as a percentage of sales and other related expenses);
- legal aspects to consider (tax, licences, etc.);
- sources of finance and other information and assistance sources; and
- publications (trade magazines of value).

Another source of information is the University of South Africa's (UNISA's) publication called *Income and Spending patterns of Households*. This was a survey done by UNISA's Bureau of Market Research and it contains a wealth of information helpful in studying the market of various commodities and its sales potential, as well as information per household income and per capita consumption for a particular line of goods (it serves as an index of consumer purchasing power). The application of the information obtained from such sources will be dealt with in a later section ('Preparing the business plan', page 92).

ASSESSING YOUR MARKET

The most important reason for assessing your market is to establish your business's sales potential. It is the only unknown figure when you draw up your business plan, and all other calculations depend on the expected turnover. Before you start to estimate you business's sales potential, first determine exactly what kind of business you want to establish. Defining the business you want is necessary because the way you view your business will provide the framework for your planning in relation to the market, trading premises, equipment and financial needs. Also, decide which kind of employees you wish to employ. Some owner-managers have gone out of business and others have wasted their savings because they did not define their businesses in detail. To explain this point, consider the following two examples:

Mr Jet on the East Coast maintained a dock where he sold and rented boats. He thought he was in the marine business, but when he got into financial trouble and asked for outside help, he learned that he was in several businesses at the same time. He was in the catering business with a dockside cafe, serving meals to boating parties. He was also in the real estate business, buying and selling stands. He was in the boat repair business, buying spares and hiring a mechanic as demand arose. Mr Jet was trying to be too many things at the same time and couldn't decide which business to put his money into and how much return to expect. Whatever resources he had were fragmented. Thus, before he could make a profit on his sales and receive a return on his investment, Mr Jet had to decide what business he really was in and concentrate on it. After much study he realized that he should stick to the marine side only — buying, selling and servicing boats.[10]

Another example is that of an owner-manager's business which made metal trash cans. When sales began to drop the owner was forced to re-examine the business. To regain lost sales the owner redefined the product as metal containers and developed a marketing plan for that product.[11]

The point is: first define your business. Write down the definition. To help you to decide, think of the answers to questions such as:

★ What do you buy?
★ What do you sell?
★ Which of your lines of goods yield the greatest profit?

★ What items do people want from you?

★ What are you trying to do better or more of, or differently from your competitors?

In assessing your market, what really matters is to have a clear idea and description of those people who can reasonably be expected to become your customers. They are the ones who will want to purchase the merchandise you have for sale or to obtain the services you can offer. Unless you assess your market, that is, define or describe it accurately and estimate its size, you run the risk of starting up a business which may never succeed. You may discover too late that there are insufficient customers and therefore insufficient sales for your business to survive. So, what you are about to evaluate is whether you have a genuine business opportunity. The steps outlined below prepared by the Small Business Development Corporation, will be most useful to you in doing this exercise.[12]

'Step 1. DEFINE YOUR MARKET

Is your market made up of consumers, that is people who use your products or services for themselves, or does your market include wholesalers and retailers, in other words, people who deal in your products?

What is the socio-economic profile of your customers? In simpler terms try to decide who your rightful customers are by answering questions about them against the following headings:

- **Age** — what is the approximate age range of your customers (remember that teenagers have different tastes and need different products and services from those which their grandparents and even parents need)?

- **Income bracket** — will your business cater for the needs of low-or middle-income people or the wealthier people in the community?

- **Sex** — are your customers male or female or both? Even although your goods may be used by male customers, who actually does the shopping? Is it the female in the family?

- **Education and culture** — these aspects frequently affect the style, fashion, pricing, etc. of merchandise which customers prefer.

- **Location** — geographical aspects of your market are important because they affect the ease with which your customers can reach you and the kind of needs they may have which arise from where they live.

- Occupation — are your customers professional people, artisans or others, and what proportion of your customers fall into the different occupational categories?

Answering these questions will enable you to define your market systematically and you will note that it is necessary constantly to bear in mind the definition of your merchandise or services and the definition of your target market. The one must determine the other to a large extent.

Step 2. HOW TO ESTIMATE THE SIZE OF YOUR MARKET

- **Where your market is an identified community living in a defined area.**
  If your market is a community of people living within say a 4 kilometre radius of your place of business or your shop, then a simple method of estimating the population is to find out the number of houses or families in the area. A good map or information from the local authority (municipality or regional service council) could be helpful. If you are able to ascertain how many households fall within your target area, then by applying the average number of people per household (which is usually available from local authorities) you can ascertain the population figure. Bear in mind of course what we said earlier regarding whether your market comprises male or female, etc.

- **Where your market is scattered over an entire city or even over the entire country.**

  In this case, it is worth seeking information from organisations such as the Bureau for Market Research at UNISA or other bureaus and institutions who carry out economic and market surveys. It may be necessary for you to pay for the literature provided by such an organisation, but this is usually worthwhile. The sort of information supplied includes data on the average percentage of income which is spent by a family on different commodities and services. The figures are available for separate regions. Economically active population figures can usually be provided by such organisations.

- **Estimating the purchasing power.**
  The main object of this research is to estimate the buying power of your market place in terms of your own merchandise or services. Having established the number of people or consumers that make up your market, you can estimate the total purchasing power provided you have information regarding the average amount spent by such consumers each year on your commodity or service. Such averages applied to the number of people whom you estimate to be your market can provide useful estimates of the total

value of the market in which you are trading. If you can afford it, it may be worthwhile consulting with some market research specialists who are able to put together such estimates with greater facility and accuracy than the average businessman.

- **Estimating your market in relation to some other known/ published information.**

  A system known as "Regression Analysis" can sometimes be used. For example, if you are selling lounge suites you could reasonably expect that the lounge suite market would grow in relation to the number of houses in that market. Since the number of houses in a given area is more easily obtained from official channels than the number of lounge suites, you may be able to draw fairly accurate conclusions about the size and potential of the market for lounge suites, by consulting market research on previous sales patterns.

- **What share of the market can you expect?**

  Having established in the previous steps, as best you can, the size of your total market, you then are faced with the challenge of deciding how much of that total you can reasonably expect as your own share. To a large extent this depends upon the effectiveness and number of your competitors, that is those people who are trading in the same services or goods to the same market. It also depends on your own competitiveness in terms of quality, price and service. To answer the question of what share you can expect, you need to begin with assessing the extent of your competition.

- Where are your potential customers getting their products or services from right now?

- How well are those suppliers (your competitors) doing their job?

- Are they inefficient, does their service lead to many complaints, does the examination of your competitors suggest ways in which you could give a better service or give better value for money?

It is also worth dividing the total market by the number of competitors that exist in that market. If for example you have decided that your market size is a total of 100 000 units selling for R300 000 annually and there are at present only four suppliers in competition with each other, you have thereby established that the average supplier at present has a market share of 25 000 units giving him revenue of R75 000 annually. The question you then need to ask yourself is whether you could in a reasonable period of say 3 years from starting, expect your business to grow to at least the average market share of 25 000 units and R75 000 annually. You will realise that to do this you will need to take some business away from the existing suppliers thus increasing the extent of the competition. Or you may have reason to believe that the total market will grow rapidly by the injection of new customers so as to allow you to reach this level in a short period of time.

You will see how market share is an important aspect of assessing your market. To obtain a market share a businessman usually has to take some share away from existing suppliers as well as to enjoy a share in the growth of that market or the new business. The more competitive the situation is the more difficult it is for any one supplier, especially a new one, to gain a share of such a market. His competitors will of course try to make it difficult for him to gain a share.'

To make the above steps more practically appropriate, consider the following example:

1. 1 500 houses (or families);
2. R15 000 (average household income);
3. R22 500 000 (1 500 × R15 000) total annual income of families;
4. 18% of the annual income is spent by every household per year on the commodities you intend selling;
5. R4 050 000 ($\frac{R22\,500\,000}{1} \times \frac{18}{100}$) is the amount the total market will spend on the commodities you will sell;
6. R1 336 500 (33% of R4 050 000) is the expected annual sales income for your business with a 33% potential market share.

THINK CREATIVELY WHEN ASSESSING YOUR BUSINESS OPPORTUNITY

When assessing the market in which you want to establish your business, it is important to think creatively. Study the existing products, merchandise assortment, services and many other business offerings for possible improvements or a combination thereof that could lead to greater customer satisfaction, convenience and attraction. Being creative may provide you with a competitive edge. But what is creative thinking in the first place, and how can it be acquired and applied? Some people think that creativity is one of life's mysteries; something bestowed — you were born blessed with creative ability, or you were not. However, research indicates that creativity is a skill that can be learned.

Herman R. Holtz in his book *Profit from your Money-making Ideas* describes creativity as follows:[13]

'Concentration — that long and deep conscious thought — is a means of transferring the problem to the human subconscious mind. In effect, it says to the subconscious: "Here is a problem for you, with all I know about it. Work on it and tell me what you think, when you are ready." During incubation, the subconscious is working on the problem — perhaps for a few hours, or a few weeks or months. The illumination, or "inspiration" as it is often referred to, is the act of the subconscious saying to the conscious mind: "Here is the best answer I have been able to come up with. Try this." '

So, the logical approach in thinking creatively starts with a well-defined problem to solve. Creativity can be most applicable and useful when a problem starts out vaguely, but during the solution-seeking process, it becomes well defined. Research psychologists are of the opinion that problem awareness and specification are critical skills that must be present for creative problem-solving to occur. Creativity is essential in the process of discovering business opportunities, evaluating the market and planning your business (collection of information and ideas that can be implemented once in business). Creativity can, furthermore, be said to be the ability to bring into existence something new and valuable. It has been said: 'Creativity is the generation of novel ideas; innovation is taking those ideas and making money with them.' In other words, creativity can also be the same thing somebody else thought of, and innovation is the use of a creative (new) idea, implementing it in your business in a different way. A business management consultant defines creativity as 'the ability to generate new options'.[14] In other words, the more creative you can learn to be, the more choices you will have. A woman once said: 'My tax consultant is creative. He consistently comes up with new ways to approach my returns and imaginative devices and solutions to stay well within the law but saves me piles of money.'[15] Judith Krantz, writer of a number of best sellers says: 'The ideas pop up from the unconscious and if anybody asks me: How can I acquire creativity?, I reply: You already have it. Everyone has it. All you have to do is develop it. Use it. Practise.'[16]

Below is some information on creativity that you can use, work on and practise to increase your own. These suggestions are compiled by the U.S. Army Management School, Fort Belvoir, Virginia, in its *Workbook for Military Creative Problem Solving:*[17]

'1. Be optimistic in your approach. Remember that for most things, somehow, somewhere, there is a better way.

2. Consider yourself a thinker as well as a learner and a doer — an idea man or woman as well as a man or woman of action.

3. Develop a honeybee mind. Gather your ideas everywhere. Don't be afraid to associate ideas fully. Let your mind buzz freely from one idea or source to another. Be "open to experience" and stimuli of all sorts — both from within and in the world around you.

4. Sharpen your nose for problems. Be curious about things that seem wrong or inadequate. Listen to the complaints of others. Jot down your own dissatisfactions with things and situations. Develop an attitude of constructive discontent — welcome problems as opportunities not only to accomplish something but to sharpen your creative abilities.

5. Learn to play with ideas. At times you must "regress" — back off from the problem and try to think about it with the naïvete and freshness of a child.

6. Look for the "elegant" answer. Don't be satisfied with just any solution to a problem.

7. Be alert for the welcome "hunches". When you get them, do something about them.

8. Be courageous and independent in your thinking and persistent in the face of frustration and difficulty — but employ an alternating type of persistence so as to invite incubation and insight.

9. Continue to acquire a growing body of knowledge about your field.

10. Schedule practice sessions with yourself, that is, conduct your own private brainstorming sessions each day. Come up with ideas — good, bad, and mediocre. Never mind the duds. Accept all ideas from yourself; don't reject any. Write them down. Unless you drill your mind regularly to produce a bag full of ideas, you haven't really decided to be creative.

11. Carry your idea trap around. A pad and pencil, that is. Keep them with you all the time. Why? Because ideas are elusive. They will drift out of your grasp as readily as they drift in. Better trap them on paper — in black and white.

12. Incubate. Relax your mind. After a hard day's work, let it wander. (Day-dream while you walk home from work. Try a hot bath or shower, restful music.) After a good night's sleep, get up an hour early, take a long walk, meditate. Take an airplane ride, play golf,

or go fishing. Use the two-day formula: set your problem aside for a day, then hit it hard after a day's rest.

13. Use idea banks and idea museums. Ideas don't fall out of the blue. Keep a dream file of clippings, notes from your idea trap, pamphlets, etc., even if you can't work on them right now. Idea museum? This is your reference library. Keep scanning it for ideas. Store them up to solve future as well as present problems.

14. Be enthusiastic, confident. Your willpower controls your imagination and is affected by your emotions. So build faith in yourself by scoring successes on little problems before you tackle big ones.

15. Find the right time of day — the time of day when you are most creative. You know the time when you are full of drive. That is the time to build up a stock-pile of ideas. The time for "red light" thinking comes when your mind is not running creatively.

16. Set a quota; and a deadline, too. Force yourself to do a little better each time. Strive for a set number of workable solutions to every problem. A deadline keeps you from putting things off from day to day.

17. Don't kid yourself with vague ideas. Force yourself to reduce them to specific propositions, thus firming up the problems your mind must solve.

18. State your problem carefully. Don't let the statement suggest the answer. For instance, if you ask a man to think up a new way to toast bread, you have already suggested a toaster. What you really want is a new way to dehydrate and brown the surface of the bread. State it this way, and you open up new idea opportunities.

19. Organize your approach. Find or devise a methodology that fits your problem and your personality. Break the process up into small step-by-step pieces ("divide and conquer"). If you don't do it in an organized way, you probably won't do it at all.

20. Be alert for the unexpected. Serendipity or the "happy discovery" happens only when you are actually seeking something. As Pasteur said, "Inspiration is the impact of a fact on a prepared mind".'

In summary, creativity can lead to new ideas that can enhance your business profits if implemented. Once you have done your market assessment and you feel enthusiastic and confident about the findings (perhaps not totally confident of success but ready to give your business idea a good try), you should be on the lookout for a suitable location for the business. Thereafter you can draw up a business plan to submit in order to finance the venture and then locate sources of finance to tap.

THE LOCATION DECISION

In a retail business, your sales potential depends largely on the location of the business. A very simple analogy to support the statement is that, like a tree, a shop has to draw its nourishment from the area around it. However, every potential small business has its own set of factors to consider and you will, of course, give priority to those that affect the business's sales potential. Your decision on where to locate the business should be based on some facts gathered during your market survey (your analysis of where and who your market is). Some questions, if answered can assist you to work through the problem of selecting a profitable location:

- What is the competition in the market area?
- How many of these businesses look prosperous?
- How many look as though they are barely getting by?
- How many similar businesses went out of business in that market?
- What price line does the competition carry?
- Which of the businesses in the area will be your biggest competitors?
- Are any highways planned for this area?
- Is the street traffic fairly heavy all day?
- Do pedestrains look like prospective customers?
- How close is the building to buses and other transportation?
- Are there adequate parking facilities convenient to your business?
- What is the occupancy history of this shopping centre?
- Why have other businesses failed in this location?
- What is the physical condition of the location?
- What services does the landlord provide?
- What are the terms of the lease?
- How much rent must you pay each month?
- What sales can you expect in this location?

- Is there adequate fire and police protection?
- Can the area serve as a source of supply of employees?
- Is the shop easily accessible?
- Is the trade area heavily dependent on seasonal business?

Once you have found a possible good location, you have only done half the job. So, before you make any serious commitment to renting the premises and moving in, you first need to re-assess several other aspects of the location to help ensure your satisfaction with — and most importantly your success in — the location (or site if you are going to erect a building) you have chosen. The decision as to where to locate is an important one if you wish to maximize profits because it will probably be your most significant investment in advertising in terms of the location, and external and internal image of the premises. Jeffrey P. Davidson, management consultant of the EMAY Corporation, Washington D.C., gives the following advice in respect of selecting a location:[18]

'Locate in haste, repent at leisure

Selection of a retail location requires time and careful consideration. It should not be done in haste just to coincide, say, with a loan approval. If you have not found a suitable location, do not plan to open until you are sure you have got what you want. Put your plans on hold, do not just settle for a location you hope might work out. A few months delay is only a minor setback compared to the massive — often fatal — problems that occur from operating a retail business in a poor location.'

Basic factors to consider in selecting the location are:

* *Accessibility.* Once you have identified your customers you must make it as convenient as possible for them to patronize your business. Accessibility has mainly to do with the flow of traffic to and from the location. You have to study its particular situation. Such elements may include parking facilities, a one-way street, on which side of the street the location is, business hours and the pattern of shoppers. For example, a particular location may be more convenient than another location in another area, because of people leaving for home in that direction and thus, passing this particular shop. If parking

facilities are available in such a situation, shopping traffic and profits can increase considerably. For some businesses a good location may be on the other side of the street, as people like to do their business when coming into town for work. It is important, therefore, to study the pattern people tend to follow.

* *Visibility.* Next in line of importance to accessibility is visibility. The two together form a handsome combination that can bring increased profits. The business must also be easily able to be seen, otherwise your advertising expenses may have to run very high. The factor of visibility is important as people do not usually like to hunt for the business. However, a business is usually quite visible within a shopping centre as the traffic flow is usually high. Therefore, when you consider the decision to locate within a shopping centre, be careful not to choose to locate in a hidden spot where customer traffic is very low. This necessitates a traffic flow study and count.

* *History of the location.* It is important to check out the history of a particular location. If the location has a history of repeat business failures, your approach should be one of caution and scepticism — it is a possible poor risk. Some businesses just don't do well in certain locations.

* *Future developments.* Business owners may want to sell their properties because of future developments they know of which could at a later stage make their properties drop in value.

* *Competition.* Location is a valuable tool with which to compete against your competitors. What have they not got that you can offer to the ultimate benefit of the customer? In other words, make a list of aspects you may capitalize on and seek for such a location — taking, of course, all the other aspects into consideration.

* *The rental contract.* This is an important legal document and you should seek legal counsel before finally signing it. It might be better for you to negotiate a one- or two-year rental period with an option on renewal after these terms. This is not always possible, but you

should try. However, the space or building you are renting must be suitable for your type of business, or such that it could be made so.

* *Proximity:* Studies have indicated that certain kinds of businesses do well when located adjacent to other businesses that are patronized by the same customers, for example: furniture stores are generally in close proximity of each other.

* *Responsiveness of the landlord.* Directly related to the appearance of a retail location is the responsiveness of the landlord to the individual's needs. They are often, in fact, responsible for the demise of their properties by restricting the placement and size of signs, by foregoing or ignoring needed maintenance and repairs, by renting adjacent retail space to incompatible — or worse, directly competing — businesses. Landlords may cripple a retailer's attempts to increase business. To find out about your landlord talk to the existing tenants before you commit yourself to moving in. Ask them; (1) Does the landlord return calls in a reasonable period and send service people quickly?; (2) Is it necessary to nag the landlord just to get routine maintenance taken care of?; (3) Does the landlord just collect the rent and disappear, or is he sympathetic to the needs of the tenants?; and (4) Does the landlord have any policies that hamper marketing innovations? In addition to speaking to existing tenants, you should also talk to previous tenants about the location you have in mind. Find out what businesses they had and why they left. Did they fail or just move? What support or hindrances did the landlord provide?

If you are to choose a location wisely, you need to estimate as accurately as possible your sales per month and what percentage of customer traffic can be converted into sales. Stop people in the street and talk to them openly about your plans. You may be surprised by the various suggestions you receive. Overall, your main consideration must be to locate where the income of people is regular and high enough for them to afford what you have to sell.

Using a traffic study The success that an excellent location can provide cannot be overemphasized, and therefore it is important to consider all possible ways and means to make sure that you will be able to get the maximum sales from the traffic flow passing your business. For calculating passing traffic, you should divide the people into different classifications according to the characteristics of those who would support your type of business. For example, a woman on her way to a hairdresser is probably a poor prospect for a gun shop, but she may be a good prospect for a pharmacy; and a men's clothing shop would obviously be more concerned with the amount of male traffic, especially those of the age group it caters for. The hours which these people pass the business will also be an indication of this purpose. For example, women passing a shop before its opening hours are probably on their way to work, and on their way home they pass the shop after its closing hours. Thus, women passing the business between say, 09h00 and 17h00, may be regarded as possible serious shoppers. Evaluation of estimated financial income of passing traffic may also have an effect (depending of course on what type of consumer you intend to cater for — convenience, shopping or speciality type of consumers; see page 210 for a description of such consumers). To determine what proportion of the passing traffic represents your potential shoppers, some of those pedestrains should be interviewed about the origin of their trip, their destination, and the business they intend to support. Such information can provide you with some valuable information and give a better estimate of the number of potential customers. James R. Lowry (Head, Department of Marketing, College of Business Ball State University, Muncie, Indiana), provides some clues as to how to go about researching traffic flows in your area that will bring business into your shop:[19]

'Pedestrian traffic count

In making a pedestrain count you must decide: *who* is to be counted; *where* the count should take place; and *when* the count should be made. In considering *who* is to be counted, determine what types of people should be included. For example, the study might count all men presumed to be between sixteen and sixty-five. The directions should be completely clear as to the individuals to be counted so the counters will be consistent and the total figure will reflect the traffic flow.

As previously indicated, it is frequently desirable to divide the pedestrian traffic into classes. Quite often separate counts of men and women and certain age categories are wanted. A trial run will indicate if there are any difficulties in identifying those to be counted or in placing them into various groupings.

You next determine the specific place *where* the count is to be taken. You decide whether all the traffic near the site should be counted or only the traffic passing directly in front of the site. Remember that if all the pedestrians passing through an area are counted, there is the possibility of double counting. Since a person must both enter and leave an area, it is important that each person be counted only once — either when entering or when leaving. Therefore, it is essential that the counter consistently counts at the same location.

When the count should be taken is influenced by the season, month, week, day and hour. For example, during the summer season there is generally an increased flow of traffic on the shady side of the street. During a holiday period such as the month before Christmas or the week before Easter, traffic is denser than it is regularly. The patronage of a store varies by day of the week, too. Store traffic usually increased during the latter part of a week. In some communities, on factory paydays and days when pension cheques are received, certain locations experience heavier than normal traffic.

The day of the week and the time of day should represent a normal period for traffic flow. Pedestrian flow accelerates around noon as office workers go out of their offices for lunch. Generally more customers enter a shop in a central business area of a town between 10 a.m. and noon and between 1 p.m. and 3 p.m. than at any other time. Local custom or other factors, however, may cause a variation in these expected traffic patterns.

After you choose the day that has normal traffic flow, the day should be divided into half-hour and hourly intervals. Traffic should be counted and recorded for each half-hour period of a shop's customary operating hours. If it is not feasible to count the traffic for each half-hour interval, the traffic flow can be sampled. Traffic in representative half-hour periods in the morning, noon, afternoon, and evening can be counted.

Motorcar traffic count

A growing number of retail businesses depend on drive-in traffic for their sales. Both the quantity and quality of motorcar traffic can be analyzed in the same way as pedestrian traffic. For information on the traffic flows for major streets, both the traffic department and town council can provide you with such data. However, you may need to modify this information to suit your special needs. For example, you should supplement data relating to total count of vehicles passing the site with actual observation in order to evaluate such influences on traffic as commercial vehicles, changing of shifts at nearby factories, through highway traffic, and increased flow caused by special events or activities.

Types of trips

Automobile traffic may be classified according to the reason for the trip. There are the *work trip,* the *shopping trip,* and the *pleasure trip.* Knowledge of the type of trip can assist you in making the correct site decision. Careful observation of the character of the traffic and even a few short interviews with drivers who are stopped for a traffic signal will reveal the nature of their trips.

Different types of retailers seek different locations although they are serving the same type of customer. For example, to serve a *work* trip customer, a drycleaner and a convenience foodstore usually desire to be located on different sides of the street. The drycleaner wants to locate on the going-to-work side of the street while the convenience foodstore wants to be on the going-home side.

A good location for a retailer seeking the customer on a planned shopping trip is along the left-hand side of the main street leading into a shopping district and adjacent to other streets carrying traffic into, out of, or across town. The beginning or end of a row of stores rather than across the street from the stores is preferable. Noting on which side the older, established stores are located provides a clue to the best side of the street. But check it out to be sure that the sales in these stores are rising rather than declining.

In smaller communities, where the major streets lead to and from the central business area of a town, the traffic pattern can be readily identified. In larger cities where there are suburban shopping centre locations, the traffic moves in many different directions. Because shopping centres tend to generate traffic, an analysis of the traffic flow to centres may show that a particular shop location is outstanding.

The person on a recreational trip is in the market for services such as those offered by motels, hotels, restaurants, and service stations. The probability of attracting this type of customer increases if the facility is located alongside a well-travelled highway and adjacent to a major entrance to the community.

Data from these traffic surveys can give you information on whether or not the location (or site) would generate a profitable sales volume for your business.

One retailer divides the people who pass a given site into three categories: those who enter a shop, those who, after looking in the windows, may become customers; and those who pass without entering or looking. Owing to prior experience, this retailer is able to estimate from the percentage falling into each classification not only the number who will make purchases but also how much the average purchase will be. If, out of 1 000 people passing each day, five per cent enter (50) and each spends an average of R5 (R250 per day turnover), a shop at that site which operates 300 days a year will have an annual sales volume of R75 000.'

A NAME FOR YOUR BUSINESS

When you purchase a business, you can keep the name of the business or you can change it. However, if you start a new business, you have to choose a name for it. Below are some simple rules to follow in choosing a name for your business:[20]

- Make it short, simple and easy to remember. 'Schlevinsky's Hardware', for example, is as difficult to remember as it is to pronounce.

- Let it tell the customers what you are offering them. 'Jones and Company' means nothing except that Mr Jones is in a business of some kind. 'Alexander, Richardson and Western Company' sounds like a law office — but what do they sell? The business's name should indicate its goods or services and its particular goals or features.

- Avoid family names or first names unless you are already well known. You may be proud of your name, but it does not say anything about your business to the customer. It is also easier to sell a business with a non-family name when the time comes that you want to dispose of it.

- Avoid worn-out words and phrases in the business's name, such as 'quality' and 'discount store'.

- Be sure you are not using a name someone else is already using.

HOW TO GET A TRADING LICENCE

Every province has its own ordinance to control trade licences, and these ordinances provide a variety of trade licences. The cost of these licences varies according to trade and province. They can be obtained from the local municipal authority. An application for a new licence must be submitted to the secretary of the licensing board. The local licensing authority then decides whether the application should be granted or rejected.

A separate licence is required for each individual fixed premises or place of business, even though they might be owned or leased by the same person or company. The premises are inspected to ascertain that they conform to the local authority's regulations, for example, health, building and fire regulations. The local authority may require you to submit a plan of the proposed business premises. It is advisable to keep in touch with the secretary of the local licensing board, who will be able to assist you in all relevant matters in obtaining a trade licence.

However, not all the provinces require every type of business to take out a licence. You should enquire from your local licensing authority whether a licence is necessary for your type of business.

Depending on the type of licence and the place from which the business is conducted (house or office) the licensing department usually requires reports from the town-planning department, health department, and fire department. The following may clarify these facets:[21]

'1. *Town Planning* will see that the zoning of the premises from which the business is to be conducted allows for the use being applied for. In certain cases *consent* has to be got from Town Planning. This is a procedure that could take up to three months and requires advertisements in Afrikaans and English daily newspapers of the intention to conduct the particular business activities. The rationale behind the consent procedure is to invite objections, and to then hear these objections before the Board.

In any event, Town Planning will have to support the application before a licence could be granted. Quite often, when Town Planning objects, the matter is heard by the Licensing Board who will then decide if it will uphold the objection.

2. *The Health Department* will see if all the stringent requirements of the Health Act are adhered to. This is especially so if the business involves the preparation of food.

3. *The Fire Department* will check the premises to see if there are any fire hazards.

If no objections are received by any of these departments, the licence can be issued without a licensing board hearing. Licensing board sittings usually take place once a month and licences are generally granted after six weeks.

The licence when granted, is valid up until the 31st December of the year during which it was issued. Licences should be renewed before the 31st March each year.

After the granting of the licence, the premises may be inspected from time to time by an authorised officer or health officer from the local authority. He may inspect the premises, vehicles, goods or records of the business to ensure that they conform to the local regulations.

Should an applicant or licence-holder object to any decision of the local licensing board, he may appeal to a licensing appeal board set up by the Administrator of the province concerned. Further details may be obtained from the local licensing authority of the area where the business is to be established.'

Licences for home industries Most urban authorities do not permit a business to operate from a residence. Some local authorities are more lenient than others, for example Johannesburg, where you do not need permission as long as:

- your home is not used as a shop, public garage, industrial building, or a noxious industry;
- goods, in a window or otherwise, are not publically displayed;
- there is no out-of-the-ordinary notice or sign to indicate your name and profession or occupation;
- you do not employ staff without the council's consent;
- vehicles other than those needed for the personal use of the occupier or employees are not regularly parked or stored on site;
- neighbourhood amenities are not interfered with;
- outbuildings are not used without the council's consent;
- nothing is stored on the site which in the council's opinion is unsightly or undesirable because of its effect on the neighbourhood;
- structures are not used to advertise;
- your business does not cause an undue increase in traffic in the area;

- anyone using the house for business purposes must live in it;
- where the council's permission is necessary — to employ others and to use an outbuilding — a formal application is made to the council and this is advertised in the prescribed manner; and
- not more than 20% of the ground floor of the house is used.

Liquor licences All licences for the sale of liquor are considered by the (National) Liquor Board, Pretoria. The prescribed procedure for any applicant is to approach a lawyer who will apply on his behalf.

The following Acts and Regulations are applicable in the consideration of a liquor licence:

- Liquor Act 87 of 1977 with special reference to clauses 9 and 37;
- *Government Gazette* 5959 dated 31 March 1979;
- *Government Gazette* 7209 dated 5 September 1980, Regulation R1847 with special reference to sections 1 – 9.

In the Transvaal the Liquor Board sits in May each year to consider applications. Applications are submitted to the local magistrate to be considered for each province at a particular time. Applicants for a liquor licence should note the following time schedule.

Province	Apply in	To be considered
Cape	October	January/February
Natal	March	June/July
Orange Free State	December	March/April
Transvaal	May	August/September

Liquor licences are issued by the Liquor Board and annual fees are payable on or before 31st December each year.

In the case of businessmen in the national states, trading rights must first be obtained. Trading rights are exactly that: 'a right to trade'. Trading rights are also often referred to as 'ministerial authority to trade'. In the national states, the establishment of businesses is controlled by the governments of the respective self-governing states. It is thus not possible to establish a business without the respective government's approval. It must, however, be stated, that in spite of this control the system of free enterprise is applicable. Trading rights are obtained through application to the local chief (in a rural area) and to the local town council (in a proclaimed town). If the local chief or town council has no objection, the applicant gets referred to the regional tribal authority (in a rural area) or to the selection committee of the respective town council. The successful applicants are then issued with a trading licence.

PREPARING THE BUSINESS PLAN

Why use a business plan? Firstly, it is used to arrange the information you gathered during the market analysis into figures, and secondly it is used to obtain financing (to present a convincing case to the lender). But what is the use of all the information gathered during the market analysis if it is only to convince the lender that you have a viable business, and once the finance is obtained it is filed away and you say, 'Now I have the money. So, let me get on with the business'?

The business plan serves the purpose of setting goals and working out the steps towards attaining them. You need to plan, and a written plan is essential to chart the course you intend taking from now on. It obliges you to face the future squarely and with certainty.

Once the information is translated, and let's say, financing is obtained, you have to work out plans of action to achieve the desired results as stipulated in the business plan. When compiling a business plan and plans of action, you should consider every matter, as it must be a thorough piece of work. Be business-minded, business-like, enthusiastic, confident and creative. Most important, believe in this plan of action and get advice on its implementation. When compiling your plan of action, constantly ask and answer the questions: who, when, what, where, why and how? Everything must be to the benefit of the business, as well as the customer.

Many a lender will out of 'interest' require some information on these aspects — how you are going to go about implementing your plans as well as the results to be achieved. You need to be well prepared so as to give convincing answers and explanations. The lender will not only ask for reasons such as safeguarding his interest in lending you the money, but also to check your entrepreneurial abilities, business-mindedness and character, and whether you did your homework. Lenders are through experience good judges of business aptitude.

As discussed throughout this chapter, every proposed new business must be put to the test of its market, and the real test of whether your idea is a 'hot' idea, only comes when you have drawn up the business plan.

Lenders normally require monthly projections for at least a year, and if possible, quarterly projections for the second year and an annual projection for the third year. But let us see what the attitude of the professionals is towards a business plan: Mr Eddie Johnston, Head of First National Bank's Small Business Unit says:[22]

'More than half of small business loan applications to banks are rejected at an early stage of negotiations. This is because many would-be small businessmen simply do not do their homework — or even understand the basics of putting a business together — before they come to us. Many applications also fail to secure bank finance because the applicants ask for too little money, while other applicants just don't have the right mental approach. In many cases a fellow applies for, say, R30 000 and wants to stage his business around the loan. That is the wrong way round. He should sort out the business he has or is aiming for, from his projections, and then the financing requirements. When the facts are all in however, the final decision by the bank rests on the banker's "gut feel" on whether the venture will succeed. That is the key. But how can they expect us to have faith in the potential business and put money up front for its success if the loan applicant hasn't a clue where to start?'

Barry Adams from Arthur Anderson and Company has this to say:[23]

'Since only one new venture in ten succeeds, venture capitalists want assurance that an entity's management team has carefully considered its weaknesses as well as its strengths, its problems as well as its opportunities and that its probability of success is high. Before the professional advisor refers a new entity to a venture capitalist, it is wise to help its management develop a business plan. A sound business plan, tailored to answer the questions venture capitalists frequently ask, is an excellent device for attracting investment capital. A business plan also is invaluable to a new company because it permits management to track and direct the growth of the business. With help from professional advisors, new entities can develop effective business plans that will interest venture capitalists and will serve as a vital management tool. The new entity's management should be actively involved in every aspect of the planning process. If an outsider prepares the business plan for the entity, the completed plan may not reflect the entrepreneur's total insight and broad concept or gain his full commitment. Instead of preparing the plan, the professional advisor's role should be to provide guidance during the planning process and to offer perspective as an experienced member of the business and financial community. As the new entity's management completes major sections of the plan, the professional advisor can offer them valuable assistance by reviewing the plan for quality, clarity, reasonableness and thoroughness. A good question the professional advisor should ask himself is whether he would invest on the basis of their business plan. If he cannot answer with an enthusiastic "yes", then the plan needs more work. The business plan is a new entity's first and perhaps best opportunity to capture the interest of a prospective investor. One prominent venture capitalist has estimated that prospective investors reject 60% of their investment opportunities within the first half hour, give serious consideration to 15%, and go as far as the negotiation stage on only 5%. To a great extent, the decision turns on the quality of the business plan which the new entity presents to support its request for funding. Even for the rare entity that does not need to seek additional capital, a business plan is a vital management tool. A sound business plan can guide an entity from start-up to maturity. Developing a business plan forces management to analyze their goals, management team, products, marketing, strategy, competition, and short and long term capital needs. If the professional advisor can help an entity's management work through these tough issues to their own, and prospective investor's satisfaction, that effort alone should increase their chances of success. After all, for each good idea that succeeds, many others just as good or better do not. The difference often lies in careful, realistic planning.'

Roger Rees, Manager, Small Business Division, Arthur Anderson and Company says:[24]

'A business must have capital. To obtain capital, a business must communicate its plans for return on the invested capital or repayment of the borrowings. The business must then maximize its return on capital, and it must generate adequate cash flow. All this requires planning. But planning often is difficult. Assumptions must be made about the future, and these assumptions must then be combined into a financial plan or model. It is this financial model which provides a means of planning for profitable operations, projecting financial results, planning cash flow and preparing and analyzing operation budgets. It thus places control of the planning process in the hands of the entrepreneur.'

Citicorp Venture Capital, Ltd, is an investment company which invests risk capital in new ventures. Its president, Rick Roesch (a University of California MBA), was once asked what might improve the chances of an applicant for new business financing. His answer stressed the importance of a well-thought-out, persuasive, written business plan:[25]

The most successful entrepreneurs have thought through their business plans. They know their strengths and weaknesses. They know what the competition is offering. The entrepreneur is doing himself a disservice to think he can go in eye-to-eye with a prospective investor and simply sell his company. It's safe to say that if it is not on paper, it is not well enough thought out for a venture capitalist to consider it.

The first step in guaranteeing sufficient capital with which to start the business is to do everything possible to ensure that your estimation of start-up expenses is accurate. Money is required for various things such as land, buildings, equipment, stock, vehicles, sufficient capital (or cash) to at least provide for the first three to six months of operation, and for debtors (if you decide to sell R1 000 on credit and your terms are three months, then you must have R3 000 saved to replace stock bought by debtors).[26] To raise enough capital, thought must be given to expenses that will be incurred in day-to-day operations for which cash must be provided. General expenses to consider are:

- insurance (fire, crime, theft, liability, disaster, etc.);
- water and electricity (plus initial deposits);
- owner's salary;
- medical scheme contributions;
- pension fund contributions;
- unemployment insurance contributions;
- registration and licence fees;
- telephone (plus initial connection fees);

- printing and stationery (letter heads, typewriter materials, paper, paper clips, etc.)
- packaging material;
- bookkeeping fees;
- travelling expenses;
- refreshment and entertainment expenses;
- advertising;
- cleaning materials;
- interest on loan or bank overdraft;
- bank charges;
- bad debts;
- maintenance on equipment, building, vehicles, etc;
- rent (and leases);
- security protection (guards);
- delivery expenses;
- uniforms (working clothes for employees);
- taxes;
- depreciation on assets;
- property taxes;
- personnel salaries;
- legal fees;
- decoration inside and outside business (signwriting, etc.)
- grand opening expenses;
- membership in business associations;
- subscriptions to trade and professional magazines and journals; and
- capital expenses such as: buildings; machinery; equipment; land; outside business improvements such as parking lots, landscaping, paving, etc.; remodelling the inside of the business structure to suit your needs, rewiring, outside windows and ventilation; typewriters, fire extinguishers, vacuum cleaner, tools; patents or copyrights necessary to the business; shelves, display counters, etc.; safes, cash registers, etc.; and vehicles needed by the business.

Steps to be followed in preparing the business plan

Step 1: Calculate sales

By now you have information on hand which was gathered during the market analysis. Say for instance, there are 12 000 people in the town, community or neighbourhood. You have also obtained the fact from the various sources mentioned earlier that their average income per household amounts to R1 000 per month. According to the index of consumer purchasing power, this indicates that the spending on commodities to be sold by your type of business is R70 per capita per annum. Therefore, the expected annual sales for your type of business amount to R840 000. Seeing that there are two other such businesses in the area or town, you can expect that they will each receive 33,3% of the market share. Therefore, you can expect for a start, sales of R279 720 per year. However, these sales must be put into monthly figures for the purpose of the cash flow budget. Obviously, you cannot just divide them by twelve, you should rather estimate the expected monthly sales based on information gained from thorough market research, experience and the economic climate (present and future). Say you are planning to open as from January 1988. These calculations could look as follows:

Sales	
January 1988	R 24 000
February	22 000
March	23 000
April	21 000
May	22 000
June	21 000
July	23 000
August	22 000
September	23 000
October	24 000
November	25 000
December	29 720
	R279 720

Step 2:   Calculate purchases

After estimated sales, estimated purchases can be calculated. Calculate the purchases of stock that you need to achieve the above sales. Estimated purchases depend on estimated sales, estimated stock turnover rate and the gross profit percentage. Here you have to consider the necessary operating ratios of related businesses which will indicate a possible stock turnover rate and gross profit percentage of the type of business in question. The location of the business is also a factor to bear in mind when estimating the stock turnover rate. Estimated purchases can be calculated as follows:

Step 1 —	estimated sales	R279 720
Step 2 —	gross profit (30% of sales)	R 83 916
Step 3 —	cost of sales (1 minus 2)	R195 804
Step 4 —	estimated stock turnover rate	7 times
Step 5 —	average stock required	
	(step 3 divided by step 4)	R 27 972

In the case of a new business the amount required for estimated purchases will be calculated as follows:

Cost of sales	R195 804
Plus: initial stock	R 27 972
Estimated purchases per year	R223 776

In the case of buying an existing business, the exercise must however continue as follows:

Step 6 —	stock on hand	R 29 000
Step 7 —	surplus/(shortage)	
	(step 6 minus step 5)	R 1 028
Step 8 —	amount to be purchased	
	(step 3 minus step 7)	R194 776

To calculate the cost of sales for every month, you take the opening stock (which is normally nil at the start of a new business), add the purchases and deduct the closing stock. In this case it may work out as shown in the table on page 95.

Initial stock, or rather, the amount needed for purchasing stock during the first month would be R44 772 (R27 972 initial stock as well as R16 800 to replenish the stock being sold during the first month). Your policy should be to hold an initial stock of R27 972 ($\pm$ R28 000 stock level). The above calculation is necessary to draw up the pro forma financial statements as well as the cash flow budget.

	Opening stock	Purchases	Closing stock	Cost of sales
January 1988	—	44 772	27 972	16 800
February	27 972	15 400	27 972	15 400
March	27 972	16 100	27 972	16 100
April	27 972	14 700	27 972	14 700
May	27 972	15 400	27 972	15 400
June	27 972	14 700	27 972	14 700
July	27 972	16 100	27 972	16 100
August	27 972	15 400	27 972	15 400
September	27 972	16 100	27 972	16 100
October	27 972	16 800	27 972	16 800
November	27 972	17 500	27 972	17 500
December	27 972	20 804	27 972	20 804
		223 776		195 804

Step 3: Determine capital expenditures

This must be done in order to determine the monthly instalments and depreciation on these assets which is an expense to the business and must appear on the income statement.

- Land and buildings: Provision is only made if you intend erecting your own building in which case a builder or architect could be of assistance. For this example we assume you are renting premises.

- Equipment: For this example we assume the total equipment needed amounts to R15 000 (including general sales tax). Depreciation on equipment is 10% per year.[27]

- Vehicles: Let us assume you need a delivery truck which will cost you R16 000 (including general sales tax). Depreciation on vehicles per year is 20%.

Step 4: Estimate operating and start-up expenses

Operating expenses are the essential recurring expenses incurred to keep the business going. Experience, the economic climate and information about existing related businesses will give a reasonable indication of what the various operating expenses of the proposed business will be. Suppose that after a thorough consideration of the expenses to be incurred in the coming year of operation, the total sum of R59 418, is made up as follows:

Salaries	R 34 000
Transport	2 800
Water and lights	780
Telephone	360
Advertising	1 600
Interest on loan	3 163
Refreshments and sundry	275
Insurance	900
Start-up expenses	1 280
Maintenance — vehicles	340
Rent	4 800
Leases: vehicles	5 640
equipment	3 480
Total	R 59 418

Some start-up expenses may for instance include R500 for your grand opening; R250 to pay for telephone, water and lights deposits (a deposit is a current asset as you will be getting the money back when you cancel the services); R120 to pay for the business licence; R500 to get invoices and receipts printed with the name of the business thereon; and R160 to buy clothing (uniforms) for your employees.

Step 5: Determine total capital requirements

So far you have determined that you need financing for the following to start your business:

Stock	R44 772	(Step 2)
Equipment	15 000	(Step 3)
Vehicles	16 000	(Step 3)
	R75 772	

Long-term loans are normally financed over various periods as follows: Stock — 5 years; equipment — 5 to 10 years; building — 15 to 20 years; and vehicles — 4 to 5 years. However, these terms (as well as interest rates) may differ from one financial institution to another. Let us further assume that such financing can be obtained at an interest rate of 15% per year. Monthly instalments on terms indicated in brackets will be as follows:

Stock	R1 065	(5 years)
Equipment	242	(10 years)
Vehicles	445	(4 years)
	R1 752	per month

Step 6: Look at your own financial resources

The time has now come to consider your own financial strength. How much can you contribute toward the loan? It is commonly known that the bank will require, at least, a 50% contribution from you. Have you got R37 886 (50% of R75 772) on hand? If you do not have it, there are other alternatives — you can lease the equipment as well as the vehicle and take a loan for the stock only. Thus, you still need to contribute 50% but now only R22 386 (50% of R44 772). It is assumed the latter is the case in this example. More assumptions and final decisions can be made from the cash flow statement. However, if we assume that you will require a loan for stock of R22 386 and lease the vehicle and equipment, then your monthly instalments and interest will obviously also be changing (from that calculated in step 5).

Step 7: Prepare a cash flow statement

From cash flow statement no. 1 (p. 98) you can see that sufficient cash will be available to the business to have a good start. It is also evident that you will be ending with a bank balance of R37 827 at the end of the first year of operation. This cash flow statement also proves that you will be able to repay the loan. However, looking at the cash flow statement from the lender's point of view, he will lend you financing as follows:

Stock needed	R44 772	
Less: surplus	R17 605	(point C on cash flow statement no. 1)
	R27 167	

The R27 167 is the 'exact' amount you need to start this business but the lender will only lend you 50% of that amount, which is R13 583. The remaining 50% (R13 584)

CASH FLOW STATEMENT NO. 1

	Jan.	Feb.	Mar.	Apr.	May	Jun.	Jul.	Aug.	Sept.	Oct.	Nov.	Dec.	Total
Receipts													
Sales: cash sales	24 000	22 000	23 000	21 000	22 000	21 000	23 000	22 000	23 000	24 000	25 000	29 720	279 720
Bank loan	22 386	—	—	—	—	—	—	—	—	—	—	—	22 386
Own contribution	22 386	—	—	—	—	—	—	—	—	—	—	—	22 386
Total receipts (A)	68 772	22 000	23 000	21 000	22 000	21 000	23 000	22 000	23 000	24 000	25 000	29 720	324 492
Purchases	44 772	15 400	16 100	14 700	15 400	14 700	16 100	15 400	16 100	16 800	17 500	20 804	223 776
Lease vehicles	470	470	470	470	470	470	470	470	470	470	470	470	5 640
Payments: equip.	290	290	290	290	290	290	290	290	290	290	290	290	3 480
Salaries	2 615	2 615	2 615	2 615	2 615	2 615	2 615	2 615	2 615	2 615	2 615	5 235	34 000
Transport	233	233	233	233	233	233	233	233	233	233	233	237	2 800
Water & lights	65	65	65	65	65	65	65	65	65	65	65	65	780
Telephone	30	30	30	30	30	30	30	30	30	30	30	30	360
Advertising	133	133	133	133	133	133	133	133	133	133	133	137	1 600
Bank loan repayments (including interest)	532	532	532	532	532	532	532	532	532	532	532	532	6 384
Refreshments & sundries	22	22	22	22	22	22	22	22	22	22	22	33	275
Maintenance — vehicles	—	—	—	—	—	—	340	—	—	—	—	—	340
Rent	400	400	400	400	400	400	400	400	400	400	400	400	4 800
Insurance	75	75	75	75	75	75	75	75	75	75	75	75	900
Other start-up expenses (Step 5)	1 530	—	—	—	—	—	—	—	—	—	—	—	1 530
TOTAL PAYMENTS (B)	51 167	20 265	20 965	19 565	20 265	19 565	21 305	20 265	20 965	21 665	22 365	28 308	286 665
Cash surplus/ (shortage) A minus B = (C)	17 605	1 735	2 035	1 435	1 735	1 435	1 695	1 735	2 035	2 335	2 635	1 412	37 827
Opening bank balance (D)	0	17 605	19 340	21 375	22 810	24 545	25 980	27 675	29 410	31 445	33 780	36 415	0
Closing bank balance (E) (C plus D)	17 605												

	Jan.	Feb.	Mar.	Apr.	May	Jun.	Jul.	Aug.	Sept.	Oct.	Nov.	Dec.	Total
Receipts													
Sales: cash sales	24 000	22 000	23 000	21 000	22 000	21 000	23 000	22 000	23 000	24 000	25 000	29 720	279 720
Bank loan	13 583	—	—	—	—	—	—	—	—	—	—	—	13 583
Own contribution	13 584	—	—	—	—	—	—	—	—	—	—	—	13 584
Total receipts (A)	51 167	22 000	23 000	21 000	22 000	21 000	23 000	22 000	23 000	24 000	25 000	29 720	306 887
Purchases	44 772	15 400	16 100	14 700	15 400	14 700	16 100	15 400	16 100	16 800	17 500	20 804	223 776
Lease vehicles	470	470	470	470	470	470	470	470	470	470	470	470	5 640
Payments: equip.	290	290	290	290	290	290	290	290	290	290	290	290	3 480
Salaries	2 615	2 615	2 615	2 615	2 615	2 615	2 615	2 615	2 615	2 615	2 615	5 235	34 000
Transport	233	233	233	233	233	233	233	233	233	233	233	230	2 800
Water & lights	65	65	65	65	65	65	65	65	65	65	65	65	780
Telephone	30	30	30	30	30	30	30	30	30	30	30	30	360
Advertising	133	133	133	133	133	133	133	133	133	133	133	137	1 600
Bank loan repayments (including interest)	323	323	323	323	323	323	323	323	323	323	323	323	3 876
Refreshments & sundries	22	22	22	22	22	22	22	22	22	22	22	33	275
Maintenance — vehicles	—	—	—	—	—	—	340	—	—	—	—	—	340
Rent	400	400	400	400	400	400	400	400	400	400	400	400	4 800
Insurance	75	75	75	75	75	75	75	75	75	75	75	75	900
Other start-up expenses (Step 5)	1 530	—	—	—	—	—	—	—	—	—	—	—	1 530
Total payments (B)	50 958	20 056	20 756	19 356	20 056	19 356	21 096	20 056	20 756	21 456	22 156	28 099	284 157
Cash surplus/ (shortage) A minus B = (C)	209	1 944	2 244	1 644	1 944	1 644	1 904	1 944	2 244	2 544	2 844	1 612	22 730
Opening bank balance (D)	0	209	2 153	4 397	6 041	17 985	9 629	11 533	13 477	15 721	18 265	21 109	0
Closing bank balance (E) (C plus D)	209	2 153	4 397	6 041	17 985	9 629	11 533	13 477	15 721	18 265	21 109	22 730	22 730

must be your own contribution. The bank will also require security for the amount borrowed by you. The final cash flow statement to be presented to the lender will be cash flow statement no. 2. Notice that your instalment on the loan of R13 583 once again changes as follows:

	Interest Rate	Term	Instalment per month	Interest per month	Capital per month
Amount of loan granted for stock R13 583	15%	5 years	323,00	160,00	163,00

Step 8: Compile financial statements

You now have to draw up financial statements to see how the real picture will look after the first year of operation and to have insight into the financial situation by means of certain ratios. (Do these ratios compare favourably to those in similar businesses?)

BALANCE SHEET AS AT 31 DECEMBER 1988

	Notes	R
Capital employed		
Capital	1	13 684
Retained profit	2	25 741
Long-term liability	3	11 627
		50 952
Employment of capital		
Cash in bank		22 730
Stock		27 972
Deposits	4	250
	5	50 952

Notes:
1. Represents initial capital invested by the owner (own contribution).
2. From profit and loss (income and expenditure) statement.
3. Bank loan (R13 583 less capital redemption of R1 956).
4. Telephone R50 plus electricity R200.
5. The amount of R50 952 represents current assets. Fixed assets like vehicles and equipment are not recorded, as they are still on lease. Ownership of items on lease can only pass to the lessee once the items are fully paid for.

INCOME STATEMENT FOR THE PERIOD 1 JANUARY 1988 TO 31 DECEMBER 1988

Sales	279 720
Cost of sales	195 804
Opening stock	—
Plus: purchases	233 776
Less: closing stock	27 972
Gross profit	83 916
Less: expenses	58 175
Salaries	34 000
Transport	2 800
Water & lights	780
Telephone	360
Advertising	1 600
Interest on loan	1 920
Refreshments and sundries	275
Maintenance — vehicles	340
Rent	4 800
Insurance	900
Leases: vehicles	5 640
equipment	3 480
Grand opening	500
Licences	120
Stationery and printing	500
Clothing	160
Net profit	R25 741

(Grand opening, Licences, Stationery and printing, Clothing) — From step 5

Ratios:	
Gross profit percentage	30%
Average mark-up	42,8%
Stock turnover rate	7 times
Net profit percentage	9,2%[28]

The business plan's main purpose may be said to be to attract capital to finance the business, and to provide the lender with information on which to make his decision. Other information apart from those mentioned that should accompany your business plan are the following:

- a brief description of the business, including operating history, if any;

- a trade name;
- the names of owners, partners, directors;
- the number of employees to be employed;
- the management team and perhaps a brief résumé covering their qualifications and relevant experience;
- the owner-manager's compensation;
- a brief description of the market — size, growth rate, names of competitors, possible new markets;
- an advertising plan;
- pricing of products or services;
- equipment which will be required;
- the owner-manager's résumé. Be aware of the fact that you will also be evaluated because lenders are of opinion that a good manager is the single most important criterion in the evaluation of any financing opportunity. When you give the lender some background of your own past experience, think about it as of writing a letter of application for a job. Its sole purpose is to sell something and an attempt is thus made to induce the lender to take some favourable action. Be honest throughout. Do not be afraid of the use of 'I' in the business plan. You are selling yourself, and your personality is the most interesting thing about which you can write. The lender needs to know about you and you need not fear that he will be antagonized by any number of modest references to yourself. The lender must also feel that you are the sort of person to whom he wants to grant a loan; and
- the organization structure (form of business).

WHAT FORM OF BUSINESS?

There are various forms of business you may wish to consider entering. Some of these forms of business are discussed below.

* *Sole proprietor.* If you have not adopted any of the other forms of ownership mentioned below, you are automatically a sole proprietor. The business and the personal assets of the owner in such a form of business

are considered as one and the owner is thus personally responsible for debts incurred by the business.

* *Partnership.* This is when two or more people decide to conduct business together. The difference between a partnership and a sole proprietor is simply that the owner of a sole proprietorship conducts business purely in his personal capacity, while the partners in a business bear equal responsibility for debts incurred. It is recommended that when you enter into a partnership, all partners consult a legal expert and a written partnership agreement is drawn up based on aspects agreed mutually by the partners.

* *Close corporation.* Introduced at the beginning of 1985, a close corporation is in essence a business with a separate legal status from its members. It is cheaper to establish, cheaper to maintain than a company, and entails limited liability to members provided the provisions of the Act are observed. Only individuals may be members and the number of members is limited to ten. Unlike the Companies Act, with its numerous articles, many of which do not apply to a small business and which are most confusing, the Closed Corporations Act is tailor-made almost specifically for the small business-man.

* *Company.* There are a number of types of companies, but the most suitable for a small business is the proprietary limited or '(Pty) Ltd' company. The number of shareholders is limited to fifty. The statutory requirements for establishing and maintaining a company are fairly onerous and relatively expensive. The most significant advantages are that its shareholders are not personally liable for its debts, and it has an indeterminate lifespan or what is known as 'perpetual succession'; it does not die when the members die.

You need to choose one of these forms of business by considering some basic factors that will influence your decision. These factors are for your consideration presented in an 'easy to choose' manner by Arthur Anderson and Co., extracted from their publication *How to run a small business successfully:*[29]

FACTOR	COMPANY	CLOSE CORPORATION	PARTNERSHIP	SOLE PROPRIETORSHIP
Life	Unlimited or perpetual, unless limited by law (insolvency), voluntary liquidation, or terms of its articles of association.	Unlimited or perpetual, unless limited by law (insolvency) or voluntary liquidation.	Generally set up for a specific, agreed term, usually will be terminated by death, withdrawal, insolvency or legal disability of a general partner, i.e. no perpetual succession.	At death, business assets pass to proprietor's estate.
Entity	Completely separate from shareholders and recognised as such.	Completely separate from members and recognised as such.	Generally recognised as separate by the business community, but not for all purposes.	Generally recognised as separate by the business community, but not for all purposes.
Liability of owners	Limited. Shareholders are generally sheltered from any liabilities of the company.	Same as company, provided certain conditions are complied with.	Each partner is fully liable as an individual for all debts. Partner has unlimited risk. Creditors can attach all personal assets for business debts.	Owner has unlimited risk. Creditors can attach all personal assets for business debts.
Ease and effect of transfer of ownership interest	Generally, shares are easily and readily transferable, subject to Companies Act, articles of association or shareholders' agreements, and transfer has no effect on the entity.	A member's interest is readily transferable, subject to Close Corporations Act, or members' agreements, and transfer has no effect on the entity.	Sale or purchase of interests require approval of all other partners and results in termination of the old partnership and creation of a new one.	Transfer terminates entity.
Availability of outside capital or financing	May sell shares to the public, provided offers to the public are supported by a prospectus, as required by the Companies Act, in addition to outside borrowing.	Limited to members' contributions and outside borrowing.	Limited to borrowing from partners or outsiders.	Limited to proprietor's personal assets and outside borrowing.
Management of business operation	Much flexibility. Control can be exercised by a small number of officers without having to consult owners, regardless of the total number of shareholders.	Active participation generally by all members since the total number of members cannot exceed ten.	Usually, all general partners will be active participants in management. However, other partners may grant management control to one or more partners by agreement.	Owner has complete control.

FACTOR	COMPANY	CLOSE CORPORATION	PARTNERSHIP	SOLE PROPRIETORSHIP
Who is the taxpayer?	The company is taxed on its taxable income, whether or not it is distributed to the shareholders.	As for company, except that all dividend receipts are taxable.	The partners are taxed on the partnership profits, whether or not profits are distributed to them.	The proprietor is taxed on the profits whether or not they are drawn by proprietor.
Distribution of earnings	Taxable in shareholders' hands as ordinary dividends.	Tax free in the hands of members.	No tax effect for partners.	No tax effect for proprietor.
Net loss	Deductible only in hands of the company.	As for company.	Deductible by partners, in their profit-sharing ratios.	Deductible by proprietor.
Salaries	When shareholders are employees, salaries are taxable in their hands and deductible by the company. Salaries must be reasonable in amount in relation to services rendered.	As for company.	Salaries together with each partner's share of profits are taxed in the partner's hands.	Sole proprietor is not an employee. Amounts paid are considered distributions of income.
Earnings accumulation	Retained earnings taxable once distributed.	Retained earnings distributed to members tax-free.	All income is taxed in hands of partners whether distributed or not.	As for partnership.
Investment	Dividend income received by company not taxable. However, undistributed profits tax may become payable.	Two thirds of dividend income earned is taxable at the company rate.	Two thirds of dividend income taxed in hands of individual partners, where individual's income exceeds R4 600 per annum.	Two-thirds of dividend income taxable, where income exceeds R4 600 per annum.
Selection of year end	No restriction; however, subject to the approval of the Registrar of Companies.	As for company.	The partners will be assessed individually according to the taxable year-end. Receiver of Revenue approval required if year-end other than last day of February.	Same as that of the proprietor.
Educational donations	Donations to qualifying institutions deductible by the company, however, limited to 5% of taxable income.	As for company.	Deducted by the partners on their individual returns subject to the limitations applicable to individuals.	Deducted by the proprietor on the individual return subject to the limitations applicable to individuals.

It is, of course of prime importance that you seek counsel from a lawyer or a management consultant when making a decision on which form of business will be best suited to your type of business. In other words, the form of business from which you can benefit the most.

Your ability to finance the business depends on your business reputation and the future potential of the business, the amount of money you need to start and operate the business and your personal resources. However, there is one thing that owner-managers of small businesses can do to improve the chances of their proposals for financial assistance and so escape the almost 90% chance of being immediately rejected — in a word: *plan.* Having financial plans demonstrates to the lender that you are a competent manager, and thus you have that special managerial edge over all other small business owners looking for finance. If you are well known in your field of business or have a product or service which others believe will be profitable, you may be able to finance your venture with a substantial amount of outside capital. But if you are starting without these advantages, you will more than likely have to depend on your own resources.

It should be clear by now that when you want to obtain finance, you have to be prepared (i.e. have a keen insight into the business you wish to open) in all aspects as well as enough enthusiasm to instil confidence for your idea. Below are some simple requirements that will inspire the lender to finance the venture:

- *Prove* that you have a reputation for paying your obligations when due.
- *Be optimistic.* The lender must 'feel' your personality. He must gather the spirit of optimism from your style and from your attitude towards your idea and what you intend to sell. If you do not really believe that you have a 'hot' idea and that no obstacles are going to obstruct the success of the business, you surely cannot make the lender believe these things. Lenders always feel safer lending capital to someone who has the will and tenacity to see his idea through, regardless of what happens. It is a semi-guarantee that they will see their money again. The matter of enthusiasm is demonstrated in this single case where a New York businessman invented a bullet-proof vest and was employing a salesman to go on the road and sell it:[30]

'The inventor interviewed a young man who applied for the job. "Put on the vest and I will show you how it works." The young man adjusted the light vest, made of thin metal plates, a trifle nervously. When the inventor drew out a police service revolver shooting a jacketed bullet, the young man turned pale. "You can't sell these vests unless you believe in them yourself", said the businessman as he placed the muzzle of the gun four inches from the heart of the salesman. I have to shoot you". The salesman was scared, but he had courage. His eyes became glassy, and as the revolver was fired, he died several deaths. An instant later he gave a yell of astonishment, relief and joy. "I ... I ... scarcely felt it!" he exclaimed. "Say ... I can go out and sell that vest now! Let me get started." He broke the sales record of the business in the next month.'

- *Know the business.* Before entering the doors of a financial institution make sure you know at least the basic 'ins and outs' of the type of business and how to apply it. You must know what you are talking about and the only way to know the field of business you are about to enter, is to observe it at first hand. Remember that the lender is not only evaluating the product but also the person with the product. He is lending the money to you and not to the product.
- *Be helpful.* The businessman who simply gives orders to the lender is foolish in his attitude towards the lender, and therefore will not have his whole-hearted co-operation. There are people in this world who think they are always right, no matter what others say. This is an incorrect attitude. Of course, there must be mutual respect if both are to retain their helpfulness, and a fair amount of dignity is necessary. As a businessman you should, where possible, accept advice from your lender. There is no other way of getting the lender's co-operation, except by being honest, frank and reasonable with him in every particular.

Communicate. You should be able to think in a business-like fashion. You will find it hard to convince the lender if your thoughts and expressions are lacking in clarity and directness. Lenders are accustomed to the use of straight, to-the-point language.

Sources of finance

Borrowing from a bank

Generally, the attitude of the commercial banks is that if someone comes to the banker with a good idea, one way or another, they will find some way to help the businessman. As said before security is important, but what is of most concern to bankers is whether the idea is sound, whether the businessman is 'right' and whether the business proposition will better serve the market he intends to enter. The integrity and ability of the entrepreneur are then as good as security.

A bank makes money by lending money and will generally lend you funds if your business reputation is good and your business is profitable or has profitable prospects. Set up a good working relationship with your bank. Look ahead to the time when you will be starting and wanting to expand your business. Bankers prefer to make loans to a problem-free business which needs funds to expand operations. A bank loan will not easily be granted if the banker (or lender) suspects that the money is needed to pay off your own personal debts. The banks want to see that the money given on loan is put to constructive use. In addition, if the motivation for your idea is poor and relevant information lacking, the banker will have no enthusiasm for the potential of your business and will be unable to put the bank's money at your disposal. Ensure that the necessary information is at your fingertips. Overall, the banker is concerned with the answer to the question: 'Will probable profits and the ability of the entrepreneur warrant the required investment?' The banker is looking for the ability in you that will ensure the success of your business.

The Development Corporations

When referring to development corporations it might be best to differentiate between the development corporations of the national states within the borders of South Africa which served the various ethnic groups and the Small Business Development Corporation (SBDC) which serves all population groups outside the borders of these national states. Their goals are the same; they differ only in the geographic areas they serve.

Before attending to the various aspects of financing your small business by either the development corporation within your national state or the SBDC, you might find a short background to the two types of development corporations of interest. Both corporations offer loan facilities (financing) to enable citizens of South Africa to establish, expand, improve or purchase their own businesses. The reasons being: firstly to promote and assist in developing and stimulating a sound, efficient and balanced small business sector with the aim of building it and maintaining it as one of the cornerstones of a free enterprise economy in South Africa (as well as in the national states), which will further assist in the country's growth; secondly, to promote entrepreneurship so that honourable men and women can perform a valuable and an important service to their communities; and thirdly, to promote a sound and competitive commercial and social structure through financing and other services in order to improve the quality of life of the people of South Africa. These corporations thus lend money to small businesses in order to achieve development goals.

It must, however, be well understood that these corporations are not welfare organizations and are not out to generate a profit by charging high interest on loans. Neither do they intend financing uneconomic business ventures. In other words, they are non-profit organizations and aim to help dynamic people to achieve success in business and thus contribute to the expansion of employment opportunities in South Africa (which will lead to the creation of wealth). Neither are these development corporations in competition with each other. In fact they co-operate with each other.

Financing is not considered for the following types of transactions:

1. speculative transactions;
2. on-lending;
3. non-profit-orientated activities;
4. community and social facilities; and
5. financing outside the Rand monetary area (in the case of the SBDC) and financing outside the respective national states (in the case of development corporations serving the national states).

The following general (though flexible) guidelines apply when financing is considered:

1. The business must be considered an economically viable proposition.

2. Relevant experience and knowledge, management ability and a spirit of entrepreneurship are considered important.
3. The applicant is expected to make a reasonable contribution towards the capital requirements of the business (in the case of the SBDC). The development corporations of the national states expect a 10% own contribution.
4. Goodwill is not normally financed. The reason being that it is an intangible asset and therefore not easy to determine, and no security can be registered on goodwill. The charging of goodwill makes sense from the seller's point of view, because he has put in a lot of time, effort and a great deal of money to bring the business where it is at the time he wants to sell it. The lenders normally feel that the proposed buyer should pay for this himself while they provide finance for the tangible assets. But lenders are always prepared to help in negotiating a price with both the seller and the buyer in order to reach a fair price if the buyer needs financing.
5. Financing the purchase of an existing business is considered only where the purchaser obtains control and either where the continuation of the business is in jeopardy or where there is a development aspect involved.
6. Replacement finance is considered only where it strengthens security, provides for the continued existence of the business and is developmental.
7. Financial assistance for the purchase of existing buildings is considered only where the applicant cannot obtain adequate finance in the open market, where the purchase is essential to the continuation of the business and where the greater portion is to be occupied by the business of the applicant.
8. Finance for the erection of commercial or industrial buildings for own occupation or partial letting is considered in areas where development is regarded as essential.
9. Finance for farming operations is considered only where processing is involved in order to market the product.

As a prospective businessman applying for financial assistance from these development corporations, you have an

110

advantage — they conduct a market survey and feasibility study in order to determine if there is 'room' for your type of business, in other words, whether it will be a viable proposition. This service creates greater confidence in the business they intend to assist financially. Commercial banks do not normally render such a service — you are required to do it.

The SBDC has developed a range of assistance programmes designed to suit the needs of small businesses at every stage of their development — programmes for informal, semi-formal, and formal businesses. Such financing programmes include: the Bank Indemnity Scheme and the General Financing Scheme (for the formal sector); The Comprehensive Assistance Programme (for the semi-formal sector); and the Mini-loan Scheme for the informal sector. Below is some information about these financing programmes:[31]

The Mini-loan scheme

The Mini-loan Scheme is designed specifically for the informal or semi-formal infant enterprise whose needs are normally of an urgent, short-term and recurring nature. Presently loans of up to R5 000 are considered and are repayable over a maximum period of 36 months at an interest rate of 1% per month. The main prerequisites to be met by the applicants are their ability to repay and evidence of a serious commitment to the business concerned. Formalities are minimised and simplified as far as possible, so that the businessman can receive the money within as short a time as possible. Two distinct schemes have been initiated in this category. The first is controlled by a locally based committee for a specific area (for example, an industrial park or local community), and the second is run by SBDC personnel who actively seek out businesses requiring this form of financial assistance.

The comprehensive assistance programme

The Comprehensive Assistance Programme for infant enterprises involves larger, formalised loans and various forms of after-care service and guidance. The maximum loan presently available from this programme is R30 000. These loans are made available on favourable terms — three or more years to repay. You can qualify for such a loan if your small business has grown to the point where you need fixed premises; if you are in need of a wider range of stock or equipment; if you are dependent on the business for your income; if you are in need of assistance to manage a more sophisticated business; or if you need finance and premises at reasonable rates.

Suppliers' Guarantee Scheme

The objectives of the Suppliers' Guarantee Scheme are twofold:

(i) to establish a credit rating for infant enterprises with suppliers; and
(ii) to allow for more competitive pricing by infant businesses.

After an infant enterprise client has been approved for this scheme, negotiations are conducted with suppliers to introduce the scheme to them. A credit limit is set for the buyer and the SBDC guarantees payment in the event of the business defaulting. Guidelines presently followed are:

1. A credit limit of R2 000 may be negotiated for a period of not more than six months.
2. A fee for this facility may be charged by the SBDC.

At the end of the credit period negotiated for the infant enterprise, the supplier should treat the infant enterprise as a normal credit customer.

Small Business Aid Fund

The Small Business Aid Fund is the SBDC's lifeline for the small business in the commercial, industrial, or service sector which have been hit by the economic downturn or other external circumstances beyond their control. Funds are only made available to small businesses which are unable to get finance from any other sources. The fund provides short-term bridging finance to tide you over. You can qualify for the Aid Fund if:

1. your gross assets are not more than R1,5 million;
2. your business is economically viable and competitive in the long term;
3. your financing problems are short term and due solely to unusual circumstances in the national or regional economy and not mismanagement;

4. you show that the loan would keep people in employment, and that your business makes an on-going contribution to employment in your area;
5. you have previously tried unsuccessfully to get a loan on the open market; and
6. your business is owned and managed independently of any other.

Should you receive assistance under this scheme, you will be able to use the money for solving short-term cash flow problems relating to:

(i) rent, or repayment of assets such as machinery, essential to the running of your business;
(ii) the reduction of overdrafts which have exceeded the limits agreed with your bank;
(iii) the payment of salaries or wages to key employees who are not owners of, or shareholders in, the business; and
(iv) the restructuring of the business to counter the effects of the economic downturn.

Only in exceptional circumstances can this SBDC loan be used to prevent the liquidation of a business by its creditors, if these creditors agree. The maximum amount of an Aid Fund loan is R50 000, loaned at an interest rate of 10% per year repayable over a maximum period of five years. Capital repayments may be deferred for up to one year. You can apply for financial assistance through your bank manager who will then refer and recommend your application to the SBDC. You could also contact any SBDC office if you have no bank account.

Bank Indemnity Scheme

Agreements have been entered into with First National Bank, Nedbank, Standard Bank, Stannic, Trust Bank, Volkskas, Investec Bank, Boland Bank, Bank of Transkei, District Bank and French Bank, whereby the SBDC will guarantee up to 80% of the facility granted by the representative bank to an entrepreneur. The guarantee operates for a maximum period of five years and the interest rate is determined by the bank. The funds can be made available, *inter alia*, through a term loan, an overdraft, an instalment sale or a lease. Presently, amounts of up to R150 000 may be covered under the scheme. Entrepreneurs seeking finance through this scheme should contact their bank managers. The SBDC only acts as the guarantor and has no direct contact with the bank client. The SBDC's fee under this scheme is 2,5% per annum.

Property Indemnity Scheme

The SBDC has negotiated with eight major South African banks a property indemnity scheme whereby small businesses are encouraged to erect their own premises. The erection of these premises will be financed by the bank. The SBDC will provide an 80% indemnity to the bank for a period not exceeding 10 years on behalf of the small business client. The small businessman is required to provide at least 20% of the purchase price or building costs involved. A mortgage bond will be registered over the property in favour of the bank concerned.

Supplier's credit Most retail businesses purchase goods for the purpose of selling again. If the supplier of goods sells on credit, you (the buyer) are actually borrowing a portion of the supplier's working capital. Those suppliers who sell on account generally quote a price for the goods, specify the time for it to be paid, and allow a discount (a reduction in price based on payment within a specified period), if payment is made within a given period, usually ten days. Supplier's credit can in some instances be more expensive than bank credit, depending on, of course, discounts, interest rates and terms of payments. Bear in mind, however, that if you buy goods on credit from a supplier, you are actually borrowing a portion of his working capital, on which he loses money. It is therefore necessary for the supplier to charge for this service.

Suppose you are planning to purchase R50 000 of stock on the following conditions: a 2% discount from the stated sales price if payment is made within ten days, and the entire amount is due 30 days from the invoice date if the discount is not taken. But you need at least a month to sell what you have bought from the supplier. Thus, you will only have the cash to pay him once the goods are sold. You purchased the goods on the first of the month. If you don't pay before the tenth, your failure to pay will cost you R1 000 (the 2% discount). An alternative is of course to borrow the R50 000 from a bank for a period of one month (the period it will take you to sell the stock) and pay the supplier in cash to take advantage of the discount. You will thus need only R49 000. Interest on R49 000 at 18% (bank interest rate) for 30 days is R724 (R49 000 × 18% ÷ 365 days × 30 days). You could also have purchased the goods from the supplier on credit on the first of the month, but only borrowed the money on the tenth of the month (date of payment to supplier) to pay the supplier. By this method you could get the advantage of the discount and your interest at the bank would be lower (for only 20 and not 30 days).

To receive discounts, you must have cash resources available or must be able to borrow promptly. Your credit standing must be good and so must your relationships with your banker and suppliers. However, be careful never to abuse the opportunity you have to buy on credit, because if you do, you could find that your suppliers refuse to supply you except on a 'cash basis', and that your record as a bad payer becomes known (to other suppliers) which will hamper your chances to obtain new sources of supply.

In summary, suppliers' credit can be useful as a source of financing purchases and it is a use of funds to the extent that it can finance debtors (credit sales to debtors). However, the cost of not taking cash discounts often exceeds the rate of interest at which the buyer can borrow. Therefore it is very important that you be cautious in using it as a source of financing — it could be quite expensive.

Working capital finance A business already in operation should consider its own resources before looking for finance elsewhere. The question is, of course, where do you look? Obviously, you should look at those items that bring in money, such as stock and debtors. Other items may be completely unproductive assets, which should be sold. When surplus, obsolete or unprofitable stock is identified, get rid of it as quickly and economically as possible. Furthermore, ensure that they are not being re-ordered — evaluate their saleability critically, according to the market you serve. Cash can also come in from debtors through the fast collection of outstanding amounts. Consideration could also be given to not selling on credit anymore, to reducing credit terms, to refusing further credit to slow payers, or to issuing statements earlier and taking prompt and vigorous action when accounts are overdue. You could also increase your stock turnover rate. Owner withdrawals can be cut considerably when capital is needed. Analyse and identify all major cost items such as staff salaries and other — reduce them if you so wish and if you can. However, the best way to secure working capital finance is to exercise financial discipline from the day the business has started — be concerned with the circulation and accumulation of money within the business. Not to do so can be a costly mistake. The old saying 'prevention is better than cure' is applicable in this situation — it is the method by which you manage the capital invested in your business, right from the beginning, that will determine your destiny.

Another source of working capital finance is a bank overdraft. An overdraft allows you to alter your financing requirements from day to day according to your cash flow. In addition, interest is calculated on your daily outstanding balance which may work out cheaper than other sources of finance. However, after a reasonable period, the business should no longer be in debt to the bank. Bankers do not like to become business partners of their clients. However, banks differ in the extent to which they will support the activities of the borrower in bad times. Some banks are active in providing counsel and in stimulating entrepreneurship, while others are less active in this regard. The personnel of these banks can provide much valuable counselling to their clients. Banks can provide you with an overdraft (short-term loan) which could allow you to expand and grow more rapidly than is possible through retained profits and trade credit. However, with the heightened competition among commercial banks, their aggressiveness has increased, and they therefore offer a wide range of financial and business services. Many of them have special departments which are out to serve the small businessman in many respects.

It is hardly possible to overemphasize the importance of getting money in without having to resort to outside finance sources. Cash on hand is vital to every business. The quicker you collect outstanding money and the longer you wait to pay obligations without damaging relations, the better will be the cash-flow situation and the less interest will have to be paid on an overdraft. The longer the money is available the better and more often it can be used productively. Of great importance is the practice of financial discipline, day by day, month after month and year after year.

Hire purchase and leasing Hire purchase and leasing are popular methods of financing certain fixed assets such as vehicles and equipment. These forms of financing are available from most commercial banks and have the advantage that you will have immediate use of the article while repayments are made monthly. The article acquired always serves as prime security as ownership rests entirely with the supplier of finance until the final instalment has been paid. A deposit is usually required if hire purchase is used, but when leasing an item no deposit is required and rental is usually paid in advance. It is very important to 'look' before you lease. A lease agreement is a legal document. It carries a long-term obligation. You must be thoroughly informed of just what you are committing yourself to. Be reasonably sure that the lease arrangements are the best you can get, that the equipment is what you need, and that the terms are what you want. Remember, once the agreement is drawn up and signed, it is almost impossible to change it.

Below follows a unique story on how leasing had benefit a business:[32]

In the early life of a business, it is difficult to show potential creditors how solid and profitable the new firm can be. This difficulty can slow down efforts to grow through the use of borrowed capital. Leasing of equipment is an alternative to waiting for profits and creditors to provide financing. Dick Moen, president of Moen Foam Corporation in Carson, CA, explains how his company used leasing to grow:

'A major reason for our annual sales volume growth,' said Moen, 'is that we lease instead of purchase or finance much of our production equipment.' The company, founded in 1977, had sales of about R4 million in its first year, increasing to approximately R8 million the second year.

What makes this growth 'astounding,' according to Moen, is that his fledgling company was almost stymied in its first efforts to expand. 'We tried umpteen different sources and got nowhere,' he recalls.

The big break came one day when Moen's stockbroker, an account executive with Bateman, Eichler, Hill, Richards, Inc., called to suggest an investment for him. The first lease arrangement with BEHR Leasing, in August, 1977, provided Moen with a R75 000 polyurethane laminating machine and platform, complete with a conveyor and slitter. Just four months later Moen leased a second piece of equipment worth R95 000. With the new equipment, Moen Foam was able to enter still another market, one which was booming.

In May, 1978, came two more leases through BEHR Leasing. One brought Moen R67 000 worth of equipment which further automated the production. That was followed by a lease with BEHR Leasing for R100 000 worth of saws and transportation and fabrication equipment to expand production capacity.

'That will bring the total value of the leased equipment to more than half a million rand,' Moen said.

What would have happened if he hadn't been able to lease the equipment?

'We would have had to wait until we generated enough profits to buy the equipment we needed,' Dick said. 'Our growth would have been delayed for years.'

Source: Ray Corob, 'Equipment Leasing — An Idea Whose Time Has Come,' *Franchising Today* (February, 1981), p. 47.

ARRANGING INSURANCE

In any business, the possibility cannot be excluded that years of hard work might be lost through a single robbery, accident or fire. However, a well-planned insurance policy can cover these losses by substituting the lost assets with insurance moneys. Always ask yourself: Without adequate insurance, what will happen to my business if a fire destroys the building, equipment and stock; or if robbers 'clear it out'? When such catastrophes hit a business whose insurance protection is inadequate or who has no cover at all, they are often forced out of business or operations are so severely damaged that the business could take years to recover. Therefore, the main objective is to be adequately covered by your insurance, avoiding both over-insurance and under-insurance. Under-insurance means that the amount you can claim does not fully replace the assets. Over-insurance, such as spending R5 000 a year on fire insurance on a building that is worth R2 000, leads to a shortage in working capital. The importance of adequate insurance cannot be over-emphasized and you must ensure that you are covered in all aspects of this significant area both in your personal capacity and with regard to your business. William H. Day puts the necessity for insurance very simply: 'To be sure ... insure!'[33]

However, the intention is not to go into all the details of insurance costs and rates because these depend on various factors such as the location of the business, the type of business, property value, value of other assets, the building's construction, the average stock level, etc., and therefore it is recommended that you consult a reputable and knowledge-able insurance agent, broker or management consultant to obtain professional advice. Such a person can be of great assistance in investigating and recommending the right insurance companies, discussing the type of insurance cover needed, giving explanations on policy terms, calculating insurance premiums and comparing different insurance company costs. You will, however, need to be able to tell the agent what you want and then let him suggest the best insurance 'package'. In general, the following types of insurance are available:

★ *Life assurance:* providing protection for a business against the death of the owner(s) or key employee(s);
★ *Fire and general property insurance:* covering fire losses, vandalism, hail, windstorms, explosions, rioting, lightning and malicious mischief;
★ *Burglary insurance:* covering forcible entry and theft of stock, cash and assets;
★ *Plate-glass insurance:* covering window breakage;
★ *Goods in transit:* covering goods damaged while being either collected from, or delivered to your customers.
★ *Public liability insurance:* covering injury to members of the public while they are on the property;
★ *Vehicle insurance:* covering vehicles in case of damage;
★ *Workmen's compensation insurance:* covering injury to employees at work or while on duty;
★ *Business interruption insurance:* insurance cover in case the business suffers losses because of fire, flood, or

any other unforeseen calamity, and where the business will need money to pay taxes, interest, utilities and salaries to employees while the facilities are being rebuilt.

★ *Product liability insurance:* covering injury to customers arising from the use of goods bought at the business.

THE GRAND OPENING

A well-planned launch of your business can be the beginning of your success or will, at least, provide you with a good start. Opening a business is, however, difficult and there will always be unexpected problems. On the day your business opens, try to learn about every problem there is in order to take corrective action for the future. Opening day can tell you a lot about how you have planned your business as a whole. Walk around, talk to customers, smile and be interested in them. You want to do well and therefore anything they say can help you. Let them know and understand that you are open to suggestions and that their comments mean a lot to you. Watch cash handling and employee relations with customers. Look for reasons to praise your employees. This builds up their desire to do good and develops team spirit. Criticize in private and praise in public. Take note of all suggestions your employees offer. You should handle mistakes by your employees on the spot — correct and train as mistakes are made. Let employees prove themselves and later, let them know how well they are doing or in what ways they can improve. You should always act in future as you did on the opening day.

You should inform the market well in advance — and remind them continuously — until the opening day. Determine exactly what you will tell the market about the business and also the method that will be used to inform potential customers, whether by newspaper advertising, hand-outs, word-of-mouth or all of these. Furthermore, you should select a few products to be 'on special' that day or during the first week. Then inform the market about these products and special prices.

Advertisements or letters of introduction that you will distribute will usually go to people who are only a group of names to you at the time of your opening. However, the first necessity is to adopt the method or approach and the tone that is most suitable and most likely to be effective in your particular case. When putting such a letter or sales talk together, consider the view of your market and remember that all customers are always interested in benefits. In other words, what is it about your business that will please its market? The letter must be closely linked with their needs, expectations and desires. The contents of an introductory letter to be distributed may be as follows:

Dear customer

How much was your clothing account last year? More than you thought it ought to be anyway. And whatever it amounted to, it was surely more than it needed to have been.

Not only do we offer a wide range of quality men's and women's clothes that will suit your personality and style for just about every occasion, but they are also available at unbeatable low prices. It is our earnest wish that your visit to our shop will result in your satisfaction. We thus invite you to discover for yourself whether our service and our clothing meet your expectations.

Please remember: We are here to serve and offer you quality goods which will be well worth your serious consideration.

We await your visit with pleasure.

Very respectfully yours

Signature

Don't forget to state the name of the business, the day of opening, where the shop is located and how to find it. Any advantage, such as free parking, must also be mentioned.

SUMMARY AND CONCLUSIONS

'An entrepreneur is a person who identifies a specific area of a market where a need for a product or service exists but has not been met' (Dr Anton Rupert). In effect, Dr Anton Rupert is saying: where there are people, there are unfilled needs and it is exactly these needs which provide you with the challenge to determine how you can satisfy them at best. As a prospective businessman you are characterized as a creative person. Use your creativity — the basic needs of people do not change, but ways and means of satisfying those needs do. If you want to succeed, those needs must have commercial potential, and if they have, your responsibility is to commit yourself to the task of satisfying them. The customers, in accepting your product or service in exchange for money, must feel they are participants in a transaction that is as profitable to them as it is to you.

This part has provided you with many questions to be answered before embarking on your 'business trip', and you cannot merely guess at the answers. Market analysis starts with identifying what the business is — what you have to sell from the prospective customer's point of view. You must make sure you have accurate answers before you make a decision to go further. The answers to these questions provide you with the opportunity to ask yourself: Based on what I know now, does it still look like a promising opportunity? Only if your new business idea passes the test posed by this question are you ready to give it a try.

When you hear the words: 'Your loan is approved', you should firstly, be enthusiastic and full of pride and joy, and secondly, you should be reminded that almost anyone can think out good business ideas like you did, but many of them never do anything with their ideas. And even the best idea is not worth a cent if not put to work. Have you ever heard of Joseph Swan? A strong case could be made for saying that he invented the electric light bulb eight months before Edison. Who got the patents? Who got the bulb to the market? Edison. Who invented the electric light bulb? Edison. Are you Edison or a Swan? You may have brilliant business ideas, but if you do not take advantage of them, somebody else might. Edison was not only an inventing genius. He was also a promotion genius, a publicity genius, a capital-raising genius, and a genius seeing potential markets for inventions. You are thus the most important element for the success of your invention.

Putting an idea to work is only the beginning of the battle. What you are now looking for is an excellent start in establishing your business with the right attitude and application of methods to head for a 'strong finish'. The fact that your application for financial assistance has been approved, means that you have selected a business opportunity that is right for you and is viable according to the investigation done — at least on paper. Furthermore it means that the lenders have faith in your ability to make a success of your venture. By approving the loan, they have in fact reminded you of the opportunity and challenge that lies ahead of you. Your challenge will be to get behind your sales and push for all they are worth during the rest of your 'stay' in business. Thus, you must utilize the money and exploit the opportunity they have given you as profitably as possible.

How much did you say you would sell in your first year of operation? Here's success to you!

BIBLIOGRAPHY

* Kenneth J. Albert. *How to Pick the Right Small Business Opportunity.* 1977. McGraw-Hill.

* Clifford M. Baumback, Kenneth Lawyer. *How to Organize and Operate a Small Business.* 1979. Prentice-Hall, Englewood Cliffs, NJ: 69–100.

* W. Tobejane. Financial feasibility study. *Small Business News* 1985; **7**(2): 12, 13. (Official journal of the University of the North, Business Advisory Bureau.)

* Anton Frank. Prepare before you apply for a loan. *Entrepreneur* 1985; **4**(2): 19.

* William H. Day. *Maximizing Small Business Profits with Precision Management.* 1978. Prentice-Hall, Englewood Cliffs, NJ: 3–44.

* Jack Gordan, Ron Zemke. Making them more creative. *Training: The Magazine of Human Resources Development.* 1986; **23**(5): 30–45.

* D. McDonough. Finding venture capital. *Entrepreneur* 1984; **3**(2): 14–15.

* Guy Macleod. *Starting Your Own Business in South Africa.* 1983. Oxford University Press, Cape Town: 10–51.

* Peat Marwick. *Starting Your Own Business.* 1985. Mitchell, Small Business Development Corporation Booklet No. 7.

* J.K. Lasser Tax Institute. *How to Run a Small Business.* 5th ed. 1982. McGraw-Hill: 7–37.

* G.G. Barnett. *Locating Your Shop: A Guide for Small Retailers.* 1986. Small Business Development Corporation, Johannesburg: Fact Sheet 5/86.

* J. Ford Laumer Jr., James R. Harris, Hugh J. Guffey Jr. Learning about your market. *Management Aids, Number 4.019.* 1979. Washington D.C., U.S. Small Business Administration.

* Michael W. Little. Marketing checklist for small retailers. *Management Aids, Number 4.012.* 1985. Washington D.C., U.S. Small Business Administration.

* John Tavela. Can you make money with your idea or invention? *Management Aids, Number 2.013.* Washington D.C., U.S. Smnall Business Administration.

* Dr Janelle C. Ashley, Dr. Danny R. Arnold. Feasibility checklist for starting a small business. *Management Aids, Number 2.026.* Washington D.C., U.S. Small Business Administration.

* Checklist for going into business. *Management Aids, Number 2.016.* Washington D.C., U.S. Small Business Administration.

* John F. Murphy. Sound cash management and borrowing. *Management Aids, Number 1.016.* 1971. Washington D.C., Small Business Administration.

NOTES

[1] J.K. Lasser Tax Institute. *How to run a Small Business.* 5th ed. 1982. McGraw-Hill: 10.

[2] H.N. Broom, J.G. Longenecker, C.W. Moore, *Small Business Management,* © 1983, South-Western Publishing Co., Cincinnati, Ohio, p. 51.

[3] Also called liquidation value (See pages 49 and 50 for an explanation.)

[4] Universiteit van Suid-Afrika. 'n Billike opbrengskoers. *Rekeningkunde IV Gids 5.* 1973: 139, 140. (Permission granted to reproduce by the University of South Africa.)

[5] *How to Buy or Sell a Business.* 1982. 8, 9. Small Business Reporter, San Francisco. (Reprinted with permission from Bank of America, NT&SA.)

[6] *How to Buy or Sell a Business.* 1982. 8, 9. Small Business Reporter, San Francisco. (Reprinted with permission from Bank of America, NT&SA.)

[7] *How to Buy or Sell a Business.* 8, 9. Small Business Reporter, San Francisco. (Reprinted with permission from Bank of America, NT&SA.)

[8] Baumback/Lawyer. *How to Organize and Operate a Small Business.* 1979. Prentice-Hall, Englewood Cliffs, NJ: 79. (Reprinted with permission.)

[9] See page 461 for details on the Small Business Development Corporation's network.

[10] Business plan for retailers. *Management Aids, Number 2.020.* 1979. U.S. Small Business Administration. Washington D.C.: 2.

[11] Raymond F. Pelissier. Planning and goal setting for small business. *Management Aids, Number 2.010.* 1978. Small Business Administration, Washington D.C.

[12] G.G. Barnett. Do you know your market? *Small Business Development Corporation,* Johannesburg, Fact Sheet 7/86 (August 1986).

[13] Herman R. Holtz. *Profit From Your Money-Making Ideas.* 1980. AMACOM, New York: 14.

[14] Source: Larry Miller. Who says you are not creative? *Cosmopolitan* 1985; June: 124.

[15] Ibid.

[16] Ibid.

[17] Source: William H. Day. *Maximizing Small Business Profits with Precision management.* 1978. Prentice-Hall, Englewood Cliffs, NJ: 156, 157.

[18] Jeffrey P. Davidson. Store location: little things mean a lot. *Management Aids, Number 2.024.* 1979. U.S. Small Business Administration, Washington D.C.: 4.

[19] James R. Lowry. Using a traffic study to select a retail site. *Management Aids, Number 2.021.* 1973. U.S. Small Business Administration, Washington D.C.: 3, 5.

[20] Baumback/Lawyer. *How to Organize and Operate a Small Business.* 1979. Prentice-Hall, Englewood Cliffs, NJ: 99, 100. (Reprinted with permission.)

[21] *Small Business Development Corporation, Fact Sheet 2/86.* Johannesburg.

[22] Eddie Johnstone. The right way to apply for a small business loan. *Entrepreneur* 1984; **3**(10): 22. (Reproduced with permission.)

[23] Barry Adams. Developing business plans to attract venture capital. *Entrepreneur* 1985; **4**(12): 10, 11. (Reproduced with permission.)

[24] Roger Rees. A financial planning system for small business. *Entrepreneur* 1985; **4**(9): 12. (Reproduced with permission.)

[25] Source: Sam Adams, "What a Venture Capitalist Looks for", MBA, Vol. 7 (June–July, 1973), p. 9.

[26] Apart from having additional money on hand for financing credit sales for an initial few months, money for living expenses, for at least three months should also be set aside in a bank savings account — not to be used for any other purpose. This will provide a cushion to help you get through the getting started period with a minimum of worry. If cash can be provided for a longer period it will add to peace of mind which will give you the opportunity to concentrate on building the business.

[27] The deduction of depreciation is not applicable when leasing assets. The monthly instalment is regarded as an expense to the business and will be treated as such (see Income Statement).

[28] This net profit ratio is determined on the net profit before tax. You should, when you compare this ratio with that of similar businesses, establish on which method their average net profit ratios were determined — before or after deducting tax.

[29] Source: *Small Business Development Corporation, Fact Sheet 1/86,* Johannesburg.

[30] Lane Flint. Nothing succeeds like enthusiasm. *Entrepreneur* 1983; May: 19. (Reproduced with permission.)

[31] The information on the SBDC and its financing schemes was obtained from SBDC booklets numbers 2 and 4. (Reproduced with permission.)

[32] Source: Ray Corob, "Equipment Leasing — An Idea Whose Time Has Come," Franchising Today (February, 1981), p. 47.

[33] William H. Day. *Maximizing Small Business Profits.* 1978. Prentice-Hall, Englewood Cliffs, NJ: 138.

3 YOUR MANAGERIAL FUNCTIONS

'To turn an entrepreneurial programme into performance requires effective management.'

Peter F. Drucker[1]

'Whatever is best managed is best.'

Frans Bekker

'The success of your business is largely dependent on the ability and enthusiasm of your people. Their competence and keenness depends on you, and your leadership and the way you manage them.'

Ron Johnson[2]

'Take a minute: Look at your goals; Look at your performance; See if your behaviour matches your goals.'

Kenneth Blanchard and Spencer Johnson[3]

INTRODUCTION

The success or failure of a business depends upon its management, and successful business management can be described as the profitable use of those factors that are necessary to conduct the business. Whatever a manager does, he does through making decisions. The actual management of the business thus consists of a series of decisions dealing with the planning function and the operation of the entire business. Thus, management begins before the business is launched and even includes such pre-operating decisions as selection of the kind of business, choice of location, provision of personnel, selection of merchandise to buy and many others. It is, furthermore, your duty as the manager (and owner) of the business to see that a satisfactory return is obtained on your investment, that the business has the opportunity to continue, and that goodwill is maintained with employees and customers.

Management is being concerned with, and paying attention to what is important. Therefore, you should be continuously involved in relating the requirements of the environment in which you operate with the resources available to you and the people you deal with — whether they are employees or customers. The quality of your management must be of a high standard as your business is dependent thereon. Your employees, customers, suppliers and any other people you deal with will be watching your every move. Not only will your reaction to various situations influence them but they will also be evaluated by them. In the private and business lives of these people, you and your business will be discussed as will your actions and decisions. You will continuously be in the spotlight. Will it be a bright or a dull spotlight? That depends entirely on you!

Entrepreneurs are doers. They are independent and action-orientated and rely on their own energy, ingenuity and motivation to plan and initiate action to accomplish the desired results. And indeed, the heart of the matter is working towards positive results. However, the key to keeping your business going is to keep it growing, which means that you need more people to help you. That is what management is all about — getting things done through people. As you become known to your market, your customers are likely to demand more from you and they will tolerate no disappointment. Thus, the business has to continue to serve the best interests of your market. Work has to be done and the resource with which to perform it is employees.

If you seek to develop professional competence, you need to begin with a clear understanding of a manager's tasks and responsibilities. Generally, a manager performs four functions to secure results: planning, organizing, leading and controlling. Although these managerial functions are shown systematically, to help you in understanding them, they are not as neatly separated in reality and you will often have to perform them together, or out of sequence. For practical purposes, however, these functions will be discussed in the order shown.

Good management is the key to success and good management starts with setting goals. Thus, planning is the basis for successful management action. 'It is the process a manager follows to think through in advance what he wants to accomplish, and how he will do it. Planning is the work a manager performs to predetermine a course of action. When you plan, you must take time to reflect and analyze, to consider alternatives, and to make sound, considered decisions. You have to decide in advance what you are going to do, why you will do it, under what conditions you will carry it out, how you will accomplish it, and what you will require to get the results you want. Because you think ahead, you must avoid the tendency to make hasty judgements and to take haphazard action' (Louis A. Allen).[4]

Types of planning Long-term planning is concerned with looking ahead for a number of years and forming a picture of the ultimate results you want to accomplish. Once you know where you want to go, the process of determining the intermediate steps to take becomes much easier.

Short-term planning involves determining the steps necessary to accomplish long-term results. Thus, this involves breaking long-range goals down into sub-goals, and deciding what you expect to achieve in, say, the next two to three months, the next six months, or the next year.

Barriers to planning The main barriers are ignorance and a lack of vision, i.e. not knowing what to plan for and believing that careful thought about the business's future will reveal new problems to face. Another barrier is the lack of specific objectives and ideals, i.e. not envisaging goals clearly. Planning cannot be done efficiently if there is a lack of information on which to make assumptions about the future. People often feel that the future seems too uncertain, and that they cannot know precisely what is going to happen in times to come. However, the fact remains that the plans made today are the best way to master the future and avoid being mastered by it.

A lack of self-discipline and the inability to 'stay close' to the goals you have set also disrupt planning. While the effort required to reach each sub-goal should be a great enough challenge to you, it should not be so great or unreasonable as to discourage you. Do not plan to reach too many goals all at one time. Establish priorities. Plan in advance how to measure results so you can know exactly how well you are doing. That is what is meant by 'measurable' goals. If you are unable to keep score as you go along, you are likely to lose motivation. Re-work your plan of action to allow for obstacles which may stand in your way. It has been said that 'effective planning is continuous planning', so try to foresee obstacles and plan ways to avert or minimize them.

It is unfortunately a fact that many businessmen prefer to do things rather than first thinking about them. The result is that operations become negative and essential planning is pushed aside, the consequences being that of becoming too involved in the day-to-day survival of the business to notice the crucial aspects for success. This cycle can only be broken by taking a firm stand and making the time to plan.

Many people question the benefit of planning. The benefit of planning is this: if you know where you are going, you are likely to end up where you want to be. The need for planning is not always seen by owner-managers because they believe that things do not work out according to plans anyway, and because they do not see the immediate results from their efforts. Yet, owner-managers of small businesses need to plan as thoroughly as — if not more thoroughly than — managers of larger businesses. The reasons for this are that small businesses do not always have sufficient resources to overcome their future problems, and often cannot afford to underwrite losses that may occur while they are adjusting to unexpected changes.

What to Plan For Primarily, a business has to plan for the following: sales; profit; costs (expenses); stock holding (or purchasing); cash flow; financial position and capital expenditures.

Above all else it is necessary that you plan for activities that stimulate the sale of goods and services such as: the image of the business; the appearance of the business (internal and external); advertising and promotion; and innovations, etc.

If planning is to enable those running the business to decide in advance what to do, how to do it, when to do it, and who is going to do it, then it is advisable that you adhere to some accepted formal decision-making process. But what exactly is meant by the word 'decision'? It is, and should be a conclusion arrived at after consideration. The emphasis is, of course, on 'after consideration'. The decisions of a businessman are in effect an effort to solve the problems confronting the business. Such decisions deal with the future in that they are commitments made today concerning where you want to be tomorrow. Thus it can be said that decision-making pervades all your functions and activities as owner-manager, but it is also the end product in the decision-making process. So, the planning process really starts by having a method to identify and solve problems. The following method may prove to be helpful:[5]

Identify the problem

A problem is an obstacle, an impediment to be overcome. It precludes the accomplishment of objectives and goals. Someone once said that the difference between getting somewhere and nowhere is the ability to make a start. The starting place in problem-solving is the definition of the problem. The executive who tries to solve problems by depending on abstract reasoning, experience, general information, memory, or a superficial survey of the problem situation is heading for disaster.

Kipling said: 'I have six faithful serving men; they taught me all I know, their names are: What, Where, When, How, Why and Who ... .' Use these six words when you try to solve the problem. By the time you can write a clear statement of the problem itself, you are halfway to a solution.

Difficulty arises in distinguishing between a bad result and the basic problem. As in the case of sickness, symptoms are often more apparent than the disease. The rather common headache is the symptom of many related diseases. For example, a headache can be symptomatic of eye strain, sinusitis, hayfever, the common cold, high blood pressure, or a brain tumour. Obviously treating the symptom with aspirin will not necessarily cure the disease.

The proverbial problem alleged by most small businessmen is 'declining sales volume'. However, declining sales are symptomatic of a problem which could be caused by a number of conditions, such as poor conduct, inappropriate pricing, inadequate promotion, insufficient selling effort, and others. As in the case of medicine, the symptoms in business are more apparent than the disease. The important thing is to narrow the problem down and get below the surface, analysing from the general to the particular and from the obvious effect to the not-so-obvious cause.

Gather data

Collect all the information that might have a bearing on the problem. Take nothing for granted where it is reasonably possible to obtain facts and figures. The amount of data gathered depends on the nature of the problem and the time available. Rarely does a man make a mistake because he knows too much; therefore, do not take shortcuts on the information-gathering phase. Also, avoid stacking the evidence by confining the search to data and facts that tend to support any preconceived ideas. To do so merely camouflages the fact that you have already jumped to a conclusion.

Next, organize the facts into usable form. For example, plot the cost-per-unit figures on a graph, which will be more meaningful than a long column of numbers. A good sales map will convey more at a glance than will an hour of reading reports.

Evaluate each item of information. Is it absolutely reliable, probably reliable, or not to be trusted too far? Is it an established fact, an expert opinion, or a guess? One of the best ways to gather reliable data is to get out of the office and to look and ask for yourself.

List possible solutions

This is the creative-thinking phase of the problem-solving process. It is a good place to utilize whatever group dynamic techniques you may have developed for joint attacks on problems by members of your company. Keep an open mind — let imagination roam freely over the facts collected. As you proceed, jot down every solution that seems possible to you or anyone else working on the problem. Resist the temptation to evaluate the proposals as you go along. Rather, list plausible and seemingly absurd ideas as well, remembering that the more possibilities you list during this phase, the less risk you will run of settling for a merely workable, rather than the best, solution. Continue studying the data as long as there seems any possibility of deriving additional ideas, solutions, explanations, or patterns from it. Try working on the problem awhile, and then stop and do other things. Let it jell in your subconscious mind. Later, return with a fresh insight and continue your efforts.

Test possible solutions

Evaluate all possible solutions. Be objective. Test each solution separately by using a common yardstick. It will be necessary to develop some criteria for the test. Criteria are best raised as questions which you ask of each possible solution. It has been suggested that they may be drawn from three general categories:

1. *Suitability:* Will this solution do the job? Will it remedy the problem situation completely or only partially? Is it a permanent or stop-gap solution?

2. *Feasibility:* Will this plan work in actual practice? Can we afford this approach? How much will it cost?
3. *Acceptability:* Will you (or the board, or partner, or employers or customers) go along with the changes required by this plan? Are you trying to drive a tack with a sledgehammer?

Rank the criteria as you formulate them on the basis of relative importance. For example, is this test one that a possible solution absolutely must pass, or is it merely something that would be nice to accomplish?

You may proceed by rating all possible solutions on the same chart, listing the solutions down the left side of the chart and the criteria across the top. Various grading methods, such as alphabetical (A through F), or numerical (0 through 100), can be used to rate the various criteria.

Select the best solution

Now you must make a decision. Sometimes one clearly superior solution will stand out; but this is not often the case. Sometimes the best solution is a combination of two or more of the better solutions tested. Your aim should be to arrive at the best solution, not just a workable one.

Put the solution into action

Solutions on paper do not always work well in practice. Scientific problem-solving does not stop with the solution that appears best in theory. Consequently, the solution should be applied and the result observed. In the process, some modifications may be suggested. If success is not achieved you may have defined the problem incorrectly in the first place and obtained the wrong solution because you tackled the wrong problem.

CHECKLIST FOR DECISION-MAKING[6]

Have you identified the causes and extent of the problem?

1. Why has the need for a decision arisen?
2. Have you identified all the factors involved in the problem?
3. Have you pin-pointed the really critical issues?
4. Is it an outward symptom of a more complex problem?
5. Is this one of a sequence of similar problems? If so, are there other factors to consider?

What circumstances will affect your method of dealing with the problem?

6. Is the problem totally within your area of responsibility?
7. How much of the work involved should you delegate, and to whom?
8. What social, ethical and environmental factors are involved?
9. Is this a priority matter when related to other work in your business?
10. What are the practical limitations of time and cost?
11. Have similar problems been successfully solved previously? If so, can you approach this problem along similar lines?
12. Can a temporary measure be brought in to ease the problem while you are finding a long-term solution?

Have you identified your long- and short-term objectives?

13. Do they cover every part of the problem?
14. Are they feasible in the light of practical and other considerations?
15. Are they in the interest of your business as a whole?
16. Have you taken into account future plans for expansion and change?

Have you collected and organized all relevant information?

17. Have you specified accurately what information you require?
18. Where can the information be obtained?
19. Do you know what the decision will cost?
20. Have you made full use of the experience within your business?
21. Could external help be profitably used?
22. Is the information presented in a suitable form?
23. Is it reliable and valid?
24. Is the information sufficient for you to base your decision on?
25. In the course of collecting information, have you altered the problem area?
26. Are your objectives still relevant and feasible?

Have you explored possible alternative solutions?

27. Have you made a list of possible lines of action?
28. Have you assessed the probable outcome in each case?
29. Can problem areas be simulated by scientific techniques of analysis?
30. Have the critical issues been obscured by minor problems which may be involved?
31. Will you need to modify your original objectives?

What action is required to implement your decision?

32. What action must be taken, and when?
33. How long should each stage take to complete?
34. Who will implement the decision? How and when should they be informed?
35. Who else should be informed of your decision?
36. What effect will your decision have on others?
37. Have you established a system of follow-through and control?

Forecasting 'The future is hidden from you. If you are to master it, you must first make reasonable assumptions about what it will be like. Once you have some confidence about what will probably happen, you can begin to take positive steps to plan those things you will want to happen. This calls for forecasting, defined as the work a manager performs to estimate and predict future conditions and events.'[7]

The key element in forecasting is to try and benefit from the lessons of the past, as it may reveal valuable clues as to what will probably happen in the future. It is, however, important that you ascertain why and how things happened in the past as well as the result. In other words: what were the causes and the effects? The other key elements are to keep the long range goals in mind as they will give you some direction in your thoughts and may result in more accurate predictions, and to be realistic about future eventualities. In forecasting there will be guesswork and assumptions, but they should be kept as realistic as possible. You will then be in a better position to make the most efficient use of resources. In addition, involve employees as they may be able to contribute in a positive way. However, in forecasting your main concern will be with answering such questions as: Will the demand for a product increase or decline? What will be the 'present value' of R1 five years from now? etc. For example, a sales forecast will result in a sales target, but before the sales target can be set, you should have done some market research to establish the size of the market and which aspects may have a bearing on changing the size of it this year, what are the needs of customers now compared with in previous years, what new products are on the market and will they sell, what have your competitors been up to, and so on. After such research a sales forecast should result in a realistic estimate of what can be sold in the forthcoming year. What will the position be if you sell only 50% of the amount estimated? Will your business be able to survive?

Developing 'The more clearly you visualize the end result you work to
objectives accomplish, the better you can determine the best route, the best timing, and the best method of achievement. Establishing objectives is the work a manager performs to predetermine the results to be accomplished.'[8] Thus, the key questions in establishing objectives are:

* Where is the business going?
* What must be done to get it there?
* How must it be done?
* Who must do it?
* When must he do it?

The first step toward getting what you want out of business is knowing exactly what it is you want out of being in business. It has been said that there are always some people who 'never seem to have anything', despite a substantial income, people who seem to have no sense of purpose about their lives. It can be concluded that such people never have anything worthwhile because they simply do not know what they want. An important distinction should be made between the objectives of the business and your own personal ones, as they are not necessarily the same. In chapter one, both these were looked at and you should consider how your personal objectives relate to the overall business objectives which are service, profit and growth. Secondly, bear in mind when setting objectives that the first objective of the business is to satisfy the needs and wants of the customer.

135

The only real way to set objectives is by determining what will be measured in each area and what the yardstick of measurement should be. Objectives should be based on past performance as it creates the platform for future achievement. To make objectives measureable they should be specific (to increase sales by, say, 16%) and realistic (challenging but achievable). Terms could be measured in money (a sales target of R250 000 for the year 1988), time (a specific date), a percentage (a 26% return on investment), or quantity (300 units). Marketing goals could include penetrating a new market with a new product or service, and a service objective could be supplying the customer with what he considers value for money in your particular line of business (seeking a 'difference' and working towards it — gaining the competitive edge). A budget must be designed to regulate expenditure for the following year (The idea is to stay within the budget or to adjust constantly to the actual situation. Any deviation must be investigated.) Furthermore all objectives should start with an action word such as: *increase* net profit, *reduce* costs, *deliver* better value, etc. To relate the above theory to practice, Ansoff suggests that every objective should contain the following four elements:[9]

1. an *attribute*: the element of performance the business wishes to measure, for example, market share;
2. a *yardstick*: the means of measuring the attribute, for example, percentage points;
3. a *goal*: the amount of the yardstick the business wishes to achieve, for example, twelve percentage points; and
4. a *time limit*: for example, two years.

Thus a full objective might be stated as '12% market share within two years.'

The growth of your business will always be accompanied by new challenges. What about five, six, seven years from now? Will your business remain healthy throughout these years? Where do you want to be in five years' time? Will you generate the necessary capital, manpower and managerial talent so that your business will grow? Growth must be planned for, not hoped for. First, however, you must be committed to pursuing a growth pattern. Then comes the actual plan for growth and thereafter the strategy and all other aspects such as practising financial discipline and adopting the marketing concept to accomplish growth. Such a 'document' should embrace all of the required elements — the specific targets set (including objectives such as the desired return on investment, the sales volume to be attained, new outlets to be opened, manpower needed, etc.) By being concerned with the circulation and accumulation of money within the business, by ploughing back profits, acquiring a new partner, keeping tight control over expenses or securing a line of credit (from a financial institution or supplier), you can generate sufficient capital to finance an appreciable degree of growth. You need to plan for accelerated progress, the strengthening of profits and of the business's position in the market, so that expansion may begin.

Developing strategies 'Developing strategies involves weighing alternatives and determining the general approach to be followed in attaining an objective.'[10] An objective is thus a significant target to be achieved. A strategy can be said to be the management of the mix of money, materials (or stock) and people-resources to achieve an agreed objective. Only through explicit attention to detail and conscious planning can those running a business increase control over its destiny. In weighing the alternative actions to take, it is not enough just to decide on the right answer or action, but is more important to make the course of action decided upon effective, to refine it. Nothing is as useless as deciding upon an action and then lacking the determination to follow it through. You must be concerned with performance, not procrastination. In developing your strategies it is necessary that the strengths and weaknesses of the business be identified and their pros and cons evaluated with regard to the overall objectives of the business. For example, a weakness might be that you do not know how to go about implementing a certain action. It would thus be necessary for you to consult a number of people who have the 'know-how', or to get the necessary training yourself in that aspect.

To develop your strategies, you need to:

1. identify the strengths, weaknesses and expected changes of your business;
2. identify external changes expected in the economy, your line of business and your customers;

3. identify your competitor's plans, strengths and weaknesses;
4. use the above findings and your objectives to develop alternative strategies;
5. evaluate the pros and cons of these strategies; and
6. select the best strategy or strategies.

Developing programmes 'Once you know where you want to go, you can determine what steps you should take to get there. In programming, you have a means of exploring the alternative routes to your proposed objective and of deciding the specific steps you will take to achieve it in the most effective and economical fashion. Programming is the work a manager performs to establish the sequence and priority of the action steps to be followed in reaching objectives.[11] An example of a programme is as follows:

GOAL	ACTION STEPS
25% increase in sales for the year 1988 (1 Jan. 1988 to 31 Dec. 1988)	— Advertising — Training of salespeople in salesmanship — Training in customer relations — Motivation of personnel — Internal and external improvement of the premises — Improve stockholding, etc.

Scheduling 'Timing is also important. Scheduling is the work managers perform to establish a time sequence for programmed steps.[12] What you have to do is to start scheduling your work (only the work that will help you build the business and achieve the objectives) into the time you have available. To schedule a task you have to know two things: how long you want to spend on the task (as determined by how important the task is), and how soon you have to get the task completed (as determined by how urgent the task is). Importance and urgency are not the same thing. An urgent task is not necessarily important. If something is important and urgent, then it must take priority in your schedule.

All important tasks must be allocated an amount of time which ensures that the work is completed within the prescribed deadline. The key elements in putting a schedule together are:[13]

1. Estimate how much space or time each main activity will need.

2. Make provision for unexpected happenings.

3. Determine time limits for the start and finish of each major action step.

4. Put time where it counts. This point is aptly described by the story of the farmer who told his wife he would plough the 'south forty'. He started early to oil the tractor. He needed more oil so he went to the shop to get it. On the way he noticed the pigs were not fed. He went to the corn crib, where he found some sacks. That reminded him that the potatoes were sprouting. He started for the potato pit. As he passed the woodpile, he remembered his wife wanted wood in the house. As he picked up a few sticks an ailing chicken passed. He dropped the wood and reached for the chicken. When evening arrived, he still had not gotten the tractor to the field! Do you find yourself having difficulties like the farmer getting to the 'south forty'?

5. Concentrate intently. You can avoid having to reconsider problems by concentrating your efforts intently and allowing sufficient time to resolve the problem. In writing on this subject, John Corson described a sales manager coming to a vice-president's office to report criticisms in handling new trainees. The two men agreed that 'something must be done'. Ten minutes were consumed as the two men exchanged opinions on sales training. They separated with a vague feeling of agreement but with no specific understanding as to who was to do what. They dismissed the problem, only to have to consider it again and again until they finally put a sufficient amount of concentrated executive brain power on it and hammered out a programme, a schedule and a budget. You can save a lot of time by disposing of problems through concentrated effort.

Budgeting 'Budgeting is an important element of planning. Through budgeting you ensure that you have the resources necessary to carry out your programmes and to reach your objectives. Budgeting is defined as the work a manager performs to allocate the resources necessary to accomplish objectives. If you simply spent money on items as the need occurs, without setting limits as to what you could afford, you could quickly find yourself spending too much. However, if you decide beforehand how much it should cost for the necessary materials, facilities, salaries, and other expenses, you can decide whether the results are worth the expense.'[14] Furthermore, you can't ride a bicycle facing backwards, and the budget gives you that vital forward view. A budget is not a forecast. A forecast is simply an opinion, however well calculated or considered, as to what might happen; for example, it might rain tomorrow. A budget by contrast, even though it will be based on forecasts, is a commitment. When you compile a budget, you commit yourself to a plan of action. One of the major benefits of a budget is that it allows for the control of expenditure before it actually takes place.

If you, who has control over approving the budget, do not approve of an extra expense, you can eliminate it from the budget. Thus, if you discover you cannot reach the objective within reasonable cost limits, you can cut back your programmed financial activities by reducing expenses, or you can change your objectives to fit the realities of the situation.

If you can do this beforehand, on paper, you can avoid committing yourself to something you cannot afford.

Budgeting is clearly a better method of controlling expenditure than sitting down after the period is over and arguing about why so much money was spent. Budgeting should not be seen as a tool for limiting expenditure but rather as a tool for obtaining the most productive and profitable use of the business's resources. Another benefit of a budgeting system is that it provides performance standards or targets that can be compared with actual results. If the actual performance of the business conforms to the budgets, the business is meeting its objectives. If performance is different, deviations must be investigated and changes can be made to adjust to the actual situation. Budgets also serve as indicators of where trouble exists or may occur in the future, and thus enable corrective steps to be executed.

For many businessmen budgeting may at times seem frustrating — a tedious exercise. You may even think it is pointless, because you always have to make so many assumptions when 'it is too early to tell'. Your management style (or attitude), is, of course, an important consideration when it comes to budgeting because budgets are worthwhile only to the extent that they are used. There will thus always be some businessmen with a negative attitude toward any kind of formalized control procedures. It is usually such attitudes which result in an unwillingness to understand how budgets can help in managing the business. On the other hand, the owner-manager who wants to improve the effectiveness of his decisions will, of course, want to learn more about budgeting and how it can help him control operations.

Lastly, but most importantly, a budget is not something you compile and then lock away. You use it frequently to manage the business.

Developing policies 'This is the work managers perform to establish standing decisions that apply to recurring questions and problems of concern to the business as a whole.[15] Policies are thus guides to action or a standard plan of action. They are set so that you can delegate work and that employees will act according to your philosophy and thinking. Policies direct the business and the people working for it to keep them in the framework of established objectives. Policies can enable you to build the particular reputation you desire in the eyes of the market. A policy is also, in effect, a sort of command from you (the owner-manager) which directs all employees to perform in certain important aspects in a prescribed manner. Therefore policies direct the business's way of doing things and general attitudes towards customers, employees, products. Customer policy should specify the attitude that is to be created and maintained toward customers. Such a policy should cover standardized procedures (which must be done uniformly) for handling troublesome customers, meeting an unusual customer request and greeting all customers. Other policies should be set for pricing products or services (which pricing method to be used, price discounts, etc.), and buying policies (from whom to buy, when to buy, whether to buy on credit or cash), credit control policies, etc.

When formulating policies, it is best to put them in writing. It is also advisable that policies should reflect objectives and plans. In other words, you should never have to say: 'There is no good reason why we do it or why we don't do it, it is our policy.' Policies should be explained to all employees, because what employees (even customers) do not understand, they cannot use correctly. Policies should also be flexible and controlled at all times —regular and careful review of policies is necessary to see whether they are up to date and if not, to make sure that they are changed in order to meet the new situation.

Your personnel policy will for example include such matters as:

★ working hours — number of hours of work per week, payment for overtime, working on holidays;

★ vacations — length, extra vacation time without pay, military leave, time of year scheduled;

★ illness — evidence of illness required, hospital benefits, etc.;

★ fringe benefits — discounts to employees, medical scheme, free life insurance, payment for studies;

★ salaries — time and method of payment; and

★ bonuses — time of payment and amounts.

Developing procedures 'In every business certain work must be done the same way wherever it is performed. In cases such as accounting and quality control, this is necessary so that uniform results can be secured. In other instances, standardization of routine may be necessary so that it can be performed quickly and efficiently. Therefore make sure that procedures always represent the best way. A procedure is a standardized method of performing specified work. Establishing procedures is the work a manager performs to develop and apply standardized methods of performing specified work.'[16] Thus, procedures and methods provide employees with instructions for performing work. The directives activate employees to do work properly. They are essential for repetitive work.

The need for organizing arises when the business starts to grow and the sort of informal arrangements found in small businesses are no longer practical. As your business grows, you will find that along with the increasing volume of business, there are increasing duties to be performed as well as increasing responsibilities. Eventually, you will reach the point where you have to seek assistance in order to be in a position to devote your energies and time most efficiently to the operations of your business. Thus, organizing basically boils down to coping with the increased volume of work. To be successful at that, you must have the right kind and number of people to assist you. Organizing implies dividing work among people. Louis A. Allen defines organizing 'as the work managers perform to arrange and relate the work to be done so it can be performed effectively by people. The function of organizing therefore includes the activities of developing an organization structure, delegating and developing relationships'.[17]

Developing an organization structure
'By developing an organization structure you can expect to get more work done with fewer people at less cost with greater satisfaction to the people doing the work. More specificially, here is what you can expect to achieve:'[18]

1. To ensure that all of the important work necessary to your objectives will be done.
2. To eliminate or minimize overlap and duplication.
3. To provide for primarily operating jobs that will be filled by people with skills in, for example, accounting and selling. The primary concern is with speciality. Quite clearly, the more a salesman can focus all his effort on selling, the more efficient he will become and the greater his productivity in selling will be. The golden rule here is: a technical specialist should be required to concentrate his major efforts on his speciality.

'Thus, developing an organization structure is the work a manager does to identify and group the work to be performed so it can be accomplished most effectively by people.'[19]

As each new employee is appointed, a post or specific job (with its duties and responsibilities) must be assigned to that person. Briefly, you must match the people with the jobs to be done. You should also be aware that the people working for you, or who will be working for you, may want a variety of benefits, each one something different, such as security of income, the feeling that they are part of a group of people, the need to be recognized as somebody important, and so on. They will work willingly towards the business's objectives, but only to the extent that their personal aims remain achievable through employment with you (as you yourself are trying to do by being in business).

Symptoms of poor organization

Poor use of time

Is most of your time taken up by operating tasks rather than managerial tasks? The more time you spend fighting fires, the less time you have to develop plans that would prevent the fires. In assigning responsibilities to employees, you may find that you have been spending more time doing things that someone else in the business — whose time is less valuable than your own — could have done. You may also find yourself doing things you like rather than things which could benefit the business. You may find that some important items were overlooked or deferred because of your preoccupation with less important matters. If you make a job analysis of each task, prepare a job specification, and assign responsibilities to each job, it will help you to see more clearly which tasks have been completed and what needs still to be done to achieve better results.

Slow decision making

Important decisions being reacted on slowly has a negative influence on customers. This happens most often because all decisions are made by owner-managers. The most likely solution is to give employees authority when you give responsibility.

High rate of customer complaints

The cause of this problem is more than likely with the organization structure. A study by Pfeiffer of the Kentse University revealed that 82% of customers do not support a particular business anymore because their complaints were not addressed immediately. Another survey indicated that the delivery performance of many businesses was poor and left considerable scope for improvement. Winning valuable orders and then failing to deliver on time remains a major area of concern which calls for closer management attention and control. Often the problem is over-committing existing capacity. Poor delivery performance is, however, no way to build or retain a reputation and is a sure way of losing repeat business. Consider this checklist in improving delivery performance:[20]

1. Do you consider that it is important to meet delivery dates?
2. Do you know what percentage of your deliveries are made on time?
3. Have you ever analysed the real costs of the business of a late delivery?
4. Have you lost customers because of unreliable deliveries?
5. Are customers alerted immediately it is known that a delay will be inevitable?
6. Is late receipt of essential materials and components the cause of your own business's failure to complete orders on time?
7. Have you visited your main suppliers to check their capacity and delivery control systems?
8. Do you get immediate warning from suppliers of any delay in their delivery schedule?
9. When you specify a date for delivery, do your suppliers know that you really mean it?
10. Do employees feel any sense of responsibility to the buyers of their products?
11. Have you got the transport and personnel to deliver on time?
12. Do all employees know their responsibilities and are they made accountable therefor?

How to organize
★ Define the goal to achieve.
★ Determine the main task to be performed to achieve each objective.
★ Determine detailed tasks. Every task normally has a number of details, i.e. steps to be followed to complete each task on time.

* ★ Assess personnel and assign tasks to employees capable of performing the job.
* ★ Employee participation in decision-making is necessary as the success of the implementation depends on a group of people working effectively together; create understanding.

Delegation of responsibility and authority 'To ensure that people have a feeling of ownership in their work, each operating decision should be delegated to the lowest organization level where the necessary facts and perspectives are available. Delegating is the work managers perform to entrust others with responsibility and authority and to create accountability for results.'[21] Delegation can be a risky business but the risks only occur if the delegation process is not properly handled. With proper planning and training a manager can minimize the risk involved, but it is essential that you overcome the feelings of fear of losing control, regret at giving up the jobs you enjoy and belief that you are the only one who can do the job properly. From a more practical point of view, delegation can be said to be the action taken to unburden yourself so that attention can be given to more profitable tasks. Never think that you will lose control if you delegate. The fact is that the reverse will take place. If delegation is done properly you will always gain overall control, and as owner-manager, you *should* be in overall control of all actions. Delegation does not mean giving someone just a task to perform, it also means that you are giving him a result to achieve. Some suggestions which may help to delegate properly are:

1. Decide which task to delegate and to whom you will delegate it (assign the task to the person best suited to do it).
2. Make clear the instructions, requirements and authority (brief and train the individual when necessary; teach him in order to save your time).
3. Don't make unreasonable demands.
4. Check on progress periodically, set a completion date and follow through on the project.
5. Provide counselling and support when asked to.

Once the tasks are assigned, you should not interfere but let it run its course as planned. A problem with managers is that they find it difficult to let go. They are like the amateur mechanic who simply refuses to leave what is in good order alone. However, the point of delegation can be well explained if it is said that you are the leader and your employees are the musicians in your band — each one has a part to play whilst you are the conductor.

Developing relationships 'Just as all of us are as important as other people make us feel, we get for ourselves just about what others are willing to give us. The manager, in particular, depends on others as the source of his accomplishment as well as of his rewards. Uniquely, his effectiveness depends on his ability to develop effective ways of working with others. The establishment of relationships is defined as the work a manager performs to create the conditions necessary for mutually co-operative efforts of people.'[22]

As you develop your organization, one of the problems you are more than likely to face is that of getting your employees to co-operate. Without co-ordination each may want to go his own direction rather than pulling together as a team. One way of getting the co-ordination you need is to form a committee wherein everyone can always be informed of what the others are doing, and that agreement can be reached on common issues.

LEADING

'Leading is the work managers perform to influence people to take effective action.'[23] The activities of leading include decision-making (already dealt with), communicating, motivating, selecting people and developing people's skills. Faulty leadership can completely nullify all the work that has gone into planning and organizing, and can also make the attainment of objectives called for by plans impossible. Leadership involves inter-action — it is a way of behaving, of persuading and inducing, of guiding and motivating. The value of human resources in any business cannot be denied, most particularly in the service business. It is the human element that can either make or break the business. But what is expected of a good manager? Below follows a list of attributes or characteristics which were developed from various studies, surveys and questionnaires completed in this particular field. It is hoped that you will be practising at least some of them daily. They are:

★ the ability to be comfortable with people in their work;
★ the ability to challenge employees to do their best;
★ being objective;
★ being empathic — sensitivity to the needs of others;
★ being a good listener — easy to talk to;
★ not letting others give up;
★ giving feedback on performance — telling people how they are doing;
★ wanting to make the business the best in the industry and in the market;
★ being firm but fair — open and honest in dealing with others;
★ focusing on the goals ahead;
★ believing it can be done;
★ not hiding bad news;
★ having a sense of humour;
★ being straightforward;
★ giving credit to others;
★ being decisive;
★ seeing mistakes as learning opportunities;
★ treating people as colleagues;
★ being enthusiastic;
★ following through;
★ insisting on training;
★ helping people to solve problems but not over-controlling;
★ trusting people;
★ ability to simplify things — make a difficult job look easy;
★ promoting from within;
★ making people confident and being supportive;
★ taking the blame at times;
★ being patient in explaining matters; and
★ criticizing in private.

You should remember that the total image of the business and its characteristics are derived from the character and leadership qualities of its founder. Your style of management will have a profound impact on the operations of the business. To be a good leader it is necessary to do the following:[24]

148

* to be really good in your trade (line of business);
* to make things really happen and to see the business taking off and doing exciting things, to seize every opportunity to develop the business;
* to see that the goods for sale or the services provided are really of good quality and fully meet the demands of the market;
* to see that the people working for you are all pulling together to do something really worthwhile for the benefit of the business;
* to see that your employees really know where you are going and what you are aiming to achieve so that they can each play their part;
* to gain the respect and support of your employees and to know that they will work well without being constantly watched; and
* to lead by example.

Communicating 'You must be able to get others to understand what you intend. In turn, you must understand your subordinates and have a keen ear for their needs and opinions. The management process at all levels depends on such understanding. Communicating is defined as the work managers perform to create understanding among people so that they can act effectively.'[25] The most essential element for successfully implementing plans, ideas and actions is communication. A business is run on communication. Customers are located, contacted and persuaded to buy products and services through communication. Similarly, employees are found, trained and motivated. Communications is thus the oil that lubricates the various parts so that they function smoothly. Communication is a four-way process — telling, asking, listening and understanding. Telling involves keeping your customers and employees informed on all aspects relating to them. Asking is the action necessary to get the communication process under way — ask for information. Listening well is the best guarantee that you will receive and understand the messages directed your way. Your main task, though, in the communication process will be to create understanding with all the people your business has dealings with. To be fully communicative requires skill and expertise in the aspects of communication mentioned, as well as in reading, speaking and writing. It was Sir Francis Bacon who said: 'Reading maketh a full man, but writing maketh an exact man.' Good communication will contribute to increasing your profits.

Motivating 'Since the most effective motivation comes from within, by motivating others you can do no more than create proper conditions that cause people to do their work with willingness and enthusiasm. Motivating is the work managers perform to inspire, encourage and impel people to take required action.'[26] Take for instance a small business selling and servicing motor cars. The service and products they sell can only be as good as the service which backs it up, and this service is delivered mainly by people. The relationship between owner and employees must be one of understanding in order for the employee to identify himself with his work and with the business he is working for. A number of symptoms may point to low morale: declining productivity; high employee turnover; increasing number of grievances; higher incidence of absenteeism and tardiness; increasing number of defective products; higher number of accidents; or a higher level of waste materials and scrap.[27] In fact, any symptom that is of significant degree (whichever way) off track might be an indication of low or high morale. You must however, try to ascertain the cause thereof as well as the genuine problem.

A motivated employee is a loyal employee and to be loyal implies that the employee supports the action and objectives of your business. In other words, from the employee's side, it is heart service that counts. Employees also expect you to be loyal. Another aspect to consider is that for five days a week an employee spends eight hours a day at his work, which is about half of the waking portion of his life. Thus one of the main desires he has for his workplace is that it should make him at ease. This is one reason why you should ensure pleasant working conditions at your business. The appearance of the business as a whole has, in fact, a bearing on the willingness and quality of an employee's performance. Some guidelines that may be helpful in improving the performance of people (and consequently your business) are the following:[28]

1. Tell and show your employees that you are interested in them and that you would be glad to hear their ideas on how conditions might be improved.
2. Treat your employees as individuals; never deal with them as impersonal variables in a working unit.
3. Improve your general understanding of human behaviour.
4. Accept the fact that others may not see things as you do.
5. Respect differences of opinion.
6. In so far as is possible, give explanations for management's actions.
7. Provide information and guidance on matters affecting employees' security.
8. Make reasonable efforts to keep jobs interesting.
9. Encourage promotion from within.
10. Express appreciation publicly for jobs well done. Offer criticism privately in the form of constructive suggestions for improvement.
11. Train supervisors to think about the people involved, in so far as is practicable, rather than just the work.
12. Keep your people up to date on all business matters affecting them, and squelch rumours with correct information.
13. Be fair.

Below is an extract from an article on 'motivation on which the late Edward Throm, Dartnell Senior Editor, has commented: 'I have never seen the case for humanistic motivation put better:'[29]

'All companies have access to the same material, machines, methods, money and markets. They even have access to the same manpower. It is the utilization of the only variable element, the workforce, that determines whether one business operates better or poorer than another.

Motivation is an abstract term. It imparts an incentive that requires a response on the part of someone else to achieve a defined goal. In business, motivation is not synonymous with salaries. Money is a means for accommodating the economic needs of workers. Motivation means an inner wholesome desire to exert effort without the external stimulus of money. To motivate the employee, the employee must be reached; to reach the employee there must be a complete understanding of the complexity of his make-up.

Motivation efforts must be directed toward improving company operations. That much is basic. To be effective, however, they must also be designed to show benefits to the employee. In fact, motivation can best be accomplished when workers are able to merge their personal ambitions with those of the company. In initial employment, for example, finding the right person for any job is only half the task. The applicant must feel that he, too, has found a job opportunity which meets or exceeds his expectations. Only when there is happy job marriage, in which both sides are satisfied, does the placement stand a chance of being successful. In such cases the company will provide the worker with the job satisfaction he needs to be happy; and he in turn, will have that built-in motivation companies look for in order to make his employment profitable.

Motivating is the ability of indoctrinating the personnel with a unity of purpose and maintaining a continuing, harmonious relationship among all people. It is a force which encourages and promotes a willingness of every employee to cooperate with every other member of the team. Basic to good motivation on the part of managers is the maintenance of conditions conducive to cooperate effort. To motivate is to create and perpetuate the climate which brings harmony and equilibruim into the entire work group for the benefit of all who are involved — the company as a whole and the employees as individuals.

Since management is accomplishing a predetermined objective through the efforts of other people, it is evident that motivation is extremely important. Stated simply, without manpower the machines would be idle, material would remain unused, and so on. Conversely, a well-staffed, carefully-selected and well-motivated workforce enhances the value of the machines, methods and other elements of business. The degree of success in motivating employees is in direct relation to the manager's ability to help employees realize personal ambitions and aspirations. Man does not live by bread alone. While money is necessary, it is not the only form of wealth, nor in the final analysis the most important.

Individuals often react differently when in groups. But always, whether alone or in league with co-workers, employees are individuals. Attempts to motivate workers are more successful when related to individuals and not to groups. It takes some doing on our part to comprehend this. In business we have been so accustomed to using mass techniques — in manufacturing, advertising, marketing — that we also apply these methods to individuals. This is what psychologists call the "fetish of symmetrical development". It is not recommended as a motivation technique for the simple reason that no two people are alike. Different people have different fears, different problems, different desires and hopes, and different ways of reacting to similar situations. They require different treatment.

A realistic approach leads to a recognition of individual strengths and weaknesses and then giving consideration accordingly. Only as people are different do they become noticed in a world of conformity. Only as we as managers and supervisors play up to this individuality, rather than the sameness, do we succeed in getting through to people with our message. We must never forget that the people whom chance has brought our way, who spend a good portion of their waking hours in our trust, are not only trying to make a living ... they are also trying to make a life.

Motivation of rank-and-file workers is becoming more of a challenge because the workforce is changing, the value system is being rearranged, and attitudes of people generally are unpredictable. There is a new breed of employee on the scene. He wants the rewards of hard work but not the trouble, strain and effort of hard work. He not only responds differently to tried-and-tested methods of motivation, but his outlook has a contaminating effect on co-workers. Workers are also more educated and this makes them impatient and dissatisfied with drudgery jobs that consists of monotonous tasks. Inspirational pep talks don't improve job content. Employees are no longer self-motivated simply out of economic necessity. It isn't easy to overcome negative attitudes toward business and work itself. The opportunity is to infuse jobs with enough spice, variety and excitement to offset the inevitable drudgery that cannot be avoided. Any manager who can make headway in this direction will get more out of the worker and out of the job.

What people expect from work

Many managers do not know as much about their employees' needs and wants as they would like to think they do. Every employee requires a certain amount of satisfaction from his or her job, and if an owner-manager knows that or can identify these basic needs and then tries to satisfy them, that manager is on his way to building a competent team to the benefit of the business. To help you cope with the identification of what employees are most likely to expect from work, the following list was compiled by a group of people after a poll to decide what motivates employees. It is of interest to note that some factors are considered least important by management but more important by employees.[30]

Bosses gave motivating factors in this order:

- good salary;
- job security;
- promotion and growth in company;
- good working conditions;
- interesting work;
- boss's loyalty to employees;
- tactful disciplining;
- full appreciation of work done;
- help with personal problems; and
- feeling of being 'in' on things.

Employees, on the other hand, listed many of the same motivations, but in a different order of priority. They said:

- full appreciation of work done;
- feeling of being 'in' on things;
- help with personal problems;
- job security;
- good salary;
- interesting work;
- promotion and growth;
- loyalty from boss;
- good working conditions; and
- tactful disciplining.

In conclusion, an aspect to be constantly aware of is that many businesses are already so competitive that it is hard to find an advantage in one over the others. There is, however, one. It has already been mentioned but it needs to be stressed in order to refresh your thinking and attitudes. The business that enjoys a more profitable position in today's competitive economy is the one which makes the best use of its resources. These resources are the six M's of business, namely: materials, machines, methods, money, markets and manpower — and all businesses have access to all of them on an almost equal basis. Also already mentioned is that management is getting results through people. So, the difference lies in the utilization of the manpower element — the human will to work, human talent, human attitude, and human competitiveness. You should employ the attitude of 'my employees can make the difference,' and you will succeed. Your job is to motivate each of them to do their best. The joy of leadership and of being in charge of people consists of spending all your management talent in order to see the people under you fulfil their greatest abilities. The more effort you put into this activity the more you will get out of it. Attitude, again, is like a two-edged sword — you may be looking for a positive attitude in your employees, but it is just as important in yourself. Be an example — a leader always has followers. Motivation is undoubtedly the best way to achieve employee co-operation.

Selecting People 'Selecting people is the work managers perform to find and choose people for positions and for advancement within the organization. Productive team results depend on selecting people who are not only qualified for their positions but who are compatible with the other members of the team.'[31]
See chapter on 'Staffing the business'.

Developing people's skills 'You can ensure top performance by training and developing the people you manage according to their aptitudes and abilities. This requires performance appraisal, counselling, and the provision of developmental opportunities. Developing people is defined as the work managers perform to help people improve their knowledge, attitudes and skills.'[32] Development can be defined as a process that consists of a combination of training programmes and practical experience, covering a wide range of knowledge, skills and attitudes, through which an individual is prepared over a relatively long period for a higher position. The term training is, however, sometimes confused with the term development. Training relates mainly to the changing of behaviour by transferring new knowledge, skills and attitudes, while development relates to the total process of which training is only a part. However, if you wish to be a success in business, the one aspect you need to give attention to is the development of your people. The other side is just as important, no training can be useful unless the person has the motivation to improve himself. Your main job is thus to create within the individual the desire to learn. Therefore, some of your first obligations are to take a real interest in your employees, to establish sound relationships with them and to be committed and dedicated to their further development. You also need to adopt the attitude that your business is here to stay.

If you don't, your attitude will probably be: What am I training my people for — to apply what they have learned from me in my competitor's business? Training in business is an unending process and must be seen as such. You are not excluded from this either; you need to learn constantly all you can about the business you are engaged in. Simply said, a business-owner who is not active in his obligation for further development may lose out to competitors.

An excellent management course: Louis A. Allen Associates has been operating in South Africa since 1958. Their expertise in the application of effective management techniques is derived from over 30 years of research and writing by the chairman, Louis Allen, and the teaching, consulting and line management experience of their associates. Louis Allen founded the firm in 1957 when he saw a need to help managers get things done; not to solve managers' problems, but rather to equip them with a system so they could solve their own. The firm specializes in management work, which is the physical and mental effort of planning, organizing, leading and controlling. When their clients have mastered the concepts, principles and techniques of management work, they are able to develop their own management system. And it is the application of such systems which results in improved management performance. Some unique features of the Allen management system are:

★ Basic concepts are defined to help you adapt to your own needs the universals of management practice that are used by successful managers in leading companies around the world.

★ Over forty management principles — cause and effect relationships developed by careful observation of real-life management situations — are used to guide managers as they perform these activities.

★ Step-by-step techniques which, like the principles, were developed by observing effective managers in action, show managers how to follow the management principles and perform their management work at a high level of effectiveness.

★ The entire system is integrated with the concept of leadership evolution, which describes the behaviour of managers.

Shortly put, all of the Louis A. Allen Associates managerial training programmes are concerned with the 'How to' of the management system. Thus, seeing that you have the potential, their courses will give you the management tools to perform with excellence. For more information on their managerial training programmes, or to enrol, write or phone:

Louis A. Allen Associates
132 Jan Smuts Avenue
Parkwood
Johannesburg
2193

Telephone: Johannesburg (011) 442-7366/7/8/70

CONTROLLING

'A plan sets forth a course of action which a manager is committed to follow in the future. While knowing where you want to go is important, equally important is the ability to stay on the predetermined course. Also, if you had to inspect every piece of work done by each of your people, you would get little else done. Control is therefore necessary. Controlling is defined as the work managers perform to assess and regulate work in progress and to assess the results secured.'[33]

Management controlling consists of the following activities: developing performance standards; measuring performance; evaluating performance; and correcting performance. As indicated earlier a budget is a tool to control. Budgeting is thus also a management tool used for both planning and control. The cash budget (or cash flow budget) in particular indicates not only the total amount of financing that is required but its timing as well. It shows the amount of funds needed month by month, week by week, or even on a daily basis. It is an owner-manager's most important financial tool as its overall purpose is to improve the operations of the business and thereby reduce costs and increase profitability. Budgeting starts with a set of performance standards (or targets). The targets constitute, in effect, the business's financial plan. The budgeted figures are compared with the actual results. This is the control phase of budgeting and it is a critical step in all well-operated businesses.

157

What to control: fraud and theft; image of the business; stock; expenses; cash; credit sales; buying; employees; quality of products or services; prices; appearance of the business; salespeople's performance; sales; advertising and promotional results; time; and productivity.

Developing performance standards 'This is the work managers perform to establish the criteria by which work and results are evaluated. You can derive standards from the objectives, programmes, schedules and budgets you have established through your planning function.'[34] See Chapter II, page 305 for criteria by which to measure sales performances. You can also make use of standard or typical ratios of your line of business to evaluate financial results, by comparing your results with theirs. Standards are also used to inform each employee of the level of performance expected, and to measure how well he does. Once the standards of performance are determined, they should be communicated to your employees who are then responsible for their performance. Standards are valuable in locating sources of inefficient as well as efficient performances.

Mearuring performance 'This is the work managers perform to record and report the work being done and the results obtained. By quantifying the observed results, you will be able to evaluate the progress of the work on hand.'[35] Information on actual performance is gained through some form of feedback, such as observation, or oral or written reports from your employees. Information about actual performance, obtained by feedback, is compared with standards to determine whether any changes are needed.

Thus, to make your plans work you need feedback. Don't wait twelve months for the 'score'. You need timely and up-to-date information, and you need to set up management controls that help you ensure that the right things are done each day and week. Such a control system should give you information about:

*Purchases (creditors) — The purpose of a record of purchases is to ensure that accounts for purchases on credit are paid on time in order to receive maximum discounts, and to preserve your creditibility record.

*Assets	— A record should be set up to include the following information: date purchased, price paid, annual depreciation, record of repairs and maintenance costs.
*Debtors (credit sales)	— Essentially credit sales represent money due to the business for sales transactions that have been made and are not yet fully paid for.
*Cash	— This enables you to control cash sales and expenses.
*Income statement	— This provides a summary of business activities for a given period of time and indicates whether a profit or loss was made from business operations.
*Balance sheet	— The balance sheet presents information on how much cash is available, how much stock is on hand, the total worth of assets, liabilities, and the owner's equity.
*Stock records	— These provide information on what to buy, when to buy and how much to buy.

The simpler these accounting control systems are, the better. Their purpose is to give you current useful information. For information to be usable it must:[36]

1. Meet the needs of the recipient. It must aid you in what you are trying to accomplish.
2. Be accurate. If the information is to be valuable to you it must be collected and processed in a manner that renders it accurate.
3. Be available at the proper time. If the information is not available when needed, it is worthless.
4. Be in the proper place. If the information is not in the right place when needed, it will not be worthwhile.
5. Be in the proper form. If the information is not in a usable form or easily adaptable by you, it is of little or no value.
6. Be understandable. Is the information clear? Do the descriptions and figures mean to you what they are supposed to? Is there a problem of misunderstanding?

To justify the expense of generating information, three important functions should be met:[37]

1. It should tell the exact story of what has happened.
2. It should explain why it happened.
3. It should suggest solutions to problems and indicate hitherto overlooked opportunities.

Evaluating performance 'This is the work managers perform to analyse, interpret and determine the worth or quality of work done and results achieved. Evaluation involves comparing results achieved with the standards set and determining whether the differences are variances or exceptions.'[38] The main tools to carry out this activity are the financial ratios. (See Chapter 15.)

Correcting performance 'This is defined as the work managers perform to rectify or improve the work being done and the results secured. You correct performance not only by eliminating current deficiencies, but also to preclude the occurrence of anticipated ones.'[39] You should approach each problem-solving situation with a view to resolving permanently.

SUMMARY AND CONCLUSIONS

The inter-relationship of management functions is put in the following manner by Louis A. Allen: 'Each management function is a product of, and closely related to, the other functions. Organizing, leading and controlling must be planned. Controls must be developed for plans, organization, and leading. Organization, plans and controls are powerless without the energizing power of people. No function is more important than the others. Their significance varies with the time, the situation, and the need. There is also no strict time sequence in which the functions are performed. Although logically, planning might be placed first. It is difficult to plan until people have been selected, trained and motivated. At the same time, planning is necessary in the selection, training and motivating of people. The best approach is to do whichever of the functions the situation requires, without trying to establish an arbitrary priority.'[40] Thus in reality, the planning and control process is a total communications system designed to convey to employees the what, how, where, who, when and why of the work to be done. It is also a check on what has been done to correct and adjust the work and the process to assure that customers receive good service and quality products at the time they need them.

In essence, planning is problem-solving and decision-making — considering alternatives, speculating on the future and setting objectives. Planning should not be regarded as a nuisance, but rather as a must. You cannot afford to make any serious mistakes — especially when you have a small business. Planning will require you to be a disciplined, creative thinker. Plans begin with an analysis of the way things are and a forecast of the way things will be. Any forecasting should begin with a full consideration of the general state of the economy, then of the conditions within the type of business you are in, and all other matters that can have a possible effect on your business, and finally of the condition your own business is in with the help of financial ratios. Action plans must be developed as they are the ultimate steps that make the business function. Action plans imply activities — people doing things, working and interacting with others inside and outside the business. Business is conducted by people and you should give your undivided attention to your 'income generators' (your people) so that your business can be competitive. Competitive management will improve your business's welfare.

BIBLIOGRAPHY

* Harold Koontz, Cyril O'Donnell. *Principles of Management*. 1968. McGraw-Hill, New York.
* J. Fred Weston, Eugene F. Brigham. *Managerial Finance*. 1977. Dryden Press, Hinsdale, Ill: 23-131.
* P.A. Miller, W.B. Roome, G.E. Staude. *Management in South Africa*. 1978. Juta, Cape Town: 29-79.
* Robert L. Katz. *Management of the Total Enterprise*. 1970. Prentice-Hall, Englewood Cliffs, NJ: 49-60.
* Thomas J. Peters, Nancy K. Austin. *A Passion for Excellence*. 1985. Collins, Glasgow: 353-362.
* Graham Rosenthal. Planning for growth. *Entrepreneur*. 1986; **5**(4): 6.
* Ian Sandler. How to run a small business successfully. *Entrepreneur*. 1986; **5**(6): 9-11.
* Louis A. Allen, *Professional Manager's Guide*. 1969. Louis A. Allen Associates, Johannesburg.
* Management by expectation: How can you become an even better supervisor? *Entrepreneur*. 1986; **5**(1): 5.
* M. R. Sareff. Strategic management for small business. *Entrepreneur*. 1986; **5**(1): 6-7.

* Walter Woeber. Delegation: an essential skill. *Management*. 1985; February 14–15.

* H. de Kock. What is management development? *Small Business News* (University of the North Business Advisory Bureau), 1984; May: 26.

* J. P. Stone. Do you budget in your business? *Small Business News* (University of the North Business Advisory Bureau) 1984; Feb: 23.

* Budgets: a management tool. *Entrepreneur*. 1982; 9–10.

* H. de Kock. Financial planning: budgets and what they can do for you. *Small Business News* (University of the North Business Advisory Bureau) 1984; November: 18.

* L. Jonker. How do you 'motivate' your workers? *Black Business News*. 1983; **5**(4): 4–5.

* Louis van Zyl. The heart of the matter: results. *Productivity SA*. 1986; **12**(3): 39–41.

* Barry Adams. Managing a business in tough times. *Management*. 1985; February: 26–29.

* William H. Day. Maximizing small business profits. 1978. Prentice-Hall, Englewood Cliffs, NJ: 154–228.

NOTES

[1] Peter F. Drucker. *Managing For Results*. 1967. Pan, London: 248. Reprinted by permission of William Heinemann Limited.

[2] R.M. Johnson. *How To Manage People*. 1985. Business Books, London: 223.

[3] Kenneth Blanchard, Spencer Johnson. *The One Minute Manager*. 1983. 6th impression. Fontana/Collins, 74.

[4] Louis A. Allen. *Professional Manager's Guide*. 1986. Louis A. Allen Associates, Johannesburg. (Used with permission.)

[5] T.F. Straton. How to simplify a problem. Reprinted with permission from *Nation's Business*. 1957. U.S. Chamber of Commerce.

[6] Checklist 19. *Decision Making*. The South African Institute of Management.

[7] Louis A. Allen. *Professional Manager's Guide*. 1986. Louis A. Allen Associates, Johannesburg. (Used with permission.)

[8] Ibid.

[9] Ansoff, H.I. *Corporate Strategy*. 1968. New York: Penguin, 44.

[10] Louis A. Allen. *Professional Manager's Guide*. 1986. Louis A. Allen Associates, (Used with permission.)

[11] Ibid.

[12] Ibid.

[13] John J. Corson. Make the time you need. *Nation's Business*, 1956; **44**: 90–93. *Source:* William H. Day. *Maximizing Small Business Profits*. 1978. Prentice-Hall, Englewood Cliffs, NJ: 162, 163.

[14] Louis A. Allen. *Professional Manager's Guide*. 1986. Louis A. Allen Associates. (Used with permission.)

[15] Ibid.

[16] Ibid.

[17] Ibid.

[18] Ibid.

[19] Ibid.

[20] Checklist 75. *Delivering On Time*. The South African Institute of Management.

[21] Louis A. Allen. *Professional Manager's Guide*. 1986. Louis A. Allen Associates. (Used with permission.)

[22] Ibid.

[23] Ibid.

[24] R.M. Johnson. *How To Manage People.* 1985. Business Books, London: 152, 153.

[25] Louis A. Allen. *Professional Manager's Guide.* 1986. Louis A. Allen Associates. (Used with permission.)

[26] Ibid.

[27] William H. Day. *Maximizing Small Business Profits.* 1978. Prentice-Hall, Englewood Cliffs NJ: 224. (Reprinted with permission.)

[28] Martin. M. Bruce. *Managing For Better Morale.* 1962. Small Marketers Aids Annual Number 4, U.S. Small Business Administration, Washington D.C.: 59-60.

[29] *Source:* Wilbert E. Scheer. *Personnel Administration Handbook.* 1979. The Dartnell Corporation, Chicago, Ill: 287-295.

[30] Wilbert E. Scheer. *Personnel Administration.* 1979. The Dartnell Corporation, Chicago, Ill: 291. (Reproduced with permission by the courtesy of the Dartnell Corporation.)

[31] Louis A. Allen. *Professional Manager's Guide.* 1986. Louis A. Allen Associates. (Used with permission.)

[32] Ibid.

[33] Ibid.

[34] Ibid.

[35] Ibid.

[36] George R. Terry. *Office Management and Control.* 5th Ed. 1966. Richard D. Irwin, Homewood Ill. 4. *Source:* William H. Day. *Maximizing Small Business Profits.* 1978. Prentice-Hall, Englewood Cliffs, NJ: 45, 46.

[37] *From:* John V. Petrof et al. *Small Business Management: Concepts and Techniques for Improving Decisions.* 1972. McGraw-Hill, New York. *Source:* William H. Day. *Maximizing Small Business Profits.* 1978. Prentice-Hall, Englewood Cliffs, NJ: 46.

[38] Louis A. Allen. *Professional Manager's Guide.* 1986. Louis A. Allen Associates. (Used with permission.)

[39] Ibid.

[40] Ibid.

4

YOUR BUSINESS TEAM

'The best minute I spend is the one I invest in people.'

The One Minute Manager[1]

'To a large extent success in your business depends on the way you deal with people. And by working to improve the motivation and ability of the people who work for you, you can improve the effectiveness of the whole operation. However, a spirit of teamwork has to be created and maintained by conscious efforts.'

Ron Johnson[2]

INTRODUCTION

When starting a new business, many a businessman is easily occupied with the thought of making money, but forgets to be concerned, or rather, is less concerned with how he is going to go about making it. In other words, he may forget that he has to manage the 'income generators' (employees) of the business in such a way as to bring out the best in them. An important fact is that the people who work in a small business can either be its greatest asset or its most serious handicap. Therefore, management expertise and personnel efficiency at all levels are important decisive factors in the success of any business. This point applies to every business, no matter how many people it employs. Even the simplest, one-man business is dependent for its success on the personality and approach of its operator. A sure way to give competitors the opportunity they need to get the extra volume of business they seek, is to employ incompetent and unfriendly personnel in your business. This is true all over, and research has proved that one of the main reasons for customers leaving one business to shop at another is because of the way they are treated by the employees of the business. Some comments from experienced managers to put what has been said into perspective are the following:

Tom Herriot, Branch Manager of OK Bazaars in Randburg, Transvaal, puts it beautifully: 'Our range is basically similar to that of our competitors, and price itself is not enough to make everyone shop at our store. So our real edge is good customer service, which also creates repeat business.'[3]

Perry Gwenossis, Branch Manager, Pick 'n Pay, Nigel, Transvaal, expresses the role employees have to play as far as customer service is concerned in the following words: 'Last impressions can do much to influence customers to shop at our store again, so we train and encourage cashiers and packers to be very courteous at the checkout.'[4]

Harold Schneemann, Branch Manager, Checkers, Queensburgh, Durban says: 'Our shelf packers always show customers where to find products rather than merely tell them. Many of our cashiers have established friendly relationships with customers. We encourage cashiers to get to know regular customers and address them by name. In our deli we have found it pays to give special attention to customers with greater purchasing potential for the department. In the past the problem with supermarkets was that customers just felt like a number; the personal care and attention of the corner grocery store, where the manager knew you by name, your children and how many dogs you had, was missing. So as part of our customer courtesy and care programme we try to make them feel welcome.'[5]

Gert Visagie, owner of Visagie Spar Foodlines, Postmasburg, Northern Cape: Good customer service is what we have built our business on over the years. We keep our customer-service levels high mainly through proper training and incentive programmes. For example, all our bakery and butchery staff receive a commission based on the department's turnover. The commission not only makes staff more productive but promotes good service. Staff know that the more friendly they are and the better service they give, the greater the turnover and the bigger the commissions. The cashier or shelf packer who gives the best service receives a small cash bonus. Our cashiers are trained to help customers promptly and thank them, and we require that they are always friendly to customers. You have to be very strict about this otherwise you lose business; people are put off at your store if the atmosphere is unfriendly.'[6]

Derek Steven, Branch Manager, Shoprite, Strand, Cape Town says: 'We constantly drive home the importance of customer service to our staff by stressing that it is the customer who pays their salaries each month. At our regular meetings with staff and supervisors we emphasize that a few polite and friendly words to customers cost nothing. Besides making the customer's day, friendliness towards them creates a congenial working environment which is important for themselves as they spend 75% of their waking lives at work. Also, if staff feel happy they are more motivated; productivity increases and so does service.'[7]

YOUR EMPLOYEES

There are many successful businesses, or rather managers, that can attest that they value their customers and their employees as more than just a number to the business. Nothing can be more disheartening to any manager than a row of bored cashiers waiting for customers, and it can happen, if managers do not supply the attention necessary to bring out the best in their 'income generators'. One of the best ways to observe the influence of service on the ultimate success of a store and on its labour productivity is to look at the impact of poor service on the shopper. Consider the example below:

The impact of poor service on customer purchases and future loyalty to a store[8]

A shopper goes out to purchase a list of ten items that she needs — in a hurry.

1. She enters the store with her shopping list and looks around. No shopping carts are to be seen. She takes a handbasket but is then lucky enough to find a trolley. Is it abandoned or is she stealing another shopper's cart? No, she quickly finds out that it has been abandoned and she knows why. One wheel is sticking and it is squeaking.

2. Moving down the aisle she has to lift her trolley over the floor-polisher's electric cord.

3. The store is badly laid out. She cannot find items where she logically would expect them to be.

4. After half-an-hour she has found just six out of the ten items she came in to buy. A shelf-packer she asked for help in locating an item said: 'Sorry, I've only been here two weeks!'

5. On her way around the store she has walked into spilt tomato sauce that has been on the floor for an hour or two. It is sticking to her shoes and she would like to go out and clean them up. Her sticky feet are distracting her from the business of shopping.

166

6. At the fish counter, the counterhand could not give her specific information on how to prepare a fish on special that caught her fancy.

7. At the front of the store just two of the ten checkouts are open and she has to queue behind another seven shoppers.

8. When her turn finally comes, two of the items are not price-marked. She complains to the cashier about not being able to find items and asks why are they not in stock. She is told by the cashier: 'We probably did not order them.' The customer then tells the cashier: 'One of the items was advertised in last night's paper.' The cashier calls the manager who is standing some six metres away loudly berating the floor cleaner. The manager says: 'Head Office didn't notify us about the item going into the ad.'

The poor service encountered by this shopper prevented her from buying as much as she might have. Items that she wanted to buy were not in stock and she was continuously distracted from concentrating on her shopping by obstructions like the electric cord and the tomato sauce sticking to her shoes. The trolley that did not run smoothly was driving her 'nuts' with its squeaking. She did not buy the fish because she did not have the confidence to cook it, and the counterhand could not give her cooking instructions. The other personal contact she had with the cashier and the store manager confirmed her impression that the store was run completely inefficiently. All in all, she wasted time, did not satisfy her needs and swore never to return to the store. The store lost a potential customer. Though some of the service problems in the example might appear to be due to factors such as poor management, poor organization or bad merchandizing, their root cause is most often poor training. Whatever the cause may be, the important point is that if operations are to run smoothly, the owner-manager cannot do all these things himself. He has to rely on others.

Although to this point the cashier of a supermarket has been used to illustrate the valuable connection that there should be between the customer, the personnel of a business and the owner-manager, it applies to all people working for a particular business. Somehow the owner-manager must do something to get this relationship between the customer and the business in shape. The question however is: Where do you start? It would probably be best to start by building up a particular set of principles and values from which the conduct policy of the business will spring. It is most important that you believe in that philosophy, live it every day, practise it every day. Practising your policy will not necessarily make it perfect, but it will make it permanent, and by being consistent in your actions as directed by your philosophy, you will create credibility. This point of 'continuity creates credibility' may need some more explanation. Probably the best way to explain it is by means of a simple, every-day example:

Take a child and its parents, and the bond of love there is between them. If the parents show their love and care for the child all the time, the child, when grown up, will believe that his parents love him and he will love them. But the reverse is also true: if the parents of a child have neglected him and did not show much love to the child, the child more than likely, will feel very lonely and neglected. He will not believe that his parents love him. Therefore be consistent in your actions because it creates credibility. (The same principle applies to other business activities such as advertising, and in your relations with customers.)

The real trick is in demonstrating to people (personnel and customers) every day, every time you come into contact with them in whichever way (personal, by mail or through advertising), where you want to take your business and that you care for them. You must take your philosophy seriously and conduct every business day accordingly. Such a philosophy should start with the omnipresent thought: respect for the individual. Help your employees to reach their full potential by providing conditions that are challenging, invigorating and fun. 'Catch them doing things right'[9] and tell them — provide positive feedback. People who feel good about themselves always produce good results.[10] Reward good performance. Allow them to be contributors, not just instruments.

If you truly want to build your business through the people working for you, then it is of absolute necessity that you have a specific 'thinking' that will be at the core of it. Think constantly of the valuable role the human resource plays in business. Consider the following:

THE VALUE OF HUMAN RESOURCES IN BUSINESS[11]

By W. F. HACHMEISTER
President
Blue Cross and Blue Shield of Texas
Dallas, Texas 75201

'Any business, particularly a service-orientated business like Blue Cross and Blue Shield, depends chiefly on the human element.

I believe that the success of a business is the sum total of the attitude of its people. A good attitude denotes effort expended, and our members sense this attitude and respond to our enthusiasm and willingness to help with their health care needs.

It's this kind of attitude on the part of Blue Cross and Blue Shield workers that has made us number one in the health care industry. Attitude is paramount in business. I can forgive lack of talent, if it's made up in attitude. If a person gives you his best effort and he has missed the mark, you can't fault him for trying.

The human element in business is what makes the difference. It is the unknown factor. Financial resources are known, technical resources are given, but the human factor in any business is what makes it or breaks it. I value employees who hustle, who get in there and do something positive about a situation. Even if what they do doesn't work well, its preferable to sitting around doing nothing.

Innovative employees are a tremendous natural resource for which no machine or financial resource can make up. If we at Blue Cross and Blue Shield cannot be innovative and come up with newer and more exciting ways of meeting people's health care needs, then our competition will.

I remember when I first came to Blue Cross and Blue Shield in the financial area. It was like a fertile field of unploughed ground. I saw what I could do, I saw that my talent and drive could make a difference. Nothing innovative was being done at the time, so I knew that anything I attempted would be better. So, I came in swinging. I like employees who have that competitive, I-can-make-a-difference feeling.

Of course, along with attitude, I look for talent, ingenuity and the willingness to take risks. When you put one company against another, the unknown quotient is its willingness to take a few risks in order to be great. The same goes for employees, who after all, are the company. I try to surround myself with people who are not afraid to stick their necks out. Sure, they'll make some mistakes, and when they do, I expect them to take the heat. But they don't have to be defensive. They'll learn to make more good decisions than bad decisions. They'll learn to be innovative and confident and to become experts in their fields.

I think what people need is simple and understandable goals, corporate goals which are reachable and concrete, but which are also set just a little beyond what is natural to attain. That way your people will grow. They will stretch and grow to accomplish their goals.

Another factor I value in my employees is a good sense of humour. I try to laugh at least once a day. If you can't find some humour in something every day, you're in pretty bad shape. It helps you put things in perspective. I think you can be light and humorous and still get 100% of the job done.

Business is a form of competition. Its like going to the first tee with a group of friends. They're friends, but when you play the game, you're in competition with each other and you will do your best to win. To me, the ideal situation would be when every person in every company was giving 100%. I'd rather lose to a company's first string team than beat its second or third string. I like good competition. Its healthy.

I like employees who are competitive. If you give people too much when they don't work for it, they get lethargic and fat. When you get fat, you get sick. Did you ever notice how it's always the lean and hungry athlete who is the best competitor? I believe in paying top salaries for good people. Good people are our most important asset, but they've got to give at least 100%. I don't expect anything out of anybody that I would not give myself. I give 110%, so I expect good people to give at least 100%. I don't mean devote 100% of one's life to one's job. No. I insist on a close family, relaxation, outside interests and vacation. But when you work, you should work hard.

I feel that running a company is like being the manager of a major league baseball team. You're too old to play third base or pinch hit. You just keep chewing out and kicking the recalcitrant players and giving the sensitive ones a pat on the head until you bring out the best in all of them. Your job is to motivate each of them to do his best. That's what makes a winning season, year after year.

Suggestions for better employee relations Below follow ten thoughts which could assist you in making your employee relations programme better and more effective:[12]

1. Can't we treat applicants as guests instead of strangers? How about simplifying the processing procedure with less cumbersome application forms, more respect for the applicant's time, more interest in each one as a person? How about following up with replies to all responses, not just the selected few? And how about reducing the indecision annoyances of unsure interviewers?

2. In employing workers, let's not try only to fill a vacancy in one of our departments. Let's at the same time try to help an applicant solve one of his own problems by finding a job to his liking. Ideally, every placement should be a happy job marriage in which both sides are satisfied.

3. When we want to transfer or promote a worker we should not only think of solving our problem. People should not be looked upon as a load of cinders moved around to fill a hole. We should be big enough to respect the worker's feelings about the new job for which he is being considered.

4. Can we arrange to give our people thorough training, a chance to increase their skills or add new ones to help them qualify for better job opportunities? This would enhance their earning power for themselves and their value to the company.

5. If we are going to establish a recognition programme for something like length of service, let's honour each worker individually on his anniversary date, the day which means something to him, rather than lumping them all together once a year, for the easy planning of a group dinner or party.

6. Let's develop a better hearing aid for business. You say you practice the 'open door' policy, but who walks in? Why don't you walk around among the workers, preferably in shirt sleeves. You'll be surprised at what you will learn.

7. Why wait until you have to announce something before you write a 'memo to all employees'? Why not write when nothing is at stake and tell your associates what a good job they're doing?

8. Instead of distributing your expensive but dull annual statements, accompanied by a mass-produced cover note full of lifeless statistics, what would be wrong with a 'personal letter from the chairman' telling each worker, at home where the family may also read it, that the company is making good progress and his job is secure.

9. Should there be a golden rule in business? Man is a sacred personality made in the image of God. If man were a machine, then it would be appropriate to use him,

depreciate him, consume him and discard him. But man is not a machine. No one, no company, no employer, no supervisor can trample with impunity upon the human personality.

10. If respecting the dignity of man in our fellow, blood-bought souls sounds altruistic, then for selfish reasons let's recognize how important other people are to us in the accomplishment of our goals. Our employees are the people through whom we do our work and through whom we attain our purpose. They are the ones who, in reality, make us look good. Let's make our personnel programmes 'people programmes'.

Your employees as contributors Years ago, businessmen used to think there was only one way to make a business grow — buy more machinery, open more businesses and borrow more money. But as time went by, they learned that their most valuable resource was people. It is people who come up with ideas to deal with customer complaints, productivity problems and marketing challenges. Businessmen started to reveal to employees the direction in which they were heading as well as that in which they wanted to go.

In this way they began to share the purpose and objectives of the business with their employees. They realized that if all the people in the business had similar goals, they would help each other to reach them, resulting in greater productivity, job satisfaction, job security and profits. Employees therefore were made full partners and contributors. Businessmen now involve people through the use of a system whereby all employees can sit around a table and work together as a team, and everybody benefits — the employee experiences increased job satisfaction and recognition; the business increases its productivity and improves operating efficiency; and the customers receive better service, greater satisfaction and more value for money. Below are a number of points that good suggestions might help to do:[13]

- Cut costs;
- save time;
- reduce errors;
- improve customer satisfaction;
- increase repeat business;

- improve employee morale;
- improve business appearance;
- help avoid misunderstanding over work;
- build greater pride in the business;
- help attract better employees;
- promote greater uniformity;
- eliminate waste;
- lessen accidents;
- lower absenteeism;
- utilize manpower to better advantage;
- prevent unnecessary wear and tear on equipment;
- create long-range advantages;
- result in significant savings;
- improve on similar suggested changes; and
- simplify the present method.

Training The kind of service a customer gets is dependent on the value attached to training by the owner-manager, and the effort invested in it. Recognition of the importance of training and some knowledge and use of certain basic techniques of instruction, which help people to learn and remember information, or to carry out instructions correctly and efficiently, can transform a business giving indifferent service and making marginal profits into one which gives first class service, with constantly improving profitability. A training need is the difference between what the employee knows now, can perform now and what his attitude is now, compared with what he should know, how he should be able to perform and what his attitude should be. Training can do much to fill the gap created by this difference. It is of great importance for you to recognize and explain the difference between an acceptable performance, an unacceptable performance and an exceptional performance. Set your standards and your guidelines in order to obtain maximum employee performance. Prepare a proper job description for each employee so that he knows what is to be done and how it must be done. A question you will probably ask at some stage is: Is investment in training worthwhile? Johann Engelbrecht of the National Productivity Institute (Human Resource Division), who's special area of involvement is productivity improvement training, aimed at providing managers with skills to measure, control and improve productivity in their areas of responsibility, sheds some light on this question.[14]

It is quite common to find that manpower, relative to other resources, is neglected when it comes to providing an infrastructure which will support high performance. Yet manpower controls all the other inputs, and therefore deserves high priority.

Training is a costly exercise and very often neglected, because even after spending money on it, it may still not give the returns hoped for if a few important factors have not been taken into consideration. These are: the focus of the training, the role of the individual (the trainee) in training and the setting of training standards.

The Focus of Training

When one talks about training, most people immediately think of training courses. However, courses are only a part of 'the systematic development of behaviour/knowledge/skills required by an individual in order to perform adequately a given task or job'. Training should therefore be very specifically geared towards improving performance on the job.

Courses, of which no fewer than 2 000 are listed in the NPI's Training Course Directory, are often of a general kind — not specific to the needs of a particular job. Therein lies a danger, because for the smaller businessman especially it is vital that the return on his investment in training should be good. General training prepares the trainee to be as productive in the next firm as in the firm which is sponsoring his training. Apprenticeship training is a good example of general training. Specific training raises the trainee's productivity less in other firms than in the firm providing the training. Training an operator to work a specialised machine is an example of specific training.

Does this imply that one should invest in specific training only? No, because we also need to train apprentices, sales staff, cashiers, etc. If this is not done, the employer will always have to compete in the open market for skilled labour. Therefore one must find a way to, from time to time, enter into general training and still make a sound business investment. This is where the role of the individual in training comes in.

The Individual's Responsibility

Theoretically, the best way to reduce the risk in investing in training is to make the trainee pay for his/her own training. This is not feasible, but in practice part of this can be achieved, sometimes indirectly. Apprentices fund part of their training themselves by accepting lower wages while learning, in anticipation of higher wages later. This is an option which can sometimes be applied.

Another is to structure the training in such a way that the trainee, at least indirectly, funds part of the training. This means that training should be on-the-job but HIGHLY structured. Certain objectives are given to the worker and whilst performing his/her normal duties, he/she also works towards achieving certain training objectives. Rather than sending people (for example cashiers) to a course away from the business or on an in-house course with a formal trainer, it is possible to use one well trained supervisor as a mentor. He/she can help trainees as and when help and guidance are required. In this way the trainee will be doing a normal job while acquiring new skills, and the supervisor will be carrying out a normal supervising job as well as being a mentor. Thereby the cost of training is reduced. It is important to note that this approach will only be productive if well planned, well structured and well controlled.

Training Standards

Training standards are very important, even more so when using the approach just mentioned. The purpose of training standards is to link the outcome of training to minimum job requirements. If standards are set too low, the trainee could perform adequately during training but still be unable to do the job to his employer's satisfaction. Very often standards are based on average performance, or on some arbitrary pass rate. The following extreme example supports this claim: A worker was trained to operate the hoist in a vehicle service garage. Because this equipment can be very dangerous if not used correctly, a pass rate of 75% was set. Even if the operator shows me his certificate for passing the course at 75%, I will still not get in underneath the car on the hoist, because the implication of passing at 75% is that there is a 25% chance (or one in four) that a car may fall on my head.

How best, then, can we set training standards? We should determine and describe the performance of our best (exemplary) performer and use his/her performance as our standard when structuring training. This may not come about in one training increment (and perhaps should not, because of the demotivating effects on a trainee of a seemingly unachievable standard) but one should not be satisfied that the training effort is complete until exemplary performance is achieved.

Small to medium sized businesses will get a lot more return out of their training effort if they make it as specific as possible and look at other alternatives than readily accepted training courses. It is also important to remember that average standards produce mediocre results, while exemplary standards produce exemplary performers.'

A very important aspect of training is reinforcement — providing positive feedback. A kind remark is a reinforcer. So is a personal compliment, or, sometimes, simply personal attention. All evidence indicates that the more frequent and prompt reinforcement is, the more effective learning will be.

The quicker the feedback, the sooner an employee learns to perform exceptionally. The main idea of training is to get the employee's performance to a certain level. Learning, on the other hand, means a lasting change in behaviour resulting from experience.[15] The best reinforcer is probably, therefore, success. Tell the employee when he is successful ('success breeds success'). The more the employee is given the opportunity to perform or practise, the more effective the learning will be. Without practice it is impossible to reinforce what the employee is doing correctly, or what needs to be improved in order to master the skills. You should not expect an employee to master a skill if you merely tell him what to do. You have to tell him what to do and why it is important to do it correctly and then show him how it must be done. Thereafter allow the employee to practise. This creates an opportunity to give him feedback; praise him for what he is doing correctly and coach him in the areas needing improvement. To provide you with some more insight into this method of training, listen to what is called 'The Dale Carnegie Method' of training (putting the aspect of positive reinforcement into perspective):[16]

'Dale Carnegie Training is presented the way golf should be taught. We believe the way to a successful golf game is to start with success. By placing the ball one or two inches from the hole, you putt it in every time — always a success. Then you move the ball back a foot and you putt it in, maybe miss a few times, but you still have lots of successful experiences. You move it back to a yard, putt it in, and putt it in again. Now you are learning to enjoy the game of golf. You may want to play it and learn to play it better. Why? Because you know what success feels like through positive feedback that encourages you to continue learning.

By contrast, the first thing done when learning to play golf is to step up on to the first tee, some 400 yards away from the hole and hit the ball off the tee into the trees. After 14 slices the only thing learned is how to slice well. Not having experienced any success, one may be ready to give up golf.

At Dale Carnegie we believe that practice makes permanent, not perfect. So the only kind of practice that makes sense is perfect practice. We help them learn an inch at a time, next a foot at a time, then a yard at a time. That is what our training is all about — reinforcing the positive. In our classrooms, the first skills we ask people to develop are the ones we know they can acquire easily. Subsequently, they become comfortable and say "I'm not afraid to try something new here, all I can do is succeed." As they acquire new techniques, they learn to succeed.'

On-the-job training provides real experience, and mistakes can be corrected before they get out of hand. Below are four simple, easy-to-follow steps when training your employees:[17]

1. Teach. Establish what your employee already knows. Take nothing for granted, even if the employee declared on the job application that he or she had similar experience. Then teach what is not known, keeping in mind that it is better to repeat some of what is already known than to have the employee waste time and material later.
2. Demonstrate. Following the job description sheet, show the trainee how to do the job. Proceed slowly, asking questions which make the trainee think about why each step is taken in the demonstrated manner. Then demonstrate at normal speed.
3. Let the trainee perform. After demonstrating, let the employee perform the job alone. Your attitude at this point should be one of encouragement. Avoid looking over shoulders. Demonstrate again, if a mistake is made.
4. Inspect. Either you or a supervisor should then check the trainee's work. Point out satisfactory progress, or explain what he or she is doing wrong and why.

Tracking down the right training course The training industry in South Africa is big and the number of training institutions is on the increase — so is the variety of training programmes they present. Some of those training programmes would meet your business's training needs, and some wouldn't. So, your main problem is not so much an availability problem as a shopping problem. The question is, how do you find the right training programme? Some advice on the matter follows.[18]

Sending employees from your business on a training programme should not be a hit-or-miss proposition. When a request from an employee comes (or you decide he needs training), you can get your money's worth by doing some careful shopping.

177

Once the employee's learning plans or goals have been agreed upon, your next step is to match his learning needs to an available training programme. Information on training programmes abounds: direct mail brochures, trade magazines' advertising, trade shows, professional conferences, suppliers, local chamber of commerce, development corporations — all are excellent resources. Examine the literature on training programme offerings; the objectives should be similar to items on the trainee's learning plans.

However, no brochure or direct mail piece can accurately cover all the information you will want to know about a training programme. If it did, you probably would not have the time to read it. So where do you get the facts and figures you need? Call the training programme organizers. Ask to speak with either the instructor or the designer or both. If you don't get the information you need, cross that organization off your list: if they are unwilling or unable to help a potential client, they are not going to do a good job with the real thing. Reputable training organizations will not see your call as an intrusion but will welcome the chance to do some informal needs analysis of their own.

Start the conversation by explaining the potential trainee's learning objectives. Tell the listener something about his needs, his background and your business. The following questions should help you get started. Add or delete to fit your needs:

*   Is any background reading recommended? For instance, has the instructor published any articles or books on the training programme topic that would be helpful?
*   What theories, models or practices form the basis of the training programme?
*   How is the training programme designed? What is the ratio of small-group work to lectures? Ask for a brief overview of the agenda. How much time will be allocated to discussions, question and answer sessions, practice and feedback?
*   How many people will be in the class? Is there an attendance limit? (The answer you want is 'yes', and the limit should make sense to you in light of the programme design. If you are told that each trainee will get individual attention from the instructor, and then that the attendance limit is 500, hang up.)

* What is the typical attendee profile? Will your business's employee feel comfortable with this group?
  What are the training programme's objectives?
* How much information will be covered? (Is the allotted time appropriate for the information? Does this sound like a half-day session stretched into a two-day programme? Or, at the other extreme, is the information too complex to be adequately discussed in one day?)
* Will the information be presented at a level appropriate for the trainees? How does the instructor define beginner, intermediate and advanced levels?
* Is the instructor willing to modify the design or content somewhat in order to meet your needs? Is the training programme totally canned or will adaptions be made based on group needs?
* What are the instructor's credentials? How about the training organization's background and the organizer's qualifications?
* Can you attend a preview free or for a nominal charge?
* How will the instructor know whether the employee has learned the material?
* Will there be a pretest? A post-test?
* What follow-up will be conducted?
* Will someone in the provider's organization (preferably the instructor) be available for help after trainees are back at work?
* Has anything been incorporated into the design of the training session to ensure transfer of training from the classroom to the workplace?
* What kind of feedback will trainees receive during the session?
* Are there any 'hidden' costs for tests or materials?
* Who can you contact for references? (Count on getting favourable responses. They will all be biased, but you can use these sources as another opportunity to get an opinion on the match between your goals and the seminar objectives. You can also ask how previous attendees applied the knowledge or skills they learned.)
* Will the provider send you sample materials, handouts or other pertinent information?

* Remember to ask questions about food (what meals are included, what type of food is offered, etc.), transportation, directions, appropriate dress, availability of accommodation facilities, etc.

In conclusion it is a good idea to take notes of your conversation with the instructor and review them with the employee who will be attending the training programme and his supervisor. At that stage you can decide if this particular training programme will be of value for your business, or if you must continue to shop around.

PRODUCTIVITY IN SMALL BUSINESS

Productivity is the relationship between input and output. The main aim of any business is profit — all actions are directed thereto — and profit is indeed the measure of performance that reflects the difference between input and output. Profit is the result of the actions a businessman takes during the year (or some other period) to reach a proper relationship between total input and output. However, the concept of productivity is much broader than this as it has to do with whether the actions taken by the businessman have had 'economic value', in other words, whether the actions (or the decisions made to take certain actions) were financially sound, profitable and useful in the production of wealth (both the business, its owner, its employees and its customers must benefit from the actions taken). Productivity is also concerned with efficiency ('Are we doing things right?') and effectiveness ('Are we doing the right thing?'). You need to ask these two key productivity questions constantly. Productivity can be increased by the following:

getting more output for the same input

or

getting the same output for less input

or

getting much more output for slightly more input

or

getting slightly less output for much less input

The abovementioned can be realized by taking 'positive actions such as:

1. better purchasing of stock (quality products at fair prices);
2. improving stock turnover rates;
3. improving methods to eliminate or cut unnecessary expenses;
4. improving fraud and theft control;
5. training of personnel;
6. improving customer, supplier, personnel and banker relations;
7. improving methods for selling on credit;
8. improving deliveries;
9. improving market research;
10. improving utilization of floor space;
11. improving personnel selection methods;
12. gaining accurate and speedier feedback on financial information;
13. improving usage of outside consultants;
14. improving stock control methods;
15. improving advertising and promotion methods;
16. improving morale building methods;
17. improving profit planning and budgeting;
18. reading and studying small business management — in other words, improving yourself; and
19. managing by setting objectives for everything to be done, etc.

To increase productivity through the methods mentioned above, action is needed. What kind of action? Action that will make all members of the staff (including the businessman) work towards the same end. Working towards the same end plans of action must be designed to reach the objectives set for the business. In essence, everybody working for the business must agree that the business's will is their will or must agree to what is to be accomplished. What then are your duties as owner-manager? Your job is to do the planning (profit-planning), assist in devising action plans, and then to act as a teacher, a coach and a counsellor. In other words, get things done through your employees and see that they get done right the first time. Doing things yourself is one thing, but getting others to do them correctly is something different and is sometimes difficult. It requires a high degree of management skill. That is why planning and directing the performance of others through skilful delegation is so important and gives an owner-manager the ability to do the planning and accomplish the objectives set through others. The business's health will also depend on how well you manage it. Therefore, you must learn to grow as a manager if your business is to grow and prosper. Your own personal growth will be reflected in the continually increasing productivity of your business — your attitude must be 'not to close the doors' of the business at night if you have not learnt something about your business that day. It boils down to improving yourself so that you can improve the performance of others and consequently, that of the business. Be more creative.

Plans are useful because they serve as a basis on which to act. But what you must not forget is that it is the action, and not so much the plan, that will ensure your success. You can spend hours planning, but if you don't get the action going, do not be astonished when your planning improves nothing.

Productivity comes about through teaching, coaching and counselling,[19] and these are, therefore, some of the actions you should employ to enhance productivity. Teaching the employee starts from the day the new employee walks through the doors of the business and says 'I'm here'. It continues for a long time — not just for a day or two or three, after which he is thrown into the deep waters and expected to contribute his best. Teaching is not about giving instructions. You must teach with the belief that the employee has the potential within him to contribute, and you should provide whatever he needs to contribute to the welfare of the business. Feedback is important — the more regular the feedback the faster the employee learns and the faster he can contribute. Only through regular feedback can the employee learn the difference between mistakes and exceptional performance, provided he has been given the opportunity to perform. Employees must also know exactly what their roles are and what is expected from them. Your role in teaching is to provide them with performance guidelines and objectives; be positive and supportive; instil confidence by your willingness and commitment to reinforce their learning; provide regular feedback and explain the difference between a mistake, an inferior performance and an exceptional performance. Coaching has mainly to do with the provision of encouragement to get employees going in spite of mistakes they have made, and the praise of exceptional performance, in order to instil confidence in the employee doing the job and to improve on his performance. Your role in coaching is to be objective about things, challenge the employee to give his best, keep his mind focused on the objectives and explain what is to be accomplished as well as how to do it as often as is necessary. Overall, coaching involves caring about the employee and his performance, being optimistic and wanting the employee to be successful. This all contributes to the welfare of the business. Counselling involves both teaching and coaching, but only when an employee is really stuck with a problem. However, counselling can only take place if your employees have free access to your office. Counselling requires that you listen and show respect, and that the employee speaks out.

People provide the most valuable input (their brain power and energy) in your business and therefore much attention must be given to them. Productivity increases with satisfying working conditions, as does morale. Your employee's morale may be judged by their attitudes towards work and their co-operation (or willingness to contribute) in trying to achieve the objectives of your business. High morale is a key factor in a well-managed business. Ask yourself these questions constantly: Do you let your employees know what is expected of them? Are you sensitive to their needs? Do they feel a sense of participation and pride in the business? Are you open and honest in dealing with them? And do you communicate clearly with them and listen actively to what they have to say? Productivity involves getting something done right the first time in order to reduce problems, wasted time through having to repeat the work, complaints and wastage of money. Productivity also involves planning and taking action — it is thinking before you act and looking before you leap, and then acting. If everybody does not move forward on the same course, the whole business will drown. Everybody must pull together to increase productivity and provide quality service and products to win the race against competitors. Profit must be the result — the result of the performance of the business in marketing, innovation, productivity, attitude of employees, continous training and many other aspects that contribute to profits.

SUMMARY AND CONCLUSIONS

When Robert Waterman, Tom Peters and later, Nancy Austin (Robert Waterman and Thomas Peters are the authors of *In Search of Excellence* and Thomas Peters and Nancy Austin are the authors of *A Passion for Excellence*[20]) set out to study America's best run companies, their goal was to find out what devices and techniques these companies had used to build and sustain their dominating competence. They were surprised to find no gimmicks, no devices and no special structures that set the top companies apart from all others. The bottom line difference was an overwhelming respect for the customer — service, courtesy and quality; a bone-deep belief in people, with the expectation that each and every one would contribute creatively and loyally; and a determination to fight off bureaucracy by maintaining person-to-person contact with customers and employees. On the one hand, these fundamentals appear obvious; we all recognize and cherish them. On the other hand, perhaps they are not so obvious, or more businesses would be successful. The problem lies in putting these ideals into practice. The businessman today who thinks that his employees are working only for a pay-cheque is blind. Only when he tries to understand that his employees are not merely staff, but human beings, is he on the right track and moving in the right direction — towards success for his people, his business and himself. Only when he recognizes his employees as people will they want to be aware of the mission and goals of the business and fulfil their role in serving the entire business.

Furthermore, you need to tell your employees what kind of behaviour you admire in them and also what you expect of them and of yourself. The main questions are of course whether you are in touch with the realities of your job (getting things done through people); and whether the objectives of the business are sharply and clearly defined.

BIBLIOGRAPHY

* Thomas J. Peters, Robert H. Waterman, Jr. *In Search of Excellence.* 1982. Harper and Row, New York.

184

* Thomas J. Peters, Nancy K. Austin. *A Passion for Excellence.* 1985. Collins, London: 203–377.
* Clifford M. Baumback, Kenneth Lawyer. *How to Organize and Operate a Small Business.* 1979. Prentice-Hall, Englewood Cliffs, NJ: 310–322.
* Lou Alberts. How we improved productivity through a total organization drive. *Productivity SA* 1986; **12**(3): 27–31.
* Immins Naudé. Job enrichment — motivator or myth? *Entrepreneur* 1982; **1**(2): 30–31.
* Wilbert E. Scheer. *Personnel Administration.* 2nd ed. 1979. The Dartnell Corporation, Chicago, Ill.
* Ron Johnson. *How To Manage People.* 1985. Business Books Limited (Hutchinson Group S.A. (Pty) Ltd), Bergvlei, South Africa.

NOTES

[1] Kenneth Blanchard, Spencer Johnson. *The One Minute Manager.* 1983. Fontana/Collins: 63. (Reproduced with permission.)

[2] Ron Johnson. *How to Manage People.* 1985. Business Books Limited (Hutchinson Group S.A. (Pty) Ltd, Bergvlei, South Africa: 13, 32.

[3] Editorial Staff. At the rock face — what have you done to get your staff to improve customer service and initiate communication with customers? *Supermarket and Retailer.* 1983; **30**(11): 15, 18.

[4] Ibid.

[5] Ibid.

[6] Ibid.

[7] Ibid.

[8] Don Munro. Why, who and how. *Supermarket and Retailer* 1982; **29**(12): 15.

[9] Kenneth Blanchard, Spencer Johnson. *The One Minute Manager.* 1983. Fontana/Collins: 39. (Reproduced with permission.)

[10] Idem, 19.

[11] Wilbert E. Scheer. *Personnel Administration.* 2nd ed. 1979. The Dartnell Corporation, Chicago, Ill.: 35, 36. (Reproduced with permission by the courtesy of the Dartnell Corporation.)

[12] Idem, 51, 52.

[13] Idem, 553, 554.

[14] Johann Engelbrecht. *Investment in Training — Is It Worthwhile?* Practical Productivity Tips (from a booklet issued by the National Productivity Institute), Pretoria: 14, 15. (See page 468 for more details on where to find the National Productivity Institute for information on the improvement of your business's productivity.) Produced with permission.

[15] Michael Renton. *You Are Training Them, But What Are They Learning?* FSA, Practical Instruction Techniques Pre-reading Booklet: 1. (Reproduced with permission.)

[16] Dale Carnegie Training.® *First an Inch, Next a Foot, Then a Yard* (The Dale Carnegie Method® of Training), Dale Carnegie & Associates, Inc. Reproduced with permission.

[17] J.K. Lasser Tax Institute. *How To Run a Small Business.* 5th ed. 1982. McGraw-Hill, New York: 192, 193. (Reproduced with permission.)

[18] How to shop for the right seminar, training, *The Magazine of Human Resources Development,* 1986; **23**(6): 17, 77, 78.

[19] As a reference concerning the aspects of teaching, coaching and counselling the source of information is: Thomas J. Peters, Nancy K. Austin. *A Passion for Excellence.* 1985. William Collins, London: 324–377.

[20] Both these two books are recommended for further reading and the studying of subjects related to the improvement of your own performance as well as those of your employees. Chapters that will interest you in this regard are 'Man waiting for motivation' and 'Productivity through people' in the book *In Search of Excellence*. And chapters such as 'People, people, people', and 'Leadership' in the book *A Passion for Excellence*. See page 471 for information on where to obtain these publications.

5 | STAFFING THE BUSINESS

'Business is transacted with people, for people, and by people.'

William H. Day[1]

'Business success depends on the quality of the human element.'

Frans Bekker

'Perfect balance in a business exists only on the organization chart.'

Peter F. Drucker[2]

INTRODUCTION

Business is a hard life with long hours and no guaranteed high income (at least in the early stages of its operation.) The people you employ must love their jobs, not hate them. If employees have a distaste in their jobs, the dice will really be loaded against you. A business that is hated by its employees is useless. Imagine yourself in this situation: You are a customer and you are entering into your business with an open mind. Now, really, do you feel a friendly greeting by the employees? Does your business say: 'Come in, welcome'? The point is that the atmosphere and the treatment customers receive by employees of your business will show. Customers can feel the attitude and atmosphere of a business the minute they set foot into it.

'Every business has a personal style of doing business attached to it, which is reflected in the attitude of its employees. One's own daily experience should convince one of the value of efficient and courteous employees. Every day you are exposed to and in contact with employees of certain businesses such as the cashier in a supermarket, a receptionist, the teller at the bank and managers. The way these people handle your affairs may encourage you to continue to do business with them, or decide never to set foot on the premises again. Naturally, what you expect from employees of other businesses, people will also expect from employees of your business. The golden rule is applicable — 'Do unto others as you want them to do unto you'. In being an example and to set the pace for your employees, your attitude is of crucial importance. Not only do you have to employ competent people but you also have to develop the necessary style of leadership that will encourage employees to give their best efforts and loyalty.[3] In other words, your business must profit from the work performed by your employees.

Although technology has advanced to the stage of computers, it still has to be operated by people and the success of any business is mostly the sum of the success of its people. In a business, all other resources are entrusted to its people resource, and it is the businessman's duty to find out how best to utilize them in the same manner as the stock and capital resources. The answer is to 'manage' the employee so that his efforts are directed towards the objectives of the business. What you need therefore is employees with skills, experience and well-rounded personalities to make a profit for you in exchange for a good salary plus other benefits. This is their source of income and ensures their family's existence.

The type of business you are in will determine the number of people to be employed. When determining your personnel requirements, you need to prepare a description for every job to be performed, and the type of employee needed for that job. It is important to bear in mind when considering the appointment of employees, that they be provided with sufficient challenging work. It can be detrimental to an employee, as well as to the business, to be in a position that does not require his service full time. Every good employee wants to be given a task which will give him the satisfaction of accomplishing something more. A salary paid to an employee is an expensive cost to the business and indeed it is your duty to see that his services are utilized in the most productive manner.

Preparing job descriptions is a paperwork exercise. Job descriptions are written statements covering the duties, responsibilities and authorities of the specific job in order to perform the task in question successfully. Many methods are used to collect information for preparing job descriptions, but most common are observation and questioning of the person performing the task. If you enter business for the first time you may just have to think logically as to what you will expect from each employee who must perform a specific job. Various books exist on this subject; you can also call in the advice of a consultant or another experienced businessman. Before employing someone in a particular job, endeavour to learn as much as possible about the job to compile the correct job description. You must be able to teach the new employee about the details of the job, to give guidance (which is always expected of a manager), and where necessary to make correct decisions concerning the tasks to be performed. It will be your responsibility to learn about the qualities, abilities and duties of those who have been successful in that job in the past.

Proper job descriptions are the basis for providing guidance to the businessman in recruiting, selecting, placing evaluating, compensating and training employees. A job description does not usually include personal characteristics. In preparing the job description, it is necessary to try and determine for every job; what must be done, how it must be done, why must it be done, and when must it be done.

Example of a job description

JOB TITLE: Assistant Accountant (also known as Bookkeeper)

DUTIES

— Preparing bank deposits, banking deposits (daily).
— Recording all daily transactions in the appropriate books (cash book, debtors, petty cash, etc.)
— Reconciling Bank statements (monthly).
— Investigating credit applications by analysing the applicant's financial status and credit record, checking references with

credit bureau. Interviewing customers, completing credit application forms, approving or disapproving credit applications (over and above a certain limit, approval is to be done by owner-manager).
— Monitoring and controlling the debtor accounts (preparing age analysis weekly).
— Following up accounts in arrears by taking care of correspondence in connection with handing over of long outstanding accounts for collection.
— Reporting weekly to the owner-manager on financial position by preparing financial statements.
— Recording of daily transactions on stock records (analysing the flow of stock).

RESPONSIBILITIES

Responsible for
— All credit functions of the business (interviewing, setting credit terms and limits, collecting outstanding accounts, handing over of accounts in arrears, reporting on credit standing).
— Writing of all credit letters (and other financial reports, etc.)
— Filing system.
— Security systems.
— Stock control function.
— Banking.
— Recording of all transactions.
— Reporting on financial position.
— Recording of sales taxes.
— Payroll records and taxes.

AUTHORITY

Financial and policy decisions are to be taken in conjunction with owner-manager, but recommendations are to be made by Assistant Accountant in writing.

OR

A job description can also be in the form illustrated in the example below. The employee can carry such a job description with him while on the job, and he will be more sure of himself for satisfactorily completing his tasks (especially when an employee has just started working for you).

STOCKER'S DUTIES[4]

1. To receive or help receive merchandise.
   (a) Assisting in unloading goods.
   (b) Assisting in opening cases.
   (c) Price marking merchandise as directed.
   (d) Separating stock into designated sections.
2. To transfer stock to sales floor by using jack and pallets, rollers, floats, hand trucks, or other equipment to move it.
3. To stock or help stock merchandise.
   (a) Checking price of new merchandise against price of stock on shelf, checking any differences in order guide or other references, and correcting price if necessary.
   (b) Rotating stock, separating damaged stock, and cleaning shelves.
   (c) Using both hands to transfer stock to shelf with labels faced out (any loose labels taped) and blocking or fronting stock in shelves according to company policy.
   (d) Removing damaged stock, surplus stock, trash (check for overlooked merchandise), and equipment from the sales floor.
4. To do miscellaneous jobs as directed.
   (a) Building displays, making price changes, maintaining cleanliness of the store, keeping aisles and floor clear by removing broken or damaged merchandise immediately, assisting customers, working in front end if needed, and ordering stock if authorized to do so.
   (b) Reporting unsafe conditions or actions and pilferage to the designated person.

Outlining the responsibilities are important to avoid the confusion amongst employees which occurs in many businesses. An example is: 'I did not do it as it was not my responsibility.' You cannot hold an employee accountable if you did not inform him about his responsibilities. Cover every angle of your business to determine who is responsible for which task in the business.

PERSONAL CHARACTERISTICS AND QUALITIES

(Person Specification)

There are certain basic characteristics a person must possess that will assist him in delivering his best performance in a specific job, so ask yourself: What are the characteristics and qualities that will make him the best candidate for that specific job? Your task as a businessman is thus to match the personal characteristics and qualities of a person with that of the job (as stated in the job description). Some of these characteristics and qualities are neatness, accuracy, being conscientious, good judgement, natural friendliness, helpfulness, sincerity, flexibility, self-confidence, decisiveness, verbal and written ability, loyalty, responsibility, willingness to work, respect for authority, honesty, punctuality, speed, energy, pleasantness, logicality, competence, emotional stability, initiative, creativeness, love of work, eagerness, ability to be innovative, tolerance, even temper, competitive spirit, business-minded, enthusiasm, maturity, self-control, reliability, self-motivation, good level of productivity, alertness, diplomatic, ability to reason and good health. It is a long list and more can be added, depending on the job and which characteristics and qualities you think are required for a person to be able to perform his tasks as you would want him to.

RECRUITING NEW EMPLOYEES

Once you have planned your personnel requirements and prepared a job description for each job and listed the characteristics and qualities needed for the performance of the job, it is your responsibility to seek them. Basically, you have two sources — from within the business through promotion or transfer in an established business, and from outside the business through recruitment. More specific sources are personnel from competing businesses of the same type, educational institutions, or family and friends. You can also make use of employment agencies or advertise in the local newspaper.

When making use of advertisements it is necessary to tell the prospective applicant what you've got to offer. Factors that may motivate the prospective applicant are better salaries, prestige, location, opportunity for advancement and pleasant working conditions. Your main objective is to advocate that your business offers more than just another job — a real opportunity which provides a challenge to a suitably hardworking person. Make use of the word 'you' in the advertisement to get the response you want — personalization.

In the advertisement, be specific as people are normally concerned with the following points (for comparing their present jobs with the one you offer): the business's activities; remuneration (compensation); working hours; benefits; location of the business; qualifications required; scope for promotion; how to apply; closing date of application; and the address, the business's name and telephone number, and the name of a contact person.

INTERVIEWING NEW EMPLOYEES

From the applications received you must eventually make a decision on who will be employed. The first step is to design an application form which should contain basic information such as outlined in the example below:

APPLICATION FOR EMPLOYMENT[5]
STRICTLY CONFIDENTIAL

Full names: _____

Surname: _____

Date of birth: _____

Identity number: _____ Sex: _____

Marital status: _____ Number of children: _____

Nationality: _____ Place of birth: _____

Present residential address: _____

Present postal address: _____

Education and training

    School attended: _____ Year: _____

Subjects passed: _____

_____

_____

Post school qualifications
   Examining authority: _____ Year: _____
   Degree or diploma obtained: _____
    Major subjects: _____

_____

Language proficiency: African Languages: _____

Speak	Read	Write
English		
Speak	Read	Write
Afrikaans		
Speak	Read	Write

Work history
   Employer: _____
   Location: _____
   Period of employment: From _____ To: _____
                  Capacity: _____
   Salary: Beginning: _____ Leaving: _____
   Reason for termination of service: _____
Have you ever been declared insolvent: _____ If husband/wife works, by whom is he/she employed and in what capacity: _____
Do you have a car? _____ Registration number: _____
Driver's licence: _____ Code: _____
Previous work experience: _____
Hobbies: _____
I declare the above particulars to be complete and correct.
Signature: _____ Date: _____

The applicant, when coming for the interview, should first complete the application form which, of course, provides you with information from which to learn more about the aplicant and to use during the interview. Interview essentials are: privacy (to communicate confidentially); comfort (to be at ease and so permit free exchange of information); understanding (decisions to be made only when mutual understanding is reached and agreed upon); and attitude (your attitude towards the applicant should be pleasant and do not try to outsmart him). Some do's and don'ts to remember are:

★ Show an interest in the person (speak about hobbies, etc).
★ Encourage the applicant to ask questions.
★ Guide the interview (draw responses from the applicant to determine if he is able to perform the tasks the job requires).
★ Listen, and let him talk freely (let nothing go unheard).
★ Don't interrupt the applicant continually (breaking the flow of thoughts leads to nervousness and frustration).
★ Don't build up false expectations (or make false promises).
★ Don't keep the applicant waiting.
★ Outline the requirements of the job clearly (in detail).
★ Don't overdo note-taking (it gives the applicant the impression that he does not have your full attention).
★ Answer all questions (be honest).
★ Thank the applicant for coming (for his time is valuable too).
★ Don't check the time frequently or stare past the applicant (it signals that you are not attentive).

The interview is certainly a determining factor in the employment process, and the success of the interview depends upon the extent to which you can create a feeling of mutual confidence and co-operation between yourself and the applicant. The purpose of the interview is also to collect information and to combine and classify it in order to assist you in making a decision concerning the applicant and whether he is able to perform the job successfully. The interview also provides the opportunity of meeting the applicant and observing his appearance, abilities, general personality and attitudes. Your task is thus to get the applicant to talk so that you may form a picture on how he will appear on the job. The real skill in interviewing is not so much in getting the information but interpreting it. Therefore it is necessary to phrase and direct the questions in such a manner as to get the applicant to talk — you just listen.

Preparation for an interview is important so that you do not forget matters that you need to find out. Questions that are normally asked are:

- Why should I employ you?
- Why do you want to work here?
- Why are you looking for a new job?
- Do you have any health problems?
- How many staff-members did you control in your last job?
- What interests you most about this position?
- How would you describe your circle of friends?
- What is your current financial position?
- What would you like to be doing five years from now?
- What type of work do you like most or least?
- Which subjects did you like most at school or university? Why?
- Do you like working closely with other people? Why?
- How do you go about making decisions?
- When are you performing at your best?
- What abilities do you have that you feel will help you reach your objectives?
- What are the things that really satisfy you in your job?
- How do other employees describe you?
- With what type of people do you get along well?
- How important is this job to you? Why?
- What do you seek most out of a job?
- Do you like many responsibilities?
- What are your hobbies?
- How long have you been planning to do this job?
- Who has had the greatest influence on you in your life?
- Are you willing to go where the business sends you?

From the answers to these questions you will have enough information to have a reasonably good chance of spotting the characteristics and qualities you are looking for and forming certain impressions in order to assist you in making a decision. Other questions can be specific, relating to the field of work in which the applicant will be performing. This will enable you to acquire information as to his knowledge, skills and experience about the job.

CHECKING REFERENCES

Many a businessman has been victimized by applicants whose credentials were not thoroughly checked, and has regretted it deeply afterwards. Therefore, reference enquiries are a very important part of the employment procedure, and cannot be over-emphasized. Enquiries must be made about prior work experience, character, education and other matters that may be considered important to help you decide whether or not to employ the person. This also provides a means of verifying the truthfulness of the applicant's statements on the application form and made during the interview. It is also an opportunity to gain additional information. When doing reference checks, be on the alert for the accuracy of dates of employment, actual salary, quality of performance, nature of the job, reasons for leaving and academic qualifications, but be careful in accepting a former employer's excessive criticism or praise. A telephone call is the quickest means of getting outside information about an applicant and is more intimate. Direct communication (by telephone) with a previous employer is preferable to written responses, as the writer of the letter may have little or no idea of your job requirements, and specific questions can be cleared up by a personal conversation. Try to uncover the real story behind the applicant's reasons for leaving his previous job.

Once all this is done and you have narrowed the number of potential employees to one or a few, the time has come to pick your man. If there is only one, he can be employed if you are convinced that he is the most suitable person. If there is more than one, you should review the information collected in order to decide which person will be the best.

The final decision rests on whether the applicant matches the job requirements concerning knowledge, proficiency, experience and characteristics. If none of them matches the job requirements, then start from scratch again. Whenever rejecting an applicant you should try and do it without hurting his feelings. This must be handled with tact, discretion and sincerity so as to let the applicant part with a feeling of goodwill towards you and your business.

COMPENSATION

Another important duty which is your responsibility is to decide on the salaries and wages of employees. Their salaries must be sufficient to motivate them to be good performers and yet low enough for your business to afford them. It should be borne in mind that employee compensation is an expense (cost) to the business, and that people work for monetary and non-monetary compensation. Non-monetary compensations are a form of physical income and often assist in motivating people when monetary compensation fails to do so. Non-monetary compensation may include certain benefits such as supplying uniforms, meals during lunch time, further education and training at the expense of the business, petrol allowances over and above salary, etc. However, both monetary and non-monetary compensations must be considered when devising the salary and wage set-up. Another aspect to bear in mind is that employees are concerned whether their absolute or net level of pay will be adequate to meet their needs. This means that you should be more concerned with monetary than non-monetary compensation. The reason being that non-monetary compensation does not necessarily contribute to the employee's family income.

Factors to consider when devising the salary and wage set-up are:
- the ability of the business to pay;
- the standard and cost of living in the area;
- the working hours;
- the rate of the job in comparison with other jobs of a similar nature; and
- qualifications and experience.

GENERAL STATUTORY POINTS ACCORDING TO THE BASIC CONDITIONS OF THE EMPLOYMENT ACT[6]

Working hours: No employer shall require or permit any employee to work for more than 46 hours in any week (except security guards — maximum 60 hours per week).

Annual leave: An employer shall grant to an employee at least 14 consecutive days leave of absence on full pay in respect of each period of 12 consecutive months of employment.

Sick leave: Employees are entitled to 30 days' paid sick leave in a 3-year period.

Public holidays and payment for work on public holidays: All public holidays are paid holidays for employees employed in or in connection with a shop or office (except an office in which work is performed in connection with or which is incidental to an activity carried out in a factory). All other employees are entitled to New Year's Day, Good Friday, Ascension Day, Republic Day, the Day of the Vow and Christmas Day as paid holidays. If an employee works on a public holiday which is a paid holiday for him, he must be paid a day plus:

(a) an amount not less than his salary rate for the time worked by him on that day, or a day's pay, whichever is the greater amount; or

(b) an amount not less than one-third of his salary rate for the time worked by him on that day, and be granted one day's leave on full pay within seven days.

Overtime: No employer shall require or permit an employee to work overtime otherwise than in terms of an agreement concluded by him with the employee and provided such overtime does not exceed three hours on any day or ten hours in any week. The maximum overtime may be increased by an inspector after consultation with the employee or employees concerned.

Payment for overtime: An employee who works overtime must be paid at not less than $1^1/_3$ times his hourly salary for the overtime worked by him.

Payment for work on Sundays: An employee who has worked on a Sunday for four hours or less, must be paid not less than a day's salary. If he has worked for longer than four hours he must—

(a) be paid salary for two days or at double his salary rate for the whole time worked by him, whichever is the greater; or

(b) be paid at $1^1/_3$ times his rate for the time worked and be granted one day's leave on full pay within seven days of such Sunday.

Prohibition of certain employment: An employer shall not employ any person under the age of 15 years and shall not require or permit a female employee to work during the period four weeks prior to the expected date of her confinement and eight weeks after that date.

Records to be kept by employers: Every employer shall at all times keep a time and salary register in respect of all employees.

TERMINATIONS

Apart from employees who terminate voluntary (through resigning), there may also be some occasions where it will be necessary to discharge employees. The important point to remember is to part on friendly terms, because if you try to hurt the employee in any way you stand a good chance of hurting your business. Be straightforward in the situation — make a fair and honest appraisal of the conditions leading up to the dismissal of the employee. Wherever possible, offer termination pay and other considerations. The act of dismissing an employee is of special importance to the individual involved, and it is therefore absolutely essential that it be done with tact, discretion and sincerity of purpose.

SUMMARY AND CONCLUSIONS

One disgruntled employee can make or break your business and to a large extent the result depends on you. Therefore, it is important for you to try not to employ the wrong people. When planning your work force, you need to consider the type and quality of employees your business needs by determining the jobs to be performed, and the qualities and characteristics needed to perform them, with proper job descriptions and personal specifications. By preparing job descriptions, you will answer such questions as: What does the job consist of (what does it do)? How should the job be performed? Why is it necessary that the job be performed? What are the standards of performance for the job to be done satisfactorily? Who is responsible for what? To whom does the employee in that job report? In a meaningful job description the duties of the job must be clearly set out to avoid misunderstanding, and the lines of authority and responsibility must be carefully drawn to eliminate confusion.

It is also of importance to determine the sources from which you can recruit employees and then search for individuals with the required qualities and characteristics, select the best available and provide fair compensation. To every employee, compensation is a very personal matter — compensation will only be fair if it is considered adequate (paid in proportion to the employee's physical and mental expenditure). Your objective must be to get the best available person for the job.

Being the owner-manager of the business, you are also a personnel manager. This personnel activity can be carried out successfully only if you handle it with the same care and give the same attention to this activity as you do with others. Your business can be successful only if you have the right kind and number of people to assist you, for on your own you cannot do everything. Carefully selected employees can become an investment of value — quality stock is always available and replaceable, but quality and loyal personnel are not always easy to find.

BIBLIOGRAPHY

* Wilbert E. Scheer. *Personnel Administration Handbook*. 2nd ed. 1979. The Dartnell Corporation, Chicago, Ill.

* Guy Macleod. *Starting Your Own Business in South Africa*. 1983. Oxford University Press, Cape Town: 86–97.

* Arthur Elkins. *Management*. 1980. Addison-Wesley, 36–83.

* Theodore Pettus. Win the interview — win the job. *Cosmopolitan* 1986; January/February: 38, 40.

* Curtis E. Tate Jr., Leon C. Megginson, Charles R. Scott Jr., Lyle R. Trueblood. *Successfull Small Business Management*. 1982. Business Publications, Plano, Texas: 173–190.

* P.L. Moolman. *Werwing en Keuring van Personeel* 1982; **1**(2): 33.

* Johan Naudé. Lei finansiële aansporing tot groter doeltreffendheid. *Entrepreneur* 1984; **3**(3): 16–17.

* J.J.L. Cronje. Recruitment — Filling a Need. *Small Business News* (University of the North's Business Advisory Bureau) 1985; **7**(3): 5, 6.

* E. van Dijk. Interviews for the right staff selection. *Small Business News* (University of the North's Business Advisory Bureau) 1985; **7**(3): 8.

* William H. Day. *Maximizing Small Business Profits.* 1978. Prentice-Hall, Englewood Cliffs, NJ.

* Ron M. Johnson. *How to Manage People.* 1985. Business Books, Hutchinson Publishing Group, London.

NOTES

[1] William H. Day. *Maximizing Small Business Profits.* 1978. Prentice-Hall, Englewood Cliffs, NJ: 226. (Reproduced with permission.)

[2] Peter F. Drucker. *Managing for Results.* 1964. Pan Books, London: 184. Reprinted by permission of William Heinemann Limited.

[3] J.K. Lasser Tax Institute. *How to Run a Small Business.* 5th ed. 1982. McGraw-Hill; New York: 189. (Reproduced with permission.)

[4] Hugh S. Peak, Ellen F. Peak. *Supermarket Merchandising and Management.* 1977. Prentice-Hall, Englewood Cliffs, NJ: 331.

[5] Although this is a very basic application form, it is also recommended that you fit the following into the application form so as to obtain more information on the applicant: employment history for at least the past four years (including the employers' name and address, period worked for him, salary and fringe benefits received, position held and description of duties, and of course the reasons for leaving each employer); any health problems (perhaps you can let the successful applicant undergo a medical test); and a list of at least three people who could be contacted as references.

[6] See: Basic Conditions of the Employment Act, 1983 (Annexure 4, Regulation 4). For more information about this Act contact the Government Printer: P.O. Box 260021, Excom, 2023.

PURCHASING

'In our organization the purchasing function is what we refer to as the hub of the wheel.'

Adrian Bellamy[1]
Managing Director, Edgars stores

'Any purchase transaction starts with the recognition of the need for an item. Once the need has been recognized, it must be so accurately described that you will know exactly what is wanted. An improperly or poorly described need can be costly. A business's profits may to a large extent measure how effectively it manages its supplies. Supplies are the very lifeblood of any functioning commercial operation. The efficiency of any business is contingent upon having them available in the proper quantity, with the proper quality, at the proper place and time, and at a proper price. Failure on any of these points adds to costs and decreased profit as surely as outmoded production methods or ineffective selling techniques.'

J.H. Westing, I.V. Fine, G.J. Zenz[2]

'Management depends on purchasing to produce profits through savings developed from well planned and carefully executed purchasing programmes.'

Alonzo Decker, President of Black and Decker[3]

INTRODUCTION

Of great importance in any business, but especially in the retail business, is the skill with which buying is done and the success with which selling efforts are carried out. Nothing is so likely to slow up turnover as the purchase of goods which do not sell. The excessive variety of goods offered for sale, pushed by the skilful merchandising activities of manufacturers and wholesalers, often leads to the purchase of stock which cannot be sold. It is very wise to let the wholesalers carry the big amounts of stock and to see that you have just enough to supply in the demand of your market. Always evaluate suppliers 'bargains' and 'specials' for their saleability in the market you serve. Good purchasing, then, is essential both to meeting the demands of customers and to keeping down the average stock in relation to sales. In general, the objective of successful purchasing can be regarded as buying the right requirements (quality stock) in the right quantities at the right time and at the right price from the right source of supply. As the owner-manager of a small business, you have to plan, organize, direct, and control all activities in the buying area. You have to decide what to buy, when to buy, from where to buy and how much to buy.

THE IMPORTANCE OF THE PURCHASING FUNCTION

In deciding how important the purchasing function for successful business operations is, the first aspect to consider should be its influence and contribution to the business's main objective, namely to reach the highest possible return on capital invested. You should recall that profit is the difference between the money that came in and the money that went out, and that your basic responsibility is to see that the difference between income and costs results in a favourable one for the business as a whole. The purchasing of goods is mainly a cost aspect and an important one too, but through efficient purchasing you can reduce costs and consequently increase net profit which again increases the return on your investment.

The second aspect to consider in deciding how important the purchasing function on business operations really is, is its impact on the stock turnover rate. Stock turnover concerns the sale and replenishment of stock in the retail business, and turnover is the rate at which this movement takes place. It can be defined as the number of times the average stock is sold (and replaced) during a certain period. The period commonly used is one year, although periods of six months or less may also be used. The common method in use for determining the turnover rate is that of dividing the cost of goods sold (cost of sales) by the average stock at cost. Thus, if the cost of goods sold is R300 000 and the average stock at cost is R30 000, then R300 000 divided by R30 000 results in a stock turnover rate of 10 times.

A rapid stock turnover is an important result of good merchandising. It is the sign which points to the effectiveness or ineffectiveness of the buying plan, the price plan and the selling plan. Net profits must be made, and may result from a rapid turnover with a small margin of net profit, or from a rapid turnover accompanied by a greater margin of net profit. There are, however, specific advantages which arise from a rapid stock turnover. With a rapid stock turnover the investment necessary to do a given volume of business is reduced. There is also a saving of interest on the investment of stock as the total stock of the business is small and insurance expenses are less. The risk of losses are reduced if the business carries a smaller amount of stock since there is less danger of physical deterioration, and a smaller amount of goods will be left to be disposed of at marked-down prices at the end of a season, or after a change in styles. Stocks are more likely to be fresh and up to date, they will occupy less storage space and the cost of handling them will be reduced. When a rapid turnover coincides with an increase in the total volume of business, certain expenses may increase and others will remain unchanged or will not change directly. The more rapid turnover and increased volume of business will always be followed by an increase in buying and selling expenses, and so cause an increase in the total expense for such items as buying, advertising, delivery costs, etc. However, when sales volume increases, the unit expenses for rent and insurance (fixed expenses) tend to decline.

Below follows an illustration as to how a rapid stock turnover rate can reduce the investment in stock:

		Stock turnover rate: 3 times per year	Stock turnover Rate: 6 times per year
(a)	Budgeted sales for 1 year	R100 000	R100 000
(b)	Budgeted gross profit (25%)	25 000	25 000
(c)	Budgeted cost of sales (a–b)	75 000	75 000
(d)	Budgeted stock turnover rate	3 times	6 times
(e)	Average amount of stock therefore required (c ÷ d)	25 000	12 500
(f)	Stock now on hand	30 000	30 000
(g)	Deficit/surplus of stock (e–f)	5 000	17 500
(h)	To be purchased (c–g)	70 000	57 500

If the stock turnover rate will be (or could be) increased to 6 times a year to generate sales of R100 000, then you will only have to buy R57 500 worth of goods during the year instead of R70 000 with a stock turnover rate of 3 times a year.

A saving of R12 500 is realized. This R12 500 will free you from sluggish stock management, and can be invested in other goods to increase your sales. It can also be used for expansion, or even applied to a reduction of any debt you have. In fact, increased stock turnover can be a valuable source of the funds you may need to finance profitable growth. Thus, you should always be alert for ways to reduce your investment in stock which will not interfere with your sales volume.

In order to secure the definite advantages of a rapid stock turnover rate, it is necessary that policies conducive to such an objective be adopted. Such a policy may be the following: Buy exactly what is needed in the proper variety and in sufficient volume; price the goods purchased within reach of customers' income; and sell the products properly to avoid the accumulation of old stock necessitating special sales efforts.

While a high stock turnover rate is very desirable, it is apparent from the above discussion that there are also certain hazards in having too fast a turnover rate. Merchandise is likely to be reduced in amount and variety until a loss in sales results or, where larger stocks are maintained and low mark-ups are used to increase the rapidity of the turnover of merchandise, it may happen that profit margins are not enough to cover expenses, and a loss results. In addition, bit-by-bit buying, when carried to extremes and over long periods, frequently brings about an increase in the cost price of merchandise and in buying and selling expenses which largely offset the savings realized through speeding up the turnover rate.

The consequences of a slow stock turnover rate are the opposite of those resulting from a rapid turnover rate. It should, however, be stressed that when larger stocks of goods are carried than are necessary to meet the reasonable demands of a business's customers, capital is tied up that could have been put to work advantageously elsewhere. For example, in contrast to tying up capital in stock, efficient purchasing can decrease the size of the investment and so increase your return on investment. To put it briefly, working towards a more profitable business starts with purchasing, and selling what you have bought at a profit as quickly as possible. Put the other way round this means: If you buy what is called for by the market, and price it in such a manner that both you and the customer benefit, the goods will sell (with the help of marketing) and profits will result.

WHAT TO BUY

Usually, it is you, the owner-manager of a small business, who must do the buying, for it might be that your business has not yet grown to the stage where you can afford a buying specialist. As a very busy individual you are at the beginning in a position with limited help and you are probably so tied to the business that you have little time to spare in order to shop around for new sources of supplies. Therefore you must rely a great deal on the representatives and salesmen who visit your shop as well as on catalogues and price lists from suppliers. Whatever the circumstances may be, you must not just buy stock in the hope that somebody will again buy it from you. Undoubtedly, the purchasing of stock must be very carefully planned. When purchasing, the most important aim is to ensure that there will be a constant flow of stock to support day-to-day sales. Without the necessary and correct merchandise at the right time, place and price, no transaction can be finalized. Neither will it help if you buy all your stock at one time — this is too expensive and it does not show good planning. Failure to provide the right merchandise will result in consumers shopping elsewhere.

Before any money is spent on purchasing stock it is again necessary to remind you that what you buy must sell. It is therefore of prime importance to find out what will sell, and whether there are any buyers for that particular product. Thus, two elements are of importance — the consumer and the product — which are dependent on each other for a sale to materialize. At the same time the consumer views you (the retailer) as his 'buying agent' and expects you to stock (or purchase) merchandise that will satisfy his tastes, preferences and needs. Your success is therefore dependent on your ability to buy correctly according to the needs of your market.

One of the first thing to do before purchasing anything is to establish your broad business mission. In other words, ask yourself: What business am I in? or What is my business? For example, if you are about to sell watches, you are not so much in the business of just selling watches, as in the 'time' business. Thus, your main objective in selling watches is to sell watches that will not make people late for appointments, among other things. You are now in the business of getting people at places on time. But before you can do so, you need to find out what product will do the job best, and that is what you are supposed to buy — quality products — watches that will conform to the requirements of the customer (whatever his reason for wanting a watch). As stated earlier in this book, people buy things that can be useful to them. They usually require the best item that they can afford.

You must also ask yourself: What is my prime objective? Obviously it is to realize a satisfactory return on your investment by satisfying the needs of your target market. Purchasing, especially, contributes hereto through availability for resale of the right products, at the right price, in the right quantity and at the right time. To sum up, among others the objects are[4]

- satisfy the needs of customers by buying products for which a need exists and selling them at prices the customers are prepared to pay;
- improve profits by buying products that will stimulate sales and result in fewer markdowns;
- optimize investment in stock by maintaining a stock level that will continually satisfy demand without using capital unnecessarily;
- keep the level of slow-moving stock to a minimum by identifying and eliminating such goods; and
- facilitate sales by constantly offering improved and fresh goods.

A number of aspects should be considered when deciding what to buy:[5]

★ Listen to the consumers in your area in order to ascertain their needs, wants, desires and preferences. They are a valuable source of information. Very often they will tell you what to stock as well as other useful information. Also, acquire a book to record all items requested which were not in stock and if further demand arises, purchase them in small quantities.

★ Check your sales records. You can then spot any definite trends in what is saleable and what is not. Such a record system could be started by preparing a list of the items the business already carries. At least once a week you can then compare the stock you have left with the original quantities of each item on your checklist. For example, if the stock on hand of an item is 20 and you originally had 40, then 20 items were sold (of a specific brand) if no other items were received of that same brand. By doing such a comparison faithfully week after week, you can quite accurately determine the demand for every item. This will also assist you in coping with the demand as you can order the right quantity and avoid being either overstocked or understocked.

★ Know what products are on the market. This can be done by asking for catalogues from suppliers and sales representatives and watching the news media for information in the same line of business as yours.

★ Ascertain attitudes towards brands. Commonly advertised brands are popular with consumers who tend to buy tried and tested brands. The same applies to items where an aspect such as 'style' is concerned.

★ Test products. Purchase only a small amount of a particular product to see whether it will sell. If it does, increase the stock gradually until a fair demand is established. Your sales records will be of great value in this exercise.

★ Find out about product availability. Will the product be readily available or is it difficult to obtain (remember, no person wants to buy a motor car only to learn that spares are difficult to obtain)? This applies to all products.

★ Take note of seasonal demand. Some products are only saleable during holiday seasons, rainy seasons, summer seasons, etc. Keep a record of these products. It is obvious that you should not buy and try to sell blankets in large quantities during summer unless you can afford to buy now for the next season, and have sufficient storage space.

★ Find out about product services. Do the products you wish to sell have to be serviced regularly and if so, can the service be carried out by you or someone nearby to the satisfaction of the customer? Will spares for the product be available?

★ Study your competitors. Perhaps one of the most important aspects to consider when deciding on a product range is to study what competitors sell. At what price do they sell it for? What products do they not stock that you could? You should always be informed on what they have and have not got as it could lead to your getting that competitive advantage. Always be innovative — supply a better product or service than your competitors in order to satisfy the demands of the customer.

★ Look carefully at shapes, sizes and colours. Some product lines come in different shapes, sizes and colours. Make sure that you purchase the correct ones. Once again your sales record can supply you with useful information if you make a study of all sizes, shapes and colours.

★ Be aware of fashion elements. Consumers associate any product (even food) with fashion. Modern packed products move faster than old-fashioned ones.

★ Standardize, as far as possible, the quality of your stock. If you are appealing to consumers who look for low-priced goods, do not stock expensive goods as well —they will only tie up money and you may have to sell them at a loss at a later stage. Beware of 'opportunities' that will lead to losses.

★ Have the correct display facilities. If you have no fridge do not stock butter and other perishables as this will only give the business a bad reputation. The same applies for, say, electrical equipment in an area where no power supply exists.

A point worth mentioning here is that in a retail market one normally finds three types of consumers — convenience consumers, speciality consumers and discerning consumers.[6] The convenience consumer is the one spending very little time deciding what to buy as he has normally made up his mind before entering the business. He buys at the cheapest price and goes to the closest or most convenient place to buy daily essentials such as bread, milk, cigarettes, etc. The speciality consumer is prepared to pay a higher price for goods and is specifically interested in the brand name. He does not necessarily go to the nearest shop but shops around until he finds what he wants. Speciality goods are such things as Parker pens, Christian Dior shirts, etc. The discerning consumer spends a lot of time deciding which is the best product. His main criterion for buying is value for money and he will shop around until he finds what he thinks will serve the purpose. The goods bought in this fashion are normally luxury articles such as furniture, clothing, fridges, etc. The brand name is of no particular importance to the discerning consumer. You should, however, try to find out which type of consumer you wish to appeal to and which type will bring more profitable business and do your buying accordingly. When you consider which product range to buy, the choice must be complimentary to the image and character of the business, and at the same time be able to compete effectively with the product range of your competitors.

WHEN TO BUY

It is important to establish when best to buy your goods. Business quantities and buying times require careful planning (and forecasting) by you. Merchandise is generally purchased in anticipation of demand, as predicted by one of two forecasting techniques: the statistical technique which uses historical data as a basis for estimating expectations; and the use of external indicators (economic, competitive and market indicators) to predict an expected future demand. A decision as to when to buy is like all other decisions that must be made; it can only be as good as the information you have available. A good system for the collection and interpretation of information received from your market is probably the most important element in sound purchasing as well as marketing. Below follow a number of points that will be of assistance in deciding when to buy:[7]

★ Past Sales. Knowing how much was sold previously will help determine the demand for the future. A simple example of this would be that on Friday 20 loaves of bread were sold which is an indication that you must anticipate buying 70

211

loaves for resale purposes next Friday. This theory can however fluctuate considerably and therefore you should consider all other points in conjunction with this one. Of valuable assistance in deciding what future demand will be, is keeping an up to date buying schedule, as follows:

BUYING SCHEDULE

Product	Last month sales	Estimated sales	Less: stock on hand	To be purchased
(1)	(2)	(3)	(4)	(5)

(1) List all products you stock in this column according to brand name and sizes.
(2) Record how many products were sold the previous month.
(3) Record how many products you expect to sell for the forthcoming period (a month, a week).
(4) Record all stock of a particular brand on hand.
(5) The difference between estimated sales and stock on hand gives you a very good indication of how much to buy.

This buying schedule also provides you with information as to what to buy and when.

★ Special Events. Watch your local press and keep an ear open for forthcoming events happening close to your business, for example, a school athletic championship. This will probably mean that there will be an increase in demand for certain related products. Any other significant event, such as another business having a special sale (or some other kind of attraction) in a shopping centre may also increase the shopping traffic for your business.

Public Holidays. These can have a considerable impact on sales and you must cater for them by purchasing sufficient stock — depending of course on the type of product line you have. For example, if you sell building material, you may even decide to close the business for the day because nobody will be working, and there will therefore be no demand. Similarly, if you have a business selling daily necessities, product demand may increase. Remember though to put up a sign, informing your market at least a few days before such a holiday whether you will be open or not. It can be very annoying to the customer if you don't do so, and the results can be detrimental — a bad reputation — as the customer may tell everybody else about his frustration.

★ Pay Days. Many an employee after being paid, goes straight to a retail shop selling daily necessities to purchase for the month ahead.

★ Advertising. Manufacturers often have large advertising campaigns on a certain product without informing you directly. Once consumers have been made aware of the product and either want it or need it, you may suddenly have a sharp demand for this product. If you are not aware of the advertising campaign, you may be caught off balance. This type of demand normally applies to new products or gimmicks.

★ Competition. Watch out for competitors opening up more outlets in your area, selling at lower prices or providing a better service; it will cause a drop in the demand for your products. Similarly, if a similar type of business near you closes down, your product or service demand will increase to fill the gap left by the previous competitor.

★ Price Changes. A drop or an increase in prices (or general sales tax) will increase or decrease respectively the demand for a product or service. A good example can be found in the motor-car market; the prices of new motor cars go up every January, and this creates a greater demand for motor cars in December.

★ Transport. Transport could be a problem with small businesses as the owner-manager is dependent on deliveries from suppliers. Some suppliers may not even deliver and in order to ensure that the goods arrive at the business, the owner should buy goods to last for at least a week or until he knows he will have another opportunity to visit his supplier. He could also make use of a group transport scheme.

HOW MUCH TO BUY

Attention has already been given to the calculation of the amount of stock to be purchased, but perhaps an even simpler approach (other than the buying schedule) might be to determine both a minimum and a maximum stock figure for every item, and order only when the items stocked approach minimum levels. Minimum levels can also represent the amount of stock you started the business with so as to keep the overall level of stock almost constant.

Problems that may arise from not having a proper buying schedule or any other method to control purchases, are understocking, overstocking and cash flow problems. Understocking will result in your being out of stock which will force the customer to go to your competitors to satisfy his needs. In addition to this, you will have lost a sale and consequently, some profits. Remember what the consequences can be of such a situation in the long run — no sale, no job. Overstocking leads to money being tied up that could have been put to better use. An example is that of stocking 30 different colours of cars, where you could have stocked only two and ordered from the manufacturer when a customer demanded another colour. Overstocking creates cash flow problems which means that you have no ready cash available to purchase products that are in demand. Again the result can be detrimental to the business.

A successful businessman tries to maximize sales by maintaining a sound customer base, but not demanding too high an investment in stock. He tries to achieve an acceptable stock turnover rate. He is most concerned about this vital aspect, not only in respect of total stock in the shop, but also for each separate category of stock he trades in. He is also concerned about measuring his stock turnover regularly — not only at the end of the year because that will be too late to make necessary improvements. The stock turnover rate should thus be a constant objective to bear in mind when deciding how much to buy. In short, buy enough stock to add to what you have to provide your business with enough to cope with your customer's estimated demands for the period ahead.

ECONOMIC EVALUATION OF RETAIL PURCHASING

The evaluation of retail buying is concerned mainly with the efficiency with which this function is carried out. To evaluate buying efficiency you may use various norms (some already mentioned) such as:[8]

- The turnover speed. The higher the turnover speed and the shorter the turnover time of stock, the more favourable it is for the business. In fact, a high turnover speed means better use of capital, which favourably influences return on the business's investment. When the turnover speed (and age of each product) is examined, the owner will be able to identify product lines selling unsatisfactorily. The examination should also show whether there is a healthy balance between stock (the quantity) and turnover.
- Turnover per square metre trading area. Generally, good product lines will result in relatively high turnover per square metre trading area. The nature of the goods will cause differences.
- The turnover per staff member. As in the case of turnover per square metre trading area, this may indicate how the relevant selling lines are performing. The good product lines will also result in a relatively higher turnover per staff member.
- Absolute sales figures and trends. These can be a further indication of the success of each product, and provide a basis for re-assessing weak product lines.
- Gross profit. The gross profit of each product influenced by buying costs provides useful information from which to establish the contribution of the relevant products in covering fixed costs and in contributing to profits. The gross profit of each product, however, must be compared with that of similar products; it does not make sense to compare groceries with hardware. In any event, the turnover speed of these goods will differ substantially.
- The number of times different products go out of stock. This may also indicate whether stock (prompt orders) or suppliers have performed according to expectations. Out-of-stock situations result in lost sales which prejudice return on investment.
- The number of goods returned to suppliers or returned by customers. This indicates how well timing and quality were attended to during purchasing.
- Inter-firm comparisons. Comparing the performance of

one retailer with that of another, may indicate the relative buying performance of a particular retailer (comparisons of stock turnover ratios).

- Price comparisons. Compare prices with similar retailers. When competitors offer lower prices for their products it is logical to ask whether their buying is not more efficient.
- Forced sales. The number and extent of forced sales of specific products may indicate the buying performance, for instance, when too much of a product is bought for which there is little or no demand.

Buy the right quality Buying the right quality does not mean buying the goods with the highest price. The higher the quality, the more you are going to pay for it, but the best quality is meant the goods your customers wish to have that will satisfy their needs personally and also know exactly what they want, and what they are willing to pay, you are then in a position to determine their standard of quality.

Quality higher than your customer's need pushes up the price of the goods unnecessarily, and they may then just as well be classified as obsolete stock or money wasted on a product that will not sell. Therefore, when you want to buy stock, ask yourself: What exactly is required by the customer in terms of the purpose for which it is intended. Some characteristics for acceptable quality may include factors such as functional suitability, reliability, durability, aesthetic advantages, safety, etc.

Selecting suppliers After decisions have been made on what and how much to buy, the next logical decision would be from whom to purchase. The most important aspect is the selection of one or more suppliers to provide what is needed in the quantity it is needed in the most economical way. Two main sources of supply are available — the manufacturer and the wholesaler (or middleman). You can buy directly from the manufacturer, and if this is possible it will save money. More likely than not, most of your purchases will come from wholesalers. Something to keep in mind however is that the wholesaler is vitally interested in keeping your business alive in order to retain you as a good customer. Some wholesalers offer valuable services which others do not. Wholesalers can be divided into two general groups — the full-service wholesaler who provides a wide range of services such as advice on merchandise, credit extension, deliveries and training, and the limited-function wholesaler who does not (he is also usually referred to as a self-service wholesaler). Below you will find a few consequences of choosing an inefficient supplier:[9]

- out of stock situations;
- unnecessarily high prices resulting in high costs that adversely affect your return on investment;
- a poor competitive position in the market and the possibility of a decline in the business's market share; and
- the loss of attractive business opportunities as a result of poor supply.

An ideal supplier is described by W.B. England[10] as 'one that provides the quality specified and delivers on time as promised; has an acceptable price; reacts to unforeseen needs such as suddenly accelerated or decelerated volumes of business, changes in specifications, service problems and any other legitimate requests. The good supplier takes the initiative in suggesting better ways of servicing customers and attempts to find new ways of developing products and services which will allow customers to perform their operations more economically. The good supplier will warn ahead of time of material shortages, strikes and anything else that may affect the purchaser's operations. It will provide technological and other expertise when requested by customers. It will remain competitive on a continuing basis.'

It may not always be easy to find an ideal supplier such as the one described above but it remains your task to find the best suppliers you can, because doing so pays in the long run. However, you are free to choose your suppliers and it is assumed that you will more than likely give preference to those who:

- can provide goods of the required quality, brand, style and sizes (the products of the supplier must be complementary to the product range your market is calling for);

- can offer goods at prices that will ensure profitability for your business (the net price of the goods must enable you to sell at an acceptable profit);
- are reliable (in respect of prompt delivery, consistent quality and continuous availability of merchandise);
- offer support services (advertising, displays, credit facilities, after sales service such as technical assistance and making adjustments, quality guarantees);
- have a convenient location; and
- employ supplier's representatives of the type with whom the business owner can co-operate (reliable, honest, sincere, helpful, and with a good knowledge about the trade).

A few methods of investigating whether the supplier will comply with your expectations can be employed, such as asking for opinions from clients (and consumers) of the potential supplier. Visiting the supplier's business will also enable you to gain insight into his capabilities and capacity, quality control methods and the general attitude of his employees. Acquire samples and compare them with products of other suppliers; look for published information such as the financial position (financial strength) and information from credit bureaus (Dun and Bradstreet credit reports). It is important to compare prices and quality of goods at all times when investigating your chosen supplier — choose the one who can offer your customers the best value for their money.

Just as important is maintaining favourable relations with the supplier by ensuring clear communications, mutual understanding of relevant matters, mutual consideration for each other's situations and regular visits to each other's businesses. Although sound relations should be developed with existing suppliers, you must nevertheless continually keep an eye and ear open for other suitable suppliers — be concerned with the continual improvement of goods you sell. A good start in ensuring sound relations is to discuss your needs regularly with the person who is authorized to make buying concessions. Be specific as to what your exact requirements and objectives are as far as price, quality, specifications and various services are concerned. Also discuss what discount can be received when payment is made before a stipulated date.

SUMMARY AND CONCLUSIONS

The purchasing function, like all other functions of a business, must be managed and remember that whatever is best managed becomes better. It is a function, that if carried out with precision, can contribute greatly to the profits of the business. It all starts with ascertaining the needs of your customers, forecasting sales, and selecting merchandise and suppliers. When negotiating your purchases, you should have a clear idea before you even begin your 'bargaining' process as to what overall average mark-up is necessary to cover all business expenses and to provide at least an acceptable profit by the year's end. If you have done your planning and maintained good stock turnover records, you will know whether or not you have been maintaining the necessary mark-up. When considering merchandise to buy, one of your first decisions must be whether or not it is merchandise which you can comfortably integrate with your present stock, which your customers would want to buy, and which is within the price range your customers are willing to pay. Only if you can answer 'yes' to these questions should you begin weighing the mark-up needed against the price asked by the supplier. If the price is too high, then be open and honest with the supplier by telling him that you can't sell it to your customers because you will not be earning enough profit. Be on the look out though, for persuasive sales talk, and rather suggest that the supplier let you try out the merchandise on a small scale. Place it in your business on consignment; sometimes it works. Relationships with suppliers are as important as relationships with customers and employees — all are needed to conduct business successfully.

BIBLIOGRAPHY

* Adrian Bellamy. The role of strategic planning in relation to purchasing. *Purchasing South Africa*. 1983; **9**(3): 6, 7.
* J. Arangies. Onderhandelinge met leweransiers. *Entrepreneur* 1983; April: 11, 12.
* D.C. van Rooyen, W.M.J. Hugo. *Purchasing Management*. 1983. Addison-Wesley, London: 236–257. C.M. Baumback, K. Lawyer. *How to Organize and Operate a Small Business*. 1979. Prentice-Hall, Englewood Cliffs, NJ: 324–340.
* J.K. Lasser Tax Institute. *How to Run a Small Business*. 1982. McGraw-Hill, New York: 103–108.

* Thomas Rodolo. *A Business Guide for African Shopkeepers.* 3rd impression. 1977. Interprint, Durban: 14–18.
* J. Arangies. Wat het opleiding met aankope te doen? *Entrepreneur* 1983; **2**(3): 28, 29.

NOTES

[1] Adrian Bellamy. The role of strategic planning in relation to purchasing. *Purchasing South Africa* 1983; **9**(3): 7. (Reproduced with permission.)

[2] J.H. Westing, I.V. Fine, Gary Joseph Zenz. *Purchasing Management.* 1976. John Wiley, New York: 13. (Reproduced with permission.)

[3] What company presidents say about purchasing. *Purchasing South Africa* 1971; December: 47. (*Source:* J.H. Westing, I.V. Fine, Gary Joseph Zenz. *Purchasing Management.* 1976. John Wiley, New York: 6. (Reproduced with permission.)

[4] D.C. van Rooyen, W.M.J. Hugo. *Purchasing Management.* 1983. Addison-Wesley Publishing Company, London: 241. (Reproduced with permission.)

[5] Kwazulu Training Trust Video. *What to Buy: KTT Retail Management Course.* Amanzimtoti, South Africa. (Reproduced with permission.)

[6] D.C. van Rooyen, W.M.J. Hugo. *Purchasing Management.* 1983. Addison-Wesley, London: 243. (Reproduced with permission.)

[7] Kwazulu Training Trust Video. *When to Buy: KTT Retail Management Course.* Amanzimtoti, South Africa. (Reproduced with permission.)

[8] D.C. van Rooyen, W.M.J. Hugo. *Purchasing Management.* 1983. Addison-Wesley, London: 255, 256. (Reproduced with permission.)

[9] Idem, 105.

[10] Idem, 106.

7 PRICING

'The best prices are those which yield the most money after being accepted by customers.'

Frans Bekker

'The "best" price for a product is not necessarily the price that will sell the most units. Nor is it always the price that will bring in the greatest number of sales. Rather the "best" price is the one that will maximize the profits of the company,'

Victor A. Lennon[1]

INTRODUCTION

The selling price of a product is that which you receive in money from the customer in return for something purchased by him. In setting the prices the goal should be to maximize profits, but at the same time, the other aims of pricing should not be forgotten — to 'outdo' competitors, to maintain or improve your market share and to acquire a reputation that brings about follow-on business. How do you decide on what to charge customers for your products? You may reason that it is easy — just charge 30 or 40 per cent more than the cost price. Many businessmen apply this sort of reasoning when pricing goods but the fallacy in this is obvious if one determines the real cause for their difficulties in business —goods sold at the wrong price. This may mean that expenses are not always covered or that the customer does not support the business because the prices are unfair. The object of this chapter is to give you guidelines as to how to arrive at a suitable mark-up of your products, and not to tell you what your mark-up should be. Small business owners normally make these two errors in setting the prices for their goods or services:

1. They charge less than bigger businesses and then consider themselves price leaders. However, because of the small business's relatively small volume of sales, product cost per item is higher than for a larger business, as small businesses do not have the capital to take advantage of large-volume discounts on their purchases.
2. They undercharge during the beginning of the operation with the idea that prices can be raised once more customers have been secured. In practice, however, it is easier to lower prices than to increase them.

SIMPLE FORMULAE TO FIND PROFITABLE MARK-UPS

To understand the relation of costs and mark-up, selling price and gross profit, it is necessary to understand retail mathematics. They are the alpha and omega of pricing. It is advisable that decisions on prices be made on a definite, daily basis. Below are a few aspects and principles to understand and to use when determining your prices:

1. Mark-up percentage is not gross profit percentage.
2. You buy goods to obtain value, but value is determined by what customers consider good. Their idea of value is relative and they compare your prices with those of other businesses — they judge whether your prices are fair or out of line.
3. Mark-up must be large enough to cover operating expenses.
4. Profit is affected by three factors — selling price, sales volume and expenses. The one affects the other. If you sell goods at a low price, you may enjoy a large sales volume but perhaps not realize sufficient income to cover the cost of selling the goods. On the other hand, if you have a high selling price, your sales volume may be so low that you will be unable to meet your operating expenses.

Mark-up is what is added to the cost price of the product to get a selling price, i.e. the difference between cost price and selling price. It is expressed both as a percentage of sales and as a percentage of cost. Thus, in the case of a product that costs R1,00 which you sell for R1,50, the mark-up is 50 cents (or 50%) which is $33^{1}/_{3}\%$ of the selling price.

$$\frac{50 \text{ cents}}{R1,50} = 33,3\% \text{ (gross profit percentage)}$$
or 50% of cost price

$$\frac{50 \text{ cents}}{R1,00} = 50\% \text{ (mark-up)}$$

This can be better illustrated by using an Income Statement (Fig. 1). This example will be used for the discussions to follow.

Fig. 1. Profit and Loss Statement	
Sales	R150 000
Cost of goods sold	100 050
Opening stock	16 000
Add: Purchases	102 050
Less: Closing Stock	18 000
Gross Profit	49 950
Less: Expenses	34 000
Salaries and Wages	21 000
Insurance	700
Water & Lights	800
Bank Charges	150
Depreciation	2 400
Maintenance — Vehicles	600
Maintaining — Building	750
Telephone	200
Transport	2 600
Advertising	900
Sundry Expenses	300
Interest on loan	3 600
Net profit	R 15 950

(a) Mark-up $= \dfrac{\text{Gross profit}}{\text{Cost of goods sold}} \times \dfrac{100}{1}$

$\quad\quad\quad\quad = \dfrac{R49\ 950}{R100\ 050} \times \dfrac{100}{1}$

$\quad\quad\quad\quad = 49,9\% \ (+/- \ 50\%)$

(b) Gross profit % = $\dfrac{\text{Gross profit}}{\text{Sales}} \times \dfrac{100}{1}$

$= \dfrac{\text{R49 950}}{\text{R150 000}} \times \dfrac{100}{1}$

$= 33,3\%$

Thus be careful not to fall into the trap of thinking that mark-up percentage is the same as gross profit percentage. From the table below you can see what your mark-up must be to achieve a certain gross profit percentage that must be high enough to cover expenses and realize a satisfactory net profit. Always remember that mark-up is calculated as a percentage of the cost price and gross profit as a percentage of the selling price.

Gross profit as a percentage of the selling price %	Mark-up as a percentage of the cost price %	Gross profit as a percentage of the selling price %	Mark-up as a percentage of the cost price %
5	5,26	28	38,89
6	6,38	29	40,85
7	7,53	30	42,86
8	8,70	31	44,93
9	9,89	32	47,06
10	11,11	33	49,25
11	12,36	34	51,52
12	13,64	35	53,85
13	14,94	36	56,25
14	16,28	37	58,73
15	17,65	38	61,29
16	19,05	39	63,93
17	20,48	40	66,67
18	21,95	41	69,49
19	23,46	42	72,41
20	25,00	43	75,44
21	26,58	44	78,57
22	28,21	45	81,82
23	29,87	46	85,19
24	31,58	47	88,68
25	33,33	48	92,31
26	35,14	49	96,08
27	36,99	50	100,00

$$\text{Mark-up} = \frac{\text{Gross Profit}}{100-\text{Gross Profit}} \times \frac{100}{1}$$

$$= \frac{33}{100-33} \times \frac{100}{1}$$

$$= 49,25$$

When setting the price of a product there are three objectives to keep in mind: (i) cover the original cost of the merchandise; (ii) cover your operating expenses; and (iii) make a profit.

Consider this example: you bought R1 000 worth of goods (100 products) from the supplier for the purpose of selling. Thus, one product cost you R10, which means that if you sell it at R10 to a customer, you have recovered the original cost of the product (your first objective) but you have not yet covered expenses or made a profit. Therefore you have not achieved the two remaining objectives of pricing. In order to cover your expenses, you need to know how much your expenses are. You can only know that if you keep up-to-date and accurate financial records (of every transaction). Now, consider the income statement in Fig. 1. You see that the expenses for the year amounted to R34 000. Your expenses thus represent 22,6% of your sales, calculated as follows:

$$\frac{\text{R34 000 (expenses)}}{\text{R150 000 (sales)}} \times \frac{100}{1} = 22,6\%.$$

We will round this off to 23%. In order to cover operating expenses (your second objective), you must then add 23% to the cost price of the product (R10). Then you will have covered the original cost of the product and expenses, but you will not yet have made a profit. Your profit will be the profit you plan to make as a percentage on the money you have invested in your business. In other words, your return on investment percentage is influenced by such factors as provision for inflation, interest you could get if you had invested your money in the bank at no risk and a reasonable salary to you. Say, you have calculated this and arrived at a return on investment percentage of 27%. This 27% is then added to the original cost price of the product. The calculation will therefore be as follows per product you bought for the purpose of selling:

Original cost	R10,00
Add: To cover operating expenses — 23%	R 2,30
Profit — 27%	R 2,70
Selling price per product	R15,00

Your mark-up on this product is thus 50% (23% plus 27%) which gives you a gross profit percentage of 33,3%.

This method of pricing can be explained in a different manner. The difference is that the 'target return', rather than a percentage, is added to the calculated costs. Let it be assumed, for example, that you have invested R60 000 in a business and that your expenses amount to R85 000. Furthermore, you wish to earn a 15% return on your investment. Total expenses plus the desired return on your investment will amount to R94 000:

Expenses	R85 000
Target return on investment	R 9 000
	R94 000

If forecasted sales are 15 000 products, then dividing R94 000 by R15 000 will give R6,26. This figure represents the expenses plus the established target return for each product. What is to remain is to add the cost price (or purchase price) of the product. Assuming the cost price per product is R8, your selling price should be R14,26. In other words, if you sell the 15 000 products at R14,26 each, you will make a profit of R9 000, a 15% return on your invested capital.

This approach is not 'market-oriented' as it puts the emphasis on your objective, that is to make a 15% return on your capital invested in the business. In addition, the realization of the 'target return' depends to a large extent on the accuracy of the sales forecast. For instance, in this example your actual sales may be only 11 000 products instead of 15 000 products. If you sell 11 000 products at R14,26 you will show a loss instead of a profit on your investment.

There is in fact a fourth objective of pricing — an important one — which can also be said to be the overall objective of pricing. It is customer acceptability of the price. The questions you should answer are: Will the selling price of

R15,00 be accepted by the customer, or rather, is he willing to pay R15,00 for that particular product? Does he consider it value for money? How much do my competitors sell this product for? It is at this point that the three factors that influence profit come into their own — price, expense and volume of sales. If the customer does not accept the price then you have to make a plan. Firstly, you could purchase the goods at a better price. Say you could get the 100 products from a supplier at R940, then the calculation would be as follows:

Original cost	R 9,40
Add: To cover operating expenses—23%	R 2,16
Profit — 27%	R 2,54
Selling price per product	R14,10

If, of course, you could purchase the goods at a better price and still sell them for R15 each, you will be making a higher profit due to good purchasing. You could also eliminate certain expenses or just controlling expenses so that they do not get out of hand. Say you got expenses down to the stage where they represent only 20% of sales (on the original example) then the calculation will look as follows:

Original cost	R10,00
Add: To cover operating expenses — 20%	R 2,00
Profit — 27%	R 2,70
Selling price per product	R14,70

If you could purchase the goods at a better price as well as lower your expenses and still sell the product at R15, you could make so much more profit. However, what is the use of determining your prices after expenses have been incurred? You need to look at the future. For example, say you have a sales goal of R200 000, an expense budget of R50 000 and a profit goal of R15 000 (before tax), then your mark-up should be:

$$\frac{\text{R50 000} + \text{R15 000}}{\text{R200 000}} = \frac{\text{R 65 000}}{\text{R200 000}} = 32,5\%.$$

It could also be profitable to increase sales by lowering the price of a product. Consider this example, where one product is sold at R1 and another at 95 cents; the product at the lower price is selling much faster (due to customer acceptability):

	Product A — R1	Product B — 95 cents
Number of products sold	10 000	15 000
Total sales (10 000 × R1) and (15 000 × 95 cents)	10 000	14 250
Total expenses	9 000	10 000
Net profit	1 000	4 250

Although some owner-managers believe that increased sales volume is needed for increased profits, it must be remembered that volume alone does not necessarily mean more profits. One must also remember that the ingredients of profit are costs, selling price, and unit sales volume. They have to be in proper proportions if the desired profit is to be obtained. It is possible to get a maximum profit for a product, but your success would depend on how well you could project unit sales volume at varying selling prices. Consider the figures below which illustrate the price–volume–contribution relationship:[2]

Selling price per product	R5	R4	R4
Projected sales in units	10 000	30 000	15 000
Projected sales in rands	R50 000	R120 000	R60 000
Costs (expenses)	R30 000	R 90 000	R45 000
Contribution to profit	R20 000	R 30 000	R15 000

In this example, assuming that you can sell 30 000 units, the R4 selling price would be the best for your product. However, if you could sell only 15 000 units at R4, the best price would be R5. The R5 selling price would bring in R20 000 profit against R15 000 from 15 000 units sold at R4. With these facts in mind, you can use a market-orientated approach to set your selling price. Your aim is to determine the combination of selling price and unit volume which will provide the greatest contribution towards profits.

Normally, when the sale of a particular product in the business increases, all other lines of products benefit. As your sales volume increases, the profit percentage increases, because the portion of sales volume that represents fixed expenses (rent, insurances, etc.) is decreasing. Likewise, as sales volume declines, the profit percentage also declines because your fixed expenses cannot easily be cut. Sales volume has to do with stock turnover rate — the ideal is to achieve the highest possible sales with the lowest possible stock. Increase your stock turnover rate by better purchasing (same quality at lower prices) and better salesmanship (what you buy, you have to sell as quickly as possible at a price the customer considers as value for money but which is still at a profit to you). Sales volume and stock turnover can at times be more important than percentage of profit. Consider the following example.[3]

The owner of a business normally buys 60 xyz products every year, which cost R50. These xyz products sell for R100, thus generating R3 000 on the original R3 000 investment. This 100% mark-up is the same as the owner makes on all similar merchandise, which he normally turns over once a year. The supplier of the xyz products offers the owner a deal — 500 xyz products for R7 500, a cost per product of only R15 (compared with the original cost of R50 each). The owner can then lower the price of an xyz product to R90, sell 50% more xyz products to achieve a mark-up of 500%. He should, however, decline this offer. Keeping cash tied up in unsold xyz stock actually costs the business money. If 75 xyz products a year are sold at a price of R90, it will take almost 7 years to sell all 500 xyz products. Total profit on the xyz products is R37 500, or about R5 350 per year. Had the R7 500 been invested in regular stock, it would have been subject to the business owner's normal 100% mark-up, generating an annual profit of R7 500. Therefore, it won't be wise for the business owner to invest a large amount of money in unsaleable xyz products. Although the percentage of profit was greater with the special deal, the resultant annual sales volume was too little and the turnover of stock too slow. Had the xyz products been priced at R40 (selling price) and sold out entirely in one year, the owner would have profited more because the profit would be greater than normal while the turnover period would not. High sales volume usually does more for profits than such stock bargains.

In applying your pricing formula to separate selling departments, your expected future expenses would be the direct expenses of that department, such as salaries of employees working in that department, advertising, etc. Your profit goal would then be the amount you expect the department to contribute to the total profit of the business, taking into consideration its projected sales. For example, you may have set one department's sales goal at R50 000, its direct expenses are R8 500, and the department must make a profit contribution of R4 000 (before tax) to the overall profit goal of the business. Thus, an appropriate mark-up for this department's products would be:

$$\frac{R8\ 500 + R4\ 000}{R50\ 000} = \frac{R12\ 500}{R50\ 000} = 25\%$$

Alternatively, the department's sales goal may be R50 000, its direct expenses R8 500, expenses for the whole business R15 000 (or 13,6% of sales), and expected sales for the business R110 000. A mark-up that will cover this department's share of expenses would be calculated as follows:

$$\frac{R8\ 500 + (13,6\%\ of\ R50\ 000)}{R50\ 000} = \frac{R15\ 300}{R50\ 000} = 30,6\%$$

Thus, a mark-up above 30,6% would be required to yield a profit to the business. The exact mark-up set by you would depend upon customer acceptability and the prices charged by competitors.

Arriving at a mark-up does not immediately solve a pricing problem, it simply gives a general guide to use in checking the adequacy of an aggregate mark-up. It is almost never a good idea to aim at the same mark-up on everything. If you have a 33,3% gross profit goal, for example, it is poor practice to mark all R1 cost items R1,50, all R2 items R3, and all R10 items R15, etc. Pricing is an art, and you must always weigh volume possibilities against customer acceptance, probable costs and expenses.

Some products require a higher mark-up than others because of the need for larger allowances for seasonal reductions. Examples of goods that require high initial mark-ups are; high-fashion goods (which have a limited or unpredictable market); seasonal and novelty items (which cannot be kept economically for another year); and goods easily damaged or which lose freshness (vegetables, etc). Some products may have high carrying costs (as mentioned above) as well as occupying more space on shelves. Some may sell rather slowly, and others might require extra storage or special installation costs. All of these factors indicate that if you are to make a profit on an item, you must have a retail price higher than that of your average mark-up. Provision must be made for any such reductions (or mark-down as it is also called), which is normally expressed as a percentage of sales. For example, you may have operating expenses of 25%, a desired profit of 15% and anticipated reductions of 8%; the mark-up percentage would be computed as follows:

$$\frac{\text{Expenses} + \text{Operating profit} + \text{Reductions}}{\text{Sales} + \text{Reductions}} = \text{Mark-up}$$

$$\frac{25\% + 15\% + 8\%}{100\% + 8\%} = \frac{48\%}{108\%} = 44,4\%$$

Competition and the sales volume you are aiming for will determine your final decision.

If you have a speciality shop, you will probably reduce your prices late in the season when you have your major clearance sale. In other types of shops, many businessmen reduce their prices a little early to attract customers to the reduced priced goods (to stay competitive in the market), and thus save the big reduction in prices for later in the season. If products do not sell even with the bigger reductions, you should consider not re-ordering it, but for the time being display it in your shop, and give it special attention or encourage your salespeople to push it. You should not assume that a reduction in price is the only means you have to get rid of sluggish stock. Customers do buy selectively and they may not need that specific product.

Apart from customer acceptability, there are three other factors that could also influence the mark-up on products. They are controlled prices, manufacturers' suggested retail prices and competition. Any product that the Government subsidises will have a laid down selling price that has to be adhered to, such as bread and milk. The mark-up on these products is restricted to the purchase price. Some manufacturers insist that you sell their products at a set price. This price normally includes a comfortable mark-up, but not always. It is a suggested price by the manufacturer, and you are not bound to sell it at that price. Unless you have a monopoly situation, your prices on certain products will have to be in the same price range as your competitors. Thus, if the product offered by a competitor is similar to yours, a competitive price must be set.

- Novelties and fashion goods. They normally carry a relatively (relative to the market — middle or upper class) high mark-up. These goods have a short selling season — prices may at first be high but will often be lowered again as the novelty wears off. The price is then reduced, and customers begin to look for new items. To cash in during the popular stage, you must anticipate your needs very carefully. If you are overstocked your profits will be reduced by the mark-downs necessary to get rid of products remaining when the novelty wears off. If the product is sold out and must be re-ordered, the re-order may not arrive before everyone has purchased elsewhere. A mark-down is a reduction of an original selling price. After the selling price is established on any item (by adding a mark-up to its cost price), the price may have to be reduced for any one of a number of reasons, such as to clear out left-overs, poor assortments and damaged goods, to get rid of poor purchases or to meet sudden changes in the market. Early mark-downs are the smallest. The sooner you discover that merchandise is not moving and you start to mark down the price, the smaller your losses will be. The time to sell is when people want to buy and not at the end of the season after everyone has bought. When you start to mark down at the end of a season or novelty period, it is best to forget about cost and continue marking down until the goods are sold. Consequently, the few accepted and still popular lines must bear the loss of less successful lines.

- Fast selling items. It is important to have competitive prices on fast-selling items such as groceries. Customers are familiar with their prices and values and are critical of small price differences on fast-selling, popular goods. Slow-selling merchandise should have a higher-than-average mark-up if it is normal for the item to sell slowly. If the item is not a normal slow-seller, it may have become unattractive to customers because of its quality or price. First check how your competitors are handling the item, as they may be causing your slow sales by a more aggressive selling effort. You may have to lower your mark-up in response. If the product is not selling anywhere, you may have to cut the price to get rid of it and consider dropping that item in the future.

- Leaders and loss leaders. A leader is an item given a special price, usually below that being charged by other businesses. The profit (or mark-up) is less than normal. It is offered as a promotional item to increase shop traffic. It can be sold at a profit or loss. A loss leader is one that is sold below its cost. A good leader sells itself. It should need no promotional effort. Items that are in everyday use and are bought frequently, and that have a well-established value make good leaders.

The same objectives for pricing apply in the service business. Every service business should have a system which accurately records operating expenses and the cost of all materials used in providing the service. When prices are fixed, your challenge is to control costs and increase operating efficiency to achieve maximum profits.

One important point to remember in determining the mark-up in your business is to remember that you must plan for it. Although in the examples discussed we have used the profit and loss statement of the previous year, that year is past — what about the future? What are your expenses going to be during the next financial year? What profit (or return on investment) do you want to achieve in the following year? The importance of forecasting and budgeting cannot be overstressed when it comes to pricing. If you do not plan for the future, how are you going to know what your expenses will be every month, and how are you going to know what to do in order to reach the profit objective you have set? All the necessary information about pricing can be obtained from the cash flow budget. (Study the chapter on 'Profit Planning and Budgeting'.)

Pricing in the service business The 'multiplier method' of pricing is a useful formula when the amount of time spent on providing the service varies from customer to customer, and if the labour cost is the most significant expense item. The multiplier is determined by dividing the annual labour costs into total sales. Three figures are then multiplied to determine the price to charge for a particular job done, namely: the employee's hourly pay, the time he spent on the job, and the multiplier. For example, if a welding service business has an annual sales figure of R100 000 and total productive labour costs of R35 000, and the average worker was paid R8 per hour, the multiplier and the price to be charged for a job that took 6 hours to complete would be as follows:

$$\frac{R100\ 000}{R3\ 500} = 2,8$$

$$\therefore\ R8 \times 6\ \text{(hours)} \times 2,8 = R134,40$$

To this amount (R134,40) would of course be added the cost of material used in completing the particular job.

Some types of businesses such as motor repair shops make use of the flat-rate pricing method which is based on the 'standard' time to do the job multiplied by the average salary rate, multiplied by the multiplier. Profits can be increased when efficient work is done by skilful people. For example, the industry might prescribe that the standard time for a particular job is 5 hours. Say your multiplier is 3, and the average hourly rate R6. Thus, the standard flat rate price would be R90 plus cost of materials used. If, however, you can do the particular job in only 4 hours, then the price will be R72 plus materials used, thus yielding a very competitive price through your efficient personnel. Or, if the price of R90 is competitive (as it might cost your competitors more in time to do the job) and accepted by the customer as fair, you can make a higher profit on that particular job.

AVOIDING PRICE COMPETITION

It has often been said, during periods when much emphasis has been placed on the promotion of small businesses and the special advantages which small business enjoy over large business, that small business has some unique advantages.

234

But, what can small business do to compete with big business? What is the best way to shield a small business from price competition? John Petrof, Peter Carusone and John McDavid provide the answers:[4]

'Although in the short run unforeseen developments may force a small businessman to engage in price competition, he should never compete on the basis of price as a matter of policy. Every time he reduces prices in order to sell an item he cuts his potential profits.

Several studies have indicated that the majority of people patronize a business for reasons other than price. Often a pleasing personality, courtesy, reliable service, an attractive shop, or a strong interest in civic affairs is the basis for choosing. A study made for Sears Roebuck discovered that for many people a personal relationship was far more important than price.* Consumers indicated a preference for shopping in stores where they were known by name. Another study found that consumers tend to patronize friendly stores.† The researchers invariably received the same answer: "X's store is friendlier." No one mentioned bargains or savings.

The above findings imply that small businesses may have a unique advantage in serving their markets. Due to structural limitations, a small business can seldom afford to engage in price competition, especially against a larger business. Cost advantages such as large-scale buying and lower rates in obtaining funds are usually not as available to smaller businesses. However, size tends to make a company inflexible. Most larger businesses tend to be bureaucratic and impersonal in dealing with their customers. On the other hand, small businesses have an advantage not enjoyed by their big brothers, namely, flexibility. This feature makes it possible for small businesses to successfully compete against larger ones without resorting to price competition. Capitalizing on their inherent comparative advantage, flexibility, will enable small businesses to better satisfy their clients by providing them with friendly and personalized service. The purpose of these paragraphs has been to emphasize the importance of non-price motives in a buying situation. Unfortunately, the typical small businessman still concentrates on price appeals.

What is a business image and why is it so important? An image may be defined as the impression that a business makes on a customer. It is the sum total of what customers think of a business. The accounting term 'goodwill' in a sense represents a quantification of this concept. Just like a human being, each business has its own personality. People tend to like or dislike businesses in the same way that they do people.

* Pierre Martineau. Motivation in Advertising 1957. McGraw-Hill, New York: 179–180.
† Idem, 181.

In other words, buyers tend to react to businesses as if they were animate rather than inanimate objects.

The concept of the business image is very important for two reasons. First, an image becomes a frame of reference within which all business activities are evaluated. A small machine tool business found that even its best customers showed resistance to new product ideas presented by its salesman. The fact was however, that the business had developed and sold some pioneering instruments in the field of boring holes through metals. As a result of its findings, the business undertook a publicity program to change the misconceptions of its clients and create the desired image. Second, a favourable image is the best way to shield a small business from price competition. Businesses that are able to create distinct images in the minds of their customers do not have to worry about each price reduction of their competitors. What is even more important is the fact that it is difficult for competition to copy a given image. This cannot be said about a policy which emphasizes the meeting of others' prices. It does take much ingenuity to match a given price.

SUMMARY AND CONCLUSIONS

Pricing is a very important aspect of management. You are in business to make a profit. You should seek that point at which, with a particular sales volume, you will make the most profit with customer acceptance of your product and its selling price as a natural consequence. Not all goods have to be priced for profit but the entire price charged on all goods should result in the desired profit.

A businessman must decide in advance on the price at which each product will be offered for sale, and therefore he must have a positive price policy. He must decide what method or methods will be used in pricing various products. There is however, no single established method for doing this, as it is very difficult to obtain all the information that could influence a pricing decision, apply a formula to it, and then come up with the best possible price. The main purpose of applying a formula, then, is to simplify pricing decisions by minimizing the need for estimation. Sound reasoning for establishing a price places a premium on managerial judgement and requires attention to a number of factors above and beyond the actual price as determined by a formula.

BIBLIOGRAPHY

* Thomas Rodolo. *A Business Guide for African Shopkeepers*. 3rd impression. 1977. Interprint, Durban: 19–25.

* William H. Day. *Maximizing Small Business Profits with Precision Management*. 1978. Prentice-Hall, Englewood Cliffs, NJ: 252–255.

* Clifford M. Baumback, Kenneth Lawyer. *How to Organize and Operate a Small Business*. Prentice-Hall, Englewood Cliffs, NJ: 373–392.

* J.K. Lasser Tax Institute. *How to Run a Small Business*. 5th ed. 1982. McGraw-Hill, New York: 108–119.

* John W. Wingate, Seymour Helfant. Small store planning for growth. *Small Business Management Series No. 33* 2nd ed, 1977. U.S. Small Business Administration, Washington D.C.

* Guy Macleod. *Starting Your Own Business in South Africa*. 1983. Oxford University Press, Cape Town: 52–62.

NOTES

[1] Victor A. Lennon. What is the best selling price? *Management Aids Number 1.002*. 1968. Small Business Administration, Washington D.C.: 2.

[2] Ibid.

[3] Example adapted from: J.K. Lasser Tax Institute. *How to Run a Small Business*. 5th ed. 1982. McGraw-Hill, New York: 111, 112. (Reproduced with permission.)

[4] John V. Petrof, Peter S. Carusone, John E. McDavid. *Small Business Management: Concepts and Techniques for Improving Decisions*. 1972. McGraw-Hill, New York: 173–175. Reproduced with permission.

8 SHOP LAYOUT, DISPLAY AND IMPROVING EXTERNAL AND INTERNAL IMAGES

'A customer is drawn into a shop by some motivated force, whether it be the attraction to an exterior display or a real need for a specific purchase. But once through the door this motivation loses impact if the interior image does not reflect your shop, or your customer's needs.'

Dina Pellegrin[1]
Advertising and Promotions Officer
Shelvit (Pty) Limited

'A business has an image whether or not the owner is aware of it. For example, throw some merchandise onto shelves and onto display tables in a dirty, dimly lit shop and you immediately have created a negative image. Shoppers think of it as a dirty, junky shop and will avoid coming into it. Your image should be concentrated enough to promote in your advertising and other promotional activities. For example, "home cooked" food might be the image of a small restaurant.'[2]

INTRODUCTION

Layout is concerned with the arranging of equipment and stock according to a predetermined plan with the objective of making the shopping experience for the customer as pleasant and convenient as possible in order to satisfy his needs. A clean, adequately stocked shop with well-arranged equipment and merchandise can awaken the buying desires of a customer and invite him to buy much more than he planned to do. Product presentation (display) includes all the techniques and skills used to display goods in a manner that will maximize attention, with one goal in mind — to maximize sales. It is once again a matter of competing, one owner tries to make his shop different from similar shops. It remains a matter of getting large numbers of customers to focus on your shop and merchandise, and being tempted into impulse buying. Impulse buying can be regarded as making unplanned purchases. The better you are catering for impulse buying, the greater the satisfaction your customers will experience and the more likely and regularly they will return to your shop. The idea is to create a certain impression or build up an image in the mind of the customer in order to get him back at your shop — even if it is just to look. Fresh, properly designed displays take advantage of customer traffic to increase sales and consequently, to help you make a larger profit. It is thus maximum sales you're after in planning the layout of your shop.

Not only does the interior reflect a great deal about the owner of the business, but it is also a key factor in shaping the total image of the business. It should be consistent with the expectations created by the business's exterior appearance or image. The interior design should match, as nearly as possible, the lifestyle of your market. Customers will immediately identify the standards you are striving for, and thus an area in which you get compared with your competitors. The image of the business has much to do with your business's attitude toward customers, employees, products and equipment and thus determines its atmosphere, its 'personality' and its way of doing business. Whether you know it or not, every business acquires a reputation of its own — be it good or bad. You should find out what your business's reputation is. However, if there is competition you can succeed if you capitalize on the principles or methods of operation in which competitors are weak.

The exterior image of your business is important. Your building must stand out from that of its competitors. The outside of the business is vitally important if you want to get the customer or even a passer-by interested (get his attention and awaken a desire) in buying from you. If your business projects an unpleasant image from the outside, you run the risk of having the public stay away. It is often the atmosphere that is the critical factor in determining whether the customer will enter your shop or not. Try to make the exterior and interior distinctive in every way. To a large extent it is a matter of personal pride towards your business, and the impression you want to create in the mind of the customer, coupled with an attention to detail. Just stop for a moment and ask yourself: What do my customers really think of me, my employees and my business? Ideally, it should be one of its kind in the immediate area.

ISSUES THAT SHOULD BE CONSIDERED IN PLANNING THE LAYOUT

Floor space Make maximum use of floor space. You must use the space available to you for selling purposes to the very best advantage, as you are probably paying a considerable amount of rent for it. The idea is not to waste space in any way, but also to consider the comfort and convenience of customers. They should be able to move easily through the shop. Aisle widths must be planned in relation to the shopping tempo in order to keep congestion at peak periods to a minimum. An orderly arrangement of equipment will permit customers to study and handle merchandise which means that they will be able to shop at ease, without being pushed or feeling hurried or to blocking other customers' progress. Aisles should be 1,5 – 2 metres wide.

Checkout area The checkout area refers to the area where payments are made for goods bought by customers and to the people operating the cash registers. This area must operate as smoothly as possible. The emphasis should be placed on convenience and comfort for the shopper and a smooth, quick flow of traffic through the checkout area. People don't like to stand in a checkout line for an excessive length of time. All customers are not equally patient and some will leave their baskets in an aisle and go to another shop. Such customers are then exposed to a competitor's shop, and if the other shop conforms to their requirements they may very well become regular customers there. The checkout area is a very sensitive area and therefore properly selected and trained cashiers are valuable employees. Impatience of customers causes this area to have much responsibility towards positive customer relations. Customers appreciate efficient checkouts operated by friendly cashiers, a fact that has an indirect effect on sales and profits.

Deciding on the exact number of checkout points (checkstands and cash registers) required by a new shop is an important decision. Too few checkout points can lead to customer impatience but on the other hand, too many will create extra expenses because of depreciation and salaries to be paid to whoever operates them. For example, a checkout point that cost R2 500 depreciated over ten years amounts to an expense of R250 (10% of the original cost) annually, not even mentioning the salary paid to the cashier operating it, if any. Too many checkout points can also lead to the misuse of valuable selling space that could rather be used to display and sell merchandise. The correct number of checkout points is usually obtained by observation over a long period of time. Therefore in the beginning it might be better to consider leasing checkout points, which in the long run may save you money.

From a security point of view checkout points should be placed so as to have a view down the aisles and from an image point of view, these checkout counters should always be kept neat and in good order. The checkout point personnel in a business such as a supermarket are often the only contact that many customers have with employees. Care must be taken in selecting staff for this position, and only persons who appear to get along well with people and who like to work with them should be employed. Once selected, these employees must be well trained in how to handle customers and operate cash register with speed and accuracy. Practice and once more practice is the answer, because in the eyes of many customers cashiers represent the management of the business. Therefore, they must be qualified to take this major responsibility on their shoulders.

Neatly dressed employees in attractive uniforms contribute substantially in enhancing the interior image of the business. It is expected of employees to look first-class at all times. At all times, you must set the pace yourself by being an example as well as maintaining a suitable working climate because customers always prefer to shop in a happy store. The job of a cashier is a boring job and can be worsened by difficult and fussy customers, sometimes unnecessary, petty and unjustified. Therefore, they should be praised for being efficient, and you should express appreciation and respect for what they do which will undoubtedly lead to the situation of them feeling proud of their jobs.

Accessibility of merchandise Whether the business is of the self-service or over-the-counter type, all merchandise must be readily accessible, either to customers or to the staff of the business. Shelves must not be constructed so high that it is impossible for the average person to reach the goods displayed on them. Not only is it inconvenient for customers and staff, but it may also be dangerous. It is logical that goods displayed far above the eye-level of customers will fail to sell. When space is limited, very high shelves may be used for reserve stocks, but care must be taken that such merchandise is also attractively displayed.

Visibility of merchandise In planning the layout of a retail shop, a very important issue is that of merchandise visibility. All goods available for sale should be presented in such a manner that they can be clearly seen by all customers. Visual barriers should be kept to a minimum and an atmosphere of openness should prevail. When displaying the goods, ensure that the correct facing of the merchandise can be seen by the customer — the front of the packaging must point in the direction of the aisles. Also, use the impact of colour where possible, group colours in blocks for maximum visibility and impact. In other words, do not use the same colour continuously, but break one colour with another for example: blue, red, green yellow, blue, red, etc. It creates interest which might lead to impulse buying.

Shelves should at all times be kept fully merchandised, especially during busy periods. When stocks are low, move merchandise to the front of the shelf. This creates the appearance of a fully stocked shop. Do not overstock shelves — avoid the extremes of looking too empty or too crowded.

The purpose of gondola ends and bargain bins is to highlight goods such as new lines, seasonal goods and specials. 'Specials' are impulse items and are normally located where traffic flow is high, such as near checkout points and around corners. Customers in checkout lines are good prospects for impulse sales. Gondola-end displays are located in the space at each end of a row of shelves. They are highly visible to the shopper making the turn while going from one aisle to another. The change from the precisely arranged display shelves to a gondola end is eye-catching. They are normally large and thus easier to see as well because they stand out against the background of the shelves. While customers may often skip an aisle, they have difficulty in not seeing the gondola ends. Low profit items should not normally be displayed on gondola ends as it would be a waste of space and the opportunity to sell higher profit items. Restrict gondola-end displays to a single item or to no more than two items at a time. A theme that is meaningful to customers can also help to draw attention and increase sales, for example: 'Here is everything you need for a beautiful skin.'

Determine the best location for demand and impulse lines. It is important to distinguish between demand and impulse lines. Demand lines are those for which customers usually plan shopping trips. These should be placed at the back of the shop and other strategic places. The reason for displaying them at the back is to draw customers to the furthermost sections and by doing so, to create a chance that you will pick up more sales through impulse buying. Two or more items that are closely associated with one another but which are normally displayed in separate sections can also be grouped together, such as teacups and tea; pots and steel wool, etc.

Such practices must, however, be limited as there is nothing more frustrating to a customer than having to 'hunt' for the goods he wishes to buy. The shop should be laid out in a logical manner. An example is not to put poisonous products between or near food products or garden equipment between cosmetic lines. Poisonous products should be put separately (for instance, in some corner of the shop) and garden equipment should be placed in the hardware section. Therefore, arrange merchandise by product type. Use platforms to display bulk items such as maize, meal, sugar, etc. Never put merchandise on the floor; it does not look healthy.

Price mark all merchandise clearly and in the correct place on the product — where the customer and the cashier can see it. This assists your customer in deciding and it helps the smooth functioning of your cashiers. Illegible price markings create many problems — the most obvious being at the checkout point. If a price is missing or cannot be read, the cashier must either guess the price or hold up the line of customers in order to obtain the correct price. During busy periods with impatient customers waiting, the cashier might be under pressure and guess the price and the customer may get the benefit of a lower price. This sort of practice creates a shrinkage problem. The cashier might also guess at a higher price. The result is just as bad — losing a customer, maybe forever. Customers appreciate a business with a good price-marking system, and are unhappy when they have to search for a price and are suspicious when a price is not clearly legible or not on the product at all.

Customers need to be able to see the goods they are buying and in many instances the brighter the lighting the better. Lighting must illuminate the true colours of the items. Such lighting reduces the return of goods by customers who have found that the colours did not look the same under normal lighting conditions. Naked light bulbs are, of course, unsuitable for any type of operation's image. Lights should be placed so as not to cause eye-strain. The best results from ceiling fluorescent lights are obtained when installed crossways rather than parallel with the aisles or gondolas. This arrangement makes displays more attractive by reducing shadows. Accent lighting can be used to highlight specific areas of the shop and can be used to great effect in corners as customers tend to avoid shopping in corners unless some special attraction pulls them there. Where artificial lighting is difficult to achieve, interiors should be painted in colours which are as light as possible, and which will reflect whatever natural light enters the premises. The idea with lighting is to present a bright and inviting atmosphere by coordinating the entire lighting system to enhance the interior appearance and image.

Security When planning the layout, you need to take into account the need for good retail security. Dead-ends, nooks and very high equipment should be avoided as they tend to provide the potential shoplifter with the ideal location and opportunity to execute his criminal activities. Privacy is the shoplifter's greatest ally and therefore the shop should be laid out in such a way that they are open to the view of staff and other customers, whose presence can discourage the potential shoplifter. The office of the management team should be raised and be supplied with big windows facing all angles of the business. This will enable the management staff to observe all activities and movements of customers and staff. Very small items, such as pens, batteries, shaving blades and others, should be placed in front where the checkout area is in order to prevent theft thereof. Not only does this discourage theft, but they are also well placed for impulse buying.

Signs Signs must be clear, attractive and informative. Too many signs are worse than no signs at all as this can create confusion and an overcrowded impression. Always make sure that the spelling is correct and that all signs are always clean and neat as they project the image of your shop. Exterior signing has the primary task of identifying the business. Such signs must therefore be designed for easy recognition. Obviously, simple identification is not enough but it should also be consistent with the desired image of the business. The customer should be aware of the nature of the business conducted, at a glance, as well as being impressed.

Housekeeping Good housekeeping does a great deal to enhance the image of the shop. No customer will enter the business eagerly if it is uncared for. Piles of rubbish and dirty pavements are not at all inviting to any potential customer. No matter whose responsibility it may be to maintain clean pavements, the businessman should do his utmost to have something done about it if he wishes to create an image of professionalism — even if it means doing it at his own expense. The mere fact that something has been done to make the shopping environment more pleasant can cause the public to look twice at your shop, which they may have passed previously. For the interior, lay down a cleaning and repair schedule to clean floors, tidy up the aisles, service shopping carts and put on price tickets. Trolleys and baskets should be tidy and in good working condition at all times.

Customer service The attitude of employees to customers is a vital factor in the creation of a good internal image. Employees who are friendly, pleasant, courteous and eager to serve can do an enormous amount to enhance the customers' impressions when entering the business as well as to put customers in a good shopping mood. Considerable attention should be given to this aspect by being an example yourself as staff will, at times, evaluate your behaviour. It is futile for the owner to drill employees in customer courtesy and then to be remiss in his own treatment of the public. The quality of your service must be personal and exceptional if you wish to acquire a bigger share of the market than competitors. The idea is to make customers feel at home and willing to buy. What employees talk about to customers should be left to their discretion as long as customers are not left thinking they are just another number to the shop. Try to be different from the normal 'Terrible weather isn't it?' kind of conversation as customers might find this boring at times, especially if it is said to the same customer every time. Try to talk about something specific or try wearing a badge saying: 'Ask me about men's clothing', etc. On conclusion of every transaction, don't forget to say 'Have a nice day', or words to that effect.

Be conscious of your image, remembering that image means personality. The personality of your product or service (or the business as a whole), can be revealed by many things — its name, its packaging, its price range and price appeal, the style of the advertising, the nature of the business, atmosphere, and generally all the aspects mentioned in this chapter. Is it unique? Does it fit and contribute to your image-building strategy? Could it be used for the next twenty years? Rate your business periodically in order to determine what kind of image it has. Be aware of danger signals and try to spot and correct them. Danger signals can be for example that customers walk out of your shop without buying; many people you know no longer visit the shop; traffic (pedestrian and vehicle) in front of your business has dropped; sales are down this month compared with the same month last year; employees are slow in greeting customers; personal appearance of employees is not neat; employees lack knowledge of the merchandise; the number of mistakes made by employees is increasing; the better employees leave for jobs with competitors; or you have a reputation of being greedy (too high prices).

Your employees are some of the 'weapons' needed to have a competitive advantage over other similar businesses. They should be trained to be effective in their respective fields.

Well-presented stock is a valuable sales tool and should be used to the best advantage. People like to do their shopping in nice surroundings and it should be obvious that it is your task to provide it for them. Time taken to plan the physical set-up carefully will pay profitable dividends. In other words, you must determine where to put the counters, shelves, checkout areas, fridges, etc. At all times you must care for the goods in the business, because if they are spoiled and unattractive looking, you cannot expect to do good business. Prevent goods from gathering dust.

Self-service shops have the advantages that they enjoy lower labour costs and higher sales from open displays of merchandise. Customers can examine items without the 'pressure' of sales people. Open displays often lead to impulse buying. Savings on wages will be considerable. Customers make their own selections and cashiers are needed only to ring up sales and wrap the merchandise. (This is applicable mostly to supermarkets.) Of course, some assistance is needed in departments where knowledge of the products must be supplied by the shop or where sizes and fittings are in question. Expensive merchandise must also be attended by sales people and much assistance is required in speciality shops.

Every square inch of your selling space is valuable. Your objective is to make a profit, which can only happen if a sale is made. Sales depend on customers and it is thus necessary that you create a demand for the products you sell in such a way as to attract the customer's attention.

Colour is an active element in the decor of the business. Use colour to accentuate or to separate departments. Colour must be used tactfully and appropriately as clashing or gaudy colours cheapen rather than enhance the image of the business. A new customer can see at a glance whether things look well organized and whether the shopping trip is likely to be a pleasant experience. Customers consider many things before they actually enter a business. They want a convenient location, easy parking, competitive prices and an image that appeals to them. The appearance of your business, both external and internal is of utmost importance if you wish to attract custom and so generate sales. Many determined businessmen have proved that money laid down to improve the appearance and image of their businesses was well spent. Their efforts have been rewarded by a better customer opinion of their operations and by the retention of their customers' continuous support.

BIBLIOGRAPHY

* Dina Pelligrin. The importance of signage in a store. *Entrepreneur* 1984; **3**(10): 16, 17.
* Willie Brewis. Is winkelmodernisering lonend? *Entrepreneur* 1983; **2**(3): 25, 26.
* Jan Visagie. Belangrikheid van goeie huishouding. *Entrepreneur* 1986; **5**(2): 14.
* Z.M. du Plessis. Die uitleg van die klein sakeonderneming. *Entrepreneur* 1983; **2**(11): 28, 29.
* Dina Pelligrin. Merchandise presentation — back to basics. *Entrepreneur* 1982; August: 14.
* Brian Rabjohn. Merchandising. *African Business* 1984; **11**(6): 12, 14, 16. (Official journal of the National African Federated Chamber of Commerce.)
* Brian Rabjohn. Merchandising. *African Business* 1984; **11**(10): 6, 8, 12. (Official journal of the National African Federated Chamber of Commerce.)
* Brian Rabjohn. Improving your internal and external images. *African Business* 1984; **11**(4): 21, 27. (Official journal of the National African Chamber of Commerce.)
* C.J. Jooste, W.J.C. van der Merwe. Die maatskappy en sy beeld na buite. *Volkshandel* 1984; August: 48, 57.
* Dirk Weideman. Aksent Beligting. *Entrepreneur* 1986; **5**(7): 14.
* Merchandising through departmental positioning and dry grocery fixturing. *Supermarket and Retailer.* **29**(11): 18–22.
* Horizontal vs. vertical block merchandising. *Supermarket and Retailer* 1983; **30**(2): 22.

NOTES

[1] Dina Pelligrin. Merchandise presentation — back to basics. *Entrepreneur* 1982; August: (Reproduced with permission.)
[2] Business plan for retailers. *Management Aids, Number 2.020.* 1979. U.S. Small Business Administration, Washington D.C.: 4.

9 CUSTOMER RELATIONS AND SERVICE

'The customer is in the middle of everything you want to accomplish in business — to be effective and earn a good return on capital invested. This can only be achieved if you do everything necessary to make people want to do business with you — repeatedly and loyally (supporting your business and remain faithful in that).'

Frans Bekker

'Service, quality, reliability are strategies aimed at loyalty and long-term revenue stream growth (and maintenance).'[1]

In Search of Excellence

'It could be a sickening spectacle if you loose one customer after the other.'[2]

D. Ogilvy

'Improper behaviour can kill a sale, an image, a reputation and overall perception of a business.'[3]

INTRODUCTION

You selected the type of business you wished to go into, you found an excellent location, you purchased the right line of goods, you priced your goods so that they are profitable and marketable, you employed personnel, you maintain tight financial controls and you are advertising. Unless, however, you build a strong and steady clientele, you will find yourself going out of business in a very short time. Business today is more than just profits and growth; it has a greater obligation to the public than ever before. Today's enlightened customers tolerate no mishandling, mislabelling, misrepresentation or misunderstanding. You must be fair in your dealings with them if you want your clientele to remain with you. Those people from among the public who are attracted to the business, who decide to buy and later to buy again, are

249

the very life of a business. Customer satisfaction is the basis for the continued success of all businesses. How to establish good customer relations should be planned as carefully as any other major objectives of the business. All employees working for you are also regarded as part of the business. In the mind of the customer, the employees are delegated by you to represent the business. Their behaviour in dealing with customers can be either constructive or destructive to the business. The same applies to you — your success as an entrepreneur is in direct proportion to your desire and motivation to serve other people. Have you ever considered the question of why do you, as a customer to other businesses, continue to patronize a specific business? It is because they know what you like, want and need.

To give a fine example of how something influenced myself and my wife as customers, listen to this: I was called up for military service for a period of two months and during that period something went mechanically wrong with our car. It was one of those cars which had just been taken off the market and there was no agent closer to us than 300 kilometres. My wife, moving from garage to garage, begged to have it looked at, no matter the cost. Despite being desperate she was turned away with such excuses as 'it's still under guarantee and therefore I'm not allowed to touch it . . .'; 'I don't like to work on that type of car . . .'; 'Maybe someone else can help you . . .'; 'You need a new engine . . .'; etc. Finally one mechanic decided to have a proper look at it and found the problem to be a minor one. He fixed it and it cost far less than was expected. He was honest, he had the know-how, he was committed to serve and he was friendly and helpful. The result — whenever that car, and our other cars give problems, we call him. We have a new favourite repair service garage — and many of our friends do too, as we have spread the word. He had gained our (and others') loyalty (and thus repeat business) for life.

Quality must come first — you must make the very best product, sell the very best product, or provide the best service you can. That is what wins customers, which in turn allows you to reap whatever benefits (profits) there are. Both you and the customer win. 'The sale merely consummates the courtship, then the marriage begins. How good the marriage is depends on how well the relationship is managed by the seller.'[4]

THE MARKETING CONCEPT

The surest way to make a great deal of money is to find out what people need and want, and then sell it to them at a profit. This statement says it all as marketing involves the selling of your business's products or services to your customers in order to satisfy their needs and to accomplish the objectives of your business. Marketing has thus two major objectives — to discover what the market wants and how that relates to what you are selling, and to discover where those people are whom you wish to serve. So, it is the process of identifying, reaching and selling to the potential customer which is called marketing, for example:[5]

'A retailer was overstocked with television sets at a time when new models were coming on the market. How to sell these suddenly outdated sets was a serious question. Finally, the retailer employed a salesman and equipped him with a hearing aid. Then the boss moved his desk to a balcony overlooking the salesroom.

When a customer came in to look at television sets, the salesman would fiddle with his hearing aid and call up to the boss on the balcony: "How much is this set?"

The boss would lean over the railing and call down: "It's just been reduced; it is R340,00!" The salesman would look a little uncertain, nod to the customer, fool with the hearing aid and then say; "It is R240,00; I think that is what he said."

Before long all the old-model television sets were sold.'

The idea of marketing is that a business ought, as far as possible, to start with its customers. The business should gear all its efforts to giving the customers what they need and want, at a profit to you. Marketing is an essential function because unless your business has a market or can develop a market for its products or services, all other business functions are futile. The small businessman normally performs all of the marketing functions, but his fundamental task is to assemble goods and services for the consumer at the latter's convenience. This constitutes the primary service of the small businessman — your community looks to you to furnish it with needed goods or services at reasonable prices at a convenient place, when they are wanted. You are consequently forced to estimate in advance what the demands of the community will be and you must be prepared to fill those needs as exactly as you

251

can. To sell successfully, you must first buy successfully. This is perhaps the most difficult retail function, since success or failure depends to a considerable degree upon your buying skill. Effective buying calls for a knowledge of the needs of customers and of the best sources of supply. You must constantly exercise judgement as to what to buy, from whom and when, and what price to pay. Selling, likewise, is an important function. In fact, assuming you have performed your buying function successfully, it is evident that your ultimate success depends on your ability to sell, and the risk arising from the ownership of goods and the necessity of selling them at a profit must be borne by you. If you do not have the products or services your market calls for, if styles change for example, you are in danger of losing the patronage of customers and of having unsaleable stock left on hand. Goods may deteriorate, or, having made sales, you may not be able to collect your money from debtors. Finally you, in common with other businessmen, may be the victim of a 'local economic depression'.

Essentially, marketing and finding a competitive edge make you different from your competitors. Your market is suggested by the nature of your product or service. Who are the logical users of what you have to offer? What is their sex? What is their age group? What is their language preference? Where do they live? What kind of jobs do they do? What is their monthly income? How much of their income do they spend on what you have to sell? In other words, choose your market by considering its potential — one which you can develop until you have dominated it and then do further planning to penetrate a new market — first a centimetre, then a metre and then a kilometre.

In order to design a marketing strategy, which is the making of careful plans and methods needed to have a competitive advantage over other similar businesses, it is firstly essential to find out what your competitors' and your own strengths, weaknesses, limitations, pressures, costs, products or services, and marketing strategies are. Probably your best opportunity is to identify a market not well served by your competitors. However, to be marketing conscious you need to be constantly concerned about the image of your business. In other words, check periodically in order to determine what kind of image the business has. You can do so by thinking of your business the way customers view it. In other words, how it is and how it should be. The difference, if any, leaves a gap that should be attended to. You could also do this by asking yourself such questions as: Is my business doing all that it possibly can to be customer orientated? Can customers find what they want, when they want it, and where they want it at a competitive price? Do my employees and myself make sure that customers' requirements are satisfied and that they leave with a feeling toward the business that will bring them back again? The necessity of being on the lookout for danger signals cannot be over-emphasized. The most commonly known ones are:

★ old customers no longer visit the business (it may happen that you found that you were wondering what happened to John as you never see him anymore. There may be a reason. Phone him up and ask him why, and do what is necessary to regain him as a customer);
★ traffic (pedestrian and vehicle) in front of your shop has lessened;
★ business sales are down this month compared to the same month of the previous year, and sales for the year to date are down from the same period last year;
★ employees are slow in greeting customers;
★ employees' personal appearance is not neat;
★ many customers walk out of the shop without buying;
★ complaints are increasing — both from customers and employees;
★ customers return goods more often than they should; and
★ sales people lack knowledge of the business's merchandise.

Once problems have been identified, the next step is to set specific marketing objectives. In other words, decide precisely what you want to achieve (or correct) and what are you going to do to achieve the objective set? Most businesses are looking for continuing success and they achieve this only through satisfying customers — and they have to do that in the face of their competitors. Marketing objectives have to be targets which can actually be achieved by advertising or promotional efforts. For example, increasing sales is not an advertising objective, although it is something to which advertising can and should contribute. Marketing rests on a simple philosophy: a business cannot succeed by selling products or services that are not aimed to serve and satisfy a particular market. You have people coming to your business and you have to keep those people happy and make sure they come back again and again. Marketing therefore focuses on what the customer wants as opposed to selling which focuses on the need of the seller. For example, if a customer needs a car serviced before 12h00 and you can satisfy his request, you will have a happy customer. Therefore, if you are marketing orientated, you are not so much concerned with what suits you, but rather with what suits the customer.

The marketing and sales concepts can be illustrated as in the table below. The sales concept starts with the business's existing products or services and involves the task of using personal selling and promotion to stimulate a profitable volume of sales. The marketing concept starts with the business's existing and potential customers and their needs and tries to build its profits by creating meaningful value satisfaction.

Concept	Focus	Means	End
Sales concept	Products services,	Personal selling, promotion, advertising	Profit through sales volume
Marketing concept	Customer needs	Service, innovation (the provision of better and more economic goods and services)	Profit through customer satisfaction

The adoption of the marketing concept in a service business is vital for success, especially when one considers that the buyer always has the option of doing the job himself, or may have a friend who can do it. He can even find a book on the shelf showing him how to perform the service you offer. On the service seller's side, most sellers think of themselves as creators, producers, professionals, or specialists — not marketers of a service. However, no matter how qualified you are to do a specific trade, you must also be an expert on the selling of your services. Thus, the special problem facing your small service business is that customers often believe they can do it themselves and your task is to convince them that they will be better off if they let you do it for them. Although you have to have a high degree of professional competence in doing the job, you also have to bend and shape your service and performance to the specific needs of the customer.

Inflexibility in serving customer needs can be disastrous, as illustrated by an entrepreneur who operated (the past tense is used because he is no longer in business) a small contracting business. He was a superior plumber, which even his competitors acknowledged. He had worked for his father and had taken over the business when his father retired. His attitude toward customers was shown by comments such as 'I don't have customers, I deal with contracts', 'I'm so good that the people will always come to me'; and 'I know what is best for them'. The result of this attitude was that he was usually late in completing work ('I'm the best, they will wait for me', he would say). He seldom took the time to explain his work or answer questions. Word went around that he was cold and indifferent toward his customers. He also failed to recognize some changes in the building industry as far as products were concerned — from steel and copper pipes to plastic pipes. And, increasingly consumers found they could do many of the plumbing jobs themselves. When he eventually found out about this, his reaction was: 'Let them, they will in the long run find out they would have been better off with a professional like me.' He did not recognize he had marketing problems and went bankrupt while waiting for the long run to arrive. Entrepreneurs of this type may be experts at solving technical problems, but their businesses fail because they refuse to adopt the correct marketing concept.

A subtle but extremely valuable promotional advantage for service businesses exists because of the personal contact they have with customers. Upon successful completion of the service — particularly if your customer sees significant value from your personal attention — you can benefit from the referral form of promotion. This offers one of the easiest, least costly and most effective tools in marketing. You simply ask the satisfied customer to recommend your service to friends who could benefit from it. You may even ask your customer personally to contact a prospective customer. After this contact has been made, you follow it up with a sales call. In contrast to product marketers, it is the personal involvement of buyer and seller in the service transaction that makes the referral form of promotion a natural and effective tool for you to use.

Remember that consumers always have the alternative of doing services themselves. However, they often perform tasks that a service business could do better or faster. And the need for the service goes unrecognized by potential buyers until the service becomes available. This is why the reaction of the consumer to a new business is often 'Why didn't I think of that idea?' However, consumers will always want more of a good service than the entrepreneur can supply. This is a 'when-it-rains-it-pours' problem unique to the service business. A product manufacturer can satisfy additional demand by adding extra shifts and a retailer can buy enough of a product to be in stock, but the capacity problem for services is not so easily solved because consumers usually buy the time of the entrepreneur. However, running into the capacity problem is a sure sign that your service fills a real need.

Some suggestions for anticipating and dealing with the capacity problem are: firstly, become an expert in the management of your own time; and secondly, schedule service work carefully and take on new clients selectively in order to prevent becoming overcommitted. Do not rush or try to be all things to all men unless you have the people to do all the jobs coming your way. Those you do serve must be completely satisfied since so much of your future business will depend on favourable word-of-mouth advertising. You should begin selecting and training a team in the early stages of operation who will be as proficient and reliable as you are in providing the service you offer. However good you want to appear in front of customers, don't make promises. In other words, don't say you will do it tomorrow or that the products ordered will be here tomorrow if you have the slightest idea or feeling that it might not happen. Rather say 'as soon as possible' and if you deliver the next day, the customer will be pleased and recommend your business to others.

Remember that a customer's dissatisfaction with one element of the service may lead to dissatisfaction with the entire service. There is a tendency for customers to remember any negative aspect of a service and to allow this to overshadow the positive satisfaction they have received. For example, an entrepreneur whose accounting practice was growing rapidly suddenly found that his volume of business was falling off. He finally found out why when a client complained about the telephone answering device he had installed. He asked other clients about it and they confirmed that, although pleased with his work, they were put off by the mechanical impersonal response and as a result hesitated to call him. Many people find it difficult to talk to a tape. In the service business, if consumers don't always have something tangible in hand to remind them of the value they received for their money, they will often recall and be guided in their relationship by their most recent personal experience with the seller. Value for money must be the alpha and omega of your actions in order to satisfy customers.

Quality and value Philip B. Crosby, in his book *Quality is Free* has two definitions of quality: firstly, 'getting people to do better all the worthwhile things they ought to be doing anyway'; and secondly, 'conformance to requirements'.[6] By 'people' he means top management (owner-manager) as well as the lower levels (employees) of the organisation. He is furthermore of opinion that the second definition enables a businessman to manage the maintenance of quality. So, whenever you see the word 'quality', read 'conformance to requirements'.[7] What it says is that quality is determined by the customer — the goods and service your customers wish to have and which will satisfy their needs. If you know your customers personally and if you know their needs, you will be able to determine their standard of quality. If you know that, you know what to provide them with, because quality is

257

what your customers are prepared to pay for. Quality higher than they need (considering their life-style and income per month) just pushes the price of the product up unnecessarily. This result in no sales and obsolete stock on hand. If a Mercedes conforms to all the requirements of a car (as determined by the customer), then it is a quality car. When someone says that something has 'low quality', question that person until you determine just exactly what he or she means. And then get the right goods or service, but first listen carefully to the customer. On the other hand, if you underestimate the quality of your customers, you are going to lose their support which is just as disadvantageous. There should be a close working relationship between yourself, the supplier and the customer. The supplier can often give you valuable advice as to the quality of the products you should sell. Furthermore, the only great quality product, by definition, is the one that sells. Sell quality goods at a reasonable profit, treat your customers like human beings and they will always come back for more. The customer is the most important person ever — whether you deal with him in person or by mail. However, quality starts by loving what you do (serving the customer). If this is not the case, the customer will remain an elusive target. Quality can be measured —just watch the effect on your business of an unhappy customer or the effect of a happy customer. Your employees need to know that poor quality in the hands of the customer will cost them their jobs — if there is no sale (repeatedly) there is no job.

Peter Drucker gives this advice: 'Find out who is your customer (the actual customer and the potential customer)? Where is he? How does he buy? How can he be reached?'[8] The question you may ask is: 'Why?' The answer is that you can get hold of the customer to show him that you are interested in doing business with him. You want and need him as your customer to stay in business. And once he has entered through the doors of your business — for the business's sake, your sake and your employees' sake — treat him as your most valuable asset (which he is). Furthermore, ask yourself what is of real value to the customer? What does he look for when he buys a product? Consider the story below:[9]

At a seminar for executives of companies that make scientific instruments, the wife of the president of one company (she is fully involved in its operations) related this tale. A friend of hers was about to buy a washing machine; she recommended that her friend buy Brand X. The reason was simple: in her long experience with Brand X machines, she had never had a problem. Her friend, also part of a die-hard engineer "rational" family, said unequivocally, "No." She was going to buy GE, as she had always done. "Why?" "Well," said the friend, "when they've broken down in the past, GE repair people have arrived immediately." The recommender of Brand X replied, "Yes, but mine has never broken down!" Her friend's last word (after all, she was the buyer): "I don't care. It might." '

This story illustrates the fact that the customer also considers service as part of the value she receives. The speed with which a customer can obtain service if something goes wrong, the quality of the service and its costs have become major determinants in the buyer's decision. The customer does not always consider price as value. In other words, quality is not just price alone — it is quality service, value for money and the best product that will satisfy the want and need of the customer. The customer is buying benefits (what the product can do for him or her as well as the relationship and service after the sale is made).

It all boils down to the fact that having well-trained employees (with product knowledge as well as the know-how in being of service to customers in all aspects), plus the right quality products, plus satisfied customers is good defence against competition (which will lead to obtaining a greater share of the market). A satisfied customer can be of great assistance to you and your business by spreading the word — provided, of course, the words are good. Always remember that you cannot be retrenched by anybody as you are your own boss, but your customers can put you out of business if they do not receive the treatment they expect from you. A customer is a person with a need and it is your 'business' to satisfy that need.

You should always be on the lookout for ways to improve your service in order to keep your loyal customers and win some new ones. One happy customer can bring many new ones.

Tony Factor, veteran discounter in South Africa, interviewed by David Pincus from the *Entrepreneur*, a monthly magazine for small business, gave quite a bit of advice concerning customer relations. Tony Factor's recipe: 'Let customers shout and scream and then give them tea.'[10]

'It costs lots of money to get customers into your shop. You have to have the right stock at the right time and your premises have to be right and be in the right spot for him to come to you. All this costs money.'

So strong is Tony Factor's belief in good customer relations that he would sooner fire a salesman for insulting a customer than for stealing R20 from the till.

'The R20 the salesman has slipped out of the till isn't even chicken feed. I am not trying to excuse theft, but viewed logically he can, if he is a good salesman, make up that R20 many times in one day, but if he insults a customer he has squandered your investment. It costs lots of money to get customers into your shop. In addition, you have spent a lot of money on advertising and invested no one knows how much in establishing your own credibility to entice him to come into your shop as a serious buyer. If a salesman then insults or antagonises your customer, and he leaves, you have lost all that; you have lost that complete investment. There is no chance of him ever coming back to you. It happened once where I told the saleswoman to go to my office to collect her cheque as it will be cheaper to replace her and the product than the customer.

Your loss does not stop here. It is compounded. Your erstwhile customer is now a very angry person who, as soon as he gets back to his office or home explodes and tells about how he was insulted — and probably embellishes the story as well. By the time he has finished telling his tale of woe there are probably twelve other people who have made a mental note to avoid coming into your shop. So, you have not lost one customer. You have now lost thirteen.

We are all guilty of kicking customers out of our shops. Everyone in retail does it. Customers leave our shops because of the things we retailers do and say and because of the things we don't do or say. We sometimes let them walk around our shops looking for someone to serve them until they get tired and leave, feeling they have been brushed off. Sometimes the goods are not up to standard or are not displayed attractively enough and they leave, mentally labelling the shop as a tatty operation. Sometimes the goods advertised have been sold out by the time they arrive, so they leave, thinking they are the victims of a confidence trick. If a customer leaves your shop with that sort of impression of you or your business, you also have no chance of getting him back. You can advertise in full colour in the most expensive newspapers and magazines. You can be genuine in claiming that you have cut your prices to below cost, but that customer won't believe a word you say. It will be something personal. He will argue that you let him down and that there will be nothing to prevent you from letting him down again. Your very name will be anathema to him. When he hears it, it will strengthen his resolve to never come into your shop again. It takes a lifetime to build a good reputation and goodwill and a single moment to destroy it.

In my operation there is a golden rule. Any complaint that cannot be satisfied by a salesman must be referred to me — and I am the only one in the organization who is allowed to be rude to a customer. But in more than 25 years of dealing with the public, I have had to be rude to only two people. The public is usually reasonable. Its complaints may be reasonable or unreasonable, but they are still complaints and must be treated as such. They are problems that must be solved if you want to stay in business. An apology, a refund or an exchange is generally all they want, and it doesn't cost all that much. It is much cheaper than losing a customer. There is no right or wrong formula in handling the public. There is only success or failure. When customers complain, they are doing you the favour of communicating with you, so listen and learn, because without your customers you do not have a business. In fact, it is our customers who teach us our business. My recipe — let them shout and scream and give them tea. The more they shout and scream the more you must smile and understand that they have a problem. Whatever went wrong probably went wrong at home. He had to travel all the way into town to shout at you. All the way to your shop he has been cooking, so let him shout at you, right or wrong, because in the end you will be friends — and if it means replacing a toaster that packed up out of its guarantee period, replace it. You can't buy goodwill for the price of the replacement of a toaster.

I believe my motivation programme is a bridge-building programme. When a customer comes in to buy a refrigerator, for example, he or she has dreamt about it, has schemed for it and has probably saved for it. It is the salesman's job to build a bridge between that dream and its realization. A motivated salesman can build that bridge. An unmotivated one builds a wall between the customer and his dream of owning a brand new fridge. The customer has fun spending his money; it is our job to help him enjoy it. That is the golden rule of selling. People cannot do anything else with their money but spend it. Even when they save, they save to spend it.

Furthermore, never yell at your number two. If I shout at my number two, he will yell at his number two and it will go all the way down the line to the salesman who will yell at the customer, who is his number two. But the customer can say "and the best of British to you" and walk out, and that comes all the way back up the line to the turnover column and the profit column.'

It is all part of commitment to deliver a fast and reliable service to every customer, every time — treat every customer as if he or she is one in a million.

Generally, all people are nice people, but everyone has 'off days' when they are bothered (especially on days when they have too much to do in town in too short a space of time). Your employees should be aware of this and must try to take full advantage of the tired and hot customer by perhaps just offering him a chair, a glass of cold water, or a cup of tea. The point is to make the customer feel better. However, employees of the business should remember that when a customer is irritated his irritation is not aimed at them. In all likelihood he is perplexed about something, and is thus not really attacking you or the employee, but the business and the situation he's upset about, or it is some problem connected with the business's products or services. The best remedy is to answer the customer with a calm and courteous response. Avoid what they call 'power games'. Get to the cause of the problem, work out a solution *with* the customer, and get agreement thereon.

When dealing with customers' problems you can of course also be unhelpful and just shrug your shoulders, but if you take it as an opportunity to get back rapport with the customer by doing something special, you form a lasting impression — one the customer will never forget, and that will increase loyalty. An example of doing something special by applying recovery skills is shown in this incident:

Someone once sent on four consequent month-ends, an account to a client whose initials and surname were identical to another client's who had a high outstanding amount. The customer kept returning the account every month with an accompanying letter saying that it was addressed to the wrong person. The employee did not believe him, until the client came in person to sort the matter out. The employee felt terrible for disbelieving the customer and not making the effort to confirm what he said. Something had to be done she felt, as he was a reputable client. She sent him a dozen roses with a note reading: 'Please forgive me: I'm terribly sorry for the inconvenience caused.' The business had many more opportunities to serve this customer.

Some Do's in dealing with customer complaints are:

- Listen carefully to the customer's complaint to make sure that you fully understand what is wrong.
- Show the customer that you understand how he feels.
- Thank the customer for taking the trouble to come and complain, and apologize for the inconvenience.
- If you can, explain to the customer what has caused the problem.
- Tell the customer what you are able to do to sort out the problem.
- Ask the customer whether your suggestions will solve the problem.
- Pass the customer on to the owner-manager if you don't know how to correct what is wrong.
- Be as pleasant as possible.
- Control yourself — do not lose your temper or be cheeky.
- If you have not got what the customer asks for, try to suggest an alternative.

Below follows a list of ideas and advice in respect of customer service. If carried out with real conviction, they can make a great deal of difference to the destiny of your business:

1. Print on all your invoices, receipts and other documents, something that will make the customer aware that you are appreciative of his business: 'We appreciate your business'; 'We enjoy selling to you'; 'Thank you for supporting us'; etc.

2. You can always render a good customer service to your clients by seeing to it that the exterior outlook of your business is clean and attractive. Customers are proud to associate themselves with a business that has a good public image. The exterior outlook of your shop can also be regarded as an 'invitation card' to potential customers.

3. The interior of the shop needs the same, if not more attention than the exterior. Purchasing is not always a pleasant experience for customers as they must part with their hard earned money. It is, therefore, important for you to create a pleasant atmosphere for customers in order to neutralize this unpleasantness. Creating a pleasant atmosphere can be done in several ways:

- Floors should be kept clean and in good condition;
- There should be good lighting in order to see the goods properly;
- Tidy up the checkout areas;
- Exits should not be congested;
- Merchandise should always be up to standard;
- Related products should be grouped together so that the customer does not have to hunt for certain items;
- Use clear price tickets and price indicators;
- All merchandise should be within reach of customers;
- Always keep shelves full, etc.

4. The equipment that is used in a business can also contribute to good customer service, such as cash registers and the effective utilization thereof by personnel, especially during peak periods. It is these small things that play an important role in establishing good customer service and relations.

5. Through advertising, you can render a special kind of customer service. An advertisement enables the customer to decide before entering the shop whether it will be worthwhile to visit your business. By advertising, you are also telling your market that you are not ashamed of your prices and products or services. If you advertise, you must be prepared. Sufficient stock of the advertised products must be available and it must be well displayed. If prices were stipulated in the advertisement, they must always correspond with those on the products in the shop.

6. Never display stock on the floor as it is regarded by the customer as inferior. As far as perishable goods are concerned it is important for you to look at the expiry dates of such products. Nothing can spoil the relationship between you and the customer more than the latter coming home with a litre of sour milk instead of fresh milk.

7. Greet as many customers as possible by name. (We all like to be called by our names and not just addressed as 'you'. Do try to remember and use their names — it adds a personal feeling.)

8. Have a personal word or two with customers when possible.[7]

9. Greet customers immediately they enter the shop even though they may have to wait for service.
10. Take the greatest care to assure the utmost courtesy in handling customers, even the difficult ones. All staff members should avoid giving a flat 'no' to a request for merchandise not in stock.
11. Give special consideration to the tired shopper.
12. Avoid the patronizing phrase 'we can let you have...'; say instead 'we will see that you get...'.
13. Express genuine regret when unable to supply customers' requirements.
14. Consult customers regarding ways of improving service.
15. Sell on quality, service, courtesy, customer listening and not merely on price. (Price will bring 'shoppers' but not 'customers' — Izzy Cohen.)
16. Always look for the good in a customer and compliment him or her thereon (a new hairstyle, a photo in the local newspaper, a new baby, etc.). Never miss an opportunity to say a word of congratulations upon anyone's achievements.
17. Listen to what customers have to say. Be genuinely interested in other people. Be a good listener as people appreciate an attentive listener. Show respect for another's opinion.
18. Provide professional working conditions if you want your employees to act like well-trained professionals. 'Looks' count a lot. You should aim for well-dressed, clean and neat people, fresh flowers in the entrance, clean floors, etc. Look for that difference from your competitors. It has been put this way: 'We don't seek to be one thousand percent better in any one thing. We seek to be one percent better at one thousand things.' You have to seek differences — a snazzier look or way of doing things, better delivery, etc. Your objective should be to differentiate.
19. Communicate with the disgruntled customer. It can be all over if you just say you are sorry — by mail, by phone or in person. The customer will become a top customer and a better friend than ever before. Spend time with him on the phone and if possible, interview him. Find out the cause of the problem and correct it immediately.

20. Find out from the customer of what quality the service was. Did anything you did bug him? How are you doing? What else can you do for him? Where does he think you can improve? Was he greeted when he arrived? Was he served in a friendly manner? Did he find what he was looking for? Design a post card with your address and a stamp on it with such questions, and enough space for the customer to comment on your service and make other general comments — feedback is important and the faster you can receive feedback from those you serve, the faster you can improve your business and rectify what is wrong. Make sure they recognize any improvements you have made.

SUMMARY AND CONCLUSION

Be alert to give service. Mark H. McCormack has a very strong point as far as aspects of service and promises are concerned:[11]

Business promises are made all the time, and almost as often they are broken — needlessly creating a horrible impression. If you say you are going to do something, do it. If you can't do it, think it is more trouble than it is worth, or don't want to do it, then don't say you will. Make up any excuse, but don't even say "I will try". At the very least, that leaves the other party with the impression that you have tried — and failed.'

What counts is what your business as a whole can do for others. Speak and act as if everything you do for your customers is a genuine pleasure. Be genuinely interested in other people. We are all given a personality, a distinctive personal identity which makes each one of us different from anyone else. Therefore, use your personality to create a personality for your business. Your business's personality will depend a great deal on your attitude towards the customer. In addition, the maturing of this personality (or individuality) of your business and better human relations is dependent on another facet — perseverance. You will need to apply the information given to you with great determination to make the most of those qualities that are already within you. Communicating with your customers is important. This means that you must tell your customers about your business's services and products, ask your customers about their needs, listen to their answers and understand them. It has been said: 'A good listener is not only popular eveywhere, but after a while he knows something.' You need to ask your customers about matters relating to your service and the products you sell. You will gain valuable information which you need to improve the performance of your business. You also have a responsibility towards your customers, and your first responsibility is to win their confidence and to serve them in the best possible way. Be careful this does not mean what *you* consider best, but what *they* consider best. Conform to their requirements. Only then will they be loyal to you, support your business and remain faithful in that. If you act in all your dealings with the customer with total integrity, the rest (increased market share, profits and growth) will follow. Try to outdo your competitors by being a bit different and that much better in everything you do for the customer, as he decides where he is going to make his next purchase. By putting effort into the 'serving of customers', your business will gain a personality which will ensure follow-on business, business success to you and job security to your employees.

It is all a matter of reciprocity (mutual agreement). In short this means: 'I (the customer) supports you (the business) because you provide what I want, need and desire.' Finally, there is sometimes panic in the 'small business's stable' because it is thought that big business has all the advantages such as strong capital reserves and specialized personnel for promotion (advertising and personal selling). There is no need to think this way because the small businessman has compensating advantages such as simplicity and flexibility. The president of a small western New York steel mill once remarked:[12]

'If we get a complaint, or a customer calls us about a problem, I am in the customer's office the next morning with my sales manager and maybe one of our technical men. By the time one of our larger competitors would have begun to study the problem or appointed a committee to look into it, we have already solved the problem or taken care of the complaint and maybe walked off with another order.'

BIBLIOGRAPHY

* Donald Currie. Sales — the life-blood of a business. *Entrepreneur* 1985; **4**(7): 10.

* David Pincus. The ability to get customers to call again. *Entrepreneur* 1984; **3**(5): 12, 13.

* Teach your customers to complain. *Entrepreneur* 1983; **2**(4): 9, 10.

* Mike Timewell. Service: the competitive edge. *Entrepreneur* 1983; **2**(4): 14.

* Franz Conradie. Klantediens is die antwoord. *Entrepreneur* 1985; **4**(2): 12, 13.

* J.K. Lasser Tax Institute. *How to Run a Small Business*. 1982. McGraw-Hill, New York: 97–102.

* Thomas J. Peters, Robert H. Waterman, Jr. *In Search of Excellence*. 1982. Harper & Row, New York: 156–199.

* Thomas J. Peters, Nancy K. Austin. *A Passion for Excellence*. 1985. Collins, Glasgow London: 8–111.

NOTES

[1] Thomas J. Peters, Robert H. Waterman, Jr. *In Search of Excellence*. 1982. Harper & Row, New York: 157.

[2] D. Ogilvy. *Confessions of an Advertising Man*. 1964. Longmans, Green, London.

[3] Advertisement words of Video Arts Inc., Illinois. Source: *Training, The Magazine of Human Resources Development* 1986; **23**(6): 16.

[4] Thomas J. Peters, Nancy K. Austin. *A Passion for Excellence*. 1985. Collins, Glasgow London: 70. (Reproduced with permission.)

[5] Ralph L. Woods. *The Modern Handbook of Humor*. 1967. McGraw-Hill, New York: 60.

[6] Phillip B. Crosby. *Quality is Free*. 1979. McGraw-Hill, New York: 17. (Reproduced with permission.)

[7] Idem, 17.

[8] Peter F. Drucker. *The Practice of Management*. 1969. Heinemann, London: 49. (Reprinted by permission of William Heinemann Limited.)

[9] Thomas J. Peters, Nancy K. Austin. *A Passion for Excellence*. 1985. Collins, Glasgow London: 72. (Reproduced with permission.)

[10] David Pincus. Let customers shout and scream and then give them tea. *Entrepreneur* 1983; October: 5, 6. (Reproduced with permission.)

10 ADVERTISING AND PROMOTIONS

'Doing business without advertisng is like winking at a girl in the dark. You know what you are doing, but nobody else does.'

Steuart Henderson Britt[1]

'You have to have something to say before advertising can be effective.'[2]

'If you believe in your business and want to build it into something to be proud of ... advertise it.'[3]

INTRODUCTION

The overall objective of advertising and sales promotional efforts is that of getting prospective customers to add 'a visit to your business' to their shopping lists. Customers are hard to get, especially for a business that has just started, because the business has not yet got credentials, a record of success (fulfilling the needs of the people or businesses your business seeks to serve), and a real reputation. Thus in a new business you will probably be underpaid for some time as it is probably struggling for its life. In order to close the gap between being underpaid and being well-paid advertising, personal selling efforts and promotional efforts should be used to place yourself, your business, your employees and your products or services in competition. It means keeping your eyes and advertising messages focused on the target market and putting whatever profits are made from increased sales to further use of the business in order to build the kind of business which would ultimately attract and hold the attention of the market you serve and wish to penetrate. As stated a few times in this book, the primary objective of business is to make sales which yield a profit — at least in the long run. Certainly sales are the lifeblood of every business, and these sales must bring a profit or the business will close or just disappear. Advertising must be fitted into this business framework of sales and profits if the business is to accomplish its objectives. Your advertising should convey your message to an area where sales will most likely result.

It should at all times be remembered that those people from among the public who are attracted, who decide to buy, and to later return for some more buying, are the very life of a business. Also, whether you know it or not, you are already advertising — your building is an advertisement, your cashiers' behaviour and their general appearance, your stationery, your delivery truck and its driver. These are all part of advertising because they contribute in forming an impression in the mind of the consumer which will lead to the ultimate decision — whether to act favourably towards the business or not. A woman who continues to buy certain goods or services from the same shop year after year and a man who always buys the same type of car from a specific garage are said to have favourable attitudes towards the business.

Remember, big businesses got big by advertising and are still advertising to maintain their position. Small businesses, therefore, need to advertise to become big, and all businesses need to advertise to stay ahead of their competitors. However, although many a small business is acting on the assumption that every business should advertise, they do so on a hit and miss basis or a little now and a little later. Such an irregular programme of advertising lacks objectives.[4] But before any objectives can be set for a programmed effort to increase sales, you need to be informed that there is a difference between advertising objectives and marketing objectives. Marketing objectives would include such objectives as to increase the market share you have, expand the whole market, achieve a sales target, and win back lost customers or gain new ones. Advertising is mainly used to inform customers (or the market) of the availability of your products or services and the use they can make of them as well as convincing the market that your products or services are superior to those of your competitors. If advertising is to be a means by which to achieve marketing objectives, the advertising objectives should be: to create, maintain or improve the image of the product or service or that of the business as a whole; to stimulate a desire to try the product or service; to reinforce or increase a feeling of loyalty to the product or service or the business as a whole; and to convey specific information of a persuasive kind.

There are various mental stages through which people usually pass on their way toward making a decision to buy, and advertising and communicating informative and persuasive ideas to prospective customers, can influence the progression from one mental stage to the next. The closer the customer then comes to the commitment stage, all other things being equal, the more likely he will be to make a buying decision with respect to a given brand or business. The stages can be said to be the following:[5]

- Ignorance — He is not aware that the business exists.
- Awareness — He knows the business exists but does not know what product or service benefits it has to offer.
- Comprehension — He is fully aware of the business and what it has to offer but has yet to formulate a firm conviction as to how these benefits can satisfy his needs.
- Conviction — He is able to relate the business's product or service benefits to his own need situation and feels certain that he has sufficient knowledge of the business to make a conclusive evaluation, either positive or negative.
- Commitment — He makes a definite buying decision in the form of a purchase, a purchase order, or a pledge to make a future purchase as the need arises.

PROMOTING SALE OF PRODUCTS AND SERVICES

The basic task of advertising is to sell, or to assist sales. However, advertising is not the only available method for making sales, nor can it do the complete job. Advertising, merchandising, sales promotion, personal selling, customer relations, public relations and publicity should be elements of any marketing strategy. Advertising then, can help to sell.

It does this to a substantial extent, by giving information — what the business is, what it does, where it can be found. A planned and continuing programme of communication with customers and the community or public should be created around a target market. It should be used to gain a competitive edge. Such communication develops awareness, interest in, and desire for a product or service.

However, the average small businessman does little advertising throughout the year and when he does advertise, he does so generally in the busy season or around holiday times. Retail advertising is 'now' advertising, designed to move stock fast and to increase floor traffic quickly. Therefore, it is important that all your retail advertising contains some kind of promotional 'hook'. If you select the right hook and bait it with a tempting offer you will reel the customers in. There should always be a time limit set so as to induce action. Your headline should appeal to the potential buyer's self-interest. In other words, it should promise a benefit. A promise of some benefit is vital as it is the main thing that will make the reader want to read on or not, and buy or not. Words that work exceptionally well for headlines in retail advertising are:

Free information/demonstration	Hurry
SALE	Last Chance
HALF-PRICE	IT'S HERE
SAVE	Just Arrived
Two for the Price of One	A magic offer
SENSATIONAL	Not to be refused
BARGAIN	QUICK
INTRODUCING	ANNOUNCING
SUDDENLY	STARTLING
How to	THE TRUTH ABOUT

How much to spend on advertising There is no easy answer to the question of how much to set aside for advertising. The decision to advertise involves a risk because it implies putting money aside now against future sales, and thus it is regarded as some form of investment. Decisions to advertise are like decisions to invest. The difference is that the result of advertising is peculiarly uncertain. What you would like to invest in advertising, and what you can afford are seldom the same. Spending too much is obviously an extravagance, but spending too little can be just as bad in terms of lost sales. This means that advertising should be approached with caution and that reserve funds should be ready to carry you over if it fails to deliver. The idea of having a reserve in the advertising budget is a valuable one. However, the fact remains: if you want to build sales, it is almost certain you will need to advertise.

A number of methods for working out an advertising budget can be used:[6]

*   *Percentage-of-sales method.* The sales budget is the foundation of all business. It affects profits and costs, including the advertising investment. By using the percentage-of-sales method, you keep your advertising in a consistent relation to your sales volume — which is what your advertising should be primarily affecting. You can guide your choice of a percentage-of-sales figure by finding out what other businesses in your line are doing, as such percentages are fairly consistent within a given type and size of business. Knowing what the ratio for your type of business is will help to assure you that you will be spending proportionately as much or more than your competitors; but remember that these industry averages are not binding. Your particular situation may dictate that you want to advertise more or less than your competition. Average may not be good enough for you. You may want to out-advertise your competitors and be willing to cut into short term profits to do so. Growth requires investment. Thus, if you want to expand your market share, you will probably need to use a larger percentage of sales than the industry average. You can calculate your advertising budget as a percentage of your anticipated sales for the next year. The most common pitfall of this method is being too optimistic that your business will continue to grow. You must always keep general business trends in mind. However, using this method is helpful, quick and easy, and it ensures that your advertising budget is not way out of proportion for your type of business.

*   *Fixed-Rand-per-unit method.* In this method you set aside a fixed sum for each unit of product to be sold, based on your experience and trade knowledge of how much

advertising it takes to sell each unit. That is, if it takes two cents worth of advertising to sell a case of canned vegetables and you want to sell 100 000 cans, you will probably plan to spend R2 000 on advertising them. You are then simply basing your budget on units of sale. This method is particularly useful in selling speciality goods such as washing machines, cars, etc. However, it becomes more difficult to apply this method when you have different kinds of products to advertise and must divide your advertising among them.

* *Matching the competitor's budget:* This assumes that you know what competitors are spending on advertising and that they know the proper amount to spend. In fact, this method is just a variation of percentage-of-sales.

Any of these methods may be used in the formulation and allocation of your advertising budget. Your advertising budget should be made flexible and you should have a reserve fund to deal with special circumstances such as the introduction of a new product, specials available, or unexpected competitive situations. All important advertising costs must be tied to results achieved.

Your first budget for advertising will be difficult to estimate in the sense that you do not have definite sales figures to base your projections on. By your next business year, however, you will have a more factual basis for budgeting than you had in your first year. Your plans will become more effective with each budget you draw up.

Media selection Every advertisement has to appear in some advertising media or other, even if it is only on a board next to the road or on the pavement. Usually you select a media by consulting your advertising budget to find out what limitations you have and what opportunities are open in various media (R30 000 won't get you very far on television, for example). Having money available is thus the limiting and deciding factor. Other factors to consider when deciding which media to use are: your own preference; the target population and size of the market; the type of product; and the activity of competitors (the media they use to compete in the same field). You should use the media that will suit the circumstances, as well as existing customers. Pay attention to the fact that some media are preferable to others for the message concerning the product or service, for example: radio carries only sound while newspapers and magazines can show pictures, radio is ideal for illiterate people. The radio follows listeners everywhere, in the home and on the road. If using the newspaper, try to place your advertisement in or close to the section in the newspaper where it will catch the eye of your kind of reader. If you are selling sport equipment, then you will place it in the sport pages, and cooking ware could go in the women's interest section. The availability of media varies. Retailers in small communities, for example, have fewer options than those in large cities. Media that could be considered are the following:

* newspapers;
* magazines;
* direct mail;
* outdoor advertising (store and outdoor signs);
* circulars (pamphlet distribution);
* radio advertising;
* speciality advertising (shopping bags, calenders, pencils, etc.);
* transport advertising (on vehicles);
* cinemas; and
* the telephone directory

Direct mail depends, primarily, on obtaining and managing effectively a selective mailing list. This offers a high degree of selectivity in a wide market. Direct mail is usually used by the businessman who can define specific markets and wishes to put a high impact campaign into operation and so influence the recipient to buy. Outdoor advertising has at times been described as the reminder medium and it reaches out to every segment of the market.

MEASURING THE RESULTS OF ADVERTISING

Measuring the results of advertising by comparing sales with advertising is a necessary function. You want to find out whether advertising is doing its job. Say your advertising is of the immediate response type with the objective to entice the potential customer to buy a particular product within a short period of time — today, tomorrow, next week, etc — it should be checked daily for results, as well as for a few weeks after the appearance of the advertisement. Other examples of immediate response advertising are: adverts which use price appeals in combination with clearance sales, special purchases, seasonal items, etc.[7]

As a small businessman you know that the money you spend on advertising must return enough sales and profits in additional business to justify the cost of advertising. It is therefore important to get a good idea about the results of your advertising. What results do you expect? Essentially, measuring results means comparing sales with advertising expenses, and thus it necessitates that you determine beforehand what you expect advertising to do for your business.

Immediate response advertising. In weighing the results of your immediate response advertisements, the following devices should be helpful:[8]

* *'Coupons brought in.* Usually these coupons represent sales of the product. When the coupons represent requests of additional information or contact with a salesperson, were enough leads obtained to pay for the ad? If the coupon is dated, you can determine the number of returns for the first, second, and third weeks.

* *Requests by phone or letter referring to the ad.* A "hidden offer" can cause people to call or write. Include — for example, in the middle of an ad — a statement that on request the product or additional information will be supplied. Results should be checked over a 1-week through 6-months or 12-months period because this type ad may have considerable carry-over effect.

* *Testing ads.* Prepare two ads (different in some way you'd like to test or set for different stations or broadcast times) and run them on the same day. Identify the ads — in the message or with a coded coupon — so you can tell them apart. Ask customers to bring in the coupon or to use a special phrase. Run two broadcast ads at different times or on different stations on the same day with different "discount phrases". Ask a newspaper to give you a "split run" — that is, to print "ad A" in part of its press run and "ad B" in the rest of the run. Count the responses to each ad.

* *Sales made of particular item.* If the ad is on a bargain or limited-time offer, you can consider that sales at the end of 1 week, 2 weeks, 3 weeks, and 4 weeks came from the ad. You may need to judge how many sales came from in-store display and personal selling.

* *Check store traffic.* An important function of advertising is to build store traffic which results in purchases of items that are not advertised. Pilot studies show, for example, that many customers who are brought to

the store by an ad for a blouse also bought a handbag. Some bought the bag in addition to the blouse, others instead of the blouse.

You may be able to use a local college or high school distributive education class to check store traffic. Class members could interview customers as they leave the store to determine: (1) which advertised items they bought, (2) what other items they bought, and (3) what they shopped for but did not buy.'

TYPES OF ADVERTISING

Attitude advertising *Attitude advertising* is the type you use to keep your business's name in the eyes of the public. Some people think of this type of advertising as 'image-building'. With this you remind people week after week about your regular merchandise or services or tell them about new or special services. Such advertising should create in the minds of your customers the attitude you want them to have about your business, merchandise, services and its policies. It is your 'reputation-builder'.

Attitude (or image-building) advertising is harder to measure than immediate response advertising because you cannot always attribute a specific sale to it. Its sales are usually created long after the advertisement appeared.

One approach in measuring attitude (or image-building) advertising is making your comparisons on a weekly basis. If you run an advertisement, for example, each week, at the end of the first week after the advertisement appears or is broadcast, compare that week's sales for the same week a year ago. At the end of the second week, compare your sales with those of the end of the first week as well as year-ago figures.[9]

'At the end of the *third week,* 1 month, 3 months, 6 months, and 12 months from the running of the ad, repeat the process even though additional ads may have appeared or been aired in the meantime. For each of these ads, you will also make the same type of comparisons. You will, of course, be measuring the "momentum" of all your ads as well as the results of a single ad.

After a time, you probably will be able to estimate how much of the results are due to the individual ad and how much to the momentum of all your advertising. You may then make changes in specific details of the ad to increase response.

277

When comparing sales increases over some preceding period, allowances must be made for situations that are not normal. For example, your experience may be that rain on the day an ad appears cuts its pulling power by 50 percent. Similarly, advertising response will be affected by the fact that your customers work in a factory that is out on strike.

Some of the techniques which you can use for keeping on top of and improving attitude advertising follow:

* *Repeat an ad.* If response to an ad is good, run it — without change — two or three times and check the responses of each appearance or broadcast against previous ones.

Keep repeating the process. Much advertising loses effectiveness because the advertiser doesn't keep reminding people. Repetition helps increase knowledge of, and interest in, the product. You can soon estimate how often you should repeat each ad — exactly or with minor changes.

* *Analyze all ads in relation to response.* Divide ads into at least two classes: high-response ads and low-response ads. Then look for differences between the two classes.

The time the ad was broadcast or run may be responsible for a particular response level. Other factors, however, may be just as influential as time or even more so, though in radio time is often crucial.

Consider the message and how well it was expressed. Did the copy stick to the theme or did it wander? If you used slogans, did they help make a point? For print, consider the effects of illustrations, type size, colour, and ad location. In broadcast, consider whether or not the voice of the person doing the ad or music used may have had an effect.

Emphasis on brand names should also be checked. Price figures should be analyzed. If price lines are involved either in the ad or in the merchandise line of which the advertised product is a part, you should consider them also.

Check the effect of the length of broadcast ads. Did you get the best results with 10-second, 30-second, or 60-second announcements?

Check the size of print ads. Size often has a bearing on response. As a general rule, the larger the ad, the larger the response.

Try to see a pattern of dominance. Your analysis of high-and-low response ads may show that certain details make the difference between a high or low response. Try to find the combinations which work best for your firm and merchandise.

Note changes occurring over time. A small retailer should never take a winning combination for granted. There is no single formula that will insure high response ads every time. Advertising changes. Therefore, you should watch the ads of others to see what changes are occurring. Continue to analyze your own ads, make small changes occasionally, and note any variations in response.

* *Listen to what people say about your ads.* In doing so, try to discover the mental framework within which any comment about your ad was made. Then try to find points which reinforce believability and a feeling that your product fulfils some wish or need.

However, you should not be misled by what people say. An ad can cause a great deal of comment and bring in practically no sales. An ad may be so beautiful or clever that as far as the customer is concerned the *sales* message is lost.'

Goodwill advertising *Goodwill advertising* is where you receive requests for advertising from all kinds of organizations including social groups, schools, churches, etc. Often, friends and relatives make these requests. From the view of maintaining good public relations, businessmen are frequently reluctant to turn them down.[10]

PLANNING FOR, AND DEVELOPING AN ADVERTISEMENT

The first step is to take a good look at the business and its customers. You will need to answer such questions as:[11]

★ What business am I in?
★ What quality of merchandise do I sell?
★ What kind of image do I want to project?
★ How do I compare with competition?
★ What customer services do I offer?
★ Who are my customers?
★ What are their income levels?
★ Why do they buy from me?

By profiling your business and your customers in this way, you will be better able to direct your sales message to those most likely to buy and thus make more effective use of your advertising money.

When you are developing an advertisement and trying to measure its effect, your success will depend on how well the advertisement has been planned. Certain things are basic essentials to planning and developing an advertisement:

279

★ Advertise products or services that have merit in themselves. Unless a product or service is good, few customers will make repeat business, no matter how much advertising the business does. Many people will not make an initial purchase of a shoddy item because of doubt or unfavourable word-of-mouth publicity. The advertisement that successfully sells inferior merchandise usually loses customers in the long run.

★ Ogilvy, Benson and Mather call your attention to the following:[12]

'Never write an advertisement which you would not want your own family to read. You wouldn't tell lies to your own family. Don't tell them to mine. If you tell lies about a product, you will be found out — either by some authority that will prosecute you or by the consumer who will punish you by not buying your product a second time. Good products can be sold by honest advertising. If you don't think the product is good, you have no business to be advertising it. If you tell lies, or weasel, you do your customer a disservice, you increase your load of guilt, and you fan the flames of public resentment against the whole business.'

★ Messages should be treated seriously: tell the people the exact facts about your merchandise and services. Ogilvy, Benson and Mather provide a few comments to put this point into perspective:[13]

'What you say is more important than how you say it. What really decides consumers to buy or not to buy is the content of your advertising. Your most important job is to decide what you are going to say about the product, what benefit you are going to promise. The selection of the right promise is so vitally important that you should never rely on guesswork to decide it. We use a number of research techniques to find out which is the most powerful. One such technique is to show consumers cards on which we have printed various promises, asking them to select the one which would be most likely to make them buy the product. Here are the results of one such test.

FACE CREAM

Cleans Deep into Pores	████████████████
Prevents Dryness	███████████████
Is a Complete Beauty Treatment	██████████
Recommended by Skin Doctors	███████████
Makes Skin Look Younger	████████

Prevents Make-up Caking
Contains Estrogenic
Hormones
Pasteurized for Purity
Prevents Skin from Ageing
Smooths Out Wrinkles

From this voting came one of Helena Rubenstein's most successful face creams. We christened it "Deep Cleanser", thus building the winning promise into the name of the product.'

★ Know exactly what you wish a particular advertisement to accomplish: in an immediate response advertisement, you want customers to come in and buy a certain item or items in the next few days. In attitude advertising, you decide what attitude you are trying to create and plan each individual advertisement to that end.

★ Plan the advertisement around one idea: each advertisement should have a single message. If the message needs reinforcing with other ideas, keep them in the background. If you have several important things to say, use a different advertisement for each one and run them on succeeding days or weeks.

★ Pick illustrations which are similar in character. Drawings, photos and layouts that are similar in character help people to recognize your advertising immediately. Give your advertising copy and layout a consistent personality and style.

★ Pick one format and stick to it. Using the same layout or the same radio format for newspapers or radio helps people to recognize your advertisements quickly. Using the same format or kind of type and illustrations also allow you to concentrate on the message when checking advertising response changes. Your layout should easily lead the reader's eye through the message from the art and headline through the copy to the price and signature.

★ Make the advertising copy easy to understand: Ogilvy gives this advice and comments; You cannot bore people into buying:[14]

'The average family is now exposed to more than 1 500 advertisements a day. No wonder they have acquired a talent for skipping the advertisements in newspapers and magazines, and going to the bathroom during television commercials.'

Show the benefit to the reader. Tell them how your product will benefit them. Consumers buy benefits not products. Get the main message in the first sentence, if you can. But do not try to pack the advertisement with reasons to buy — give the customers one primary reason, then back it up with two secondary reasons. Sentences should be short. Be direct. Go straight to the point.

Try out your script on somebody else or read it into a tape recorder. When you play the tape back, you will easily spot the phrases that are hard to understand (or believe): Your ears are better than your eyes at judging.

★ Use coupons for direct mail advertising response as often as possible: coupons give an immediate sales check. One food chain asked listeners to hand draw a coupon and bring it in for a free hamburger.

★ State a price or range of prices: Do not be afraid to quote high prices. If the price is low, support it with a statement which creates belief, such as clearance or special purchase.

★ Include the business's name, address, telephone numbers and business hours in the advert.

★ Make each word count: You could build the winning promise into the name of the product or service, or even the name of the business, for example: 'Speedy Exhaust'. People will only read the rest if the headline arouses their curiosity. End your headline with a lure to read on.

★ Back up your advertising with identifying material: If you are talking about a sale in your advertisement, make sure that it looks like it inside and outside your business. Use posters from manufacturers, create interesting displays and signwriting that ties in with your advertising theme. Make sure all else is ready for the sale — a well-lit business, clean products, clean floors, neat personnel with smiling faces, and sufficient products or enough people to carry out the service at good prices.

★ Timing is important. People get paid at the last week of the month — a good time to run an advertisement.

★ Photographs that do work are those which arouse the reader's curiosity. They are more believable than illustrations and more compelling. The customer may glance at the photograph and say to himself: 'What goes on here?' Then he reads your advertising copy to find out.

★ In your advertisement, depending on the nature of your product or service and the image you wish to create, you should be stressing quality, reliability, integrity and service rather than lower prices. A good example of such an advertisement is that of Sandown Motors:

Our Philosophy is simple: When you sell extraordinary cars you'd better have extraordinary back-up.

Simple to say. But very demanding in practice.
Because it means that we must be on our toes all the time. In every department.
From the time a vehicle is prepared prior to customer delivery to the times we service and maintain it.
And of course, all of that depends on the quality and dedication of the people we employ.
Our workshops are laid out and equipped to the stringent standards demanded by both Mercedes-Benz and Honda. Our staff, from service manager to workshop mechanics are kept abreast of the latest technical developments by constant updates and on-going training programmes.
All of which means you can rest assured of service back-up that is extraordinarily good.

 SANDOWN MOTORS Star Service is the least you can expect

PASSENGER CAR SERVICE CENTRES AT SANDTON CITY, 5C RIVONIA ROAD. ☎ 783-4675
AND MORNINGSIDE SHOPPING CENTRE, OUTSPAN AND RIVONIA ROADS. ☎ 783-7467

(Reproduced by the courtesy of Sandown Motors)

★ Use promotional ideas in your advertising: Retailers featuring products without the benefit of low prices, novelty or new features have found promotional techniques an excellent basis for their advertising. Action is the keynote for sales promotion, while merchandising ideas is the necessary prelude to action. If you can co-ordinate promotion with advertising and personal selling, you can usually increase shop traffic and thus produce good sales results. The first requirement is a sound selling idea such as a 'special sales' event. Ideas can be obtained by watching other businesses. However, creative potency is what counts in developing a promotional idea into sales results, for example:[15]

'Blumberg did such a fine business in his variety store that two rivals —Weinstein and Blitzburg — opened up establishments on either side. Moreover, the two new stores both erected massive signs offering extraordinary bargains. Blumberg thought it over for a few days and then simply put a still larger sign over his store. It read: MAIN ENTRANCE.'

SALES PROMOTION

Sales promotion consists of activities that have the purpose of making other sales efforts more effective. Creativity is probably the key to effective promotional efforts. One has to do some very creative thinking in order to come up with promotions which will really produce traffic and increase sales volume. However, promotional efforts all start with the preparation of a detailed three- to six-month promotion calender. Simply draw, for example, six columns (for six months) on a sheet of paper. At the top of each column write the name of each of the next six months then break down each column into four or five sections (Week 1, 2, 3, 4, 5). From your regular yearly calender enter in all the holidays for which you normally plan promotions. You will then find that there are many open weeks for which there is no ready-made theme. Your task now is to fill in all those empty spots on your promotion calender, choosing from a wide range of possibilities, including the more obvious ones, such as back-to-school or Christmas themes. You should also try to actually go beyond these obvious days and dig into the potential of your own distinctive promotions, for example: 'Secretaries' Week'; 'Bankers' Day' (target population will be all people working in the bank — or others in your market).

Once you have determined your themes, the next step is to fill in all the details — the amount of money to be spent on each promotion, the products or services you will feature, the advertising (if any) you will do and in which media it will be done, when and what stock will be bought, specific instructions to your sales people, etc. From such an effort a thorough promotional blueprint can be derived for boosting your sales. If it is all down on paper well in advance, you will have excellent directions to follow. There is no doubt that, early and thorough planning and co-ordination of all elements and involving all staff for ideas in each promotion are a definite 'yes' to promotional success. Remember, nothing ventured, nothing gained.

Below follows a number of promotional efforts to 'hook' people:[16]

★ Free theatre tickets if purchasing more than R50 worth of goods.
★ Treasure hunt promotion. In every department there are a few hidden items which have been knocked down to 20 cents. Come and find them.
★ Free gifts. A related gift like a tin of coffee with every set of cups and saucers is a good hook.
★ Two for the price of one. Buy one and get one for your best friend absolutely free. (This makes the customer feel like he is doing the friend a favour as well as getting a bargain.)
★ Short-term offers at a discount price are given added urgency if the customer must buy before a certain date.
★ The preview sale. Offers selected customers with well-kept accounts the chance to come along and buy before the new season's stock is announced.
★ The find-a-reason sale. Sales must have a reason to be believable: stocktaking, clearance, birthday, anniversary.
★ Free demonstration. This always attracts people, and a crowd draws others. Many people normally buy what is being demonstrated or disperse around the business to buy something else. Bring customers in to see something particular — a new vacuum cleaner for example.

Opportunities for retail and service promotions are as endless as your imagination and form a vital ingredient of advertising. Always think in terms of novel ways of offering what you already have for sale — price promotions are not always the answer, you also need a good 'hook'. Service businesses should however, concentrate mostly on refining their present offerings to their customers as clients tend to change service businesses mostly because of a dissatisfaction of some sort. Therefore, it is vital to pay strict attention to reliability, quality, availability of service, convenience, friendliness of personnel, promptness of delivery, etc.

PUBLICITY

The use of publicity to obtain favourable public opinion must be clearly understood as being a part of the whole public relations process. A widely known opinion of many people, within and outside the trade, is that public relations is regarded as the 'bulldust' business. This concept has probably been developed as the result of communications which contain 'false' information pertaining to the business and its actual performance within a particular area, town or country. So, words are as important as actions in determining what people think. This does not mean that there is anything unethical about publicity, but the point is that, when every business is saying 'Our products or services are best', there is a tendency amongst consumers to treat such a message with some scepticism and doubt. Probably from what they have heard from others who had dealings with the business before or what they have themselves experienced, or something the owner or employees themselves have said on occasion. It can be said that public opinion is made up of impressions which individuals form in their daily contacts with the owner-manager and his business. Therefore, it must be emphasized that you should be most concerned when people do not think highly of your business as a whole. And a sure fact to remember is that publicity cannot compensate for a poor product or service. What must be understood clearly is that people tend to interpret 'what is said' in the context of 'what is done'. Ethics, after all, is the fulfilment or violation of people's expectations. Therefore, you should always strive to put forward the kind of publicity that will accurately portray the true situation and any kind of 'trade puffery' should be avoided. The groups to be concerned about within the process of forming a positive public opinion are usually customers, employees, investors, members of educational institutions, government authorities, fellow businessmen (competitors and non-competitors), and the community at large. However, the only way to ensure lasting positive public opinion is consistently to pursue a policy of fair dealings and open communication with all you come in contact with during your stay in business. Much has been said about the need for good employee relations, customer relations, and investor relations (involving all who have a stake in the business such as creditors, partners, and lenders), in other chapters. In this section, there are two groups to be discussed, namely: fellow businessmen and the community.

★ *Fellow businessmen.* John Petrof, Peter Carusone and John McDavid provide some valuable information on this topic:[17]

'Small businessmen have many opportunities to cultivate mutually beneficial relations with their colleagues, that is, with other businessmen who share the same or similar problems. This includes fellow members of trade and business associations, owners and managers of neighbouring businesses, and even one's own competitors. It is generally a good idea to join the appropriate trade and business associations because their primary purpose is to promote the goals which members have in common. When it comes to publicity, such associations are usually assured of obtaining good coverage in the news media. This is one of those situations in which a dozen or so businesses pulling together can exert far greater impact than if each one worked independently toward the same goals. An actual case by which two businessmen benefited through sharing is where one owner of a business became great friends with two other owners from nearby towns. Their wives also became good friends, and once a month, the three couples exchanged visits. By sharing their experiences and common problems, each man learned quite a bit about the deficiencies of his own operation. Moreover, each man helped to publicize the other's business to customers who were moving by referring them to his friends' stores.'

★ *The community.* As an owner of a small business, you have a social objective pertaining to people in the community other than customers. People within a community usually expect businesses to show a sincere interest in the welfare of its surrounding community which of course, if you are aware of it, provides you with an opportunity for an attempt to work at a good track record of community participation. This can definitely enhance your reputation for being progressive and co-operative, and establish a climate for future business. Publicity can be regarded as free advertising and anything that is newsworthy can be publicized through the appropriate media. Thus, for any community service performed, you should attempt to obtain publicity. Scott Cutlip and Allan Center provide you with a few excellent examples of how small businessmen can invest in community progress:[18]

'1. Retail store windows should be available for charity campaign posters and displays, for civic undertakings, for community holiday features.

2. Officials should be available for counsel and committee work in school projects, city improvement programs, and lobbying for the community at the county and state levels.

3. Facilities of small plants and stores should be available for the reception of guests from out of town, for meetings of local groups, and for use in citywide events.

4. Membership should be maintained in worthwhile associations for which each business is eligible. In this way the hometown can be alerted to developments on the national level likely to affect it. There often is something that can be of benefit locally. For example, the Small Business Men's Association alerts its members to pending legislation that might be unfavourable to the community.

5. Property maintenance and improvements are contagious. The small businessman who remodels his place, paints the front, installs new showcases, or enlarges his merchandise lines does a real service. That is often the first step in a beneficial process. First, his competitors do likewise. Second, their neighbours follow suit. Third, the whole downtown spruces itself up. Fourth, real estate developers gamble on new home sites. Fifth, new business likes the new look of the community. Sixth, transients stop more to shop more, and residents don't go as much to the "big" city for their needs. It is a long way from Step One to Step Six, but the sequence is normal.

6. Businessmen should buy supplies locally as long as the price is right or nearly right. That keeps the money in the local stream moving back and forth from purchase to payroll and back to purchase. More than that, it expresses confidence in other businessmen locally, which will pay itself back.'

Some other ways to obtain favourable public opinion through publicity are to have some social event with employees periodically, in order to establish some sort of rapport with them; or to make a presentation on some topic you feel qualified to discuss considering your areas of competence and knowledgeability. For example, one owner of a garden shop held many seminars on topics related to his trade such as: how to plant trees, how to prune trees, where to plant trees, how to lay out a garden, etc. Of course, once you have spoken before a few groups and have won their confidence in your ability to 'know what you are talking about', the word will get around.

Favourable public opinion does not happen overnight, neither can it be bought, it must be worked at. Favourable public opinion comes only from maintaining good relations with people on a consistent ethical basis.

SUMMARY AND CONCLUSIONS

Customers' confidence is of little value if people don't know that your business is 'around' and ready to serve them. Keep reminding people — out of sight is out of mind. A small advertisement in the classified section of the telephone directory won't do the job if your competitors are constantly reminding people about the advantages of their offerings. A general rule of advertising is that the advertisement should embody a clear, straightforward, proposition to the buyer; in other words, at least one good and clear reason to purchase. It will take only a bit of thinking to figure out a reason for purchasing or making use of the service, as any product or service has some characteristic which makes it unique in its class otherwise it would not be on the market at all. Other general rules of advertising are that you must say what you have to say (provide the facts); put the promise in the headline; put other key words in the headline; keep the headline short; and provide photographs. Having good advertising ideas depends, above all, on being steeped in knowledge of the product.

As far as promotional efforts are concerned, some good advice is not only to want to see your market (i e the people in the 'territory' you serve) at times of crisis. This is a big mistake. Do not just advertise or have promotional events when you are really in trouble or during bad economic times, because everybody does it then and this reduces your chances of getting the business. This sort of attitude is the same as your being a 'friend' who only visits your friends when you want something from them (one normally does get tired of such a situation and as a rule this results in a less positive attitude towards the 'friend'). Rather get into the habit of seeing your market when the 'weather is calm' (throughout the year) in order to establish a good relationship with your customers which may save your business when the storm comes up again. This calls for devoting your brains to the service of your market by being creative and putting your ideas on your programme of promotion. It is one thing to draw up an advertising programme and quite another to ensure that it is implemented. So do not neglect to execute your plans in order to improve the results of your business.

BIBLIOGRAPHY

* Roderich White. *Advertising — What It Is and How To Do It.* 1980. McGraw-Hill, Berkshire, England: 67-69.
* William H. Day. *Maximizing Small Business Profits with Precision Management.* 1978. Prentice-Hall, Englewood Cliffs, NJ: 287-293.
* John Naylor, Alan Wood. *Practical Marketing Audits.* 1978. Associated Business Programmes, London: 91-104.
* Curtis E. Tate Jr., Leon C. Megginson, Charles R. Scott Jr., Lyle R. Trueblood. *Successful Small Business Management.* 1982. Business Publications, Plano, Texas: 303-351.
* J.K. Lasser Tax Institute. *How to Run a Small Business.* 1982. McGraw-Hill, New York: 235-241.
* Mike Timewell. Service: the new competitive edge. *Entrepreneur* 1983; **2**(4): 14.
* J.H. Steyn. Waarom moet ek adverteer? *Entrepreneur* 1983; **2**(1): 14, 15.
* L. Radder. Informal market research for the small retailer. *Entrepreneur* 1984; **3**(4): 10, 11.

NOTES

[1] Ralph L. Woods, *The Modern Handbook of Humor.* 1967. McGraw-Hill, New York: 64.

[2] Business Plan for Retailers. *Management Aids,* Number 2. 020. 1979. U.S. Small Business Administration, Washington D.C.: 4.

[3] Why businesses should advertise. *Small Business News.* 1986; **8**(4): 5. (Official journal of the University of the North, Business Advisory Bureau.)

[4] William H. Day. *Maximizing Small Business Profits with Precision Management*. 1978. Prentice-Hall, Englewood Cliffs, NJ: 277.

[5] John V. Petrof, Peter S. Carusone, John E. McDavid. *Small Business Management: Concepts and Techniques for Improving Decisions*. 1972. McGraw-Hill, New York: 309. Reproduced with permission.

[6] Steuart Henderson Britt. Plan your advertising budget. *Management Aids, Number 4.018*. 1978. US Small Business Administration, Washington D.C.: 2,3.

[7] Elizabeth M. Sorbet. Do you know the results of your advertising? *Management Aids, Number 4.020*. 1979. U.S. Small Business Administration, Washington D.C.: 2.

[8] Idem, 3, 4.

[9] Idem, 4, 5.

[10] Ovid Riso. Advertising guidelines for small retail firms. *Management Aids, Number 4.015*. 1977. U.S. Small Business Administration, Washington D.C.: 4.

[11] Idem, 3.

[12] D. Ogilvy. *Confessions of an Advertising Man*. 1964. Longmans, Green, London: 99.

[13] Idem, 93, 94.

[14] Idem, 97.

[15] Ralph L. Woods. *The Modern Handbook of Humor*. 1967. McGraw-Hill, New York: 60.

[16] *Advertising and Business Promotion Manual*. 1984. Incentive Marketing, Cape Town: 25, 27. This manual has been designed to equip the businessman with a fast reference and basic layout of rules and approaches that will enable him to do-it-himself, or work in closer harmony with advertising professionals who can do it for him. It is a manual to be recommended as it provides the small businessman with many valuable ideas that can be implemented to maximize profits. It can be obtained from: Incentive Marketing (Pty) Ltd, Box 10131, Cape Town, 8000. Telephone (021) 7901624. Reproduced with permission.

[17] John V. Petrof, Peter S. Carusone, John E. McDavid. *Small Business Management: Concepts and Techniques for Improving Decisions*. 1972. McGraw-Hill, New York: 355. Reproduced with permission.

[18] Scott M. Cutlip, Allan H. Center. *Effective Public Relations*. 2nd ed. 1958. Prentice-Hall, Englewood Cliffs, NJ: 302–303.

11 SALESMANSHIP AND SELLING

'Good sales people, like good cooks, create an appetite when the buyer does not seem hungry.'

Statesman

INTRODUCTION

Expertise in selling is necessary in retailing and in the service enterprise, even if it means that customers purchase relatively small quantities. A customer walking into your shop expects and appreciates good service. Advertising and promotional activities may draw the customer into the shop, but it is not usually sufficient to create and complete a sale. Selling is, as they say, 'the name of the game' and therefore vital to every business's success as increased sales lead to increased profits, which again enhance growth possibilities. Selling is vital in order to outdo competitors. When competing shops carry the same range of stock as you do, the main reason why you or they could out-perform each other, can be attributed to the expertise of the sales people. Sales people are not necessarily those who are well qualified as salesmen. They can also be the ordinary shelf packer or cashier who understands the principles of selling. Remember the saying: 'If there is no sale, there is no job.' It means that you and your employees must be able to sell effectively, because the income of the business is solely dependent on maximum turnover. Sales results are tangible and measurable. The desire to create a sale is a positive motivation in business — your desire for creating a sale must be strong because your fear of failure is so strong. If you are not afraid of failure then you probably don't care enough. When you have failed to reach the required sales target, you will feel pained if you care. The reasons for not reaching sales targets as set out in your budgets should be found immediately through investigation so that appropriate remedial action can be promptly taken.

Selling is mainly an activity for arousing desire for satisfaction and the better the efforts to arouse desire for satisfaction, the greater profits are generated as you cannot make profit without sales. You need to bring the products to the attention of consumers and you need to meet competition by knowing more about your products than your competitor knows about his. Good service and good selling lead to word-of-mouth advertising, which again may lead to increased business. Know your product, and if you don't you can forget being effective because you cannot give the customer the sales assistance he expects. The process of personal selling, whether oral or written, can be described as an 'argument' to persuade another man (the buyer) to your way of thinking; that is, to bring him to believe, as you believe, that he wants to buy your goods, or use your services, or do something else that you want him to do. This 'argument's' purpose is to increase sales and it should be conducted in such a friendly, honest, intelligent and creative manner that it makes the customer want to do business with you.

THE SALESMAN

As mentioned, the salesman can be anybody who works for you — the shelf packer, the cashier, the tea girl, the storeman or yourself. There are many characteristics and qualities one will be looking for, but here are a few key ones as outlined by Mr M. A. Motsoeneng, a Small Business Advisory Bureau consultant:[1]

★ Sociability — best described as the ability to 'get along with people'. The desire to associate with others.

★ Effectiveness in speaking — the use of understandable language. In the case of a sales situation, the seller must state the case simply and straightforwardly. A way of accomplishing this is to assess the use of words for accuracy, logic and comprehensibility. If people frequently ask for an explanation of what the sales person is driving at, it means that he is not using sales language comprehensively and effectively. Therefore, a sales person must always try to be brief, direct and to the point.

★ Curiosity — to be a good sales person one should be a 'why' and 'how' person. Curiosity leads to an interest in things and people. The more curious the seller is, the more he learns about the many products he sells, and the greater are his chances of effecting a sale.

★ Thinker and doer — creative and imaginative.

★ Genuinely sincere and reliable — a sales person should know that pretence does not last long. Sincerity is a factor which mostly distinguishes truth from falsehood. In all selling situations, the sales person should strive to give firm evidence of sincerity. This is particularly shown by the manner in which he treats customers, and by what he says. Reliability is the corollary of sincerity. If a sales person is sincere, it is certain that he is dependable.

Another important quality is undoubtedly enthusiasm for the product or service. The ability to call customers by name and to show a personal interest in them is extremely important. Probably, the most important qualities are the sales person's personality, his knowledge, his judgement ability and his power of persuasion. Persuasion can be described as the act of convincing people that the product or service meets their requirements and that it will satisfy their particular needs. For persuasion to be successful, it is essential to establish the true needs of the buyer by getting the answers to the questions: 'Who are my customers?' 'What do they want?' and 'How can they be best satisfied?' Then the persuasion phase can be completed by demonstrating the benefits of the product or service with one aim in mind — to satisfy the need. In getting business, service and satisfaction are the fundamental appeals. Without them very little can be accomplished, for unless the customer feels certain that the goods will render him service and that the deal will be personally satisfying, he will ignore all selling efforts. The customer may be perfectly convinced that your goods are all right and that if he bought them he would be satisfied, but still he does not buy. The customer needs his emotions awakened and his desires aroused before he will take action. He must see the item with a heightened interest which will carry him over the painful moment of parting with his money. Persuasion should also never exist without conviction, for unless solid reasons and benefits are given, limited action will be secured.

The knowledge salesmen must have A salesman needs knowledge (or information) as a tool as much as he needs the right characteristics and qualities in order to create a sale. His knowledge should include the following:

* *Business knowledge*
  He should know the background of your business and in particular the circumstances which led to the establishment of the business (where the business has come from and what it is presently striving to accomplish) as well as the 'personality' (image in the mind of the public) the business is to develop in the market it is serving.

* *Product knowledge*
  It is difficult to sell without knowing something about the products. Sales can be noticeably increased if the sales person knows what the product can do for the customer. The customer needs only to ask a single question about a product that cannot be answered, in order to lose confidence. The importance of having product knowledge is that it helps the sales person to instil confidence in the customer and it keeps the sales presentation alive. The more product knowledge you have, the more confidently will you be able to sell, and that will lead to your enjoying your work (this is also applicable to your employees) which is an important ingredient for success. You will also be able to show the customer how the product will satisfy his needs. When customers feel that they can confide in you, they also feel confident that the product in question is really worth buying. Product knowledge can be obtained from the label on the product itself, brochures from the suppliers or manufacturers, representatives, newspaper advertisements, trade shows and even feedback received from previous buyers of the product. Look out for the good points — its uses, advantages, serviceability, and quality. You should also know how to care for the product. It is important that you know these things as many customers are reluctant to buy new products because they do not always know how to use them. For

example, customers want to know such things as: 'How many kilometres will I get out of these tyres?' 'For how many years can I expect this paint to last?' 'How can I benefit from reading this book?' 'Will it be better to buy this product or that one?' etc. To have any success, the facts of the product must be translated into specific benefits that will satisfy a need. The customer is very much interested in benefits, advantages, and lasting satisfaction. Customers want to know these things as it convinces them that they will be getting value for their money.

The importance of having product knowledge cannot be over-emphasized as it is pretty obvious that a salesman should have reasonably complete knowledge of the goods he is presenting, and at least enough thereof to be able to describe every feature, demonstrate its correct use and be able to answer any question the buyer may reasonably raise. The salesman who is about to sell a product should study it so that he is aware of every feature necessary to enable him to present it effectively, and can satisfy the customer on any point he may bring forward. If hunting equipment is being sold, for instance, the salesman should make it a point to learn all about the hunting sport industry and trade. This calls for the study of magazines, trade journals, newspaper articles, as well as attending local conventions and conferences sponsored by the industry or trade. Details on more specific product knowledge are the following:

* *Background and history of the product.*
Knowledge of the history of furniture, for instance, gives the furniture salesman an appreciation of the fine designs and skilled work in both antique and modern furniture, and this can be passed on to customers. It is important for the salesman, and of interest and value to the customer, that you get the 'story behind the product'.

Uses of the product. The salesman must have a complete understanding of how the article is used, and the purpose for which it was produced. For example, a salesman selling hunting equipment should be able to explain and show the customer how to aim, how to take the rifle apart for cleaning purposes, what game can be shot with the rifle, whether it can be used for self-defence, how to load and unload the rifle, etc. If the salesman is awkward or clumsy in demonstrating these operations, the customer may easily get the impression that the rifle is difficult to operate. Furthermore, very few products are used on their own. Most are consumed or used in association with other articles. If you are selling tinned tomatoes, you could stress the fact that they are ideal with fried bacon — display tinned tomatoes with bacon and maybe give a recipe with it all. This could increase sales of both products.

Serviceability of the product. The product can be supported by a certain service to influence customers in favour of purchase. Such a service may be a delivery service or a promise of speedy delivery. A business selling 'complicated' equipment may include a training service to ensure satisfactory results. Another service which can support a product is a guarantee given to the customer in order to ensure a full and satisfactory service from the purchase. Notice how the salesman in the following example assures the customer about the serviceability of the shirts being sold.

Customer: But will this shirt wear well?

Salesman: This shirt will last twice as long as the less expensive brand you were looking at, Sir. It is made of pure silk which is the best material. Take for instance, the silk shirt I have on. I have been wearing it for five years, twice a week. It is as new as the day I bought it.

Care of the Product. A customer's decision can be influenced by how difficult it seems to take care of the product. You can assist the customer by showing how to take care of the product properly as well as how proper care could contribute to the serviceability of the product. Such information can be obtained from the supplier or manufacturer from whom the product was bought or made. Such knowledge instils confidence. Just the other day I cleaned out my cupboard and sold some of the old shirts, the aim being to use the money to obtain new ones. With certain shirts I had unpleasant experiences because of ignorance in how to care for them properly. In the process of considering certain brands of shirts and opening the packet to have a closer look, I found a note inside the shirt which said the following:

Thank you for buying this **XYZ** *shirt ...*

*Great care is taken in the making of our shirts and
we would like you to enjoy them to the full.*

*Please pay careful attention to the washing instruction
tag sewn into the bottom of the shirt.*
Spin dry is dangerous for fine fabrics.

*Remember that all dark colours tend to carry
excess dye initially and should be washed on
their own.*

*Fabrics containing silk, linen and wool are the most
luxurious shirtings available and sometimes require
gentle handling. Please take care in washing and
ironing luxury garments and they will give you
great pleasure.*

Although this was inserted by the manufacturer, there is no
reason why the retailer can't do it if the manufacturer does
not. Not only did it make me feel special in purchasing these
shirts, but it has provided me with all the information I
needed to care for it. Do you see the point of importance?
Make the customer special and provide him with correct
information to take care of or use the product.

* Customer knowledge
In retailing, buying is the complement of selling. It is thus
obvious that you first have to buy the right stock in order to
be sure that it will sell. But before any right stock can be
bought, you first have to determine what your market's
needs are, who they are and where they are. Any improvement can come from only two directions: increasing your
sales, and lowering your costs and expenses. However, a
combination of the two produces the best results. Selling
more is primarily the outcome of improvements made in
such areas of your business as buying, stock presentation,
promotion and personal selling. Thus, you must know your
customers so as to be able to ascertain easily what products
to buy which are within their price range. Useful suggest-

ions in order to give customers a satisfactory shopping experience are; to be friendly and courteous; make them feel at home and important; provide sales demonstrations in which you demonstrate the benefits of the products or services; assist the customer to make a decision to buy — why he should buy it, what type brand, size or style he should buy; be a 'sportsman', whether you made the sale or not (refer customer to competitor's shop) and show through your actions and words (tone of voice and use of language) that it was a genuine pleasure to be of service to him. A customer who received service which came up to his expectations will always return for more.

BUYING BEHAVIOUR

In retail selling, prospecting is not as necessary as it is in other types of business with something to sell. Your shop windows, the interior displays, your advertising and sales promotion, and the words from the mouths of your customers take care of this. For example, a man walking down the street may see a product displayed in the window with a note attached to it which says: 'Do you know that this quality hammer is on sale this week only? Please come in and test it.' The man stops to examine it more closely. He likes what he sees. So his interest has been aroused. As a result of the invitation to a demonstration and testing, his feelings are intensified to the point of desire to possess such a hammer and is thus seriously considering whether to buy it. In this example we see that it takes two people or two things to make a sale — the buyer and the salesman who gives the demonstration, or the buyer and the note in the window, or the buyer and the visibility of the product. This is more or less the buying sequence which invites the buyer's (or customer') attention to the product: arouse interest; develop interest into desire; and develop desire into action taken to possess the product.

This brings us to the question of why do people buy? When people buy something, they have a reason for doing so. Take the case of a person who decides to spend R500 on a correspondence degree course. What makes the person decide to spend his money that way? Is it a desire for more education?

More education might be desired by the person because he seeks an improvement in personal development. The buying motive might thus be dissatisfaction with a low-paying job and a desire to earn a higher income. It is for these reasons that you need to be a 'why' person — a why person in the sense that you must identify the selling points of a product or service and translate them into values that explain its worth from the customer's viewpoint.

When people buy something, they have one thing in common: they buy things for the satisfaction of owning them or using them. They buy things that represent advantages and benefits to them. For example: Lorette may buy a new dress because she wants to make an impression on others; Edward may buy a leather jacket because the other fellows wear leather jackets (he desires to belong to the crowd); and Timothy may buy a pair of comfortable shoes because he has to do a lot of walking. The difference between a need and a want is that a need is a lack of something that is essential, and a want is a desire or a longing for something that is not necessarily essential.

As a businessman, you do not really create the need for a product, but it is possible for you to make the customer aware of a need and persuade him to act on it. Therefore, your job is to locate a need, want or desire and make a sale out of it. Buying motives normally include desires for the following satisfactions:[2]

- *comfort* — the desire for physical or mental ease and well-being.
- *convenience* — the desire for a minimum of effort, for saving of time and energy.
- *security* — the desire to know that the future is provided and one's welfare assured.
- *prestige* — recognition of the individual as personally outstanding or a member of a desirable group.
- *health* — the desire to feel and look physically fit.
- *economy* — the desire to secure full value for each cent spent, to save money.

Your main concern should be to study your market and to find out which type of shoppers there are, as some may be more interested in prices, values and quality of the goods (buying motive: economy); others may enjoy personal relationships with sales people and prefer to shop where they are recognized and feel welcome (buying motive: prestige); some people again avoid large businesses as they are of the opinion that they are very impersonal, and prefer to do business with a smaller business since they believe that it also needs to make a living (buying motives: prestige and convenience); others dislike shopping and only shop because they must and therefore the most important attribute to them is the convenience of the location (buying motive: convenience); etc. If you can identify the market's type of shoppers and their buying motives, you can begin to organize your business so that it appeals to most shoppers. For example, if your prices and quality of products are right for any economic consideration of the people in the market and you have the calibre sales persons with whom people get along and, to top it all, a convenient location, there is little doubt that you will have quite a high volume of buying traffic — 'stealing' them away from your competition.

SALES PRESENTATION AND DEMONSTRATION

You may have been successful in getting a customer's attention focused on a certain product or on the shop as a whole, and you may have aroused interest, but if you have not translated the interest into desire to possess the product, you stand a good chance of losing the sale. Do not be shy or stand there with a mouth full of teeth when you come to this stage. Remember the saying; 'Nothing ventured, nothing gained.' You can translate interest into a desire to possess with confidence if you are well informed about the product. You need to show the customer how the product will satisfy his needs and therefore you have to explain the merits of the product from the customer's point of view. This particular part of the sale, where you attempt to turn the customer's attention and interest into a desire to own the product, is the heart of the selling process and is called the sales presentation. The presentation is the 'talking' part and the demonstration is the 'doing' part — both are necessary. Through the presentation and demonstration, the customer thus gets the opportunity to experience or come to know what the product is like and what benefits are conferred by owning it. He has a chance to handle, try on, or feel the product as well as to listen to the salesman, and he has the opportunity to ask questions. In fact, the presentation and demonstration appeals to all senses — smell, taste, hearing, touch and sight — depending of course, on the particular product. The demonstration in particular, serves to provide 'living proof' that the product is all the salesman says it is — it gives substance to the facts mentioned about the product.

One of your main tasks is to buy and display the right goods and thus help the customer come to a buying decision. Often a customer will enter a business and ask to see some merchandise that the shop carries in several different price ranges. The question you may ask yourself is: 'What goods should I show first?' The best procedure might be to start showing goods in the middle price range and then carefully watch the customer's reactions. A customer who indicates an interest in something better can then be shown the more expensive, higher-priced (and presumably better-quality) merchandise. It is just as easy to step down to the less expensive items. If you start showing the highest-priced goods and the customer happens to be a bargain-minded shopper, you may scare him away.

It is generally a rule in retail selling that the specific requests of a customer be honoured. Nothing is more upsetting to a customer than being shown everything but the item that was requested. However, suppose a customer is quite determined and the desired item is not in stock. Is there anything the salesman can do? Yes, he can handle a determined customer by explaining the reason for not having the item in stock. If, for example, a customer in a hardware business says: 'I want some X paint remover', you can reply: 'I'm sorry, we don't carry that brand because we found that while it is very effective in getting off the old paint, one must use it several times before it does the job properly. We carry Y paint remover. It is every bit as effective as X paint remover, but much easier to work with and one uses about twenty percent less of this to do the job properly compared with X paint remover. It is a cost-saver as well as a time-saver.' The customer will be grateful for this kind of frank answer and will probably accept the substitute. By doing it this way the salesman has shown eagerness to serve the best interests of the customer.

The salesman dealing with the man who specifically wants to buy a black jacket, extra large with white stripes, can also indicate a real desire to be of service. This might not pay off in an immediate sale, but it will make the customer think well of the salesman and the business. The salesman can say tactfully: 'I am terribly sorry, we don't have a jacket like that. In fact, I think you may have a hard time finding one, because black is not one of the big colours this spring. While you are here, why don't you just look at what else we have and then if you don't find elsewhere what you have in mind, you can always come back.' This kind of information saves the customer's pride and makes it easier to return to the shop if necessary.

The way goods are displayed plays an important part in making merchandise seem desirable to a customer. A sales person should also handle goods as if they are very valuable. Take for instance the case of a person selling handbags: if she reaches for the bags on top of a shelf, grabs a few and throws them down on the counter, the customer will think that they are not worth much, but if she, the saleslady, handles the handbags with care from start to finish customers will get the impression that the bags must be something special. The saleslady should also give a brief sales talk about each bag to increase the desire for it, for instance: 'Just feel the leather of this handbag. It is the softest and finest leather on the market. Please look at the construction — perfection and top quality. You will surely have people turning their heads. It is really the quality anyone desires. They are going to envy you.'

A salesman should be able to make this type of brief but interesting and specific comments about any piece of merchandise shown. This means identifying the main selling features of merchandise. After making an interesting comment about each item shown, back it up with something more substantial — the story behind the product. Customers should know what the products are made of, how they are made, what their uses are, how they should be cared for, what they cost and how the products compare with competing items. There are certainly times when you won't need all this information, but you must have it in case questions arise. For example, suppose a lady is shopping for trousers for her child and she says: 'These are nice trousers, but I don't dare buy anything that can't be washed in a washing machine.' A sales person who does not know the stock will lose the sale. One who does may say: 'That is polyester that can be washed. It couldn't be easier to care for as it does not even need ironing, and I think it is so much better looking than that one (showing another type of trousers), don't you?'

SELLING BENEFITS

Once again, it must be emphasized that people do not buy goods because of what they are, but far more important, because of the benefits they hope to gain from possession; in other words, because of what the product will do for them. As the title of an article on selling once said: 'Sell the shade, not the garden umbrella.' The salesman must always endeavour to prove, as far as this is possible, what advantages the customer can hope to enjoy by acquiring the article or service under consideration, and in so doing, he builds up in the customer's mind a strong desire to purchase. Some examples of 'selling benefits' are as follows:

★ 'Because of the speed at which the motor revolves it does the job ten times better and ten times faster than by hand.'

★ 'That concludes the demonstration of this machine. Now let us see how much profit will be returned to you from its use in your business.'

★ 'An unusual feature of this curtain is that it is made of flameproof material. I have a square of the material here. Watch the effect when I put the flame of my lighter under it. See! the material absolutely refuses to burst into flames.'

It should also be remembered that one of the main purposes in selling is to communicate ideas to customers. To do this, you have to speak in terms that are familiar to the customers. For the average customer, technical terms should be translated into everyday language. Short, simple words should be used in preference to more complicated words that may be over the customer's head.

Some businessmen find it difficult to measure the performance of their sales people because customers and business conditions vary, as do the many criteria that can be used for measuring. Experts are of opinion that owner-managers make one of the following five errors:[3]

1. They evaluate their sales representatives primarily on the basis of sales volume, and sales volume by itself won't tell you how much profit or loss you are making on each sales representative. Unless you know this fact, a sales representative can cost you money without your realizing it. For example, one businessman was losing money until he analysed the profitability of the sales volume brought in by each member of the sales team. He found that one of them created a loss on almost every order. This representative was concentrating on a market that had become so competitive that mark-ups had to be drastically reduced to effect sales.

2. They rely too much on the number of sales calls made by each of their sales representatives. Making calls on customers and prospects is important, but a sales representative should also make calls on accounts in relation to their sales and profit potential. Paying sales representatives to do routine visits, for example, can be expensive.

3. They compare each sales representative's present sales results with past sales for a corresponding period — for instance, May one year against May of the previous year. That can be very misleading. Some months have more working days than others, changes in products, prices, and competition all have influences on the result of the measuring. It is much better to measure cumulative progress — quarterly, half-yearly, or annually — toward goals.

4. They expect their sales representatives to follow explicitly the selling methods that worked for them when they were selling. Why criticize a sales representative for spending too much time in the office if that brings in profitable sales?

5. They may give their sales representatives too much freedom. They do not really know what they should expect from their sales representatives.

Sound Criteria for Measuring Performance

The following are sound criteria for measuring the performance of sales representatives. Some of them are usable for measuring the performance of sales representatives. The important aspect is to use the yardsticks that can be expressed in numbers and those that can be accompanied with target dates such as month-end, year-end, etc. Some of the other criteria will need some judgement in these areas (through observation):[4]

1. volume of sales (in rands);
2. amount of time spent in office;
3. personal appearance: for example, clothes, hair cleanliness and neatness;
4. number of calls made on existing accounts;
5. number of new accounts opened;
6. completeness and accuracy of sales orders;
7. promptness in submitting reports;
8. money spent in entertaining customers;
9. extent to which sales representatives sell the business;
10. accuracy in quoting prices and deliveries to customers; and
11. knowledge of the business.

After sales performance has been measured, the next thing to do is to plan for better performance in those areas with which you are not satisfied. The three steps necessary to bring about improvement when it is needed are:[5]

Planning: Get the sales representative's agreement about goals to attain for a period. Goals should be measurable, for example; suppose that the sales representative has to sell 10 products in the coming month which cost R1 000 each, then the sales target is R10 000 or 10 units. If the costs in selling these 10 units amounts to R4 000, then you would add his contribution to the 'profit' made, namely, R6 000. Also get the sales representative's agreement about expenses to stay within certain limits for the month he will be 'selling' his target set.

Measuring: Review sales representative's progress and provide direction. The sales representative can also submit a report weekly, fortnightly, or monthly.

Correcting. Meet regularly with sales representatives to

find out the problems and accomplishments experienced. In addition, you may need to do some of the following to help improve performance:

★ give more day-to-day assistance and direction;
★ increase sales promotion activities;
★ transfer accounts (or certain customers) to other sales representatives if there is insufficient effort or progress;
★ increase or reduce selling prices;
★ ask sales representatives to provide suggestions for improvements;
★ add new products or services;
★ increase incentives;
★ transfer, replace or discharge; and
★ provide training.

The foundation of measuring and correcting of your sales representative's performance is planning, by defining the yardsticks that are profit-orientated.

SALES LETTERS

As seen so many times through this book, it is imperative for the small businessman to know his customers personally and to deal with them face-to-face. Although your business is restricted to a comparatively small area, you would do well to increase the number of your customers and extend your business beyond your particular area, if you make use of writing sales letters. What you need when writing sales letters are names and addresses of people in the total market you are serving or want to penetrate. This information can be obtained in many ways, such as: by taking the numbers of cars from a nearby shopping centre and acquiring their owners' names and addresses from the Traffic Department or Town Council's office; from friends and relatives; from other businesses who are not in competition with you; from a doctor's consulting rooms; from a customer register book in the business; by telephone analysis.

True salesmanship never slumbers. It is always selling goods as well as the business itself. It means that every letter is a selling letter. The volume of advertising and the amounts expended for advertising stagger one whenever they are mentioned, but expenses incurred by sending sales letters are comparitively low. It is indeed a more economical, personal and effective method to get a sale. The strength of a letter as a medium for selling goods can be very well supported by carefully choosing material; for instance, not the old stereotyped brown envelope which just about everybody throws away without opening. In a conversation with a customer, a salesman might also forget to mention certain advantages, but the letter can express, after careful thought and selected words, just those points that are best for the given situation. Another advantage of a letter is that it can start with a tactful introduction and build up to a climax which could eventually secure a sale, whereas in a conversation the pre-arranged order is bound to be shattered by the interruptions of the customer, the questions he asks, the comments he makes, etc. A further advantage of a sales letter is that the writer can carefully select the wording in order to make it attractive and compelling — words seen are words remembered. Another advantage of the sales letter is that it can be read when the recipient has time to do so, and if it is a courteous and individually directed letter, the recipient may like it and will probably read it more than once. Still another advantage is that the sales letter is much cheaper than a salesman's visit.

All these facts make the art of salesmanship by letter an important one for study and consideration. Every day a businessman should enter into his diary a note reminding him that he must write at least five letters that day to customers which are well known or not well known to him, about a special product in stock (especially in a speciality shop), which that particular customer might consider buying.

When selecting the material and product to offer in your sales letter, you must become thoroughly acquainted with that specific product from every possible angle. Study the product, not only by yourself, but also by virtue of a testimony from others. Find out who has used it and what they think about it. You could also contact the manufacturer or suppliers, and ask them to send a list of their best talking points and, if they can, to tell you which they usually select, and in what order. All such sales material should be listed, studied, improved, revised and arranged. Then look for the most attractive combination of points that will appeal to the intended recipient (customer). The next step is to study the customer. Put yourself in his place. See him in his surroundings, in his business, in his home and determine why he needs this product or service.

Let us then consider a product — a small vacuum cleaner — from the point of view of the product itself and the customer. The main talking point is its light weight, only 3 kilograms. It will be easy to put the vacuum cleaner on a scale and so prove to the customer that it does in fact, weigh so little. It will be just as easy to show the customer why the article is so light, because it is small and made of aluminium. Now consider the customer. Who will be using the vacuum cleaner? Probably the woman of the house — she may have a servant doing the actual work, but the woman of the house must be reached. Now, why is this article made so light? So that she can easily move it or carry it around — up and down the stairs (the selling point of lightness here is beginning to have persuasive power). Other aspects to consider this way are the effectiveness of the cleaner, the guarantee, the excellent service after the sale, how economical it is on electrical power, how it takes up less storage space, etc. In the sales letter you could also provide the customer with the exact measurements of the vacuum cleaner. If you could bring all these benefits together in a letter that will get the woman of the house's attention, interest and desire, the only thing left for her is to take action — to come to your shop for a demonstration and possibly to buy the product. In the letter, make the prominent ideas stand out on the page by using words that are most likely to strike the reader's eye. When the reader opens the envelope and pulls the letter out, her eye must at once glance upon a statement which shows her that the letter is worth reading. Such headings signal what is to come. Not only do they announce the topic but they also stimulate interest. A question heading can be effective as it stimulates curious readers — they will want to see the question answered in the letter. Such a sales letter will then be mostly directed to a group of people and not so much to an individual whose needs, wants and desires are specific and known to you. Examples of getting attention are:

- Let me save you from the mistake a friend of mine made last year ... .
- Your comfort and convenience have been consulted first of all in designing our new shop ... .
- Did you ever stop to think what ... .
- Take a trip through our shop ... .
- This is the shop for you ... .
- We will tell you about and show you our new ... .
- Have foresight. Do not ... . (or Do ... .)
- You are special because ... .
- An easy way of solving your Christmas problem ... .
- How to maximize your return on investment ... .
- Yes, it is possible, triple your savings with ... .
- Ensuring performance ... .
- The right choice ... .
- Three of 1986s best opportunities for you ... .

Something that is a definite must in a sales letter is the clincher as it induces action. Its main objective is to make the purchase much easier for the customer — so easy that it will actually be harder not to buy the product at all. A common form of clincher is that which asks the customer to fill in a form or coupon and send it back in the enclosed envelope, either to ask for further information or to order. If you forget the enclosed envelope or postcard or the clincher, the buyer's interest will fade and the golden moment for making a sale will be lost. Another good policy concerning periodic letters with clinchers is to place a final date thereon, the reason being that it leads to action and it is also a persuasive technique. However, if you do not put a final or closing date on, in effect you are saying: 'Whenever you have made up your mind about these products, please feel free to pay us a visit at our shop.'

Answers to enquiries An enquiry is different from an order. When receiving an enquiry, your first task is to identify the enquirer's interest — what exactly does he want to know and how much. The answer to an enquiry is usually written in support of an accompanying booklet or catalogue. The mistake to be avoided is to write too brief a response such as this one:

Sir,

Your letter of 15 May 1985 refers. In reply thereto we send you under separate cover our catalogue describing our line of goods.

Yours faithfully
(Signature)

One of the worst mistakes you can make in business is failing to answer enquiries. Many a person has had the experience of being interested in an advertisement and of asking for specific information about the offer made by a business, only to find that the desired information was not given in reply by the business who advertised. This can be very annoying. In business, where your income is dependent on sales, there is no excuse for failure to give specific answers to every question asked by potential customers. A longer letter is required when the enquiry contains several detailed questions. Even if some questions are answered in an accompanying catalogue or booklet, your letter should still refer definitely to the pages of the booklet where the questions are answered. If the desired information is not given in the accompanying material, the sales letter itself should provide it in complete detail, and should answer every question carefully. Consider this letter in reply to an enquiry concerning accommodation at a resort:

Dear Sir

We thank you for your interest and we take pleasure in replying to your letter of 16 June 1985 concerning accommodation at Sun Valley Inn. We have some very desirable cottages still available for the period you have mentioned. They are all close to the hotel, and are rented in conjunction with it.

We are sending you, under separate cover, some pictures of Sun Valley Inn as well as a booklet which will show you just what these cottages look like. Also included is a list of places worth seeing in the surrounding area within a radius of 150 kilometres of the hotel.

There is a dam close to the hotel, but no fishing is allowed. A much larger dam is but a short distance away (6 kilometres), and the fishing is well above average all through the year and there it is very seldom that the fisherman is not rewarded for his efforts. Enclosed is the name of a person to contact in order to find out more specific information about the types of fish available.

As you know, the hotel is situated right next to a game reserve and the pleasure of watching and hearing the wild animals, is one of the main attractions of the place. Regular hotel tours are to your advantage as they are conducted at a very special rate to our visitors. These tours also include visiting observation posts where you can watch the animals drinking and they put you in an excellent position for taking photos.

We should be glad to have your application for accommodation as soon as you can send it, since we do not have many cottages at our disposal. We include a picture of a one-roomed cottage near the hotel, which we believe you will find particularly desirable.

Please do not hesitate to call us if there is anything else you wish to know. We assure you of our best service and await your stay in our beautiful area with pleasure.

Yours truly,
(Signature)

Most points in this letter answer points in the letter of enquiry, and an effort was made to make the reply interesting at every point. When negative information is given, an attempt has been made to remove the disappointment which it might cause. It is a fairly long letter, but its attractiveness and its persuasive quality justify its length.

An enquiry from a person (potential customer) is valuable and is to be treated as such. It takes hard work (or rather, hard thinking) to design a letter in order to get the market's attention and interest in what you have to say. If you have achieved that, the sale is partly made, but to fail to give the enquiry due attention is like shutting the door in the face of a person who wants to enter a shop and do some business. The enquiry should be answered promptly — not after a week or longer period has gone by.

In a speech, Maxwell C. Ross, a well-known sales promotion expert, listed fifteen ways letters can be used to create goodwill, and eventually sales. He said: 'There is just one prerequisite; the person using them has to be a nice guy, courteous, friendly, and above all, sincere.' Each of these fifteen is simply a friendly, personal letter that you may use of some occasion when you would not be expected to send a letter at all. They create a tremendously favourable impression.[6]

'1. You can use a letter to follow up a salesman's call. You could start something like this: "John Smith told me today of the pleasant visit he had with you about your insurance program. I know that John will do a fine job for you." Then finish off in your own words.

2. You can use letters to make appointments. You say, "It's about time for me to sit down with you, Jim, and go over your insurance in the light of the new tax changes. I suggest that we get together late Friday afternoon. How would four o'clock be?" You don't need to say much more, but you'll be surprised at the nice reception you get when you arrive.

3. Whenever a customer or client has been promoted or has changed jobs, it's a nice gesture to send a letter like this: "Congratulations on your appointment to District Sales Manager. This is fine news, and I know you'll do a great job."

4. When a customer is ill all you need to say is: "I'm certainly sorry to hear that you are laid up. I hope it won't be many days before you're back at your desk."

5. When there is a death in the family. If it's tactfully done a short message of sympathy can mean much.

6. When a daughter or son gets married, or a new baby arrives. These letters make no tangible effort to sell; they're simply goodwill builders—the kind that some day will bring something nice to you because you went out of your way to do something nice for somebody else.

7. When people buy a home, write to them. Your letter doesn't need to be long or fancy. Perhaps: "I hope you are enjoying getting settled in your new home." If you have something to sell, tell these folks you'd appreciate a chance to call when things are squared away. In some cases, an inexpensive gift like a small rosebush or a young tree helps to create goodwill.

8. When a customer has a birthday. Quite a few successful salesmen make a practice of keeping birthday lists and sending cards or letters. If you use a card, write something in longhand on it.

9. When people move to your town a letter of welcome is an excellent source of new business. They don't know where to go for dry cleaning, laundry, milk—what service station to trade with, where to do their banking, or the nicer places to eat. So you write: "Welcome to Centerville. We know you'll like it here. If there is any way we can help you get settled, please let us know."

10. When you read about a customer in the newspaper, send him a letter. Clip the article, send it to him, and say: "I don't know whether your children keep a scrapbook of the nice things that happen to you, but just in case they do, here's an extra copy."

11. When a customer is elected or honoured in some way, perhaps you would say: "I've heard some nice things about the work you've done for the Chamber of Commerce, so I was not surprised to see that you have been elected vice president."

12. When someone has done you a favour he will appreciate a note from you. "Thank you for those two extra tickets. I hope I can repay the favour soon."

13. When some product or service pleases you, take time to write about it. "I wanted you to know how pleased I am with our new floor furnance, and with the courteous and efficient way your men installed it."

14. When a serviceman comes home write to him or to his parents if he lives at home. That's a small way to show your appreciation of all he has done for you and his country.

15. Thank new and old customers for their orders with letters. In Des Moines, a filling station operator sends a post card to new customers. All the card says is, "It was nice of you to stop at our station. I hope you'll come back often." '

HOW TO CORRESPOND BY LETTER

This section attempts to enlighten you on how to correspond by letter — a skill you will need if it is your intention to make use of the ideas mentioned in the previous section. A businessman should be able to write a letter which is effective and makes people do things. Each letter must be written with a definite purpose and to accomplish that particular purpose, the message as a whole must be expressed clearly and correctly. In every letter you write, your personality and that of the business must come to the fore. This calls for individuality in writing business letters, and individuality in writing letters means avoiding those modes of expression that have become worn-out. A letter is not good just because it is like other stereotyped letters. Try to avoid the use of words that have been employed so often by others that they have almost ceased to possess any power and image. Words must be selected for their special aptness in expressing exactly your idea or purpose. In addition to all other purposes your letter may have, every letter must have the purpose of creating goodwill built into it. You also need to develop your own particular style of writing letters. By style is meant the combination of thought and method of expression that indicates your attitude towards the matter concerned and towards the recipient of the letter. The recipient can sense a particular attitude or to put it in a sharper manner — the customer can 'smell' you. Your letters must use a language of respect for the recipient of the letter as well as of friendliness. The letter is a valuable tool to serve the customer with humaneness in today's very automated world where impersonality has been the all-too-frequent norm. The small business is in a unique situation to capitalize on this impersonality and make it more personal through his own individuality and particular style. You therefore need to put everything into the letter that ought to be put in — individuality, style, correctness, clearness, conciseness and courtesy.

Mark McCormack, author of 'What they don't teach you at Harvard Business School' put the matter this way,[7]

'Correspondence — both internal and external — is one of the most frequent opportunities you have for presenting yourself to the business community. I'm a real stickler about any written communication that goes out over my name. I insist that it be neatly typed ("pleasing to the eye") and contain no spelling errors or typos. There are few things in business that you can easily make stick, but this is one of them. It frustrates me to hear a secretary say "It is almost right". Correspondence forms a strong subliminal impression about how you run your business, and I don't want someone to think I run it "almost right" when I have such a simple, obvious opportunity to impress otherwise.'

Business can at times be compared with an engine: there is always friction between the moving parts and courtesy can be compared to the oil that lubricates the moving parts in order to make it operate smoothly. Courtesy is as essential in written form as it is in personal conversation — it gains goodwill. Courtesy is important in the sense that every business transaction should thus be advantageous to both parties. If mutual benefits are not exchanged, then one party is defrauded. Courtesy is a very large consideration for others. And if you are discourteous in your letters, it will stand out in the letter that you have little consideration for others. Discourtesy justifies a suspicion that you don't care about the recipient of the letter. Rather be different and show consideration through the written word — think enough of the reader's business and treat him in such a way as to justify his continued support for your business.

Courtesy also gains favours as they are more easily granted if they are asked for courteously than if they are demanded. Do your asking in a courteous manner. Courtesy is undoubtedly the mark of a successful gentleman. This does not mean that a letter may not be sharp, but the sharpness must be courteous. See the following two examples, the first one being sharp but not courteous. The second one being an improvement:

1. Sir

   While you were employed by us, you promised to change your attitude and habits. You have not done so, and we don't want people like you around in our organization. You have twenty-four hours to leave our premises and please, do not return.

   Yours truly
   (Signature)

2. Sir

   While you were employed by us, the agreement was that your continuance of employment was subject to the fulfilment of certain conditions, which you were well aware of. Those conditions have not been complied with and thus we have no alternative but to terminate your service.

   We sincerely regret the necessity for this action but we are confident that your opportunities for success will be greater than they have proved to be with us. We wish you success in any work you undertake.

   Yours very truly
   (Signature)

Courtesy in writing letters (or in business) is simply the possession and expression of good manners. It involves a mental attitude of consideration toward the recipient of the letter. Discourtesy invites discourtesy, which you cannot allow to happen in business. Once you have put the recipient of the letter in an attitude of opposition to the writer instead of consideration for him, the letter is going to fail in its purpose and defeat the object of being in business — to win not only one customer, but many. Although courtesy is an absolute necessity in all business letters, it is particularly essential in complaints and answers, enquiries, acknowledgements of orders and letters to women. A discourteous letter can only damage relations which could result in the business losing sales. Never write when angry as you might later regret what you have said in the letter. The point is: first cool off and then think objectively about the matter concerned, as a letter once posted is tough to recall. The successful correspondent does not write discourteous letters because he never thinks discourteously.

Clearness involves understanding. If the person for whom the letter is meant is not able to understand what it tries to say, the writing of that letter has been a waste of time and energy. A waste of time in the sense that some 'detective work' needs to be carried out in order to get the correct message. The meaning must be clearly understood by the recipient as he cannot always read your mind. The words before him are his only means of finding out what you intended to say.

When a letter is concise it says everything that needs to be said and in the briefest possible way. Conciseness means that the letter should be as short as possible, but that it should also say everything that is necessary and that the number of words is less important than the number of thoughts and the manner in which they are expressed. Consider these two letters in reply to an enquiry received from a consumer about whether the businessman is selling furniture made from a certain type of wood:

1. Dear Sir

    We don't sell furniture made of kiaat wood.

    Yours truly
    (Signature)

2. Dear Sir

    We are sorry to say, in response of your enquiry of June 4 1986, that we do not sell furniture made of kiaat wood. We suggest, however, that you communicate with Mr MacLaren of Fides Furnishers, PO Box 2744, Nelspruit, 1200. They have for many years manufactured kiaat furniture of good quality and we are sure they will take pleasure in serving you in every way.

    As an authority on good furniture you might be interested in our range of furniture made of stinkwood. We take pleasure in forwarding our catalogue together with a price list. Our furniture is excellent value for money and we are confident that it will be to your advantage to examine our range. We regret that we are unable to be of immediate service to you.

    Yours very truly
    (Signature)

The first letter is very clear as it answers the enquiry fully, but it is not concise as there is a lack of all the other essentials such as courtesy, individuality and so on. The second letter is much better as it gains the goodwill of the recipient by telling him where to find what he wants. Furthermore, the second letter introduces the products you are selling, which is likely to be to your benefit.

Correctness has to do with various things such as the quality of the paper, the layout of the letter, grammar, spelling and general neatness and appearance.

Correctness, conciseness, courtesy and neatness are the essential qualities of all successful business letters. The main necessity, however, is individuality or character. Individuality has to do with personality, which means that the letter must be written by yourself rather than by somebody working for you. What is meant by the latter statement is that the business has a personality and this desired personality must be expressed in every business letter. It also means the avoidance of the common letter. In other words, if the letter or expression sound common or familiar, try to change it to something that will project your personality and that of the business. As a small businessman you must identify this personality and move away from the stereotyped in everything. Make your letters represent your personality and your business alone.

SUMMARY AND CONCLUSIONS

Having a capable, well-trained sales personnel is one decided advantage which the small business can enjoy over larger businesses. As a general rule, these larger retailers rely mostly on fully stocked shelves and low prices, and therefore the singular potential of the small business as far as competing is concerned, rests on the calibre of your personal selling efforts. Customers will judge your business by the way they are treated by you and your employees. Courtesy and tact are always expected. It is indeed very important to both the retail or service business to make certain your employees are knowledgeable, continually informed and technically proficient. Training ought to be a continuous process. The service business, particularly, demands mastery of the area of specialization. Learn all you can and encourage employees to do the same — be an example. In whatever you do to make a sale, demonstrate a professional, proprietary attitude.

Sales people often confuse the approach of 'Good morning, madam. How can I help you?' with selling. Although necessary, it has little to do with selling. The approach ought to be the beginning of the sales presentation wherein the attention, interest and desire of the customer is awakened. A 'guest register' in which your customers can record their names and addresses would be helpful when you run occasional special promotions. However, when shoppers seem to be 'just looking', the salesman should at least greet the customer and comment on the fact that she is available if the customer needs assistance. Where a shopper (potential customer) is evidently interested in a displayed item, the salesman should approach the person, introduce himself, and point out some of the interesting features of the product or, better still, some benefit which the product can bring to the customer.

As far as sales letters are concerned, it is necessary first to attract the reader's (customer's) attention and show him that the remainder of the letter is worthy of being read. Study the subject of writing sales letters. As a businessman you will receive many of them. Look for mistakes and then let those mistakes guide you in avoiding similar faults in your own letters. The basis of successful sales letters is conviction and solid facts presented with the needs of the customer in mind. These should be arranged and worded so as to lead to the precise action that will result in a sale. Make the difference between yourself and your competition so much bigger by being so much more personal than they are by applying sound selling techniques.

BIBLIOGRAPHY

* The world's greatest salesman. *Entrepreneur* 1984; **3**(9): 16, 17.
* Donald Currie. Sales — The Life Blood of a Business. *Entrepreneur* 1985; **3**(7): 10.
* D. Moeletsi. Why do customers behave the way they do? *Small Business News* (University of the North Business Advisory Bureau) 1985; **7**(2): 22-24.
* Dr. R. Abratt. The selling process in retailing. *Entrepreneur* 1984; June: 12, 13.
* Charles Attwood. *The Sales Representative's Handbook*. 1969. Business Books, London: 1-96.
* Willie Gerter. *Selling Is My Game*. 1984. W.H. Allen, London: 19-34.
* B. Howard Elvy. *Salesmanship Made Simple*. 1979. W.H. Allen, London: 141-154.
* Mark H. McCormack. *What They Don't Teach You at Harvard Business School*. 1984. William Collins, London: 95-99.
* J.W. Ernest, R.D. Ashmun. *Selling Principles and Practices*. 1973.
* Sandt Claasen. Sporthandelaar — Verkoop die skaduwee, nie die sambreel. *Entrepreneur*. 1983; **2**(7): 13.
* Tom Prinsloo. Eienskappe van die suksesvolle verkoper. *Volkshandel* 1984; July: 83.
* Reader's Digest. *Write Better, Speak Better*. 1977. The Reader's Digest Association, Pleasantville, New York.

* Herman R. Holtz. *Profit From Your Money Making Ideas.* 1980. AMACOM (A division of American Management Associations), New York.
* Ralph Starr Butler, Henry A. Burd. *Commercial Correspondence.* 1919. D. Appleton, New York.
* William H. Day. *Maximizing Small Business Profits.* 1978. Prentice-Hall, Englewood Cliffs, NJ: 242–276.
* J.K. Lasser Tax Institute. *How To Run a Small Business.* 5th ed. 1982. McGraw-Hill, New York: 229–243.

NOTES

[1] M.A. Motsoeneng. The Salesman. *Entrepreneur* 1982; July: 20. (Reproduced with permission.)

[2] Baumback/Lawyer. *How to Organize and Operate a Small Business.* 1979. Prentice-Hall, Englewood Cliffs, NJ: 406. (Reproduced by permission of Prentice-Hall.)

[3] Measuring Sales Performance. *Management Aids Number 4.003.* 1967. U.S. Small Business Administration, Washington, D.C.: 2, 3.

[4] Idem, 2.

[5] Idem, 4, 5.

[6] Reader's Digest. *Write Better, Speak Better.* 1977. The Reader's Digest Association, Pleasantville, New York: 242, 243. (Reproduced with permission.)

[7] Mark H. McCormack. *What They Don't Teach You at Harvard Business School.* 1984. William Collins, London: 41. Reproduced with permission.

12 STOCK CONTROL

'In the case of many small business undertakings, the stock represents up to 80%, and even more of the total assets. Due to the extent of the investment in stock it is essential that every small businessman pays attention to stock control, that is, the purchasing and administration of, as well as supervision over the physical movement of stock.'

Small Business Advisory Bureau
of Potchefstroom University
for Christian Higher Education

INTRODUCTION

Stock control in effect, implies the right goods, at the right time, in the right place, at the right price and displayed in the right manner. It is thus the primary purpose of stock control to maintain a balance between these aspects in order to bring about some profitable operations for the business. Putting it another way: stock control is the supervision of stock to avoid overstocking or understocking. If the stock is too large in relation to the demand for it, the cost of carrying the stock will be higher than it needs to be which leads to a shortage of cash on hand. Consider the parallel below in explaining the point of being overstocked:

Twenty family members are coming to have dinner with you. After considering what their tastes are and how much each of them will be eating, you figured out the goods to be bought to prepare for dinner and calculated that it will cost R25. However, you have R50 on you to buy goods. Are you going to buy the amount of goods you need with the R25 or are you going to spend the whole R50 budgeted for the dinner? If you choose to do the latter, you may end up with excess goods worth R25, and may not have a further opportunity to use them in the next year — you will then have the

321

'stock' but not the money which could perhaps have been used on other more important matters. (In effect, you are overstocked.)

The costs involved in having a larger amount of stock than necessary (also known as carrying costs) include such items as interest on money borrowed or laid out to obtain stock, handling costs involved, insurance costs, storing costs and obsolescence. The main question of course is what the answer is to such a situation. The answer is the main objective of stock control: reduce the investment in stock by increasing its turnover speed.

The point of increasing the stock turnover speed is always an important one in business. Many businessmen have ignored it, and the consequences are usually disasterous. I know of one businessman who opened a clothing shop in a shopping centre. The market research done indicated a great future, but he was not there for long and then sold it to someone who knew what the problem was and could solve it. Why didn't he make it? He stocked too many high profit, slow-moving and expensive clothes (the market could not afford it) and not sufficient stock of fast-moving items for the trade he was in. Thus, turnover and sales income were not adequate to sustain the business. He did not do his purchasing right from the beginning, and therefore suffered the endless struggle to generate income so as to replace existing stock with lower priced goods and faster moving items.

Now the other side: If there is not enough in relation to the demand called for by the market, an out-of-stock situation will result. The ultimate result goes further however — dissatisfied customers and the loss of profits from sales which could have been made if the items requested by the customer were available at the time required. The time factor is of utmost importance because when a business is constantly out of stock, even if the missing line will be available the next day, it soon begins to lose its customers who prefer to do their shopping at a more reliable business. In such a situation you might be responsible for creating the reputation of being out-of-stock if perhaps, you did not establish what it is your market wants in as much detail as possible, or had no records to inform you how much they usually buy. Rather concentrate on the service image you seek so as to force you to be competitive and always to be aware of the total needs of your customer.

It was mentioned earlier that one of the essentials for business growth is to increase its stock assortment in breadth and depth, but before going ahead, matters to consider are:

- Are the additional products you wish to introduce called for by the market? In other words: will it sell?
- Would it not be more feasible rather to stick to a more specialized line of goods?

Both the above matters of concern depend on the type of business you are in. Having in stock a wide and large variety of items (many styles, brands, colours, sizes) will project a very broad line to your market, but you can't be everything to everyone although customers may think you should be. The fact still remains that if it is your money that is invested in the business, it should be spent wisely on stock assortment. Say for instance that both your available space to sell and your funds are on the 'short' side, you must still make productive use of money already invested in stock. Meaning, in a situation of limited space and funds, you cannot stock every item available from manufacturers and wholesalers, but you can balance your stock assortment to include most of the items that the majority of your customers need.

To grow also means to attract a specific type of consumer group from a wide market instead of from just the immediate territory — even if you still offer only a narrow line of goods (stock in depth). Such a group of consumers can be attracted through advertising and other sales promotional means. However, the control of stock is not always easy as it has to do with knowing 'what goes for what' and there are many decisions to be made in this particular field. To be successful at stock control requires experience and information concerning the market you serve. Generally, stock control enables you to:

- obtain control over the financial investment in stock and thus save interest on other costs;
- institute scientifically and practically a simplified method of purchasing;

- diminish stock shortages due to administrative errors and pilfering;
- diminish losses due to obsolete stock, over-purchasing;
- determine the movement as well as the profitability of various stock lines;
- utilize space more efficiently;
- obtain management information which facilitates decision-making;
- Turn the asset (stock) into sales repeatedly in order to make a profit.

HAVING THE RIGHT GOODS

Although having the right goods in stock has mainly to do with the purchasing of initial stock and thereafter continuous purchasing to maintain a certain level of items, and was more specifically discussed in an earlier chapter, there may still be a few valuable points worthy of mention in this section. One such point may be that of 'assortment planning'. One of the main differences among businesses stocking the same major lines is the difference in the assortments available — differences in brands, qualities, varieties of styles, in prices and sizes. This makes one business's image very different from another. However, if you have a growing business and wish to create an image that will attract and keep customers from a wider area, you have two alternatives:[1]

1. You can work out exclusive or selective dealerships. If you can do this, your store may become a central headquarter for certain famous brands which you will stock in both breadth and depth. Or you might become an agency for one manufacturer or wholesale distributor. More commonly, however, you will probably want to make a number of dealership arrangements with a number of key resources in various lines.

2. You can free yourself from manufacturer domination by introducing shopping lines where brands are not as important as design, quality, exclusiveness, colour, and so on. You may also be able gradually to introduce private brands, as you will have a better mark-up on them, and more assurance of repeat business if a customer's purchase is satisfactory.

However, as far as a stock control system is concerned which is reliable, the simplest form of stock control is probably the 'model stock system' where stock on hand is never permitted to fall below a certain level, nor to exceed that level for any significant period unless there is a good business reason for doing so, such as a particularly attractive discount offered by a supplier on a sure-sell line for a certain period provided a minimum quantity is purchased. Businessmen need to be particularly careful of the dangers of the over-utilization of this practice. It is false economy to overstock on one or two lines in this way if one has problems with cashflow, or if storage facilities are very limited. Whatever systems are in use, regular calculation or physical counting of stock on hand is necessary for the maintenance of the system. Many a business owner will say that this is too time-consuming, but it is only time-consuming until it becomes a matter of routine. However, it is worth the effort because without doing this it is not possible to have an accurate picture of one's stock on hand and one's purchasing needs. Accurate counting of stock is of absolute necessity if you wish to establish purchasing needs and ascertain the rate of sale per item, which is helpful in allocating the amount of space to each line of product, in relationship to the demand. It also helps establishing the product's 'best point of sale'. On page 326 is a simple example of a 'model stock system:'[2]

In this very simple example sales were calculated in arrears. Before deciding how many items to buy on 12/3/86, the businessman calculated sales for the period before, as follows:

Stock on hand (4/3/86) + stock purchased (5/3/86)
— stock on hand (11/3/86)

A model stock was not established until a pattern of sales began to emerge after 5 weeks' history. It became obvious at this time that slightly more than 144 items were selling per week. As the packs contained 48 units the businessman decided to make his model 192 and see how sales went. When he saw what the trend was for increasing sales of that line, he increased his model by a further 48 to bring it to 240.

Once a model is established, deciding what to purchase and how much to purchase becomes much easier as it is only

ITEM: XXX Baked Beans			SIZE: 440g		PACK: 48
Model	Date	Stock on hand	Date	Stock Purchased	Sales
?	4/3/86	23	5/3/86	144	
?	11/3/86	53	12/3/86	96	23+144-53=114
?	13/3/86	5	19/3/86	144	53+96-5=144
?	25/3/86	0	26/3/86	144	5+144-0=149
?	1/6/86	0	2/6/86	192	0+144-0=144
192	8/6/85	50	9/6/86	144	0+192-50=142
192	15/6/86	35	16/6/86	192	50+144-35=159
192	22/6/86	64	23/6/86	144	35+192-64=163
192	29/6/86	17	30/6/86	192	64+144-17=191
192	6/7/86	0	7/7/86	240	17+192-0=209
192	13/7/86	18	14/7/86	240	0+240-53=222

necessary to subtract stock on hand from the model quantity and to order to the closest pack.

Information provided by a good system of merchandise control that will improve both buying and selling activities, includes the following:[3]

- price preferences of customers;
- items no longer popular;
- right quantities to buy;
- amount of a given item sold;
- season or time a given item sells;
- time to stop buying seasonable goods;
- kind and style of goods customers want;
- time to display and promote certain items;
- slow movers;
- particular items for which demand is falling off;
- best buying sources;
- best buying prices;
- possibilities for new lines or kinds of goods; and
- whether stock is properly balanced.

The following table illustrates how the retailer can order sizes, colours, or styles of merchandise in proper proportion:

	Size or Style Number					
	1	2	3	4	5	Total
On hand, July 1	20	21	20	14	17	92
Received (purchased during July	—	13	—	4	12	29
	20	34	20	18	29	121
On hand, Aug. 1	12	14	18	16	21	81
Sold during July	8	20	2	2	8	40

The quantity sold is obtained by adding the number on hand at the beginning of the period and the number received or purchased, and deducting the number on hand at the end of the period. The amount needed to bring stock up to normal is then estimated according to demand for it the next month.

In establishing how long an item has been on the shelf (or by when it was to be sold) the 'dating code' method can be used. By means of the code, the older stock can be sold first (on a first-in, first-out basis), and items can be kept from being too long on the shelf and losing their freshness. For example: the code number written on the item might read '5104' which means that the item should be sold before 10 September. The actual date is determined by adding the first (5) and the last (4) digits to get the month, while the middle two digits indicate the day of the month.

HAVING THE GOODS AT THE RIGHT TIME

Having the goods at the right time means having the stock available for sale when desired by the customer. A particular example is seasonal merchandise, such as easter eggs during Easter time, Mother's Day cards on Mother's Day, etc. These items will however only sell at the time of the year for which they are intended. Clothing and certain food merchandise are also seasonal, for example, soup in winter and cooldrinks in summer, and blankets will sell better in winter than in summer. Care must therefore, be exercised to provide sufficient space for such merchandise during its high demand periods. Also remember that stock in the storeroom does not sell, so if space is available rather bring it forward to the selling area. Your stock control system (or buying schedule[4]) will provide you with the information of 'when to buy' if it is kept up to date regularly.

HAVING THE GOODS AT THE RIGHT PLACE

As far as the 'place' aspect is concerned there are several issues[5] which the businessman needs to be aware of, of which the important ones are: a logical layout (departmentalization); a pleasant shopping environment (interesting); visibility and accessibility of merchandises and security. Customer convenience must always take precedence over all other factors. This requires some ingenuity on the businessman's side when he decides where he will place his high demand lines to create maximum traffic flow inside the business that may lead to increased impulse buying. Making maximum use of space is also important, and as a rule of thumb, the fastest selling products should be allocated the most space, and the 80/20 rule should apply, that is, that 80% of sales probably come from 20% of the lines of merchandise stocked. This 80/20 rule is also known as 'Pareto's Law'.[6] Although this rule cannot be presented as an absolute norm, as the specific figure will differ from business to business, it is a useful rule to apply when you are to decide which items (or products) should always be stocked. In effect this rule implies that 80% of your sales will derive from 20% of the stock you have. You can categorize your stock in the following manner (to find out which 20% of your stock is responsible for 80% of your sales income):

A — the top sellers;
B — the average sellers;
C — the poor sellers;

They can be categorized by using your 'Model Stock System' or other observation methods. The 'A' group products are obviously your fast movers (and should always be stocked), while the 'C' group products do not have to be stocked (or you could stock them in smaller quantities at least to fulfil the little demand there is), and can also be phased out at some stage by replacing it with a better demand group. It is however also important to establish whether the real problem with the 'C' group sellers is not the brand.

The 80/20 rule is also applicable on the selling aspect; that is, that 80% of your business is done with 20% of the customers in your market. Experienced businessmen who use this rule say that it does make sense to focus four-fifths of your time and effort getting to know the one-fifth of your customers who are the most important to you. They say: focus on the interests and tastes of your top 20% and take the time to figure out what you can do to keep them there.

HAVING THE GOODS AT THE RIGHT PRICE

When setting the prices, your objective should be to maximize profit. The essentials of making a profit are to cover the original cost, to cover expenses and to provide a margin of profit. The best selling price should, however, be high enough to cover your costs and help you make a profit, but also low enough to attract customers and build sales volume. Remember though that no customer is prepared to be cheated, and asking too high a price is one way of cheating. Many loyal customers will lose their loyalty once it is costing them too much.

The question to decide upon is whether to make your profits through a relatively high mark-up and small sales volume or a low mark-up and a large sales volume. This decision has of course a great bearing on the image you wish to create, for example: bargain prices are not compatible with exclusive merchandise, and so is the reverse: high prices are not compatible with low quality merchandise.

Suppose your mark-up is too high and you wish to reduce it and want to know what increase in sales volume you will need to provide at least as large a gross margin as you have now. You will calculate it in the following manner: suppose your business is operating at a 40% gross margin and you wish to lower it to 36%, then you divide your present mark-up percentage by the one you contemplate: 40% ÷ 36% = 1,11. Thus for every R1,00 of present sales, you will need R1,11 volume, or 10% ($\frac{4}{40} \times \frac{100}{1}$ = 10%) more. In another example, suppose you wish to reduce your mark-up from 40% to 25%, then for every R1,00 of present sales, you will need R1,60 volume, or 37,5% ($\frac{15}{40} \times \frac{100}{1}$ = 37,5%) more. In the first example, if you have good reason to believe that the lower mark-up would increase your sales considerably more than 10%, the reduction in price is justified. Such a policy of concentrating on low mark-ups with an accompanied high sales volume should be 'pushed' by an improvement in your marketing programme — become more aggressive in all aspects of marketing which will boost sales.

HAVING THE GOODS DISPLAYED IN THE RIGHT MANNER

Having the goods displayed in the right manner involves showing the goods that are for sale in a fashion appealing to customers as well as arranging them in an orderly fashion. Some points relating to this aspect of stock control have been discussed, but below follows a more precise list of things that will contribute thereto:[7]

- Put impulse goods near the front of your shop, and intersperse them with demand products so that as many people as possible will see them.
- Customers like to see bright, interesting, clean and well-cared-for shops when they go shopping. They like to think that the business people (personnel and owner) have taken the trouble to prepare the place properly.
- Place larger sizes and heavy, bulky goods near the floor (on lower shelves).
- Arrange your stock so that customers are drawn towards the back and sides of the shop.
- Every item of merchandise must be clearly price-marked.
- Every item must have only one price-ticket.
- Merchandise must be classified into departments to make it easier for customers to find what they are looking for.
- When a product is out of stock, do not leave the space empty but fill it with a suitable product (in keeping with the department) until new stock arrives.

- Don't hide one line of merchandise behind another.
- Remove all damaged merchandise.
- Keep shelves full.
- Sell older stock first (first-in, first-out).
- Use signage selectively.
- Make use of colour-blocking.
- All goods must be within the reach of most customers (top shelves must not be packed too high as this can cause injuries).
- Institute a general housekeeping programme — cleaning of shop floor and merchandise.
- Equipment must be in good order.

Generally, having the goods displayed in the right manner is like saying welcome to the customer. To illustrate: when people (friends) visit your home, you of course prepare for their visit — almost as if you want to show off a little. You put clean towels in the bathroom, you spend hours cleaning out the house, the bed is made up with clean sheets, flowers are put in the guest's room and you prepare some delicious food. The same attitude and care should be the order of the day when your customers are visiting your shop. They must feel they are getting the best.

HOW TO INCREASE YOUR RANGE OF STOCK

Increasing your range of stock has to do with ways of manipulating your investment in stock in order to make a profit. One of the factors that causes customers to do business (their shopping) at other businesses, is that they do not find an adequate range of products at the business they no longer patronize. Such a situation can be reversed if businessmen persevere in widening the choice of merchandise, quality, price, styles, brands, etc. The range is, however, not the only issue to be concerned with. Other factors that go along with steps to improve the range are: improved physical facilities (a 'new look' or modernization); improved salesmanship; and the provision of other services that will enhance the favourable image you want to create. In agreeing that your range does require an improvement, you may not have the know-how to effect it and attempting to cater to everyone can be the first step toward failure as the assortment may become a collection of odds and ends that will only be wasted money, and you then may have to offer so many services that none are well performed (Jack of all trades, but master of none). Ill-advised buying can very well result in such a situation. Thus, you should rather discover what your customers wish to buy, accepting that you cannot be all things to all people, and do your best to provide these items if there is demand therefor. Furthermore, rather select a few characteristics in which you have the ability to excel, and develop them creatively. Your business's image will be distinct, and interested customers will be attracted. Below follow some techniques developed by Brian Rabjohn for increasing your range:[8]

★ Overstocking: By establishing a rate of sale for the products on hand the businessman can establish whether or not he is overstocked in certain lines. Not only is overstocking unacceptable from a financial point of view, but it also takes up space that could be better utilized. Once a rate of sale for products is established, the slow-sellers of which there are too many in stock should be given back to suppliers or sold at cost in order to use the credit or money received to further advantage. Simultaneously, you should be taking steps to ensure that you will in future carry the balanced range which customers desire.

★ Customer suggestions: Acquire a book wherein all requests of product lines not in stock can be recorded and if there proves to be reasonable demand for it, it should be purchased in small quantities and customers should also be informed (through putting it in a promotional position) that you have it in stock. All personnel can greatly contribute by asking customers whether they found everything they needed.

★ Range review: Another method is that of scanning or looking, and the best place to start doing so is in the shops of your competitors, especially those who have 'stolen' your customers. Using this method has its advantages such as what is being stocked in those businesses, who is buying there and what you can stock. Other places to scan are wholesalers; in the homes of friends and family; what is advertised in newpapers, magazines, television, catalogues; etc.

★ Complimentary items: Develop a list of complimentary items such as 'curry and rice'. This concept can however be extended by the alert businessman if he is to maximize sales and satisfy customers. Take the example of 'school exercise books' as a base item; complimentary or related items would then be other items such as pens, pencils, rulers, covering materials, school cases, lunch boxes, etc. The skill in handling this is the application of logical thought and imagination. In limited space it is however not always possible to stock everything and you must use your experience, knowledge and intelligence in defining the parameters of your range. The important things are to be creative, adventurous, flexible and interesting.

★ Taking action: In order to obtain the best results it is essential to develop an action plan (procedures) once it has been decided how the range will be improved. Below is an example of the kind of steps which should be taken, in a logical sequence, when implementing the project:

* physically check current stock on hand;
* establish market demand;
* establish profit potential;
* check legal restrictions (trading licence);
* consider equipment required;
* consider staff knowledge/skills required;
* consider seasonal demand;
* check for competition dominating the market;
* establish source of supply;
* check supplier's prices/terms;
* ensure continuity of supply;
* investigate supplier's promotion and advertising plans;
* arrange test marketing if possible;
* establish minimum order quantities;
* consider shelf space required;
* consider storage space required;
* decide on quantity to order;
* check availability of finance; and
* order stock.

STOCKTAKING

Stock is generally regarded as comprising those items or products that are for resale purposes in the ordinary course of business. It thus represents all stock on the shelves as well as that in storerooms. Various methods can be used to determine the stock on hand at any given moment, but the most accurate is by actually counting the stock. Although many retailers regard this method as a waste of time, it is actually the reverse as it provides him with an opportunity to clean out old stocks and to reduce excess stocks. It is important to remember that all stock on hand should be recorded at cost (cost price) in the financial statements. Some other methods will be discussed below.

Stock can be estimated by the gross profit method. Under
this method, you assume that the gross profit margin for the
period is going to be a certain percentage of your sales.
Normally, the gross profit margin for the period between the
last two physical stocktakings is used. The cost of sales for
the current period will then be the cost of the sales percent
(100% less the gross profit) times the sales for the period.
Closing stock is then computed as in the following
example:

Suppose that your sales for the month are R12 000, your
stock at the beginning of the month was R8 000 and your
merchandise purchases during the month amount to R7 000.
You calculate your gross profit and find it is 25% of sales.
Your closing stock is then as follows:

1.	Opening stock	R 8 000
2.	Merchandise purchases	R 7 000
3.	Merchandise available for sale	R15 000
4.	Estimated gross profit	25%
5.	Cost of sales (100% – 25%)	75%
6.	Sales for the month	R12 000
7.	Cost of goods sold	
	(75% of R12 000)	R 9 000
8.	Closing stock	
	(step 3 minus step 7)	R 6 000

When using the gross profit method of calculating your
stock, it should be applied separately to each department
because of different mark-ups. This method can give you
fairly accurate results for monthly financial statements
under some circumstances, but the fact remains that it is
only an estimated stock figure. As often as is practicable,
you should make a physical count rather than an
estimate.

Coded cost
method Another method of determining cost prices for stock valuation is to have the merchandise marked with a coded cost as
well as a retail price at the time it is put on sale. A letter code
can be devised by using any 10-letter key word with no letter
repeated, for example:

1	2	3	4	5	6	7	8	9	0
P	U	R	C	H	A	S	I	N	G

Thus, a product that cost R4,20 and sells for R5,00 would be marked 'CUG R5,00'. In taking stock, you use the coded cost on the price tag to arrive at the original cost price of the merchandise in the shop. Such a system can also help sales people in bargaining with customers — they cannot then sell the product below cost, as they know what the cost price is.

To ensure accuracy in stock counting, care should be taken to see that merchandise is in good order on shelves and other display areas. If any 'unusable' merchandise is on hand, it should not be included in the computation, but should be valued at scrap value, if any.

INFLATION

In recent times (1986/1987), the inflation rate has averaged more than 16% per annum, and is now recognized as a critical problem. This 'double digit inflation' has a tremendous impact on businesses, especially on their financial operations. Although no one knows what the full impact of continued inflation will be, one thing is clear — if double digit inflation continues, many financial policies and practices will have to be modified to meet this new situation, apart from its being disturbing and challenging to the business owner. However, we all know the effects of inflation on our pockets, and in the business world its effects on costs and prices is no exception. In small and large businesses, dramatic price rises have upset everybody's budgets, and they have taken big bites out of business capital and profits.

But what has inflation to do with stock control? Consider the following explanations. Say for instance you bought 1 200 watches at R11,00 each. So, the total cost of the purchase was R13 200. Say you sold all 1 200 watches at R15,40 each. Income (sales turnover) is therefore R18 480. Say it costs the business about R3 400 to operate. Deduct running and purchase costs from income and the result is a profit of R1 880.

Let us assume now that you are about to order a new consignment of watches and, of course, you are going to pay them with the R13 200 you have recovered from selling the first 1 200 watches. But, to your surprise, they don't cost

R11,00 any more. The price has gone up and they now cost R12,20 each. You can still buy R13 200 worth of watches. But, you can only buy 1 081 watches this time, instead of 1 200 watches. The next year, you will again get fewer watches for R13 200, as the prices go up every year. What has happened is that prices have been rising steadily whilst profits have shrunk, due to inflation as follows:

First consignment

Sales	R18 480
Less: Purchases (1200 at R11,00 each)	R13 200
Less: Operating costs (Expenses)	R 3 400
Net profit	R 1 880

Second consignment

Sales	R18 480
Less: Purchases (1200 at R12,20 each)	R14 640
Less: Operating costs (Expenses)	R 3 400
Net profit	R 440

The R13 200 may be what the previous lot of watches cost, but what your main concern should be what the next lot of watches will cost — what you have to pay in order to replace stock. In the first situation there was a net profit of R1 880. In the second situation you would have made a net profit of only R440, that is, if you had to buy 1 200 watches at the new, increased price and sell them at the same price (R15,40 each). Thus, R1 440 (R14 640 less R13 200) is needed for stock replacement next year.

The point is always to keep track of the prices of merchandise. Beware of inflation and adjust prices accordingly. Especially, to determine the correct cost per product and calculate the mark-up that will be sufficient to cover expenses and provide you with a reasonable net profit. It should be borne in mind that costs (expenses) are also on the increase every year, such as salaries to personnel (increases), transport (rise in petrol price), water and electricity, telephone, postage, interest rates, etc.

The question is, how does one cope with inflation? One has to look firstly at your expenses and see whether you can reduce them and in which ways. This can be done if you look with great concern at such aspects as budgets — the important thing is to keep within the budget. Other ways can be to motivate employees to a higher level of performance. See where and how you can improve the productivity of your business. Before buying a new vehicle, first re-consider this decision as the one you have at present may still be of use for another year or more.

The best way to beat inflation is by improving the stock turnover. Say for instance that the average inflation rate is 15%, then stock that cost you R80 000 at the beginning of the year will cost you R92 000 at the end of the year. Let us look at an example which will support this theory. Say for instance your trading account looked as follows at the end of 1988:

Sales	R200 000
Cost of sales	R146 000
Opening stock (1 Janurary 1988)	R 28 000
Add: Purchases	R151 000
Less: Closing stock (31 December 1988)	R 33 000
Gross profit	R 54 000

$$\text{Gross profit percentage} = 27\% \quad \frac{\text{Gross profit}}{\text{Sales}} \times \frac{100}{1}$$

$$\text{Stock turnover rate} = 4{,}7 \text{ times} \quad \frac{\text{Cost of sales}}{\text{Average stock}}$$

(Average stock is computed by adding the opening stock to the closing stock and dividing by two.)

Suppose the present average inflation rate is 15%. Thus, the minimum sales for the next accounting period (1 January 1987 to 31 December 1987) in order to keep up with inflation, would be R230 000 (R200 000 plus 15% = R230 000). If the same gross profit percentage and stock turnover rate are applicable, then the cost of sales would be R167 900 in 1987 (100% minus 27% gross profit is 73%. 73% of R230 000 is R167 900). The average stock needed is thus R35 723 (R167 900 ÷ 4,7 times).

However, the ideal of any business is to achieve the highest possible sales with the lowest possible stock, and this can be achieved mainly by improving the stock turnover rate. Say you could improve the stock turnover rate from 4,7 times per year to 6 times per year (during the 1989 accounting period), then the average stock needed for a turnover (sales) of R230 000 would be only R27 983 (cost of sales [R167 900] divided by stock turnover rate [6]). This desired stock turnover rate can be achieved by effective stock control, better stock presentation, better purchasing by establishing the needs of your market, more effective advertising and sales promotional efforts, good relations with suppliers, better customer relations, etc.

Thus, what you buy you have to sell, and as quickly as possible (at a profit) as stock is just another form of money. Inflation can thus be coped with if you concentrate on two major aspects — correct purchasing and good salesmanship. Correct purchasing involves purchasing the goods your market will buy at a profit to you. Let the wholesalers carry the big amounts of stock — just see that you have enough to cater for the needs of your customers. Selling means getting rid of the stock you bought at a price the customer considers as value for money at a profit to you — and as quickly as possible.

CHECKLIST FOR THE ADMINISTRATION OF STOCK

Below is a checklist to help in increasing profitable operations and especially managing the flow of stock with more precision. The checklist is simple and topics are presented in the form of questions intended to stimulate analysis with regard to various important matters relating to the flow and control of stock. The checklist will help you not to overlook important matters caused by a busy day which may have the tendency to reduce the application of the best practices and decisions to be made as far as stock control is concerned. The checklist is compiled by Dr John W. Wingate and Mr Seymour Helfant.[10]

Control ★ Do you have an effective system for checking on slow-selling stock?

★ Do you have an effective system for spotting potential fast-selling stock?

★ Do you keep a close check on customer demand with a want-slip system?

★ Do you keep adequate records to help you plan for next year's purchases?

★ Do you plan your stock so that you will always be 'in stock' at peak periods?

★ Do you maintain a basic stock assortment even in dull months?

★ Do you have any opportunities to increase your stock turnover and reduce the length of time goods are on hand before being sold?

★ Do you make your mark-downs early enough?

★ Do you set the first mark-down low enough to move most of the goods marked down?

★ Have you established mark-down prices?

★ Do you re-order well enough in advance to avoid being out of best sellers?

Buying[11] ★ Do you avoid stocking items from different suppliers and in different brands that virtually duplicate one another?

★ Do you select each item in stock with a distinct customer group or target in mind?

★ Do you choose items for promotion that have outstanding merit in price, fashion, or utility?

★ Do the characteristics of the stock give your store a clearly defined personality or image that attracts people in the trading area?

★ Will your mark-downs be reduced by rising wholesale prices?

★ Do you overbuy promotional merchandise frequently which can later force you to take heavy mark-downs on remainders?

★ Are your stocks peaked well in advance of the sales peak?

★ Do you curtail reorders at the peak of the selling season?

★ Are you developing classic lines with a long life?

★ Do you take advantage of discount opportunities?

★ Do you keep your transportation costs to a minimum?

★ Do you concentrate your purchases with key suppliers?

★ Do you actually use the facilities of a resident buying office to obtain better values?

★ Could you realize savings by placing orders further ahead?

★ Have you an undeveloped opportunity to use private brands to compete with national brands?

★ Do you resist special quantity price concessions for merchandise that will not turn over for a long period of time?

★ Do you keep in close touch with all new market developments by co-operating with a buying office or voluntary group and by seeing all salesmen who call?

★ Do you select the lines you carry carefully since you can't be all things to all people?

★ Do you know your competition, their strengths and their weaknesses?

★ Are merchandise shortcomings leading to customer returns and mark-downs? (If so, demand higher quality standards.)

★ Do you place your orders on time so that you will have the proper merchandise in your store when the demand is great?

★ Do you concentrate your buying on what you know will sell instead of experimenting with fringe sizes, colours, fabrics and types of merchandise?

★ Do you 'test' new merchandise in small quantities before the beginning of a season and then concentrate heavily on the items that were successful?

★ Do you follow up your orders carefully to check for better deliveries?

★ Do you refuse to accept past-due merchandise when the demands fall off?

★ Are you getting the largest possible cash discounts from your suppliers?

★ Do you pay all your bills on time so as to obtain the discounts offered?

Publicity *Outside publicity*

★ Do you promote best sellers?

★ Do you make adequate use of the appropriate media: newspapers, direct mail, signs, radio, television, press publicity, house to house selling, mail and telephone selling?

★ Do you use the most appropriate newspapers?
★ Do you have adequate promotion each month of the year?
★ Do you advertise on the right days of the week?
★ Are your advertisement layouts eye-catching?
★ Does the advertisement inspire interest, desire and action and above all, is the copy believable?
★ Are your employees made aware of what you are advertising?
★ Does your store have adequate window space?
★ Are your show windows well planned and compelling?
★ Do you promote your store as the type of store you want it to be to the kind of customers you want to attract?
★ Do you promote your strong points in the types of merchandise you carry and the services you offer?
★ Do you maintain an excellent relationship with your regular customers, while still going after new customers?
★ Does your advertising copy sell your store as well as the item?
★ Do you include related merchandise, when possible, in all your advertisements?
★ Do you present clearly the main merchandise you advertise?
★ Do you include your store's name and address in all your advertising?

In-store publicity

★ Do you maintain adequate ensemble displays that co-ordinate items?
★ Are your signs effective?
★ Do you use handbills at the store entrance to attract customers to specials in the store?
★ Are the merchandise lines properly located in your store and easily accessible?
★ Is each merchandise line adequately serviced?
★ Are your fixtures up to date?
★ Is the lighting good?
★ Is the majority of your fast-selling merchandise always on display and available for customer inspection without the intervention of a salesperson?
★ Are informative labels listing major selling points

attached to all items for which customers may need the information?

★ Are your impulse goods so placed as to be seen by customers shopping for demand items?

★ Do you limit your reserve stock area if you are paying a high rental?

★ Are your counters and aisle shelves not overcrowded with merchandise?

★ Are your checkout areas kept free of boxes, unneeded wrapping materials and odds and ends?

★ Do your aisle and counter arrangements tend to stimulate a circular traffic flow through the store?

★ For your advertised goods, do you have prominent signs to inform and guide customers to their exact location in the store?

★ Do you prominently display both advertised and non-advertised specials at the ends of counters as well as at the point of sale?

★ Wherever feasible, do you give the more colourful merchandise in your stock preference in display?

★ In locating merchandise in your store, do you always consider the productivity of space?

★ Do you keep your fixtures and windows clean and dust free?

★ Do you replace burned out light bulbs immediately?

★ Do garments fit properly on mannequins and fixtures?

★ Do your displays reflect the image of your store?

Sales ★ Is your sales force well chosen?

★ Is your sales force adequately trained in merchandise information and in customer handling?

★ Do your salespeople get adequate merchandise information?

★ Do you provide your salespeople with sufficient premiums, rewards, and contests to maintain their interest?

★ Do you train your sales force to substitute items when styles and sizes are sold out?

★ Do you get on the floor often enough to stimulate your sales force — and learn what your customers are demanding?

★ Do you motivate your sales force to do an outstanding job?
★ Do you take every opportunity to buy exclusive merchandise?
★ Do you price every item on its merits (rather than applying an average mark-up on most goods)?
★ Could you raise price line endings slightly without detracting from your sales volume?
★ Do you know the mark-up of each price line and in each classification?
★ Do you make an adequate effort to feature in your advertising those price lines and items that bear a high mark-up?
★ Is your high mark-up merchandise adequately displayed in the store?
★ Are your salespeople trained to give special attention to higher mark-up goods in stock?
★ Do you give rewards for selling high mark-up goods?
★ Do you avoid giving valuable space to slow sellers?
★ Are your salespeople adequately presenting the older goods in your stock?
★ Do you have a good follow-up system to ensure that goods don't become slow sellers?
★ Do you carefully instruct your salespeople in the selling points of merchandise that is slow moving?

Customer services
★ Do you make it convenient for customers to exchange merchandise or obtain refunds?
★ Do you have a liberal refund policy?
★ Do you offer gift wrapping?
★ Do you accept telephone orders?
★ Do you encourage credit accounts?

SUMMARY AND CONCLUSIONS

Your stock control system keeps you informed of the quantity of each kind of merchandise on hand. An effective system will provide you with the information on what, when and how much to buy of each style, colour, price, size, and brand. An effective system will curtail the number of lost sales resulting from out of stock on merchandise in popular demand and it will also identify slow-selling items and provide you with an indication whether there are any changes in the preferences of customers. Simply, an effective stock control system will provide you with the information needed to take appropriate action as far as having the right goods, at the right time, and in the right quantity. Another important point in achieving the above is to have good supplier relations (fair treatment of suppliers and prompt payment of accounts), for example: an emergency arises and a certain line of products needs to be replaced quickly. In such a critical situation, your relations with suppliers can prove to be invaluable.

BIBLIOGRAPHY

* Hugh S. Peak and Ellen F. Peak, *Supermarket Merchandising and Management*, 1979, Prentice-Hall, Englewood Cliffs, NJ.
* Guy Macleod, *Starting your own Business in South Africa*, 1983. Oxford University Press, Cape Town: 119–128.
* Mark H. McCormack. *What They don't Teach You at Harvard Business School*, William Collins, London: 122.
* Clifford M. Baumback, Kenneth Lawyer. *How to Organize and Operate a Small Business*. 1979. Prentice-Hall Englewood Cliffs, NJ: 342–372.
* J. Fred Weston, Eugene F. Brigham. *Managerial Finance*. 1978. 6th ed. The Dryden Press, Hinsdale, Ill.: 14–16.
* Mervyn Hills, Gavin Barnett, John Hensley. *Small Retailer's Kit.* July 1986. (Small Business Development Corporation, Johannesburg, Booklet no. 8.)
* Emile Woolf. *Depreciation and Inflation*. 1980. Video Arts Limited, London. (A briefcase booklet.)
* John W. Wingate, Seymour Helfant. Small store planning for growth. *Small Business Management Series no. 33*. 1977. (U.S. Small Business Administration. Washington D.C.)

NOTES

[1] John W. Wingate, Seymour Helfant. Small store planning for growth. *Small Business Management Series no. 33*. 2nd ed. 1977 U.S. Small Business Administration, Washington D.C.: 59, 60.
[2] Brian Rabjohn. Merchandising: part 1. *African Business* (official journal of the National African Federated Chamber of Commerce) 1984; **11**(6), 14. (Reproduced with permission.)
[3] Controlling merchandise (Dayton, Ohio: NCR Corp.), 5. *Source:* Clifford Baumback, Kenneth Lawyer. *How to Organize and Operate a Small Business* 1979. Prentice-Hall, Englewood Cliffs, NJ: 346, 347.
[4] See page 212 for an explanation on the buying schedule.
[5] See page 243 for more information on these aspects.

⁶ Vilfredo Pareto (1848–1923), a French born economist and sociologist whose Italian parents fled their native country in search of political freedom. That familial backdrop presumably was what led Pareto to study the distribution of wealth in Italy instead of France, which led in turn to his listing in many references as an Italian economist and sociologist instead of a French one. In the course of that study, he discovered that a small percentage of Italy's population controlled most of the country's wealth. From his studies comes Pareto's Law. Pareto's Law says that in any series of elements or variables, a small fraction of the elements account for most of the effect; you can get a lot of outcome from very little effort if you know where to concentrate your effort. In the workaday world, Pareto's Law is known colloquially as the 80/20 Rule. It has become a popular rule of thumb that suggests such clichés as: 80% of the money deposited in a bank comes from 20% of the customers; 80% of the profit comes from 20% of the products; 80% of the griping comes from 20% of the employees; 80% of the value of your work comes from 20% of your activities, etc. The problem is of course in figuring out which 20% gives you the 80%. (Adapted from: Ron Zemke. *Training, The Magazine of Human Resources Development* 1986; **23**(7): 59.

⁷ Self-Service Merchandising Methods. A training programme designed by the Centre for Developing Business Graduate School of Business Administration, University of the Witwatersrand, Johannesburg. Sponsored by Kodak (South Africa) (Pty) Ltd.

⁸ Brian Rabjohn. Techniques for increasing your range. *African Business* (official journal of the National African Federated Chamber of Commerce) 1984; **11**(3): 19–25. (Reproduced with permission.)

⁹ Method adapted from: Robert C. Ragan, Jack Zwick. *Fundamentals of Recordkeeping and Finance for Small Business.* 1978. Reston Publishing Company, Reston, Va: 42, 43. (Reprinted by permission of Prentice-Hall, Inc., Englewood Cliffs, New Jersey.)

¹⁰ John W. Wingate, Seymour Helfant. Small store planning for Growth. *Small Business Management Series no. 33.* 2nd ed. 1977. U.S. Small Business Administration, Washington D.C.: 90–102.

¹¹ These questions also serve as a checklist for some other functions related to the ultimate movement of stock, such as purchasing, shop layout and improving the external and internal images, salesmanship and selling, customer relations and service, advertising and promotions, and pricing.

13 | SECURITY

'Any retail store that is not addressing the problem of theft today is being unrealistic.

Jane Letzler
Manager of Training and Development for
Nieman-Marcus Department stores, U.S.A.[1]

INTRODUCTION

It would be inadvisable not to provide information on security as the profits of small businesses each year are substantially cut by theft. In other words, the effect of theft is money right off the bottom line and it is indeed a matter to deal with if the business is to survive. The statistics are eye-opening and can only prompt one to declare that we are in the midst of an epidemic of workplace dishonesty and theft. If you wish to continue making profits, you have to take this matter seriously. Mr A. L. Hughes, group loss controller of Metro Cash and Carry says that staff are the major culprits. He continues by saying: 'Let me tell you a terrible fact about the retail trade. It is so that 80% of all stealing in a shop is committed by staff. It is by the receiving clerk, signing for goods that are not received. They have a "fiddle" going with the driver of the delivery vehicle, where only part of the load is received, although the whole load is then sold to some dishonest person, and the parties concerned share out the cash. It is by the cashier, stealing money or not charging customers the correct price for the goods. This underringing for friends and relatives is a major problem. It is by the cashier making out false refund slips. She puts this document into her till and steals the money, so that to all intents her takings balance at the end of the day. Staff take their lead from their managers. In most cases, if he sets a good example in his behaviour and work, they will follow his lead.'

A wise security man once said that 10% of the people you employ are honest, a further 10% will steal regardless of what you do, and the remaining 80% will stay honest if you create an environment that discourages and detects theft. Mr Hughes: 'Your job therefore is to keep the honest 10%, to identify and get rid of the dishonest 10% before they do much more damage, and to protect the remaining 80% from themselves by making sure that they obey the rules and systems that discourage them from stealing. Your problem is similar to that of every businessman throughout the world, so be smart, look for the loopholes and plug them, but remember, as you close one, another one might open. It is an ongoing task, but being aware of the problem is halfway to solving it.[2]

The South African statistics for 1982/83 reveal that 8 757 women, and a staggering 11 770 men were convicted for shoplifting during that time. It is interesting to note that 52% of shoplifters caught are under 21 years old, the majority being male, but among adults the majority of shoplifters are female.[3] It has also been said that 80% of all cases of shoplifting are never discovered and of those discovered another 80% are not reported. In South African super-markets alone there is an annual loss of some R3 million due to shoplifting. An estimate was made in 1983 that shoplifting in South Africa accounted for over R100 million in stock losses during 1981, and this figure could approach R300 million per annum by the end of 1984. It was also noticed that some relatively modest retail businesses are losing between R2 000 and R3 000 per month to shoplifters. One can, however, only obtain a meaningful picture of stock losses by expressing the losses as a percentage of sales (turnover), and losses as small as 2% or 3% can threaten the future existence of many a small business. Shoplifting can never be prevented altogether, but it can be reduced by taking certain preventative measures. Sometime or other your business is also going to become the victim of shop-lifters. Be prepared and aware, and remember that prevention is better than cure.

WHY DO PEOPLE STEAL?

A loss-prevention manager with 20 years' experience says: 'As long as you have people and as long as you have merchandise, you are going to have employee theft. Some of the Egyptians working on the pyramids probably took some flagstones home to put in their patios.' Just the idea of theft from outsiders and those working for you is an uncomfortable one, but here are some reasons why people steal as gathered from various literature reviews:

★ People rationalize that everyone else steals, so they are acting according to accepted norms. This indicates a lack of values. The old absolute of 'Thou shalt not steal' is rationalized out of existence.

★ Economic factors are involved: People are more likely to steal in highly inflationary periods, when their budgets are being stretched, or because they live a life-style that outstrips their income.

★ Some personality-related factors found in people who are prone to steal from an employer are: stubborness, sensation-seeking and aggressiveness. They are often undependable quitters who are habitual rule breakers. They have few strong ties and a happy-go-lucky attitude toward life.

★ Perpetrators are more likely to continue stealing when they think management does not know or care about theft.

★ Some people just want a few extras in life. The thieves believe that the taking of money or other things may help them to reach living standards which they have set for themselves.

★ Revenge is sometimes a reason (low and inadequate salary), or the thief believes that he has been wronged, and to get even, he steals.

★ The thrill compels many people.

★ Temptation is a frequent factor: Place temptation in front of an employee and he may weaken and yield to the chance of taking something. You can create the opportunity through inadequate measures of control.

★ People may steal because of need and hunger, out of desperation.

★ Stealing can be for resale purposes (to finance a 'private venture').

★ The thieves may feel that they are not appreciated by superiors.

348

Shoplifters Shoplifters use many techniques to steal merchandise or money.

The most common shoplifting method is to conceal the merchandise in an innocent-looking object such as a handbag, shopping bag, box, briefcase, etc. The shoplifters normally also leave through the checkout point in a normal manner. The second common method is to conceal merchandise in clothing. A raincoat draped over one arm can be useful for stealing. Other useful features are pockets, and professional shoplifters normally wear specially designed or prepared clothes with extra large pockets underneath. Amateur shoplifters conceal merchandise under their clothing by tucking it in the waistbands of pants, slipping it inside a blouse, or using long sleeves to collect and conceal small-size, high-price items. Some female shoplifters conceal merchandise beneath their skirts by holding it between their legs (crotch-walking) as they pass through the checkout area. Others wear slings around their necks apparently to support broken arms but actually to be used as a depository for stolen goods. Baby carriages can also serve as hiding places. Young people sometimes pre-arrange to enter the shop in a crowd and deliberately confuse attention. Any disturbance is a favourite cover for theft. Returning an item for refund that was in fact taken from a shelf is another method, or switching price tags on bottle tops. Never put the price of an item on the lid of a product as some products' lids can be swopped.

The business's own merchandise packages can hide other merchandise: shoplifters empty the original contents of a package and refill it with more expensive merchandise. Fruit, vegetables and drinks whet the appetites of 'grazers' — those who eat within the shop and do not pay for what they eat. Professional shoplifters may carry shopping bags and an old cash-register tape into the shop, fill the bags with expensive items, and walk out, waving the slip at the cashier. A customer may go into fitting rooms taking four dresses in, steal by putting one dress over her clothing and then walk out, handing only three dresses back. Shoplifters are quick to use these and other techniques to take advantage of any weakness in a shop's security.

Employees Employees may steal from the petty cash box (or from the cash register) and cover theft by false vouchers, or they may steal cash payments from incoming mail. Another relatively simple method for employees is to send goods to non-existent customers that are then sold for personal profit. Employees sometimes steal directly from the shop's suppliers or stock.

The stealing of cash by employees usually involves the front-end personnel. Typically, the cashier points out a 'mistake' to a customer after the merchandise has been rung up and for which the customer has paid. Using the slip, the cashier shows a ,99 cent ring-up that should have been a R5,99 ring-up, or a similar combination. The customer then pays the additional R5,00, which the cashier puts in the cash register to be pocketed later.

Collusion or working with other people, is another method of theft. For example, a cashier can operate together with other people by not ringing up merchandise when helping friends, relatives or fellow employees. Employees then overcharge customers to make up for shortages. Employees sometimes even have a key to the business made, and steal after hours.

Suppliers Another form of robbery, especially applicable to businesses that buy merchandise in weights, such as a butchery, is that the incoming delivered goods do not weigh up to what is indicated on the invoice. Say for instance, you pay R3,50 per kilogram and you ordered 60 kilograms from a supplier. When it gets delivered, weigh before paying the supplier for it because it might only weigh 55 kilograms. If you don't weigh it, you may be robbed of R17,50. Note the difference on the invoice and sign there together with the delivery man.

Honest shoppers seldom if ever knowingly witness the commission of a shoplifting offence. There are three reasons for this:[4]

(a) They are pre-occupied with their own business and are not looking for this type of activity;

(b) Assuming they were interested in spotting a shoplifter, they do not know what to look for; and

(c) Their attention spans, in this regard, are short-lived.

The efficient floor-walker, on the other hand, is constantly on watch and knows the signs of theft. The following list, although not exhaustive, contains many of the things to watch for:[5]

1. Shoppers who wander aimlessly about the store, handling pieces of merchandise.
2. Groups of teenagers who spend considerable amounts of time in the store without making purchases.
3. Shoppers who appear nervous and glance about without moving their heads.
4. Shoppers who leave the store, then immediately return.
5. Shoppers who continually drop articles on the floor.
6. Shoppers who place their packages, coats and purses on top of or near merchandise.
7. Shoppers who carry large purses, knitting bags, briefcases, umbrellas and newspapers into the store.
8. Shoppers who bring garments to others who are in the dressing room.
9. Shoppers appearing hard to fit or difficult to please, who make repeated trips to the fitting room.
10. Shoppers who distract the attention of sales personnel by engaging them in long conversations or arguments.
11. Shoppers who wear coats with bulging pockets.
12. Shoppers who are dressed out of season.
13. Shoppers who wear loose-fitting garments.
14. The female shopper who repeatedly opens her handbag for a handkerchief, handles merchandise with the same hand, then places the handkerchief back in her purse (along with the merchandise).
15. Shoppers who wear large boots that are loose-fitting or open at the top.

16. Customers pushing shopping carts containing open purses.
17. Shoppers pushing baby carriages and strollers.

ANTI-SHOPLIFTING METHODS AND SAFEGUARD PROCEDURES

In general, the possibility of theft and fraud in a business can be cut by instituting some of the following meaures:

- The interior arrangement and layout should provide maximum visibility. If you have the necessary finance available put wall mirrors up as they will enable personnel to watch movements between the aisles. Locked display cabinets should be used for small and expensive merchandise. Display small items such as pens, pencils, razor blades, batteries and so on at check-out areas. You can, if you feel it is absolutely necessary, put signs up warning against shoplifting, but this can give a negative impression. A customer going to a fitting room should be handed a tag corresponding with the number of clothes being taken in. When the customer leaves the fitting room, a staff member should check that the number on the tag and the number of clothes are the same. Doors not in regular use should be locked. Fast service is recommended as a deterrent to shoplifting. It reduces the customer's privacy by the presence of a salesman. Courteous attention is welcomed by honest customers, and it also keeps potential shoplifters honest. When shoplifters are suspected in a shop, the staff should be able to alert one another by using the prearranged signal or code. The arrangement of merchandise and its tidiness are important. Do not stack goods so that they obscure the view or make it easy for a thief to sweep items into a bag or pocket.

- Lifting money from the cash register, a type of theft known as 'till tapping' can be discouraged by placing cash registers away from customer access and keeping the amount of cash at a low level (bank regularly). Close the cash register drawers immediately after giving change. Employees should avoid being distracted by a customer while the drawer is open. A cash register not in use must be locked. Confront shoplifters only as they leave the shop so as to make sure there is no intention to pay and no opportunity to get rid of stolen goods. Say something like: 'I believe you forgot to pay for something.' Always remember that you have to prove intent to steal. Intent is only shown if the customer has deliberately taken the goods past the cash register or has secreted the item inside his or her clothing.

- Cashiers should not serve friends and relatives, keep their purses or their own money at the check-out points, allow goods to accumulate at the check-out area, ask customers the price of any article that is not price-marked (rather call a shelf-packer) and accept payment by cheque unless authorized by the floor manager to do so.

- 'Walk the floor' regularly and look specifically for suspicious actions.

- Cashiers must also check their cash floats before they start to operate for the day to ensure that they are correct. At the end of each day place the empty till drawer next to the till so that if a burglary takes place at night, the thief can see that the till is empty and thus will not cause damage to the till by forcing it open.

- Look out for damaged price tags as it is an indication that a swop has taken place.

- Keep a record of each day's takings separately for each till as it is essential to establish differences.

- Authorize only one person to sign for petty cash (or till) withdrawals; even better, an authorized person plus yourself or only yourself (business owner).

- All mail be opened under competent supervision and away from other staff.

- Customer complaints of the nature that accounts have been paid should be investigated immediately. If complaints make you suspect something, you might want to send a few pieces of mail containing cash in the incoming mail and so try to catch the culprit.

- Let employees know that you are watchful.

- Provide an adequate safe room. Make certain that the safe is burglar proof and fireproof. Permit only authorized people to know the combination codes of safes and change combinations periodically. Keep a record of the dates on which changes in combinations were made. A key system is needed when you have issued keys. This may come in handy when an employee leaves your service (with the key). Before the employee leaves, you can make certain that the key has been returned to you. It is suggested that an employee be issued with a receipt when a key has been entrusted to him and it be put in his personal file. Below is a typical receipt:[6]

KEY RECEIPT

I have received this date a key to _____ (door[7]). This key is the property of _____ company and must be returned on request, transfer to another job, or when leaving the service of the company. Any abuse of this key, unauthorized loan or duplication may be grounds for discharge, and I understand my responsibility in this regard.

Signed: _____

Date of Issue: _____ Key No: _____

Employee Name: _____

- Make bank deposit slips in duplicate to receive bank proof and so be in a position to follow up any forgery. Check daily deposits through bank records. If possible, have this done by someone other than the person banking the money.

- Reconcile all bank statements regularly. If possible, have the reconciliation done by someone other than the person banking the money.

- Permissive use of cheques provides an opportunity for forgers. Install a sound verification system in the writing of cheques. Keep cheque books locked in a safe place. Remember that in too many cases a trusted, long-time employee has proved to be an embezzler. Blank cheques must always be locked up safely.

- Employees must not park cars in the stock-receiving area.

- Make sure the receiving door for goods is closed and locked when not in use. An alarm should ring when it is opened, and only managerial or authorized employees should have a key to turn the alarm off.

- Educate customers. They must know that they are entitled to a receipt. Advise them that subsequent adjustments depend on their showing their receipts.

- Do not cash cheques for customers or any other outsiders. The person who has fraudulent intentions might just be the one who wants to cash his cheque at your shop.

- When people pay by cheque see to it that their full names, address, phone number, identity number and perhaps also car registration number, are written on the back of the cheque. Also check that the cheque is completed in detail. Compare signature, if possible, with that of the shopper's credit card, or any other document that may serve as proof. A cheque has several key items such as the name and location of the bank, date, amount (in figures and words) and signature. Close examination of such key items can sometimes tip you off to a worthless cheque. Before accepting a cheque, look for the following as advised by Leonard Kolodny, Manager, Retail Bureau Metropolitan Washington Board of Trade:[8]

Date: Examine the date for accuracy of day, month and year. Do not accept the cheque if it is not dated, if it is post-dated, or if it is more than 30 days old.

Non-local banks: Use extra care in examining a cheque that is drawn on a non-local bank and ask for positive identification. List the customer's local and out-of-town address and phone number on the back of the cheque.

Location: Look first to be sure that the cheque shows the name, branch, town and province where the bank is located.

Amount: Be sure that the numerical amount agrees with the written amount.

Legibility: Do not accept a cheque that is not written

legibly. It should be written and signed in ink and must not have any erasures or written-over amounts.

Payee: When you take a personal cheque on your selling floor, have the customer make it payable to the business (name of business).

Amount of purchase: Personal cheques should be for the exact amount of purchase. The customer should receive no change.

Cheques over your limit: Set a limit on the amount — depending on the amount of your average sale — you will accept on a cheque. When a customer wants to go beyond that limit, your sales clerk should refer the customer to you.

Low sequence numbers: Be more cautious with low sequence numbers. Experience indicates that there seems to be a higher number of these cheques that are returned. Most banks who issue personalized cheques begin the numbering system with 0001 and number in sequence when a customer re-orders new cheques.

Amount of cheque: Most bad-cheque passers pass cheques in the R25 to R35 range on the assumption that the retailer will be more cautious when accepting a larger cheque.

Types of merchandise purchased: Be watchful of the types of merchandise purchased. Random sizes, selections, lack of concern about prices by customers should indicate to you that a little more caution should be exercised when a cheque is offered as payment.

- Offer rewards for catching thieves.
- Employ security guards at night. A guard's basic responsibility is to provide security for the property he is hired to protect. The use of security guards cannot alone provide adequate protection against criminals, but they can be very useful by reacting on threats immediately. Mostly, their presence is enough to deter intruders and criminals and guards are well-trained to respond accordingly with appropriate action. However, the guard's effectiveness depends a great deal on the presence and nature of other security measures on the premises, such as alarms, good lighting, protective fencing, etc. Using these measures in combination can be very effective. It would be less expensive if your business is situated in a large shopping centre, if you could share the costs with

other businessmen (such an arrangement can also be made with the landlord of the property).

- Install alarms with the intention of giving a warning or calling attention to a situation; in other words, a device that will draw immediate response by guards or other security personnel who are on or close to the premises. An alarm is a psychological deterrent, convincing most criminals to leave the business alone. Another aspect to consider is to advise criminals that you have an alarm by means of appropriate signs, otherwise the criminal may try to enter the business in the mistaken belief that the property is not protected and so cause damage that might not have happened in the first place.
- Almost all shop break-ins occur at night and good lighting on the outside is also a good preventer of a burglary, because darkness conceals the burglar and provides him with much time to do his 'business'. Indoor lighting is also important because when the shop is dark, the burglar can spot the police but the police or guard can't see the burglar.
- No safe is too heavy to be stolen. The best solution is to bolt it to the building structure. When closing your safe at night, be sure to check that all moneys and valuable documents have been put into the safe and that it is properly locked.

APPREHENSION AND PROSECUTION

When you catch a person who shoplifts, you must make very sure that he did indeed steal the goods and had no intention of paying for them. One important point that needs to be emphasized is that when a person's guilt is not proved, good judgement requires that the suspect go free. This is a safe policy, as false arrests can be very costly and have after-effects that can cost the business dearly as far as word-of-mouth advertising is concerned. A person is guilty of theft only if he takes possession of merchandise offered for sale with the intention of using it for himself without paying for the value thereof; or alters, transfers or removes any label, price tag or marking upon any merchandise offered for sale; or transfers any merchandise from one container to another with the intention of avoiding paying its full value. However, to give your charges a chance of succeeding, you must be able to do the following, otherwise you leave yourself open to counter-charges for false arrest:[9]

- see the person take or conceal merchandise;
- identify the merchandise as yours;
- testify that it was taken with the intent to steal;
- prove that the merchandise was not paid for; and
- call at least one or two other employees as witnesses.

It is wisest to apprehend shoplifters outside the store. You then have a better case if you can show that the shoplifter left the store with stolen merchandise. Outside apprehension always eliminates unpleasant scenes which might disrupt normal store operations. You may prefer to apprehend a shoplifter inside the store, if the merchandise involved is of considerable value or if you feel that the thief may be able to elude you outside the store premises. In either case, avoid verbal accusation of the suspect. One recommended procedure is to identify yourself, then say: 'I believe you have some merchandise which you have forgotten to pay for. Would you mind coming with me to straighten things out?' When cornered, the first thing most shoplifters — impulsive thieves or professionals — will say is: 'I have never done this before.' In general, this is all the more reason, if your evidence is sufficient, to call the police and proceed with prosecution. Failure to prosecute first offenders encourages them to try stealing again. Word also gets around that your store is an 'easy hit'.

Juvenile shoplifters require special handling. A strict, no-nonsense demeanor often makes a lasting impression on young offenders and may deter him from future theft. While many stores choose to contact the parents of young shoplifters rather than the police, remember that juveniles perpetrate about half of all shoplifting. The parents of troubled youngsters may be ineffective in handling the situation. Whom are you helping if you let the young shoplifter go free to steal again?

Some advantages of prosecution (the bringing of formal criminal charges against an offender in court) are that shoplifters normally avoid stores that have reputations for prosecuting apprehended thieves which will bring about the detection of more crime and the recovery of more merchandise. A good policy is always to prosecute those who are caught, even if your preferred approach is to prevent the offence rather than to catch the thief. Some disadvantages of prosecution are that it is a costly and time-consuming affair.

BURGLARY AND ROBBERY

Crime prevention begins with very elementary measures. One of them is to make it physically difficult for any burglar to get into the building. Another is not to be careless —doors, windows and safes must be locked at all times and especially after closing hours. Be sure that no unauthorized people are on, or locked into the premises at closing time, and that you keep certain lights on inside and outside the business. Bank at irregular times and change money bags frequently. If possible, always send a second person with the messenger going to the bank. If you lose keys, change the locks. Changing locks from time to time is one method of preventing the use of old keys by former employees or other people. Install an alarm system, preferably connected to the nearest police station.

Whatever happens with a robbery, observation of the robber's appearance, methods of robbery and get-away car can provide the police with very necessary clues, such as the colour of the car, its model and type, registration number, dents in the car, whether it was with or without certain wheel caps, scars on a person's face, sex, race, estimated age, approximate height and build, etc. A mark placed, say, six feet high on a doorframe may be useful in judging a robber's approximate height as he leaves the store. If robbers look dangerous keep a cool head and try to memorize clues that can lead to the arrest and eventual prosecution of the person by the police. Do not try to attack — your safety and that of your employees may be at stake if the robber is armed. Always report every case of theft to the police immediately as confirmation thereof by the police will come in handy when claiming back from insurance companies — they will want to know the circumstances and case number.

A police consultant Margaret Kenda, in her book *Crime Prevention Manual for Business Owners and Managers* (American Management Associations, New York), warns that 'a given business may be losing as much as a third of its profits to internal crime. Perhaps as many as 30% of all business failures are the direct result of inside theft'.[10] *The Small Business Reporter,* a publication by the Bank of America in San Francisco, says: 'Most businesses that fail are small businesses that are particularly vulnerable because of lax controls.'[11] Saul D. Astor, a security consultant, says: 'Internal dishonesty has many faces, but whatever form it takes, some deviation from normal patterns must appear. It is to these deviations and signals, that company executives must be sensitive and must react.'[12] Security experts are of the opinion that the most distressing thing about employee theft is that companies make it so easy. They leave valuable items unlocked or do not check to see that supplies actually exist. They put resources into catching thieves as opposed to preventing theft. Richard Fisher, vice-president of Brock International Security Corporation of Middlebury, Vermont, says: 'Employees take from the company for four reasons — need, greed, temptation and opportunity. A company can control the last two.'[13]

Care in screening job applicants is the first step in preventing inside theft. You should follow up on personal and business references as indicated on the application form. Previous employees and personnel managers can always give some indication as to the applicant's background, habits, personality and employment record. Consider the story below in this regard:[14]

Last April the Gaithersburg, Maryland, branch of Manpower Temporary Service, the nation's largest supplier of secretaries, honoured a smiling Kathy Cody, 29, as its 'secretary of the year'. Forty-eight hours later, Cody was sentenced to three years in prison and put on probation after she tearfully pleaded guilty to embezzling R8 762 from a former employer, the Gaithersburg Health Centre.

Cody's conviction came as a shock to the people at Manpower Temporary. That company had first telephoned and then mailed a reference request to the Gaithersburg Health Centre, but the health centre had made no reply.

'When she applied for a job with us', said Mitchell S. Fromstein, president of Manpower Temporary, 'she was asked a number of questions on a form. One was whether she had ever been convicted of a crime. Her reply was no, which was correct because she had not been convicted of anything at that point.'

Fromstein says the Cody episode was 'a bizarre and unpredictable happening'. However bizarre, Cody's case was not really that unusual. In fact, it was typical. She told the Montgomery County Circuit Court Judge, James McAuliffe, that in 1982, when she was working at the health centre, she was having money problems. She pocket small amounts paid in cash by clients, fully intending to pay back the money, yet never doing it.

SCREENING THE APPLICANT

Saul D. Aster, President of Management Safeguards, Inc., New York, comments as follows on screening applicants:[15]

Upgrading the level of retail personnel is largely a matter of careful personnel screening and selection, including careful reference checks, credit checks, psychological tests, polygraph lie-detector tests, and personal character examinations. Doing these things and sticking to the basic tenets of employee motivation can help you to generate a store atmosphere that discourages employee theft.

Just like a book, a job applicant can't be judged by outward appearance alone. Don't let the 'front' he or she puts on dull your caution. Appearances, experience and personality may all be striking points in the applicant's favour. And he or she may still be a thief. Or an alcoholic, drug addict, or other high security risk. Remember that the person you easily pick may just be looking for easy pickings.

One hiring mistake could prove to be a devastating profit drain for months or years to come. No matter how urgently you may need additional personnel, it does not pay to loosen your screening and hiring procedures. When you compromise on your standards of character and integrity, you also compromise on your profit position.

Don't take chances. Run a concientious reference check on every new employee. No security measure is more important than this.

Lack of knowledge about the store's routine usually restricts new employees' stealing to what they can slip from the cash register or conceal on their persons. You can detect either by closely watching daily receipts and personal scrutiny of new employees until you are satisfied that you can trust them.

SET THE TONE

Checking out new employees is only the beginning of upgrading your personnel. Another important step is setting a tone or atmosphere which will encourage honesty in your store.

In doing it, watch for excellence of good conduct and performance. Because people respect high standards, you should not settle for less. They also tend to copy the individuals who set such standards and require that they be met. It is important to adopt a 'Zero Shortage' attitude. If you feel that a 'reasonable write-off' due to pilferage is all right, keep it a secret and always hammer at shortage control, even when losses diminish.

Owner-managers should avoid setting a double standard of moral and ethical conduct. If an employee sees a supervisor in even a minor dishonest act, he or she will be encouraged in the same direction. Return over-shipments or overpayments promptly. When you set rules, have them apply to everyone. Owner-managers cannot expect their employees to set standards that are any higher than those they set for themselves.

Preserving the dignity of your employees is essential if you expect your people to respect you and the business. Employees should be treated with courtesy and consideration. Show an interest in them as individuals. Then back that interest — to mention an example or two — by keeping restrooms and other areas clean and attractive, and by providing fresh uniforms, if your business uses them. Respecting employees may not reform the hardcore thief. But it will help keep many others from straying.

Finally, owner-managers should not expect their people to achieve the impossible. Giving employees unrealistic goals is an invitation to cheat. When you do, you give no alternative. It is either cheat or admit failure and risk of losing their jobs.

PROVIDE INCENTIVES

A third step in upgrading personnel is to enable employees to live up to your expectations. The following practices can be helpful:

Make certain each person is suitably matched to his or her job. Employees should not be put in a position where they are forced to lie or cheat about performance because they are unable to do their work. Lying and cheating, even on a small scale, are just a step away from theft.

Set reasonable rules and enforce them rigidly. Loosely administered rules are more harmful than no rules at all.

Set clear lines of authority and responsibility. Each employee needs a yardstick by which to measure his or her progress and improve performance. To fill this basic need, duties should be spelled out — preferably a job description in writing. When employees do not know who does what, there will be error, waste, and the kind of indifferent performance that breeds dishonesty.

Employees should be given the resources they need to achieve success. Whether they are buyers, salespeople or stock clerks, nothing is more frustrating to employees than to see their goals blocked by circumstances beyond their control. To perform well, an employee needs the proper tools, the right information and guidance when it is required. Denying such support and expecting him or her to produce certain results is a sure way to weaken morale.

Be fair in rewarding outstanding performance. The top producing salesperson who receives the same treatment as the mediocre employee is apt to become resentful. Individuals who make a worthwhile profit contribution are entitled to, and expect, a fair share of ego and financial satisfaction. Honest recognition of merit by the owner-manager triggers more honest effort on the part of the employee. Various types of incentives for special achievements should be available.

Finally, you should remove the temptation to steal. One organization of counter service restaurants is noted for its good employee relations. It treats people fairly. It displays faith in their integrity and ability. But it also provides uniforms without pockets.

Remove the opportunity to steal and half the battle is won. There is no substitute for rigid, well-implemented preventive measures.

In addition, owner-managers should use a continuing programme of investigation and training. They should train employees on ways to eliminate stock shortage and shrinkage. One small retailer, for example, trains employees to record items, such as floor cleaner, which they take out of stock for use in the store: "Otherwise, its an inventory loss even though its a legitimate store expense." Above all, never stop letting your people know that you are always aware and that you always care.'

To protect what belongs to the business, you need to become almost fanatical in encouraging awareness of the threats of robbery, fraud and theft. Pilfering from both internal and external sources seems to be on the increase which results in shrinking profit. Therefore, an awareness of the seriousness of the evil should be cultivated amongst staff and all security controls should be tightened.

Many security experts are of the opinion that the best way to reduce shrinkage in general, and employee theft as well, is by concentrating on good customer service. They say that when you are on your toes, trying to do your best for the customer, you set a positive image, and have a positive presence in the shop. For employees, the anti-theft message begins with orientation programmes for new employees, to let employees know right from the beginning how you feel about theft. Henry Sobinski, vice-president for loss prevention at AMES, Inc., a chain of 458 discount and variety shops, based in Rick Hill, puts the matter this way: 'We are very up front about it. We don't whisper about it in the halls. We tell our associates that, yes, we know theft exists, that is part of the business and that we want to make it an unnecessary option for them. On the other hand, we, as management, have to be examples of concern about the issue. We have to pay the associates adequate salaries and treat people with respect and dignity. If we do that, and keep on doing it, we can control losses.'[16]

Saul D. Astor also makes the following very interesting statements:[17]

'"Shrinking controls is the result of shrinking profits"; One reason for pilferage is misplaced trust. Many owner-managers of small companies feel close to their employees. Some regard their employees as partners. These owner-managers trust their people with keys, a safe combination, cash and records. Thus, these employees have at hand the tools which a thief or embezzler needs for a successful crime. Unfortunately, some of the "trusted" employees in many small businesses are larger partners than their bosses anticipate. Unless you are taking active steps to prevent loss from internal pilferage, some are probably trying to steal your business, little by little, right from under your nose. Few indeed are the businesses in which dishonest employees are not busily at work. Usually, these employees are protected by management's indifference or ineptitude as they steal a little, steal a lot, but nevertheless, steal first the profit, and then the business itself.

One of the first steps in preventing pilferage is for the owner-manager to examine the trust he or she puts in employees. Is it blind trust that grew from close friendships? Or is it trust built on an accountability that reduces opportunities for thefts?

In addition to misplaced trust, it is easy for an owner-manager to create an environment in which dishonesty takes root and thrives. Just relax your accounting and stock control procedures. Nothing deters would-be thieves like the knowledge that stock is so closely controlled that stolen goods will be missed immediately. The owner-manager who does not exercise tight control over stock, cash, invoices, purchase orders, removals (for example, tools, materials and finished goods), and credits, is asking for embezzlement, fraud, and unbridled theft. Crooked office workers and production and maintenance personnel dream about sloppily kept records and unwatched stock. Why make their dreams come true?

Let people know you care. Make them aware of the stress you place on loss-prevention. This point must be driven home again and again. And with every restatement of it — whether by a security check, a change of locks, the testing of alarms, a systems audit, a notice on the bulletin board — you can be assured that you are influencing that moment of decision when an employee is faced with the choice — to steal or not to steal.'

Christopher, J. Moran, C.P.A. Partner, A.M. Pullen and Company, Greensborough, North California, comments on the subject as follows:[18]

'The first and one of the most important things an owner-manager should do is to set a good example. Your employees watch what you do and are prone to imitate your habits — good or bad. An employer who dips into petty cash, fudges on an expense account, uses company funds for personal items, or sets other examples of loose business behaviour will find employees rationalizing dishonest actions with the attitude "if it's good enough for the boss, it's good enough for me".

Another important way an owner-manager can discourage embezzle-ment is by establishing a climate of accountability. Employees should know their jobs well and feel trusted. But they should also realize that they are held accountable for their actions. To some people manage-ment indifference in financial administration is a licence to steal. That is why it is important for you to examine your procedures and determine what controls can be added to forestall any dishonest practices.'

SUMMARY AND CONCLUSIONS

Methods of dealing with internal and external security raise critical questions for any small business owner. In addition

365

to being alert to outside factors continually affecting the business, the modern owner-manager of a small business is increasingly faced with the need to pay greater attention to internal security. You should have seen that message in this chapter — it was intended to stimulate you to consider and implement security measures for protecting your profits and consequently, your business.

BIBLIOGRAPHY

* Errol Ashman, Shrinking Controls results in Shrinking Profits, *Entrepreneur*, Volume 5 Number 2 (February 1986), p. 24 and 25.
* Ben Barone, Store Detectives? Security Guards? — or an Article Surveillance System?, *Entrepreneur*, Volume 2 Number 11 (November 1983), pp. 13 and 15.
* George Schutte, The Adverse Effect of Shoplifting on Your Profits, *Small Business News*, Business Advisory Bureau of the University of the North, Volume 8 Number 3 (August 1986), pp. 5 and 6.
* L.M Gwangwa, Improved Office and Data Security is a Must to Every Businessman, *Small Business News*, Business Advisory Bureau of the University of the North, Volume 8 Number 3 (August 1986), p. 8.
* P.R. Mehlape, Seeking the Soft Target, *Small Business News*, Business Advisory Bureau of the North, Volume 8 Number 3 (August 1986), p. 10.
* Ron Zemke, Employee Theft: How to Cut Your Losses, *Training, The Magazine of Human Resources Development*, Volume 23 Number 5 (May 1986), pp. 74–78.
* J.K. Lasser Tax Institute, *How to Run a Small Business*, 5th Edition, 1982, McGraw-Hill Book Company, pp. 199-214.
* Lynne Adkins, The High Cost of Employee Theft, Employee Theft Resource Centre, American Hardware Mutual Insurance Company, Minneapolis. An article that appeared in the *Dun's Business Month*, October 1982.
* A.L. Hughes, Shrinkage can Cost You Your Business, *Entrepreneur*, June 1984, pp. 16–17.
* A James Fisher, *Security for Business and Industry*, 1979, Prentice-Hall, Inc., Englewood Cliffs, New Jersey.
* Charles F. Hemphill, Jr., *Modern Security Methods*, 1979, Prentice-Hall, Inc., Englewood Cliffs, New Jersey.
* Addison H. Verrill, Reducing Shoplifting Losses, *Management Aids Number 3.006* (Washington, D.C.: U.S. Small Business Administration, 1967).
* S.J. Curtis, Preventing Burglary and Robbery Loss, *Management Aids Number 3.007* (Washington, D.C.: U.S. Small Business Administration, 1968).
* W.C. Odendaal, Hoe Seker is u dat u nie Besteel word nie?, *Entrepreneur*, Volume 3 Number 11 (November 1984), p. 6.
* Editorial, Security and Management, *Entrepreneur*, Volume 5 Number 2 (February 1986), p. 4.
* Hugh S. Peak and Ellen F. Peak, *Supermarket Merchandising and Management*, 1977, Prentice-Hall, Inc., Englewood Cliffs, New Jersey.

[1] Ron Zemke. Employee theft: How to cut your Losses. *Training, The Magazine of Human Resources Development* 1986; **23**(5): 75. (Reproduced with permission.)

[2] A.L. Hughes. Shrinkage can cost you your business. *Entrepreneur* 1984; June: 16, 17. (Reproduced with permission.)

[3] *Source:* Myron Brenton. Women who steal. *Cosmopolitan* 1986; April: 158.

[4] A. James Fisher. *Security for Business and Industry.* 1979. Prentice-Hall, Englewood Cliffs, NJ: 196–197. (Reprinted with permission.)

[5] Ibid.

[6] Charles F. Hemphill, Jr. *Modern Security Methods.* 1979. Prentice-Hall, Englewood Cliffs, NJ: 48.

[7] You could also number your doors or identify them by allocating some code. Also number the key to correspond with the number on the door. A similar method can be used when issuing tools to employees.

[8] Leonard Kolodny, Outwitting bad-cheque Passers. *Management Aids, Number 3.008.* 1983. U.S. Small Business Administration, Washington D.C.

[9] Addison H. Verrill. Reducing Shoplifting Losses. *Management Aids, Number 3.006.* 1967. U.S. Small Business Administration, Washington, D.C.

[10] Seth Kantor. How to foil employee crime. Quoted by permission from *Nation's Business.* July 1983; U.S. Chamber of Commerce.

[11] Ibid.

[12] Ibid.

[13] Ibid.

[14] Ibid.

[15] Saul D. Aster. Preventing retail theft. *Management Aids, Number 3.004.* 1966. U.S. Small Business Administration, Washington, D.C.

[16] Ron Zemke, Employee theft: how to cut your losses. *Training, The Magazine of Human Resources Development,* 1986; **23**(5): 78. (Reproduced with permission.)

[17] Saul D. Aster. Preventing employee pilferage. *Management Aids Number 5.005.* 1970. U.S. Small Business Administration, Washington, D.C.

[18] Christopher J. Moran. Preventing embezzlement. *Management Aids Number 3.009.* 1973. U.S. Small Business Administration, Washington, D.C.

14 SETTING UP A RECORD-KEEPING SYSTEM

'Accounting information is regarded by some as the language of the businessman.'

William H. Day[1]

'Information provided by the recordkeeping system is management information.'

F. Bekker

'A set of books is like a roll of exposed film. The latter must be developed before you can see the picture.'

Irving M. Cooper[2]

INTRODUCTION

Why must you keep records? If you are a businessman who's business is not performing as you would like it to, your attitude and answer to this question is more than likely 'because the government requires me to'. Not only does good business practice dictate that you keep good records that can provide you with information to aid you in managing the finances of the business as well as the business as a whole, but also, seeing that you are being granted a licence to trade, you are required by law to provide a summary of all business transactions in the form of financial statements to be compiled at the end of every year. If it is only for the government, it shouldn't be. However, if it were not for this annual financial requirement, many a business owner would never know whether he was making a profit or a loss, and obviously that is of vital interest to you. If you look upon record-keeping being a nuisance imposed by the government, you will never be successful. You will never know how your business is performing and you will never be able to plan for the future.

Record-keeping (better known as accounting) has two distinct objectives: the provision of information to aid you in planning the future activities of the business based on accurate data of the past by measuring actual results against predetermined results; and recording, classifying, analysing and interpreting day-to-day transactions. However, it should be borne in mind that record-keeping is not financial management, but only an instrument to make financial management possible. Accounting records will not provide you with ready-made answers to your financial problems, but they will help you in shaping sound decisions, as it is the facts of the past that form the decisions to be made in the future. You don't have to go to the extent of implementing a 'fancy' record-keeping system. What you need is a system patterned after basic accounting principles that gives you all the information necessary.[3] You need a system from which you can obtain the answers to such basic questions as:

- What was my income last year, last month, last week, yesterday?
- What were my expenses last year, last month, last week, yesterday?
- In what way can I increase my income (through sales)?
- In what way can I cut down or eliminate some of my expenses?
- What is the value of my building, equipment and other fixed assets after depreciation?
- How much did I receive in cash business and by selling on credit?
- How much do my debtors owe me? How many of their payments are overdue and how long overdue?
- How much money did I invest in my business?
- What was my gross profit? Was it sufficient to cover expenses?
- What was my net profit? How does it compare to other similar businesses?
- How much do I owe my creditors?

Money is constantly moving in a business. As it comes in, some of it has to go out again, and, unless strict control is kept of its movements it will be difficult to know whether the business is being managed at a loss or a profit. What makes record-keeping so important is the fact that no memory can remember all the transactions of the day never mind all the transactions for the whole month or year. It is for this reason that a cash book is employed to record all the transactions of a business—all cash coming in and all cash going out.

It is not the intention here to explain a complicated accounting set-up in full, but the following very basic record-keeping system is a minimum requirement in every small business: a cash book, a cash control system, an asset register, and records of debtors and creditors. It is furthermore a legal requirement that you have a wages and salary analysis book to show how your calculations of these amounts were made up for each employee. In addition, every employee must be provided with a pay slip.

THE CASH BOOK

The cash book has two identically divided sides—one for receipts (debit side) and one for payments (credit side). The cash book is in effect a summary of a single day's business transactions. This provides a good permanent record and makes the information easier to work as mentioned below. On the debit side is recorded all money received through the sale of goods (cash and credit sales), capital paid into the business by the owner, sale of assets, interest received and the bank balance brought forward (if the business has a credit balance at the bank). The credit side is used for recording all payments of goods bought for resale (purchasing of stock), buying of assets, business expenses such as salaries, rent, stationery, donations, water and lights, personal drawings, telephone, insurance, bank charges and many more. The income received and payments made should be analysed into headings appropriate to your business, for example: divide receipts into those from debtors and cash sales, and payments into those concerning stock purchases, salaries and wages, transport, etc. (See Fig. 1 for an example of the cash book.)

The debit side In the 'details' column a description is given of what the income was for. The 'bank' column represents the total income of that particular day. It also represents the money you should be banking every day. In the 'cash sales' column the total cash sales for the day are recorded, which information is obtained from the cash register slip (an explanation of this can be found under the 'cash control system' — Fig. 2). In the 'debtors' column all money received from debtors (credit sales) are recorded for that particular day. In the 'sundry' column all other income is recorded, such as that for the sale of an asset, or any other income received not through the sale of normal stock. Notice that the balance brought forward is recorded in the 'bank' column as well as the 'sundry' column. It is done in this manner so that the totals will balance at the end of the month.

The credit side In the 'details' column a description is given of what the payment made was; in other words, to whom the cheque was made out. The 'total' column represents the total payments of that particular day. In the 'stock purchases' and 'small stock purchases' columns are recorded all payments made to suppliers who delivered goods to your shop. However, if you purchase stock on credit from a supplier, only the payments made to the supplier will be recorded in the cash book and not the total amount of stock received. For example, you bought goods on credit worth R800 on 1 July 1986 and you pay this supplier R400 on 26 July 1986. Then it will be the R400 that you record in the cash book on 26 July 1985 (cheque number also to be recorded). It is, however, important that a creditors record book' be introduced so that you always know how much you owe your creditors on any particular date. All payments made must be allocated to a specific expense column such as petrol costs under the 'transport' column, wages and salaries under its appropriate column in the cash book, and so forth. The 'sundry expense' column is mostly used for those payments for which you have no other column available, for example: you buy an asset such as a cash register during April 1985, or you had a vehicle repaired. Thus, the 'sundry expense' column is used for payments that do not appear frequently and saves using the limited space in the cash book to provide such an expense with a column of its own. It is important that you make a note next to the amount in the 'sundry expense' column explaining what it was for in order to get the correct

Fig. 1

CASH BOOK FOR XYZ STORES — APRIL 1986

(Debit Side)

Date	Details	Bank	Cash Sales	Debtors	Sundry Income
1	Balance brought forward	1636,00			1636,00
1	Sales	364,20	364,20		
2	Sales	82,86	82,86		
4	Sales	364,00	364,00		
5	Sales & debtors	934,00	740,00	194,00	
6	Sales	450,00	450,00		
7	Sales	230,00	230,00		
8	Sales & debtors	521,00	310,00	211,00	
9	Sales	299,00	299,00		
10	Sales	340,00	340,00		
		16801,00	14760,00	405,00	1636,00

(Credit Side)

Date	Details	Cheque No.	Total	Stock Purchases	Small Stock Purchases	Transport	Salary & Wages	Sundry Expenses
1	Vinto Minerals	40106	374,00	364,00		10,00		
2	Metro	40107	220,00	210,00		10,00		
3	Cash	40108	116,00		16,00			100,00 (personal drawings)
4	A & C Wholesalers	40109	870,00	850,00	20,00	20,00		
5	Spar Wholesalers	40110	705,00	660,00	25,00	20,00		
6	Vinto Minerals	40111	260,00	240,00				
7	B and B Office Machines	40112	504,00		24,00			480,00 (purchase of new cash register)
8	Altec Garage	40113	113,00		13,00			95,00 (repair of vehicle)
10	Metro	40115	370,00	340,00	20,00	10,00		
11	Mr J Lubisi	40116	2100,00				2100,00	
			11034,00	7254,00	620,00	170,00	2100,00	890,00

description. This will be of assistance in preparing the financial statements (balance sheet and income statement).

A word of caution: do not include your own personal expenses in the cash book of the business. Don't mix the two as this will cause problems in preparing financial statements. They will not truly reflect the operations of your business. Furthermore, you must not forget to record deductions by the bank (to be obtained from the bank statement) on the credit side of the cash book. Such deductions can be for bank charges and other service charges, insurance payments and stop orders.

Fig. 2

CASH CONTROL SYSTEM — APRIL 1986

CASH REGISTER 1

Date	Cash Reading	Small Expenses	Balance	Cash (Bank)	Surplus	Shortage	Notes to small expenses
1	364,20	10,00	354,20	354,20	—	—	Petrol
2	82,86	10,00	72,86	75,86	3,00	—	Petrol
3	210,40	16,00	194,40	194,40	—	—	Stock
4	364,00	20,00	344,00	344,20	0,20	—	Stock
5	740,00	45,00	695,00	693,00	—	2,00	R20,00 Petrol/R25 Stock
6	450,00	20,00	430,00	430,00	—	—	Petrol
7	230,00	24,00	206,00	206,00	—	—	Stock
8	310,00	18,00	292,00	292,00	—	—	Stock
9	299,00	16,00	283,00	283,00	—	—	Stock
10	340,00	30,00	310,00	310,00	—	—	R10,00 petrol/R20,00 Stock
11	260,00	24,00	236,00	236,00	—	—	Stock
31	450,00	24,00	426,00	426,00	—	—	Stock
TOTAL 14760,00							

CASH CONTROL SYSTEM (Fig. 2)

The cash control system is necessary as it gives you an indication of what is happening at the cash registers during the day. For example, the second day of April can be interpreted in the following way: you sold R82,86 worth of goods, you took R10 from the till for petrol, which is supposed to leave you with R72,86 in the till but when you actually counted the cash in the till and subtracted your daily float, you had a surplus of R3,00 for the day. The surplus could be the result of giving a customer too little change, neglecting to record or ring up a transaction or recording or ringing up a transaction for too small an amount.

373

When we consider the 5th of April where you had a shortage of R2,00. This shortage could be the result of giving the customer too much change, the cashier taking R2,00 for himself from the till, yourself taking money out which you did not record, or recording or ringing up too large an amount for a transaction. When you find these variations in your daily operations, you can immediately take action to correct the matter. However, first determine which one of these factors caused the problem before demanding an explanation from the cashiers as it might be a sensitive matter. People can and do make mistakes and therefore you need to use your own discretion concerning the difference being picked up every day. Don't constantly pick on someone who has a shortage or surplus every day, as it might damage his morale as well as that of others. They might feel they are not trusted. Be careful in your aproach—use tact. Once cashiers know that they can be caught out and have to give account of the shortages (and surpluses), they will constantly strive to do their best in order to balance every day—providing you handled the incidents with tact. Explain the consequences of 'cheating' customers. If you have more than one cash register in operation, there should be a system of control for each cash register. Assign cash registers to cashiers for the day. This will encourage the cashiers to be responsible for the money in the till and gives no opportunity to blame another cashier if there was any mismanagement of the money.

The figures in the 'cash reading' column reflects your cash sales for the day and are transferred to the debit side of the cash book to be recorded in the 'cash sales' (turnover) column. The figure is obtained from the cash register slip.

The figures in the 'small expenses' column represent those cash payments made for various small purchases, such as milk, bread, petrol, tea for personnel, cleaning materials or paying a labourer who helped with the unloading of your truck, etc. Make sure that for each small expense there is a slip saying what it was for, the date and bearing your signature or that of any other person authorised by you.

The figures in the 'balance' column are calculated by subtracting small expenses from the actual sales made on that day. The 'balance' is what should be in the till—excluding the daily float.

The figures in the 'cash' column are ascertained by actually counting the money, subtracting the daily float and writing down what cash you have left. You now compare this with the amount in the 'balance' column—the amount that you should have in cash. You can now determine whether there is a shortage or surplus for the day.

In the 'notes to small expenses' column, you can make notes of what the small expenses were for in order to do the correct allocation in the cash book (credit side).

ASSET REGISTER

It is also very important to keep an asset register for all assets in your business. This is so as to know what each asset's original cost was, and other details for information when necessary, for example:

Fridge
Product: Zero Freezer
Model: 141639
Serial number: 004163973
Original cost: R630,00
Invoice number: 63101
Date bought: 12.12.1983
Supplier: Zero Manufacturers
Address: P.O. Box 1416   *Tel.:* (011) 676367
                Johannesburg 2000
Contact person: Mr R. P. Hanekom

Say for instance you sold this particular freezer for R300 to a Mr P. Nkosi on 14 March 1986, then you can draw a line across the page indicating that you sold it and it is no longer on your list of assets (see below).

Sold to P. Nkosi for R300 on
14 March 1986

You should have similar information recorded in your 'asset register' for every asset. This will enable you to prepare the financial statements and calculate depreciation. All improvements to buildings and other assets should also be recorded as this will have an influence on their value, which again affects the depreciation of the respective assets. It is further recommended that you include columns for recording depreciation for every year and for every single asset individually.

DEBTORS RECORD

Debtors are known as the people who bought goods from you (the business) on credit. They thus owe you money and when payments from them are received, they are recorded on the debit side of the cash book as well as on their individual accounts.

An example follows:

Acc No.: 6006		Name: Mr. J. Jones			
Date	Invoice No.	Amount of goods bought	Receipt No.	Amount Paid	Balance
26/3/86	1436	R450,00	—	—	R450,00
5/4/86	—	—	304	194,00	R256,00

Acc No.: 6007		Name: Mr. R. Nkosi			
Date	Invoice No.	Amount of goods bought	Receipt No.	Amount Paid	Balance
21/3/86	1448	R260,00	—	—	R260,00
8/4/86	—	—	326	211,00	R 49,00

Do not forget to issue each credit customer with an invoice specifying the goods the customer bought from you. File the copies in a neat fashion.

CREDITORS RECORD

Creditors are the suppliers from whom you (the business) bought goods on credit for resale purposes. You thus owe them money. All payments made to these suppliers (or creditors) must be recorded on the credit side of the cash book. It is advisable that you have a separate book in which you record this information so as to know at any particular date what you owe any creditor. Furthermore, this will assist you in preparing financial statements and in times where there is doubt about whether payments have been made to suppliers:

A AND A WHOLESALERS (CREDITOR)					
Invoice No.	Date goods Received	Amount per Invoice	Amount Paid	Payment Date	Balance Owing
1006314	1/4/86	R461,00			R461,00
1006419	4/4/86	R744,00	R850,00	4/4/86	R355,00

BANK RECONCILIATION

The bank will periodically send you your paid-out cheques and a statement of your bank account. Normally banks send out statements at the end of each month so that you can reconcile your records with the bank statement—that is compare the two records and account for any differences. Reconciling your bank statement every month without fail is an important step in keeping accurate records.

Before starting to check, or reconcile your bank statement, you should check your own figures. When you are sure that the balance in your cash book is mathematically correct, you are ready to reconcile your records with that of the bank. The actual procedure of reconciliation is very straightforward and you proceed according to the steps discussed below. Before you close off your cash book at the end of the month, you must compare the entries in your cash book with the entries on the bank statement. Certain entries on the bank statement will not appear in the cash book and you must use this information (from the bank statement) to complete the cash book. Such cases may be: (i) bank commission, ledger fees and other bank charges; (ii) interest which may be debited by the bank in the case of a bank overdraft; and (iii) cheques received by the business which were banked, but which were not cashed by the bank and were returned as 'dishonoured cheques'.

Steps in completing reconciliation

1. You first determine your cash book balance by subtracting the total payments from the total income.
2. You then turn to the bank reconciliation of the previous month and check whether there were any outstanding cheques noted in that month's bank reconciliation. If there were, these cheques should have come through the bank during the current month. Now you start ticking off the outstanding cheques listed in the previous bank reconciliation that have now come through the bank. When you have finished ticking off the outstanding cheques of last month, you may find that a few of them are still outstanding. Those which are still outstanding remain, of course, outstanding for the current month as well. You then turn to the credit side of your cash book and next to each cheque that has gone through the bank, put a tick mark. Those cheques which have not as yet gone through the bank, and are outstanding, will have no tick mark next to them.
4. You make a list of your outstanding cheques, keeping them in numerical sequence.
5. On the debit side of the cash book you tick off the deposits listed on the bank statement. You should also turn to the bank reconciliation made for the previous month to see if there were any outstanding deposits. If there were, the first deposit listed on the bank statement should be the record of that outstanding deposit. You may find, near the end of the month, that there is an outstanding deposit not yet recorded by the bank for the current month. You know this because it is not ticked off in your cash book on the debit side. If, however, you find that you have a deposit listed on the bank statement and not in the debit side of the cash book or the previous

bank reconciliation, you know that it has been deposited in the bank but has not been recorded in your books.

6. After you have done the above and have a list of all outstanding cheques and outstanding deposits, you proceed to do your bank reconciliation as in the following example (based on the cash book in Fig. 1).

Your cash book balance is R5 767,00 (R16 801 minus R11 034) and your bank statement shows a balance of R8 207,00. Your books indicate that there are two outstanding cheques: Numbers 40115 and 40116, issued for R340,00 and R2 100,00 respectively. There are no outstanding deposits.

Bank balance as per cash book		R5 767,00
Add: Outstanding cheques		
No. 40115	R340,00	
No. 40116	R2 100,00	R2 440,00
Balance per bank statement		R8 207,00

The balance that gets carried forward to the following month is that of the 'balance as per cash book', R5 767,00.

In this example, if you had a credit bank balance (overdraft at the bank or the total expenses were more than the income), then you would have deducted the outstanding cheques and added outstanding deposits to the bank balance per cash book in order to reconcile it with the bank statement.

SUMMARY AND CONCLUSIONS

Your books and records are not only the tools with which to measure your success, but they also form the basis from which you can make assumptions about the future and thus plan for profit. They will, furthermore, assist you in compiling financial statements at the end of every day, month or year. You dare not operate without an accurate summary of all transactions, as this is the foundation on which sound financial management is based. A simple, well-organized system of records, regularly kept up to date can actually save you time and money in the long run and, most importantly, it will provide you with the exact financial position of your business on a daily basis.

BIBLIOGRAPHY

* Robert C. Ragan, Jack Zwick. *Fundamentals of Record-keeping and Finance for the Small Business.* 1978. Reston Publishing Company, Reston, Virginia.
* R. Keith Yorston, E. Bryan Smyth, S. R. Brown. *Accounting Fundamentals.* 1961. 4th Ed. Taw Book Company, Australia.
* Dan Snyder. Finansiële state as bron van inligting. *Entrepreneur* 1983.

NOTES

[1] William H. Day. *Maximizing Small Business Profits with precision management.* 1978. Prentice-Hall, Englewood Cliffs, NJ: 50.

[2] Irving M. Cooper, Accounting services for small service firms. *Management Aids, Number 1.010.* 1967 Washington D.C.: 1. U.S. Small Business Administration.

[3] An accountant or an accounting service can assist in keeping the business on a sound basis. They can set up a record-keeping system for you, as well as interpret your financial statements and provide financial advice on such an interpretation by relating it to a profitable operation. When selecting an accounting service, make sure it has the ability to provide you with timely information.

15 FINANCIAL FUNDAMENTALS

'A business is a business is a business. If you can read the financial statements, you can manage anything. The people, the products, and the services are simply those resources you have to align to get good financial results.'

Thomas J. Peters and Robert H. Waterman, Jr.[1]

INTRODUCTION

A most vital area of your responsibilities is the management of the business's finances. What you need to do is to keep the business liquid, profitable and solvent. Without realizing a profit, there is little incentive to stay in business; without liquidity the business will be on search for cash to pay creditors, expenses and various other commitments; and without solvency, the business would not have sufficient assets to meet its liabilities and creditors could take legal action to put it into liquidation (i.e. force a sale of assets in order to pay at least something). In difficult times, liquidity and solvency are almost more important than profits.

In the widest sense your task as a businessman is to eliminate uncertainties by knowing constantly where the funds have come from, where they are going to come from in the future, how those funds are going to be utilized, and what the actions are going to be when funds are not sufficient. Thus, your task is to know whether the business is financially sound and if not, what corrective actions need to be taken. The financial statements can only be useful to you if transactions were accurately recorded in the books, otherwise they are useless as no sound decisions can be taken on false facts. At the end of the accounting period and after the preparation of the financial statements, it is necessary to analyse such statements for the purpose of ascertaining how far the results from the period concerned were from being satisfactory. Financial ratios are used for this analysis.

FINANCIAL STATEMENTS

The two most important financial statements are the balance sheet and the income statement. The difference between the two is often explained by comparing the balance sheet to a 'snapshot' of the business as it stood on the last day of the accounting period. The balance sheet answers the question: 'How did I stand financially at that time?' The income statement is regarded as a 'moving picture'. It is also a summary of business transactions that have taken place during the year (or a period) resulting in either a profit or a loss. The balance sheet presents a financial picture of the business at any given moment—its assets, liabilities and ownership (equity). In short, the balance sheet shows where the business is and the income statement shows how it got there.

INCOME STATEMENT
1 January 1986 to 31 December 1986

1. Sales	176 310	
2. Less: Cost of sales	131 409	(3+4−5=2)
3. Opening stock	28 680	(Closing stock of previous accounting period)
4. Plus: Purchases	136 960	
5. Less: Closing stock	34 231	(Stock physically counted on 31 December 1986)
6. Gross profit	44 901	(1−2=6)
7. Less: Expenses	23 885	
8. Salary and wages	12 600	
9. Water and lights	760	
10. Telephone	460	
11. Transport	1 870	
12. Depreciation	2 820	
13. Interest on loan	3 600	
14. Bank charges	195	
15. Maintenance—vehicles	660	
16. Maintenance—building	240	
17. Advertising	680	
18. Net profit	21 016	(6−7=18)

BALANCE SHEET AS AT 31 DECEMBER 1986		
19. **Employment of capital**	**R84 832**	(20+24=19)
20. *Fixed assets*	*R41 380*	
21. Building	28 000	
22. Equipment R4 200 less depreciation of 10%)	3 780	
23. Vehicles (R12 000 less depreciation of 20%)	9 600	
24. *Current assets*	*R43 452*	
25. Cash on hand	760	
26. Cash in bank	4 300	
27. Debtors	4 161	
28. Stock	34 231	
29. **Capital employed**	**R84 832**	(30+33+35 =29)
30. *Equity*	*R62 955*	
31. Capital	41 939	(19−32−33 −35=31)
32. Net Profit	21 016	
33. *Long-term liabilities*	*R18 716*	
34. Bank loan	18 716	
35. *Current liabilities*	*R3 161*	
36. Creditors	3 161	

RATIO ANALYSIS

In order to analyse and interpret financial statements, use is usually made of certain financial ratios. Ratio analysis employs financial data taken from the financial statements of a business and provides clues for spotting trends towards better or poorer performance. Ratio analysis is thus the conversion of financial statement figures into simple ratios, which can be compared from one accounting period to another. When a series of balance sheets for regular intervals are compared, the changes in certain items begin to disclose trends. Similarly, comparitive income statements reveal significant changes in what took place. It is only by comparing these financial data from one period to another that revealing answers are found. Ratios are normally classified into four fundamental types:
1. liquidity ratios, which measure the ability of the business to meet its liabilities (or obligations).

2. leverage ratios, which measures the extent to which the business has been financed by debt, and show the relationship of owner-supplier funds to those furnished by creditors.
3. activity ratios, which measure how effectively the business is using its resources.
4. profitability ratios, which measure management's overall effectiveness in operating the business.

Specific examples of each ratio are given in the following sections, in which the financial statements in this part are used to illustrate their calculation and use.

LIQUIDITY RATIOS

Liquidity may be thought of simply as the ability to pay your bills on time. It is the very first objective of financial management. Measures of liquidity are intended to help you answer questions such as: Do you have enough cash, plus assets that can be readily turned into cash, to be sure of being able to pay the debts that will fall due during the accounting period? A sensitive indicator is the ratio of current assets to current liabilities. When this ratio falls continuously, it is a sign of deterioration.

Current Ratio The current ratio is computed by dividing current assets by current liabilities. It is the most commonly used measure of short-term solvency, since it indicates the extent to which the claims of short-term creditors are covered by assets that are expected to be converted to cash in a relatively short period.

$$\frac{\text{Current assets}}{\text{Current liabilities}} = \frac{\text{R43 452}}{\text{R3 161}} = 13,7:1$$

Thus, for every R1,00 of current liabilities, there is R13,70 in current assets to cover it. Conservative bank practices look for a ratio of 2:1. Therefore, although the ratio of 13,7:1 is well above the standard set through conservative bank practices, there should be some concern as to what caused it or what can be done with the excess funds. The standard ratio of 2:1 is usually considered adequate because theoretically it provides for the current liabilities with a 100% margin of safety. An excessively high ratio may, however, indicate poor credit control over debtors. Excess liquidity is just as undesirable, because it may have been caused by too many credit sales or by maintaining an unnecessary credit balance in a current account at the bank. An excessively high ratio can also mean that the business is not making full use of its current borrowing power. It should be borne in mind that credit sales on paper are not yet money in the bank. What is meant by maintaining an unnecessary credit balance in your current account at the bank is that you receive an income at a much lower interest rate than you could get by investing the money at a higher interest rate. By doing so, you could make use of your borrowing power.

A business which maintains current assets barely equal to its current liabilities will be in a weak financial position if half or more of the current assets consist of merchandise and debtors. In an emergency requiring payment of all current debt, the merchandise and debtors would have to be sacrificed, and the assets turned into cash would not meet its debts. Therefore, the business might find itself in the hands of its creditors. If you decide that your current ratio is too low (below the ratio 2:1), you may be able to raise it by:

1. increasing your current assets from loans or other borrowings with a maturity of more than a year;
2. converting non-current assets into current assets (selling off assets such as equipment, vehicles, etc.);
3. increasing your current assets from new equity contributions;
4. ploughing back profits; or
5. increasing sales efforts.

Consider the following example on page 386:

If this business buys R15 000 worth of merchandise on account (column 2), stock will be increased to R35 000 and total current assets to R65 000. At the same time, creditors will be increased to R35 000 and total current liabilities to R40 000. The current ratio will drop from the present 2:1 to 1,6:1.

	1 Original current assets & liabilities	2 Merchandise bought on account R15 000	3 Cash paid to creditors R7 000	4 Capital invested R10 000
Current assets				
Cash............................	10 000	10 000	3 000	20 000
Debtors....................	20 000	20 000	20 000	20 000
Stock.........................	20 000	35 000	20 000	20 000
Total current assets	50 000	65 000	43 000	60 000
Current liabilities				
Creditors..................	20 000	35 000	13 000	20 000
Other........................	5 000	5 000	5 000	5 000
Total current liabilities...............	25 000	40 000	18 000	25 000
Net working capital*...................	25 000	25 000	25 000	35 000
Current ratio.............	2:1	1,6:1	2,4:1	2,4:1

* Difference between current assets and current liabilities is the net working capital.

Going back now to the original figures (column 1): Suppose that the company instead of buying more merchandise on account, pays creditors amounting to R7 000 with cash (column 3). Current assets will then be reduced to R43 000 and current liabilities to R18 000. The current ratio will be increased to 2,4:1.

Suppose the businessman, instead of taking either of these steps, invests an additional R10 000 in his business (column 4). This time current liabilities will not be affected, but current assets will be increased to R60 000 and the current ratio will rise to 2,4:1.

The above examples show what the effect of various actions can be on the current ratio of the business. They also illustrate how to obtain the best solution (most workable solution to your problem) in correcting the position if the current ratio is lower than the standard of 2:1. The current ratio is also known as the 'working capital' ratio.

Survival during a liquidity crisis period It is possible that a business can operate profitably but still have some liquidity problems because cash outflow does not synchronize with cash inflow. This is normally the case where there is insufficient control over current capital, viz. debtors, creditors, stock and expenses.[2]

Debtors For most businesses debtors are a valuable source of cash and if there are too many outstanding debtors there should be a planned action to build up some cash again such as:

1. issuing statements earlier;
2. trying to collect long-outstanding debts sooner;
3. evaluating the credit policy of the business (terms and limits);
4. refusing further credit sales to slow payers; or
5. improving the accounting system to get better information more quickly to management concerning debtors so that immediate action can be taken on present outstanding debtors, and plans can be made for future debtors.

Creditors A good creditor's payment scheme must be one in which payments to creditors are delayed as long as possible without damaging the good relationship with suppliers. When a business has a liquidity problem, it might be necessary to hold back payment as long as possible. This delaying tactic must be handled carefully.

1. Negotiate with creditors and offer payments on specific set dates.
2. Make early partial payments to cause the minimum dissatisfaction to suppliers.

387

3. Make enquiries concerning wrong supplier's invoices.
4. Make payments by post-dated cheques to satisfy creditors.
5. Return a certain amount of stock to suppliers.
6. Pay invoices when suppliers expect payment, which is $\pm$ 15 days after specified terms, for example: pay 30-day accounts after 45 days.

Stock Where the stock the business carries is higher than needed, it will be best to get rid of dead stock (at cost price) so that it does not influence your sales volume negatively. Identify unprofitable, slow-moving and obsolete items in your product range. Have a sale and then do not re-order these items. When purchasing stock on credit, aim for maximum credit terms. Evaluate the cost benefits of cash discounts and evaluate all 'bargains' of suppliers as to their saleability according to the market you serve. Don't accept deliveries of goods which have not been ordered.

Expenses During a crisis it is imperative to reduce costs (variable expenses) such as travelling, entertainment, etc. Analyse and identify major cost items such as salaries—try to reduce or eliminate them.

In the evaluation of financial analysis, there has been much speculation as to what the current assets to current liabilities ratio should be. Experience has taught that no single ratio can give a complete picture of a business's financial position, but the current ratio does tell a story—it is an item of evidence. Richard Sanzo[3] says that the story can be deceptive:

'A 4 to 1 ratio in a seasonal business might go down to 1,5 to 1 at the height of the season. Or it might be high because of large amounts of accumulated unsold stock such as a shoeshop that had a current ratio of 4 to 1 largely because of a stock of R20 000 in high button shoes— which would never be sold. Thus, a 2 to 1 current ratio is not necessarily a guarantee of sound financial condition, but it is not a bad idea to have one most of the time. Most managers recognize, however, that a current ratio less than 2 to 1 is a symptom of possible trouble. It is an outward sign that financial stress is occurring.'

Quick ratio or acid test Quick assets are current assets less stock. The quick ratio is calculated by deducting stock from current assets and dividing the remainder by current liabilities. If a business has R1 of quick assets for every R1 of current liabilities, it has sufficient working capital to support the business and enable it to cope with most emergencies—i.e. it has a quick ratio of 1:1.

$$\frac{\text{Current assets minus stock}}{\text{Current liabilities}} = \frac{\text{R9 221,00}}{\text{R2,9 : 1}} \times \frac{100}{1}$$
$$= \text{R3 161,00}$$

But not including stock, it concentrates on the really liquid assets, whose values are always fairly certain. It helps to answer the question: If all sales income should disappear, could my business meet its current obligations with the readily convertible quick funds on hand? In the example, the quick ratio compares favourably with the standard of 1:1. If the ratio is lower than 1:1, debtor accounts should be collected in order to pay off current liabilities, or you should consider not granting credit for a certain period, and concentrate on selling for cash only. Whatever you decide to do when the ratio is below the standard of 1:1, money must 'enter' the business. Remember, cash on hand (or in the bank) is the best current asset.

Current liabilities to tangible net worth ratio Like the current ratio, this is another means of evaluating a financial condition by comparing what is owed to what is owned. If this ratio exceeds 80%, it is considered a danger sign. Net worth is usually calculated by subtracting liabilities from the total assets, and it generally includes ownership equity, retained profits, and undivided profits. A large current liabilities to net worth ratio indicates a business which is top-heavy with liabilities. Such a situation is bound to undermine business judgement, because if you are constantly worried about your debts, it is always difficult to have the analytical objectivity that is needed to plan a sound and progressive programme for the business's advancement.

$$\frac{\text{Current liabilities}}{\text{Tangible net worth}} = \frac{\text{R3 161}}{\text{R62 955}} \times \frac{100}{1}$$
$$= 5,02\%$$

389

When the current liabilities to the tangible net worth ratio is moving too much in the direction of 80%, analysts are of the opinion that the equity of creditors is coming too close to equating the equity of the owners. For a small retail business, they would argue that current liabilities should seldom come to more than 50% of the tangible net worth. Why? A retailer, they say, usually has most of his current assets in stock. Stock must be sold to realize cash. If heavily obligated, the retailer may find a sudden letdown in stock turnover embarrassing. If the creditors' equity in the business nearly equals the owner's equity, the situation can be rectified by investing more capital and/or liquidating some assets. A third alternative might be to build up ownership equity from retained earnings (profits). Richard Sanzo, an expert on financial ratios and former Dun & Bradstreet executive, give this advice:[4]

'There are only three ways to reduce debt. One is to invest more capital—not always available. The second is to liquidate assets—not always practical. The third is build up capital from earnings—not possible overnight. So watch those debts.'

Net sales to working capital ratio This is also known as 'turnover of working capital'. This ratio measures how actively the working cash in a business is being put to work in terms of sales. A low ratio shows unprofitable use of working capital and a high one vulnerability to creditors. Just about all businesses require a margin of current assets over and above current liabilities to provide for stock and to carry debtor accounts between when the goods are sold and when money is collected. The importance of maintaining an adequate amount of working capital in relation to the amount of annual sales being financed cannot be overemphasized. And it is this degree of adequacy which the ratio of net sales to working capital measures.

$$\frac{\text{Net sales}}{\text{Working capital}} = \frac{\text{Net sales}}{\text{Current assets--current liabilities}}$$

$$= \frac{\text{R176 310}}{\text{R40 291}}$$

$$= 4,3 \text{ times}$$

LEVERAGE RATIOS

Fixed assets to tangible net worth ratio This ratio, which shows the relationship between investment in total assets (land, buildings, lease-hold improvements, furniture, machinery, equipment, etc. less depreciation) and the owner's capital, indicates how liquid the net worth is. The higher this ratio, the less owner's capital is available for use as working capital, to meet debts, carry debtors, meet salary obligations to employees, or pay creditors. Generally it is advisable for a small business to have less than 75% of its tangible net worth represented by fixed assets.

$$\frac{\text{Fixed Assets}}{\text{Tangible net worth}} = \frac{\text{R41 380}}{\text{R62 955}} \times \frac{100}{1}$$
$$= 65\%$$

As Richard Sanzo puts it: 'If fixed assets exceed 75% of net worth, they may become unmanageable because bills cannot be paid with brick or mortar.'[5]

Total debt to tangible net worth ratio This ratio also measures 'what is owed to what is owned'. As this figure approaches 100%, the creditors' interest in the business's assets approach the owner's. Total debt is the sum of all obligations owed by the business.

$$\frac{\text{Total debt}}{\text{Tangible net worth}} = \frac{\text{Current liabilities + long term debt}}{\text{Tangible net worth}}$$
$$= \frac{\text{R21 877}}{\text{R62 955}} \times \frac{100}{1}$$
$$= 34,7\%$$

This ratio complements the total debt/total assets ratio; that is, the two ratios tend to move in opposite directions to point out a given situation. For example, a debt-heavy business will have a high total debt/total assets ratio, but its total net worth/total debt ratio will be rather low. The question of how much debt a businessman should incur is difficult to answer as there are no rigid rules to answer this question. But common sense tells that an established business with favourable prospects may feel justified in using debt financing to a larger extent than a new business that is faced with plenty of uncertainties. Although a low percentage of debt may mean fewer headaches for management, it may also mean that management is neglecting opportunities to use more low-cost funds to enhance the return on the owner's equity. It is however possible to increase the rate of return on owner's equity by using funds from sources external to the business. This is because successful businessmen can use borrowed funds in such a manner that the return on the funds exceeds the cost of using them. The following example may help to clarify this point:

Business A		Business B	
Owner's investment	R100 000	Owner's investment	R40 000
Net profit	R 10 000	Term loan	R60 000
Return on		Net Profit	R10 000
investment	10%	Cost on borrowing at 8%....	R 4 800
		Return on investment	13%

Although both businesses have capital of R100 000 and earn the same amount of profit, R10 000, the return on owner's equity is higher for Business B because it takes advantage of financial leverage. By borrowing part of its capital at an 8% interest rate and earning a higher rate on it elsewhere, Business B is able to obtain a greater return for its owner. The 13% is calculated as follows: the net profit of R10 000 brings about a 25% return on an investment of R40 000, and the cost of borrowing at 8% represents 12% of the owner's investment of R40 000. Thus, the return on the owner's investment is 13% (25% minus 12%).

ACTIVITY RATIOS

Activity ratios measure how effectively the business employs the resources at its command. These ratios all involve comparisons between the level of sales and the investment of various assets. The activity ratios presume that a proper balance should exist between sales and the respective assets — stock, debtors and fixed assets.

Stock turnover ratio The stock turnover ratio is defined as cost of sales divided by average stock. Average stock is computed by adding the opening stock to the closing stock and dividing by two. The rate of stock turnover is the number of times stock is sold during a given accounting period. The average stock should represent the typical value of stock (for resale) carried by the business throughout the year. Very often opening and closing stocks are the only figures available and these should be used and averaged. Should, however, monthly stock figures be available then these should be used and averaged as the resultant figure is more accurate.

$$\frac{\text{Cost of sales}}{\text{Average stock}} = \frac{\text{R131 409}}{\text{R31 455}} = 4,1 \text{ times}$$

This means that you have 'turned' your stock 4,1 times during the year — that is you used up, through operations, merchandise totalling 4,1 times its average investment in stock.

The rapidity of the turnover of stock varies considerably according to the type of business. Although a high stock turnover rate is usually considered to be favourable, its importance may be exaggerated, as a stock turnover rate that is too high may be just as unfavourable as one that is too low. Too much attention to high turnover of stock can lead to stock shortages and customer dissatisfaction. A very high stock turnover rate usually indicates that the businessman has concentrated on carrying small stocks of 'fast movers'. This practice may result in the loss of potential sales because of the risk of being 'out of stock' and because of the lack of an adequate variety of goods to satisfy the needs of customers. A low stock turnover rate may be the result of bad buying, the accumulation of obsolete stock or the carrying of too much stock. These are the danger signals. Thus, stock that turns over too slowly is probably loaded with slow-moving products that may not only tie up needed working capital but also lead to loss of sales because of the lack of continuous fresh stocks of merchandise. To find the desired turnover rate of your business, a study of turnover rates of businesses similar to yours will help answer the question.

The stock turnover rate varies greatly with different types of businesses (stock turnover will be much higher in concerns dealing with, say, food, than those dealing with, say, motor cars) and with different degrees of management efficiency in terms of purchasing, stock and sales techniques. A new business, especially, should keep a record of this ratio for its operations, preferably for periods of three to six months. All changes in the turnover rate should be closely watched. You can then determine what the typical stock turnover rate is and whether it can be improved.

Average The average collection period, or number of days' sales tied
collection up in debtors, can be computed from the balance sheet and
period ratio profit and loss statement. This ratio is computed in two
steps — annual sales on credit are divided by 365 to get the
average daily credit sales, and debtors outstanding are taken
account of to find the number of days' sales tied up in
debtors. This is defined as the average collection period,
because it represents the average length of time the business
must wait after making a sale before receiving the cash.
Assume credit sales amounted to R18 000 and debtors
outstanding are R4 161 (from balance sheet).

$$\text{Average sales per day} = \frac{\text{Sales}}{365} \quad \text{(Credit sales)}$$

$$= \frac{\text{R18 000}}{365}$$

= R49,31 (average credit sales per day)

$$\text{Average collection period} = \frac{\text{Debtors}}{\text{Average credit sales per day}}$$

$$= \frac{\text{R4 161}}{\text{R49,31}}$$

= 84 (number of days' sales tied up in debtors, or average collection period)

Knowing the average collection period helps you answer the
question: 'How promptly are my outstanding accounts being
collected considering the credit terms I extend as measured
against my credit policies?' This tells you how well you are
handling the job of collecting outstanding accounts.
Accounts are now being collected, on the average, in approximately 84 days. For example, say your sales terms call for
payment within 90 days, thus the 84-day collection period
indicates that customers, on the average, are paying their
accounts on time. If the length of time for which debts are
outstanding is excessive in comparison with the normal
period of credit allowed (90 days), an investigation should be
made into the reasons for slow paying by customers. This
credit collection period is in fact only a medium for
comparison as it does not pinpoint the condition of

individual accounts. If the collection period is high, it may mean that there are perhaps an overdependence on too many slow-paying customers. Too low a collection period might justify taking a few more credit risks.

This ratio gives some indication of the efficiency or otherwise of the credit and collection policies of the business. An alternative method of calculating the turnover of debtors is to divide the total credit sales by the total debtors outstanding as at say 31 December 1986. This gives the turnover as 'so many times a year', which may be converted to 'days outstanding' by dividing the turnover rate into 365.

$$\text{Turnover of debtors} = \frac{\text{Credit sales}}{\text{Debtors}}$$

$$= \frac{\text{R18 000}}{\text{R4 161}}$$

$$= 4,3 \text{ times per year}$$

$$\text{Number of days credit is outstanding} = \frac{365}{4,3 \text{ times per year}}$$

$$= 84 \text{ days}$$

To calculate the average credit sales per day, the actual number of business days during the accounting period can also be used for greater accuracy. Thus, say 250 days for the year instead of 365 days. However, credit management implies selectivity. Too lax a credit policy can turn the collection of outstanding accounts into a nightmare, and too rigid a policy can lead to loss of sales.

Total assets turnover The final activity ratio measures the turnover of all the assets of the business. It is calculated by dividing sales by total assets.

$$\text{Total asset turnover} = \frac{\text{Sales}}{\text{Total assets}}$$

$$= \frac{\text{R176 310}}{\text{R84 832}}$$

$$= 2,0 \text{ times}$$

To find the desired average ratio, it is necessary to compare your rate with that of similar businesses. If this ratio is well below the average of those businesses, then your business is simply not generating a sufficient volume of sales for the size of its investment in assets. Sales should then be increased or some assets should be disposed of. Both steps should be considered.

PROFITABILITY RATIOS

Is your business earning as much profit as it should, considering the amount of money invested in it? Profitability must be your main objective and can only be achieved through proper financial management. A number of ratios can help you measure the success of your business in achieving profitability. These ratios can reveal some interesting particulars about the manner in which the business is operating. They can also reveal how effectively the business is being managed.

Gross profit ratio Probably the most important of all ratios in the analysis of the profit and loss statement is that known as the gross profit ratio. This is the ratio of gross profit in relation to sales (or turnover). Basically, gross profit is conceived as the difference between the selling price and the cost price of a given product which has been sold, and it is the gross profit, and not the sales proceeds, which gives you an indication of the operating income of a business.

The percentage gross profit (on turnover) affords you insight into the efficiency of the management of the business in respect of its buying policy and the general administration of merchandise being purchased in respect of its control of stock, and also in respect of its selling activities. It is computed as follows:

$$\text{Gross profit ratio} = \frac{\text{Gross profit}}{\text{Sales}} \times \frac{100}{1}$$

$$= \frac{\text{R44 901}}{\text{R176 310}} \times \frac{100}{1}$$

$$= 25,4\%$$

The above result is equivalent to declaring that for every R1 worth of goods sold the business makes a gross profit of 25 cents. This ratio, besides being extremely valuable in itself, is very useful when compared with that for previous accounting periods. A high gross profit ratio may indicate either purchases at low prices or sales at high prices, or both. A low gross profit ratio, may on the other hand indicate either low mark-ups or high merchandise costs as a result of poor buying practices. It may even be the result of a campaign of selling at low prices in order to obtain a large sales volume. To be profitable, such a selling practice must result in a large sales volume and be accompanied by low operating expenses. This gross profit percentage on turnover is an average figure resulting from different mark-ups and subsequent gross profits on different products in the product mix.

An increase in this ratio as compared with that for the previous period may indicate:
1. an increase in the selling price of the goods sold without any corresponding increase in cost of sales.
2. a decrease in cost of sales which was not reflected in the selling price of the goods.
3. stock at the beginning valued at a figure lower than it should have been.
4. stock at the end valued at prices which were too high.

On the other hand, a decrease in the gross profit ratio as compared with that for the previous period may indicate:
1. a decrease in the selling price of goods sold without any corresponding decrease in cost of sales.
2. an increase in cost of sales without a corresponding increase in the selling price of the goods sold.
3. stock at the end valued at too low a figure.
4. stock at the beginning valued at a figure higher than it should have been.

Below are a few other possible reasons for an unsatisfactory gross profit which may considerably affect the gross profit ratio.
1. All purchases have not been received even though they have been paid for. Thus, you might have forgotten to include them in the stock figure while including them in the purchase figure.
2. products are incorrectly price-marked or prices are too low.

3. There are too many sales to personnel (or customers) at a discount.
4. There is shoplifting or pilfering.
5. Stock and cash are taken by the owner without being recorded.
6. Stock damaged or obsolete is affecting the selling thereof.

The effect shoplifting has on your gross profit can be illustrated by the following example: Suppose you bought 10 jackets of which one got stolen. The cost price is R10 and the selling price R12. The result will be as follows:

Sales (9 jackets × R12,00)	R108,00
Cost of sales	R100,00
Opening stock	
Plus: Purchases (10 jackets × R10,00)	R100,00
	R100,00
Less: Closing stock	Nil
Gross profit	R8,00

From this example you can see that you only made R8 gross profit instead of the projected R20. Shoplifting decreases your gross profit and eventually also your net profit.

The effect of cash discounts on gross profit can be illustrated by the following example:[6]

Mark-up on cost price	Discount	% increase in turnover necessary to keep gross profit constant
50%	5%	17,6%
	10%	42,9%
	15%	81,8%
	20%	150,0%
33,3%	2,5%	11,11%
	10,0%	66,7%
25%	5%	33,3%
	10%	100,0%

The following table shows the percentage increase in turnover necessary to keep gross profit constant, when giving discount:

It is calculated as follows:

Without Discount		With Discount	
Cost price	R100,00	Cost price	R100,00
Mark-up 50%	50,00	Mark-up 50%	50,00
Selling price	150,00	Selling price	150,00
		Less: 10% Disc.	15,00
			135,00
Gross profit is	R50,00	Gross profit is	R35,00

The difference in gross profit is R15,00. To realise the same gross profit of R50,00 the turnover (sales) must increase by

$$\frac{R15,00}{R35,00} \times \frac{100}{1} = 42,9\%$$

It is important to remember that by giving discount, you are not increasing your sales and you are not making more profit. It is also important to let the customer know your business policy as far as discount is concerned. One customer should preferably never receive discount if others are refused the facility. This may confuse public relations.

It is also important that a business keep up its margin of gross profit, otherwise it may not cover its operating expenses and thus provide a smaller or no return to the owner. With purchasing the aim is to keep the investment in stock as low as possible. Too much investment in stock is just as disadvantageous as having too little stock. Both these extremes can cause high and unnecessary costs. This can be prevented through good planning and proper stock control. However, the minimum investment in stock does not mean that you must have a low amount of stock, but that the stock you have should be in line with your normal business performance and the service you want to maintain.

However, for all businesses there exists a more or less recognized gross profit ratio. Experience and comparisons will indicate whether the ratio of your business is satisfactory or not.

Net profit ratio This ratio measures the difference between what your business receives in gross income and what it spends in the process of conducting business. This ratio depends mainly on two factors — operating expenses and pricing policies. If your net profit on sales goes down, it might be that you have lowered prices in the hope of increasing sales volume, or it might be that your expenses have been increased while prices have remained the same. This ratio is computed as follows:

$$\text{Net profit ratio} = \frac{\text{Net profit}}{\text{sales}} \times \frac{100}{1}$$

$$= \frac{\text{R21 016}}{\text{R176 310}} \times \frac{100}{1}$$

$$= 11{,}9\%$$

The above result is equivalent to declaring that for every R1 worth of goods sold the business makes a net profit of 11,9 cents. This ratio reflects the net results of the operation of the business, thus it indicates the effectiveness of the management of the business and measures the efficiency of its operation. A profitable business is usually the result of efficient management which, on the one hand, succeeds in maintaining a satisfactory gross profit from purchases at low prices and from prices that are neither too high nor too low, and, on the other hand, succeeds in keeping all expenses under control.

The net profit ratio is most useful when you compare it with those of businesses similar to yours, or when you study the trends in your own business through several accounting periods.

Return on investment ratio This ratio shows the return you received on your own investment in the business. In calculating this ratio total equity is customarily used, but there are arguments as to what specific items from the financial statements are to be used for 'profit' and 'investment'. For example, 'profit' might be considered to mean net profit before taxes or net profit after taxes. 'Investment' could mean total assets employed or equity (or net worth) alone. It is important to decide which of these values you are going to use in computing return on investment and then to be consistent. The example here uses net profit before taxes and total equity.

$$\text{Return on investment} = \frac{\text{Net profit}}{\text{Equity}} \times \frac{100}{1}$$

$$= \frac{\text{R21 016}}{\text{R62 955}} \times \frac{100}{1}$$

$$= 33,3\%$$

The rate of return on investment is probably the most useful measure of profitability for the small business owner as it is this rate of return that compensates the businessman for the risk he has taken to enter business and it provides him with sufficient incentive. This, after all, is why you went into business. The nearer this percentage is to 100%, the greater the return on your investment. But be careful — Richard Sanzo explains:[7]

'In 1928 and 1929, radio manufacturing was tremendously profitable. One particular manufacturer made over R5 million in net profits in a single year on an initial capital of the same amount. A 100% net profit on capital in one year is very good. Next year, the entire capital, including the previous year's profit was spent in enlarging the plant. Then, the following year, the bottom fell out of radio manufacturing and the company went insolvent. When net profits are large in relation to tangible net worth over a very short period, they can lead to a very warm self-appreciative glow. They are like meat to a hungry hunter, and they lure plenty of wolves out of the forests of competition.'

In planning for the forthcoming years, you will probably want to set a return on investment objective that will compare favourably with the average profit potential for your type of business. By using the rate of return figure you decide upon, and given a knowledge of the market in which you plan to operate, you can compute what sales will be needed to provide a satisfactory return:[8]

For example, suppose you invest R25 000 in a small business and your objective is to receive a 12% return on investment. You could earn R12 000 a year working for someone else. You should then expect to receive an annual income from the business of at least R15 000, which is the equivalent of R12 000 salary plus R3 000 return on investment (12% of R25 000). You further estimate your market to consist of 5 000 people spending an average of R1 000 per year on the items you will sell. This represents a total market potential of R5 million. The typical profit-to-sales ratio for the industry is about 6%. By dividing your hoped-for earnings of

R15 000 by the profit margin of 6%, you find that you must have sales of R250 000 (R15 000 ÷ 0,06) in order to achieve your profit objective. This means you would need at least a

5% share of the market $\left(\dfrac{R250\ 000}{R5\ \text{million}} \times \dfrac{100}{1}\right)$ for your products.

However, earlier in this book it was mentioned that there is no general agreement between accountants concerning the return on investment rate and the meaning of the terms that are used to compute this ratio. Generally, the *basic* return on investment (ROI) rate is expressed as follows:

$$\text{ROI rate} = \frac{\text{Sales}}{\text{Capital employed}} \times \frac{\text{Net income}}{\text{Sales}}$$

This basic ROI-rate formula takes into consideration most of the items that appear on a balance sheet and income statement. The application of this basic formula can be illustrated with the balance sheet and income statement used in this chapter:

Sales (net)	R176 310
Less: Costs and expenses	R155 294
Net income (or profit)	R21 016
Working capital	R40 291
Fixed assets	R41 380
Total capital employed	R81 671

As far as the terms used in this ROI formula are concerned, opinions vary:[9]

Sales: The term 'sales' usually means either credit sales or net sales (credit sales plus cash sales less general sales tax). You can use either but not both of these terms in your computations.

Net Income: 'Net income' is a term to denote 'net income after tax'. When taxes are deducted, they are considered an expense of the business just as any other business expense. Also used is 'net income before taxes' to eliminate the effect of changes in tax rates. This usage may be advisable in instances where rates of return are being compared during a period of fluctuating tax rates. Other refinements in the use of the 'net income' figure include: (i) net income before depreciation; (ii) net income before interest charges; and (iii) average net income for a number of accounting periods.

Capital employed: The most significant area of differing opinions with respect to the components of the ROI formula is found when an attempt is made to define capital employed. The difference arises primarily from two problems: (i) which assets should you consider as capital employed? and (ii) what valuation basis should be placed on these assets? Among the various opinions concerning what should be included in the basic ROI formula as 'capital employed', three are most generally considered acceptable:

1. Equity. If ROI is to be interpreted as the return on an amount invested by the owner, capital employed in the formula can be defined as the owner's equity[10] in the business. This approach excludes investments by creditors.

2. Total assets, including those that are current (i.e. cash, debtors, and stock) and those that are permanent capital (i.e. plant and machinery, property, equipment).

3. Total assets less current liabilities. Those who accept this concept combine what is generally referred to as net working capital (current assets minus current liabilities) with permanent capital (fixed assets). This interpretation stresses the importance of long-term debt and the owner's equity as the investment upon which a return is to be based.

Whichever of these terms and definitions of capital employed you use in your computation, the same definitions of net income, sales, and capital employed should be applied in all your computations to validate your comparisons. Thus, it is imperative that you express them consistently when calculations involving comparisons are made.

Other ratios Other ratios that are necessary in managing the finances of the business are the total operating expense ratio and individual expense ratios to sales. Both these ratios are valuable for the purpose of ascertaining whether, and to what extent, expenses vary between different trading periods.

$$\text{Total operating expense ratio} = \frac{\text{Total operating expenses}}{\text{Sales}} \times \frac{100}{1}$$

$$= \frac{\text{R23 885}}{\text{R176 310}} \times \frac{100}{1}$$

$$= 13,5\%$$

The above result is equivalent to declaring that 13,5 cents out of every R1,00 of turnover (sales) represent operating expenses. Net profit could thus be increased by increasing sales without an increase in expenses, or by keeping sales constant and at the same time, decreasing (or eliminating) expenses, or a combination of both methods. It is, however, important that this percentage be included in your mark-up on products in order to cover expenses when a sale is made.

Another type of ratio which is invariably calculated, is that of each different item of expense to sales. A few will be discussed below:

$$\text{Salary and wage ratio} = \frac{\text{Salary and wages}}{\text{Sales}} \times \frac{100}{1}$$

$$= \frac{\text{R12 600}}{\text{R176 310}} \times \frac{100}{1}$$

$$= 7,1\%$$

This ratio indicates the percentage for every R1,00 of sales allocated to labour. It is a valuable measure of productivity in the total staff component. The 7,1% implies that 7,1 cents has been spent on personnel expenses in respect of each R1,00 in sales. It is thus logical that, should a higher sales figure be reached for the same amount of salaries and wages, a higher net profit will be realized. For example, should sales increase to R190 000 per annum, but the personnel remuneration remain at R12 900, the salary and wage ratio will be 6,7%. This implies an increase in productivity of 0,4%. However, a high salary and wage ratio is ordinarily an unfavourable sign. A high salary and wage ratio may be the result of inefficient use of labour, a poor arrangement of the shop's activities, or the employment of too many employees in relation to the sales volume obtained. A low salary and wage ratio is usually evidence of efficient management, especially if it is accompanied by a low total operating expense ratio and a satisfactory net profit ratio. It could also mean that the business is not employing enough workers or not the right people for the right jobs.

The salary of an owner-manager is another item to be concerned about, and it is worthy of analysis. When it is too high, it may indicate that an excessive part of profits, which should be retained for future growth, is being drained from the business. Something of this sort can only invite trouble, for every business should create some kind of cushion, either for expansion or to meet unforseen situations. A business must have reserves for almost any emergency!

Where an expense is a fixed amount, such as rent, the ratio of the item should decrease as the volume of sales increases. A high rent expense ratio may also be the result of the business being larger than is necessary to handle the present sales volume. On the other hand, a high rent expense ratio may also mean that a favourable location has been obtained which makes it possible to obtain sales without high expenditure for advertising which might otherwise be necessary. A low rent expense ratio may mean that the businessman has been able to secure the shop building at a favourable rental.

Advertising expense is another operating expense that needs to be closely watched. Consider this explanation on controlling advertising expenses by Richard Sanzo:[11]

'Improperly used, of course, advertising may prove to be something less than a cure for competitive problems. The incident may be recalled of a small manufacturer of underwear who spent relatively large sums to bring its products before the public. The advertising was in good taste, and the campaign was well planned. Sales did go up. But so much capital has been laid out in publicity that the business was unable to pay its bills. It went bankrupt before earnings could catch up. The point is that advertising expenses must be subjected to careful planning just as are other costs.'

However, a less expensive way of advertising could be the sales letter and any other actions to improve word-of-mouth advertising. If the latter can be done effectively, it will certainly lower advertising expenses far below the trade average which means that you have been more productive in this particular area.

By comparing each of the expenses with sales in this way, valuable conclusions can be reached and problems can be identified and solved by looking at the effect this has on sales volume and general business operations. Higher-than-standard ratios for any of the other expense items on the income statement usually indicate a necessity for expense reduction. Standards can be obtained over a period by comparing ratios in similar businesses.

MEASURING AGAINST STANDARD RATIOS

It is also very useful in ratio analysis to compare your business's performance with that of an industry or line of business similar to yours. Such ratios are referred to as standard or typical ratios, and they have caused many small businessmen to make some worthwhile reappraisals of their business thinking. If you know such ratios, you may be able to answer such questions as: How much rent should my type of business pay? What should the advertising to sales ratio be?; How much should my business earn on invested capital?; etc. Thus they serve valuable purposes, such as enabling you to allocate, budget and plan.

Those managers that regularly compare ratios in the normal conduct of their businesses will be well repaid for their efforts by the greater profits that will ultimately result from the right decisions and the correct actions taken. A thing to bear in mind, though, is that when you compare your business's results with that of similar businesses, you have to do with averages. The main question is then: Do you want to be just average? You should try to be at least as good as the average, but better operating results are desirable. You should also be consistent in comparing similar time periods — monthly, two-monthly, quarterly, yearly, etc.

Ratios are useful in giving guidance and pinpointing actual or potential trouble spots. When properly interpreted and related to a given business and/or industry, ratios can provide effective guidelines for the small business owner. But like any other tool, ratios also have their disadvantages. So in order to use them properly you must be aware of their limitations. If misused, they can be harmful. If ratios are to be used as a tool for managing the finances effectively so as to produce optimum results, they must be used correctly. It is the purpose of the following paragraphs to explain some of the inherent pitfalls of ratio analysis:[12]

'Never use a single ratio

Ratios are generally more effective when used collectively as decisions being made on the basis of a single ratio could prove disastrous. This point can best be demonstrated by an example.

The figure on page 408 shows a set of ratio charts for a men's clothing store. The business's net profit/net sales ratio has been steadily increasing. Taken by itself, this is a desirable condition. The upward trend of total debt to total assets indicates the possibility of excessive debt; however, in itself this could mean an astute usage of financial leverage. The constant decline in the current ratio indicates that the business has been headed for liquidity problems since 1968. A look at the trend in accounts receivable (debtors) points out the fact that during the last few years the business's debtors as a percentage of sales have practically skyrocketed. This has been due primarily to a change in policy; management decided to increase volume by emphasizing credit sales. It is thus evident that management embarked upon a growth policy without making adequate provisions for ensuring solvency. The ratios clearly indicate that if financial embarrassment is to be avoided, the business must finance its growth through a long-term loan or additional ownership funds. As the result of such a clear visual description the manager of the business saw the need to supply additional funds, and he arranged for a five-year term loan with a bank. Thus, thanks to a simple analytical tool, a disastrous future development was avoided.

In conclusion, although the business in the example was definitely headed for trouble, this could not be determined on the basis of any one single ratio. Indeed, if only the net profit/net sales ratio were used, an entirely different conclusion would have been arrived at from the one indicated in the example.

Examine the sample

Before comparing a business's ratios with those of the industry, a small businessman should raise several questions. How many businesses are there in the industry? How many of them were included in the sample? Are the sampled outfits comparable with this business? If not, have the published ratios been broken down by business size, geographic location, etc.? Do most businesses in the industry use accounting methods comparable to that of yours? Answers to such questions will indicate whether or not the businessman should engage in such a comparison at all. If industry figures are obtained from an

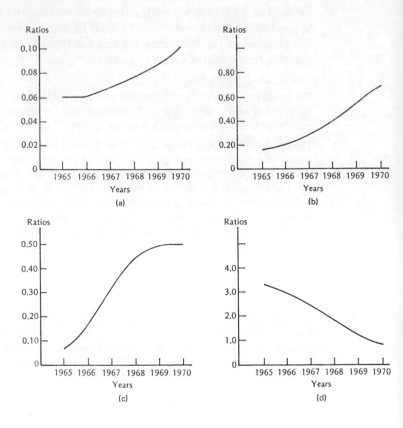

Fig. 1. *(a)* Net profit/Net sales; *(b)* Total debt/Total assets (a useful and simple way of determining the extent of debt financing is to compute the ratio of total debt to total assets. This indicates the percentage of the total assets that are financed by creditors. The higher the ratio, the more debt-heavy are the assets.); *(c)* Debtors/Net sales; *(d)* Current ratio.

unrepresentative sample or if there are variations caused by different accounting methods, there would be no justification for comparing figures with those of the industry. This is also true when industry averages are not broken down by business size and when geographical differences make the ratios different from those of the average business in the industry. If the business is located further away from sources of supply, the cost/sales and stock relationships will differ from those of the average business in the industry. The prudent businessman will also want to know what kind of computations were used in figuring the published industry averages.

Industry ratios indicate a guide and not a specific course of action

Published ratios for an industry indicate averages. After making a comparison, many small businessmen tend to take drastic action if their figures differ substantially from industry averages. Although the businessman should always keep in touch with developments in his field of endeavour, he must also realize that industry averages alone do not necessarily contain the key to success; they are simply averages.

The first question to be answered by a businessman is: "Do I want to be just average?" The ambitious small businessman may wish to employ industry averages as standards to be exceeded rather than merely complied with. Also, if a business's figures are out of line with those of the industry, this does not necessarily mean that they must be changed. The question to be answered is: "Why are my ratios different from those of the industry?" There have been many successful businessmen who's selling expenses were higher than average because of some unusual services that they provided for their customers. However, because these services were greatly appreciated by the customers, the owners were able to charge higher-than-average prices. Therefore, when comparing his ratios to those of an industry, a businessman should consider taking corrective action in relation to the overall picture and not on the basis of a simple comparison.

No substitute for managerial judgement

Ratio analysis is a tool to assist in decision making and is not a substitute for it. No analytical tool will substitute for managerial judgement. Ratios cannot give the final answers to final questions of operating policy, and by themselves they cannot transform a business into success. They can, however, help in measuring performance, and they can be useful in raising questions for further inquiry. The knowledge of what other businesses in the same industry are doing can be very valuable for making decisions and locating potential trouble. Marked differences in a businesses' ratios from those in the past or in its line of business may indicate the need for important changes in operational policy and practice.

A businessman who is not using all available tools, ratios included, is certainly remiss in his duties. Unless he is exceptionally lucky or is one of the very few who has the gift of clairvoyance, he cannot control the various functions of his business effectively. To paraphrase an old adage, a businessman's best friend at home might be his dog, but at work it is best not to let a slipping ratio lie.'

Depreciation can be seen as that proportion of an expenditure charged to an asset for the accounting period under review. It is an operating expense. Depreciation is thus the loss in value of an asset because of the wear and tear caused by its use. This affects particularly such assets as machines, motor vehicles, furniture and equipment. Friction and vibration are aspects of wear and tear. Although repairs and maintenance may offset the process of wear and tear to some extent, they can never indefinitely keep the asset in perfect working order.

Depreciation is a cost which must be accounted for because of its use in the business to earn income. To take a simple example, assume your business uses a particular piece of equipment, costing R1 000, for the purpose of keeping products which it sells fresh. If this piece of equipment were to have an estimated life of, say, 10 years, it is clear that it may be costing the business (among other things), R100 per year over that period for the use of such a piece of equipment, and therefore the profit-and-loss statement should reflect such a cost. It is probable that, in this instance, the cost of utilizing the piece of equipment is just as much an expense of running the business as are, say, the salaries paid to employees. When fixed assets are used in this and other ways, it is generally known that such fixed assets depreciate. This is so because, in effect, what happens when an asset of that nature is purchased, is that you charge its cost to an asset account (or asset register[13]). Then, as it is used over the period of its life, a proportionate amount is charged in each accounting period against the operating results as representing the proportion of the original cost to be matched against the income generated during that period. The amount charged for each accounting period is termed depreciation.

A depreciation charge is thus necessary because it is a cost which must be matched against the income as are other costs incurred in earning that income, and by making provision for such a charge, you are adopting a means of writing the asset off by the time its useful span of life has expired.

There is, however, a further reason for the necessity of keeping track of depreciation. Let us assume you bought a vehicle for R10 000 when you started your business. After five years it won't of course, be valued at R10 000 and neither will a new vehicle cost you R10 000. If you have not made provision to replace the vehicle in five years' time, or something happens unexpectedly (a complete break down, for example), you then have to find enough capital to replace this asset.

Why was no money designated in the business to replace the asset? It may be because you had spent what you earned as well as the money you had put in, in the form of capital to purchase the asset. You could also have used the profits to invest in other fixed or current assets. What is of importance is that you may have spent the profits generated by the business either on yourself or for other uses. However, the time for replacement of the vehicle as an asset has arrived (after the break down) in order for the business operations to continue, but the problem is that the same asset now costs far more than it did originally. So, what must you do, or rather, what were you supposed to do to be able to replace that vehicle? Assume it does not cost R10 000 anymore after five years, but R17 622. Firstly, you should have ploughed back enough profit into the business and restricted your personal drawings, or provided for its replacement by putting money aside. This is necessary so that you will be able to replace the vehicle to continue doing business. You also need to keep track of by what percentage the price of such a vehicle is increasing every year, so as to make provision for replacing the vehicle after five years, or to be at least prepared when the vehicle gets completely damaged in an accident. Remember though, that prices don't remain the same, so the first thing to forget is the original cost of the vehicle. It is irrelevant. With inflation and improvements by the manufacturers of these assets, the prices go up every year and you have got to keep making money to stay in business. Consider this example on page 412.

Say you want to replace the vehicle in January 1986. A new one at that time will cost you R17 622. For a trade-in of your present vehicle you will receive, let's say not less than the

VEHICLE		Replacement cost (12% increase per year)
Original Cost (1 January 1981)	R10 000	R10 000
Less: 20% Depreciation (31 December 1981)	R2 000	
Value as at 1 January 1982	R8 000	R11 200
Less: Depreciation (31 December 1982)	R1 600	
Value as at 1 January 1983	R6 400	R12 544
Less: Depreciation (31 December 1983)	R1 280	
Value as at 1 January 1984	R5 120	R14 049
Less: Depreciation (31 December 1984)	R1 024	
Value as at 1 January 1985	R4 096	R15 734
Less: Depreciation (31 December 1985)	R819	
Value as at 1 January 1986	R3 277	R17 622

reduced value of R3 277. The calculation is as follows:

Replacement cost	R17 622
Less: Trade-in	R3 277
Difference	R14 345

This means that you were supposed to have put R14 345 (an average of R2 869 per year, or an average of R239,83 per month) aside over the five years (from profits), to be able to pay the difference that will be sufficient to meet the replacement cost when required, without having to seek expensive finance elsewhere.

There are several methods of apportioning depreciation between all the financial periods which constitute the anticipated useful life of the asset. The method most commonly used in commercial concerns is the fixed instalment method (also known as the straight-line method). By this method of depreciation a fixed amount is charged against profits each year by way of depreciation. The fixed amount charged each year represents a proportion of the original cost, so that if it is estimated that the asset will last 10 years, then 10% of the original cost of the asset will be written off each year for 10 years. When an asset is sold during the accounting period, then it is necessary to compute the profit or loss on the sale and adjust the asset account (asset register), and the profit or loss made must be reflected in your books (to be recorded in a journal or the assets register). For instance, you bought a piece of equipment for R800 on 1 January 1981 and sell it on 1 January 1986 for R450. Depreciation on equipment with an expected life span of 10 years is 10% per year (thus R80 per year). The value of the piece of equipment is then R400 after 5 years. You thus made a profit of R50 which must appear in the profit-and-loss statement (if, of course, this R50 was reinvested in the business) as an income. Its proper heading would be 'other income' and it would be shown separately from sales income. However, the balance sheet will no longer show this asset's value and no further depreciation will be charged against income for this particular asset.

Although depreciation is computed on an annual basis, you need to know each month's depreciation for use in preparing monthly financial statements. This monthly depreciation can be computed by dividing the total depreciation for the accounting period by twelve. When additional assets are purchased during the year, depreciation should be calculated from the date the item was bought onwards. If your accounting period were from 1 January to 31 December and you purchased a new piece of equipment on 1 March for R700, depreciation would be R70 (10% of original cost) per year (in this instance, as from 1 March to 31 December) or R5,83 per month. Depreciation is continuous until the asset is written off completely — at least in your books.

Whatever the nature of fixed assets or the type of business in which they are used, they have the fundamental characteristics that they are kept in the business with the object of earning income and not for the purpose of sale in the ordinary course of business. The amount at which they are shown in the balance sheet does not necessarily reflect their realizable value or their replacement value, but is normally a record of their cost less amounts provided in respect of depreciation. Depreciation represents that part of the cost of a fixed asset to its owner which is not recoverable when the asset is finally put out of use by him. The assessment of depreciation involves the consideration of two factors: the cost of the asset; and the length of time during which the asset will be commercially useful to the business. Various life spans are allocated to different assets: equipment 10 years (thus 10% depreciation per year); and motor vehicles 5 years (thus 20% depreciation per year).

SUMMARY AND CONCLUSIONS

Probably the best way to explain the function of ratio analysis is, as stated by Fred Weston and Eugene Brigham:[14] 'Financial analysis can actually be compared to a detective story investigation. What one ratio will not indicate, another may do so.' If warning signs appear, look for the causes and for possible remedies. Immediately though because the sheer passage of time can aggravate any problem that may exist. All capital invested in the business should be put to use in the most economical and profitable way. Ratio analysis will greatly assist you in making sound decisions concerning the operation and growth of the business. It is of fundamental importance to have accurate and up-to-date information with which to compile financial statements.

BIBLIOGRAPHY

* J. A. Cilliers, Introduction to Analysis and Interpretation of Financial Statements, 1967, J. L. van Schaik (Pty.) Ltd., Pretoria, SA, pp. 11–24.
* R. G. J. Mackintosh, How to read Financial Statements, 1984, Juta & Co., Ltd., Cape Town, SA, pp. 5–20.
* J. K. Lasser Tax Institute, How to run a Small Business, 1982, McGraw-Hill Book Company, pp. 60–66.
* Clifford M. Baumback and Kenneth Lawyer, How to Organize and Operate a Small Business, 1979, Prentice-Hall, Inc., Englewood Cliffs, New Jersey, pp. 496–498.
* Richard Sanzo, Ratio Analysis for Small Business, Small Business Management Series Number 20 (Fourth Edition). Washington D.C.: U.S. Small Business Administration, 1977.

* Guy Macleod, *Starting your own Business in South Africa*, 1983, Oxford University Press, Cape Town, pp. 111–118.

* Robert C. Ragan and Jack Zwick, *Fundamentals of Recordkeeping and Finance for the Small Business*, 1978, Reston Publishing Company, Inc., Reston, Virginia, pp. 1–30.

* R. Keith Yorston, E. Bryan Smyth, S. R. Brown, *Accounting Fundamentals*, 1961 (4th ed), The Law Book Co. of Australia (Pty.) Ltd., Sydney, pp. 546–572.

NOTES

[1] Thomas J. Peters, Robert H. Waterman, Jr. *In Search of Excellence*. 1982. Harper & Row Publishers, New York: 44.

[2] P. C. Bierman. Die oorlewing van 'n likwiditeitskrisis. *Entrepreneur* 1983; **2**(11): 5. (Reproduced with permission.)

[3] Richard Sanzo. Ratio analysis for small business. *Small Business Management Series* No. 20. 1977. U.S. Small Business Administration, Washington D.C.: 000.

[4] Idem, 59.

[5] Idem, 63.

[6] Die effek van kontantkorting op wins. *Entrepreneur* 1983: **2**(4): 13. (Reproduced with permission.)

[7] Richard Sanzo. Ratio analysis for small business. *Small Business Management Series* No. 20. 1977. U.S. Small Business Administration, Washington D.C.: 60.

[8] Curtis E. Tate, Jr., Leon C. Megginson, Charles R. Scott, Jr., Lyle R. Trueblood. *Successful Small Business Management*. 1985. Business Publications, Plano Texas: 48. (Reproduced with permission.)

[9] Dr. Charles J. Woelfel. Guides for profit planning. *Small Business Management Series Number 25*, 0000. U.S. Small Business Administration, Washington D.C.: 45–47.

[10] The term 'return on investment' may be misleading. In reality it is 'return on equity'.

[11] Richard Sanzo. Ratio analysis for small business. *Small Business Management Series* No. 20. 1977. U.S. Small Business Administration, Washington D.C.: 56.

[12] John V. Petrof, Peter S. Carusone, John E. McDavid. *Small Business Management: Concepts and Techniques for Improving Decisions*. 1972. McGraw-Hill, New York: 115–118. Reproduced with permission.

[13] See page 375 for an explanation of the asset register.

[14] J. Fred Weston, Eugene F. Brigham. *Managerial Finance*. 1978. The Dryden Press, Hinsdale, Ill.: 45.

16 PROFIT PLANNING AND BUDGETING

'Forecasts and budgets should not be regarded as wishful thinking but rather as attainable objectives.'

Frans Bekker

'Profit is the major motivating force in your business. Some businesses do make a profit without planning, but those are exceptions. And even then such businesses probably do not realize their full potential. To operate successfully, you need planning based on reliable information and proven techniques. Planning is your most effective method for obtaining the best possible results.'

Dr Charles J. Woelfel,[1] Professor of
Accountancy at Southern Illinois University,
Carbondale

INTRODUCTION

Budgeting, as already mentioned, has to do with the functions of planning and control. Planning deals with the establishment or setting of a specific and desired profit objective and control measures to monitor the performance. Well-considered planning is necessary before control can be effected. Forecasting has to do with well-considered planning, as it is the making of reasonable assumptions about what will probably happen in the future—thinking ahead, looking to the future and providing for it. Little can be done about the past, but you can certainly do something about the future, although it is hidden from you. The greater the uncertainty, the greater the necessity for planning.

The most important budget, the cash flow budget, is the compass by which your business must keep as closely as possible to a charted course that will enable you to make the most economical and effective use of the capital in your business—the results must be profits. And many unsuccessful business owners will tell you what they would do if they could be given a second chance in business. The fact is that they no longer have the capital to begin again. Forecasting and budgeting could have given them that chance by showing them in detail, as well as on paper, how they could have avoided committing themselves to something they could not afford.

Failure to meet expectations as expressed by the budgets immediately points to the need for corrective action. When planning is done in advance, many problems can be anticipated long before they arise and solutions can be sought through deliberate study. Budgets will thus inform you whether sufficient cash will be available in a certain month to meet all estimated needs and whether corrective steps can be taken before it is too late. These corrective steps may take the form of arranging for a temporary bank loan, or, if the need for cash will greatly exceed the supply and a bank loan cannot be obtained, the corrective step will be to revise your plans for the future—again, before it is too late and before the financial condition of your business is endangered.

PROFIT PLANNING

The important thing is to have a specific goal to aim for—a financial goal. Your profit goal is usually expressed as a rate of return on investment. By using the 'return on investment rate', your attention is drawn to a combination of factors needed for successful operations.[2]

The steps to take in planning for profit are as follows:[3]

1 establish your profit goal;
2 determine the planned volume of sales;
3 estimate expenses for planned volume of sales;
4 determine estimated profit based on steps 2 and 3; and
5 compare estimated profit with your profit goal.

These steps will be explained by an example. Below are an income statement and a balance sheet, on which the example will be based.

417

INCOME STATEMENT —
1 JANUARY 1986 to 31 DECEMBER 1986

Sales	280 000
Less: Cost of sales	201 600
Opening stock	32 000
Plus: Purchases	203 600
Less: Closing stock	34 000
Gross profit	78 400
Less: Expenses	54 800
Salaries	32 000
Depreciation	7 600
Maintenance on Building	2 600
Insurance	780
Interest (long-term loan)	3 200
Stationery	700
Sales promotion & advertising	3 600
Transport	2 600
Water & lights	1 000
Telephone	480
Bank charges	240
Net profit (before tax)	R23 600

BALANCE SHEET AS AT 31 DECEMBER 1986

Employment of capital	R190 100
Fixed Assets	139 400
Building	95 000
Equipment	25 200
Vehicles	19 200
Current Assets	50 700
Bank balance	7 500
Cash on hand	700
Debtors	8 500
Stock	34 000
Capital employed	190 100
Equity	158 400
Capital	134 800
Net Profit	23 600
Long-term liability	23 000
Bank loan	23 000
Current liabilities	8 700
Creditors	R8 700

Consider the following application of the profit-planning steps:

Planning for profit for 1987[4]

Step 1: *Establish your profit goal*

Capital invested	134 800
Net profit	23 600
Capital employed (or equity)	158 400
Return desired	33 264 (21% × 158 400)
Profit needed before tax[5]	33 264

Step 2: *Determine your planned volume of sales*

Estimated sales income	324 800 (16% increase over 1986)

Step 3: *Estimated expenses for planned volume of sale*

	Actual 1986	Estimate 1987
Cost of sales	201 600	233 856
Salaries	32 000	35 840
Depreciation	7 600	7 600
Maintenance building	2 600	400
Insurance	780	780
Interest (bank loan)	3 200	2 640
Stationery	700	785
Sales promotion and advertising	3 600	4 800
Transport	2 600	2 910
Water & lights	1 000	1 100
Telephone	480	510
Bank charges	240	260
	R256 400	R291 481

Step 4: *Determine estimated profit based on steps 2 and 3*

Estimated sales income	324 800
Estimated expenses	291 481
Estimated net profit before tax	33 319

Step 5:   Compare estimated profit with profit goal

Estimated net profit before tax	33 319
Desired profit needed before tax	33 264
Difference	55

Step 1:   The return on investment achieved in 1986 was 14,8%. The businessman decided that this return on investment was too low and calculated that a return on investment of 21% would be more desirable for 1987, after taking into consideration the inflation rate, a reasonable salary, and other investment possibilities of similar risk.

Step 2:   To reach his objective, he calculated that he need to increase his sales by 16% in 1987 (or forthcoming year).

Step 3:   Expenses must be adjusted for the planned volume of sales. The cost of sales represented 72% of sales in 1986. Therefore he uses this percentage to determine the new cost of sales, which will more than likely also be 72% of the new volume of sales as determined in step 2. Other expenses will increase more or less in line with the percentage increase in sales volume, except for fixed expenses. It is however, also important to remember to budget for any additional expenses which you might incur in 1987 (or forthcoming year).

Step 4:   Deduct estimated expenses from estimated sales income to derive at an estimated net profit figure before tax.

Step 5:   Deduct the desired profit goal as determined in step 1 from the estimated net profit (before tax) as determined in step 4. The difference being R55. The idea is of course, to get the difference as close as possible to nil. If you find that the difference is a negative figure than the profit goal, you can decrease your return on investment goal; increase your sales; decrease expenses; or increase your prices.

From the above exercise it perhaps looks on paper as if you can reach your desired profit objective, but this is not yet possible in reality. What you now have to do is preparing budgets for 1987 and work out action plans in order to reach your desired profit target for 1987. It does not all stop here either, you still need to implement these action programmes. It is recommended that, after careful thought has been given to the action steps to be taken, he needs to discuss them with a knowledgeable consultant and develop a schedule for their implementation. Make sure first that you know how to implement these actions.

BUDGETING

Budgets should now be drawn up for sales, purchasing, capital expenditure, expenses and cash flow.

Sales Budget

SALES BUDGET FOR 1987 (16% increase over 1986)	1986	1987
January	R24 000	R27 840
February	23 000	26 680
March	22 000	25 520
April	21 000	24 360
May	25 000	29 000
June	20 000	23 200
July	22 000	25 520
August	21 000	24 360
September	22 000	25 520
October	23 000	26 680
November	24 000	27 840
December	32 000	38 280
	R280 000	R324 800

Purchasing budget

AMOUNT OF STOCK TO BUY FOR 1987   R

1. Budgeted sales (from final profit planning for 1987)   324 800
2. Gross profit percentage – (28%)   90 944
3. Cost of sales: (1) minus (2); or 72% of sales   233 856
4. Budgeted stock turnover rate   7 times
5. Average stock needed: (3) divided by (4)   33 408
6. Present stock level (closing stock for 1986)   34 000
7. Surplus (shortage:) (6) minus (5)   592
8. Stock to buy (capital needed for purchases): (3) minus (7)   233 264

In order to arrive at the monthly amount of stock to purchase for the volume of sales, the calculation is as follows:

$$\frac{\text{1986 monthly purchases}}{\text{Total purchases in 1986}} \times \frac{\text{Stock to buy}}{1} = \text{Monthly purchases}$$

$$\frac{\text{(January 1986) R17 450}}{\text{R203 600}} \times \frac{\text{R233 264}}{1} = \text{R19 992}$$

MONTHLY PURCHASES		
	1986	*1987*
January	R17 450	R19 992
February	16 725	19 161
March	16 000	18 331
April	15 270	17 495
May	18 180	20 830
June	14 540	16 660
July	16 000	18 331
August	15 270	17 495
September	16 000	18 331
October	16 725	19 161
November	17 450	19 992
December	23 990	27 485
	R203 600	R233 264

Capital budget The capital budget is used to budget for assets to be purchased such as vehicles, equipment, modernization, building extensions, etc. For this example it is assumed that you want to buy another vehicle in April 1987 which is going to cost you R13 600 (taking into consideration price increases and general sales tax inclusive). The capital budget is also used to budget for payments on long-term loans. We assume your capital redemption is R650 on this loan and the interest is R220 per month. The interest payments are recorded in the income statement as an expense to the business.

Expense budget The expense budget is a control device to be used in order to aid you in conducting the business in line with these expenses as planned. You can also now determine what percentage each expense represents of the monthly sales and adjust your mark-up on products to sell accordingly.

In the capital budget you decided to purchase an additional vehicle in April 1987, and the depreciation involved is 20% annually. The depreciation from 1 April 1987 to 31 March 1988 will proportionally be R2 720 (R226,66 per month). This monthly figure is to be recorded in the expense budget.

Cash flow budget The information on all other budgets is transferred to this budget in order to give an overall picture of the financial position of the business for 1987 (see cash flow budget on page 425).

The cash flow budget serves as both a motivational and a control tool. It is motivation in the sense that you must try to adhere to the figures at all times and try not to exceed any expenses on the budget — monitor progress almost daily. The actual figures realized must be compared with those budgeted, deviations must be calculated and the reasons for deviations correctly established. An example of how such a system of control may look is shown on page 426:

ACTION PLANS

An action plan is necessary to achieve the desired results as budgeted. The action plan may be as follows to increase sales volume in 1987:

Objective for 1987. To increase sales by 16%.

Actions to be taken are the following:

1. Design an advertisement to be featured in an appropriate media regularly.
2. Design a promotional plan that will attract customers selectively.
3. Apply better stock presentation techniques.
4. Provide incentives for salespeople.
5. Become obsessed with giving customers excellent service.
6. Write 10 sales letters to known or unknown customers per day.
7. Strive for savings in the purchasing function and search for better quality products.
8. Maintain good relations with suppliers.
9. Prevent shoplifting losses by creating bigger awareness and implementing appropriate measures.

COST (EXPENSE) BUDGET FOR 1987

	Total	Jan.	Feb.	Mar.	Apr.	May	Jun.	Jul.	Aug.	Sept.	Oct.	Nov.	Dec.
	R	R	R	R	R	R	R	R	R	R	R	R	R
Salaries	35 840	2 756	2 756	2 756	2 756	2 756	2 756	2 756	2 756	2 756	2 756	2 756	5 524*
Depreciation	9 643	633	633	633	860	860	860	860	860	860	860	860	864
Maintenance on building	400	33	33	33	33	33	33	33	33	33	33	33	37
Insurance	780	65	65	65	65	65	65	65	65	65	65	65	65
Interest	2 640	220	220	220	220	220	220	220	220	220	220	220	220
Stationery	785	65	65	65	65	65	65	65	65	65	65	65	70
Sales promotion	4 800	400	400	400	400	400	400	400	400	400	400	400	400
Transport	2 910	242	242	242	242	242	242	242	242	242	242	242	248
Water & lights	1 100	92	92	92	92	92	92	92	92	92	92	93	88
Telephone	510	42	42	42	42	42	42	42	42	42	42	42	48
Bank charges	260	21	21	21	21	21	21	21	21	21	21	21	29
TOTAL	59 668	4 569	4 569	4 569	4 796	4 796	4 796	4 796	4 796	4 796	4 796	4 796	7 593

*Bonuses for 1987.

CASH FLOW BUDGET FOR 1987

	Jan. R	Feb. R	Mar. R	Apr. R	May. R	Jun. R	Jul. R	Aug. R	Sept. R	Oct. R	Nov. R	Dec. R
1. Opening balance	7 500*	10 129	12 429	14 399	2 218	4 942	6 036	7 779	9 198	10 941	13 014	15 416
Income												
2. Sales	27 840	26 680	25 520	24 360	29 000	23 200	25 520	24 360	25 520	26 680	27 840	38 280
3. Other income	—	—	—	—	—	—	—	—	—	—	—	—
4. Total (2 + 3)	27 840	26 680	25 520	24 360	29 000	23 200	25 520	24 360	25 520	26 680	27 840	38 280
Expenses												
5. Operating costs	4 569	4 569	4 569	4 796	4 796	4 796	4 796	4 796	4 796	4 796	4 796	7 593
6. Capital expenses	650	650	650	14 250	650	650	650	650	650	650	650	650
7. Purchases	19 992	19 161	18 331	17 495	20 830	16 660	18 331	17 495	18 331	19 161	19 991	27 485
8. Total (5 + 6 + 7)	25 211	24 380	23 550	36 541	26 276	22 106	23 777	22 941	23 777	24 607	25 438	35 728
9. Cash increase/decrease (4 − 8)	2 629	2 300	1 970	(12 181)	2 724	1 094	1 743	1 419	1 743	2 073	2 402	2 552
10. Bank balance (1 + (or −) 9)	10 129	12 429	14 399	2 218	4 942	6 036	7 779	9 198	10 941	13 014	15 416	17 968

*From balance sheet of 1986.

BUDGET/ACTUAL SYSTEM

	January 1987		February 1987		March 1987	
	Budget	Actual	Budget	Actual	Budget	Actual
Sales						
Purchases						
Salaries						
Depreciation						
Maintenance of building						
Insurance						
Interest						
Stationery						
Sales promotion						
Transport						
Water & lights						
Telephone						
Bank charges						
Maintenance on vehicles						
Maintenance on equip.						
Capital redemption						
Other						
Totals						

10. Train sales personnel.
11. Stay open for longer hours to create convenience for late shoppers (if possible).
12. Sell on credit, but control it effectively.
13. Boost employee morale with better relations, etc.

This section is concerned with how break-even analysis apply to the management of a small business. This analytical approach can be financially rewarding to the business if used regularly, because it will assist you in having a better understanding of the elements that affect profitability.

Break-even analysis has to do with the determination of the cost-volume-profit relationship. In effect the break-even analysis will reveal that cost and profit vary with the volume of sales. But before a break-even analysis can be done, it is first necessary to know your fixed and variable costs. This information then, can be used to graphically express the relationship between cost, profit and sales.

Fixed Costs: Known as those costs that exist regardless of the volume of sales. In other words, costs that are constant over the entire range of output for a given capacity. Fixed costs usually are rent, property tax, salary expenses not related to sales, insurance, leased machinery and equipment, etc. These expense items may vary somewhat, but the variations are not caused by output. Your rent, for instance, stays the same for the year whether you sell R100 000,00 or R100,00 worth of goods. Fixed costs as they would appear on a break-even chart is shown below.

Variable Costs: These are costs which vary directly and proportionately with output. Thus, an increase in sales volume of 15 per cent causes an increase in cost of about 15 per cent. Basically then, variable costs are your cost of sales — you have to buy more or expend more if you sell more. If you pay commission to your salesmen, you would be paying them more for more sales. The figure below shows how variable costs would appear on a break-even chart.

427

Semivariable Costs: These are costs which are fixed over limited ranges of output but change over the wider range. In other words, costs that seem to be part variable, part fixed. Examples of semivariable costs are maintainance, delivery expenses, etc. You should use your good business judgement and split them between fixed and variable costs proportionately.

Step 1: Classify expenses into fixed costs and variable costs.

Item of expense:	Total estimated expenses	Fixed expenses	Variable expenses
Cost of sales	233 856		233 856
Salaries	35 840	18 000	17 840
Depreciation	7 600	7 600	
Maintenance—building	400		400
Insurance	780	780	
Interest (Bank loan)	2 460		2 640
Stationery	785		785
Sales promotion and advertising	4 800		4 800
Transport	2 910		2 910
Water and lights	1 100		1 100
Telephone	510		510
Bank Charges	260		260
	291 481	26 380	265 101

Step 2: Draw the Break-even Chart.

The break-even chart is a square with a 45-degree sales income line drawn from the lower left to the upper right of the chart. The scale on which the total costs are plotted is located on the vertical axis; the volume scale, which is located on the horizontal axis. On the break-even chart the measure of volume may be based on the number of units sold or on Rand sales. The total-cost line on the chart actually starts on the vertical axis at the point of intersection with the fixed-cost line. The point at which the total-cost line intersects the sales income line is called the "break-even" point. It is the point at which cost is equal to income and profit is equal to "zero".

The area between the total cost and sales income line above the break-even point is the "profit area"; below the break-even point is the "loss area". The break-even chart on page 430 is based on the following data (imaginary figures for explanatory purposes):

Sales Income for a year		R80 000
Total Cost at that Sales volume:		
Fixed Costs	20 000	
Variable Costs	40 000	60 000
Profit		R20 000

The total cost line in the figure below was drawn by first plotting two points: fixed costs of R20 000 at zero sales volume; and total cost of R60 000 at R80 000 sales volume (the difference between the two figures, of course, is the variable cost at the indicated volume; in this case, R60 000 minus R20 000, or R40 000). These points were then connected and the line extrapolated to the edge of the chart on the right. By inspection of the chart it can be seen that the break-even point is R40 000.

Of course, it is not necessary for you to draw a picture to determine your break-even point because the break-even chart is merely a graphic representation of your cost-volume-profit relationship. However the major significance of the break-even chart for profit planning purposes is that it clearly shows that above the break-even point the business is able to make increasingly higher profits. Conversely, the business suffers increasingly greater losses with a decrease in sales. The break-even point can however also be determined as follows:

Step 1: Express the variable expenses as a percentage of sales. In the condensed income statement, sales are R324 800. Variable expenses amount to R265 101. Therefore, variable expenses are 81% (R265 101 ÷ R324 800) of sales. This means that 81 cents of every rand in sales are required to cover variable expenses. The remainder — 19 cents of every rand — is available for fixed expenses and profit.

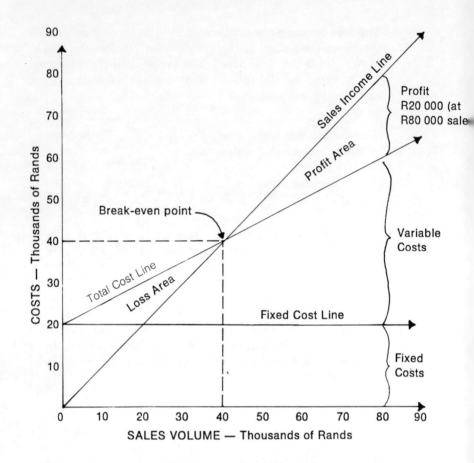

Step 2: Substitute the information gathered in the following basic break-even formula to calculate the break-even point:

$$S = F + V$$

Where S = Sales at the break-even point
F = Fixed Expenses
V = Variable expenses expressed as a percentage of sales.

This formula states that when sales equal the fixed expenses and variable expenses, there will be neither profit nor loss. At this point, sales income is just sufficient to cover the fixed and the variable expenses. In other words, the break-even point.

Step 3: Calculate the break-even point by using the basic algebraic formula:

$$S = F + V$$
$$S = R26\ 380 + 0,81S$$
$$10S = R263\ 800 + 8,1S \text{ (Multiplied equation by 10 to get rid of decimal fraction).}$$
$$10S - 8,1S = R263\ 800$$
$$1,9S = R263\ 800$$
$$S = R138\ 842 \text{ (Sales needed to break even).}$$

Proof of this calculation is as follows:

Sales at break-even point per calculations	R138 842
Less: Variable expenses (81% of sales)	R112 462
Marginal Income	R26 380
Less: Fixed Expenses	R26 380
Equals neither profit nor loss	R0

The basic break-even formula can also be modified to show the sales required to obtain a certain amount of net profit. In this case, let S mean the sales required to obtain a certain amount of net profit, say R33 319. The formula then reads as follows:

$$S = F + V + \text{Net profit}$$
$$S = R26\ 380 + 0,81S + R33\ 319$$
$$10S = R263\ 800 + 8,1S + R333\ 190 \text{ (Multiplied equation by 10)}$$
$$10S - 8,1S = R263\ 800 + R333\ 190$$
$$1,9S = R596\ 990$$
$$S = R314\ 205$$

Proof of this calculation is as follows:

Sales	R314 205
Less: Variable Expenses	R254 506 (81% of Sales)
Gross Profit	R59 699
Less: Fixed Expenses	R26 380
Net Profit	R33 319

You can now see how these formulas can be used to help in finding out how much you need to sell to break even or make a given profit. Also, you may have noticed that the sales figures in the formulas used differ from the profit planning exercise on page 419. The reason being that the sales in the profit planning exercise was determined to achieve a net profit for a return on investment objective, whilst the basic break-even formula was used to determine the sales for a specific net profit objective. The difference then in the two objectives set.

Returning now to our simplified break-even exercise (Figure 1), we have noticed that the break-even point occurs at a volume of R40 000 sales, at the point where both expected sales income and total costs are equal (R40 000). The amount of profit or loss is expressed as the difference between the total cost and expected sales income lines. As sales volume increases past the break-even point, expected profit rises rapidly. In other words, if a sales volume of R90 000 is forecasted, for example, the relationships depicted in figure 1 tell us that the business would incur total costs of R60 000 on sales income of R90 000, for a profit of R25 000. If you are alert, you will note that by increasing sales volume with 12,5% (from R80 000 to R90 000), the business would be able to increase profits by 25% (from R20 000 to R25 000).

As a businessman then, you will do well to consider alternative courses of action that could be implemented, for example, to increase sales volume. If sales volume could be increased from R80 000 to R90 000 by simply spending more—an additional R4 000—on advertising, should you go ahead? And what if it would require an additional R8 000 in advertising to reach the desired increase in sales? In other words, the key question is: How much can you afford to lay out for additional promotional activities in this particular case?

Returning now to the profit planning exercise's figures, we will analyse a few alternative action plans from a profit standpoint. You have seen that you have to sell R314 205 worth of goods to make a profit of R33 319, and variable expenses and fixed expenses amount to R291 481 (total costs).

Therefore, each Rand of sales will incur a cost of R0,92 (R291 481 ÷ R314 205). However, if you increase your sales to R1,00, the extra sales should not cost you R0,92. The fixed costs will stay constant, and only the variable cost should increase. So, your cost should increase only by the variable portion. For R1,00 of sales increase, your cost should increase by only R0,843 [R265 101 (Variable costs) ÷ R314 205 (Sales)]. So, your increase in profit per Rand of increase in sales volume, often called marginal income, is R0,157 (R1,00 – R0,843).

This concept of marginal income (also referred to as "contribution margin") can be explained in simpler terms.

The concept of marginal income is an important one because it represents the proportion of sales income that is left over after all the variable costs have been paid for, and tells you the margin (or amount) available to contribute to fixed costs. For example, if variable costs varies in amount with volume of business, while fixed costs is the same regardless of the volume of the business, then the difference between 100 per cent and the variable cost proportion may be called the "marginal income". In other words, if variable cost is 60 per cent (or 60 cents) out of each rand of business, there must be 40 per cent (or 40 cents) out of each rand of business applicable to fixed cost until it is offset, and thereafter, to profit. By way of an example, suppose you sell a product that cost R60,00, for R100,00. The marginal income is R40,00 or, expressed as a percentage, 40% (R40,00 ÷ R100,00). This marginal income (sales income minus variable costs) can be used to offset fixed costs, and anything left over is regarded as profit.

You can now compute your cost and profit at several sales volumes and so get a picture of the related changes in profit. What you have also seen in the break-even analysis done, is that the sales volume where the business makes no profit is between 0 and R138 842. Thus, the business can make the desired profit only if sales increase from R138 842 to R314 205. However, the marginal income analysis done above can help you in your decision making concerning alternative courses of action as follows:

1. Will it be profitable to increase your layout for promotional activities with R4 000, which, you estimate, would increase your sales with R14 000. You should then obtain additional profits of R2 198 [R0,157 (marginal income) × R14 000] for the R4 000 paid out. This would then result in a loss of R1 802 (R2 198 minus R4 000). Thus, the R4 000 that you want to lay out for promotional activities should at least increase sales with R26 000 before a profit of R4 082 [0,157 (marginal income) × R26 000] can be realized. However, this would only give you an added profit of R82,00 (R4 082 minus R4 000). From these calculations you can see clearly why it is so important to be selective in your advertising, to pick your spots, and to make your "ad dollars" count. Your promotional activities should be well planned to get the most "mileage" — profits do not just happen.

2. Will it be profitable to increase the price by 10% if you can expect a drop of 12% in sales? The price increase would result in a marginal

income of about R0,257 [R0,157 (marginal income) + R0,10], and the profit would change to about R38 995, [R0,257 (raised marginal income) × R0,92 (cost per Rand sales) × R276 500 (12 % decrease in sales) – R26 380 (fixed) costs)], which would be better than the present expected profit of R33 319. However, the market's acceptance to the price increases of 10 % should be seriously considered.

3. What would happen to the profit picture should you plan to reduce variable costs by 5 %? The marginal income should increase to R0,224 [R1,00 – (0,843 × R0,92)], and the profit at R314 205 sales volume would be R44 001 [R314 205 (sales) × R0,224 – R26 380 (fixed costs)]. This profit looks promising should ways be found to reduce the variable costs without any damage to other operations.

The basic break-even formula can also be used to consider alternative action plans:

4. You are planning to expand by modernizing your business as you think that it will attract more customers. Thus, this change in equipment to be bought will add R10 000 to fixed costs (raising them to R36 380 per year). The variable expenses will remain at 81 % of sales. What will happen to the break-even point if your modernization plans are carried out?

Basic formula: Sales at break-even point = Fixed expenses + Variable expenses expressed as a percentage of sales.

$$S = R36\ 380 + 0,81S$$
$$10S = R363\ 800 + 8,1S \text{ (Multiplied by 10 to get rid of decimal fraction).}$$
$$10S - 8,1S = R363\ 800$$
$$1,95 = R191\ 473 \text{ (Sales needed to break even).}$$

Under the proposed plan of modernizing the business, the new break-even point is R191 473. Before the proposed modernizing plan, it took sales of R138 842 to break even. Profit will obviously reduce under the proposed plan of modernizing the business, but it can be increased if prices can be increased or variable costs be reduced, or sales can be increased significantly.

You now would want to know how much sales are required to make the same profit (R33 319) after the shop has been modernized. To solve the problem, we modify the basic break-even formula to show sales required to make R33 319 profit when fixed expenses are now R36 380. Let S equal sales required to make the desired profit under the proposed plan.

S = Fixed expenses + Variable expenses expressed as a percentage of sales + required profit.

S = R36 380 + 0,81S + R33 319

10S = R363 800 + 8,1S + R333 190 (Multiplied equation by 10)

10S – 8,1S = R363 800 + R333 190

1,9S = R696 990

S = R366 836 (Sales required to make profit of R33 319 after modernization of business).

Other alternatives can be evaluated in much the same manner as discussed. Once you have made such an economic analysis, a final plan of action can then be decided upon and objectives can be set to achieve the desired results. Your choice as to selecting an action plan would of course be what would be most beneficial to the business. However, let us assume that you have decided to make it your objective to reduce costs (variable costs) with 5 % during 1987 and to aim for sales of R314 205. As already calculated, your net profit would be about R44 001 (before tax) which gives you a return on investment of 27,7 %.

In conclusion then, break-even analysis can provide you with a flexible set of income and expense projections under assumed conditions and alternative managerial programmes. It enables you to study information concerning sales volumes, selling prices, and expenses. Probably the greatest limitations of break-even analysis are related to the difficulties encountered in obtaining reliable and realistic estimates of income and expenses; and the assumptions made in carrying out the analysis. Thus, your business judgement plays a large role and is very necessary, but at least one sure thing break-even analysis gives you is that you have a starting point — a technique to help you attack your problems and help point you toward rational decisions. That is what break-even analysis is all about.

SUMMARY AND CONCLUSIONS

Healthy financial practices are a major factor in business. By not preparing budgets in advance, you might realize too late that your business is failing. What matters in business is how you handle and control the money you've got, and you will never impose control over your financial affairs without a budget. To practice the best kind of pro-active management, you should compare your figures (actual against budgeted) on a regular basis. The feedback you receive will enable you to correct deviations quickly. It will also point out to you what you are doing well, and what you should be doing more of, and better.

NOTES

[1] Dr. Charles Woelfel. Guides for profit planning. *Small Business Management Series Number 25.* U.S. Small Business Administration, Washington D.C.: 1.

[2] These factors (or 'profit-making opportunities') needed for successful operations and associated with the return on investment rate are mainly the following: increasing the planned volume of sales (or volume of units sold) by applying more aggressive sales promotional techniques, purchasing better quality products and improving the service, making the product more available; increasing or decreasing the planned prices of the goods or services —the best price may not be the ones you planned; perhaps a combination of both the actions mentioned above is justified because it may not be good to sell on the basis of price alone, but you should price for profit and sell quality, better service, reliability, and integrity; decrease expenses by implementing various control systems to avoid shoplifting losses and loss of money from the cash register, reduce poor scheduling of work, and avoid having too much money tied up in stock; increasing the productivity of people and assets through improved methods, employing the right kind and number of people, further training; etc. All these actions and many others have an effect on the outcome of your return on investment rate.

[3] Profit Planning Steps adapted from Curtis E. Tate, Jr., Leon C. Megginson, Charles R. Scott, Jr., Lyle R. Trueblood. *Successful Small Business Management.* 1985. Business Publications, Plano, Texas: 488. (Used with permission.)

[4] Ibid.

[5] It should be borne in mind that the desired return on investment in this example is computed without considering the payment of tax. In planning for the forthcoming year, you should make provision for tax, for example: if you want to realize a desired return on investment rate of 21%, and you have estimated that your tax on this profit (R33 264, that is, 21% of R158 400) is R10 000, then the profits to be planned for before income tax are as follows:

436

Return desired	R33 264
Estimated tax on profit	10 000
Profit needed before income tax	R43 000

A volume of sales should then be determined and planned for that will enable you to reach this profit objective.

17 | CREDIT CONTROLLING

'The purpose of credit extension is to help the customer to buy; but the purpose of business is to make a profit. Difficulties arise when the temptation to sell at all costs makes the seller forget there must be a "day of reckoning". A transaction is profitable only if the bill for the goods or services is paid promptly. To say that profitable credit decisions often call for "nerves of steel" is no great exaggeration. If we criticize the banker's traditional "coldness" in lending situations, we must remember that friendly enthusiasm and blood ties have been an expensive luxury for many a business owner; better to be rational and objective and profitable in business than emotional and subjective and bankrupt. Those who have suffered believe that it is better to lose a friend quickly through refusal of credit to him or her, than slowly through the long trials surrounding this person's refusal to pay.'

Clifford M. Baumback and Kenneth Lawyer[1]

INTRODUCTION

Many an established businessman will agree that the above is very true. Credit makes the economy go round and while 'buy now, pay later' is the 'in thing' today, your perspective as a business owner must be somewhat more conservative when you have decided to sell on credit. A 'cash only' policy is undoubtedly the least expensive method of selling as cash flow tends to be high, records and personnel expenses are minimized, and there are no bad debts. Overdue debtors can play havoc with your cash flow, but sales are not always stimulated by selling just for cash. People do not like to carry large amounts of money and many therefore prefer to buy ahead of payment. You may sell entirely on credit, which helps your business to maintain a level of sales volume. Such a service is usually preferred by customers, but it can be very risky as not all people to whom you grant credit will honour their debts prompty. In order to stimulate sales, you can provide credit to your customers, but your objective should always be to reduce your risk while benefiting from the buying power of the credit society. You must know what it costs you to extend credit as businesses lose far more from slow accounts than from bad debts — the cost related to slow accounts is the most important item in the total cost of doing business on credit.

Giving credit can increase sales but if the sales are only on paper you will be forced to borrow money in order to replace the stock purchased by the customer. In extending credit, your working capital must be sufficient to carry the credit accounts, to buy stock, and to pay for operating expenses. Giving credit is, therefore, not simply a snap decision. Facts and information must supplement your personal judgement. You cannot just make a decision on face value alone. Selling on credit allows you to select your own customers but you must first investigate the customer's ability to pay and his credit rating to minimize bad debts. When bad times come, slow-paying customers may force your business to seek credit elsewhere and if you are over-extended, they may even jeopardize your business. 'A sound credit system is one in which (1) credit applicants are thoroughly investigated; (2) limits are placed on the amount of credit extended; (3) accounts are systematically monitored or "controlled"; and (4) delinquent accounts are followed up promptly.'[2] To say that 'time is money' is no lie, especially when selling on credit.

MAKING A DECISION ON EXTENDING CREDIT TO CUSTOMERS

Should you or should you not sell on credit to your customers? The more new accounts you open, the better your business, providing the new accounts are not bad ones! How do you know? How can you recognize an eventual credit risk? Granting credit facilities to your customers always involves an element of risk and to minimize this risk and make a sound credit decision you need to know the facts. Can they pay? Will they pay? Some business owners simply judge the customer by appearance and on face value and take a name and address, only to regret having made the sale. When such a lax attitude on the part of your debtors towards making prompt payments make cash flow a problem, it is time to step into the picture and draw up a credit policy or revise your credit policy. If this is adhered to it will ensure profitability for your business, and allow credit to be used to stimulate and promote sales with minimum risk. A sound credit policy will prevent customers from using your money indiscriminately.

The first decision to be made is: Why do you want to sell on credit to your customers? You first have to look at your financial statements. Have the sales declined or increased? If your sales have dropped, then it might be wise to sell on credit in order to increase sales. If your sales have not dropped, then it might still be a wise decision to increase credit sales, in order to generate further sales and consequently, a higher profit. You thus have to analyse your financial statements regularly. A requirement is of course that you have the correct figures in your books. Remember, your judgement is as good as your information. Other reasons to sell on credit are to increase your profit or, if you are already selling on credit, to implement a sound credit control system in order to minimize the risk of losing money. To enable you to make a decision whether or not to sell on credit it is also necessary that you weigh both the advantages and disadvantages of granting credit. Advantages (in addition to increased sales) are:[3]

1. A more personal relationship can be maintained with credit customers who feel a bond with the business.

2. Credit customers are likely to be more regular than cash customers who tend to go where bargains are greatest.

3. Credit customers are more likely to be interested in quality and service than in price.

4. Goodwill is built up and maintained more easily.

5. Goods can be exchanged and adjustments made with greater ease. If necessary, goods can also be sent out on approval.

6. A list of credit customers provides a permanent mailing list for special sales promotions.

Some disadvantages are:

1. Capital is tied up in merchandise bought by credit customers.
2. If you have borrowed the extra money required when credit is granted, the interest must be added to the cost of goods sold.
3. Some losses from bad debts and customers with fraudulent intentions are bound to occur.
4. Some credit customers pay slowly because they over-estimate their ability to pay in the future.
5. Credit customers are more likely to abuse the privileges of returning goods and having goods sent out on approval.
6. Credit increases operating and overhead costs by adding the expenses of investigation and of the bookkeeping entailed in keeping accounts, sending out statements, and collecting payments.

In most cases, the advantages of selling on credit outweigh the disadvantages, as most disadvantages can be eliminated through a proper credit control system.

CREDIT POLICY

In setting up a credit policy, you need to answer the following questions:

1. Who will be responsible for extending credit? It will usually be yourself or an employee authorized by you.

2. What percentage of your turnover (sales) should be allowed for credit extension? It is always wise to start with a low percentage of about 10% (even lower if you wish) of your turnover in order to minimize the risk involved in granting credit. You can then increase the percentage periodically if it proves to be profitable. Say for instance your turnover for the coming year is R150 000 (as planned), then your total sales on credit must not exceed R15 000 per year (10% of turnover). This means that you can grant credit of R1 250 per month (R15 000 ÷ 12 months = R1 250). It also means that total credit outstanding at the end of the first month must not exceed R1 250. Also remember that if your terms are three months, then you need at least R3 750 (three times R1 250) in extra cash to replace stock being bought by credit customers, to pay for operating expenses and to carry the accounts outstanding.

3. When an application for credit is received, who will be responsible for interviewing the applicant? It will normally be yourself or an employee authorized by you. Do not forget to inform all your employees to refer credit customers to yourself or the authorized person.

4. What percentage of the applicant's salary will determine his credit limit? Normally, twenty percent of the applicant's net salary is acceptable. You have to take into account his net earnings and not his gross salary, as the money he will have available per month to repay you will be what is left after deductions. If the applicant's net salary is R600 and you have decided that 20% of it will be his credit limit, your responsibility will be to see that he does not buy goods for more than R120 at any time until his limit can be increased because of an increase in salary. You also need to inform other employees about the amount of goods that can be bought by credit customers so that no over extension takes place. Credit limits are allocated to ensure that customers do not buy beyond their capacity to pay and by doing so, jeopardize their credit record and create the possibility of severe cash flow problems for your business. Limits must be revised continuously — upward (to prompt-paying customers) and downward (to slow-paying customers) if necessary.

5. What will the terms of payment be? It could be two months, three months or more. If you decide to make it three months and the customer's credit limit is R120, then his monthly instalment will be R40.

6. Before or on what date of the month must payments be made? Normally, sound practice is payment before or on the 10th day of each month. If a customer has bought goods during January 1985, then it is expected of him to pay his first instalment on or before the 10th of February 1985.

7. Who will be responsible for controlling credit accounts? It could be yourself or an employee authorized to do so. Such responsibilities will include following up accounts in arrears, collecting outstanding money, and handing over of long outstanding accounts to an attorney (or collection agency).

8. What about a delinquency charge for late payers? Such a charge can discourage customers from allowing their accounts to become long past due. The delinquency charge normally involves a finance charge or service charge of 1% or 2 per cent per month on all balances more than 30 days past due. For example, if a customer's statement at the end of May indicates a total balance due of R630,00, of which R417,00 is more than 30 days past due, the finance charge for May would be calculated as follows (assuming a 1% delinquency charge):

$$R417 \times .01 = R4,17$$

Most people recognize that a charge of 1% per month represents an annual interest expense of 12% (12 × .01). A charge of 2% per month represents an annual interest charge of 24% (12 × .02).

A policy such as that outlined above and the answers to the questions asked need to be closely studied before any credit can be granted to customers. The policy will serve as your guide as far as credit extension is concerned. Having now decided what the conditions will be, it is of utmost importance to adhere to them yourself in order to be successful in controlling credit extended to customers.

PREPARING A CREDIT APPLICATION FORM

Credit information about customers can usually be obtained from the contents of credit application forms completed by the applicants. Every day you may be confronted with potential customers asking for credit. No one can be expected to obtain all the particulars about every applicant, and therefore the information on the credit application forms will supplement your personal judgement. In order to obtain a record of the desired information, you should ask the customer to fill in and sign a credit application form. It is also advisable to have the credit application forms neatly typed (or printed) as this creates a good first impression — a professional one. Preferably, the customer should complete the form himself with your guidance. See Fig. 1 for an example of a credit application form.

A business needing daily credit information should consider joining at a nominal fee the services of a reputable credit

Telephone number: _____ Address of business: _____

_____

_____

CREDIT APPLICATION FORM: XYZ STORE

1. Surname: .... Christian names: ....
2. Marital status: .... Married/Single/Divorced/Widowed
3. Residential address: ....
4. For how long: ....
    (Owner/Renting/Stay with parents/Boarding)
5. Previous address: .... How long? ....
6. Home phone no.: .... No of dependants: ....
7. I.D. Number: .... Nationality: ....
8. Name of employer: .... How long? ....
    Address of employer: ....

    ....
9. Occupation: .... Office phone no.: ....
10. Previous employer: .... How long? ....
11. Husband/wife — Full names: .... Date of birth: ....
12. Monthly salary: .... Net salary after deductions: ....
13. Name of bank or building society: ....
    Branch: ....
14. Car registration number: ....
15. Trade references:

Name of business	Address	Tel. No.	Acc. No.	Amount Owing

16. Personal references:

Name	Res. Address	Employer	Relationship
1			
2			

I certify that the above information is true and correct

Signature of customer: _____ Date: _____

Fig. 1. A credit application form.

bureau. Normally such a bureau is particularly effective in rating persons living in the local trading area, and its effectiveness is extended through its co-operation with other national and even international credit bureaus. All these associations compile credit information on persons who have moved from one town to another, or even from one country to another.

INVESTIGATING THE CREDIT APPLICATION

Your main objective in investigating the credit applicant is to reduce losses from bad debts and slow payments. After completion of the credit application form, the next step should be an interview with the applicant. During the interview your friendliness and way of obtaining information can help a great deal in gaining the applicant's goodwill and confidence. Since the applicant will speak more freely when relaxed, the interview should be in complete privacy if possible, and in a pleasant atmosphere. It is important to bear in mind that the client expects you to keep his matters confidential, and he also expects you to listen to him confidentially and in complete privacy.

The question you need to answer in evaluating the credit application is: Can he pay, or will he be able to pay and how does he manage his money? This brings us to the commonly known three C's of credit — Character (willingness to pay), Capital and Capacity (the applicant's capital resources and the capacity to manage them well). Character refers to the probability that a customer will try to honour his obligations. This factor is of considerable importance, because every credit transaction implies a promise to pay. Will the debtor make an honest effort to pay his debts, or is he likely to try to get away with something? The capacity of a debtor is evaluated by his past record. Capital is measured by the general financial position of the debtor. A convenient formulation using the three C's in order to recognize a good credit risk is as follows:[4]

Character + Capacity + Capital = Good credit risk
Character + Capacity + insufficient Capital = fair credit risk

Character + Capital + insufficient Capacity = fair credit risk

Capacity + Capital + impaired Character = doubtful credit risk

Character + Capacity − Capital = limited success

Capacity + Capital − Character = dangerous risk

Character + Capital − Capacity = inferior credit risk

Capital − Character − Capacity = distinctly poor risk

Character − Capacity − Capital = inferior credit risk

Capacity − Character − Capital = fraudulent credit risk

If circumstances allow, the correctness of the information supplied by the applicant should be confirmed with credit bureaus, the applicant's other creditors, and his salary and address with his employer. As a safeguard against bad debt losses, you should also inform and have a definite understanding with the customer as to the terms of payment, credit limit, date of payment and other relevant information. Try not to give credit to jobless people and do not give credit to contract workers. They normally buy goods on credit just before leaving for another contract somewhere else. They are very difficult to get hold of, although when a debtor changes his address, he does not usually deliberately do so to avoid payment. He may, however, be tempted to sit back and wait for you to find him — which costs money.

Once you have accepted the customer as a credit customer and he has agreed to the conditions and terms, you can write a friendly letter telling how pleased you are to welcome him as a customer to your business, and at the same time make use of the opportunity to confirm the conditions with the customer. An example of such a letter is as follows:

Dear Mr ....

We are happy to advise you that we have decided to open a credit account for you, and we would like to take this opportunity to welcome you as a client to our business. Since you have not purchased goods on credit with us before, we would like to explain our policy in handling customers' accounts.

At the end of each month we send a detailed statement showing all purchases for the preceding 30 days and amounts due. Normally we would expect to receive payment within ten days from date of statement.

From time to time we will send you advance news of special sales and campaigns we have planned and also furnish you with other helpful information. If at any time, you have any queries or complaints to make about our services, we should be glad to hear from you personally.

We are looking forward to being of service to you.

Yours very truly

(Signature)

MONITORING ACCOUNTS

When the customer receives the account, the 'day of reckoning' has arrived. As you may already know, some people seldom realize the true consequences of buying on credit. They love the idea of 'buy now', but the 'pay later' is not as easily done as the purchasing was. These are usually the impulsive buyers who over-commit themselves without pausing to think about the implications. The answer for them would have been to buy for cash only, which is still the best way to avoid over-committing oneself. The problem at times is not so much as how to live within your means, but how to control your buying on credit. From the day the customer makes his first purchase on credit, you must watch the account carefully to see whether he honours his share of the obligation. Credit control has mainly to do with the keeping of adequate records and prompt collections. Keeping a tight control on the settlement of debts by the people you do business with, is essential for good financial management. The sooner you collect outstanding debts, the less money it costs you.

At the end of each month (about the 25th to the 30th of every month), you must send out the debtors accounts and your attention should be focused on those accounts that have become overdue. Also, check the total sales and the total amounts outstanding to see whether your customers are still within their limits as determined by the credit policy. The longer an account is carried on the books, the less likely it becomes that it will be collected, which is the main reason for monitoring every account very carefully so that quick action can be taken.

Don't be reluctant. Many businessmen are reluctant to enforce strict collection procedures. The reasons for this are several, and none of them are valid. Some people simply are embarrassed to ask for money even though it is owed to them. Others express concern that they might alienate a "good customer" and perhaps loose an account. The opposite is true. How good is an account if the bills are not paid? Even more important, the customer owing you a large balance may be reluctant to do more business with you until the account is cleared. You not only lost your money, you have also lost a customer. Other businesses feel that rigorous enforcement of a collection policy can damage their reputation. Viewed logically, would you conclude that a person who owes you money is likely to spread this news around town?

FOLLOWING UP ACCOUNTS IN ARREARS

The ability to collect accounts punctually may spell the difference between the success or failure of your business. Until the cash for goods bought is actually received, the money cannot be used for paying expenses or buying other goods and generally, funding the business with additional working capital. As time passes and an account is not paid, the probability of collection decreases. Once an account becomes overdue, two actions are important — collecting the money and retaining the goodwill of the customer for future business. Care must be taken not to harass debtors with continual or untimely phone calls and not to employ bad language. If the customer is slow in paying, prod gently at first in order to retain his goodwill, and become increasingly firm. The first approach should be gentle as the customer may have been ill or have had other urgent matters to attend to. If such a problem develops and the customer shows co-operation, you can accept from him a token payment to get collection under way (a mutually agreeable plan). The same debtor may in future still be a good customer.

THE CREDIT COLLECTION LETTER

The collection letter calls for very careful preparation. It is important to employ a positive approach that will assist in

448

collecting the outstanding money. Much success can be achieved by keeping the letters and notices current. However, the letters must be characterized by perfect frankness and the desire to be of service, which will lead to building and returning a solid foundation for repeat business. It is also of absolute necessity not to write a letter in such a manner that it will make the debtor think he is a dishonest person. This will only worsen the situation and you could lose his business for ever. Almost all people will try to be honest if they are treated with confidence. Normally, the procedure of sending letters is as follows:

- suggesting settlement of account;
- urging settlement of account;
- insisting on settlement of account; and finally
- demanding settlement of account.

You can also have a rubber stamp made to endorse accounts sent with such words as:

> The enclosed account has probably escaped your attention. Prompt remittance will be appreciated.

It should be borne in mind that such a letter is a very personal and confidential communication, which derives its force from the fact that it is directed at a special individual. Individuality must be kept as far as possible in order to build up the 'personality' of business and personal contact with the customer. The letter may look like this:

Dear Sir

My attention was drawn to the fact that your account, which fell due on April 25, has not been settled within the terms agreed upon. I am sure the remittance was delayed for a good reason, but am now looking forward to prompt settlement. I also want you to know that a new range of trousers is to be on display as from next week. Please do come to view them as they may be just the style you were looking for.

Yours very truly

(Signature of business owner)

The above letter has a natural beginning — not a formal one. It was sent in a friendly spirit. It makes the debtor think: 'If I want those trousers in that particular style, I better pay my account.' The fact is that very few people are annoyed by letters concerning their accounts if the reminders are prompt, regular and courteous. Your relationship with the customer is entirely friendly and nothing was put in words that would put the customer off. Another way of putting the 'suggesting settlement of account' letter is as follows:

Dear Sir

May we remind you of the balance of R ... on your account. We are sure that you have overlooked this matter and hope you will now find it convenient to send us your remittance.

Yours very truly

(Signature of business owner)

When you write a letter like this, you are determined to get a friendly reply. Payment may, or may not be immediately forthcoming, but it would be a 'difficult' person who would not see that it was to his benefit to keep on the right side of the businessman who treated him so humanly. Such a letter ought to bring a response and will probably result in settlement. It can also establish a basis for more sound relations in the future. Always be careful not to assume automatically that a person is dishonest even when he does not reply to your first or second letter.

If no reply has been received to the second letter in which you still demonstrate an air of friendliness, and the customer has sent no payment or word of explanation, then your further action will depend on what you suspect, and you can now take a different step from before. Whereas your second letter has explained your side of the circumstances, that you wish to serve, your third letter must point out to the customer that he still has an obligation. You must now definitely insist on immediate settlement of the account, as follows:

Dear Sir

We are sorry to note that although we wrote to you on May 1 and June 1, we have had no response to our requests. We are surprised that we have had no reply, and we therefore now insist that you immediately meet your obligation. The enclosed copy of your account shows an unpaid balance of R ..., and we trust you will admit this is a very unsatisfactory situation. Prompt settlement is requested within seven days from date.

Yours very truly

(Signature of business owner)

This letter is rather urgent, but a customer (debtor) who has not replied to the previous letters evidently needs a sharp reminder. To set the customer a date for settlement is fairly severe treatment. When a large and important customer's account is involved, and he has always been a good payer by promptly meeting his obligations, but suddenly fails to reply to courteous letters, the sensible approach will hardly be to take harsh measures until you have satisfied yourself about the reasons why the customer does not respond. You will surely not run the risk of losing the customer's further support if there is any possibility of a mistake or misunderstanding. However, if silence prevails, it is justifiable to assume that the customer is not able to pay. Failure to answer one or two letters may mean inability to pay, but after no reply to a third friendly letter, more purposeful action is necessary. Always be definite in your third letter. Imply or state that the amount must be paid in full — this has the effect of the words becoming a definite request to the debtor. Always try to find a reason for non-payment, before you insist on settlement. Keep copies of all letters written for proof in case of further legal action.

The fourth letter demanding settlement of account, should almost contain an element of threat and should be short compared with previous letters. Time is now past for more friendly letters offering to assist the debtor. You must now resort to quick efforts in order to get the money by a certain date for the continuation of your business. The account has been outstanding too long and your main concern now must be to get the money rather than soothe the feelings of this debtor. A final letter of demand may look as follows:

Dear Sir

Although we have waited for a reply to our letter none has so far been received. You have already enjoyed the maximum extension we are able to grant. If, therefore, full settlement of your account is not forthcoming by return of post, we shall have no other choice but to resort to legal action to recover this long outstanding debt.

(Businessman's signature)

The reference to legal action means that the next letter will come from your attorney. You could also have stated: 'We shall be obliged to place your account in the hands of our attorney for collection.' For the customer this letter means the end of his credibility record; his delinquency will be advertised and he will be regarded as unreliable — no character, no capacity and no capital. It is this fear of unpleasant publicity that you wish to awaken in him. A court case might be expensive for you. You thus hope the threat will bring about action. However, many debtors hang on until the last possible moment before paying the account. Suppose this is the case, you must then adjust the matter by adopting a tone similar to that which follows:

Dear Sir

Thank you very much for your cheque of R ... which reached us this morning, in full settlement of your account.

I am sorry our last letter was displeasing to you. I deeply regret what seemed to threaten a termination to our pleasant relations, and felt sure there was some mistake which stood in our way. Let me further suggest that the best way to prevent any misunderstanding is to write to us frankly when you are in difficulties and need our assistance, because we consider ourselves privileged to assist our customers to the limit of our capacities. Matters will then never again reach such an unfortunate stage.

Your future business with us will be very much appreciated.

Yours faithfully

(Businessman's signature)

Should your last letter to the debtor bring neither a reply nor payment, then there remains only one thing to do — carry out your threat. Never let the debtor think you are 'bluffing'. Of course, if the last letter brings a reply but without payment, your further actions will depend on the nature of the reply. The circumstances may justify an extension of time or some other adjustments that will ease the situation.

If the customer comes to see you after the threat, it will be necessary to talk frankly about his obligation and to arrange a plan of payment that will enable him to settle his account as soon as possible. As a businessman your attempt should always be to get personally in touch with the debtor. What you will be looking for with such an interview will be an explanation and mutual arrangement for further friendly relations if possible. Your objective should thus always be to retain the customer.

Sound advice is to vary your methods. In your letters, try not to treat the same customer twice in exactly the same manner as before. Change your tactics so that they will lead to action on the debtor's side. Such variation will bring out that personal contact as well as the 'difference' you are looking for to compete successfully with other businesses. It will make your customers feel they are dealing with a live businessman rather than a routine clerk with whom they can afford to play around if they want to. It is going to be hard work, but in the end it will be worth it.

BANK'S CREDIT CARDS

Many problems associated with credit can be avoided through the use of bank credit cards. In many businesses, particularly in the retail and consumer service fields, credit arrangements for customers are available through the use of these cards. Under these plans, there is little or no commitment of the business' own capital, and the costs and risks of administration and collection are almost entirely the responsibility of the credit card company or bank. Credit card service is available from your regular commercial bank. Receipts from bank credit card purchases can be deposited daily and are immediately credited to your current cheque account. The bank assumes all credit risks provided that you follow instructions for approval of credit card purchases.

Accepting credit cards can work to your advantage as far as selling is concerned. They eliminate the need for credit approval, invoice preparation, record maintenance, and collections. They also minimize your commitment of capital and virtually eliminate the risk of uncollectable accounts. From a marketing standpoint, the availability of instant credit could often encourage a customer to buy immediately, rather than postpone the decision to a later date or bypass it completely.

SUMMARY AND CONCLUSIONS

The best control of losses on outstanding accounts starts with the prevention thereof. You will enhance your position if you investigate the customer's ability and willingness to pay, provide clear terms, and set limits on the total amounts of monthly purchases on credit. However, most businesses sell on credit not only to increase sales but also to be competitive within their line of business. Therefore, if you are fighting for a share of the market, selling on credit may favourably influence the market. The prime objective of all businesses is to make and maximize profit, but a sale is only profitable when the cash is received. Cash sales obviously require no collection costs and there is no time delay between selling and collecting, but more profitable sales may be made if credit terms are available as you will obviously charge more for products. The credit function must, however, be carefully controlled if its use is to be a profitable one for the business.

BIBLIOGRAPHY

* F.D Greyling. A closer look at credit. *Growth* 1986; Autumn: 19.
* F.D. Greyling. Credit control: a more realistic approach. *Entrepreneur* 1985; 4(2): 10.
* *A Business of Your Own.* A Standard Bank publication: 18.
* I.W. Modisha. Credit: a sales tool. *Small Business News* 1984; 6(2): 30-31.
* *Making the Most of Your Money: A Guide to Basic Budgeting.* Standard Bank of South Africa Limited.
* William H. Day. *Maximizing Small Business Profits with Precision Management.* 1978. Prentice-Hall, Englewood Cliffs, NJ: 291-307.
* Tate, Megginson, Scott, Trueblood. *Successful Small Business Management.* 1982. 3rd ed. Business Publications, Plano, Texas: 310-312.
* Thomas Rodolo. *A Business Guide for African Shopkeepers.* 1977. Interprint, Durban: 45-47.
* Clifford M. Baumback, Kenneth Lawyer. *How to Organize and Operate a Small Business.* 1979. Prentice-Hall, Englewood Cliffs, NJ: 418-449.

* R.S. Butler, H.A. Burd. *Commercial Correspondence.* 1919. D. Appleton, London: 302–349.

* J.K. Lasser Tax Institute. *How to Run a Small Business.* 1982. McGraw-Hill, New York: 245–257.

NOTES

[1] Baumback/Lawyer. *How to Organize and Operate a Small Business.* 1979. Prentice-Hall, Englewood Cliffs, NJ: 448, 449. (Reproduced with permission.)

[2] Idem, 432.

[3] Idem, 421.

[4] Theodore N. Beckman, Ronald S. Foster. *Credit and Collections: Management Theory.* 1969. McGraw-Hill, New York: 90, 91. (Reprinted by permission of McGraw-Hill Book Company.)

18 | DEVELOPMENT OF ENTREPRENEURSHIP

'If you listen to advice and are willing to learn, one day you will be wise.'

Proverbs 19:20[1]

'Get all the advice you can, and you will succeed; without it you will fail.'

Proverbs 15:22[2]

'You must make careful plans before you fight a battle, and the more good advice you get, the more likely you are to win.'

Proverbs 24:6[3]

INTRODUCTION

Wherever you are in South Africa, there are institutions that are awaiting your application for starting your own business and are willing to assist you in keeping your business on the road to success. But why are they all in Southern Africa? Because this country is in need of entrepreneurs like you and many others who can exploit their talents and those entrepeneurs again need assistance in the form of training, advice, financing, guidance and information in order to become successful businessmen. Problems are to be found every day and anywhere, and the small business owner is not exempt therefrom. A consultant's true reward does not lie only in monetary emoluments but also in the service and assistance he renders, in the satisfaction of assisting other small businessmen, and in seeing that the desired economic progress takes place. These institutions cater for about every need the small businessman has — no matter how small the business may be. What counts is that you can be put on to the 'map' simply by seeking information and accepting the advice given by these consultants (also known as business advisers[4]). The assistance of a consultant can be considered to be an investment in the business. However, to get the best assistance and advice from a consultant, you need to brief him accurately to ensure that the problem can be clearly defined. Remember though, that a decrease in profits, a declining market share, over-extension of credit, etc, are not always the causes of problems but merely the symptoms. A positive, honest, mutual trust and regular contact in good faith between you and the consultant, could greatly contribute to the eventual success of your business (and consequently your future). If you are unsure of the nature of the underlying problem, allow the consultants to try and identify and define the problem. In this way he can help you to solve the problem and not waste any effort in trying to eradicate the symptoms while the real cause goes untouched. Be frank and helpful, and provide as much relevant and accurate information as is needed. Always remember that you are still the owner-manager of the business, thus, you can accept or reject, in part or in totality, the findings and recommendations of the consultant. It might, however, be good insurance to accept their advice, as they do not just advise upon the best solution to be taken, but the most workable solution for the situation in question. The objective of this chapter is to enlighten you on what a consultation involves and where to find such assistance.

CONSULTATION SERVICES

The characteristic of the human race to assist others through consultation and advice is part of the social order in which we live. Man has, on the one hand, an inherent fear of the unknown and a desire to acquire the opinion of others on matters unknown to him, and on the other hand, a desire to share their knowledge and experience with others. Man is also conditioned from birth, into a learning process in which he is being prescribed to, counselled and advised in almost every aspect of his education and life in general. Consultation, therefore, forms a natural part of the human existence.

It therefore follows logically that consultation and the rendering of advice will play a similar and important role in the economic life of a nation. The optimum economic application of factors of production and scarce goods, place demands on man that are not usually within the scope of knowledge and experience of the individual. Exchange of experience, consultation, deliberation and collective decision-making are essential emanations of individual human limitations. It is in these fields that consultation services contribute to the economy of a country.

Meaning of a consultation service Probably the first thing a businessman needs to know, is that he must learn not only in order to be a success in business, but also to cope with the competition in his immediate territory and in the business arena in general. For this reason, the need for consultations is mainly centred around the need to help the owner-manager, as experience has shown that it is management which determines the success or failure of a business. Technical aspects such as the site, the financial means and cost effectiveness do play an important role, but management is the key-note. It is a fact that any business must keep abreast of what is happening in the business world and a consultation can make a special contribution by bringing such know-how into the business. The advice of a consultant could help to limit the risks involved in running your business. It facilitates your decision-making, because you get a better idea of the achievements, potential and future prospects of your business from an experienced outsider (a second opinion).

A consultation service is not just limited to managerial skills but covers the entire spectrum of knowledge and skills required in operating your business successfully. The advantages in making use of a consultation service are many, but two very important ones are that it stimulates action and helps to remove uncertainties (the sharing of knowledge promotes self-confidence that leads to action), and it could partially or entirely free you from problems which may arise.

A consultation service may be described as a comprehensive service to you (the individual businessman) and your business, as well as to the commercial sector as a whole. The primary objective of a consultation service may be said to be the promotion, stimulation and development of small businesses as an important element in the economy of Southern Africa. A consultation service assists you in making decisions and organizing your thoughts, and aids you in solving your business problems by suggesting possible, the best and the most workable solutions you may have overlooked in the course of a busy workday. The definition of a consultation service could thus be: to guide your business with close attention, advice and training with respect to its total operation, before and through the period from establishment to maturity (economically viable or profitable).

The role of the consultant It is a strong recommendation that the services of an experienced business consultant be obtained to assist the smaller business to develop a periodic reporting package as it is imperative that the accumulation of unnecessary data is avoided. This package should contain meaningful financial information only.

It has been proved that a regular management meeting (attended by the consultant), which formalizes the review of these performance indicators, can improve management's efficiency. Decisions taken should be documented in such a way that it is clear where the responsibility lies and when the deadlines fall due. Other items to be dealt with at the periodic management meetings are the fixing of marketing targets and the reviewing of cash flow forecasts to determine financing needs.

Operation of a consultation service A consultation service does five things — it evaluates, it identifies, it seeks solutions, it educates and it creates contact. But before any of these activities can be carried out by the consultant, you and the consultant must make initial contact with each other, either at his office or in the actual physical environment and circumstances within which the business operates. It is of vital importance that there should be mutual confidence right from the start between the consultant and yourself. You should collaborate as equals in your attempts to find solutions to the problems of the business.

The consultation service continually evaluates your business as it is at present, comparing it and its potential with similar businesses. It is impossible to solve problems without identifying them. Therefore, it is necessary that the consultant identify the problems of the business in conjunction with yourself as you are the one who understands fully the consequences of the problem. Solutions are then sought in collaboration and in agreement between the consultant and yourself. Corrective measures for their implementation are then considered. Practical assistance is available in implementing these solutions. The consultation service is also an important educational opportunity since it brings you into contact with certain knowledge, skills and attitudes which may have been lacking or vague in the past. The foregoing four aspects concerning the operations of a consultation service have one thing in common — communication. The consultation enables you to communicate confidentially about your business and its problems. There might not even be major problems but the fact that communication (or contact) has taken place can greatly boost your confidence by the mere confirmation that your business is being managed along the right lines. Sometimes you may be lonely and just need someone to talk to about your business in your own language — who better than your consultant whom you have come to trust, who shares your dreams and is always available to give sound advice, encouragement and inspiration. It is for such reasons that specific consultation services are definitely justified. You should make use thereof to your own advantage and you will need such assistance particularly when you start your business. Remember, the poorly operated business will fail and the well-managed one will succeed. A consultant can greatly contribute to the latter.

WHERE TO FIND ASSISTANCE

1. *The Small Business Development Corporation (SBDC)*

   The Small Business Development Corporation is the leader in South Africa as far as the advancement of small business entrepreneurship is concerned. They provide for just about every need the small businessman may have. Their activities include financing, provision of business facilities, information, advisory services, and the development and promotion of small business interests. Contact points for the SBDC offices are as follows:

Head Office: Small Business Centre,
5 Wellington Road,
Parktown, Johannesburg.
P.O. Box 7780, Johannesburg, 2000.
Telephone: (011) 643-7351.

Cape Regional Office: 701 Foretrust Building,
Martin Hammerschlag Way,
Foreshore, Cape Town.
P.O. Box 4295,
Cape Town, 8000.
Telephone: (021) 212480.

Natal Regional Office: 1901 Trust Bank Centre,
475 Smith Street, Durban.
P.O. Box 1035,
Durban, 4000.
Telephone: (031) 31-3666.

Branch Office: 8th Floor, Golden Mile Centre,
655 Main Street, North End,
Port Elizabeth.
P.O. Box 1745, Port Elizabeth, 6000.
Telephone: (041) 54-5494.

Information Offices: Bloemfontein — (051) 7-8380/97.
Durban — (031) 86-7130.
Johannesburg — (011) 643-7351.
Cape Town — (021) 21-2480.
Middelburg (Transvaal)
— (01321) 29156/29164.
Newcastle — (03431) 2-7949.
East London — (0431) 3-1363.
Pietersburg — (01521)
54-5494/5, 54-4408/9.
Pretoria — (012) 26-8671/2.
Soshanguve — (01214) 2031/2.
Soweto — (011) 949-0705.
Upington — (0541) 7751.

2. *Small Business Advisory Bureau (SBAB)*

The Small Business Advisory Bureau is an institution which forms part of the Potchefstroom University for

Christian Higher Education, and is committed to rendering a quality service to the South African small business sector. Their services are many, but the main ones include:

- **Consultations:**

General management consultations; Specific management consultations; follow-up consultations; advice per telephone and letter; and analysis of financial results.

- **Training Courses:**[5]

General management; financial management; marketing management; profitability in the motor trade; driveway efficiency; workshop management; customer relations and selling techniques; practical small business management; practical financial management; practical marketing management; office management; personnel management; sales promotion; profit control; manufacturing; specific management courses for general dealers, garages, pharmacies, professional concerns and hotels; factory planning; in-store sale training; costing for small manufacturers; practical bookkeeping; and practical management for building contractors.

- **Planning Services:**

The concentration of this service lies mainly in advice and assistance with the planning of business premises, the lay-out and internal finishing of premises, modernization, merchandising, general sales promotion methods as well as courses to promote sales. Technical advice is given with regard to furnishing, equipment, refrigeration, lighting and related matters. After the on-site investigation, the businessman is provided with a complete set of sketches and lay-out plans for the lay-out and furnishing of the business with the necessary technical details. Further discussion takes place and, where necessary, changes and adaptions are made to the suggested plans until mutual satisfaction has been reached. The plans can then be sent to various shopfitters for quotations. In all cases plans are modified until the owner is satisfied that they are what he wants. During the installation of equipment and furnishings, or the modernization of the existing businesses, constant contact is maintained and follow-up work is done to eliminate any possible problems.

• Monthly Publication:

The *Entrepreneur* is a monthly magazine you cannot afford to go without. This magazine is compiled and published by the Small Business Advisory Bureau. It is from the *Entrepreneur* that understandable information can be acquired to enable you to improve the efficiency and success of your business. *Entrepreneur* aims at providing information by means of articles on all aspects of small business management, finance, marketing, planning, general information (information on developments; modern tendencies and technical information), general news of vital importance to the small businessman, success stories (which give you inspiration and inform you about how it is done), information on courses you may attend to join dealing with a wide range of business-related subjects, and general news of importance to you (you may be able to spot some business opportunities).

For subscription write to:
The Editor
Entrepreneur
P.O. Box 1880
Potchefstroom
2520
or telephone:
(0148) 99-1002 as from 1/1/88.

For more information about the services of the Small Business Advisory Bureau, contact:
The Director
Small Business Advisory Bureau
Potchefstroom University for CHE
Potchefstroom
2520
Telephone: (0148) 99-1002 as from 1/1/88.

3. *Commercial Banks*

• Barclays Small Business Unit:

This unit was established in 1979 to provide finance and expert advice to entrepreneurs who have sound business ideas but who would not normally qualify for

463

a bank loan. It is based in Johannesburg but has business development offices operating from Barclays offices in all the main centres of Southern Africa.

They can help you in several ways, such as:

(i) by establishing, through research, the viability or otherwise of an entrepreneur's business idea;

(ii) by helping an aspirant businessman, who might not have the security normally required by a bank, to obtain finance. They are able to do this as a result of an indemnity agreement between the Small Business Development Corporation (SBDC) and Barclays, in terms of which the SBDC shares the risk with the Small Business Unit on loans to a maximum of R150 000 by guaranteeing up to 80% of the amount lent;

(iii) by giving the new entrepreneur initial training in aspects of financial management;

(iv) by ensuring that the entrepreneur has sufficient finance to enable the new venture to succeed; and

(v) by keeping regular contact with the new venture and assisting the new entrepreneur wherever possible to keep the new business on the road to success.

Address: 9th Floor
           Barclays Insurance House
           73 Loveday Street
           Johannesburg
           P.O. Box 8785
           Johannesburg
           2000

Telephone: (011) 632-9111

- **Standard Bank Small Business Development and Advisory Department**[6]
  P.O. Box 6702
  Johannesburg
  2000
  Telephone: (011) 636-4600 or 636-9112
- **Trust Bank Bureau for Business/Management**
  P.O. Box 7694
  Johannesburg
  2000

4. Other Development Corporations

- **Development Bank of Southern Africa.**
  P.O. Box 784433, Sandton 2146.
  Tel. (011) 445-9111 Telex: 4-22666 SA
  Teletex: 450087
- **South African Development Trust
  Corporation Limited, Pretoria.**
  P.O. Box 213, Pretoria 0001.
  Tel: (012) 21-5911 Telex: 3-22125 SA
- **Bophuthatswana National
  Development Corporation, Mmabatho.**
  P.O. Box 3011, Mmabatho 8691.
  Tel. (01401) 22151 Telex: 0937 3055 BP
- **Transkei Development Corporation
  Limited, Umtata.**
  P.O. Box 103, Umtata 5100.
  Tel. (0471) 26881 Telex: 711
- **Ciskei Peoples Development Bank
  Limited, Bisho.**
  P.O. Box 66, Bisho.
  Tel. (0433) 21540 Telex: 25-0134
- **Venda Development Corporation,
  Thohoyandou.**
  P.O. Box 9, Sibasa 0970.
  Tel. (01559) 21131 or 21314 Telex: 3-22682 VM
- **Lebowa Development Corporation
  Limited, Pietersburg.**
  P.O. Box 951, Pietersburg 0700.
  Tel. (01521) 7-2221 Telex: 3-22738
  Office also at
  Sheshego Tel. (01527) 6311
- **Kangwane Economic Development
  Corporation Limited, White River.**
  P.O. Box 935, White River 1240.
  Tel. (01311) 31101 Telex: 4-84929
- **Kwandebele National Development
  Corporation Limited, Bronkhorstspruit.**
  P.O. Box 1300, Bronkhorstspruit 1020.
  Tel. (012121) 2074 or 2084 Telex: 3-21427 SA
- **Kwazulu Finance and Investment
  Corporation Limited.**
  P.O. Box 2801, Durban 4000.
  Tel. (031) 907-1055 Telex: 6-4406
  Office also at
  Newcastle Tel. (03431) 92078

- **Shangaan/Tsonga Development Corporation Limited, Giyani.**
  P.O. Box 222, Giyani 0826.
  Tel. (01526) 3225 or 3213 Telex: 3-22615

- **Qwaqwa Development Corporation Limited, Phuthaditjhaba.**
  P.O. Box 5063, Phuthaditjhaba 9866.
  Tel. (01432) 9311

5. Some other institutions that can be helpful in many aspects related to the establishment of your business and provide advice and general information needed to operate a business are:

   - Small Business Development Services (Bekker & Partners)
     Services include:
     Economic Viability Studies
     Financial Applications
     Cashflow projections
     Small Business Management Advice
     Tax consultants
     Investment advice
     Accounting services
     1st Floor, Nedbank Centre, Brown Street, Nelspruit
     P.O. Box 207, Nelspruit, 1200
     Telephone (01311) 53808/9.

   - Unit for Entrepreneurship and Small Business Management (Graduate School of Business, University of Stellenbosch)
     P.O. Box 610
     Bellville
     7530

   - Centre for Developing Business (Wits Business School)
     P.O. Box 31170
     Braamfontein
     2017

   - Centre for Businessmen
     University of Zululand
     Private Bag X1001
     Kwadlangezwa
     3886

   - School for Business Leadership
     University of South Africa
     P.O. Box 392
     Pretoria
     0001

- Institute for Small Business
  University of the Western Cape
  Private Bag X17
  Bellville
  7530

- Afrikaanse Handelsinstituut
  P.O. Box 1741
  Pretoria
  0001

- Business Advisory Bureau (University of the North)
  Private Bag X1106
  Sovenga
  0727

- National African Federated Chamber of Commerce
  P.O. Box 2901
  Johannesburg
  2000
  Tel: (011) 337-4847/9

6. *For information on personnel matters:*

- Institute of Personnel Management
  Libridge House
  25 Ameshoff Street
  P.O. Box 31390
  Braamfontein
  2017
  (011) 339-6411

- Association of Personnel Service Organizations of
  South Africa
  P.O. Box 1598
  Johannesburg
  2000
  (011) 726-8090

  Employment agencies
  (see Yellow Pages)

- UIF and Workmen's Compensation
  Unemployment Insurance Fund
  310 Paul Kruger Street
  Pretoria
  0002
  P.O. Box 1851
  (012) 28-3928

Workmen's Compensation Commissioner
Marais Viljoen Building
Cnr Hamilton and Soutpansberg Roads
Arcadia
0083
P.O. Box 955
Pretoria
0001
(012) 323-9911

7. *For Advice on increasing your productivity:*

National Productivity Institute

Head Office: P.O. Box 3971
Pretoria
0001
(012) 42-3022/44-2263/44-4376
Telex: 3-20485 SA

Cape Town: P.O. Box 6575
Roggebaai
8012
(012) 21-1743

Durban: P.O. Box 10828
Marine Parade
4056
(031) 32-8111

8. *For advice on insurance:*

• Your insurance broker (or agent)

• S.A. Insurance Association
Harland House
Loveday Street
Johannesburg
P.O. Box 2163
Johannesburg
2000
(011) 838-4881

• S.A. Insurance Brokers Association
Swiss House
86 Main Street
Johannesburg
P.O. Box 62155
Marshalltown
2107
(011) 834-8401

9. *For information and advice on legal matters:*
   - Your attorney
   - Your auditor or accountant
   - Your bank manager
   - The Registrar of Companies or Close Corporations
     Zanza Building
     116 Proes Street
     Pretoria
     0002
     P.O. Box 429
     Pretoria
     0001
     (012) 235-2350
   - Association of Law Societies
     Volkskas Centre
     Van Der Walt Street
     Pretoria
     0002
     (012) 21-1931

10. *For information on taxation:*[7]
    - Your auditor or accountant
    - Your local Receiver of Revenue
    - Your attorney

11. *For information on advertising:*
    - Advertising agencies (see Yellow Pages)

12. *For information on marketing research:*
    - Central Statistical Services
      Steyn's Building
      Private Bag X44
      Pretoria
      0001
      (012) 325-2400
    - Bureau for Economic Research, University of Stellenbosch
    - Institute for Marketing Management
      Delvers Square
      Kerk Street
      Johannesburg
      P.O. Box 8377
      Johannesburg
      2000
      (011) 337-4455

13. For information on starting a franchised business:[8]

- S.A. Franchise Association
  P.O. Box 18398
  Hillbrow
  Johannesburg
  2038
  (011) 642-2921

14. For information on choosing a location for the business:[10]

- A reputable estate agent
  (see Yellow Pages)

- Institute of Estate Agents of South Africa
  Auction House
  Fox Street
  Johannesburg
  (011) 838-6429

SELF DEVELOPMENT

Self-development implies self-study on the aspects relating to the type of business (or trade) you are in — keeping up with the latest technology on products you sell or use. But self-development involves more. It also means that you must improve your own knowledge and general proficiency in management-related aspects in order to bring about personal growth that can lead to a more successful business wherein you will ultimately be the beneficiary. However, the only real requirements to an effective self-development programme are self-discipline, making the time to study, getting the information and perseverance.

Self-development is a must, and mainly for two reasons:

1. not all problems or circumstances of any two businesses are the same and not all courses or seminars are directed to solve your specific problems; and

2. you need to keep up with the times and not become obsolete in management techniques, get new ideas and methods to improve the performance of the business as a whole.

The aspect that should deserve the most emphasis under this section, is that self-development is your responsibility and that it can be done through various ways and means, such as studying books and articles related to small business management, the use of consultants, attending courses and seminars and studying publications related to your line of business. An important point is that you should develop a regular programme of study because, unless you set aside a specific amount of time each week, you will never be able to find enough time to pursue self-study. Below follow a few publications recommended for further self-development:[11]

Author, Title	Where to Obtain
• Clifford M Baumback and Kenneth Lawyer. *How to Organize and Operate a Small Business.* 1979.	• Prentice-Hall, Inc. Englewood Cliffs New Jersey, 07362 United States of America
• J.K. Lasser Tax Institute, *How to run a Small Business.* 1982.	• McGraw-Hill Book Company (S.A.) P.O. Box 371 Isando, 1600, Tel. (011) 974-1181
• Thomas J. Peters and Nancy K. Austin. *A Passion for Excellence.* 1985.	• William Collins Sons and Co. Ltd 8 Grafton Street, London Great Britain, W1
• Thomas J. Peters and Robert H. Waterman Jr. *In Search of Excellence.* 1982.	• Harper and Row Publishers, Inc. 10 East 53rd Street, New York NY 10022, United States of America
• Louis A Allen. *Professional Manager's Guide.* 1975.	• Louis A. Allen Associates, Inc., 132 Jan Smuts Avenue, Parkwood Johannesburg, 2193 Tel. (011) 442-7366
• William H. Day. *Maximizing Small Business Profits with Precision Management.* 1978.	• Prentice-Hall Inc. Englewood Cliffs, New Jersey 07362, United States of America
• *Advertising and Business Promotion Manual.*	• Incentive Marketing (Pty) Ltd. P.O. Box 10131, Cape Town 8000 Tel. (021) 7901624
• Wilbert E. Scheer. *The Dartnell Personnel Administration Handbook.* 1979.	• The Dartnell Corporation 4660 Ravenswood Avenue, Chicago, Illinois 60640, United States of America
• Peter F. Drucker. *The Practice of Management.* 1969.	• William Heinemann Ltd. 15-16 Queen Street, Mayfair WIX 8BE Great Britain

471

- *Entrepreneur,* The Monthly Magazine for Small Business, Small Business Advisory Bureau, Potchefstroom University for CHE

- The *Entrepreneur* SBAB University of Potchefstroom P.O. Box 1880, Potchefstroom, 2520 Tel. (0148) 99-1002 as from 1/1/88

- David Ogilvy. *Ogilvy on Advertising.* 1983.

- Pan Books Limited, Cavaye Place, London SW 10 9PG

- Peter F. Drucker. *Managing for Results.* 1967.

- Pan Books Limited, Cavaye Place, London, SW 10 9PG, Great Britain

- Guy Macleod. *Starting Your Own Business in South Africa.* 1983.

- Oxford University Press, Harrington House, Barrack Street, Cape Town, 8001

- P.A. Miller, W.B. Roome, G.E. Staude, *Management in South Africa,* Juta and Co. Ltd.

- Juta and Company Limited, P.O. Box 123, Kenwyn, 7790

SUMMARY AND CONCLUSIONS

People have always been fascinated by the financial success of certain individuals, but do they ever stop to ask how they did it? Firstly, it is because they know what they want and are willing to work for it. They set goals that are realistic, they recognize their strengths and their weaknesses, then they decide how these goals can be achieved and what training and experience are necessary. They make use of the type of services outlined in this chapter. They seek, listen to and accept the advice of others, then they act on it by using the abilities and qualities they possess. It is because consultants have assisted them in setting things up so that they (the entrepreneurs) can come through as winners. It is because they were taught the what, why and how on all aspects of business. The real reason for teaching businessmen is so that they can become self-sufficient. They are encouraged and inspired and can help themselves after the consultation — they are given the 'tools' and the confidence to move ahead. And they are given regular feedback on their performance — the more regular the feedback the faster the learning. Entrepreneurs have developed through continuous advice, guidance, creation of a certain attitude for the businessman towards conducting business and the operating of the business, training, private study, provision of information, financing, follow up and regular feedback. If you can understand that to be an entrepreneur is not a position but a function, and you can then say: 'I am willing to learn from and accept the advice of consultants', then there will be no doubt about your being a winner in the long run.

Below are a few suggestions to enable you to get the most out of the services rendered by these institutions:

1. Develop a deep, driving desire to master the principles of operating a business.
2. Stop frequently to ask yourself: How can I apply the knowledge and skills acquired?
3. Review each week's progress. Determine what mistakes you have made, what improvements took place and what knowledge and skills you have learned for the future.
4. Keep a diary showing how and when you have applied this knowledge and these skills. What were the results?
5. Ask questions. Don't hesitate to call upon the consultant if you do not know what to do and how to do it.

NOTES

[1] Quotations from the Holy Bible, Good News Edition. 1976: 633. (Reprinted with permission of the American Bible Society.)

[2] Idem, 637.

[3] Idem, 641.

[4] In some organizations business advisors or consultants are also referred to as aftercare officers.

[5] Recently the Small Business Advisory Bureau of the Potchefstroom University introduced a one-year diploma course on small business management that can be completed part-time. For more information contact the Bureau.

[6] The institutions mentioned in points 4, 5, 6 and 7 also provide some or all of the services mentioned in this chapter.

[7] Information such as the following can be obtained from these sources: Preparing your tax records, submitting your return—when and where, tax computations, deductions, special allowances, tax on fringe benefits, etc.

[8] Many small business owners have been helped to a sound start in business by investing in a franchise. You may wish to consider doing the same. Franchising can minimize your risk as it will enable you to start your

business under a name and trade-mark which already have public acceptance. You will also receive training and management assistance from experienced people in the line of business you choose. You could also obtain financial assistance that will permit you to start with less cash than you would otherwise need. However, the one major disadvantage is that you will loose a certain amount of control of your business, you may have to pay a fee or share profits with the franchisor. From the S.A. Franchise Association you should obtain some information such as: advantages and disadvantages of franchising; your rights and limitations; how to evaluate a franchise opportunity; a typical franchisee/franchisor contract, etc. You should study these documents and information, as well as discussing them with your lawyer before committing yourself.

[10] For information and advice on choosing a location, it might be a good idea to speak to consultants at the Small Business Advisory Bureau of the University of Potchefstroom as they have done much research on where to locate a specific type of business. Also contact the SBDC's Information Bank for such information.

[11] The list is necessarily selective and no discourtesy is intended toward authors whose works are not mentioned in this section.

19 | MAINTAINING A DYNAMIC BUSINESS

'If nothing else, entrepreneurship is a simple concept kept alive by a few old-fashioned practices. I have worked with entrepreneurs and entrepreneurial managers in more than 25 countries, and what most impresses an international observer is not the difference in entrepreneurial behaviour around the world, but the striking similarities.'

Larry Farrell
President of the Farrell Consulting Corporation
of Princeton, New Jersey [1]

'Starting a business is risky at best; but your chances of making it go will be better if you understand the problems you will meet and work out as many of them as you can before you start.'

U.S. Small Business Administration,
Washington D.C.
Management Aids No. 2.016

'Successful businesses are run by people who have their priorities straight, their values clear, and their directions tight.'

Donald K. Clifford, Jr. and Richard E. Cavanagh,
The Winning Performance [2]

INTRODUCTION

This part may be seen as a broad summary of what has been dealt with up to now in this book. However, not only is it a summary, but it also contains valuable information and advice that will certainly deserve your attention. This part is mainly concerned with three aspects, namely: Why does a business succeed?; Why does a business fail?; and the quest for growth. The section on why a business succeeds deals specifically with 10 points of advice that one can offer someone who wants to get into business (or is already in business) and wants to stay there. The section on why a business fails tries to highlight the aspects that contribute to failure in business with the objective of informing you so that you can avoid the pitfalls that the unprepared so easily fall into. The section on growth provides you with information as to when you are ready for growth, routes to follow if you wish to exploit an opportunity to grow in business, as well as what to do in planning for growth.

WHY DOES A BUSINESS SUCCEED?

Many a person will give his 'eye teeth' in exchange for a prescription which he can use as a guide as to how to become successful in business. Although there are many such books to find on the shelves of libraries and book shops, they do not provide one with the complete recipe although they are helpful, necessary and absorbing to read and study. The closest one may come to such a recipe might be to observe and learn from those who have been successful. Donald K. Clifford (Jr.) and Richard E. Cavanagh in their book, *The Winning Performance*, share a similar point of view which in fact strengthens this aspect. They say on p. xix:

'Example is a powerful way to learn. Children learn through example, observing the successes and failures of their parents, brothers and sisters, playmates, teachers, classmates, and neighbours. Craftsmen serve apprenticeships. Lawyers and business students study by the case method. Physicians serve internships and residencies. Almost all of us have profited from mentors — successful practitioners who share the wisdom of their experience and serve as examples for us. Learning by example is simple in concept but difficult in execution. It is the process of discovering what works and doing more of it, and discovering what does not work and doing less of it. Learning by example is not mindless imitation. To learn by example, one must understand best practices, applying them selectively, always testing and challenging.'

However, there seems to be some common ground in what successful businessmen say are the factors for their successfulness:

'Believe in yourself and be successful. Plan with pen and paper — it's like making a promise to yourself. Visualize what you want to achieve. Do not procrastinate. Procrastination is an illness. Do it now. Persevere — A winner never quits; a quitter never wins. Action — do something. Immediately. Apply your plans — otherwise you are stillborn. Behave like a winner. Success is achieved by those who try, and maintained by those who keep on trying with a positive mental attitude. All growth involves risk — it takes courage, energy and determination to tackle the business world. Furthermore, believe in your product!'

(Annequè Theron) [3]

'The ability to get customers to call again. If you know your product and you know it well, you will always be a good salesman. People will come back to you for advice, again and again, because they believe you know what you are talking about. You will get a reputation of knowing what you are talking about and will lead to your business being recommended to others.'

(Alan van Heerden) [4]

'Decide what you want to sell and who you want to sell it to. Don't try to become a giant overnight. Grow gradually. We believe our business is unique. We train our personnel. We don't want a bunch of trained puppets oohing and aahing over their customers while trying to remember what the sales manual said about clinching sales, but people to whom selling comes naturally and who can learn our way by watching how we do things. Our philosophy — quality, style, value and suitability. Whenever we make a sale it must measure up to all those requirements. Above all, if you want to develop a sound small business, realize your limitations and always plough money back into your business. Your business is only as good as your stock. When doing a promotion, make sure nothing can detract from your products. If for example, there is a possibility that the sandwiches at a cocktail party will be soggy, don't serve sandwiches; Your soggy sandwiches, not your merchandise, will be remembered.'

(Lesley and Jaye Derber) [5]

'We make a point of talking to our customers. As a result we have almost reached the stage where we know everyone on first name terms. We make a special effort to learn retailing. Everytime a member of the family enters another retail or competitor's store, they may not leave until they have learned at least two new merchandising ideas. Our success is also due to a team effort based on innovative merchandising and the implementation of proven principles of good supermarket management. Our formula for super performance is fresh, friendly, fastidious. Consult outside expertise for advice when making decisions which have financial implications. We are meticulous about detail.'

(Bill and Shirley Buxton) [6]

'Be prepared to work hard for a long period. Control the cash flow. Do a proper and detailed investigation of the market before starting the

477

business. Implement administrative systems to supply you with management information.'

(Johann Smit)[7]

There are many successful businessmen who can provide you with such sound advice. There are also not-so-successful businessmen who can provide you with just as sound advice. Their advice will normally be: 'Don't do this and that', 'If only I knew more before I started', 'If I had only listened to the advice of others', 'Watch out for that', etc. Many unsuccessful owners can tell you how they would manage the business. However, to have a chance of success, there must be a genuine business opportunity, for if there is none, no amount of extraordinary spirit or intellect, nor capital, can overcome this lack.

Opportunities are sometimes hard to visualize, but it becomes less difficult if you will only make the effort to think objectively. Peter Drucker comments as follows: 'Weaknesses indicate where to look for business potential. To convert them from problems into opportunities brings extraordinary returns. And sometimes all that is needed to accomplish this transformation is a change in the attitude of the executives.'[8] For example: a well-known saying is: 'The rich get richer and the poor become poorer.' And, because of this saying the question often arises: Why are some rich and why are some poor? Why does the one make money and the other not? The answer is undoubtedly in spotting an opportunity and reacting on it in order to create wealth. It is a matter of looking upon money, not as an end in itself but as a tool to help you in accomplishing life-long dreams. It is business-mindedness as demonstrated in this example:

Mr White is advised by a reliable source that a certain type of business is badly needed in a certain town or area. Mr White knows that he can be of assistance in some way or other in satisfying the particular needs — so, react he does. This reaction to an opportunity that creates wealth is the difference between Mr White, who sees potential and acts, and let's say, another type, Mr Johnson, who sees potential but lets it go because of fear and doubt. There is a big difference in wanting to make money, and wishing to make money. Mr White wants to and does. Mr Johnson wishes to but doesn't. Thus, the secret to good fortune can be said to be: think right, do right and act right.

On the matter of business-mindedness Earl Nightingale offers the following set of basic business rules for the owner manager of a small business (From his radio programme 'Our changing world'):[9]

'Do you have good business sense? Well — let's see. More than 200 successful businessmen were asked: "What advice can you offer to someone who wants to get into business and stay there?" From their composite answers here are the ten basic rules that have topped the list.'

The rules are set out here with explanation and comment.

1. *Be more concerned with the accumulation of money than with what money can buy. Most people are never able to go into business for themselves simply because they lack the self-discipline to acquire the necessary capital. And thousands fail because they started on a shoestring that was too short. To succeed in business takes time; prepare for twice the time you think it will take you.* One can also add to the first part of the statement that to be more concerned with the circulation and accumulation of money within the business. This point can be illustrated as follows:

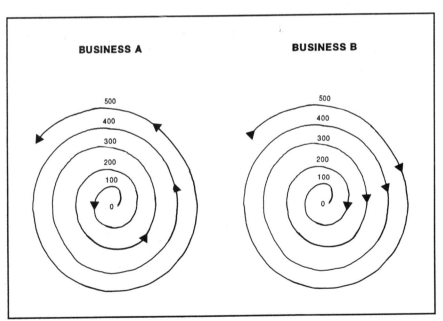

By looking at the two illustrations one can clearly see that business A is circulating its money (ploughing back profits) which leads to the accumulation thereof. Business B, on the other hand, is doing the opposite (taking profits out of the business; not re-investing the money, but spending it) and the eventual result is that the business shrinks in size and value (heading for bankruptcy).

Once your capital is invested in your business it is not easy to withdraw it again. It is thus a long-term commitment and a challenge to you as a businessman to ensure that the capital invested in your business is managed profitably. If the purpose of business is to turn an amount of cash into a larger amount of cash, and you end with less cash than you started with, you have lost money and if you continue to lose money, you are heading for bankruptcy. Of course, this explanation may be over-simplified because, 'cash' may be represented by stock or additional equipment. However simplified, the point of importance is to re-invest and re-invest and re-invest (plough back profits) — keep the money in the business. A sure way to ruin your business is to extract from the business more than it is earning, that is: to draw money from operating capital (also known as working capital) rather than from profits. That is what the rules say — if the cash stops going around, you go out of business. If you think that business has to do with expensive cars and other luxuries, you will never understand business. You can only have them if the business grows. And there is only one way a business can grow, and that is by making a profit. It is as has been said: 'Profit is like health. You need it, and the more the better.'

Keeping the business going will depend on how well you have started it and how well you manage its operations. Mark McCormack said that being self-employed is the purest form of capitalism and the best way of getting paid what you are truly worth.[10] However much truth that statement may hold, you should avoid being in a hurry to prove your worth. Do not try to get simple success, instant success, and down-hill success. If you want to enter business to get instant success, you will more than likely never succeed, however relevent the term success may be to each individual. Success does not come on a platter and neither is it a formula being sold like merchandise. You must rather say to yourself: In order to succeed I have to sweat, I have to work hard, I have to plan, and I have to devote my full attention to doing the right thing in the right manner. The only way in which you can hope to achieve anything successfully in business is by constantly striving for success in everything you do and then constantly trying to achieve bigger successes. Persevere in your actions. Success is not that you cannot fail, it is more a case of not accepting failure. Nothing is over unless you have decided to throw in the towel. One thing you have to do is realize your potential, put your unique talents to use and apply sound basic business principles (develop a deep, driving desire to master the principles of business; apply them at every opportunity; and monitor the progress you are making). It is what you do and how well you do it that establishes the difference between success and failure — the difference must be your reward.

For the majority, a successful person in business is one who has achieved his goals. Of a person that failed can be said that his abilities should have enabled him to achieve certain goals, but he tried and failed. Too many businessmen do not do their best. Many could do better by putting more of their hearts and minds into the business that is supporting their families. Many of them know what they must do, but they don't do it. It might be that they don't know how to go about implementing some necessary action to rectify the problem on hand, but then they should put their pride in their pockets and obtain the know-how from a knowledgeable or qualified and experienced adviser in the field of business. However, the very first thing to do in such a situation is to define the problem and to determine its underlying cause. (See page 130 for more details on problem-solving.)

The fact that many businessmen fail because they started on a shoestring that was too short, might need some explanation. When either starting a new business from scratch, or buying an already established business, one of the first questions you need to answer is: How much money will I need? This question cannot be answered before a number of other questions are answered, and some decisions are made. These other questions and decisions are to do with assessing your market — and essential they are because unless you assess your market (that is, define or describe it accurately

481

and estimate its size) you run the risk of starting a business which may never succeed, and you may discover too late that there are insufficient customers, and therefore inadequate sales for your business to survive.

If you overestimate sales, you are likely to invest too much in equipment and initial stock and commit yourself to bigger operating expenses than your actual sales volume will be able to carry. It is right here that many a potential business owner makes his first crucial mistake. He does not assess his market, and estimates sales way above the real demand. You must remember that all other capital requirements are dependent on the sales figure.

You should always ask yourself the question (and do the calculation) once you have prepared your cash flow statement: Will I survive if sales drop by 50%? Since you are just starting, you may have low sales, or even no sales for the first month. Consider this example in determining your capital requirements to start the business (assuming that you have estimated your income, expenses, equipment to be purchased, and have decided to put R4 000 into the business as initial capital).

		January R	February R	March R	April R
1.	Cash on hand	4 000	1 500	500	(500)
2.	Income	0	1 500	1 500	3 200
3.	Total cash available (1 + 2)	4 000	3 000	2 000	2 700
4.	Cash paid out	2 500	2 500	2 500	2 500
	Purchases	2 000	2 000	2 000	2 000
	Rent	200	200	200	200
	Salaries	300	300	300	300
5.	Cash position (3 − 4)	1 500	500	(500)	200

If you continue this method of operation for the entire year, you will find you have negative figures, or a negative cash flow. Oliver Galbraith III, Professor of Management, San Diego State University remarks as follows: 'About this time (April) you will also realize that you should be working on your cash flow statement with a pencil that has a good eraser.'

Although a very simplified illustration, you can see that at the end of March you are minus R500 in cash. Some solutions can be tried — reduce your purchases in January by R500, or start with R500 more. You may not be able to reduce expenses as they may go up once in operation. So you will have to put in R500 more to start with. If R4 000 is all you have, then the additional R500 you need represents capital you must get from somewhere else, i.e. borrow it.

Don't be misled by this simple illustration. Many small businesses start with R500, and try to get the R4 000 from somewhere else. A major reason for failure in the early stages of a business is under-capitalization, so be very careful in your planning at this stage. You can almost always plan for some unexpected expenses and some delays in expected income.[11]

There is virtually nothing as important in business as assessing your market in order to determine your exact capital requirements. Thus, even though you may feel it is a complicated exercise, it is still the best to get started with this approach — putting the figures down on paper. The same approach must be followed when buying an established business. Perhaps the best advice is: seek assistance with this crucial and essential aspect of your business. Peat Marwick puts this point of seeking advice as follows:[12]

'Don't forget that there is no substitute for good professional advice — whatever your field or activities. Although professional fees are sometimes expensive, it is generally far cheaper to get professional help at the outset than to have to call in professional assistance to sort out the mess afterwards.'

See Chapter 18 for more details on where to find professional assistance. Chapter 2 ('Entering the business world'), deals with aspects of planning your financing requirements in more detail.

2. *Keep your mark-up higher than your overheads (expenses). The number one cause of business failure is a matter of buying for too much, or selling for too little. This can lead to a terrible treadmill where every day is a frantic attempt to keep your chin above water. A few bad days . . . and . . . you are under. But the quality of your product or service must fully justify your prices. When a sale is made properly, it is not a game where somebody wins and somebody loses.*

Everybody wins. The product must be worth more in use value than its cost. Good management is the key to success and your competitors will require you to be a good manager, if you are to survive. This statement is especially true when it comes to the matter of delivering value to your customers. However, probably ranked as one of the top ingredients of success in business is your continued ability to satisfy (and anticipate) the wants, needs and desires of your market. In some instances (depending on the type of business, its location and the appearance of your business, the nature of the products or services you sell, the image you wish to create, and other additional services you wish to offer), it may necessitate that you should be stressing quality, reliability and service, rather than lower prices. In other words, before opening your business or even while in business you must decide upon the general price level you expect to maintain. Will you cater or are you catering to people buying in the high, medium, or low price range? Your price will much depend on the customers you hope to attract.

Much of your success in business will depend on how you price your products or services. If your prices are too low, you will not cover expenses and if they are too high, you will lose sales volume. In both cases, a profit will not be realized. (See the chapter on Pricing which deals with the method of pricing and factors influencing prices).

Regarding the statement that 'the quality of your products or services must fully justify your prices', an important point of view to stress is that it is the customer who is the foundation of your business, and keeps it in existence. It is as simple as this: If there is no sale, there is no job. 'Customers alone provide employment through being willing to pay for the goods and services you sell and in so doing, create wealth for you. What the customer needs and wants at any given moment must be adopted by you as an objective. What the customer thinks he is buying, what he considers value, is decisive and determines whether the business will prosper.' [13] It is a known fact that the most innovative, prosperous and growth-orientated businessmen get their information as to what to sell from the customer, through observing, questioning and listening intently. You have to be aware of this fact if you wish to give the customer what he wants and needs. Frankly, that is what you get paid for by your customers — greater value satisfaction. (See the chapter on customer relations, for details on how to satisfy customers.) But before you do turn to this chapter, note the story (stressing the point of listening to customers):

'In 1918, Konosuke Matsushita invested his life savings of 100 yen (about R150) in an electrical socket. According to his own account, he was unsuccessful because he was thinking too much about selling and not enough about what customers wanted to buy. He went back and listened carefully for the first time to customers and retailers, and developed a new two-way electrical socket. That's when the Matsushita legend was born. By 1937, Matsushita was 150 000 employees strong and operating in 130 countries.'[14]

3. *Be liberal in your standards of friendship. Winning business and keeping it depends to a great extent on cordial personal relations. I know of a case where the wife of the businessman thought he was too lenient with his employees. Finally, after years of heckling, he let her become personnel manager. Before long, all employees quit. This is a two way street.* No matter what you think of yourself and your business, it is important to know what your customers and your personnel really think of you and your business. Maybe your customers only come to your business because of easy parking facilities, but what if another shop opens with easy parking facilities? If customers are not satisfied with the general treatment received (and all other aspects that have a bearing on their decision to support your business or not) from your business, you will probably lose them forever. But if they are satisfied, they will continue to buy from you and recommend your business to others. Don't fool yourself about how your customers and employees feel.

In business, it is important not to forget those who have assisted. If an employee working for you makes a substantial contribution to the ultimate success of your business, he is entitled to considerably more than the satisfaction of a job well done. It is important that employees feel they are participating directly and commensurately with their contributions in the form of labour and expertise to your business. If you want your employees to be creative, you must manage in such a manner that they have the opportunity to contribute their ideas. Such a management style may lead you to gaining better knowledge and even exploiting opportunities that can prove to be valuable for the continuation of the business. It should be remembered that the prosperity of your business can be enhanced through the contributions of employees. They may help you turn your business's weaknesses into strengths measured against your competitors, and turning problems into solutions. It is, however, of absolute necessity that, when you do get such contributions, you evaluate them in terms of whether the business as a whole will benefit by implementing whatever suggestions are recommended by employees (What would happen to the business should the implementation of the idea succeed?; What will the consequences be of not implementing the idea?). After all, the business thrives through sales, and you and your employees benefit from the profits of the business. It is by increasing sales that you and your employees are ensured of a prosperous future. You are all part of the same business. (Study Chapter 11.)

4. *Stay with it. Long hours are an inevitable part of the job. You can forget about the eight-hour day and the five-day week.* What you have begun must be carried through to completion. It is better not to start at all than to tackle business half-heartedly and abandon it halfway. A business is an ongoing activity that doesn't run by itself. As the owner-manager you will have to set goals, determine how to reach those goals and make all the necessary decisions. As mentioned already, it is mostly a matter of how you fill your hours in business that makes the difference between success and failure. Your daily tasks should be as productive as possible. Organize each day to ensure you devote most of your time and attention to those aspects deserving the highest priority. Business success is dependent on you. You are the one who must think right, make the right decisions and act right. Therefore, you need a clear mind, calm attitude and sound reasoning.

Your business needs you to take care of it. It requires your undivided attention in order to operate smoothly and grow. Remember that management is 'doing', and success is an accomplishment. The toughest competition is yourself, and you are working to achieve your greatest aspirations. You need ceaseless and inexhaustible courage to become and remain successful in business.

5. *Be prepared for the unexpected. Don't leave yourself financially unprotected against possible emergencies. This applies to the family as well as the business. A good reserve of operating capital (working capital) has saved thousands of businesses from going under. It is insurance against mistakes . . . and bad times.* To be prepared for the unexpected necessitates the building up of reserve funds. Exercise strict control over your working capital and cash resources, to ensure that a healthy financial position is maintained at all times. However, to control working capital you must consciously control each of its components. This can be done through control of the following components:

Debtors Prepare a credit policy which serves as a standard plan of action, including as far as extending credit is concerned. Such a policy will direct and control the activity of extending credit. For such a policy to be effective, it should be based on adequate information, definite though flexible to be adjusted to meet fundamental changes, and be adhered to at all times. If you apply to the management of your business the techniques you learnt about in the chapter dealing with 'credit control', your money tied up in debtor accounts should be reduced, thus allowing it to be used profitably elsewhere.

Allocate credit limits to your debtors and ensure that they comply with agreed payment terms.

Insist on trade references for new customers and do credit checks. Many potential 'bad payers' can be eliminated through investigation and prudent judgement when extending credit to customers. The need for sound judgement is particularly critical since credit extension policies should be neither too liberal nor too restrictive. Too liberal credit policies invite excessive uncollectible accounts, while restrictive credit policies can cause loss of sales.

Do invoicing promptly and specify the terms of payment (for example: payment within 30 days of invoice date). Re-evaluate credit terms once a debtor falls into the habit of paying late on a regular basis.

Send out statements as soon as possible after month ends. Make sure invoices and statements are accurate and easy to understand. Errors and confusion regarding accounts give customers excuses to delay payment.

Charge interest on overdue accounts. Avoid becoming a cheap source of finance for other people.

Stock Keep stock levels down to a practical minimum. Do not overstock as this can tie up much needed cash. At the beginning, how much to buy could be speculative. The best policy is to be frugal until you have enough experience to judge your needs. On the other hand, you cannot sell merchandise if you do not have enough of it. (See chapters on Purchasing and on Stock control.)

Exercise strict control over the movement of stock by keeping accurate stock records in order to determine appropriate re-order levels, and to identify obsolete and slow-moving stock items. This will assist you in solving buying problems.

Listen to your customers in order to buy the correct goods.

Stock on hand should be examined regularly, so as to ascertain that stock levels are in line with current trends.

Creditors Establish favourable terms of payment with suppliers, as well as advantageous relations. Take full advantage of credit terms and discounts made available by suppliers, and negotiate more favourable terms with them.

Do not overtrade (or overbuy); that is, do not trade in excess of your financial resources. Take advantage of 'specials', but make sure there is a ready and needy market to sell to. Remember that what you buy, you have to sell. Thus, evaluate suppliers 'specials' according to their saleability. Try to buy directly from manufacturers whenever possible.

Cash Monitor capital expenditure. Do not spend good money on unnecessary or unproductive assets.

One of your most important duties as an owner-manager, is to keep the assets of the business working hard and productively. It is easy for a small business to slip into the practice of having larger stocks. Dank finance or other investments will then be needed. 'Bigger' is often equated with 'better'. The sales manager wants larger stock and more liberal credit terms from his suppliers. These added investments will improve his sales efforts. The production manager wants newer and faster machines and tools, larger stock of raw materials and supplies. These investments will enable him to cut costs, and meet delivery dates. The financial manager wants larger cash balances to make his job easier. Office management needs new equipment. It often seems that the opportunities to spend money are unlimited!

The aim of asset management is to make certain that new or increased assets pay their way. The added profits these new assets bring in, should total more than the cost of the resources involved. The return on investment measure can be used to show the expected effect on profits of an investment you may be thinking about making. Thus, it is a useful tool in judging and comparing various investment opportunities.

Often, unfortunately, opportunities that promise satisfactory returns on investment, must be put aside because of lack of capital. This is especially true in small businesses, where financing new investments can be a real problem. When such a problem arises, good asset management may come to the rescue in two ways. Firstly, it may improve a small business's chances of getting a loan, by emphasizing to the lender the financial competence and alertness of the would-be-borrower. Secondly, additional cash can sometimes be raised by reducing unnecessary investments in existing assets. It may be possible to produce funds for one area of the business by avoiding or reducing their use in other areas.[15]

Have additional short-term finance available in case of emergencies, for example: additional overdraft facilities or a line of credit.

Do not distribute after-tax profits in the form of dividends or personal drawings, unless the working capital needs of the business can bear the outflow of funds.

Invest excess short-term funds in more profitable short-term investments. It is an important responsibility to see that a shortage of cash does not occur, or that excess cash is not retained uneconomically.

489

Prepare short- and long-term cash flow forecasts, and regularly monitor these against actual performance.

Bank income regularly and promptly. It brings about a saving in interest when operating on an overdraft.

Control expenses In the long run your gross margin must exceed operating expenses if your business wants any chance of survival (see chapter on Pricing). In the short run, however, you may deliberately plan an operating loss in order to carry out a sales expansion programme, or to keep essential services and personnel you need during temporary times of trouble. Nevertheless, you should make every reasonable effort to keep expenses below estimated margins. Examine all proposed expenses for their contribution to growth and profit. Even so-called fixed expenses, such as insurance, can be reduced by careful analyses.[16] (See page 118 for details on how insurance can be reduced.) Through growth you can reduce the ratio of your fixed expenses to sales. Expense planning and control are more fully discussed in Chapter 16.

Control losses — both cash and stock losses. (See chapter 13.)

6. *Be ruthless with people who want to cash in on your success. Prosperity always draws parasites. Tell those relatives and old friends who would love to go on a permanent vacation on your payroll that you are just not hiring this year.* Such an attitude will help in controlling expenses. A businessman must be able to say 'NO' — even when it hurts. Rather follow the method of employing the 'right man' for the job, as outlined in the chapter on 'Staffing the business'. Careful selection of personnel is essential for the welfare of the business. To select the right employees you need to determine beforehand what you want each one to do. Checking references is a must before any final appointment can be made. Knowledge, ability, experience and personality are important considerations in choosing the right person.

7. *Become an expert on the products or services you sell.* To establish your business on a firm footing requires a great deal of aggressive personal selling. You may have established competition to overcome; or, if your product or service is new with little or no competition, you have the extra problem of convincing people of the value of the new product or service. Personal selling is necessary to overcome the problem, but it then requires thorough knowledge of the product or service by the salesman as this can make all the difference between clinching the sale or not. Selling skills are very necessary, and if you are not a good salesman, appoint an employee who is. (See the chapter on 'Salesmanship and selling'.)

Selling requires action — you need to set the ball rolling by being a marketer, a salesman and a sales promoter, for the life-blood of your business is its sales volume. Below follows a particularly striking example of a person who is a marketer, a salesman and a sales promoter (engaged in creative customer contact). This article by Robert Bearson, Managing Director, ABM, California, appeared in the February 1984 issue of *Shopping Centre World* as well as in the *Entrepreneur*.[17]

'CRUISERS INTO CUSTOMERS

Susan is a professional retail saleswoman. She has been selling in a houseware speciality store for over three years. She understands her customers and their buying behaviour, and she knows how to cater for their needs. When she is not working, a typical customer is likely to spend no more than three minutes in the store.

There is a fascination with housewares and cookware. It is not easy for a woman to walk by the shop without coming in just to look around to see what is new. This "just looking" normally takes somewhere between three and five minutes. When Susan is in the store, the customer almost always stays in the shop longer, sees more, considers more and buys more. Susan never greets the customer with "May I help you?" or "Are you looking for something special?" Instead, she greets the customer with "Hi", or "Good afternoon", or a personal comment like "I love your haircut". She does not approach the customer at the same time she greets the customer.

After having greeted the customer, she allows the customer to wander through the store. Although Susan appears to be pre-occupied with straightening and dusting, her eye is on the customer. As soon as the customer touches an item or something seems to catch her eye, Susan is prepared. She immediately volunteers a selling fact, something of interest about the item: "That's a coffee bean roaster from Ecuador."

"These stainless steel items are completely dishwasher safe." "I have one of these at home and am just amazed at how much I use it."

This kind of knowledge does not come about by accident. Susan has put forth a special effort to be prepared, and often tests herself by walking around the store, picking up any item and asking herself if she can cite three facts she will tell about the item if a customer shows interest in it. There are very few items about which there is not something worth saying: the name of the manufacturer, country of origin, unusual uses, wearability, time-saving features or safety. Susan is ready to volunteer information on almost any item in the store.

A secret weapon: There are times, though not very many of them, when the customer does not reveal an interest in a particular item. In these cases Susan is prepared to offer the "item of the day". Each morning she selects a piece of merchandise to be the "item of the day", usually something new, interesting, well-stocked and preferably something suitable for demonstration and small enough to carry around. She then decides what she wants people to know about the item.

In each instance when she does not have the opportunity to approach the customer based on her revealed area of interest or when the customer is on her way out, Susan positions herself between the customer and the door. As the customer approaches her (she does not approach the customer), she volunteers, "This just came in, what do you think of it?" or "This is General Electric's newest appliance. Have you seen how it works?" When she does this, nobody says "I will call if I need you". Invariably there is at least a brief conversation, inducing the customer to remain in the store longer.

Again, this is what it is all about. When the customer spends more time with Susan, she sees more of what the store has to offer. She considers more and she buys more.

Susan is a professional who knows her customer. She knows how to separate her greeting from her approach and she understands how to use "the item of the day" to establish rapport with customers, encouraging them to see what the store has to offer, turning customers who are "just looking" into customers who buy.'

One crucial point in selling is that of measuring the performance of your salespeople. In the early operation of your business at least, you will have to fulfil the duties of a sales manager until you can afford to employ one. Thus, the task may be complicated because of the many criteria that can be used for measuring such a performance. (See page 306 for such criteria.) But why measure sales performance? Consider this question by a consultant to an owner-manager.[18]

| Consultant: | But tell me, why do you want to measure the performance of your sales force? |
| Owner-manager: | Because one sales visit can cost up to R200. I don't want to spend that kind of money unless it is a good investment. |

8. *Deal primarily in fast-moving items. Look at your stock from the customer's point of view. Make sure there is a sufficient market for what you are selling.* What this is actually saying is that your viewpoint is of little importance in so far as the needs and preferences of the customers are concerned. The customer, not you, decides from whom to buy and what to buy. Clifford Baumback and Kenneth Lawyer put this into perspective:[19]

'It is unfortunate that beginners in business are inclined to choose the business they like, and the goods or production methods or standards of service they like, and the location they like without enough objective thinking in terms of what the customer likes and wants and is willing to buy.'

Be careful not to fall into this trap. Effective marketing starts by identifying, understanding, influencing and predicting what your customers require. To do this you need to know your customers; their requirements; characteristics; the type and volume of their business; the scope and range of their activities; and how they purchase goods and services.

Selling mainly fast-moving items is a case of establishing what to buy for the purpose of selling, but before you can buy, you have to assess what is demanded by your market and when it is required. This aspect of assessing your market receives much attention in chapter 2 as the decision to go into business is only sound if you can satisfy a need for profit, and if you cannot do this over a reasonable period of time, you create the opportunity for another businessman to try and do the job properly.

9. *Be selective in your advertising. Pick your spots. Make your ad 'dollars' count.* Another way to build sales is by advertising which should not be seen as just another business expense but rather as an investment in building your sales. Whenever you want to initiate a programme for the future growth of your business, your successfulness will be greatly influenced by your ability to execute an effective advertising programme. Such an advertising programme is especially essential for long range planning so as to build not only sales, but also on the characteristics and image you want your business to develop.

When you are just starting a business, your advertising budget might be limited and it is your task to see that your advertising does the job you want it to, even with the limited amount of funds available. As with all other business activities, measuring the results on a continuing basis can help you to see whether your advertising keeps the business's name in the minds of the public, and whether it contributes to increasing sales. (See chapter 10 for more details.) More light on the subject is provided by John W. Wingate and Seymour Helfant:[20]

'People used to believe that even the small merchant should advertise regularly every day or week, though he took only a small space for his message. Attitudes are changing, however. Nowadays, it is considered more important to have a compelling story to tell, and to tell it dramatically in ample space, than merely to "chirp-me-to" at regular intervals.

If you have a growing business, you can make a greater impact on your community by mounting a well-conceived promotion — requiring full page advertisements every month at important dates in each season — than by making run-of-the-mill little announcements every day. What you need is massive impact, not a repetitive tap.

This of course, means that you should make a continuing search for special promotional goods to supplement your regular stock assortment. If your store is a headquarter for national brands, you should be able to get specials from these sources late in the season. If you stress fashion and shopping goods, you will have to alert yourself to stay on the lookout for outstanding buys. Your promotional goods won't be limited to seasonal clearances. Merchandise with unusual fashion and quality interest may be available at the start of a season when the timeliness of the product rather than its price is the important factor.

One very successful merchant says he gets his ideas for special promotional goods by checking on the special offerings of stores in large cities. From a trade service and direct contact, he learns of the public's response to these promotions. It is not difficult to locate the suppliers of such goods; and he has bought and successfully promoted many "hot" items this way.'

10. *Don't expand too quickly. Other things being equal, you will do well to wait for that second location or branch store until you can afford to gamble at least twice the sum spent on your original location.* Take one step at a time and learn as you earn. A Chinese proverb states: 'The journey of a thousand miles starts with a single step', then of course, step by step towards the objective. First become well experienced in your line of business and assess your own strengths and weaknesses before going ahead with greater intentions. When you intend to expand your business, it is time to eliminate some day-to-day operations and become a manager. Management, as understood today, is composed of four functions with some twenty activities. (See chapter 3 for more information.) Management does not include doing the work yourself, but getting it done through your business team (your employees). To help you make the transition from being the person who has carried out most of the duties to being a manager as your business grows, it is recommended that you acquire the know-how through a practical training course. (See page 177 for knowing how to go about finding such a suitable course.) Clifford Baumback and Kenneth Lawyer motivate the need for training yourself and acquiring business experience before going into business or approaching the expansion phase as follows:[21]

'By going into business, it is difficult to predict what problems you will be facing, but an ability to anticipate them, to surmount them, and to make the right decisions and to do the right things at the right time, will mostly depend on your expertise and business experience.'

Knowing what to do is very different from knowing how to do it. Even more difficult is knowing how to do it the best way. Therefore, training, or rather preparation, before going into business or entering the expansion phase is essential because it is doing things wrongly that costs money. Doing things correctly is what will boost the successful operations of your business.

There are many institutions that provide training courses to small businessmen in all aspects of operating the business. These courses are geared towards improving your proficiency. When you return from such courses and after you have applied what you have learned and after a few successes, a new and better attitude will emerge that will boost your confidence in going ahead with your plans to expand. Self-study is a must. (See page 470 for further details). Also obtain professional advice. Larry Farrell gives the following advice for improving your chances of success in business.[22]

'Learn all you can about entrepreneurs and translate your findings into language appropriate to your own business. Discover and get to know successful entrepreneurs in your area, and review the extensive literature available on the subject. In your "spare time", learn how to read a balance sheet, an income statement, and a cash flow statement. Become knowledgeable about business.

Demand entrepreneurial behaviour of yourself, and be a living model of the behaviour you are advocating.

Get hands on experience with external customers. Work periodically in any job that involves face-to-face contact with customers. Sales, service and customer-complaint departments are obvious choices. Become a customer expert. Work periodically in any job that involves the design, production or distribution of the organization's products or services. Become a product expert.'

The above is but one aspect of getting prepared to expand. As you grow, you will need additional funds for the future implementation of your expansion plans. The amount of money you will need to secure in the interim for further growth will depend on the purpose for which you need the funds. Although there is no one best way to finance a business under all conditions, great care should be exercised in determining capital requirements, the ways in which the capital will be used, and the sources from which the funds are to be secured.

Calculating the amount of money needed for expansion (business construction, conversion or modernization) is relatively easy as equipment manufacturers, architects, estate agents, builders and suppliers will readily supply you with cost estimates. It is furthermore important to determine the exact route you wish to follow by expanding, and to determine the likely action steps to be followed in working towards your expansion objective. The worth of such predetermined projections is that they force you to consider the results of your actions and the money needed to implement them in the best and most workable way. Your estimates must be explicit and must present your business's case persuasively to the financial institution if you are to succeed in obtaining the needed capital. Careful projections should thus enable you to explain fully to the lender how the projected financial statements and the cash flow budget have been prepared, and the underlying assumptions on which the figures are based. Obviously, these assumptions must be supportable in order to instil some confidence in the lender for your plans — demonstrating to the lender that you are a competent manager.

The money needed for expansion will have to be made up by retained earnings (profit kept in the business) and growth capital. However, when you set out to borrow money to finance this expansion phase, it is important to know the types of money available. There are basically three types: equity capital, working capital and growth capital. Deciding what type of money to use is not always easy and an important distinction between the types of money is the source of repayment. Generally equity capital does not have to be repaid, working capital loans are repaid from the liquidation of current assets which it financed, and growth capital (or long-term capital) is usually paid from accumulated (or retained) profit. A fourth source of money is trade credit, but this type of 'money' is not borrowed — it is money you owe your suppliers who permit you to carry your fast-moving stock on account. Although trade credit is relatively easy to obtain, it is often very costly.

Growth capital is extended for fairly long periods of time — two to ten, or even twenty years. It is logical that growth capital loans require collateral as security for the protection of the lender's money lent to you. Even if you have sufficient collateral, you still need to demonstrate to the lender how the borrowed money will be utilized. Any general business ideas you wish to obtain money for is eligible, as long as it promises possibilities of success.

Lenders are generally more interested in the potential income of your business than the present profit potential in considering lending you growth capital. That is because the lender wants to be sure you can repay the loan over the period agreed upon. Some common requirements of growth financing are:

The money to be lent to you will more than likely not exceed one-third of your total business capital. Thus, you will have to have twice as much equity in your business as the amount you will borrow. One important point to stress is that equity capital provides a basis for obtaining money, and it establishes a greater net worth for your business which can be helpful if you plan on borrowing. Such an equity cushion enables you to present a stronger picture to the lender. The greater the net worth of your business, the more growth capital can be obtained. However, your net worth can only become greater if you plough back profits into the business, and do not withdraw profits from the business — at least not for careless utilization thereof.

Your business profits should be great enough to pay off your loan, plus interset, during the period agreed upon.

Your business must have shown a favourable profit trend over the past few years. In other words, if you plan to enter some expansion phase in, say three years' time, you better see that your business is being managed profitably in the interim period.

The crux of the matter is that you will be better off if you can determine your future capital requirements, and do the things now (the circulation and accumulation of money within the business) that will secure the availability or acquisition of funds for the future in order to finance your growth plans.

A serious mistake many an entrepreneur easily makes is to under-estimate the amount of capital required. Another pitfall is that as soon as the volume of operations becomes larger, the increased flow of funds may give the businessman a false sense of richness, for example: He buys an expensive vehicle, a new house, builds a swimming pool or buys some expensive jewellery. Since his business is growing, he feels it can afford all these things, and thus engage in some more debt. He is in effect bleeding the business by removing retained earnings that are needed to finance growth.

Money, your own or borrowed, is the key to a profitable business if it is utilized efficiently. To be ready for the growth phase finance wise, accept this advice from the insurance people: 'It is better to have it and not need it, than to need it and not have it.' Rather be patient until you are ready for growth—financially and in the managerial skills that are requisites for greater things—than rush into a rather risky situation. Once your timing is correct and you have a taste for risk-taking, go ahead and execute your plans. Remember, every tycoon had to start small and followed the same principles in order to grow.

So there you have them. Ten tips that are part of the good business sense of the successful businessman or woman. By reading to this point, most of the advice may sound very familiar to you, and also logical. Indeed, these business principles are pure common sense, and thus not difficult to grasp. But it is important for the welfare of your business to remember it, and apply it all in practice.

Under all circumstances, you are responsible for the vision and pace of the business. Larry Farrell (President of the Farrell Consulting Corporation of Princeton, New Jersey) describes an entrepreneurial organization as follows (this will assist you in understanding what is meant by 'vision'):[23]

'Label them visions, values, beliefs or priorities, but most entrepreneurs seem driven by a personal and business philosophy. They rarely have time in the early days of their enterprises to spell them out, but their philosophies are clear from their actions.

For entrepreneurs, the number one priority is the customer. Every entrepreneur learns on day one that a business's first need is a real, live customer who will actually pay some money for something. The lesson you learn very quickly when you start your own business is that if you don't have a customer, your children don't eat. You *understand*, not in an abstract way, but on a gut level, that your pay cheque does not come from a corporate payroll department; it comes from your customers.

Build the customer-product vision: Every book ever written about entrepreneurs says they must have vision. But vision of what? In the mundane world of day-to-day entrepreneurship, this vague notion can only mean one thing. The single critical vision all entrepreneurs must have, is a clear picture of a specific set of likely customers who need, and will pay for a specific set of products and services. Nothing could be more basic to the entrepreneur. The integrated vision of customer and product is the *sine qua non** of entrepreneurism. The vision is precise. It is intense. All else revolves around it.

* An indispensable condition.

Academic debates over whether an organization should be driven strategically by product or by market, are symptomatic of business theory too sophisticated for the entrepreneur. A customer without a product is not a customer. A product without a customer is not a product. What counts is the entrepreneur's vision of the connection between the two. Below are some practical suggestions that can help you to become more service minded:

1. Simply identify the business's customers and the product or service provided, and set a few standards to measure customer satisfaction.

2. Publicize, through any vehicle available, your version of the customer-product vision. Let people know that being a customer expert and a product expert is a rare and valuable combination.

3. Foster the realization that customers are the only source of salaries, and the only reason for the continued existence of the business. Do anything to raise this awareness amongst employees.

4. Include in virtually all training programmes, sections covering key entrepreneurial behaviours towards customers. Three of the most powerful are: *(a)* immediacy of response, always demonstrating that customer needs are more important than company plans, or employee schedules; *(b)* old-fashioned courtesy; *(c)* working directly with customers to develop or improve products and services.'

Imagine you are watching a 125 cc motorcycle race. In relating this particular race to business, it might be a good example of explaining the point that it is only the best that win, although some may also make it, but more slowly, and some don't make it at all. All motorcycles in the race are the same size and have the same power, but the race depends on those who can handle it best, as well as those who have the confidence to ride, and those who are the most daring. Those who don't make it at all are normally those who have made some crucial mistake along the way (perhaps right at the start of the race) — crashed or fallen down, because of their own negligence or carelessness. Others again, have been more careful by concentrating on doing the right things and not making any mistakes, and they do finish the race and are also winners (in the sense that they did not fall out of the race completely).

The above example is illustrative of the fact that it is not necessarily the business itself, but the businessman with the best performance and highest ability, that will win. Simply put: 'When the man is right, the business is right.' (See section on the characteristics of a successful entrepreneur, page 8.)

Another important aspect is never to underestimate your competition. How you get on with your competition is one of the best yardsticks for measuring your success. And if you want to be a serious competitor, you better be sure which competitive modes will give you the greatest competitive advantage, and develop an optimizing strategy for achievement. Such modes may for example include differentiation (a complete quality range of products with the best back-up service) and focusing on a specific market so as to attract and hold their business (the best value for money, for a specific customer target group with special requirements). Such modes and actions to achieve it, should be effectively communicated to the 'business team' (your employees) and your customers (through purposeful advertising means).

Last, but not least, the decision to go into business, and being in business, can be exciting but it must also be supported by the rest of your family. The 'starting up' phase can be particularly time-consuming and there are many things to do which require constant concentration. At times your family might feel that you are married to the business instead of to them. Your family needs to be patient, supportive and encouraging. After all, the business is not just for your own benefit but for theirs as well.

Many a sound business principle has been outlined in this section — all of which were practised by those who are still in business (and successfully so). They are for you to apply in order to enhance your profits as well as your career as an entrepreneur. Only then will you be able to fight the disease called 'business failure'.

WHY A BUSINESS FAILS

Most of the discussions up to this point have been centred around the reasons why a business succeeds, but it is just as important to know, and to be aware of, why a business fails. Business is a hard competitive struggle, and business failures are on the increase in stringent economic conditions which provide only hardship to the businessman, his family and his personnel. The question of course, could these lost hopes, lost dreams, the lost money and these lost jobs have been prevented? And if so, by whom, and how? A true fact in business is that if there is no sale, there is no job. In other words, there is no income because a need was not satisfied, and therefore no transaction could be made. However, having no sales is not always the cause of business failure. A question that should be addressed is: Is it always poor economic conditions that lead to the failure of a business, or are there other causes as well?

Studies of the financial troubles of businesses emphasize two general types of difficulties: those that arise from factors outside the business; and those that arise from the unwise decisions of management. The former affects all businesses in varying degrees simultaneously. The truth is that the real causes of financial difficulty probably originate from internal factors, but are revealed whenever external factors make internal defects apparent. This type of reasoning is seldom used by the businessman who faces financial difficulty. It is easier to look for a scapegoat, than to engage in soul-searching.

The real causes are often hidden within the character of management. Based on my own observations and experience, and by reading various articles in magazines, books and reviews of studies,[24] and talking to people in the same field, it seems that there is little doubt that business failure is attributed mostly to the incompetence of the owner-manager of the business. This is also the opinion of those who had dealt with failing businesses before, such as creditors, lenders and others (even honest businessmen), mostly because it is management's vision — or lack thereof — in a business that is responsible for the pacing. Successful business management can be summarized as the profitable use of the six Ms of business and, therefore, management's vision or lack thereof may best be illustrated by means of an example: A rugby team with an excellent coach and excellent players will have a number of victories whilst another coach, using the same players, may only have losses. The two are inseparable and as true in business as in rugby — the best team with the best coach will win.

Competition has much to do with this, as the real competition is not so much business against business, but businessman against businessman — how the business is managed by the owner-manager. 'Poor management is thus attributable to the owner's lack of expertise (lack of "know-how") and lack of how to mobilize the knowledge they have in sales, purchasing, personnel administration, finance and marketing.'[25] It is thus obvious that success in business demands knowledge and expertise. Business management ability or success is not self-evident, but requires training and much assistance in order to achieve entrepreneurial success.

Some reasons why owner-managers get into trouble

- Mismanagement of stock. Poor stock control leads to over- or understocking. The result is overspending, or underspending. Overspending leads to a shortage of working capital, and underspending to loss of sales.
- Over-investment in fixed assets (too much money going into fixed assets, which leads to a shortage of working capital).
- Owner taking too much out for himself (excessive personal drawings for luxuries, which leads to a shortage of working capital).
- Starting off without enough capital (poor planning of financial requirements. The saying: 'It takes money to make money', means that a business must start with enough capital if it is to operate profitably.)
- Lack of adequate information and expense controls (lack of business records and how to use, analyse and interpret the information).
- Improper mark-up (mark-up not high enough to cover expenses and to realize a profit. Making the mistake of wanting to be too competitive.)
- Inadequate sales (poor advertising, customer service and sales-promotion efforts). See chapters on 'Advertising' (page 269), 'Customer relations' (page 249), and 'Salesmanship and selling' (page 292).
- Employees don't deliver good work (lack of motivation, training and leadership). See chapters 'Your managerial functions' (page 126); 'Your business team' (page 164).
- Businessmen are easily discouraged when conditions get tough (lack of motivation to achieve). See sections on

'Why do you want to enter a business?' and 'The characteristics of successful entrepreneurs' on pages 2 and 8 respectively.

- Having a poor attitude and failing to ask for advice (too proud to admit own mistakes, implement solutions recommended, or seek and accept advice). See Chapter on 'Development of entrepreneurship', page 456.
- Businessmen are so tied up in the day-to-day survival of their businesses, that they cannot fully analyse the problems on hand. (The crucial obstacles went unnoticed, they did not give attention to details, they procrastinate.)
- Businessmen do not do proper profit planning. They fail to set a profit goal. (Feedback comes too late as businessmen let financial statements be compiled once a year by a bookkeeper or auditor. Usually, therefore, feedback is received when the previous financial year is long forgotten. Too much is left to chance.) See chapters on 'Profit planning and budgeting', and 'Record-keeping', pages 416 and 368 respectively.
- Over-extension of credit (poor credit-granting practices lead to a shortage of working capital).

If you were to ask any unsuccessful businessman, and those who dealt with failing businesses, which result of poor management practices 'scores the highest', the answer will undoubtedly be the situation where working capital is too short to pay the obligations of a business. If you run out of the cash necessary to pay suppliers and lenders on time, they may force you into bankruptcy. Not everyone has the patience of Job. It is also such shortage of capital situations that lead to some other difficulties such as: getting discouraged when things begin to turn sour; poor attitude towards others; and poor performance by employees. The one affects the other.

Whatever the causes may be for failure, one should differentiate between what the owner says, and what others say. The reason for this is that unsuccessful business owners tend not to regard themselves in the same way as others do, and therefore assign causes for their failures to many other reasons — rarely personal mistakes. It is as if they become 'colour-blind' to their own mistakes. Their perspective of the 'real cause' differs almost invariably from what the real cause is found to be, after investigation into the matters of the business. Normally, when the business fails, the owner-manager blames everything and everyone — the equipment, the location, the employees, the financial institution by whom he was financed, the consultants, his competitors and even the government but never himself. The truth is that many a business fails because the owner-manager: never took the time to study a book on the subject of business; had little knowledge about the type of business and its products; was not able to communicate with people; did not stay abreast of aspects relating to the type of business; did not understand what profit really is; and did not really watch the business. Retailing is mostly a cash business, and most of the time you will have a great deal of money in your possession. The biggest mistake you can ever make is to believe that it is all your money, when in reality, the money is there to pay the obligations of the business, and supply it with operating capital. Incurring debts in excess of your ability to pay, is no longer looked upon as a crime. It represents a risk which every business runs, and which every creditor takes into consideration when examining the ability of the potential debtor to pay whatever debts he intends to incur, before extending credit. Before entering into excessive debt, remember the risks involved — not only may you lose your business, but you may never recover from the blot on your creditworthiness.

The basic difficulty in business is poor management, and the number of business owners who are prepared to admit that they are poor managers is small. One wonders whether they admit it at least to themselves. What may be described by the failing businessman as 'too many competitors', may in reality be insufficient attention to efforts to improve sales. It is because the 'poor small businessman' fears competition (from other, similar businesses, and the giants) that he gives up trying to do better. What may be called 'bad debts', may in reality be careless credit-granting practices. 'Insufficient capital' could mean anything from too expensive assets, to too many employees being unproductive, who must nevertheless be paid, or excessive personal drawings in order to purchase expensive cars and other luxuries.[26] 'Employees that don't perform as they should', could in reality mean that they perform according to the attitude and behaviour of management. It is a known fact that people create most of their problems through their attitudes. Negative attitudes when things turn sour, always seem to be stronger than positive ones. However, motivating or training employees may be of little benefit to the business if employees have a strong negative attitude towards the owner-manager, or management of the business. See the sections on 'Training' (page 173) and 'Motivating employees' (page 150). Larry Farrell comments on the second priority of entrepreneurial managers (the first priority being the customer) as follows:[27]

'Priority number two for entrepreneurial managers, is employees. If you start your own business, and you have two or three of those wonderful customers who pay you money to feed your family, you might need some help in keeping them happy, or finding some more of them. You need a partner, a helper, an employee. Are you concerned about your first employee? Are you concerned about your second, third and fourth employee? You bet. You know they will make the difference between prosperity and bankruptcy. Entrepreneurs recognize employees as the primary instrument in serving and pleasing customers. The challenge is to keep the employee's performance environment simple and customer-focused.'

In today's competitive market, businessmen cannot afford many mistakes, neither will they progress if they constantly treat the symptoms of their problems, and leave the underlying causes untouched. It is virtually impossible to deal with the real cause of the problem if the businessman is not prepared to admit that he can also be reponsible for making mistakes. It is important from an entrepreneurial development point of view that failing businessmen admit, at least to themselves, that they can also make mistakes. Only then will the businessman be able to do something about his failure in business, by trying to correct it through whatever means are applicable to his problem. All people have weaknesses, even successful leaders. The difference between a successful person, and a less successful person can be said to be that the successful person recognized his weaknesses and applied all his abilities to correct them, and at the same time built on to his strengths. They involve others, they seek advice, ask for information, and seek solutions to problems. The 'illnesses' from which some businesses suffer, such as 'lack of money', and others, are mainly caused by their owners not taking precautionary measures, and once in business, such a businessman realizes too late the managerial ability required for a successful operation, and as a result of that, he loses his faith in what he is doing, his confidence in himself, and any belief in future success.

In other words, he loses that spark for achieving, which is one of his greatest assets. The businessman who loses his enthusiasm and motivation for achieving, is no longer a businessman, as they are the driving forces in a business, and no man can manage a business without those qualities. These are the qualities that laugh at obstacles, carry the businessman over the hard places, enable him to forget a day of disappointments and go out with renewed determination to succeed.

The best way out of difficulty is through it, by seeking sound advice in order to identify the problems, and to devise and implement ways and means to improve the efficiency of the business. The seeking of expertise concerning the problem applicable, should be part and parcel of a failing entrepreneur's plan of action if he wants to get back on the road to success. It is also a known fact that those who accept the advice of others, are far more successful than those who refuse. Donald K. Clifford, Jr., and Richard E. Cavanagh put the aspect of responding to trouble as follows in their book *The Winning Performance*:[28]

'The best responses to adversity are reminiscent of the response of a golfer whose game is off; single-minded commitment, a tremendous sense of urgency, and a redoubling of time and attention to the basics (a true championship golfer does not, for example, blame his caddie, or claim that the rules are unfair). The underlying attitude of each is the same: I am a winner. I not only will solve this problem, but I will be even stronger and better as a result.

Furthermore, the high-performance businesses come to grips with their problems and resolve them by being alert enough to recognize the existence of a problem at an early enough point to do something about it before it becomes cataclysmic. Once they have identified the problem, they don't hesitate to bite the bullet. In other words, once they sensed things were awry, they conduct a complete investigation to make sure they catch all the things that contribute to the disfunction, and as in any life-and-death situation, there is no higher priority than

507

the rescue. Dealing with the problem is everybody's top priority and they move quickly to address it in a substantive way.'

THE QUEST FOR GROWTH

Growth means expansion. Growth is the process of growing towards full size or maturity. Growth is an increase in size, importance and power and it creates additional profit. In the long run, growth is essential to the well-being of a business and so is continuity in management. The owner-manager has to get stuck in and be active when he is concerned with the growth of his business. It is the management of the business that is responsible for establishing the purpose of the business, setting the objectives, deciding on the actions necessary to accomplish growth, and directing operations according to predetermined and well-considered methods. Growth also requires investment — and continuous reinvestment of profits into the business. In other words, the business must be managed for cash flow to avoid a liquidity crisis that can be a major stumbling block in its growth. Let's therefore 'talk growth'.

Survival comes first Most businesses have some sort of problem(s) that require immediate attention and as mentioned a number of times in this book, the owner-managers of failing businesses have proved themselves incapable of coping with the immediate problems that must be resolved in order to sustain a financially viable business. The businessman who is capable of handling such problems will be in a better position to pursue the opportunities of growth as his full attention will not be devoted to 'killing fires' all the time and therefore he will have more time on hand and more objectivity to concentrate on the future. So the most important requirement for maintaining a dynamic business is to be knowledgeable about the possible causes of failure so that the managerial concepts and techniques concentrated on within this book can be applied judicially. In other words, know the causes of business failures and manage according to the rule 'prevention is better than cure'. More specifically, it is important to be able to recognize the common causes of business failure, to be alert for the underlying difficulties which might contribute to such causes, and to have the acumen necessary (or consult someone with such acumen) for making the correct diagnoses of such problems. John Petrof, Peter Carusone and John McDavid put this matter of immediate attention to problems as a requisite for survival in business into perspective, as well as providing some valuable information on the development of essential decision-making habits:[29]

'Stop! Look! Listen!

Recognition of problems that might be serious enough to cause the stagnation and death of a business is the most important requirement for maintaining a dynamic enterprise. It is, however, only a first step in the right direction. Once management has been alerted to certain deficiencies in the business's operations, more precise diagnoses still have to be made, and finally, appropriate remedies have to be prescribed. If the sales of a certain product are unsatisfactory in relation to potential, is it promotion that is lacking, or is the product itself deficient in the eyes of your customers? Or is the price too high? More important, what action should be taken? If a poor location is causing inadequate traffic flow for your business, should you do more advertising to try to attract more people? Or should the business be relocated? What to do?

Unfortunately, there is no magic formula for answering such questions. Whatever the problem may be — or seems to be — the only intelligent way to find an appropriate solution is to make judicious and strategic use of the managerial tools which the small businessman has at his disposal. By "strategic use" we mean selecting the right tools and techniques for use at the right time and applying them in the right way.

This can usually be accomplished through a problem-solving approach such as to be found on page 130. By "judicious use" we refer to the exercise of sound judgement in making sensible, prudent decisions, that is, decisions which will maximize the chances of achieving some degree of success while minimizing the risk of disastrous failure. This puts the emphasis on deliberate, research-minded, and analytical management methods. In other words, the need to cultivate good decision-making habits. The following suggestions should be helpful in developing such habits:

Research habit. Look for as much relevant information as you can reasonably afford to obtain in order to shed more light on a given problem. Never be content to accept the superficial aspects of a problem as being indicative of the real underlying difficulty. Consider the fact that each of the concepts and techniques we have discussed

509

may seem fairly simple and logical when studied separately but that overall implementation in the context of a real business situation can be quite complex. Problems are likely to be interrelated. Underlying causes are often hidden from immediate view. Do not hesitate to probe for new answers to old questions. Assumptions based on dated or tenuous information can be dangerous. Listen to what people have to say about you and your business operation. A receptive attitude is more likely to evoke helpful constructive criticism than a recalcitrant posture.

Analytical-thinking habit. Insights into complex problems are not likely to suddenly blossom from your research information. Insights are the result of careful scrutiny of available data and serious analytical thinking. Try to put things into perspective. Do not become panicky when problems arise. Consider all the ramifications of what has transpired. What are the implications for the long run as well as for the immediate situation? What are the implications of social, economic, and competitive trends? It is often possible to take what seems to be a major business problem and turn it into a lucrative business opportunity.

A small general-merchandise retailer was experiencing inventory and sales difficulties in 1970 when women's fashions began to shift from the "mini" to the "midi" length skirts. He had followed the lead of his major competitors, who were putting more emphasis on midiskirts. Since his store was much smaller than those of his competitors, he found it almost impossible to carry a complete assortment of both midis and minis. As a result, customers could not find what they wanted, sales dropped, and inventory continued to accumulate.

After much careful deliberation, this small retailer turned things around by deciding to specialize in a wide assortment of miniskirts, promoting them heavily while completely dropping the midiskirt line.'

As we approach our discussion of the opportunities for growth and the aspects that could give you an indication as to when your business is ready for growth the challenge to you should be clear. That is, first deal with the problems that commonly cause a business to fail.

Your business is ready for growth when: 1. The business purchase for resale good quality products and offers them for sale at reasonable prices and provide an excellent service using quality products. It has been said: 'You either make the very best product or provide the very best service.' Providing an excellent service also means being conscious of the fact that the sale really begins after the sale — not before. Consider the following advice in an illustration of closeness to the customer:[30]

510

Although he is not a company, our favourite illustration of closeness to the customer is car salesman Joe Girard. He sold more new cars and trucks, each year, for eleven years running, than any other human being. In fact, in a typical year, Joe sold more than twice as many units as whoever was in second place. In explaining his secret of success, Joe said: "I send out over thirteen thousand cards every month."

Why start with Joe? Because his magic is the magic of IBM and many of the rest of the excellent companies. It is simply service, overpowering service, especially after-sales service. Joe noted: "There is one thing that I do that a lot of salesmen don't, and that is believing the sale really begins after the sale — not before. The customer ain't out the door, and my son has made up a thank-you note." Joe would intercede personally, a year later, with the service manager on behalf of his customer. Meanwhile he would keep the communications flowing.

Joe's customers won't forget him once they buy a car from him; he won't let them! Every month throughout the year they get a letter from him. It arrives in a plain envelope, always a different size or colour. "It doesn't look like that junk mail which is thrown out before it is even opened", Joe confides. And they open it up and the front of it reads, "I like you". Inside it says "Happy New Year from Joe Girard". He sends a card in February wishing the customers a "Happy George Washington's Birthday". In March it is "Happy St. Patrick's Day". They love the cards, Joe boasts. "You should hear the comments I get on them."

Out of context, Joe's 13 000 cards sound like just another sales gimmick. But like the top companies, Joe seems genuinely to care. Said Joe: "The great restaurants in the country have love and care coming out of their kitchens . . . and when I sell a car, my customer's gonna have the same feeling that he will get when he walks out of a great restaurant." Joe's sense of caring continues to shine through after the sale: "When the customer comes back for service, I fight for him all the way to get him the best. . . . You've got to be like a doctor. Something is wrong with his car, so feel hurt for him." Moreover, Joe has cared about every customer as an individual.

He doesn't think statistically, but emphasizes that he has sold "one at a time, face-to-face, belly-to-belly". "They are not", he said, "an interruption or pain in the neck. They are my bread and butter." We introduce this section with Joe because he has acted, as well as anyone, as if the customer really does count.'

2. *Everybody takes pride in the operations of the business.* Pride in the operations can however mainly be established by creating loyalty to the business, that is, employees believe

511

in and support the actions decided upon by management as far as (i) the external operations of the business, and (ii) matters relating to internal personnel policies, are concerned. Three basic ways of establishing this pride in the operations of the business are:

- Demand entrepreneurial behaviour of yourself and of your employees. Be a living model of the behaviour you are advocating.
- Almost all employees have a latent entrepreneurial drive, but they are just waiting to be inspired. And many spend one-third to one-half of their lives at work. When given the opportunity to become 'contributors', they will find it more interesting, challenging and fun to spend this huge chunk of their lives in an environment of enterprise. Moreover, they will be dedicated to persevere in their actions to succeed in whatever they have recommended. (See page 172 for details on what are regarded as good suggestions from employees.)
- In order to win their confidence, you have to show confidence; meaning, you have to know what you are doing and talking about under all circumstances. For example: you must be able to handle difficult customers, as they will more than likely be referred to you by employees. If a customer walks out of your office without a smile on his face, you have failed to satisfy the customer as well as the employee. Remember, the employee will expect you to solve the problem. If you are unable to solve the customer's problem, do not take your frustrations out on the employee. Rather reassess the problem as well as the underlying cause and rectify it by the appropriate action. Remember, for every problem there is a solution or at least, a simple method to follow in solving such a problem.

3. The management (yourself as owner-manager as well as the key employees) is growth-minded, business-minded, flexible and orientated towards creativity (thinking up new ideas, for example: to satisfy customers, or solving a problem) and innovation (implementing those ideas). When Thomas Peters and Robert Waterman studied the attributes that characterize the successful innovative businesses, they found that one such quality was a strongly favoured feeling

512

towards getting on with implementing constructive ideas that will bring results. This vision is expressed as follows in *In Search of Excellence*:[31]

'... A bias for action, for getting on with it. Even though these businesses may be analytical in their approach to decision making, they are not paralyzed by that fact (as so many others seem to be). In many of these businesses the standard operating procedure is: "Do it, try it, fix it." Says a senior executive for example: "When we have got a big problem here, we grab ten senior guys and stick them in a room for a week. They come up with an answer and implement it."'

4. *Sales are moving steadily upwards.* A growth in sales from year to year at least equal to the inflation rate for the period under review is desirable, but more preferable is a growth in sales higher than the inflation rate. This is a rule of thumb, but experts are of opinion that growth is more accurately measured by what they call 'the transaction trend'. This is what they say:[32]

'Growth is measured in rand sales; but don't forget that rand sales are the product of transactions and average sales. For many businesses price increases have boosted the amount of average sale (thus causing rand sales to rise), but the number of transactions has shown only a sluggish increase. For example: department store sales from 1960 to 1970 rose 62 per cent, but transactions gained only 7,5 per cent. Growth such as this is not a healthy kind. Population and real incomes are growing rapidly, and yet many businesses—thinking they are progressing because of higher sales—are really standing still.

Increased transactions are a better measure of real growth than are greater rand sales. You will need to make organized efforts to stimulate them. Here are some ways that will help:

• Improve your stock assortment in breadth, depth, quality and fashion rightness.
• Do more effective advertising both outside and inside the business.
• Improve your shop layout.
• Stimulate better personal salesmanship.

The checklist from page 338 to page 343 can indicate to you in more detail where the major opportunities are for increasing transactions. Pick a few of the methods that seem to offer the best prospects and concentrate on them. Also study the following chapters carefully:

513

- Stock control.
- Advertising and sales promotions.
- Shop layout, display and improving external and internal images.
- Salesmanship and selling.

Of interest to you might be a study of retail survival done in nine Illinois communities. The criteria for measuring the success of these businesses were:[33]

- rate of employee growth;
- rate of increase in the owner's investment;
- rate of return on the investment; and
- rate of return on sales.

Using these considerations, the study analysed 419 retail businesses to determine the operating practices associated with success. Here are the major findings of this study:

- Successful businesses encourage salespeople to increase their sales by organized efforts.
- Successful retailers add new items for sale more frequently than others do.
- Successful retailers conduct more special sales and are specially active in community promotion campaigns.
- Successful retailers advertise more consistently.
- Successful retailers maintain more frequent and detailed merchandise and operating data, but depend on their accountants to collect them.
- Successful retailers are better educated, are well-informed about their business's financial data, and are aggressive yet friendly.

5. *Business expenses are carefully monitored and kept under control by means of 'budget control'.* Budgeting is a simple process whereby you detail your income and expenditure and see that for the foreseeable future your income is on the average greater than your expenditure. It is essential that you consult your budgets before laying any money out for whatever purpose. For more details see chapter 16.

The owner of a manufacturing company, which managed to survive for only fourteen months, made the following remarks: 'My biggest problem, now that I have had a chance to think about it, was in estimating our income and outgo. Actually, my sales projections were pretty realistic. It's the unexpected expenses that killed us. We should have had at least 50 per cent more capital going in than we did. That's what it boils down to!'[34]

6. *Employee morale is high and they are motivated to provide their best efforts.* To succeed in business, not only you, but the whole business team have to perform consistently at their best. One other attribute — productivity through people — that emerged to characterize the distinction of the excellent, innovative businesses was noted as follows in the book *In Search of Excellence:*[35]

'Every worker is seen as a source of ideas, not just acting as a pair of hands. (Mark Shephard, Texas Instruments' Chairman).'

It has also been noted that if you are a leader, you have followers — even if only one. A leader is somebody who can actively pursue goals and inspire others to action. If an improvement in your competitive edge is to be achieved, it is required of you to adopt this vision called leadership. However, in developing leadership qualities, it is first required of you to understand your role within your business (your managerial functions) and thereafter to acquire the skills to transform this understanding into action. Some leadership skills needed to achieve not only personal success but also business success are: Managing the performance of your employees; initiating and influencing action; gaining commitment and follow-through; working as a team and handling change. You should be on the lookout for a suitable, performance-orientated training course for yourself by following the procedures outlined on page 177.

7. *There exists considerable talent among employees and the owner-manager.* It should be obvious by now as well as after you have worked through the book that how well your employees perform affects the performance of the business. William Day puts this into perspective:[36]

'Management is directing people, not directing things. Put in other words, success is people. Your profits will be affected by your ability to successfully handle your personnel. Typically, there are two ways of using people. One is to keep them in the dark so they cannot learn your job. The other is to train them well so you can delegate more responsibility. The failure of a business to grow is often linked to a lack of developed personnel. To be effective your people must be informed of your plans and the progress of these plans, to enable them to make

515

a maximum contribution. Give them exercise in thinking for themselves. Teach them to save your time. Place responsibility gradually and build feelings of responsibility. Give complete responsibility for certain parts of the work. Make them accountable for responsibilities, and evaluate them frequently. Encourage the assignment of new responsibilities as fast as they are able to take them on.'

Thus, to do better in business all the time, everybody needs the skills that will enable him to meet increased responsibilities and personal growth. The heading of an advertisement states the following: 'We don't underestimate your intelligence, we count on it.'[37] You should therefore utilize the 'brains' of your employees to the best advantage of the business, and not underestimate what they are really capable of doing. Provide them with the opportunity to contribute. However, that you ought to bring out the best in your employees seems a benign enough message, but the important point to stress in this section is not to regard your employees as a 'nuisance' as so many businessmen do. Rene McPherson comments as follows on the above matter: 'Almost everybody in business agrees that people are their most important asset, yet almost none really lives it.'[38] Below follows a particularly good example of what one employee (being an ordinary employee) can do to enhance the performance of a business:[39]

'Our business day had taken us beyond the last convenient flight out. We had no hotel reservations, but we were near the Four Seasons Hotel, had stayed there before and liked it. As we walked through the lobby wondering how best to plead our case for a room, we braced for the usual chilly shoulder accorded to latecomers. To our astonishment the concierge looked up, smiled, called us by name, and asked how we were. She remembered our names! We knew in a flash why in the space of a brief year the Four Seasons had become the "place to stay" in the District and was a rare first-year holder of the venerated four star rating.

Good for them, you are thinking, but why the big deal? Well, the incident hit us with some force because for the past several years we have been studying business excellence. For us, one of the main clues to business excellence has come to be just such incidents of unusual effort on the part of apparently ordinary employees. What's more, we were fairly sure we would find sustained financial performance that was as exceptional as the employee's performance.'

Not only is it one of your functions to attend to the matter of bringing about service back-up, which is dependent on the quality and dedication of the people you employ, but also to employ the right people. Below follow a few comments on employee selection in order to obtain talent:

Excellent customer service demands excellent employees. Businesses live on the money of customers. So, any business is people business. Thus, the selection of service people is to be taken seriously. Who you employ to deal with the customer is of utmost importance. When screening applicants, give them customer problems to solve. The purpose thereof is to see whether they have the ability to satisfy the customer in the real situation. You know your customers, and you know what they expect from your business, and such a role play gives you the opportunity to look at the applicant from your customer's perspective. Will *they* accept this employee?

An assistant of considerable talent means firstly, the right person with the right personality, attitude, qualities, and know-how ability to do the job, and secondly someone in whom you can build on his strengths and improve his skills through appropriate and purposeful means in order to secure maximum performance. Advice on means to achieve maximal performance from employees can be obtained from chapter 4.

8. *You as owner-manager consult expert advice.* In the recent times more and more consultants and financial institutions are tailoring their services to the needs of small businesses. What most small businesses need is specialized assistance when some serious difficulty is encountered and periodic checkups to detect hidden pitfalls that may be avoided if discovered in time. When you do seek the advice of consultants or other professionals, it is of the utmost importance to co-operate with them in every possible manner, both during and after their assistance. Their work consists of two major parts: (i) diagnoses of the trouble areas or weaknesses; and (ii) recommendations for improvement. Their recommendations are of no value unless followed. However, a major problem experienced by such small business management consultants is that some business-men seek advice but don't follow it, and others just simply refuse to seek advice in spite of the fact that they are in serious difficulties. Clifford Baumback and Kenneth Lawyer provide some clarity on this subject:[40]

'No matter how extensive the owner-manager's personal experience may be, it is no longer possible for many to operate a small business successfully if it is insulated or detached from the information and assistance available from "outsiders".

Small business consultants, or "business doctors", may save a business life just as a physician or surgeon may save a human life. However, it has been said that the chief problem of independent owners is their independence. Small business ownership does attract an independent, self-reliant type of person — one who is less likely to seek advice and assistance from those of greater experience and know-how. Often the biggest problem is to get the independent to appreciate the need for outside assistance, and then to be willing and able to take the time to profit by it.'

When you are considering expanding your business, you need to ask yourself this question at some stage in your thinking process of how you are going to go about things: How can I devise a growth strategy to help me and my employees and my business as a whole in competing more effectively? Simply answered: consult the best to teach you what you don't know. And if you have got yourself a consultant and you are not taking his advice — fire him. The consultant may even give you the best advice you can ever wish for, but if you are not following it you are wasting his time and your money.

9. You as owner-manager must manage for profit and being concerned with the circulation and accumulation of profits within the business. Reference has already been made to both the above matters. Some points which should be stressed are sound cash management and borrowing, because the lack of capital for growth in total or even for the first step towards growth (for example: employment of an additional salesman, or the purchase of a machine, or additional merchandise, or for modernization, etc.), has been one of the major obstacles facing the small businessman. However, today many sources of capital are readily available, provided of course you have a well-conceived business plan (and idea). But sound management must be practised from the day the doors are thrown open if loans are to be

518

obtained and used profitably. Such management includes: knowing the business's cash flow, forecasting cash needs, planning to borrow at the appropriate time, and sustaining the business's payback ability. For more details on sound cash management and borrowing, refer to chapters 2 and 16. For the purpose of demonstrating how a goal can be achieved through sound management and by borrowing only a nominal amount, the experience of two partners in a Southeast business are provided as a sound management success story.[41]

'They obtained a contract to manufacture and install kitchen cabinets for a builder. The contract called for installation in 4 months. To meet this deadline, the partners figured that they needed R56,500 in extra working capital.

Because this amount was more than they wanted to borrow, they asked for help from S.B.A.'s Score* Programme. The Score counsellor helped the partners to come up with a borrowing requirement of only R16,000. This solution was arrived at by:

1. Arranging with their suppliers to deliver and bill for the materials monthly over a 3-month period.
2. Contracting with the builder to make an initial payment and 4 monthly payments.
3. Agreeing not to take any drawings from the business until the cash flow forecast indicated it was free and available.

Based on these facts, the partners estimated that during the 5 months (July to November) the firm should take in R88,000, pay out R56,500, and have a balance of R31,500 at the end of November. However, the problem was in July and August when expenses would run far ahead of the business's income. To determine how a loan of R16,000 (including interest) could see the business through these months, the following estimates were made:

Estimate Of Borrowing Requirements To Take On Additional Contract

	July	Aug.	Sept.	Oct.	Nov.
Cash Requirements					
Inventory (Stock)	15,000	10,000	7,000		
Operating Expenses	4,000	6,000	6,000	4,000	2,000
Extra Equipment	2,500				
Total	21,500	16,000	13,000	4,000	2,000

* Score is an acronym for the Service Corps of Retired Executives, a counselling service sponsored by the U.S. Small Business Administration to improve a businessman's chances of success.

Cash Available

Cash on Hand	2,000			2,000	18,000
Collections	10,000	10,000	15,000	20,000	31,000
Total	12,000	10,000	15,000	22,000	49,000
Excess Cash Over Receipts	0	0	2,000	18,000	47,000
Additional Cash Required	9,500	6,000	0	0	0

According to these estimates, at the end of November, the partners would have cash on hand amounting to R47,000. Certain obligations would be outstanding against this cash. The first one would be the repayment of the loan of R16,000. Other obligations would be those which the partners planned to accumulate during the early months of the contract when cash on hand was at a premium, such as reserve for taxes and the partners' drawings.

These estimates convinced the partners that they could perform the contract if they could get a loan. The next step was to convince the bank that their plan was sound.

For the bank lending officer's benefit, as well as their own, the partners projected the loan funds through a cash flow plan for the entire business. The cash flow schedule that was prepared is shown below. It showed: (1) that the amount of money requested would be adequate for the business's needs and (2) the margin of cash that was expected to be available both during the contract and at the end of the contract.

Cash Flow Schedule— Period of Contract to Repayment of Loan

	July R	Aug. R	Sept. R	Oct. R	Nov. R
Estimated Receipts					
Cash Sales	800	600	700	1,200	2,800
Accounts Receivable	10,000	10,200	15,800	20,000	31,600
Other Income	200	400	200	480	250
Total Receipts	11,000	11,200	16,700	21,680	34,650
Estimated Disbursements					
Accounts Payable	17,000	11,000	8,200	2,700	2,200
Payroll & Drawing	2,600	4,200	4,200	7,900	5,800
Expenses	1,200	1,800	2,000	2,700	600
Interest Expense	130	130	130	130	130
Plant & Equipment	2,500	460	600	800	100
Reserve for Taxes				3,800*	3,800*
Total Disbursements	23,430	17,590	15,130	18,030	12,630

* To be allotted in October and November so that available cash can be kept at the maximum during the months of heavy cash outflows.

	July	Aug.	Sept.	Oct.	Nov.
	R	R	R	R	R
Estimated Excess Receipts over Disbursements	(12,430)	(6,39)	1,570	3,650	22,020
Estimated Cash Balance at Start of Month	4,200	7,770	1,380	2,950	6,600
Borrowings	16,000				
Loan Repayment					16,000
Estimated Cash Balance at End of Month	7,770	1,380	2,950	6,600	12,620

Good managers recognize that occasional borrowing is one of the accepted business tools. Your long range plan for borrowing should be based on the fact that each of the various types of money in your business has its specific and appropriate purpose.

Recognizing this fact is important in preventing the misuse of funds. Keep in mind that misuse can cause a shaky financial condition. This point is especially true when operating cash seeps into long term investment in the business. As a result, the business requires a constant renewal of short term borrowings. Such borrowing indicates a capital deficiency in the business and the need for additional permanent capital.

Bear in mind that financial planning is the first step when borrowing. Such planning must be based on facts that come from your records if you are to secure loans and use them profitably.'

Growth by means of retaining and investing profits is usually a slower process than combining with other businesses or getting new partners, but where the expansion projects are small and relative to the income-producing capacity of the business, this method (ploughing back profits) is feasible and very desirable. A business may also expand by making use of short-term credit (trade credit). Any one supplier of goods on credit expects to have his account paid within the limits of the credit terms. But he also expects to be a regular supplier over a long period of time. Thus, initial credit will be paid off and replaced with new credit. The business that uses short-term credit may come to count on credit transactions and accounts payable as a more or less permanent source of funds. Both creditor and debtor may be satisfied with such an arrangement as long as current accounts are alternately paid off and incurred. In this way, the debtor (businessman) demonstrates his willingness (character), ability (capital) and capacity to pay. He has a good credit record

record with the supplier. When a business makes use of more short-term credit in this way, obtaining and utilizing funds effectively, it brings about growth.

In summary of the 9 points mentioned, new businesses will always experience some birth and growing pains, but as employees get accustomed to doing things as you want them done, and when you want them done, the work will be easier and everyone, including yourself, will find the working days going more smoothly as time goes on. As everyone becomes more proficient in doing their respective jobs, they will become more efficient and self-assured, and confidence will become apparent to customers in the way they are served. This will also help the profit picture and therefore lead to growth.

Basically, the life cycle of a small business consists of two stages which can be said to be the experimentation stage and the exploitation stage. All small businesses have the opportunity to grow (move step by step through these development stages) if they have the potential (pro-active management). The experimentation stage concerns getting the business firmly entrenched in its market. During this stage the owner must lay the foundation for future growth—realizing that growth occurs by increasing the business's share of the market. It is important that the businessman identify the ways needed to succeed in the line of business he is in (and applies sound business principles). Financial planning and control processes are especially important. Financial ratio analysis should be used to develop standards in the particular field of business to help isolate developing problem areas. If you expect growth, you must plan for it. Devise a thorough plan for future growth and profits. But don't put it quickly aside—refer to it frequently. With luck the businessman who has no plan may survive, but the closed and empty businesses all over testify that this does not often happen.

A successful business with growth potential will enter stage two, which is further exploitation. In this stage, the business has achieved initial success. It is reasonably profitable and economically viable. Sound working capital management can bring a business to this stage. Working capital management is critical to you as a businessman. If you fail here, you will not remain solvent, and if the financial position worsens continuously the business will run into serious difficulties. The exploitation stage is the stage where the business expands its services to other markets not yet satisfied or inadequately served.

A particularly striking example of a business owner who went through the stages mentioned (and who is probably still on the move) is that of Mr Louis Röntgen. He is a pharmacist and this story appeared in the magazine *Finansies en Tegniek* (31 January 1986, page 14), under the heading of 'A Bank overdraft was Röntgen's first step to success':

'Mr Louis Röntgen, now thirty-eight years of age, had used the money (which he earned through doing part time jobs whilst at school and at the Technikon of Cape Town), to complete his studies in pharmacy. Thereafter he opened a chemist in Citrusdal, of which his only source of finance was a bank overdraft of R3 000.

He did not wait for better days to come after he started in 1975, but took action and in 1977 he went into partnership and opened another pharmacy at Lamberts Bay. In 1979 he went into another partnership and opened yet another pharmacy in Clanwilliam, and in 1981, he and his partners opened another in Porterville. In this time the annual turnover increased from R50 000 to R2,5 million in February 1986. Their share of the respective markets are 100 % in Citrusdal, Clanwilliam and Lamberts Bay, and 60 % in Porterville.'

Mr Louis Röntgen is an outstanding example of what can be accomplished through perseverance and desire. He had that key ingredient — the motivation to face the situation and see it through. Sure, he had a lot of help from his partners; Mr Louis Röntgen ascribes their (he and his partners) success to specialization — he is responsible for the general administration, another director for cosmetics, another for photography and another for purchases, etc. Success is also a matter of thinking big and starting small — which they did. He says that they perform together as a team to bring about results, and in the final analysis, they made it work. They went through the stages. A business was conceived and born and grew with purpose. The business was viable in the first place, well-managed in the second place which brought about a bottom-line figure registered in black ink instead of in red. The major business functions were under the control of all the directors. Sales grew and tight reins were held on spending, profits were ploughed back and the businesses continued to prosper. They hold a sizeable share of the market. Growth has taken place. It was planned, organized, then guided and nurtured. Top management coveted growth. They were highly motivated and possessed the ability to make growth possible.

You too can accomplish a great deal of growth by developing your capabilities through self-motivation and desire to succeed. Don't underestimate what can be accomplished. After all, you have already demonstrated enough initiative to read this book. And there are many things you can do right now to prepare yourself better for a business of your own. You should be gathering information about the key aspects of running a business. Material relating to management, finance, accounting, marketing, and so forth will be invaluable when you get started on your own. Learn all you can — attend seminars and courses, consult consultants and talk to people with small business experience. You need to be directed in a positive and fruitful manner in selecting the right business opportunity and in preparing to manage it effectively.

Thinking about growth The growth and expansion of a business is not necessarily an automatic process, but rather the result of progressive management. There are, however, positive reasons for stimulating the growth of a business of which the first one is the opportunity for increasing profits. The sound reason is that growth is usually associated with greater strength. Thus, growth is encouraged as a means of becoming more capable in warding off economic fluctuations. The third reason for stimulating growth is to avoid stagnation (becoming dull through lack of variety of activity). Sometimes the only way a businessman can improve sales is by introducing a new product (or service) as some may have reached their sales peak. By introducing new products or services, you can help ensure that your business's net profits are increased over time. However, innovations may not occur too frequently, if at all, although they may help your business to become more competitive in the market (increase your market share). Therefore, keep your eyes and ears open for any improved products or services required by customers. Mostly, it becomes a question of knowing where to look for new products that can be sold at a profit, or finding out which services can be improved or introduced, or which promotional techniques will attract customers more regularly. Peter Drucker put the aspect of innovation as follows:[42]

'It is not good enough to provide just any economic goods and services, but rather to provide better and more economic ones. It is more important for a business to become constantly better in whatever economic performance it is engaged in than to go bigger.'

You should be aware of the fact that the environment in which you operate is continuously changing and therefore the demands on you will also change. You have to try and do better than yesterday and you have to become cleverer every day in order to cope with the challenging world around you. Innovation can take on various forms, and there is no area within any business where innovation cannot be applied. As Peter Drucker puts it:[43]

'Innovation goes right through all phases of business. It may be innovation in design, in product, in marketing techniques. It may be innovation in price or in service to the customer. It may be innovation in management organization or in management methods. Or it may be a new insurance policy that makes it possible for a businessman to assume risks.'

Donald K. Clifford, Jr. and Richard E. Cavanagh stress the importance of innovation in their book *The Winning Performance* as follows:[44]

'Innovation — the applied art of the new and better — underpins the strategies and successes of the winning performers. These businesses innovate early and often by creating new markets, new products and services, and new ways of doing business.

Almost by definition, innovation means breaking the rules and overturning conventional wisdom. It's the opposite of imitation and of business-as-usual. For the new competitor who seeks to survive and succeed in a market where established competitors have the advantage of scale, longstanding customer relationships, reputation, and financial staying power, innovation isn't just a nice-to-have. It is a necessity. Innovation — your best competitive edge.'

One important point to stress is that any business is fragile in the sense that the question of continuity is ever-present, and this is dependent mostly on the owner-manager and the way he manages and utilizes the resources available in order to reach certain objectives. Furthermore, even though it is a business truth that any business cannot stay the same size in order to survive, you should resist the temptation to grow too fast. Rather grow steadily at a healthy rate than double in size. Peter Drucker puts this point into perspective:[45]

'Finding the potential and developing the opportunities of a business are prerequisites for survival and growth. This does not mean that every business has a hidden potential and can turn weaknesses into opportunities. But a business that has no potential cannot survive. And a business that fails to search for its potential leaves its survival to chance.'

Mark H. McCormack, one of the most successful entrepreneurs in business today, the man who founded IMG (the International Management Group) and guided its growth to a multi-million-dollar worldwide corporation, and who started with less than R2 000, provides you with his formula for growth. It is: 'Start with the best; learn from the best; expand slowly and solidify your position; then horizontally diversify your expertise.' He also places much emphasis on 'becoming better before going bigger' as there is much still to learn before you can go ahead with bigger things. He is furthermore of the opinion that too many businesses are not prepared to do this. He says: 'They would rather grow quickly than profit quickly. If these businesses would just slow down a little, take some time to analyse their success, and allow their depth of management to catch up, they would see that they could have both — a healthy growth rate and healthy profitability.'[46]

But even businesses that intend to grow can fail. The reason of course, is that although the will to grow is necessary, it is not sufficient by itself. Most of the businesses that have the will, lack the skill. Donald K. Clifford, Jr. and Richard E. Cavanagh investigated the factors that have a bearing on this inability of businesses to grow. Here are their findings:[47]

'*Faulty design.* Sometimes a successful small business fails when it tries to expand because the business is not designed to be operated on a broad scale. Plenty of chain restaurant marketers who did not develop standardized menu items and operating guidelines (to ensure consistent quality-control, food-preparation, and service policies in all locations) have gone out of business. Still other businesses have been stopped because their products were designed for too narrow a market, as with high-priced electric automobiles. And some never developed the marketing programmes to substitute for business owner's personal relationships in his local community—the frequent cause of collapse among personal service businesses that try to expand geographically.

Financial over-extension. Most small businesses that fail financially do so because they lack the fundamental disciplines and controls to manage growth. Some employ staff and build stock too far in advance of income, which drives them broke. Others take on too much business too fast and find themselves unable to keep up with demand without running out of cash. Either way, growth must stop or the business fails.

Human frailty. In at least as many instances, small businesses that seek to grow seem to snatch defeat from the jaws of victory because they cannot achieve the co-operative climate or sustain the personal motivation to continue the journey toward further growth. Sometimes the problem is that the owner himself loses his driving interest in the business; sometimes he does not sense the importance early enough of dedicated personal follow-through; sometimes egos get in the way and lead to family or employee squabbles; sometimes the problem is downright dishonesty. Perhaps most frequently, the business owner finds that he really wants to do it all himself rather than manage others, and so the growth potential of the business is strictly limited by his personal energy and capability.'

But growth, of all things, is the result of initial success — of offering what the market wants, buys and pays for, of utilizing resources effectively, and of reinvesting profits into the business for expansion and to provide for the risks of the future. If these factors are in a state of total imbalance, the business's existence will be threatened. The point is: be aware of the factors that provide for balanced operations and try by all means to keep them in balance so as to ensure a profitable outcome. You should always be concerned with practising the few right things in business and should perform them with excellence so that you can maintain the business on a continuing basis. Thus, the real challenge is in maintaining a profitable business over time. Keep in mind Ecclesiastes 9:11 (paraphrase): 'The race is not to the swift and strong, but to those who endure to the end.'[48] The parallel which follows emphasizes the need for balance facilities and effort in the operation of a business which will assist you to understand the above points more clearly:[49]

'Link your business to a motorcar. A smooth-running motorcar, one that gives its driver comfortable, dependable, and economical performance mile after mile, is a well-balanced mechanism. The engine has just the right compression ratio and spark timing. The chassis has just the right strength and resiliency, the body is the right size. Wheels and tyres are engineered to co-ordinate with engine power and speed and with road conditions.

Most poorly designed, unsatisfactory cars lack this balance, this co-ordination of mechanical elements and effort. An oversized engine or undersized tyres will immediately cause trouble, as will insufficient battery power or a malfunctioning distributor. These facts are familiar to all of us. A motorcar fails because its engineers did not provide for balance elements and effort.

Balanced facilities and effort in the operation of a business is a necessity. Offerings to the community, to the market, must be in proportion to its needs. The money supply must be adequate to carry it safely over the early rough roads. The advertising appropriation must be one that will give the most "mileage", one where the results will justify the cost. The payroll must be paid to people who are achieving results, who are not a drag on the business's progress. So on and on, the parallels are seemingly endless.'

Attention has been given to many such factors, but the real aspects to be concerned about in this section are: What are the essentials to accomplish growth?; Where would one begin to accomplish growth?; and what should be planned for to accomplish growth? The second question is a difficult one if you want to follow a sequence of steps to accomplish growth, because factors for growth interact and influence one another all the time. Therefore one cannot in a logical sequence spell out the steps, but merely the aspects that are essential in accomplishing growth. The object of this section is then: how to think 'growth' in general.

Capability of the owner-manager: Before you consider following a growth strategy, you should ask yourself the following questions, and answer them honestly. Do I have more know-how in the functions of management than when I started? What, exactly, does this know-how entail? What have I learned in these years? In which business functions do I need more experience? What are my weaknesses and strengths? In other words, you should make an objective self-analysis concerning your proficiency. In general, your experience as owner-manager should be balanced and should include managerial responsibilities. Balance refers principally to the acquiring of experience in all major business functions and activities.

Apart from being proficient in the management functions and activities of the business, you also have to know your line of business and its products as well as have some technical abilities (skills necessary to sell or to perform a service). Sometimes an owner-manager knows the technical side but is a poor manager. Such an owner-manager often fails to plan ahead. Because of his enthusiasm for the operating side of his business he does the jobs himself. However, before you can with reasonable prospects of success put the process of growth in motion, you need to become balanced in your 'capability' as a manager. In other words, first learn to be a manager — the number one prerequisite for stimulating growth. Clifford Baumback and Kenneth Lawyer put this point of view into perspective:[50]

'Although it is growing increasingly important, formal education has never been a prime requisite of the successful entrepreneur. Yet recognition of the many facets of business — of the importance of each as a functional part of business operation — and a willingness to respect each enough to master it, either personally or with the help of associates, have ever been a requisite.

Individuals should first learn to manage their own life well. This in itself is preparation for business management. Among the qualities they should develop and practise are self-reliance, good use of time, and wise money management.

All are as important to successful business management as to well organized living.'

Petrof, Carusone and McDavid emphasize the need for personal growth and leadership by relating an old story about a college professor who continued to lecture from notes that he had compiled twenty-five years earlier:[51]

'His classes were characterized by students as being dull, out of touch with reality, and largely irrelevant. But these were simply reflections of a much more serious malady. The underlying problem was that the man had almost totally neglected the opportunities to stimulate his personal growth and development — opportunities which most teachers view as being essential to effective and responsible teaching. There are too many small businessmen who, unknowingly perhaps, are guilty of the same neglect. And, as in the case of the college professor, their lacklustre performance reflects it. Whatever his capabilities may be, the manager who wants to maintain a dynamic enterprise must continuously try to improve them. To fully appreciate the need for personal growth and leadership, let us consider what might be a perfect example of a small businessman who conscientiously tries to build on his strong points and to improve his weak spots where he can. Ideally, such a man would be described as follows:

He is constantly trying to improve himself. He knows he can never attain perfection, but that by striving for it, he will be moving in the right direction. He is receptive to new ideas, open-minded at all times. He tries to learn something from each new experience. He has the ability to adapt to change. When new management tools and techniques become available, he is among the first to use them. He recognizes the need to be "future-oriented" and "outward-oriented". He is able to relate to people — both inside and outside the business. He learns from them, and they learn from him. He has the ability to inspire and direct his employees, to lead them in new directions. He is willing to subordinate his independence to the interests of others, realizing that in the long run, this will also serve his best interests.'

For more information on self-study (developing yourself), see page 470. This section is an important one to read as it will help you to see that nobody else is responsible for your development, except yourself.

William Day, Professor of Management at North-eastern Oklahoma State University provides you with another idea:[52]

'A very productive way of stimulating growth is to employ proficient management. By means of proficient management, the business may receive some dynamic inputs, fresh ideas, new approaches, or "new blood" to energize the growth possibilities for the business. Keep your eyes peeled for such an individual who may be brought into the business.'

Planned growth Successful business owners have *first* determined where they want to go and how they want to get there. How did they do it? Every year, year after year, they plan by establishing realistic and measurable objectives and then devise action plans to reach them. In order to make their plans work, that is to know whether they have 'arrived', they expect feedback all the time. For example, the year-end income statement shows whether your business made a profit or a loss for the past twelve months. But you can't wait twelve months for the score. To keep your plan on target you need this information at regular intervals. An income statement at the end of each month or quarter is but one type of regular feedback. In addition your cash flow projection must be continuously updated and revised as necessary. You also need to set up management controls which will help you to ensure that the right things are being done from day to day and from week to week. However, planning is as important as controlling the achievement. Planning, for both the short term and the long term is an important, if not the most important job you have in directing the growth of your business. Short-term planning is normally for one year ahead, or shorter. More specifically, a short-term planning is used to get you from 'here' to 'there' in a number of very specific steps. It is the implementation of action plans through effective business actions and behaviour according to proven business principles. Details concerning short-term planning is discussed fully in chapter 16. For the purpose of this section, some aspects of long-range planning will be dealt with.

Long-range planning covers a wide spectrum of activities, but it basically boils down to deciding what will be done, by whom, and at what time. In planning, your attention to detail is required for one reason, that is to assist you in making good decisions that will result in the right actions at the right time in the future. Common sense with a purpose in mind must be the order of the day when you are doing long-range planning.

In devising a deliberate plan for the growth of the business, you should take your time to project where you want your business to be in, say, three years, five years, or even ten years in the future. The question to ask is: What routes are there to follow in accomplishing growth? Basically there are the following possibilities:

- modernizing existing space (perhaps with some expansion of selling space);
- opening a branch or relocating your business in the same metropolitan area; and
- relocating the business itself or establishing a branch in another community.

One or a combination of these routes can be considered as your long-range goals. Some factors have already been mentioned concerning how you know whether your business

531

is growing, or factors which will assist you to determine whether you are ready to grow (see page 510). One can almost say that *if* you can positively associate (or identify) those factors with your operations, you are ready to grow. The important thing to remember is: If your business is growing, you have to know the direction of that growth:

For example,[53] if you think you are going to need to set up a suburban branch in another four years and you will need at least two years to get it ready to operate, then you have only the intervening two years to the needed planning. One handy rule to keep in mind is: If you are unable to prepare for development more than five years away, there is no point in peering ten years into the future.

Your long-range planning will probably attempt to assess important changes in the following factors: population, purchasing power, customer-spending habits (with specific information on various classes of goods and services), government regulations, and competitive pressures. Getting projections on all these factors may well lead you to make plans to modernize, to open branches, or even move your business to a new location — all of which entail important financial considerations. Or you may decide to change the breadth and depth of lines you now handle, to add new lines and drop others, to revise your customer services set up, to start new advertising and selling techniques, to update your personnel policies, to start a manpower development programme for tomorrow's business. All of these decisions are important, and the changes they bring about must be planned for.

However, as far as forecasting is concerned, no one can foretell future events with certainty. Louis A. Allen has a good point concerning the 'uncertainties of forecasting' (stressing the importance of forecasting):[54]

'Since you must look ahead in order to plan at all, forecasting of some kind must take place. The question is not whether to forecast, but whether to move ahead haphazardly and fortuitously, or in terms of a logical and systematic assessment of the future.'

Predicting future events is futile and, therefore, probably the best you can do is to anticipate the future effects of events. The future cannot be predicted and therefore you should rather be concerned with what should be done today in your business for it to have a future.

Below are some hints that can assist you in making a reasonably sound decision when thinking about which route to follow for growth:[55]

'Modernization is probably your best choice under the following conditions:

1. Your present location is readily accessible to an expanding customer market.
2. Improved public transportation facilities are being planned.
3. Your city or town is improving its traffic arteries in ways which will keep your business readily accessible to existing and new customers.
4. Adequate parking facilities are available.

To help you decide about expanding, you will want to make a careful analysis of the statistical and qualitative data you can get from local estate agents, chamber of commerce, your bank, municipality and other services. What you will hope to find is evidence (1) that the group from which you are drawing your existing customers is increasing in numbers and purchasing power, and (2) that new customers can be attracted frequently to your location in considerable numbers. If you can determine these two factors, you may decide to stay put and to modernize your business to attract the new customer mix.

If you want to move to a new location* that has better prospects for growth, you have three major choices:

1. You can seek admission to a planned shopping centre.
2. You can locate in an established (though unplanned) suburban business centre.
3. You can develop a store with its own parking facilities on or off an artery of traffic.

A *second* aspect to be concerned about in long-range planning is that of 'shaping the image of the business'. In other words, deciding now the characteristics you want your business to have in the minds of customers. If you have a growing business, you should select two or three features in which your business has the capacity to excel, and then place major emphasis on developing and projecting them throughout the community. By having decided on these features, you will be more able to direct your sales message

---

* In locating in another community, your main consideration is the growth trend of the customer group, or target your type of operation is best fitted to serve.' See section on 'The location decision'. p. 77, for more information.

to those most likely to support your business and thus make more effective use of your advertising.

David Ogilvy in his book *Confessions of an Advertising Man* (p. 100–101), shares some of his experience with you on the aspect of building (or creating) an image through advertising:

'Every advertisement should be thought of as a contribution to the complex symbol which is the brand image.* If you take that long view, a great many day-to-day problems solve themselves. Most manufacturers are reluctant to accept any limitation on the image of their brand. They want it to be all things to all people. They want their brand to be a male brand and a female brand. An upper-crust brand and a plebeian brand. They generally end up with a brand which has no personality of any kind, a wishy-washy neuter. It takes uncommon guts to stick to one style in the face of all the pressures to "come up with something new" every six months. It is tragically easy to be stamped into change. But golden rewards await the man who has the brains to create a coherent image, and the stability to stick with it over a long period. The men who have been responsible for advertising hardy perennials have understood that every advertisement, every radio commercial, every TV commercial, is not a one-time shot, but a long-term investment in the total personality of their brands.* They have presented a consistent image to the world, and grown rich in the process.'

David Ogilvy, in his book *Ogilvy on Advertising* [Pan Books (Orbis Publishing Ltd, London—original publisher) 1983, p. 14–15, reproduced by permission], further elaborates on and supports the arguments in the above paragraph with an example:

'It pays to give most products an image of quality—a first class ticket. This is particularly true of products whose brand-name is visible to your friends, like beer, cigarettes and motorcars: products you "wear". If your advertising looks cheap and shoddy, it will rub off on your product. Who wants to be seen using shoddy products? Take whiskey. Why do some people choose Jack Daniel's, while others choose Grand Dad or Taylor? Have they tried all three and compared the taste? Don't make me laugh. The reality is that these three brands have different images which appeal to different kinds of people. It is not the whiskey they choose, it is the image. I have always been hypnotized by Jack Daniel's. The label and the advertising convey an image of homespun honesty, and the high price makes me assume that Jack Daniel's must be superior. Next time an apostle of hard-sell questions the importance of brand images, ask him how Marlboro climbed from obscurity to become the biggest-selling cigarette in the world. Leo

---

* The 'brand image' referred to here is applicable to manufacturers, but it can also be seen as the business's image as a whole.

Burnett's cowboy campaign, started 25 years ago and continued to this day, has given the brand an image which appeals to smokers all over the world.'

Everything you and your employees do and the way you behave in general towards customers will and must contribute to an image — you have to have the capacity to behave in such a manner as to 'create' the excellence you are striving for, that will characterize your business as a leader in the market you serve. See chapter 10 and 8 for more information on advertising and image-building.

Your detailed advertising and promotion plan should be communicated to all your employees, especially your image-building 'recipe', so that they can take an appropriate action within their powers to further what has been planned. See that the following is not happening in your business:

'I see you have a notice: "We aim to please", remarked an irritated customer to the store manager. "Yes", replied the manager, "that is our motto". "Well", said the customer, "you ought to take a little time off for target practice".' [56]

The *third* aspect to be concerned about in long-range planning is that of getting the work done through people. In other words, you need employees to assist the business in carrying out its action plans to accomplish growth. In the beginning you may not have a formal personnel policy, but in the process of growth you should think seriously of putting one together; the reason being, of course, to attract people that are fitted for the job you intend them to perform. Such a policy must include some or all of the matters employees are concerned about (employee fringe benefits, etc.) if you wish to attract the best, because they are going to ask you about these matters in order to see whether it is going to be beneficial for them to work for you. They thus evaluate what your business can offer against what they now have. If you are serious about growth, even go as far as employing someone 'smarter than yourself' — one who can handle the work you have in mind, as well as be of additional value to the business. Before employing someone, consider his experience, abilities, past performances and other necessary qualities, and then ask the question: Does he measure up to to your expectations? In other words, is he competent enough to play for your business team?

The degree of detail of your personnel policy will increase as your business team becomes enlarged. The business team concept should be adopted in the selection process, for example:

You are the coach as well as the selector of a rugby team. Of course, you are aiming at winning the rugby league in your particular district. In order to do so, you need the best players in every position. In order to know who the best ones are, you have to look at their past performances and on that basis select the best players. But also, before you can begin to select the players, you have to know what qualities of a player are required by the positions in order to match the players with the positions.

The process is no different in a business than in selecting a rugby team. You should first make a job analysis of each position you are to establish, and from it develop job specifications to help you fit the right person to the right job.

In long-range planning, the exact personnel policies will differ with the location of the business (or future businesses), the image you are trying to create, and the size and financial ability of the business. Furthermore, you should also devise some training programme for whomever you have in mind to run your second business. As a business grows, specialization becomes necessary:[57]

'Modern business organization is built upon the concept of specialization. More and better work is performed at less cost when it is done by specialists than when it is done by general workers who shift from one job to another and who continually improvise.

Specialization is of two kinds: Tasks and People. Specialization narrows a person's activities to simple, repetitive routines. Thus a relatively untrained employee can quickly become proficient at a narrow specialty and turn out more work with fewer mistakes. Because they develop routines and don't have to keep jumping from one job to the next, they don't waste time and effort in a constant change of activity. This type of specialization is typical of the factory operation where, on an assembly line, each person performs a narrow and relatively simple task — tightening bolts, for example.

Specialization of people involves not simplifying the job, but developing a person to perform a certain job better than someone else can. Training and experience improve the quality and quantity of the particular type of work.

In the small retail business, most of the specialization is of the second type; but in larger businesses there is more and more need for narrow task specialization. For example, certain special records must be kept, and certain phases of merchandise handling must be done by a well-trained person. Remember that if you have a small growing business, your first need is to develop people who are specialists in handling a major function.'

Always remember that a business is run by people and it can be broken by the inferior quality of its people and the inferior quality of work they produce, which is dependent on the knowledge they possess (knowledge being the ability to apply information to specific work and performance). Therefore, develop your people to become specialists in handling major functions in order to obtain that 'leadership position' in the market. That competitive edge or the differentiation you are striving for, can only be obtained through the distinct knowledge possessed by your people and to the degree of excellence to which they apply their knowledge. To do something as well as others is not enough as it only brings about a marginal performance, while excellence is associated with doing a few things superbly well and it can only be achieved by people using their brains and skills. For accomplishing growth, long-range plans should take into account those areas wherein you wish to specialize and specifically, who is needed to perform superbly (or who can be developed to perform with excellence); and what the means are, in the interim through which such people will be recruited or developed to reach the projected level of excellence.

The *fourth* factor to be concerned about in long-range planning is the investment of profits now that will enable you to carry out future growth plans, for example: For replacing machinery (or equipment and vehicles); the acquisition of improved facilities (modernization); the opening of another branch; or employing proficient people, etc. To understand the impact investing profits can have on future operations, it is necessary to be aware of the meaning of 'present value':

A rand today is worth more than a rand in the future. Assuming no change in the price level, you would obviously prefer to have R10,00 today instead of R10,00 a year from today when you consider the interest possibilities associated with money. Money does not have time value. However, the present value of a rand is the amount that must be invested now to produce a rand at a specific time in the future. Present value is shown for determining present values of future amounts. (See page 539 for such a table.) A selection from this table is shown here:

PRESENT VALUE OF R1,00 AT COMPOUND INTEREST

Period	Compound Rate			
	4%	6%	8%	10%
1	0,962	0,943	0,926	0,929
2	0.925	0,890	0,857	0,826
3	0,889	0,840	0,794	0,751
4	0,855	0,792	0,735	0,683
5	0,822	0,747	0,681	0,621

To illustrate the meaning of this table, you can determine that the present value (i.e. the value today) of R1,00 two years in the future discounted at 10 per cent is R0,83 (rounded). The present value of R100,00 two years in the future discounted at 10% is R82,60. How much must you invest today at 10% if you desire to accumulate a fund of R100,00 two years in the future? The answer is the present value of R100,00 two years in the future discounted at 10%, i.e., R82,60.

The importance of this is that if, for example, you need R20 000 to open another business in two years' time, you have to invest today (according to the 'present value' table) at 10%, R16 520.* See also the workings of similar concepts in the sections dealing with aspects of inflation (page 335) and depreciation (page 410).

* Or invest R688 per month for 24 months from profits.

PRESENT VALUE TABLE

Present value of R1,00 at compound interest

PERIODS	4%	6%	8%	10%	12%	14%	16%	18%	20%	22%	24%	26%	28%	30%	40%
1	.962	.943	.926	.909	.893	.877	.862	.847	.833	.820	.806	.794	.781	.769	.714
2	.925	.890	.857	.826	.797	.769	.743	.718	.694	.672	.650	.630	.610	.592	.510
3	.889	.840	.794	.751	.712	.675	.641	.609	.579	.551	.524	.500	.477	.455	.364
4	.855	.792	.735	.683	.636	.592	.552	.516	.482	.451	.423	.397	.373	.350	.260
5	.822	.747	.681	.621	.567	.519	.476	.437	.402	.370	.341	.315	.291	.269	.186
6	.790	.705	.630	.564	.507	.456	.410	.370	.335	.303	.275	.250	.227	.207	.133
7	.760	.665	.583	.513	.452	.400	.354	.314	.279	.249	.222	.198	.178	.159	.095
8	.731	.627	.540	.467	.404	.351	.305	.266	.233	.204	.179	.157	.139	.123	.068
9	.703	.592	.500	.424	.361	.308	.263	.225	.194	.167	.144	.125	.108	.094	.048
10	.676	.558	.463	.386	.322	.270	.227	.191	.162	.137	.116	.099	.085	.073	.035
11	.650	.527	.429	.350	.287	.237	.195	.162	.135	.112	.094	.079	.066	.056	.025
12	.625	.497	.397	.319	.257	.208	.168	.137	.112	.092	.076	.062	.052	.043	.018
13	.601	.469	.368	.290	.229	.182	.145	.116	.093	.075	.061	.050	.040	.033	.013
14	.577	.442	.340	.263	.205	.160	.125	.099	.078	.062	.049	.039	.032	.025	.009
15	.555	.417	.315	.239	.183	.140	.108	.084	.065	.051	.040	.031	.025	.020	.006
16	.534	.394	.292	.218	.163	.123	.093	.071	.054	.042	.032	.025	.019	.015	.005
17	.513	.371	.270	.198	.146	.108	.080	.060	.045	.034	.026	.020	.015	.012	.003
18	.494	.350	.250	.180	.130	.095	.069	.051	.038	.028	.021	.016	.012	.009	.002
19	.475	.331	.232	.164	.116	.083	.060	.043	.031	.023	.017	.012	.009	.007	.002
20	.456	.312	.215	.149	.104	.073	.051	.037	.026	.019	.014	.010	.007	.005	.001
21	.439	.294	.199	.135	.093	.064	.044	.031	.022	.015	.011	.008	.006	.004	.001
22	.422	.278	.184	.123	.083	.056	.038	.026	.018	.013	.009	.006	.004	.003	.001
23	.406	.262	.170	.112	.074	.049	.033	.022	.015	.010	.007	.005	.003	.002	
24	.390	.247	.158	.102	.066	.043	.028	.019	.013	.008	.006	.004	.003	.002	
25	.375	.233	.146	.092	.059	.038	.024	.016	.010	.007	.005	.003	.002	.001	
26	.361	.220	.135	.084	.053	.033	.021	.014	.009	.006	.004	.002	.002	.001	
27	.347	.207	.125	.076	.047	.029	.018	.011	.007	.005	.003	.002	.001	.001	
28	.333	.196	.116	.069	.042	.026	.016	.010	.006	.004	.002	.002	.001	.001	
29	.321	.185	.107	.063	.037	.022	.014	.008	.005	.003	.002	.001	.001	.001	
30	.308	.174	.099	.057	.033	.020	.012	.007	.004	.003	.002	.001	.001	.001	
40	.208	.097	.046	.022	.011	.005	.003	.001	.001						

Merger. Another growth opportunity factor is that of two businesses deciding to combine their efforts by merging. By means of a merger, a more complete and competitive business may result.

Partnership. If you lack either technical or management skills which are of major importance to the growth of your business, a partner with such skills may be a satisfactory way to cover the deficiency, 'two heads are better than one'. Although the viewpoints of the partners may clash, the outcome can be a desirable compromise. Furthermore, personal abilities are complemented — the salesperson and the bookkeeper with different personalities and abilities may succeed together when neither could alone. In addition, if you need money to finance growth (or even a new business), added capital can be made available by combining assets of two or more partners and therefore less borrowing is necessary. However, great care should be taken in choosing the right partner. Personality and character, as well as the ability to assist with technical or managerial matters, affect the success of a partnership, and consequently the performance of the business. Careful consideration should be given to your motives for taking on a partner because not all partners will perform to the other partner's expectations which can cause unnecessary stress. It has therefore been said: 'No wonder so many successes are achieved by solo entrepreneurs.'

Among the disadvantages of a partnership are: each partner is liable for all debts incurred by the business; each partner is responsible for the actions of all other partners that create an obligation for the business; and profits must be shared among the partners. In other words, if you bring in another person who has capital to invest in your business, it affects your ownership. You will have less say in operating the business. If you decide to take on a partner, work out an exact agreement that specifies the responsibilities of both or all the partners. You should also protect your business against the financial chaos that can result from the death of one partner by taking out life insurance for each partner, which is ceded to the business on any such partner's death. A purchase and sale agreement should accompany such a policy by which each partner agrees that his or her share of the business is to be sold to the surviving partner(s) and wherein he/they agree to buy the deceased partner's share.

Below is a success story which is illustrative of how two people can assist each other in turning a hobby into big business:[59]

'Biggie Best — a South African success story

Port Elizabeth-born Lynn McAdam comes from a family of doers. "My parents were very practical people. In our home, if you want something you make it yourself." Lynn's artistic parents instilled in her a strong work ethic; a will to strive and to succeed.

She stumbled into the retail business when she started selling clothing from a small store in Cape Town. Success eluded her, and to prevent herself slipping even further into the red, she started sewing patchwork. Her timing was perfect. The quaint charm of cottage crafts and furnishings had captured the South African imagination. Everyone was doing patchwork, quilting, and smocking. Lynn had timeously tapped a well of great demand.

She created two simple cottage designs in three mix-and-match colourways — and Capetonians loved what they saw. The good news travelled fast, and it wasn't long before Lynn had enough work to keep herself and a team of seamstresses busy, full time.

Patchwork enthusiasts came to her small shop in Claremont, seeking fabric, and few left without useful hints and tips to help make their patchwork perfect.

Lynn's one-woman enterprise flourished, and she began to supply other outlets in the Cape Town area. The time had come to find new premises, and the turning point came when Lynn moved into a bigger and better shop in the prestigious Cavendish Square shopping centre. Soon thereafter she opened a second shop in Port Elizabeth, and the Claremont shop soon became a mecca for patchwork purists.

Demand for Lynn's inexpensive all-cotton fabrics grew and she expanded her workforce, so that she could devote more time and energy to the design of her whimsically-romantic fabrics.

The time had come to adopt a more professional approach — she needed to rationalize the whole business. Fortunately her friend Prudence Phul had all the right credentials to tackle the marketing and financial side of things.

Lynn and Prudence complement each other in every way. Together they make a formidable team. Prudence's practical approach towards the dynamics of business provides a perfect foil for Lynn's creative and innovative input. They share common goals — "Our motto is:

541

where there is a will, there is a way." And although they had their set-backs, they have never been known to give up. They have always believed that nothing is impossible. "And things don't come easy, but if you cultivate a positive outlook, you will find it all works out at the end."

According to Lynn, patience is your biggest asset in business. She says: "I have waited for years for some of my ideas to materialize. And I have come to realize that to succeed in business, you need 50 per cent talent . . . hard work and lots of motivation make up the other 50 per cent."

The Biggie Best enterprise has blossomed and borne fruit since Lynn and Prudence pooled their talents. They now have stockists all over the country—with more to come in the future. "In just one year we have grown by 200 per cent and we still can't quite believe how it snowballed", says Prudence. Their stockists rely on them for products and innovations. "We feel terribly responsible—a kind of personal obligation to the people who work for us," Prudence says.

"There is an interesting story behind each woman or husband-and-wife-team that runs the many Biggie Best outlets," according to Lynn. "Some are astute business women; some are talented interior decorators. They all have a tremendous enthusiasm for our products, and motivation is always high. We do our best to encourage them to give their stores that distinctive Biggie Best look, and make sure that they get all fabrics, accessories and gifts in bulk, to cut and eliminate waste."

Quality is an overworked adjective these days, but it certainly applies to the unique Biggie Best product range. Fabric is all locally manufactured, pure cotton.

Soon the original Biggie Best shop will move once more. This time, to a Victorian-style townhouse, where customers will be able to fulfil their decorating fantasies as they wander through Biggie Best-style rooms. Lynn's husband will owner-build this ultimate Biggie Best Shop, and Lynn and Prudence will decorate to their heart's content, "to show how everything works". There will be a Victorian coffee-shoppe, too, where shoppers and "just lookers" can sample the sweeter things in life. The idea is to have a centre—"a place from which to generate ideas", says Prudence. "We want to encourage people to pop in whenever they want to. We will tell them whatever they want to know about crafts, or sewing, or decorating. They can use or adapt our ideas."

Although Lynn's Biggie Best Shop has changed and grown beyond even her wildest dreams, the original concept remains just the same. "We are middle-of-the-road, and affordable and we have proved that you can offer an all-South African product that is both stylish and good value for money."'

Long-range goals are necessary for growth and must be established. No businessman who wants to remain in business can afford to leave the future destination of his business to chance and hope that everything will turn out for the best. There are too many demands from the future, and if attention is not given to them early, future problems can be expected. The amount of profit you made a few years ago is not sufficient to offset today's rising costs. Another demand from the future is that you must learn to become a manager of work rather than simply a doer thereof (that is, give up doing the technical things you know and enjoy, and focus on the managerial aspects). Either you work towards this transition or you stand a good chance of losing out to more alert competitors.

Your determination to succeed and the extraordinary energy you possess as an entrepreneur will certainly come in handy when you want to grow, and you are definitely going to use these qualities in the process of making this transition. Succeeding in the implementation of your growth plans will require nothing less than your personal evolution from doer to manager to leader.

Once long-range goals are established, targets can be set for each year which lead towards the attainment of the long-range goals. In other words, try to determine the steps you should take now to work towards the long-range goals. However, the best of plans can get out of hand when conditions change. Such changes may even happen within your business. For example: a number of employees may leave the business. The change could also be with customers — their needs, desires and tastes shift. To adjust your plans to account for such changes, you should be alert and recognize any changes in your line of business, your market, and community. Check your plans against such changes, and determine what corrective steps, if any, are needed to get the action in motion again. A weekly, monthly, or quarterly review of progress towards these goals will help you determine when progress is below expectations.

Every year a considerable number of people in Southern Africa ask for financial assistance from various financial institutions and some invest a considerable amount of their own money in their ventures. Some of them are successful and others are less so. The question is why? The reasons given are supplemented by factors such as managerial ignorance, limited managerial experience, limited attention to detail and other incompetencies in management. Existence of a genuine business opportunity, adequate capital, managerial as well as technical abilities are prerequisites for success in business. Getting money to set yourself up in business may be difficult; keeping it is even more difficult. Having money does not guarantee making money, that is, making a profit. You not only have to have money, you have to utilize it well. That is, rather manage it than let it manage you. So, firstly, for a business to be successful it must be controlled. A businessman who is in proper control of the business watches carefully every rand that comes in and goes out, and understands how capital is to be safeguarded and utilized, and how to keep part of the profits for expansion.

There is no magic formula for success in business, and neither is success achieved by luck or accident. Success is planned and the benefit is efficient allocation of resources. The result of this is a profitable business. If your business is ill-conceived and ill-planned, and its activities ill-conducted, it will be of no long-term benefit to you, but may in fact be harmful. In business, you will be successful or effective only to the degree that you accomplish what you have planned to achieve. The application of modern and sound business principles (as outlined in this book), with purpose, direction and method is essential to success, for business success is a philosophy, a point of view, and an approach that must permeate your mind thoroughly if you are to master the business. Much of developing a business has to do with careful planning and then taking the necessary steps to turn the theories in practice.

Success is achieved when you do something about things constructively. Courage is being aware of the risks and the pitfalls but going on anyhow, to make it worthwhile. Only through taking risks are there profits, growth and rewards. And to take a risk, takes guts. To have courage is to have a personal commitment to getting things done — stick your neck out and face the future of your business idea in spite of doubt. It is believing that something can be done and that there is a benefit in it, and as has been said: 'If I screw up, I pay the price, but if I succeed, I reap the benefits.' Mr Ray Eppert, president of Burroughs Corporation has expressed it as follows:[60]

'Freedom of enterprise is more than the freedom to succeed. At the core, it is the freedom to fail. This country owes its greatness to men who are free to take chances and who dare. We can stick our chins out, we can take risks . . . and we get the reward for doing it if we are right.'

A good definition then of a businessman is: He is the kind of fellow who knows how to do things his community (or market) needs to have done. He has the energy and the courage to go ahead and do them. He does more than dream. He wastes no time blaming others. He is without fear. He does not worry — he risks. By virtue of these characteristics, he is a man of good business.

Some people talk about going into business incessantly, but they never take the step. Why? It may be that they do not want to take the risk. Or perhaps they do not have the confidence. Of course, everyone can experience periods of doubt. But also, one can overcome anything. As someone said: "Don't sweat the small stuff. Put everything into the proper perspective. How important is business next to life? Not very. That's what I mean by saying don't worry".

Those businessmen who like their businesses best, grow the most. And growing businessmen know where they are going. How would you react for instance to this question: Do you expect your sales to increase this year over last? The growers would say, "Yes, sure". The non-growers would say, "I hope so; I don't know; I really can't say." Growth in business requires the forward look.

"Would you tell me, please, which way I ought to walk from here?"
"That depends a great deal on where you want to get to," said the cat.

545

"I don't much care where," said Alice.
"Then it doesn't matter which way you go", said the cat.
Lewis Carroll's Alice's Adventures in Wonderland.

Probably the greatest resource of your business is under your hat. Business is the extension of education. Without education there would be no business as we know it. Education raises men's aspirations, widens their vision, makes them look forward. One has written: "Creative thought — imaginative study — courageous experiment by men of education and business offer the greatest hope for our future". Education makes people want better, wealthier, happier, more useful lives. The prosperity and happiness of any community is directly related to the extent and character of its education. Simply, if you want to earn more you have to learn more. Look around you. You see (or know) many successful businessmen. They all started where you are today with one difference, they tied theory into the reality of practice.

I would like to end this book with the words of an anonymous bullfighter:[61]

'To fight a bull when you are not scared is nothing. And to not fight a bull when you are scared is nothing.

But to fight a bull when you are scared — that is something.'

BIBLIOGRAPHY

* Starting a Small Business in Ontario: A Sound Business Approach to Setting Up Your Own Company. 1985. Ontario Ministry of Industry and Trade: 1–7.

* Clifford M. Baumback, Kenneth Lawyer. How to Organize and Operate a Small Business. 1979. Prentice Hall, Englewood Cliffs, NJ: 43, 49, 50.

* Curtis E. Tate, Jr., Leon C. Megginson, Charles R. Scott, Jr., Lyle R. Trueblood. Successful Small Business Management. 1982. Third Ed. Business Publications, Plano, Texas: 1, 18, 20, 21, 22.

* J. Fred Weston, Eugene F. Brigham. Managerial Finance. 1977. The Dryden Press, Hinsdale, Ill.: 950–962.

* Victor Kiam. Are you an entrepreneur? Reader's Digest, p. 186; **129** (771): 64–66.

* M. R. Sareff. Strategic management for small business. Entrepreneur 1986; **5**(1): 6–7.

* M. J. Crous, C. J. Jooste, J. D. Nortje. Konsultasie- en nasorgbehoeftes van kleinsakeondernemers. Entrepreneur 1986, **5**(1): 8.

* Tobie de Coning. Entrepreneurskap: sleutel tot voortgesette ekonomiese groei. 1985; **4**(9): 6–7.

* Willie Conradie. The strength of small business. *Entrepreneur* 1982; **1**(6): 5.
* Willie Conradie. What is a consultant worth to small businessmen? *Entrepreneur* 1984; **3**(4): 5.
* Roy Polkinghorne. How small businessmen can survive. *Entrepreneur* 1985; **4**(1): 18.
* Bill Siebenhagen. Eagles or vultures? *Entrepreneur* 1982; **1**(2): 18.
* Tommy Brand. Is business management self-evident? *Entrepreneur* 1982; **1**(2): 34.
* Planning for growth in small business. *Entrepreneur* 1983; **2**(7): 17.
* Thomas J. Peters, Nancy K. Austin. *A Passion for Excellence: The Leadership Difference.* 1985. Collins, London: 415–419.
* Lane Flint. Nothing succeeds like enthusiasm. *Entrepreneur* 1983; 19.
* Immins Naudé. Job enrichment: motivation or myth? *Entrepreneur* 1982; **1**(2): 30–31.
* Peter F. Drucker. *Managing for Results.* Pan Books, London: 1967.
* Mark H. McCormack. *What They Don't Teach You at Harvard Business School.* William Collins: 1984.
* *Managing Money for Profit.* Small Business Development Corporation, Johannesburg: Fact Sheet 10/86.

NOTES

[1] Larry Farrell. Building entrepreneurship: a global perspective. *Training, The Magazine of Human Resources Development* 1986; July: 46. (Adapted with permission.)
[2] Donald K. Clifford Jr., Richard E. Cavanagh. *The Winning Performance.* 1985. Sidgwick & Jackson, London: 17.
[3] See: Fransien du Plessis. Small business success story. *Entrepreneur* 1984; **3**(4): 18–19 for further information. (Reprinted with permission.)
[4] See: David Pincus. Small business success story; *Entrepeneur* 1984; **3**(5): 12–13 for further information. (Reprinted with permission.)
[5] See: David Pincus. Small business success story. *Entrepreneur* 1985; **3**(1): 6–7 for further information. (Reprinted with permission.)
[6] See: Buxtons — the small one that made it. *Entrepreneur* 1982; **1**(6): 10–12 for further information. (Reprinted with permission.)
[7] Die resultate van doeltreffende bestuur. *Entrepreneur* 1985; **4**(11): 28–29 for further information. (Reprinted with permission.)
[8] Peter F. Drucker. *Managing for Results.* 1964. Pan Books, London: 175. (Reprinted by permission of William Heinemann Limited.)
[9] *How's Your Business Sense?* Programme 1302. Nightingale-Conant Corporation.
[10] Mark H. McCormack. *What They Don't Teach You at Harvard Business School.* 1984. Collins, London: 244. (Reproduced with permission.)
[11] Wendell O. Metcalf. Starting and managing a small business of your own. *Starting and Managing Series* Vol. 1. 1982. U.S. Small Business Administration, Washington D.C.: 17–18.
[12] Peat Marwick. *Starting Your Own Business.* 1985. Mitchell, Johannesburg: 2. (Small Business Development Corporation, Johannesburg: Booklet Number 7).
[13] Peter F. Drucker. *The Practice of Management.* 1969. Heinemann, London: 35. (Reprinted by permission of William Heinemann Limited.)

[14] Larry Farrell. Building entrepreneurship: a global perspective: *Training, The Magazine of Human Resources Development* 1986, July; 46. (Adapted with permission.)

[15] Robert C. Ragan, Jack Zwick. *Fundamentals of Recordkeeping and Finance for the Small Business.* 1978. Entrepreneur's Press, Reston Publishing Company, Reston, Virginia: 2-3. (Reproduced with permission.)

[16] John W. Wingate, Seymour Helfant. Small store planning for growth. *Small Business Management Series Number 33.* 1977. U.S. Small Business Administration, Washington D.C.: 8.

[17] *Entrepreneur*, a monthly magazine published by the Small Business Advisory Bureau, Potchefstroom University for CHE. (Reproduced with permission.)

[18] Measuring salesforce performance. *Management Aids Number 4.003.* 1067. U.S. Small Business Administration, Washington D.C.: 2.

[19] Baumback, Lawyer. *How to Organize and Operate a Small Business.* 1979. Prentice-Hall, Englewood Cliffs, NJ: 88.

[20] John W. Wingate, Seymour Helfant. Small store planning for growth. *Small Business Management Series Number 33.* 1977. U.S. Small Business Administration, Washington D.C.: 71-72.

[21] Baumback, Lawyer. *How to Organize and Operate a Small Business.* 1979. Prentice Hall, Englewood Cliffs, NJ: 39. (Reprinted by permission of Prentice-Hall, Inc., Englewood Cliffs, New Jersey.)

[22] Larry Farrell. Building entrepreneurship: a global perspective: *Training, The Magazine of Human Resources Development* 1986, July; 50. (Adapted with permission.)

[23] Idem, 43-49.

[24] See W. H. Kuehn. *The Pitfalls in Managing a Small Business.* 1973. Dun & Bradstreet, New York, and *The Business Failure Record through 1976 and 1979.* 1977. Dun & Bradstreet, New York, as sources.

[25] Baumback, Lawyer. *How to Organize and Operate a Small Business.* 1979. Prentice Hall, Englewood Cliffs, NJ: 20. (Reprinted by permission of Prentice-Hall, Inc., Englewood Cliffs, New Jersey.)

[26] Idem, 21.

[27] Larry Farrell. Building entrepreneurship: a global perspective: *Training, The Magazine of Human Resources Development* 1986, July; 46. (Adapted with permission.)

[28] Donald K. Clifford Jr., Richard E. Cavanagh. *The Winning Performance.* 1985. Sidgwick & Jackson, London: 154, 168.

[29] John V. Petrof, Peter S. Carusone, John E. McDavid. *Small Business Management: Concepts and techniques for improving decisions.* 1972. McGraw-Hill, New York: 379-380. (Reproduced with permission.)

[30] From Thomas J. Peters, Robert H. Waterman, Jr., *In Search of Excellence.* 1982. Harper & Row, New York: 157-158.

[31] Idem, 13.

[32] John W. Wingate, Seymour Helfant. Small store planning for growth. *Small Business Management Series Number 33.* 1977. U.S. Small Business Administration, Washington D.C.: 3-4. Dr. Wingate is Chairman Emeritus, Marketing Department, Baruch School of Business and Public Administration, City College of New York. Mr. Helfant was Vice-President and Manager of the Independent Stores Division of the National Retail Merchants Association and is currently Director of Education of the International Council of Shopping Centers.

[33] Idem, 9-10.

[34] John V. Petrof, Peter S. Carusone, John E. McDavid. *Small Business Management: Concepts and techniques for improving decisions.* 1972. McGraw-Hill, New York: 377. (Reproduced with permission.)

[35] Thomas J. Peters, Robert H. Waterman, Jr. *In Search of Excellence.* 1982. Harper & Row Pubishers, New York: 14–15.

[36] William H. Day. *Maximizing Small Business Profits.* 1978. Prentice-Hall, Englewood Cliffs, NJ: 155.

[37] Advertisement headline of Human Synergistics, Plymouth, Michigan. (*Source: Training, The Magazine of Human Resources Development* 1986; June: 95.)

[38] Thomas J. Peters, Robert H. Waterman, Jr. *In Search of Excellence.* 1982. Harper and Row, New York: 16.

[39] Idem, xv.

[40] Baumback, Lawyer. *How to Organize and Operate a Small Business.* 1979. Prentice-Hall, Englewood Cliffs, NJ: 274, 284. (Reprinted by permission of Prentice-Hall, Inc., Englewood Cliffs, New Jersey.)

[41] John F. Murphy. Sound cash management and borrowing. *Management Aids Number 1.016.* 1971. U.S. Small Business Administration, Washington D.C.: 4–5.

[42] Peter F. Drucker. *The Practice of Management.* 1969. Heinemann, London: 37. (Reprinted by permission of William Heinemann Limited.)

[43] Idem, 38.

[44] Donald K. Clifford Jr., Richard E. Cavanagh. *The Winning Performance.* 1985. Sidgwick & Jackson, London: 7.

[45] Peter F. Drucker. *Managing for Results.* 1964. Pan Books, London: 198. (Reproduced by permission of William Heinemann Limited.)

[46] Mark H. McCormack. *What They Don't Teach You at Harvard Business School.* 1984. Collins Publishers, London: 163–164.

[47] Donald K. Clifford Jr., Richard E. Cavanagh. *The Winning Performance.* 1985. Sidgwick & Jackson, London: 23–24.

[48] Source: William H. Day. *Maximizing Small Business Profits.* 1978. Prentice-Hall, Englewood Cliffs, NJ: 311.

[49] Baumback, Lawyer. *How to Organize and Operate a Small Business.* Prentice Hall, Englewood Cliffs, NJ: 42. (Reprinted by permission of Prentice-Hall, Inc., Englewood Cliffs, New Jersey.)

[50] Idem, 62, 64.

[51] John V. Petrof, Peter S. Carusone, John E. McDavid. *Small Business Management: Concepts and Techniques for Improving Decisions.* 1972. McGraw-Hill, New York: 388–389.

[52] William H. Day. *Maximizing Small Business Profits.* 1978. Prentice-Hall, Englewood Cliffs, NJ: 324.

[53] John W. Wingate, Seymour Helfant. Small store planning for growth. *Small Business Management Series Number 33* 1977. U.S. Small Business Administration, Washington D.C.: 40.

[54] Louis A. Allen. *Professional Manager's Guide.* 1969. 4th ed. Louis A. Allen Associates, Johannesburg: 45.

[55] John W. Wingate, Seymour Helfant. Small store planning for growth. *Small Business Management Series Number 33.* 1977. U.S. Small Business Administration, Washington D.C.: 40–44.

[56] Source: *Small Business News* 1984; **6**(3): 31. (Journal of the University of the North, Business Advisory Bureau.)

[57] John W. Wingate, Seymour Helfant. Small store planning for growth. *Small Business Management Series Number 33.* 1977. U.S. Small Business Administration, Washington D.C.: 26.

[58] Charles Woelfel. Guides for profit planning. *Small Business Management Series Number 25.* 1985. U.S. Small Business Administration, Washington D.C.: 53–54.

[59] Ingrid Hoffman. *Your Family* 1987; January: 98–100.

[60] Ray R. Eppert in an address before the Boston Conference on Distribution. (*Source:* Baumback, Lawyer. *How to Organize and Operate a Small Business.* 1979. Prentice-Hall, Englewood Cliffs, NJ: 50. (Reproduced with permission.)

[61] Thomas J. Peters, Nancy K. Austen. *A Passion for Excellence.* 1985. 414. (Reprinted by permission of Collins Publishers, London.)

INDEX

A

Absenteeism (employees): 43
Acceptability: 132
Accessibility of merchandise: 242
Accounting control system: 159, 160
Acid Test Ratio: 389
Action Plans: 138, 161, 423, 426
Activity Ratios: 384, 392–396
Advertising: 65, 120, 213, 269,
  493, 494
Advertising budget: 273, 274
Advertising (media selection): 274
Advertising (measuring results): 275
Advertising (developing an
  advertisement): 279–284
Advertising objectives: 269, 270, 271
Analytical thinking: 510
Anti-shoplifting methods: 352–357
Apprehension (shoplifting): 357, 358
Asset appraisal methods: 49, 50
Asset Register (recording assets):
  375, 376
Assets: 159
Attitude advertising: 277, 278, 279
Attorney (consult): 50
Auditor (consult): 51
Average collection period (ratio)
  394, 395
Average credit sales per day
  (computation): 394
Average stock: 393
Awareness (a buying decision
  stage): 271

B

Balance sheet: 100, 159, 382, 383
Bank Reconciliation: 354, 377–379
Bankruptcy: 480
Barclays Small Business Unit: 463,
  464
Book value: 49
Break-even analysis: 427–435
Break-even chart: 428, 430
Budgeting 139–141, 157, 416–435
Burglary: 359
Burglary insurance: 119

Business (a definition): 16
  (a name for it): 84
Business failure (causes): 501–508
Business interruption insurance: 119
Business knowledge (the salesman):
  295
Businessman (definition): 546
Business mission: 208
Business objectives: 19–22
Business opportunity: 16, 25,
  478, 479
Business plan: 88–102
Business problems (responding to):
  507, 508
Business success (10 points of
  importance): 479–501
Buying behaviour: 299, 300
Buying (checklist): 339
Buying a business (advantages
  and disadvantages): 31–33
Buying a business: 28–51

C

C's of credit control: 445, 446
Capital requirements (determination
  thereof) 482, 483
Capital budget: 422
Capital employed: 403
Cash book: 370–373
Cash control (a system): 373–375
Cash control: 159, 488, 489, 505
Cash flow budget: 97, 98, 99, 423,
  425, 519, 520, 521
Close Corporation: 103, 104, 105
Coaching: 182–183
Coded cost method (in stocktaking):
  334
Commitment (a buying decision
  stage): 271
Communication: 10, 149, 150
Company (a form of business): 103,
  104, 105
Competitiveness 154, 169, 213, 234,
  235, 236
Comprehension (a buying decision
  stage): 271

Consult advice (the necessity): 517, 518
Consultants (their role in business): 459
Consultation services: 457, 458
Controlling (a management function): 157–160
Convenience (a buying motive): 300, 301
Convenience customers: 210
Conviction (a buying decision stage): 271
Correctness (in written correspondence): 317
Cost of borrowing: 392
Creativity: 3, 73–79, 161, 192, 284
Creditors: 387, 488
Creditors (recording transactions): 377
Creditors application form: 443, 444
Credit collection letters: 448–453
Credit controlling (advantages and disadvantages): 440, 441
Credit controlling: 438–454
Credit policy: 441–443
Credit sales: 159
Curiosity (a salesman quality): 294
Current assets: 383–386
Current liabilities to tangible net worth ratio: 389, 390
Current liabilities: 383–386
Current ratio: 384–388
Customer complaints (dealing with it): 144, 262, 263
Customer knowledge (the salesman): 298
Customer loyalty: 249, 250
Customer relations: 165–168, 245, 246, 250, 263–266
Customer relations (danger signals): 253

D

Debtors: 38, 159, 376, 387, 487, 488
Decisions: 126, 144
Decisiveness (entrepreneurial characteristic): 9
Delegation: 146
Delivery performance checklist: 145

Departmental pricing: 230
Depreciation: 410–414
Development Corporation: 108, 465, 466
Discerning consumers: 210
Discounts (its effect on gross profit): 398, 399

E

Economy (a buying motive): 300, 301
Education: 546
Employee compensation: 198
Employee interviewing: 193–197
Employee morale: 515
Employee motivation: 506
Employee relations: 170–172
Employee terminations: 200
Entrepreneur (a definition): 121
Entrepreneurial behaviour: 512
Entrepreneurial characteristics: 3, 4, 8–11
Entrepreneurial instinct (an example): 3
Entrepreneurial learning: 496
Entrepreneurial vision: 499, 500
Equity: 392, 403
Equity capital: 497
Evaluating a business for sale: 31–34
Expenses: 91–92
Expense budget: 422, 423, 424
Expense control: 490

F

Fast-moving stock: 493, 494
Financing (sources): 106–118
Financial over-extension: 527
Financial planning: 519, 520, 521
Financial ratios: 37, 383–409
Financial statements (verify its validity): 35, 382, 383
Fixed assets to tangible net worth ratio: 391
Fixed costs: 205, 427
Fixed-rand-per-unit method (in advertising): 273

Forced sales: 216
Forecasting: 134, 161, 211, 532
Franchise agreement, the: 63-65
Franchising: 52-57
Franchise fees: 65

G

Geographic distribution: 44
Goodwill: 32, 39-40, 127
Goodwill advertising: 279
Growth (business): 477, 508-546
Growth capital: 497
Growth financing: 497, 498, 499
Growth objective: 21, 22
Growth stages: 522, 523

H

Hire purchase: 37, 117
Human relations (an entrepreneurial
ability): 10

I

Ideas (their worth): 16
Image: 235, 236, 239, 245, 246, 253,
533, 534, 535
Immediate response advertising: 276
Impulse buying: 242, 243
Income statement: 101, 223, 382
Inflation: 21, 22, 335-338
Innovation: 74, 525, 526
Insurance: 118
Inter-firm comparisons: 215, 216

J

Job application form: 193-195
Job descriptions: 189-191

L

Leading: 147-157
Leaders (pricing): 233
Learning by example: 476

Lease agreements: 37
Leasing: 117, 241
Leverage ratios: 384,
391-392
Liquidation (definition):
381
Liquidation value: 381
Liquidity crises (survival
measures): 387-388
Liquidity ratios: 383, 384-390
Location: 32, 42, 70, 77-84
Long-range planning: 532-
540
Long-term loans: 96
Loss leaders (pricing): 233

M

M's of business: 18
Mark-down (pricing): 231, 232
Market analysis: 66, 67, 70-73,
92-102
Market assessment: 483
Marketing concept, the: 251-257
Marketing information: 252
Marketing objectives: 251, 252, 253
Mark-up: 221, 222, 225, 226, 230,
483, 484
Market share (computation): 72-73,
401-402
Market value: 40
Minimum levels (stock): 214
Modernization: 533
Morale (symptons of low morale):
150
Motivating: 150-155
Motorcar traffic count: 82
Myths (of business): 2, 8

O

Organizing (management function):
143
Organizing (symptoms of poor): 144
Organization structure: 143
Overdraft facilities: 116
Overstocking: 214
Owner-manager (capabilities): 528,
529, 530

Owner's salary: 45

P

Pareto's Law: 328
Partnership: 540–543
Pedestrian traffic count: 81
Percentage-of-sale method (advertising budget): 273
Person specification: 192
Planning: 128, 129
Plate-glass insurance: 119
Policies: 141–142
Positive thinking: 7, 17, 18
Present value: 537–539
Price (business for sale): 40–50
Price leaders: 222
Price-marking: 243, 244
Pricing objectives: 225
Product knowledge (the salesman): 295
Productivity: 172, 180–183
Profit planning: 416–435
Profitability ratios: 384, 396–406
Profit objective: 19–21
Promotional calender: 284–285
Prosecution (shoplifting): 357, 358
Public holidays (employees): 199
Public liability insurance: 119
Publicity: 286–289
Purchasing: 203–219
Purchasing power: 71

R

Ratio analysis (pitfalls) 407–409
Record-keeping: 368–380
Rental contract, the: 79–80
Replacement finance: 110
Retained earnings: 497
Return on investment: 46, 226, 392, 400–404
Risk-factor: 40–44

S

Salary and wage ratio: 404, 405
Sales demonstrations: 301–304
Sales letters: 307–313

Sales presentations: 301–304
Salesmanship: 292, 293, 294, 513
SBDC (Small Business Development Corporation): 460, 461
SBAB (Small Business Advisory Bureau): 461, 462, 463
Scheduling: 138, 139
Security: 346–366
Self-confidence: 5, 10, 11
Self-development: 470–472
Self-motivation: 192
Semi-variable costs: 428
Shop-layout: 238–248, 352
Short-term planning: 531
Signage (shop layout): 245
South African Franchise Association: 52, 66
Speciality goods: 274
Staff selection: 155
Standard ratios: 406–409
Stock (administration checklist): 338–343
Stock control: 321–344
Stock records: 159
Stocktaking: 333–335
Stock turnover ratio: 392–393
Success (definition): 480, 481
Suppliers credit: 114
Supplier selection: 216, 217, 218

T

Tangible assets: 44
Teaching: 182, 183
Theft control (general comments): 360–365
Total assets turnover ratio: 395, 396
Total operating expense ratio: 404
Trading rights: 39, 87, 88
Training: 155–157, 173–180
Treasure hunt promotion: 285
Trust Bank Bureau for Business/ Management: 464

U

Understocking: 322

V

Variable costs: 427
Vehicle Insurance: 119
Venture capitalists: 89, 90
Visibility (location): 79

W

Working Capital finance: 115
Workmen's compensation insurance: 119

MANAGEMENT TITLES FROM JUTA

ASSESSING MANAGERIAL COMPETENCE
HERMANN SPANGENBERG
This book is based upon research results and years of experience which show that the tasks and roles of managers at various organisational levels differ substantially, calling for different success criteria and, consequently, differences in the required competencies. Competencies in themselves are complex differing in type and level and this work should prove to be indispensable in the assessment of the potential of managers and supervisors.

GETTING IT RIGHT — THE MANAGER'S GUIDE TO BUSINESS COMMUNICATION
ADEY & ANDREW
This work is more an introduction to business practice than a book about theoretical communication and management, marketing, advertising, and industrial relations are approached from the perspective of business communication. Each chapter has a summary of concepts and terms, as well as case studies that test the understanding of these concepts. The syllabi of the diplomas of various professional institutes, including that of the Communication Course of the Diploma in Business Administration as examined by the SA Institute of Management, are covered.

MARKETING MANAGEMENT
MARX & VAN DER WALT
Written to suit South African conditions, the style of this text is easy, while figures and tables are used liberally to explain complicated concepts. While characterised by a practical approach, the content is scientifically founded. The twenty chapters are divided into four parts. The first is a general introduction providing a broad perspective; the second deals with the marketing environment; the third with marketing decisions and the fourth part, including topics such as the product life cycle, marketing warfare, strategic marketing, product portfolio etc, deals with the integrated marketing strategy. This work is also available in Afrikaans.

PROFIT FROM DYNAMIC PEOPLE MANAGEMENT

BRIAN ANGUS

Business organisations depend wholly on the ability of their employees to produce more value than they consume in costs—to add value during the process which will enable the organisation to operate at a profit. This book is aimed at those managers and supervisors who want to learn, not only how to apply routine people management techniques but also, more importantly, how to implement dynamic as opposed to static human resources management to the ultimate benefit of their employees, their organisation and themselves.

PROFIT FROM PRODUCTIVITY

HUMPHREY & HALSE

This book lays bare the opportunities for productivity improvement in any organisation. It is written in a style that is simple, thorough and practical, and managers, trainers and supervisors will have no trouble in implementing and maintaining the strategies contained in this important work.

PROFIT FROM PERSONAL PRODUCTIVITY

HUMPHREY & HALSE

Most of us think of productivity as something that goes on in factories and businesses, and it's therefore of little general interest. Productivity is in fact something which greatly affects all of us in both our business and our personal lives. Knowing how to measure and improve your personal productivity is to be able to take charge of your life and start to direct it in the way that you wish it to go. The insights offered by this book will enable anyone to realise their full potential.

PROFIT FROM EFFECTIVE COMMUNICATION

NEAL DuBREY

Professional and business people know that personal communication skills determine the success or failure of any venture. But very few do anything to address their own shortcomings in this area. This book is a goldmine of practical, helpful advice that will enable the reader to develop his or her personal communication skills—to listen effectively—to formulate thoughts into words—to write clearly and to benefit from the use of sound argument and persuasion.

INDUSTRIAL RELATIONS TITLES FROM JUTA

INDUSTRIAL RELATIONS HANDBOOK
Policies, Procedures and Practices for South African Managers
ANDREW PONS

This loose-leaf publication assists the management team to promote successful relationships with employees in order to continue to develop in the medium to long term. It has been designed to take cognisance of developments both in labour law and the current practice of industrial relations in South Africa. Practical guidelines are set out in detail ensuring the value of this book as a "hands-on" text suitable for all levels of management.

INDUSTRIAL RELATIONS IN SOUTH AFRICA
SONIA BENDIX
In some 600 concise and informative pages, frequently punctuated by tables, figures and charts, Sonia Bendix skilfully analyses international industrial relations principles and specifically gives in-depth insight into our own. It includes the 1988 Amendments to the Labour Relations Act and a chapter is devoted solely to dispute settlement machinery in South Africa, dealing with the question of fairness, unfair labour practice and the Industrial Court.

PERSONNEL MANAGEMENT: THE BUSINESS OWNER'S HANDBOOK FOR SMALL AND MEDIUM SIZED COMPANIES
JULIA HOLDEN
Written specifically for any business that is operating without in-house personnel management staff, this easy-to-read, subscription publication provides a working system that is quick to implement and provides the procedural 'knowledge' required to deal with employees. It is the only publication available that provides vital working documents that the subscriber is free to copy and to use. The only entrepreneur who can afford to be without this handbook is the specialist who consults and works alone.

WORKER PARTICIPATION — SOUTH AFRICAN OPTIONS AND EXPERIENCES
MARK ANSTEY (Editor)
A future South Africa will demand industrial relations that operate beyond the adversarialism of strikes and stayaways, dismissals and litigation. This text comprises a unique collection of papers by South African and international industrial relations practitioners and academics — all experts in their field. The book contains not only theoretical insights, but practical guidelines for implementing various approaches, and helpful of South African initiatives.

NEGOTIATION—THEORY, STRATEGIES AND SKILLS
PROFESSORS M SPOELSTRA & W PIENAAR
Although various approaches and theories of negotiation are acknowledged, the authors of this test clearly view negotiation as a process wherein the development of alternatives to strongly emphasised. Verbal and non-verbal strategies and skills in negotiation receive detailed attention. The book explains how power can be deployed during negotiation and how attitudes and behaviours can be changed through the use of a few step-by-step recipes.

CONFLICT MANAGEMENT
PROFESSOR D DE VILLIERS
This is a pathbreaking text on one of the most important aspects of industrial relations written by one of South Africa's leading academics from the School of Business Leadership at UNISA. It is of value to anyone affected in any way by employer–employee relationships and, indeed, interpersonal relationships in every sphere of their lives.

THE McGREGOR LIBRARY

INDUSTRIAL RELATIONS HANDBOOK
McGREGOR'S WHO OWNS WHOM—The Investors' Handbook

A thorough, exhaustive and easy-to-use analysis of relevant data on over 700 companies listed on the JSE. The most comprehensive work on any stock exchange in the world.

"Few publications relating to Diagonal Street provide more valuable references than Robin McGregor's annual offering."
FINANCE WEEK June 1987.

McGREGOR'S QUICK REFERENCE TO THE JSE

This six-monthly publication provides a detailed summary of listed companies' annual reports. Graphic reflections of performance over fifteen months and performance relative to each company's sector are included to give the subscriber an instant appreciation of the relevant share's trend.

McGREGOR'S TAKEOVER TALK

A companion volume to WHO OWNS WHOM—THE INVESTORS' HANDBOOK, this loose-leaf publication keeps you up to date on a monthly basis on a whole range of related and pertinent topics, takeovers, mergers and other important company changes.

McGREGOR'S PRIVATISATION IN SOUTH AFRICA

Including schedules of State owned bodies the book pinpoints where privatisation and de-regulation can assist in regeneration and revitalisation. Of value to all decision-makers in both the public and the private sector, and for the academic.

McGREGOR'S THE MECHANICS OF THE JOHANNESBURG STOCK EXCHANGE

Not only does this volume provide the reader with a detailed account of exactly how the Johannesburg Stock Exchange works, its history, who it belongs to and where it is going, but it also gives authoritative opinions on such subjects as the various investment philosophies, the merits and demerits of unit trusts, debentures, gilts etc and the value and usage of indicators. There is also a chapter on the concentration of control of the JSE explaining in full the methodology and rationale behind this concept. It is an essential reference work for the big and small investor, the student and the businessman.

McGREGOR'S CYNIC'S GUIDE TO THE STOCK EXCHANGE

Although related in a relaxed, witty and droll style, Dr Jannie Hofmeyr's on-going tryst with the stock exchange reveals a set of incisive strategies of use to the serious investor, the dabbler or for those who merely dream of tilting at the JSE. A wealth of research data, historical precedent and anecdote all serve to address the basic questions, fears and forebodings of every investor, especially after the Great Crash.

McGREGOR'S DICTIONARY OF STOCK MARKET TERMS

The main problem in learning any subject is its nomenclature. As more private investors start to learn about shares and the stock market, the greater the room for misunderstanding. Yet, with the greater specialisation of the financial markets, the greater is the need for a specialised language and a dedicated glossary of terms. This dictionary by Ciaran Ryan will help in the understanding of these markets, and their peculiar languages.